Ray Folk
3441 Biscayne Rd
LI-6-7144

895

W9-ABD-349

OFFICE AND ADMINISTRATIVE MANAGEMENT

PRENTICE-HALL INTERNATIONAL, INC., *London*
PRENTICE-HALL OF AUSTRALIA, PTY., LTD., *Sydney*
PRENTICE-HALL OF CANADA, LTD., *Toronto*
PRENTICE-HALL FRANCE, S.A.R.L., *Paris*
PRENTICE-HALL OF INDIA PRIVATE LIMITED, *New Delhi*
PRENTICE-HALL OF JAPAN, INC., *Tokyo*
PRENTICE-HALL DE MEXICO, S.A., *Mexico City*

OFFICE AND ADMINISTRATIVE MANAGEMENT

Systems Analysis, Data Processing, and Office Services

C. L. LITTLEFIELD   *Chairman, Department of Management*
North Texas State University

FRANK RACHEL   *Assistant Professor of Management*
North Texas State University

SECOND EDITION

Prentice-Hall, Inc., Englewood Cliffs, N.J.

OFFICE AND ADMINISTRATIVE MANAGEMENT, SECOND EDITION
formerly MODERN OFFICE MANAGEMENT

© 1956, 1964 by Prentice-Hall, Inc.
Englewood Cliffs, N.J.

Library of Congress Catalog Card No.: 64-10058

Printed in the United States of America

[C]

PREFACE

The field known traditionally as office management has probably undergone more change during the past decade than any other field or function of management. Pressures of ever keener competition have forced executives to seek fresher, more accurate, and more complete information upon which to base decisions, yet to do so through means which meet a rising tide of office costs.

A revolution in data-processing technology has occurred and has made information available in forms and at speeds previously undreamed of. These advances have triggered other developments of even greater long-range significance—a mushrooming science of decision-making, the emergence of the systems concept as the key approach in linking separate and specialized activities into a coherent whole, and the appearance of professional administrators who are primarily concerned with coordinating the diverse activities of specialists and directing them toward over-all objectives.

New concepts and patterns of thought are demanded. A new generation of office administrators, information technologists, systems analysts, programmers, and other persons having fresh viewpoints and trained minds is called for. A reorientation of thinking on the part of top executives and functional managers, such as those in sales, production, finance, accounting, and personnel, is necessary if the new tools are to be utilized and if the separate parts of an enterprise are to fit together.

The office management field is being rapidly transformed (or absorbed) into a much broader and more significant field—as documented by such changes as the redesignation of the Office Management Division of the American Management Association as the Administrative Services Division, the merging of the official publications of the National Office Management Association and the Society for Advancement of Management, and the change in title of a leading professional journal from *Office Management to Administrative Management.*

This new edition of this book is a carefully designed attempt to incorporate the significant developments which are occurring, yet to contribute to the balanced perspective needed both by persons soon to join enterprises and those already employed who seek sharper tools to meet the new demands.

Many of the newer concepts are somewhat more complex than those presented in the original edition; they could hardly be otherwise in view of the rapid evolution of the field. More rigorous study is required to understand the evolving concepts and to grasp their implications. Yet the learning process may be aided by greater clarity of descriptive material, liberal use of illustrations, and greatly improved study questions and case problems.

The authors are deeply grateful to the many writers and researchers, professors, and executives who have contributed ideas upon which this book is based. Particularly helpful was Professor Martin B. Carter of the School of Commerce, Accounts, and Finance, New York University, who read the entire manuscript and made many constructive suggestions. Sincere appreciation is hereby expressed to all other persons who provided assistance and encouragement.

CONTENTS

I

INTRODUCTION

1

THE DEVELOPING ROLE
OF THE OFFICE

Management as a professional endeavor · The management process · The need for information · Brief history and perspective · A broadening field · Increasing clerical and professional employment · Problems and challenges · Career opportunities

Management as a Professional Endeavor

The roots of modern management reach far backward, but management as we know it today is a product of the twentieth century. During its brief existence, management has become one of the leading institutions of our society. It holds promise of becoming the most influential of all for it cuts across all others, from small shop to world government, and provides the leadership which largely shapes their present and future roles.

The central focus of managerial attention is upon the primary mission of the individual enterprise. A business enterprise, for example, must justify its existence by supplying a particular group of consumers with certain lines of goods or services. The management of the firm must perceive clearly this primary service objective, and it must guide activities in a manner that will insure success and keep the enterprise strong and healthy. The first responsibility of the management of a business firm, thus, is *internal*. The same obligation holds for the management of any other type of enterprise.

Any management quickly finds that *external* responsibilities also demand recognition, however. A business must earn profits sufficient to

3

compensate the owners for the use and risk of capital, must serve varied needs of employees, and must contribute to the stability and progress of the community. What starts as an economic venture soon takes on social and even political dimensions. And in an economy such as that of the United States, where more than two million separate businesses create more than three-fourths of the nation's wealth, income, and employment, it is easy to see that the collective impact of business decisions is very great indeed.

The Management Process

Described simply, the management process is one of setting objectives for an enterprise and of taking steps to insure that these objectives are achieved. Management carries on this process by making decisions—decisions required in planning, organizing, directing, and controlling the activities of the enterprise.

The Need for Information

The information for decisions is gathered, processed, recorded, and communicated by means of a network of office activities which extends into every corner of an enterprise, and includes many outside relationships as well. When information is complete, accurate, and timely, the batting average of executive decisions can be very respectable, assuming that the information is used logically. When information is inadequate, inaccurate, or out of date, decisions can be no better.

Quite easily seen is the dependence of day-to-day operating decisions upon the availability of information. Errors or slowness in information-handling with reference to a customer's order may mean loss of the customer, as may lack of consideration on the part of an employee in communicating with him regarding the order. One department may initiate a purchase order for a year's supply of an item and another department may be overstocked with the item. A costly machine may, without management notice, reach the stage of excessive downtime and maintenance expense, or it may be rendered obsolete by a later model. A trusted employee may leave the firm because a verbal promise of a salary increase has been forgotten.

Less easy to see, but no less significant, is management dependence upon pertinent information in long-range planning and policy decisions. Changing patterns of customer demand, trends in income and expenses by product lines, impact of new technology, population and other social trends, state of the general economy, emerging patterns of international competition—these and other significant types of information should influence long-range decisions fully as much as the more specific types of information should guide current operating decisions.

Brief History and Perspective

Through most of his recorded existence, man has based his decisions upon knowledge accumulated through experience, and he has relied heavily upon individual shrewdness and intuition in interpreting his experience. He preserved and guarded his accumulated knowledge.

The merchant of less than a century ago placed much emphasis upon trade and house secrets which might give him competitive advantage. He kept few records except those required for legal documentation and protection (of course, there have been taxes as long as there have been governments!). His informational tools and techniques were simple but adequate for his needs.

The first strong winds of change came with the Industrial Revolution, first in England, later in other nations and the United States. Rapid improvements in production technology, introduction of the factory system, and emergence of the corporate form of ownership required numerous management adjustments. Business firms developed quickly in size and scope of operations, with profit the chief incentive. Supply began to catch up with demand and competition grew steadily keener, causing the functions of marketing and finance to vie with production for management attention. An awareness of responsibilities to employees and to society generally, emerged—an awareness of external as well as internal obligations.

The new problems have been, and are continuing to be, met with varying degrees of success. Perhaps the most significant general development has been a growing awareness of need for *professional management*—for competent and responsible leadership which can cope with increasingly complex problems, coordinate diverse activities, serve both internal and external needs, and make things happen.

With the coming of awareness that management is "something special" —not an offshoot of technical knowledge, and not a process that can be carried out successfully in a dynamic environment by means of intuition and individual shrewdness—developments in managerial knowledge and skill began to accelerate. To attempt to classify these developments in a brief treatment is to over-simplify; however, we can recognize three general movements:

The scientific management movement, through which Taylor, the Gilbreths, Gantt, and many others brought the "logic of efficiency" to management, beginning shortly before the turn of the century and continuing today. Involved have been the search for principles of efficient operation, measurement and standardization of performance, and substitution of facts and orderly thinking for guesswork in the making of all sorts of decisions.

The human relations movement, given strong early impetus by Mayo and his associates in the Hawthorne Experiments in the late 1920's but furthered by many others, chiefly in the social sciences. The general direction of this movement has been toward recognition of the importance of employee attitudes—such as understanding, voluntary cooperation, and willing dedication—in the accomplishment of enterprise objectives.

The information technology movement, now gaining momentum, which strives to reduce management uncertainty through careful analysis of elements bearing upon decisions, design of systems, and utilization of computers and other greatly improved information-handling methods. Whether this movement is merely an extension of the scientific and human relations movements, or whether it cuts across and goes beyond the others, cannot yet be answered with assurance because there has not been enough time to assess its full impact.

Individuals and groups contributing to the rapid accumulation of managerial knowledge and skill have included leaders in business, government, and other organizations; professors in business, economics, government, and other social science fields; and physical scientists who have contributed to technological innovations. Special mention should be made of the strong influence of professional associations, including the American Management Association and the Society for Advancement of Management, in the broad field of general management; the National Office Management Association and the Systems and Procedures Association of America, in the office management and systems fields; and several associations in the business automation and equipment fields, which are now gaining rapidly in size and influence.

A Broadening Field

Office activities, contributing information needed to coordinate and administer other activities, have been among the last to come under the spotlight of management analysis. Progress has been rapid during the past decade, however, and is now accelerating at such a pace that an "information revolution" appears to be in the making.

Although triggered by technological breakthroughs in electronic computers and other giant steps in mechanization, the information revolution must be attributed to underlying forces, such as the increased complexity of modern enterprise and ever-keener competition. Size, diversification, specialization of function, and decentralization are among the forces which make coordination both more imperative and more difficult. Domestic and international competition in product, service, and price have contributed to a profit squeeze which leaves little margin for error in managerial decisions.

A significant managerial response would be to strive for greater unity among the parts of an organization: finer focus upon overall and common goals, and reduced interdepartmental conflict. As we shall note later, this need for *unity* and coordination has important implications for organization structure, systems design, and executive qualifications.

Several developments during very recent years may indicate an evolving pattern. In 1960, the American Management Association changed the name of its Office Management Division to Administrative Services and expanded the scope of its activities. Also in 1960, the magazine, *Office Management,* merged with the magazine, *American Business;* in 1961, the name of this publication was changed to *Administrative Management.* In 1962, the official publications of the Society for Advancement of Management and the National Office Management Association were merged, under the tentative title of *Advanced Management-Office Executive.* The Controllers Institute of America has become the Financial Executives' Institute; the National Machine Accountants' Association has become the Data Processing Management Association; the Office Equipment Manufacturers' Institute has become the Business Equipment Manufacturers' Institute. These and similar developments may provide the following clues: (1) the general field which we have referred to as "information technology" is in a state of flux; (2) groups and publications, formerly specialized, are sensing a need to broaden their perspectives and services; (3) efforts to reach beyond former limits are frequently finding common ground in an area being tentatively named "administrative management" or "management information services" or some other similar title.

Equally impressive is the tendency of a growing number of firms (notably insurance companies, but others as well) to create a position of "Administrative Vice-President" or "Vice-President of Management Services" and to place under it such functions as Operations Research, Systems and Procedures Analysis, Data Processing, and Office Services Management. All of these functions are concerned with the analysis of informational requirements, the coordination of activities through master systems plans, and the design of methods with an eye on total enterprise requirements rather than merely isolated tasks.

The Increase in Clerical and Professional Employment

One gets a real "eye-opener" when confronted with the fact that despite the amazing advances in computer technology and other "labor-saving" devices associated with office activities, the clerical and kindred worker group has been the fastest growing major segment of the working force during the past decade. The only group now increasing more rapidly, while still much smaller, is the professional and technical group. Many members of this group are involved in planning, programming, and other activities closely related to the development of information for management decisions. These two groups combined with the sales group, also increasing rapidly, compose most of the "white-collar" group, which in 1956 passed the "blue-collar" group in numbers for the first time and is expected to more than double that group in size in little more than a decade.

About one in six of all employed persons is now in the clerical and kindred worker group; this ratio compares with one in ten in 1950, and one in forty in 1900. In addition to full-time office workers, most employees engaged in sales work, factory work, and other occupations are "part-time office workers" in the sense that they devote substantial portions of their time to office phases of their jobs.

How can this trend exist, in the face of swift introduction of labor-saving devices in the office field? The answers seem to lie in such factors as the following:

1. *Larger, more complex enterprises* require more coordination. Planning and control must be more highly developed; records and reports are depended upon increasingly; communication of information among managers and employees becomes an increasing problem.

2. *More office-type enterprises* have swelled the number of office employees. These include insurance companies, banks, and a wide variety of other service-type businesses predominantly office in nature.

3. *Expanding governmental services* at federal, state, county, and municipal levels have furnished a two-fold stimulus—more clerical employees within government service, and more within private firms to interpret and apply regulations, maintain records, and make reports.

4. *Scientific management* is drawing nearer to reality, as management attempts to reduce to a minimum uncertainty in decisions, and as it develops new tools for gathering and analyzing information needed in decision making. Management's appetite for more, better, and fresher information seems insatiable.

While not a directly-contributing factor to increased office employment, the decline in "blue-collar" job opportunities has obvious influence on the general proportions. Mechanization of many tasks formerly done manually and rising requirements for technical skill, are upgrading many such jobs to technical and professional categories. Other jobs are being eliminated, forcing more and more persons to prepare themselves for careers in the faster-growing "white-collar" segment.

Problems and Challenges

It should be helpful at this point to note certain problems of fundamental current importance in office and administrative management. Doing so may clarify some of the concepts mentioned briefly thus far, and provide a preview of later sections. The following list of subjects is far from complete; it is intended to be suggestive rather than exhaustive:

1. Need for optimization of the general goals of the enterprise rather than special departmental and personal goals—in order to achieve the maximum of coordination and unity of effort.

2. Need for management to define informational requirements more carefully—in order to pinpoint information which *is* needed, and to eliminate that which is *not* needed.

3. Need for a master systems plan, or plan of integrated systems, which links the operating subsystems, procedures, and methods in a coordinated whole.

4. Need for careful reappraisal of organization structure in the light of new demands—it is probable that few arrangements should stand without modification.

5. Need for extreme care in transition to automation—care in making sure of needs, in preparing thoroughly in advance of changeover, and in meeting responsibilities to employees as well as to the enterprise.

6. Need for improved measures, standards, and controls—but without excessive rigidity or loss of individual initiative.

7. Need for administrative cost reduction where possible without impairing services actually needed—through management by objectives, management by exception, streamlining of procedures, modernizing of methods, subcontracting to outside service agencies, improving evaluative techniques, strengthening supervision, etc., while being careful not to fall into the trap of false economy by cutting back on programs or services really needed.

8. Need to look unceasingly for ways to integrate employee and enterprise interests—to provide opportunities for employees to meet their basic needs such as security, social acceptance, and self-expression, while working in the best interests of the enterprise.

Career Opportunities

The days of the chief clerk or office manager of old are numbered. The detailed work to which he gave close supervision is being sifted for truly significant information, and much of what is significant is rapidly being converted to machine handling.

New careers are springing up in such specialized areas as planning informational requirements, systems analysis, computer programming, and a wide variety of staff services dependent upon organizational requirements.

The future seems particularly bright for the person who has a firm grasp of general management, thorough familiarity with the various operating areas in an enterprise, *and* thorough appreciation of the potentialities of systems and data processing. Clearly, such a person must have breadth of perspective, analytical ability, and familiarity with the new tools of management.

For such a person—who comes about as close to warranting the title of "professional administrator" as anyone—the outlook was described recently by a high-ranking executive of a major corporation, in the following terms:

> In previous periods of corporate growth it was the production genius—the man who could make things better and faster—who occupied the center of the management stage. In later years, as production problems were solved, the sales and marketing specialist—the man who could develop new markets to receive the company's products—pre-empted the spotlight. The post-war era saw the research scientist and the engineer—men who could create new markets and revitalize old ones through new products and product improvements—emerge as key figures in the corporate drama, and their role will undoubtedly continue to grow in importance.
>
> But from today on, as expenses increase, as the pace of competition quickens, and as the risks attending management decisions mount, it will be the men who can organize all of their companies' resources and efforts for greater profitability and growth who will gain top billing. These are the men of business: the coordinators and administrators. Their opportunities for service will lie primarily in the basic design of the business: in determining where it is going, in devising a total scheme of operations for getting there, and in coordinating the activities of all its parts.[1]

QUESTIONS FOR STUDY AND DISCUSSION

1. Appraise the following statement: "Management has existed as long as man has existed, and the process of managing has remained virtually unchanged. It is true that most of the writings on management have appeared during the past half century, but these writings merely record the principles and techniques which good managers have always followed."

2. How important is it that the management of any given business be competent today and in the years ahead? What is at stake? To what different groups is any given management responsible?—why should it be responsible to each of these groups?

3. A speaker at an office management convention recently declared, "The office *is* management." Do you agree? Explain.

4. Give several illustrations of how management must depend upon informa-

---

[1] George W. Chane, "Centralized Administrative Management: The Need, The Promise, and the Challenge," *Shaping a New Concept of Administrative Management*, AMA Management Report 56 (New York: American Management Association, Inc., 1961), pp. 14-15.

tion in making: (a) day-to-day operating decisions and (b) long-range planning and policy decisions.

5. Trace what seem to be the major phases in the development of managerial skills to their present levels. Does management now seem to have reached a state of maturity?

6. Are we now experiencing an "information revolution"? Suggest several forces which have increased management desires for fresher and more complete information.

7. What conclusions may be drawn from the numerous mergers of professional magazines and the changes in titles of professional associations in fields closely related to office activities of various sorts?

8. There is an old saying: "If I give a man a dollar and he gives me a dollar, each of us still has a dollar; but if I give him an idea and he gives me an idea, each of us then has two ideas." Does this simple concept help to explain the contribution of professional associations? Do you see any limits in how far the concept can be carried in such associations?—think about one specific association in considering this possibility.

9. The trend in the proportion of clerical employees continues to rise, despite rapid extension of mechanization and automation in the office field. How can this apparent contradiction be explained? What do you predict for the future?

10. Consider each of the "problems and challenges" said to be of current importance to office and administrative management. Does each seem valid? Can you suggest others which might be added to the list?

11. What are several examples of career opportunities now developing in the office and administrative fields? Do many of these opportunities seem to offer high ceilings for advancement, or are they typically "dead end"?—what factors may bear upon the answer to this question?

12. What does the term "professional administrator" seem to suggest in terms of functions performed and qualifications required?

Case 1-1. Some Case Experiences in Administration

Several experiences reported recently by a sampling of business firms and governmental agencies are summarized below:

1. A maker of industrial engines established a centralized, network-type system for dictating and transcription, and reduced stenographic costs by 70 per cent while making instant dictating possible for executives.

2. An oilwell supply house combined a purchase order form and a receiving report form, simplifying the procedures involved, and saving $32,000 annually.

3. An industrial distributor replaced a system of transcribing information from customer orders to internal forms by one of making five photographic copies of incoming orders, thus eliminating a serious error problem and getting most orders out within half a day from the time received in contrast to the two or more days formerly required.

4. An electrical products manufacturer converted inventory and billing records to magnetic tape and computer processing, thereby cutting time for shipping from five days to one day, closing five warehouses no longer needed, and reducing inventory investment by 25 per cent.

5. A chemical manufacturing firm installed an integrated system of order processing, making it possible to reduce delivery time by 50 per cent, handle greatly increased volume with no increase in personnel, reduce errors substantially, and produce reports which provide swift and accurate production of facts needed for management forecasting and analysis.

6. A municipality invested $10,000 in microfilm equipment and now saves some $6000 a year in direct storage costs alone, while reducing greatly the processing time required to make duplicate copies of records when requested.

7. A state drivers' license bureau motorized its files, installing 50 electrically operated file units in a central location, and speeded up service greatly while realizing an annual saving of $225,000.

Problems and questions:

a. Appraise the effects of each of the administrative improvements described upon the success of the enterprise in achieving its objectives.

b. In the business enterprises cited, compare the net effects of the advantages realized with those of higher sales volume produced through aggressive sales efforts. What general conclusions can be drawn?

Case 1-2. The Need for Professional Skills in Providing Management Information

Certain provocative and challenging observations regarding the present state of professionalism in the area of providing management information were made recently by a prominent consultant.[1]

> Where are the professionals in the use and processing of data? In very short supply. There are technicians who can specify data analysis and data processing techniques. There are generalists who can define the management jobs. But in all this populous field of data processing there are few who have the combination of skills that marks the true professional: a sound grasp of company-wide operations to serve as a basis for developing patterns of information and information use, plus an equally sound grasp of data analysis and data-processing techniques.
>
> Today we use a team approach to the problem of developing information. Our teams are staffed with narrow experts and facile coordinators. What is

[2] Milton M. Stone, "Data Processing and the Management Information System," *Data Processing Today: A Progress Report,* AMA Management Report Number 46 (New York: American Management Association, Inc., 1960), pp. 21-22.

wrong with this approach? Two things are wrong with it. First, expert members of teams reinforce their claims to expertness in specific fields by becoming "no-men." (What better way to prove expertness or to preserve status based on expertness than to become a debunker—to throw cold technical water on each bright new idea?) Second, we are approaching the time when professionals in the use and processing of data should be out selling new information products. Teams don't sell, individual professionals can and will.

Aren't these professionals now in the controller's office? I doubt it—again for two reasons: First, with some notable exceptions, there has been little in the actions . . . of those in the controller's office to indicate widening interest in and understanding of the non-financial, operating areas of business. Second, and more important, this new profession of information development and use depends quite heavily on communication skills . . . which are quite new to controllership. Information must be interpreted, in operating terms as well as in financial terms. Presentations must stimulate action. Decision-making information must clearly illustrate the implications and the risks of each alternative. These communication requirements will inevitably introduce the skills of graphic arts and expository prose into what has thus far been a world of neat columns of numbers and not-so-neat interpretations of those numbers.

Certainly the controller is in a fine tactical position to become a broad-gauge professional in the development and use of information, a counterpart to the high-level military staff intelligence officer. He now controls part of the contents of the company's bucket of facts, and in most cases the bucket itself: that is, the data-processing equipment. To exploit this beginning fully, today's controller must teach himself to temper the habits, the attitudes, the prejudices born of a lifetime of education and practice in the world of fine-ruled yellow analysis pads.

But from whatever source this new management professional emerges, his arrival will herald the next exciting phase in the use and processing of data: the practical realization of the concept of the management informational system.

Problems and questions:

Appraise the views expressed with regard to the skills needed by the management information professional, the limitations of the team approach to developing information, and the potentialities of the controller's department for meeting the new needs. Are certain alternative sources for the new management professional implied? If so, which sources may these include, and what reasoning seems to support each?

II

THE ADMINISTRATIVE
ORGANIZATION

The evolution which has characterized the field of administrative management during the past decade calls for substantial realignment of the organizational arrangement of the typical enterprise. Concepts once adequate will no longer serve the needs.

Increased demands for informational services, coordination through well-designed systems, methods which will be both effective and economical, revolutionary developments in data processing—all call for fresh thinking, for willingness to question established arrangements, and for ingenuity needed to devise new arrangements.

In Part II we shall briefly examine certain principles of organization which have special application to the changed administrative requirements. We shall then look specifically at alternative arrangements for administrative management, and shall consider criteria for selecting an appropriate arrangement. We shall delve into one area which appears to have immense potential but has been generally overlooked by managements—that of organization of work at the individual job level. Finally, we shall study carefully some techniques of organizational analysis which can serve any management in deciding upon an effective administrative arrangement.

2

ORGANIZATIONAL PRINCIPLES

Chief organizational decisions · Need for definite organizational plan · Principles of organization: primary role of objectives; functions; responsibility and authority; dividing and grouping work; delegation; line and staff; balance, stability, and flexibility; place of specific functions; informal organization

The process of management anywhere consists of planning, organizing, and controlling activities in a manner that will achieve objectives.

The matter of first concern in any plan must be the *objectives* or purposes sought. Objectives can be attained most effectively if *policies* are formulated carefully and made known to all who can be guided.

But objectives and policies are merely ideas. They must be translated into reality—into tangible products or service. This means that an *organization* must be planned and developed that can carry ideas to final completion. This holds true for a business firm, for an army, for a university, for a church, for a governmental agency, or for any other form of group endeavor.

Chief Organizational Decisions

Planning a suitable organizational arrangement involves three principal types of decision, which are closely related:

What types of work, or *functions,* are necessary to attain objectives?

How may these be broken down most effectively into departments and individual jobs?

What personal qualifications, and therefore types of *personnel,* are needed for performing these functions?

What *physical facilities* would enable personnel to perform functions effectively and economically?

The actual work of organizing puts the plan into effect. It involves assigning necessary functions or duties to specific individuals, and taking steps to insure that personnel are properly trained and equipped for performing these activities. The third management process—controlling —makes use of appropriate parts of the organization in getting day-to-day work done and in insuring that it follows planned lines.

Need for Definite Organizational Plan

When you see a group of people working effectively together for a common goal, you may be sure that their activities fit into a well-defined pattern. One person may do only selling, another may operate a lathe, and another may post accounts receivable. But the contribution of each of these persons, and those of their fellow employees, together make up the end product or service.

The organizational plan is thus the basis for teamwork. It accomplishes a tie-in of all separate activities with the common goals or objectives which justify the existence of the enterprise. It is the basis for informing personnel of their individual responsibilities.

As an enterprise becomes larger, it becomes more and more important that the organizational plan be set up in definite, written form. Organization charts are the most common device for accomplishing this. They show groupings of activities into departments and other units, and they show basic relationships of the different departments with each other. If more detailed descriptions are desired, these are written up in organizational manuals. Charts, manuals, and other devices for planning organizational arrangements will be considered further in the chapter on techniques of organizational analysis.

Each enterprise must devise its own plan of organization. There can be no standard arrangement that will be suitable for all banks, all department stores, or all firms in any other industry or trade. The obvious reason for this is that purposes and conditions are certain to vary somewhat from firm to firm.

But there are certain principles of organization that may serve as highly valuable guides in working out any individual arrangement. So helpful can these be that the remainder of this chapter will be devoted to discussing them. To use them blindly and unquestioningly would be very unwise; to ignore them would be to pass up the combined thinking and experience of leaders of all types throughout the history of mankind.

Principles of Organization

A principle is a general rule or truth that may be expected to apply under similar conditions anywhere. Since organizing is a universal problem in enterprises of all sorts, many principles have been found to underlie successful organizational relationships. Together, they form the framework of a science of organization—admittedly a young science and far from an exact one.

An exhaustive study of principles of organization is neither possible nor desirable here, but a brief treatment of principles that seem to have particular significance in the organizing of office activities should furnish valuable background for analyzing such problems in specific enterprises.

Accordingly, a select group of organizational principles will now be considered, following the outline below:

- The primary role of objectives
- Relationship of functions, personnel, and physical facilities
- Responsibility and authority
- Dividing and grouping work
- Effective delegation
- Line and staff relationships
- Balance, stability, and flexibility
- Place of specific functions
- Informal organization

The primary role of objectives

Management must try to determine and assign responsibility for all types of work actually needed for attaining objectives. "If there is a real need for something in an organization, you will pay for it whether you buy it or not." The pay may be in the form of low productivity, customer dissatisfaction, or employee turnover, rather than direct cash expenditure; it is nevertheless a real cost to the enterprise.

Only those types of activity actually needed should be provided. Any specific type of work should be performed only if it makes a definite and justifiable contribution to customer satisfaction, employee well-being, or some other objective of the enterprise.

In answering the question "Is this activity necessary?" one must often look beyond the immediate product of the activity. This is a consideration of special importance in managing office activities, where contribution to overall objectives is more often indirect than direct. A given office job, for example, may be concerned with assembling information and working up a certain type of report for higher management. The immediate purpose of the job may be satisfied if the information is compiled by efficient methods and if the report is in a concise, understandable form. But what if no one reads or uses the information in the report after it is completed? If this is true, no justifiable purpose is being served and the report clearly should be eliminated.

If, to turn the illustration around, a genuine need for this information exists and if it is not being met, the weakness is again a failure to perceive objectives clearly and to take steps necessary to achieve them.

There is a special need for management to make frequent reappraisals of both the objectives and the organizational arrangements being used, for both probably will need to change from time to time, and they should be kept in close relationship with each other. This requires vision, alertness, and adaptability in high degree.

Not only must management itself try to see as clear a picture of objectives as possible, it must also help to produce a clear picture of these objectives in workers' minds. In answer to a question by an analyst, a statistical clerk in a certain insurance company made it clear that he considered his principal objective to be that of clearing his desk of one stack of policy applications after another. Actually, the tabulations he was making were serving as the basis for premium rates charged. When a little time was taken to explain this to the clerk, what had seemed a monotonous, somewhat futile undertaking was made to take on interest; beneficial effects on quality and promptness of work were immediately noticeable.

Relationship of functions, personnel, and physical facilities

Objectives should determine functions or types of work performed, as just indicated. Types of work necessary, in turn, ordinarily should determine types of personnel and physical facilities needed. This basic relationship is illustrated in Figure 2-1; an effort should be made to follow it in all organizational planning, even though exceptions may sometimes be necessary.

Just as an athletic team must be built around certain positions or basic assignments, an organization must be built around the types of work to be performed. It would be considered quite ridiculous for a coach to decide that, available material being what it is this year, he will play one center and ten quarterbacks. It would be equally short-sighted for the management of an enterprise to hire a motley assortment of individuals and then attempt to devise jobs for them.

This in no way denies the importance and the rights of the individual.

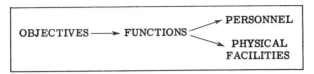

Figure 2-1. Relationship of basic components of organization

It merely recognizes that individual well-being depends upon organizational well-being, and that this relationship is dependent upon team-play pointed toward a common objective.

Sometimes it is clear that a specific program or activity would be beneficial, but it may be out of the question because personnel or facilities are lacking. In other cases it may be necessary to combine unlike activities in one department or one job in order to make full use of existing personnel and facilities, to take advantage of special abilities of personnel, or for some other reason. Although such expedients may be necessary from time to time, it is well to keep in mind the basic goal of fitting personnel and facilities to the needs of the work to be done.

Responsibility and authority

Functions become responsibilities when assigned to individual employees. Each employee assumes an obligation to perform certain duties, in other words.

In order that all necessary work will be performed, it is highly desirable that work assignments be clear-cut and unmistakable. Special tools in defining responsibility for the different types of work include the organization charts and manuals already mentioned, charts of work distribution within departments, and job descriptions. These need to be supplemented by adequate training and personal consultation to insure understanding by each employee of the nature and scope of his responsibilities.

If an individual is to carry out a responsibility, he must be able to take necessary action and he may need to require action of others—he should have authority in proportion to his responsibility.

The process of assigning responsibility and authority starts at the top of the organization, where the head of the firm is held finally responsible by the owners for performance of all necessary functions, and is given authority over all separate divisions. For each division and department, the same pattern of responsibility and authority applies.

The ideal arrangement, then, is one providing a definite chain of responsibility and authority from the top executive to each employee, even though there may be several levels or layers in between. It is desirable for each employee to take direct orders from only one superior, although, as will be considered in connection with line and staff relationships, many of his actions may be influenced strongly by staff specialists.

Two qualifying statements, or corollaries, require consideration along with the general principles governing responsibility and authority just presented.

Responsibility assigned to one's subordinates (discussed further in relation to delegation) does not relieve the superior of the final responsibility and obligation. A good analogy is with the familiar concepts of "contracting" and "sub-contracting." The superior is the prime contractor for getting certain work done and fulfilling a certain responsibility. When he sub-contracts work to assistants, as he usually must do, he retains final responsibility for carrying out the duties and accomplishing the mission assigned to him by his own superiors.

Authority of a formal nature, while essential to insure coordination, is by no means the *only* management tool for getting work done. Best results follow from keeping authority in the background and relying, instead, upon interesting work assignments, two-way communication, effective use of employee participation in decision-making, and other means of motivation which result in voluntary cooperation and a sense of personal responsibility.

Dividing and grouping work

The process of assigning responsibility for work has just been reviewed briefly. The specific activities provided will of course vary with the nature and the objectives of the organization. An insurance company, for example, will determine the protection and savings plans which it will offer, sell through some agency arrangement, underwrite service policies in force, handle claims, invest surplus funds in income-producing properties or loans, and provide for supporting activities. Other enterprises will need a different assortment of activities. We can generalize by saying that any organization must *create* something of value (either product or service), *distribute* to users, and *finance* its operations.

The process of grouping work is commonly referred to as *departmentation*. Departmentation is essential for specialization and coordination. Specialization may be in terms of function, product, process, or some other basis; it is necessary for attaining familiarity and proficiency within some areas of activities. Coordination is then required to hold the specialized parts together, and to have "one big team instead of a lot of little teams."

Early departmentation is usually by *functional* specialty. This arrangement allows for concentration and development of proficiency in sales, production, accounting, or other necessary fields of specialization. It is most successful for single-product, single-region operations.

If the enterprise grows and, particularly, if it expands in product or service lines, or territory, or both, it is likely sooner or later to move to a *divisional* structure—with either product divisions or territorial divisions, each operating much as an independent enterprise, subject to the general objectives and policies set by the top management. The degree of freedom allowed to divisions may vary considerably from firm to firm, of course. Generally, however, divisions provide closer working relationships among functional groups within the same division. In the insurance example, agency, underwriting, claims, and service personnel would work in close proximity in serving the same policyholders. Divisions provide a broader perspective and a greater sense of responsibility on the part of personnel, more clear-cut control over profits and other criteria of success, and other benefits.

Divisionalization normally carries with it a high degree of *decentralization* of authority; each division head and his group have a considerable amount of freedom to act and to adapt to local needs. We shall note particularly the impact of decentralized and centralized arrangements upon administrative management in Chapter 3.

Effective delegation

A problem of special importance to any executive—president, first-line supervisor, or one between—is that of how best to delegate responsibility and authority for work to his assistants. Management authorities generally regard this as one of the most important requirements for executive success.

Good delegation exists when decisions are made at the lowest level capable of making them. The head of any given organizational unit does not try to do all the thinking for the unit. Instead, he passes down any tasks which could be learned and performed effectively by certain of his assistants. At the same time that he assigns responsibility for the duties involved, he also assigns the authority to make all ordinary decisions regarding them.

Two benefits seem to result from good delegation:

The executive is relieved of detail and given more time for the managerial responsibilities of his position.

The employees of the unit are given an opportunity to think and to develop. This is important both to their own satisfaction and to the future success of the organization.

An analysis of how the executives in an organization spend their time will usually reveal that some are skillful at delegation but that others never seem to be able or willing to release responsibility and authority even for routine duties. Good executives manage to pass down most types of routine tasks, and thus keep most of their time free for assigning and coordinating work, handling special problems that arise, planning improvements, taking personal interest in employees, working closely with fellow executives and superiors, and dealing with exceptional or non-routine matters.

Those who have not learned the art of delegation spend much of their time on such tasks as filling out routine reports and forms, handling routine contacts with customers and suppliers, making detailed checks on work done by employees in the unit, and similar tasks. Such a person may be reluctant to delegate because of uncertainty as to how to break down and assign the work of his unit, lack of confidence in assistants, desire for personal credit, feeling of security through being a "master of detail," belief that it is easier to do something himself than to train another, superabundance of energy, or other reasons. Whatever the reasons, such an executive penalizes himself, his employees, and the organization. The superman on whom everyone else must depend is a bad security risk for everyone concerned.

It is highly important to realize, however, that good delegation means more than merely dividing work up and dumping it into the laps of employees supervised. An effective approach to delegation will usually reflect these considerations:

> Systematic appraisal of all duties performed in the unit with a view to assigning them at the lowest job level capable of handling them effectively. Exceptions or adaptations may be necessary where cross-training, work flow sequences, and other special factors must be considered in grouping duties.
>
> Careful choice of the person who will be delegated each specific duty. This requires knowing the strengths, limitations, and background of each individual in the unit.
>
> Clear explanation to the person involved concerning what will be expected, a clear definition of responsibility and authority. The employee involved should understand just what types of decisions he should make personally and what types he should refer to his superior. Others in the unit should also know about the new responsibility for the employee.
>
> Adequate training in the new work, including thorough familiarization with policies and procedures to be followed and development of specific skills needed.
>
> Delegation of current work in a manner that specifies *results* expected, or targets or goals to be achieved, insofar as possible.
>
> Adequate follow-up and control by the head of the unit. This should include checkups actually necessary to insure that work stays under control, but a good general rule is to place as much trust in the employee as he can carry. This probably should allow some freedom to fail or to make mistakes, since only in this way will he grow and learn to do things on his own initiative.

As soon as the assistant seems ready, the executive will turn the activity over to him; for no type or amount of training can take the place of actually bearing the responsibility and making the decisions involved in carrying it out.

Ability to delegate responsibility effectively can be developed, and its importance is such that it represents one of the greatest of challenges to any executive or potential executive.

Line and staff relationships

Management's need to delegate responsibility and authority to assistants becomes more pressing as an organization grows. The volume of work mounts and problems become more complex.

Study of possibilities for delegation by any given management suggests that the activities to be performed may fall into two broad groupings: (1) the *primary* activities which contribute most directly and vitally to the objectives of the particular enterprise, and (2) the *supporting* activities which are needed to keep primary functions in operation.

Primary functions, commonly called *line* functions, typically include production and sales in a manufacturing firm, with research added if a vital determinant of success. Their equivalents can be found in service-type firms and other organizations. Supporting, or *staff* functions, include a wide array of activities which are split apart either because of their technical nature or to relieve line executives and personnel. Illustrative of staff functions often present are personnel management, engineering, accounting, production control, and administrative services.

The line and staff concept has been a valuable one in organizational planning. It provides only one head and a single line of authority over operations in each division, and it provides that any staff specialists will work for and through the executive given line authority. The effect is to place emphasis upon common purposes, concentrate efforts in certain primary channels, lay a basis for teamwork, and avoid having a great many specialists who are working at cross-purposes and "going off in all directions."

The concept of *staff* now seems to be undergoing substantial change, at least in the minds of many academic scholars and some managers. Staff persons, particularly in technical fields, exercise what is often called "the authority of ideas." Even though they are not in the chain of command, their recommendations may carry so much weight that the effect is virtually the same. Staff specialists are being relied upon increasingly by top management for aid in planning. They frequently play influential roles in committees.

Of some special interest in administrative management is the impact of *systems* (to be studied in detail later) in leading to job groupings according to the logic of work flow. If a particular project calls for performance of successive operations by a marketing analyst, an engineer, a computer programmer, and an operating department head, a *project team* may be formed in which line and staff distinctions are virtually meaningless. Closely related, although often concerned with smaller-scale undertakings, may be a "self-sufficient" *task team*. If volume of work handled by either a project team or a task team becomes sufficiently heavy and continuous, the organizational arrangement may become permanent rather than temporary.

How are office activities, as such, related to the line and staff concept? Office activities are parts of *all* functions, line and staff alike. To illustrate: in submitting budgetary proposals to a corporate board of directors, the president of the firm may present statistical summaries, reports, estimates, and other documents. While negotiating a purchase, a purchasing agent depends upon files for information regarding commodities and suppliers; he communicates with prospective suppliers by mail, telephone, or other means; he makes computations; he prepares numerous forms in the process of completing the transaction. The fundamental nature of these office activities is not changed in the least when some of them are performed by office specialists who help the president or the purchasing agent, even in cases where they are performed in a separate office department. When office work is separated physically, it may justify being called staff, although in the special sense just indicated. In such cases, the objective of contributing to the basic operations of the departments being served should continue to be the foremost consideration; the office portions are merely performed in a different place and by different personnel, for reasons of convenience.

Balance, stability, and flexibility

The concept of _organizational balance_ suggests that each organizational unit should be developed in proportion to its contribution to the overall success of the enterprise. It should be large and strong enough to perform its functions adequately, but no larger. If one unit is either seriously underdeveloped or overdeveloped with reference to others, all will be handicapped. Weak cost accounting, buying, or advertising can seriously handicap a firm that is strong in other respects. An engineering, sales, or controller's department that dominates other important functions can do just as much harm.

There probably is no way of determining the exact number of personnel and the amount of equipment that a given unit justifies. Much may depend upon such variables as the competitive situation, the stage of growth reached, and future plans. And one department head may be more aggressive than others, or may be under a top executive who has special interest in his area; he may build an empire while others go begging. The best general approach seems to be either top-executive group thinking with various special fields adequately represented and with objective data on critical factors available; or impartial study by well-qualified independent consultants, particularly where there is good reason to believe a serious problem exists.

Organizational stability refers to the capacity to withstand losses of specific personnel without serious loss of effectiveness. A key need, here, is for long-range planning with regard to manpower needs, accompanied by a positive program for developing executives and other key personnel. Current interest in manpower inventories and executive development programs indicates management concern for the problem. Even more likely to be influential is a general climate which draws upon the thinking ability of large numbers of persons, provides challenge and encouragement and, in various ways, makes personal development a continuing process.

Organizational flexibility measures the capacity to adjust work assignments, personnel, and facilities to temporary changes in work volume. Nearly all firms face this problem in greater or lesser degree. Office activities are especially susceptible to peaks and valleys in work volume. We shall study a variety of organizational adjustments which may aid in coping with such problems—parallel service agencies, taking full advantage of flexibility in work schedules, and other approaches.

Place of specific functions

Even where the need for a type of work is unmistakable, there remains the problem of deciding where to place it in the organizational framework. This problem is important to the management of office activities since such activities facilitate all others. Below are certain factors which frequently bear upon such a decision.

1. *Relative importance in accomplishing objectives.* Both the level and the scope of any given activity are indicated. Functions most vital may justify representation in the top echelon of management. Operating divisions ordinarily should report to an executive vice-president or vice-president of operations rather than to any functional head. A specific function, such as inventory control, might be placed in purchasing, production control, or accounting—depending upon need and emphasis desired.

2. *Specialization.* By holding down the variety and scope of activities for which any given unit is to be responsible, greater operating proficiency, greater ease of training, justification of special equipment, and other benefits may be realized. Specialization may be a mixed blessing, however, for it also may result in limited

perspective, monotony, difficulty in coordinating numerous specialists, and other management problems.

3. *Place in work flow.* Increasingly, extension of the systems concept—aided, as we shall see, by vastly improved data processing—is drawing more attention to horizontal relationships of operations as they fit together in normal work flow. Project and task teams have been suggested as being early evidences of a pattern which seems likely to gain much wider use in the future.

4. *Portion of organization served by staff specialists.* Earlier discussion of changing concepts of the role of staff point to further and perhaps even more significant developments. It is highly desirable to determine just what the field of service for any staff unit should be, then to place the unit in a position in which it can render the best possible service. If a particular function is to serve all portions of the organization (such as a personnel department, for example), there will be good reason for placing it either in the top echelon or under the top executive, where it will have maximum encouragement to serve all other units. Placed under a functional department, the scope of its activities probably would be limited. We shall need to refer to this principle specifically when examining provisions for administrative management in Chapter 3.

5. *Span of control.* A practical consideration is the number of employees under the direct supervision of any single superior. There are now two quite distinct schools of thought—each having merit, dependent upon how interpreted and applied. The traditional view, and the one still most widely held, would place the limit at a number that could be actually *supervised,* with some flexibility according to level, complexity of work, geographical dispersion, and caliber of subordinates and superior. The newer school of thought would place the limit at the number that the superior could *guide* in directing their own activities. This implies a higher degree of delegation, and a greater sense of responsibility. Thus, the span might be much broader than under former assumptions.

Such considerations as the above may demonstrate the rather high degree of flexibility which exists in specific placement of a given function. In capable hands, and where a cooperative spirit prevails, it is true that some functions can be carried out effectively in different spots in an organization. Interest in the function and desire to do something with it may be more important than slight theoretical or logical advantage for a given location. But the principles stated can serve as basic guides, and deviations should be made consciously and with the intention of working toward a more satisfactory arrangement later, particularly if the present arrangement is highly dependent upon the special abilities of a single individual.

Informal organization

The preceding discussion of organizational principles has dealt mainly with officially designated lines of authority and responsibility which make up the formal organization of an enterprise. Every enterprise requires such a structure or framework in order to coordinate the efforts of specialists in accomplishing needed work.

In every enterprise there also comes into being a set of informal relationships through which employees attempt to fill needs which are largely *personal* in nature. Recognition of these relationships is important to management because they influence both the motivation of individuals and the effectiveness of formal organization. Certain of the more significant informal relationships will now be considered.

Employees tend to band together in small, *informal groups,* drawn by common interests and harmonious personality traits. Such groups commonly take coffee breaks and lunch together, engage in personal contacts as work permits through the day, and, in many cases, have social contacts away from work. Alert managers have come to accept and even encourage such relationships, recognizing that they fill employee needs for social acceptance, increase satisfaction with the general working environment and loyalty to the enterprise, and provide needed diversion from work pressures.

Of special importance, also, are *informal leaders* among employees, in whom others have confidence and to whom they turn for advice and example. Management will do well to spot these key people and recognize their influence upon other employees—keeping them well informed, consulting them frequently in making decisions which influence employee interests, and observing them as prospects for promotion to positions of formal leadership.

There are many other unofficial relationships and standards of behavior which arise to fill personal needs. Included are *status symbols* such as a desk that is larger in size or of a different color, a private secretary, a private office, and many other evidences of personal achievement and recognition. There are *group standards of behavior,* illustrated by the frequent tendency to produce at or near the output achieved by most other members of the group, the critical view of any member who appears to be striving for special consideration by management through devices not approved by others, and the attitude (good or poor) toward cooperation with certain other units and departments. There is of course always the *grapevine,* or informal communications channel, through which persons try to get information on all sorts of matters which arouse their interest or curiosity.

Informal relationships such as those mentioned previously can be highly influential. The challenge to management can be summed up as one of seeking a blend of formal and informal relationships which furthers the objectives of the firm and fills the personal needs of employees. In some instances, the formal organization can be modified to promote better understanding and cooperation among individuals and groups; in others, better formal communications can lessen dependence by employees upon the grapevine for factual information which they desire and need; and group standards of behavior can be influenced by efforts to win acceptance of new programs by informal leaders, by more democratic techniques of leadership, and by other means. We shall make further note of certain of these possibilities at numerous points in later chapters, giving them particular attention in the section on leadership.

QUESTIONS FOR STUDY AND DISCUSSION

1. Which managerial function logically comes first—planning or organizing? Suggest possible reasons for placing each first, then draw conclusions and justify them.

2. A clerk in the rate unit of a billing department answered a question regarding the purpose of his job by saying, "I enter the code number of each item of a customer's order in the proper space on his worksheet, referring to the rate table when necessary although I have most of the rates memorized. Then I place the completed worksheets in the key puncher's basket." Was this an adequate statement of the purpose of the job? If you were the supervisor of the rate unit and learned of the clerk's response, would you feel that you should take any action?—if so, what?

3. In what ways may the managerial technique of delegating be related to "sub-contracting" in the construction of a building? What similarities and what differences can you suggest?

4. Is formal authority necessary in progressive management?—why or why not? To what extent, if any, should employee motivation depend upon use of authority by higher management?—discuss.

5. What principle can best guide in dividing and grouping work? Trace the pattern of departmentation which usually evolves in a growing enterprise and explain the main stages.

6. What "spade work" must be done before delegation can be carried out effectively? What seem to be the major obstacles to effective delegation—the reasons why so many bosses do not delegate and achieve good results? What remedy can you suggest for each obstacle mentioned?

7. Distinguish as clearly as you can between line functions and staff functions. In what ways, and for what reasons, does the role of staff now seem to be changing? Are office activities line or staff?—explain.

8. Explain the concepts of organizational balance, stability, and flexibility, and suggest managerial approaches which may aid in achieving each of these attributes.

9. Does the function of inventory control belong to accounting, purchasing, production control, or some other function? Would you need certain types of information before attempting to decide this question?—if so, what types?

10. Does extension of the systems concept seem likely to alter the placement of certain functions and jobs, or is it more likely to use them in different combinations and leave their location unchanged?

11. What opposing schools of thought now exist with reference to the span of control? Explain each. Are they really in opposition?

12. Is informal organization a threat to management, a challenge, or some thing that can be ignored? Support your reasoning with specific examples of informal organization often found.

Case 2-1. The Longdale Company

In the Longdale Company, the president was very careful to inform his executives of changing plans and ideas, but this distribution of knowledge did not seem to lead to positive action by the various executives involved. Nor did it bring ideas up from the other executives to the president.

A study by a prominent consulting firm revealed that the executives heard and noted the information given by the president, but no one seemed to know who was expected to act on this information. Sometimes two executives would take opposing actions that would cancel each other out, or no one would do anything at all.

Problems and questions:

a. What, in your judgment, should the representatives of the consulting firm recommend to the Longdale Company?

Case 2-2. Jack Bainbridge

Jack Bainbridge is a senior clerk in the tabulating department of the Marston Distributing Company. Because of mounting work volume, the supervisor of the department recently asked Jack to take over much of the work of training new employees in the department, preparing certain control reports, and assisting with certain other supervisory duties. The supervisor thought it better not to say anything to Jack's fellow employees about any official change in duties for him since some had been with the company longer than Jack and they might resent it. He felt that Jack could take over the new responsibilities gradually and that in this way the other employees would soon become accustomed to the arrangement.

A few days later, Jack came to the supervisor in a disturbed frame of mind and said that, even though he was doing his best to help some of the younger employees with their work, they seemed to resent his efforts, and that he had overheard one accuse him of meddling.

Problems and questions:

a. What seems to be the root of the trouble, and how should it be corrected?
b. What action, if any, should be taken to prevent reoccurrence of similar situations?

Case 2-3. Line and Staff Organization

The following quotation is taken from an article in a magazine which deals chiefly with physical facilities and layout of offices.

"The functional purpose of a separate executive suite is to recognize and emphasize the separation of Staff and Line administration. In very large firms, policy people are often isolated on a separate floor, or even at a different location from the operating departments. It can be expected that the decor of the executive suite will be more plush than at Line levels."

Problems and questions:

a. Without attempting to analyze the primary conclusion of this statement regarding the need for an executive suite, appraise the concept of line and staff organization reflected in the statement.

3

ORGANIZATIONAL ARRANGEMENTS FOR ADMINISTRATIVE MANAGEMENT

The evolving role of administrative management · Traditional problems in organizing office activities · The administrative management concept · Responsibility for administrative services · Informational analysis · Systems analysis · Data processing · Central office services · The position of office manager · Control of office production

---

The Evolving Role of Administrative Management

We have considered certain sweeping changes that have occurred in the field traditionally regarded as office management. We have noted the evolving role of administrative management, and the approach to meeting management needs for (1) better information, and (2) improved coordination, in increasingly complex enterprises.

In Chapter 2, we studied principles or fundamentals of organization which apply to the entire structure of an enterprise, in order to emphasize principles which have particular application to administrative management and to set the stage for considering specific organizational arrangements for this developing area within the general framework.

The field of administrative management is in a formative stage of development. During the next several years, clearer definition of the role to be filled will undoubtedly be seen. Certain patterns are emerging, however, and in this chapter we shall consider the need for specific functions, which are now quite distinct, and the problem of suitable organizational provisions for these functions.

Traditional problems in organizing office activities

A good way to acquire insight into the problems involved in organizing office activities is to try to answer the question, "Just where is 'the office' in a typical organization?" The inevitable conclusion is that the office is never found in one location. Instead, office activities are found in all parts of the organization. Actually, they are *processes* which are necessary to carry on separate functions—sales, production, accounting, personnel, and other functions—and to coordinate the work of the separate functions where systems and procedures require cooperative effort, as is normally the case. Office activities provide information necessary to perform these functions and link them together.

As suggested in Chapter 1, the necessity for office activities in every part of an organization poses an organizational dilemma. Clearly, they should facilitate and be an integral part of each function (such as the recording of a sale on an order form and subsequent processing of both the order-filling activities and the information which guides them).

But it is normal for functional specialists to have primary interest and knowledge of their own areas, and usually office activities are neglected if planned and supervised entirely by functional heads. Poorly-designed systems, obsolete or inappropriate equipment, duplicate records, ineffective layout arrangements, and a resulting surplus of personnel are conditions typical of such arrangements.

It is obvious that *some* form of specialized attention to office activities is esssential.

The Administrative Management Concept

There is no single answer to the problems described above which will satisfy all needs. One approach now rapidly gaining acceptance, however, is that of viewing office activities as but a part of the broader concept of administrative management. Office activities, as suggested earlier, should provide better information at lower costs, and promote coordination of various specialized groups.

Understanding the concept and the organizational relationships which may be involved can be facilitated by study of Figure 3-1.

The organizational arrangement suggested in Figure 3-1 is representative of trends of thinking with regard to administrative management.

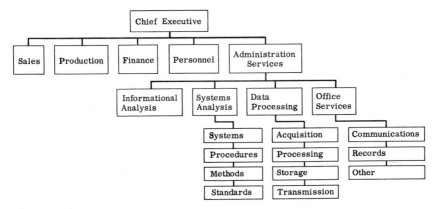

Figure 3-1. Administrative services in the organization structure

Many firms have changed to structures strikingly similar to this arrangement during very recent years. Others, preferring variations to fit particular needs, may find the conceptual framework helpful in working out their own adaptations.

We shall now consider (1) general responsibility for administrative services, (2) informational analysis, (3) systems analysis, (4) data processing, (5) central office services, (6) the position of office manager, and (7) organizational arrangements for controlling office production.

General responsibility for administrative services

A magazine article, "Enter—The Administrative Manager," published a few years ago, gave notice of a new and significant development in organizational structures.

Reference to the functions included under the administrative services section of Figure 3-1 will indicate that they have a great deal to offer *all* specialized functions of an organization.

Traditionally, and presently in many organizations, these functions have been placed under a controller. There have been good reasons for such arrangements, and in some firms they may continue to be quite adequate. The controller, being responsible for accounting, budgeting, and other internal financial control, has headed the functions in which the heaviest volume of paperwork has been necessary. Moreover, the controller functions in a staff capacity in serving all departments. His concern with keeping costs under control is another significant factor. Even today, if a controller is sufficiently "broad-gauge" in his thinking, and if the general concept of administrative services is understood throughout the organization, such an arrangement may be quite satisfactory.

But the controller is primarily concerned with *financial* matters—as evidenced, perhaps, by the recent change in title of the professional group called The Controllers Institute to The Financial Executives Institute. This primary interest and preoccupation makes it difficult for the top financial executive, or *any* other functional specialist, to provide administrative services now increasingly needed by sales, production, research and development, public relations, personnel management, and other functions.

An administrative vice-president, in contrast, can be a key staff executive who serves all functions impartially and assists top management in coordination by providing information needed to mold all groups into a closely-knit team.

It is unquestionably true that many controllers are increasingly "broad-gauge" in viewpoint, and are concerned with enlarging the scope of their services. It is somewhat doubtful, however, that even under such an executive, staff services such as systems analysis and data processing would ever be fully utilized for, let us say, sales forecasting, production scheduling, or study of personnel turnover. What seems to be needed is a "neutral," service-minded executive who is dedicated to development of administrative management to truly *professional* status; one who can work with maximum effectiveness with all departments and, at the same time, serve top management needs for coordinating the separate functional units.

Informational analysis

There is growing recognition of the dependence of sound decisions upon careful study of factors which bear upon results desired, and upon determining information needed to understand each pertinent factor. Greater complexity of organizations, keener competition, and more knowledgeable management have contributed to a building up of pressure for fresher, more forward-looking, and more complete information from both internal and external sources. The field of operations research, dealing with just such informational needs, has developed rapidly and has been extended to a wider range of uses in the management of business and other enterprises. The vast improvement of data processing and communications technology has made possible many types of information-gathering and processing not available before.

This rapidly-developing field will be considered further in Chapter 6.

Systems analysis

A system, broadly defined, is a planned approach to the activities needed to attain desired objectives. Any enterprise operates through a network of systems (for carrying through with sales transactions, purchases, credit investigations, employee appraisals, and many other work sequences). Indeed, the entire enterprise is being viewed increasingly as one complex system, made up of subsystems, procedures, and methods.

Systems analysis definitely has become a field of specialization. Large organizations may have different persons concentrating on master systems planning, procedures improvement, data processing analysis, forms design and control, communications analysis, records and reports analysis, equipment selection, and other areas within systems planning. Each area requires *technical familiarity, objectivity, analytical ability,* and *time for concentrated study*—all in greater measure than the person primarily interested in a functional field of specialization is likely to have.

With impetus from new tools such as operations research and computers, the concept of total systems or master systems planning for an entire enterprise seems likely to increasingly serve as a general model. Breadth of perspective, general familiarity with operations, understanding of the tools for getting work done, and basic commitment to the goal of coordinating all activities to best advantage will be special needs in making "total systems" a reality.

The normal mode of operation of systems analysts (general or specialized) is to serve individual department heads on request, when problems involving systems are encountered. Thus the head of a trust department in a bank might call for assistance in working out a better layout if his department is crowded, or if he suspects that excessive movement or delay is occurring because of the present equipment arrangement.

In many instances, however, systems analysis will cut across departmental lines, and will call for joint study by a number of departmental representatives with the guidance of one or more members of the systems staff. This is now occurring frequently when firms convert to data processing. Top management will often initiate large-scale or especially significant systems studies. In other cases, systems personnel may initiate action by suggesting possibilities for improvement which they have observed.

Also typical of functions assigned to systems specialists are determination of standards of operating methods, and standards of performance sought in terms of time, quantity, quality, and cost.

Data processing

Some of the most impressive developments in management during the past decade can be attributed, wholly or in part, to tremendous developments in data processing technology.

Mechanization has progressed remarkably in nearly all types of office operations. The most outstanding, at least in the public mind, have been developments in the electronic computer field. Processing of data at extremely high speeds, data transmission (machines talking to machines), vast storage or file capacity linked with computers, information retrieval (quick retrieval of information for reference), and equipment linked and automated by "common language" media such as punched tape or magnetic tape, are some of the most significant developments.

In a sense, data processing could be classified as one of the office services and grouped with other processes in that section, because it involves actual performance of administrative operations, just as they do. So great has been the impact of computers and related equipment, however, and so specialized has become much of the work associated with computers, that we have separated data processing from other service units. We shall devote a series of chapters to data processing because of its present and potential effects.

Central office services

We have noted that one means of providing specialized attention to the effectiveness of office work, wherever it is needed, is through staff assistance by systems specialists. The other principal means of achieving specialization in office activities is by establishing centralized office service units. In Figure 3-1, communications, records, and other services are indicated as areas for possible centralization. Communications services include the composing, dictating, and transcribing of correspondence; mailing; message transmission by means other than mail; data transmission; receptionist service; and other services for special communications needs. Records management, broadly defined, includes forms, reports, reproduction of written materials, filing, records retention, microfilming, and related services. Other services which may be centralized include supplies and building services management.

We shall describe and analyze means of providing services in a series of later chapters. The basic question of *whether* to centralize such services is one common to all of them. We shall, therefore, delve more deeply into it at this point.

To illustrate the nature of a central office service unit, let us consider a central file unit.

Under such an arrangement, a large portion of all filed material for the organization is pulled together and maintained in a central location, under a file supervisor. When anyone in another department desires a given item from the file, he fills out a simple requisition for it. The requisition is delivered to the central file by messenger (or other delivery system); the item requested is pulled from the file, charged out to the person desiring it, and delivered on the next messenger schedule unless immediate delivery is specified.

Other central service units function somewhat differently, of course, but the relationship between the service unit and the departments served is ordinarily quite similar to the pattern illustrated.

Two limitations in actual use of such central units should be noted. In the first place, it is not likely that all of the office activities mentioned above would be centralized in any given organization. Of those suggested, filing and transcribing are probably centralized least, although central units for these are quite common. The other office activities listed are usually centralized, although in small organizations their volume may be so limited as to permit combination with other activities in a single unit or even in a single job.

Secondly, the centralization of any single office service, such as one of those mentioned, may be partial rather than complete. There will still be a great amount of office activity going on in the various departments—often more than in the central service units. The latter may be thought of as the nucleus of office services but no more than that.

To centralize or not to centralize?

Enthusiasts for centralization of office services often claim overwhelming advantages for this organizational arrangement. But some of the supposed advantages may not be realized in practice.

As a general principle, we can say that if the quality, promptness, and economy of office service to departments can be improved by centralization, and if the cooperation of the personnel involved can be secured, the change will probably be warranted. But in order to decide the problem in a given situation, a painstaking analysis of a rather large number of specific factors is called for.

This analysis may well consist of a point-by-point check of the extent to which the usual advantages and disadvantages of centralization would apply in the light of conditions prevailing in the particular organization.

For any specific office activity it would be well to try to determine how many of the *typical advantages of centralization* listed below would actually be realized and how significant each would be:

Fuller utilization of personnel through more constant and more even work flow (this is especially likely when peak loads of work come at different times in different departments and when these will offset each other when assigned to a central department)

Greater employee proficiency on specific clerical operations

More specialized supervision

Feasibility of hiring people with limited backgrounds and of training them quickly in specific clerical operations

Greater ease of measuring, standardizing, and controlling individual output

More equitable salary administration

More justification of special purpose machines through concentration of sufficient work volume—and better utilization of machines generally

More uniformity in clerical methods and procedures

Less duplication of effort among departments, hence:

> Fewer copies of records
> Less equipment required
> Less space required

More continuous service—less possibility of the interruptions and delays that may arise when specific persons in primary departments must be depended upon

For the office activity being considered, how many of the *typical disadvantages or limitations of centralization* as listed below would be confronted? How important would each be?

Requirement on some work of technical familiarity with subject matter, hence need for performance of the activity in the department needing it

Greater difficulty in communicating between service unit and primary departments being served—problems in making needed explanations, time required for delivery of materials, and other difficulties

Difficulty in insuring that the most important work items are given priority

Given phase of office activity may be needed in only one department and may need to be readily accessible there (such as special files)

Confidential work or records may need to be left in using departments

Possible resistance of executives and of clerical personnel accustomed to decentralized arrangement

If advantages of centralization should seem to outweigh disadvantages, for any given office activity:

How, specifically, could we cope with the problem of resistance from executives and clerical personnel involved as mentioned above?

How completely would we try to centralize the activity involved? How much, if any, of it should be left in each department served?

What specific steps would we take in installing the new arrangement?

Just how would we follow up to be sure that the supposed advantages are actually being realized?

The position of office manager

The reader may have noticed that, thus far, the title of Office Manager has not been used to describe the head of administrative services or any section of this department. A part of the reason for this omission is the wide range of responsibilities assigned to persons bearing this title in different organizations. In some situations (typically small firms) the office manager is over certain functional departments such as accounting, budgeting, credit, and billing. In others, he is in charge of certain office services. In others, he is chief clerk for a division; and he may fill still other roles.

We shall be concerned throughout this book with effective and economical management of office work, wherever located and by whomever performed.

We may note in passing that the office manager of the past is fading from the picture; many of his duties have been absorbed by other specialists and some have been converted to mechanical processing. *But* a new type of office manager—whom we have chosen to refer to as Administrative Manager—is evolving. The successor to the old office manager, whatever title he may bear, is faced with many new and challenging opportunities, and may eventually justify more fully than any other executive the designation of "professional manager."

Organizational Arrangements for Controlling Office Production

Before leaving the subject of office organizational arrangements, it seems wise to examine briefly the problem of controlling the current performance of office work as it relates to organization. This problem was given introductory mention in Chapter 2, and it will be analyzed carefully in later chapters.

In a typical factory, a separate production control department usually will be set up rather early in a firm's development. The express purpose of such a department is to coordinate the work done by all departments, and in doing this it contributes greatly to the overall success of the organization. Such a central department sets overall plans and schedules; then it takes steps to insure that each department does its work at the right time and in the right order so that final delivery can be made when desired by the customer. It may be noted in passing that the work of such a control unit is almost entirely office in character; it consists of preparing written orders and instructions, releasing these at scheduled times, receiving reports on work in progress, and related activities.

Most of the experience thus far in applying production control to office operations has been within single departments. A department head or a unit supervisor, with the help of any procedures and standards supplied him by methods units or higher line heads, usually will do his own controlling in a very informal way. He will assign work personally, give most instructions regarding procedure and time requirements verbally, and follow up on work progress through personal supervision. In some situations, the control may be considerably more formal and precise, but the situation just described is typical.

The idea of a central production control unit for office-type organizations has not yet caught on on any wide scale, although some firms have made encouraging beginnings. Among reasons for this are the frequent lack of time standards for office tasks, the variety in items handled, the fact that single items often take only small amounts of time, and irregular work flow. Moreover, it is frequently possible to establish procedures and thus routinize office operations to the point where detailed controls over current performance are unnecessary. The basic need for central coordination as to time and order of performance is just as clear-cut in office situations as in factories, and one seems justified in concluding that in this area lies one of the major frontiers of office management. For this reason, production control at both central and departmental levels is treated more thoroughly in the chapter on control of office production.

QUESTIONS FOR STUDY AND DISCUSSION

1. What distinctions can you suggest between general management and administrative management?—between administrative management and office management? Are these distinctions important?—why or why not?

2. Why has the field of administrative management developed so rapidly during the past decade? What future do you predict for administrative management? What knowledge, skill, and other qualifications will be needed for administrative management?

3. Where is "the office" in a typical enterprise? What organizational dilemma is posed by this situation? What alternative solutions seem possible?—which do you recommend and why?

4. Since a sales manager is responsible for achieving satisfactory sales results, does it not follow that he should have the authority to determine the information that he needs in making sales plans, to design his own systems (including procedures, forms, equipment, etc.), to process current sales data, to communicate by whatever means he wishes to use (telephone, teletype, personally dictated letters, etc.), to maintain whatever records he may find helpful in his work? And will not the same hold true for the production (or operations) manager, and for other department heads? Analyze carefully with reference to the needs of each such department and the best interests of the entire enterprise.

5. Distinguish informational analysis, systems analysis, data processing, and central office services. Do you find this difficult at certain points? Explain.

6. Build the best possible case for placing the administrative services just noted under the Controller. Then do the same for placing them under an Administrative Vice-President, assuming that either would report to the President. Does it seem likely that both arrangements will continue to find extensive use? —why or why not?

7. What different problem areas are sometimes studied by systems analysts? Why may systems analysts be able to contribute greatly in these areas? At this point of our studies, what do you understand the "total systems" concept to include?

8. Name as many as possible of the types of office services. Does it seem likely that we will see increased use of central office services? Consider the conditions which ordinarily favor such centralization, those which oppose it, and any general trends in organization which may influence the outcome.

9. Should the Office Manager always report to the President? Discuss.

10. Contrast the conditions which influence production control arrangements in factories with those in offices, and suggest organizational arrangements which may be indicated for controlling office production.

Case 3-1. The Childers Manufacturing Company

The Childers Manufacturing Company is a large manufacturer of industrial products, which are distributed both commercially and under government contracts. Its top management organization includes research and development, engineering, production, sales, a controller's department, and an administrative staff department. The company has long been recognized for its progressive management policies.

Within the organization, systems work and other administrative services are performed by three departments: the electronic data processing department which is under the Administrative Vice-President, the industrial engineering department which is under the Vice-President of Engineering, and the office services department which is under the Controller along with accounting and budgeting functions.

The electronic data processing department was established to design and implement a totally integrated information system. A master plan was developed during several months of careful study, and the executive committee, made up of top management personnel, approved it for implementation in several stages. Within the EDP department, each systems and procedures analyst has full responsibility for carrying any given project all the way through—reviewing the present or proposed procedures, establishing new procedures, designing related forms, writing and testing the program, and supervising the installation of the new procedures in actual operation.

The industrial engineering department has authority for general systems and procedures, factory methods improvement, labor performance and standards, master scheduling, and governmental reporting. In practice, the systems and procedures unit of this department devotes its efforts mainly to those methods, procedures, and systems which are not involved or planned for EDP application. Specific functions of the latter group include procedures analysis and manuals, forms design and control, reports control, and methods improvement in non-EDP clerical operations. On some projects this group has worked jointly with EDP systems personnel, but it tends to follow what is believed to be top management's desire to leave to EDP any project which might have potentialities for conversion to that equipment in the near future.

The office services department provides a variety of clerical services to all other departments. These include technical publications, reproduction services, central stenographic service, and a central file unit. The office services manager has experienced difficulty in obtaining support for mechanization of a number of activities for which he is responsible. Reasons usually given are the possibility of rather early conversion to EDP or possible conflict with the implementation of the master systems plan to which the management has committed itself. The industrial engineering department makes some studies of possibilities for office mechanization but tends to shy away from any project that seems to have much potential for EDP conversion.

Problems and questions:

a. What problems if any now seem to exist in the provision for systems analysis and office services in the Childers company?

b. Are the problems mentioned of a nature that they can be "lived with" until full implementation of the master systems plan?

c. Would you recommend certain changes in the manner in which the functions involved are now being performed or in the responsibility for them? If so, what changes?

Case 3-2. The Melton Manufacturing Company

All files of the Melton Manufacturing Company are now decentralized; this has been the situation for many years.

Recently a combination of crowded conditions and mounting costs have caused management to explore various avenues for possible relief. One such avenue that is being considered is centralization of a number of office services, among them filing.

The work of studying the files organization has been made a project of a special committee of junior executives. The chief action taken at the first meeting of the committee was the preparation of a statement that the principal objectives with regard to filing must be to maintain high standards of service to departments, to reduce the costs and crowded conditions that led to the investigation, and to consider supervisory and employee reactions to any changes that might be proposed. Individual assignments to members of the committee also were made.

The following tentative findings were reported at the second meeting of the committee:

Some space formerly used for a stockroom could be converted for use as filing space adequate to house about seventy-five per cent of the file cabinets now in use in different departments. The stockroom could be moved to a basement area which could be easily adapted.

A rough appraisal of labor requirements indicates that while many office employees in the various departments would be relieved of filing responsibilities, the need for these employees to perform other duties and to handle expanding volume would make it difficult to release many of them for the proposed new filing departments.

File service to the various departments probably could actually be improved except in certain departments which make heavy and constant use of files.

Opportunity to reduce duplicate filing of multiple copies of material seems great; on many of the forms in use the practice has been to send duplicate copies to several departments.

The initial reactions of department heads and of departmental clerks who now do some filing were not highly enthusiastic when the possibility of centralization of files was mentioned to them by members of the study committee.

Problems and questions:

a. Based on the preliminary analysis by the committee, does centralization of files seem warranted?

b. Should the committee attempt to obtain further information? If you think so, indicate specific types of information needed.

Case 3-3. Comparison of Organizational Arrangements

In the organization of a medium-sized food manufacturing concern, the Controller heads up a department which includes the following sections: Accounting, Budgeting, Taxes, Internal Auditing and Systems (combined), Data Processing, and Office Services.

In a medium-sized insurance company, the Administrative Vice-President heads up a department which includes: Planning and Research, Systems and Procedures, Data Processing, Office Services, and Personnel Management.

Problems and questions:

a. Suggest probable reasons for the arrangement found in each of these firms for Systems, Data Processing, and Office Services. Can the variations be explained by the differences in type of firm? How adequately are these services likely to be provided for in each arrangement?

b. In the food manufacturing firm, the head of the combined Internal Auditing and Systems section has noted that in most firms, internal auditing is a separate department to encourage independent checking and appraisal, but he asks, "Who else is in a better position to spot systems defects than the Internal Auditors?" Do you believe this arrangement to be a sound one, and do you agree with the reasoning of the section head?

c. In the insurance company, how can you explain the presence of Personnel and Planning and Research under the Administrative Vice-President? Can you see advantages?—disadvantages?

4

OFFICE JOB DESIGN

Individual job content · Job enlargement · Basic patterns of work subdivision and conditions justifying each

Individual Job Content

The treatment of organization in the two preceding chapters dealt mainly with the structure of the entire organization and with the place of office work in the structure. The principles considered were for the most part those involved in setting up and coordinating entire departments and other units of organization.

Management must also organize work at the individual job level; it must break departmental functions down into man-sized jobs. In most firms, this phase of organizing has received only scant attention. This is unfortunate because at the job level may lie some of the best "pay dirt" in terms of motivation and work flow.

One of the axioms of business in the United States has been that efficiency is increased by specialization. Accordingly, many jobs have been broken down into simple, repetitive tasks that workers can learn easily and perform rapidly. Each employee does a single operation and then passes the work on to the person who is to handle the next operation. The "production-line" approach was originated in factories, but offices probably now use it almost as extensively as factories.

The benefits of specialization are real and significant. Complex undertakings can be broken down and accomplished effectively by joint effort. Skill and dexterity usually can be increased when employees specialize in single operations. Employment and training problems tend to be simplified, and this may be especially desirable when business is booming and when qualified clerical workers are at a premium. The trend toward increased mechanization is generally favorable to specialization, for the more costly equipment often can be justified only when work of a given type is concentrated and specialized.

However, some executives are beginning to have doubts. They have found that in many operations there is a point at which specialization ceases to pay. Benefits such as those described may be outweighed by loss of worker interest and understanding, and by the introduction of work flow problems such as excessive work movement, delay, checking, and familiarization time required for each employee to become acquainted with each work item processed.

The basic problem, as more and more executives see it, is not whether to accept or reject specialization but how far to carry it.

One of the most promising approaches to job design lies in recent and current experiments with *job enlargement* or deliberate broadening of narrowly specialized jobs to a degree where they become more challenging and meaningful while retaining specialization actually needed.

Job Enlargement

In recent years several firms have conducted enlightening studies with regard to job enlargement, and some have gone so far as to broaden the scope of most of their jobs. It is likely that many other firms have broadened particular jobs which caused problems, without consciously viewing their efforts as job enlargement.

The International Business Machines Corporation conducted pioneering experiments with job enlargement in manufacturing operations during the late 1940's. The jobs of machine operators were broadened to include sharpening their own tools, setting up machines, operating machines, and inspecting finished work. Other jobs were similarly enlarged. Results included lower costs, better quality work, less idle time for machines and operators, and enriched jobs for workers through the introduction of interest, variety, and responsibility not present before.[1]

The Detroit Edison Company conducted some of the first and most comprehensive studies of job enlargement in the office field. Illustrative of early efforts to broaden jobs were a change in a procedure wherein billing machine operators checked their completed bills and assumed final responsibility instead of having separate people do the checking, a revised procedure in which typists would run a section of past-due bills on a tabulating machine in addition to basic typing duties, and establish-

[1] Charles R. Walker, "The Problem of the Repetitive Job," *Harvard Business Review*, May, 1950. Descriptions of the IBM experience and of later experiences of several other enterprises with job enlargement are presented in Charles R. Walker, *Modern Technology and Civilization* (New York: McGraw-Hill Book Company, Inc., 1962), pp. 119-136.

ment of a machine-job classification which required each operator to learn to perform any job in the group. Results included renewed interest, better teamwork, improved quality, greater flexibility, and lower average billing costs per customer.[2]

The Colonial Life Insurance Company has utilized job enlargement in a number of departments. Faced with a high error rate and high personnel turnover in a highly fragmented underwriting clerical procedure, they established a job title of application control clerk and assigned to each clerk an alphabetical portion of applications received, for complete processing of all steps except that of approval by a professional underwriter. Salary upgrading was then necessary. The reduction in turnover alone was found to more than offset the differential in salary, however, and errors have been reduced, a better grade of employee attracted, job satisfaction increased, and other benefits realized.[3]

The aircraft carrier, *USS Franklin D. Roosevelt,* had a staff of 17 personnel men and trainees who processed transfers, re-enlistments, receipts, separations, leaves, and other personnel services for 2400 enlisted crew members. Work was divided into 12 separate jobs, all quite routine; crew men had to go from desk to desk to have papers processed, morale of personnel men was low, and workload varied greatly among the jobs from time to time. The personnel office was reorganized into four identical record units, each staffed by a personnel man and a trainee who were responsible for processing all personnel transactions for an alphabetical segment of about 600 crew members. Results included better service to crew members, less coordination required, more equitable work load, and greatly increased enthusiasm and sense of responsibility on the part of the personnel men—as evidenced by more frequent reference to "my men" rather than seeing crew members merely as names on pieces of paper.[4]

Evidence such as that gained from these and other experiences suggests strongly that traditional ideas regarding specialization need to be reconsidered. Most enterprises probably have suffered in some measure from the disease of overspecialization.

Job enlargement is not without its costs, and these will be examined in succeeding pages. As suggested previously, the problem is not whether to accept or discard specialization in its entirety. Rather it is a matter of being willing to take a fresh look at former assumptions of the more

[2] J. Douglas Elliott, "Increasing Office Productivity Through Job Enlargement," *AMA Office Management Series, No. 134.*

[3] Robert H. Guest, "Job Enlargement—A Revolution in Job Design," *Personnel Administration,* Vol. 20, No. 2.

[4] William E. Pink, "Wearing Five Hats in Place of Two!" *Office Executive,* September, 1961.

specialization the better, and of finding more effective means of determining the form and degree of specialization to be provided.

The decision in what form and to what degree to specialize must be made separately for each job. Much additional research is needed before generalizations can be made with confidence, but sufficient experience has been accumulated to indicate certain patterns and guiding principles. These will now be considered.

Basic Patterns of Work Subdivision and Conditions Justifying Each

In order to decide both the form and the degree of job specialization appropriate, it is helpful to think in terms of basic patterns by which work may be subdivided. For office work, these may be classified under two principal headings—*serial* and *parallel*.[5] Other arrangements seem to be merely modifications of these basic types.

The serial plan of work subdivision involves breaking work down into a series of small jobs and having each unit of work (customer's order, policy, and so forth) move progressively from job to job until final completion. All work of the same general type follows the same channel; each worker is a specialist on his small segment of work. This is the production-line approach—the same basic plan used in factory mass production. It is not uncommon in a large office for a single customer's order to pass through the hands of fifty or more people; perhaps one types the order, another records the information on punch cards, another checks the invoice, and others make various separate contributions.

The parallel plan divides total cases to be processed into two or more parts and assigns each part to a separate unit or work team, which completes all steps on that group of cases. Each worker will normally perform a series of work steps on the cases assigned to his unit rather than just one step on all such cases as called for under a serial arrangement. Cases may be split up either on the basis of distinguishing features of the work itself (by territory, clientele, type of case, size of case) or on a purely arbitrary basis (by chance, order number, letter of the alphabet, and so forth).

The two basic arrangements are illustrated in Figure 4-1, using the example of a computer programming procedure that is divided into three principal steps. Under the serial arrangement, each person does only one of the programming steps on a project before sending the work

[5] For what is probably the best discussion of these and other possible bases for work subdivision, see Henry E. Niles, Mary Cushing Niles, and James C. Stephens, *The Office Supervisor* (3rd ed.) (New York: John Wiley & Sons, Inc., 1959), Ch. 16. Another useful source is the U. S. Bureau of the Budget bulletin, *Production Planning and Control in Office Operations, Part I.*

along—but he performs this step on all projects. Under the parallel arrangement, each person does the full series of programming steps on projects arising in one of the three divisions of the enterprise. While Figure 4-1 shows the separate work steps as being performed by single individuals, the principle would be the same if Martin (for example) headed a small unit of employees instead of doing all the work himself. Under the parallel plan, each individual would still perform a wider range of work steps than under the serial plan—usually a series of steps constituting one stage, coordinated closely with the steps performed by other members of his unit.

| | | Work Subdivision Arrangement | | |
| | | Parallel Plan | | |
Programming Step	Serial Plan	Western Division	Central Division	Eastern Division
Problem Definition	Martin	Martin	Bailey	Tucker
Flow Charting Block Diagramming	Bailey	Martin	Bailey	Tucker
Coding Testing	Tucker	Martin	Bailey	Tucker

Figure 4-1. Comparison of individual assignments in a computer programming unit under serial and parallel plans

A special application of the parallel plan which can sometimes have great value is that of setting up one or more units for "clear track" or routine cases and a separate unit for difficult or problem cases. Niles compares this approach to the use of fast and slow lanes on a highway which make it less likely that a slow truck can hold up fast traffic.[6] Routine cases can move rapidly over the "clear track" without being held up by problem cases; the result can be much faster processing of the majority of cases handled since most are routine. Another important value of the "clear track" unit can be its use in training new employees.

Despite what may be an impending shift in emphasis toward enlarging jobs, as considered earlier in the chapter, the choice between serial and parallel plans of subdividing work is seldom easy. Each arrangement has distinct advantages.

The matter of chief concern probably should be the firm's own objectives, particularly with regard to the relative importance of the features

[6] Henry E. Niles, M. C. H. Niles, and James C. Stephens, *op. cit.*, p. 179.

of quality, costs, and promptness of service to customers, and with regard to the satisfaction of employee interests, stockholder interests, and any other interests recognized. Only a firm's own management can determine the importance of these factors in a given situation.

With its own purposes and needs in mind, the management of a firm can derive much guidance from examining general conditions which seem to point toward the use of one or the other of the basic arrangements. These conditions will now be summarized for both serial and parallel arrangements.

Conditions pointing toward use of serial plan

Subdividing work on a serial—or production-line—basis may be desirable where one or more of the following conditions are considered to be of key importance:

1. Where skill and dexterity on specific clerical operations are considered more important than possession of an overall picture, and where a high degree of specialization is necessary to acquire the desired clerical skill.

2. Where training must be kept simple and brief, perhaps because of either a desire for training economies, a scarcity of high-grade employees who could absorb more, or a need that is only temporary.

3. Where job content is so complex as to discourage employees and keep turnover high, and where simplifying job duties would increase the employee's feelings of self-confidence and personal security in the job.

4. Where scarce or highly-rated skills are required for certain phases of the work and where it is advantageous to use specialists full-time on these phases, while assigning newcomers and persons with lower-grade skills to other phases.

5. Where concentrating the work volume for a given type of work is necessary to justify mechanizing it, and where mechanizing would be clearly advantageous, or where machine costs are so great that constant utilization must be sought.

6. Where assurance of uniformity in handling certain phases of work is so important as to justify making them the sole responsibility of specific individuals.

7. Where there would be a serious problem of loss of time in changing from one operation to another.

8. Where fluctuations in volume of different work flows would offset each other if combined into a single flow—such as that formed by setting up a central filing unit on which some departments would make heaviest demands on Monday, others on Tuesday, etc., with the overall result of full utilization of filing personnel and equipment.

9. Where volume of single operations is ample to keep separate employees fully occupied in performing them. (This factor *must* be present if operations are to be completely serialized.)

Conditions pointing toward use of parallel plan

Subdividing work on a parallel basis may be desirable when one or more of the following conditions are considered to be of key importance:

1. Where single operations are so routine and repetitive in nature as to be monotonous, and where greater variety in duties would increase worker interest.

2. Where thorough understanding and familiarity with subject matter being handled (orders, adjustments, credit approval, and so forth) are desired more than higher skill on specific clerical operations (such as typing).

3. Where "compartmentalized thinking" has been a problem, either on the part of workers or supervisors, or both—and where a better overall picture would be likely to improve relationships among departments, increase feeling of responsibility for overall results, provide better background for promotions, or bring other advantages.

4. Where errors caused by narrow view or lack of understanding have been a problem.

5. Where the elapsed time from the beginning to the end of a transaction needs to be reduced—through less delay and less travel time from work station to work station, and through less familiarization time since only one person must take the time to become familiar with a case being processed.

6. Where elaborate controls and much duplicate checking between steps have been the practice.

7. Where it is felt that individual satisfaction could be increased through association with others in a small, closely-knit unit which would foster team spirit and group solidarity.

8. Where friendly rivalry or competition among parallel units could have strong motivating effect.

9. Where fluctuations in volume of different work flows can be dealt with most effectively through flexible work assignments and versatile employees who can be shifted about as needed.

General considerations in work subdivision

In addition to conditions such as these, which seem to point rather directly toward either the serial plan or the parallel plan, there are other factors that probably should be considered.

The trend in progressive thinking toward job enlargement is only one facet of a broader trend—that of more employee-centered thinking on the part of management generally. Experience has shown that employee morale and the will to work are the major determinants in productivity, quality, dependability, waste, turnover, and absenteeism. To the extent that employee morale can be improved by modification of job content, this factor probably should be heavily weighted in any analysis of pros and cons of a given method of work subdivision. This probably suggests that the parallel plan would justify much wider use than it has yet found in the typical organization.

In situations where a rather high degree of serialization seems justified, a firm may be able to combat monotony and compartmentalized thinking by such means as job rotation, better acquainting of employees with other phases of work, and better communication regarding the progress of the company and of the particular employee. Better selection can minimize the number who are dead-ended in routine jobs although they have the capacity to move on to higher jobs. Better programs of training, performance rating, transfer, and promotion can make it unlikely that any employee will be forgotten.

It was suggested earlier that any given firm is likely to find uses for both the serial and the parallel arrangements. Certain large-volume operations may be serialized, while the volume on others may be so small that they must be combined with other operations in order to constitute a full-time job. Some steps may be serialized in order to justify the purchase of expensive machines, even though the general pattern may be parallel; the same action may be taken in order to justify centralizing a particular office service such as filing or mailing. Beginners, temporary workers, and workers having limited ability may be given assignments on a serial basis; experienced career employees and others who show promise may be given parallel assignments which include a rather wide range of work steps and responsibilities. Still other combinations are likely to appear logical after careful analysis.

There are other management decisions which must be made at the same time with those on work subdivision. Layout must be made to fit; a serial plan calls for a straight-line layout in which, at least ideally, work can be passed from desk to desk with a minimum of travel and delay; a parallel plan, in contrast, will usually require that each work station be located and equipped as a single, complete unit with everything needed for the sequence of work steps involved.

Form and procedure changes may point the way for eliminating, combining, or rearranging work steps; in any case, needed alterations in forms and procedures should be made when work assignments are changed —whatever the reason.

Performance standards may be materially affected by changes in work subdivision. Techniques for checking both the quantity and the quality of work may have to be changed. It may be noted in passing that with greater use of the parallel plan, these techniques tend to be simplified; this arises from the fact that duplicate checking is avoided and that broader work units can be checked.

The content of supervisory jobs

Before leaving the subject of work subdivision, brief attention to the problem as it appears at the supervisory job level seems warranted.

The job enlargement movement, mentioned in connection with operative jobs, which is still struggling for a foothold at that level in most organizations, is much more firmly established at the supervisory level. In an effort to make the supervisor a real part of management, progressive concerns of all types are widening the responsibilities assigned to him.

This may be due in part to the possibility of unionization of supervisors and foremen; but it probably should be attributed in a greater degree to management realization that many decisions are best made near the point of performance and that supervisors can hardly be expected to represent company interests unless they are drawn all the way into the management partnership.

Whatever the reasons, supervisors more and more are being given increased responsibility in such areas as hiring, training, counseling, salary administration, handling of grievances, budgeting, work simplification, and even limited policy determination. Many of these functions were well on the way to being taken over by staff or functional departments such as personnel and methods. In recent years, the emphasis has changed. The staff unit still has a vital role to play, but this role, increasingly, is one of developing and assisting supervisors and department heads to assume greater direct responsibility for operations in their own units.

If the trend toward greater use of parallel subdivision of work continues, the effect is certain to be that of developing broader-gauge supervisors. This is particularly true where units are made responsible for carrying all cases for a certain territory (or product class, order number group, or the like) through a full sequence of work steps, thus enabling supervisor and employees to see the complete picture.

Closing observations on overspecialization

An interesting discussion of the compartmentalized thinking that accompanies overspecialization at any level was included in an article by R. C. Davis.[7] In this article, Professor Davis reproduced a group of sketches of "Dream Airplanes" which were circulated at Wright Field during World War II. The sketches showed one person's impressions of how an airplane might look if each of the special groups participating in design had its way. The stress group would make the frame out of I-beams; the plane might never get off the ground but at least no "hot" pilot could crack it up. The production engineering group would build the design

---

[7] R. C. Davis, "The Specialist," *Advanced Management,* June, 1951.

around a two-by-four for the body and a couple of slats for the tail—and there would be little question regarding ability to produce 50,000 planes of that particular design in a day. The armament group wanted fire power; the plane might become a permanent fortification and a sitting duck, but in any event it would bristle with guns. Other special groups had similarly exaggerated ideas about the importance of their own specialties.

It takes only a little imagination to see how the same tendency to magnify one's special field is just as characteristic of office operations and office management. To a file supervisor, the main reason for the firm's existence may seem to be the creation, storage, and disposal of records; production, sales, finance, and other departments should accommodate themselves to the convenience of the records department. To a statistical clerk, the epitome of success for the firm may be the installation of punched card equipment. To the credit man, all accounts receivable should be strictly of the blue chip variety—whether the firm has many credit customers is relatively unimportant.

The joint efforts of a large number of specialists at work have been compared by Peter Drucker with a symphony orchestra. The similarity is striking if one thinks about the systems that unite the efforts of group members—but the analogy may end there. While the tympani player must be able to read the score and must know it well enough so that he can come in at the right moment, the assembly worker or the records clerk has no more than a superficial knowledge of the next job in line and may find it difficult to see any sense, order, and purpose in what he does.

It is therefore heartening to see the attention now being given to the problem of overspecialization. Some of the keys to this problem have been examined in this chapter. Much additional research is needed, both in increasing general understanding of the problem and in reaching satisfactory solutions to it in individual firms.

QUESTIONS FOR STUDY AND DISCUSSION

1. Which logically should be planned first—the functions of entire departments or the duties of individual jobs? Give reasons.

2. Is the problem of how far to carry specialization on individual jobs a difficult one? Why or why not?

3. To what extent does it seem that each of the following measures could help in solving the problems of monotony and lack of job interest: rest periods, color dynamics, music, job rotation, and efforts to acquaint new employees with overall company operations? How does job enlargement seem to compare with these measures in potential effectiveness?—Explain.

4. Briefly describe the experiences with job enlargement in IBM, Detroit Edison, Colonial Life Insurance, and the *USS Franklin D. Roosevelt*. What gen-

eral conclusions seem to be justified? Can you suggest other conditions in which job enlargement would appear to have little if any application?

5. Distinguish serial work subdivision from parallel work subdivision. On what different bases may work be split up in a parallel plan? Explain the "clear track" variation of the parallel plan.

6. Examine the general conditions which were said in this chapter to point toward use of serial plans and those which point toward use of parallel plans. Is each a valid justification? Can you think of others? How can a given firm weigh and decide between the plans?

7. Does work subdivision (including job design) have both a *human relations dimension* and a *work floor dimension?*—Explain.

8. What other management decisions need to be made at the same time as that on work subdivision?

9. What has been happening to the scope of supervisory jobs? Why?

10. What areas for further research seem to need attention in the related areas of job design and work sub-division?

11. Mark Twain once said, "The law of work does seem utterly unfair—but there it is, and nothing can change it: the higher the pay in enjoyment the worker gets out of it, the higher shall be his pay in money also." Do you agree with Mr. Twain? Why?

Case 4-1. Organizational Planning

Mr. L. T. Miller was recently placed in the position of planning supervisor for the Wright Manufacturing Company. During the several months just ahead he hopes to carry out a systematic improvement program which will include study of the content of individual jobs, study of the distribution of work to different jobs within each department, and study of the allocation of major functions to entire departments.

Problems and questions:

a. What would be the most logical sequence for study of these three phases of organization? Give reasons.

Case 4-2. The Bradley Manufacturing Company

The Bradley Manufacturing Company used a "bookless bookkeeping plan" in which copies of invoices to customers are filed and matched with cash remittances when these are received, thus eliminating the use of the usual accounts receivable ledger.

The company is a large one, and one group of clerks is assigned to filing the invoice copies by customer, another to handling and applying cash remittances, another to preparing statements, and another to handling collection follow-up.

The system is not working out satisfactorily. General ledger controls are often out of balance, cash is frequently applied to the wrong accounts, and errors are hard to trace. The department manager, Mr. Bruce, has attempted to impress the clerks with the importance of accuracy; but he has been unable to arouse much interest and there is much passing the buck regarding responsibility for errors.

Mr. Bruce is convinced that the "bookless" plan is sound for companies such as the Bradley Company, and he knows that many companies use variations of the plan successfully. What he is not so sure about, however, is the way in which work is now split up among the groups of employees.

Problems and questions:

a. Suggest a plan of revised work assignments that should remedy most of the difficulties now encountered.

b. Would the plan suggested be likely to create any new problems? If you believe so, list these.

Case 4-3. Applications of the Clear Track Plan

The clear track variation of the parallel plan of work subdivision was illustrated by use of a fast lane and a slow lane for highway traffic. Another example is the use of an express checkout counter in a supermarket for persons buying a limited number of items.

Problems and questions:

a. Would the clear track plan be applicable to bank teller operations—to automobile repair—to medical practice? Can you suggest other types of operations in which the principle might warrant careful consideration?

b. Draw up a brief statement of the general conditions which may point toward use, or at least careful consideration, of the clear track plan in various types of operations.

Case 4-4. Do They All Want Larger Jobs?

A number of surveys have been reported in which factory workers were asked such questions as, "Would you like to have more responsibility than you now have in your work?" and "Would you like to have a wider range of duties?"

A tabulation of the responses to such surveys usually shows that a majority of workers say that they do *not* want larger jobs.

Problems and questions:

a. Are these findings surprising? Why, in your opinion, do so many workers answer such questions in the negative? Would you expect similar results from a survey of office employee attitudes?

b. Does it seem possible that a very large portion of employees might raise their levels of aspiration if encouraged to do so? Can you suggest certain managerial practices which might lead to changes in employee views toward their jobs?

c. How strongly do you feel that management should be influenced by findings such as those developed from the surveys described? Should any criteria other than the survey responses of employees be considered? What general course of action do you recommend that a given management take in resolving the issues presented, in its own situation?

5

TECHNIQUES
OF ORGANIZATIONAL
ANALYSIS

General approach · Techniques of analysis: organization charts, manuals, and principles check lists; work distribution charts; job analysis; analysis of informal organization

---

The earlier chapters have presented basic principles or fundamentals of organization, with particular reference to the office activities of business firms. Together, these fundamentals constitute what might be called "standard parts" in a theoretically ideal organization. Seldom can such principles be followed blindly. However, when used as general guides or benchmarks, they can have the effect of placing the research and the accumulated experience of many firms at the fingertips of the executive who faces a specific problem in organization.

General Approach in Organizational Analysis

In studying any particular organizational problem, it is helpful to follow a sound analytical approach. Major steps in such an approach, whether applied to organization, systems, or other problem areas, include the following:

State the problem clearly. This step, when dealing with an organizational problem, consists basically of perceiving company and departmental objectives clearly and of stating the problem *in terms of objec-*

tives. Objectives dictate types of work necessary; types of work (or functions) dictate personnel and equipment requirements.

Determine alternative solutions—different ways in which the problem *might* be solved. Try to overlook no good possibilities. In the organizational field this calls for thorough familiarity with organizational arrangements and types, and with general principles such as those discussed in preceding chapters. It also points up the value of using related experiences of other firms in building the list of "possibles." Published material, exchange of ideas in professional associations, and visits to other firms are some of the ways of turning up such ideas. It should be re-emphasized, however, that such leads should be treated as "thought-starters" rather than "thought-finishers."

Get and analyze pertinent facts and determine the best of the possible solutions. Special tools and techniques have been devised for use in organizational analysis. These include organization charts and manuals, work distribution charts, job descriptions, checklists of general principles of organization, and others. These special techniques have much the same effect as that obtained when telescopic sights are put on a rifle; they show the facts of a situation in bold relief and make it easier to determine action needed. Most of the detail in this chapter will be devoted to a description of these useful techniques.

Install the plan decided upon. No plan is a good one unless it is understood, accepted, and made to work smoothly. Problems involved in winning acceptance for organizational changes will be considered briefly in a later section of this chapter.

Follow up and evaluate results, modifying plan where indicated. This important phase will be considered in the final section of the chapter.

Techniques of Organizational Analysis

Basic tools of organizational analysis will now be examined. These can be grouped conveniently as follows:

1. Analysis of formal organization.
   a. Organization charts, manuals, and principles checklists for analysis of the structure of the entire organization and of the relationships among separate departments.
   b. Work distribution analysis for study of work assignments made to individual employees within a single organizational unit, considered individually and as a group.
   c. Job analysis for study of the content and requirements of individual jobs.
2. Analysis of the informal organization.

These techniques will now be considered in the order outlined. In the discussion of each, the question of *who* may use the particular technique will be analyzed.

Organization charts

The most commonly used technique for studying and planning organizational arrangements is the organization chart. Such a chart ordinarily shows the groupings of major activities into departments and other units, and it shows main lines of authority and responsibility among these departments and units. Either functions or position titles may be charted.

Organization charts range from very simple drawings which merely outline the structure of major units to very complex drawings which attempt to include all minor units as well and which purport to show minor variations in level of authority, cross-relationships among departments, and sometimes other features.

The main purpose of an organization chart is to aid understanding of organizational relationships. Experience usually favors keeping such charts simple and not trying to show every possible relationship. A complex chart can confuse more than it helps, and it is impossible to chart *all* relationships in any case. An organization chart, at best, is much more comparable to a still, two-dimensional picture in black and white, than to a moving, three-dimensional picture in color.

One feature of importance in keeping charts simple is the form used. Some flexibility in choice among the many possible arrangements is desirable; the decision probably should be based upon such considerations as clearness, emphasis, and economy of space. Study of many *forms* of charts in use seems to support the following ratings of some of the more common types:

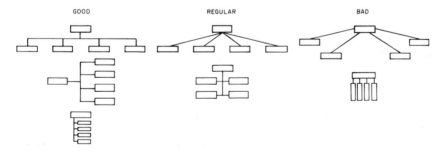

GOOD   REGULAR   BAD

Figure 5-1. Comparison of organization chart forms

Advantages and limitations of organizational charts will be considered at the same time as those for organizational manuals.

Organizational manuals

Where a detailed description of organizational relationships is desired, manuals are used. These ordinarily are made up of organizational charts accompanied by descriptions of the different positions charted. A common breakdown of headings in organization manuals is by general function, responsibilities and authority, and relationships with others. Such manuals are generally kept in loose-leaf form to facilitate revision. They have come into wide use, particularly in large organizations.

To illustrate, an organizational manual might include a chart such as that presented earlier in Figure 3-1, followed by a position description for the head of each major department such as the one for Vice-President, Administrative Services, which is shown in Figure 5-2. Later sections of the manual would present smaller organizational units, first charted, then with each position described.

Advantages and limitations of organization charts and manuals. Principal advantages or uses of organization charts and manuals seem to be the following:

Lines of responsibility and authority made definite and formal. Personnel know what is expected of them, and management can better control results.

Valuable in training new personnel and in assuring continued handling of basic responsibilities when turnover occurs.

Constructive and critical thought required in preparation. Gaps and overlaps in responsibility can be reduced, misunderstandings can be cleared up, and emphasis can be properly placed in line and staff relationships. Also, those participating learn more about the organization.

Principal disadvantages or limitations of organization charts and manuals include:

May increase "compartmentalized thinking" of various specialists and may discourage informal cooperation among personnel in different departments and units.

Give only a limited picture. Do not show, for example, the many informal relationships which must take place daily, and do not show whether the executives involved use democratic or autocratic leadership in discharging the responsibilities charted.

Not easy to keep up to date and tend to establish a status quo which resists change.

The preponderance of management opinion and practice seems to indicate that organization charts and manuals can serve as useful tools of management. This can be particularly true if they are treated only as

VICE-PRESIDENT, ADMINISTRATIVE SERVICES

General Function: To provide information needed in decision-making by personnel at all levels and in all departments, and to promote coordination of decisions and actions of the various specialized groups.

Responsibilities

1. To determine the informational requirements of individual executives and employees in making decisions, drawing upon personnel served for specification of needs and assisting in the development of an overall management information system which coordinates separate decisions and focuses upon the general objectives of the enterprise.

2. To provide specialized study and guidance in the design and improvement of all systems which involve two or more departments, and to provide similar assistance when requested with regard to procedures and methods utilized within single departments and units.

3. To administer a full range of data processing and communicating services as needed by different departments and individuals.

4. To administer central office services as needed—including mail and other forms of message communication, filing and records management, reception of visitors, provision of office supplies, and other services which may be centralized.

5. To assist in establishing standards of performance which will facilitate the setting of goals and the use of controls needed to assure attainment of goals.

Relationships

1. To work with the top management of the enterprise in clarifying general objectives, and in determining information needed for top-level decisions, general systems design, and standards of accomplishment to be sought.

2. To work with managerial and operative personnel at all levels in providing services of information, systems design and improvement, standardization, and other services as requested.

3. To administer data processing and central office services and to provide these services in a manner that best facilitates the work of all other departments.

4. To develop, maintain, and utilize external sources of information which may be needed to support and extend internal sources.

Figure 5-2. Illustration of position description

ıns for securing better understanding and if their limitations are
ıized. The belief that compartmentalized thinking may be increased is being minimized in many organizations by training courses to
broaden familiarity with the work of other departments, regularly scheduled conferences, job rotation, and general emphasis on interdepartmental cooperation.

It probably is wise to regard the work of preparing organization
charts and manuals as a direct responsibility of top management, since
organizing is one of the most vital functions of executive leadership.
Some of the actual work of preparation, however, may be delegated.
Staff specialists who are familiar with organizational principles and types
and with the techniques of chart preparation may be called upon for
technical help; these sometimes include organizational analysts, methods
analysts, personnel department representatives, special assistants to the
top executive, and outside consultants. There is also a growing tendency
to have line executives participate. Each department head may be asked
to make a preliminary draft of the section of the chart or manual covering
his own department. This draft will then be reviewed, discussed with
the department head where desirable, and consolidated with the drafts
prepared in other departments.

Checklists of principles of organization

Another worthwhile technique of organizational analysis is that of
systematic checking of present and proposed arrangements against accepted principles of organization. Checkpoints are usually expressed in
question form.

Such a checklist may be a valuable aid when used in conjunction with
charts and manuals of organization, or on any occasion when an appraisal
or audit of an organizational arrangement is desired. If the user of such
a list has an open mind and a questioning attitude, he can check the
situation in his own firm against the combined experience of a great
many others—experience which led to the recognition of the general
principles involved.

One such checklist is presented in Figure 5-3; the items included were
all considered in Chapter 2; they are merely expressed in question form
here.

Work distribution charts

One of the newest and most promising tools in organizational analysis
is the work distribution chart. This chart is designed for study of work
assignments and job content *within* any single unit or work group. It
shows who does what and for how long or—viewed differently—it shows
how employees in a unit spend their time.

ORGANIZATION CHECKLIST

1. Have objectives been formulated carefully? Does each person understand clearly the objectives of his unit and his own position, and does he have the needed degree of familiarity with broader objectives?

2. Is each of the present organizational units justified at the present stage of growth? Should any be combined or organized on a different basis, and should any new units be added in the period ahead?

3. Is centralization of responsibility and authority at an optimum degree? Is there sufficient decentralization to utilize the thinking ability of all company personnel?

4. Is responsibility delegated effectively at departmental and job levels?

5. Does each person have a clear understanding of his responsibilities and is he given sufficient authority to carry them out?

6. Have line and staff relationships been thought out clearly, and are they understood clearly by individuals involved?

7. Are departments and units in balance? Is each developed in proportion to the need for it in meeting the goals of the organization?

8. Is adequate provision made for "executive succession"—for development of future management personnel?

9. Is there sufficient flexibility in organizational units and personnel to permit ready adjustment to temporary changes in work volume?

10. Does each organizational unit occupy the most logical place in the organization? Consider its relative importance, form and degree of specialization needed, span of control of superior executives, portion of organization served if a staff unit, abilities and preferences of personnel.

Figure 5-3. Checklist of principles of organization

A preliminary understanding of the nature of the work distribution chart may be obtained by reference to Figure 5-4. On this chart, the vertical column on the left lists the major activities for which the entire unit is responsible. The other vertical columns are assigned to the employees of the unit in descending order of job rank, from left to right. For each employee, the separate tasks performed and the number of hours devoted to each task during a standard time period, in this case a week, are entered. The tasks are classified by the major activities in the left-hand column and totaled by major activity.

WORK DISTRIBUTION CHART (ONE WEEK)

MAJOR ACTIVITY	Total Man Hours	Marvin Lincoln, Supervisor	Man Hours	Lucy Kregel, Stenographer	Man Hours	May Robinson, Ledger Clerk	Man Hours	Joe Howard, General Clerk	Man Hours	Melvin Hay, Mail and File Clerk	Man Hours
CORRE-SPONDENCE	44	Give dictation	12	Take dictation / Transcribe	12 / 16					Open and route incoming mail	4
MAILING AND FILING	38	Supervise mail and file	2							File / Follow up / Handle out-going mail / Check file informations	15 / 4 / 11 / 6
POSTING	36	Assign and check posting / Post accounts receivable	2 / 5			Post accounts receivable / Post accounts payable	13 / 9	Post accounts receivable	7		
BILLING	35	Assign and check billing	2	Prepare invoices	4	Prepare invoices / Handle customer questions on items billed	9 / 4	Prepare invoices	16		
MISCEL-LANEOUS	47	Attend meetings / General super-vising and answering questions	8 / 9	Check "hunt list" for misplaced file items / Type stencils	4 / 4	Check credit applications	5	Operate ditto and mimeograph / Replenish supplies and keep stock records / Do messenger work	5 / 6 / 6		
TOTAL	200		40		40		40		40		40

Figure 5-4.

66

The distribution of tasks among the employees in any given work group is likely to have serious weaknesses, particularly if it has never been studied critically. Analysis may reveal that a surprisingly great amount of time is being devoted to an activity that is obviously of minor importance, while at the same time a surprisingly small amount of time is being allowed for an activity of key importance. Specialization may be either too much or too little, or it may not be of the type needed. Such factors as worker interest, utilization of rare skills, familiarization and travel time requirements, and logical training sequence for beginners may be largely ignored. Some employees may be overloaded while others are not carrying their share. (Do any of these weaknesses or others show from casual inspection of Figure 5-4?)

The work distribution chart lays out work assignments in a form that facilitates critical questioning of the existing distribution. It does not provide solutions, but it makes finding them a great deal easier.

Steps in preparation and use of the work distribution chart

The work distribution charting technique is a basically simple, though potentially powerful tool of analysis, and it is particularly well adapted to study of office activities. For these reasons, and because the technique is not yet widely used or known, a detailed description of the steps involved in charting work distribution will be presented.

Instructing supervisors in purposes and manner of work distribution charting. The supervisors of units to be studied can play a key role in work distribution analysis, and both their morale and the specific results obtained from the program are likely to be improved when they are given such a role.

Accordingly, a good introduction will usually include one or more group meetings at which the supervisors involved are present. As a highly desirable first step, a representative of top management may give his blessing and enthusiastic backing for the program. Then an instructor who knows the technique thoroughly and can present it effectively (preferably a company employee but, if necessary, an outside consultant) should explain the approach carefully, using sample forms, visual aids, problem assignments for practice, and any other materials helpful in explaining and selling the program. Ample opportunity for questions and discussion should be provided. Some firms devote as many as five or six sessions to familiarizing supervisors with the technique and with the approach to be followed.

An effective closing for the training sessions may be that of having the same executive who launched the program indicate his confidence in the results of the program, announce at least a rough time schedule, and request a report on results obtained—perhaps one that will show *before* and *after* versions of work distribution charts for each unit, with improvements specifically noted.

Gathering basic data on tasks performed by employees. Results from work distribution analysis can be no better than the facts on which they are based; this phase will be examined in some detail.

The usual source of information about tasks performed and the time spent on each is the employee himself. Each supervisor, after being thoroughly instructed, guides his employees in preparation of a task list.

The task list is an itemized list of the different tasks performed by an employee during the time period selected for the study, and the total amount of time devoted to each task during this period. Some firms use a preliminary worksheet or log such as the daily task list illustrated in Figure 5-5 for daily recording of tasks by each employee. A refinement would be the addition of vertical columns for standard tasks which would merely be checked at times during the day when they are performed, with a column for special tasks, where unusual tasks would be written at times performed.

The task list proper or task summary sheet, such as that illustrated in Figure 5-6, is then used to summarize and total the amount of time devoted to each task during the entire period.

DAILY LOG OF TASKS PERFORMED

Name of employee *Lucy Kregel*   Day or days included _10/3_

Time Period	Task Performed
8:00 – 8:15	*Type stencils*
8:15 – 8:30	"
8:30 – 8:45	"
8:45 – 9:00	*Take dictation*

Figure 5-5. Daily log kept by employee as basis for task list

The period used is most often a week—usually a particular week likely to be typical in terms of volume and work assignments. The primary reason a week is ordinarily used is the assumption that this is long enough to include substantially all tasks employees will ever perform. This assumption may be a reasonable one for most jobs, but in some

TASK LIST	
Name of employee *Lucy Kregel* Week ending *10/6*	
Task Performed	**Hours**
Take dictation	*12*
Transcribe	*16*
Prepare invoices	*4*
Check "hunt list" for *misplaced file items*	*4*
Type stencils	*4*
Total	*40*

Figure 5-6. Task list of an employee summarizing work assignments for one week

there are month-end peaks, and in others there are seasonal highs, lows, and other fluctuations. Where the regular cycle of work results in large swings in volume that occur at intervals of more than a week, it may be desirable to include a longer period, or it may be desirable to make two charts, one for a normal week and one for a peak week, with work assignments altered on a planned basis during the peak or abnormal period.

The major reason for having employees record their own times on task lists is the ease of getting the needed data in this manner. The most serious objection is the possibility of not getting completely reliable information. Proper explanation of the program can minimize this possibility, as can a standard procedure of having the supervisor check task list data, discuss questionable allocations of time with the employee, and draw upon supplementary sources of information for checking purposes.

If more accurate time values are sought, tasks may be time-studied and the standard time-per-unit arrived at for each task, then volume-multiplied to determine how much time *should* be required for the tasks performed, suitable allowance being made for fatigue, delay, and other factors. Time study is still little used in most offices, however. Where it is used, chief attention is given to high-volume, repetitive tasks. Since the typical office job includes a variety of tasks, time study data are likely to be available only for a portion of tasks, if any.

Another approach that may result in time values more accurate than those obtained by task lists filled out by employees is that of work sampling. One simple, non-technical approach [1] consists of having a supervisor make an observation about every fifteen minutes to see what activity each employee is working on currently. The observations are entered on a sampling form by type of activity involved. A statistically adequate number of observations must be accumulated—probably a total of 2500 single observations, or the equivalent of an observation of sixteen employees every fifteen minutes for five eight-hour days. Then the *percentage* of observations when all clerks, and each separately, were found to be engaged on each activity can be determined. This percentage can be applied with confidence to total time expenditure during any comparable week; if eleven per cent of the observations found people on the activity of filing index cards, then eleven per cent of the total time for the week may be predicted for that activity. Results can be quite dependable if a sufficient number of observations have been made, if the observations are on a random basis, and if classes of activity are broad enough to include a range of minor tasks.

The basic source of information probably will continue to be the task list filled out by employees, because of the ease of securing data in this manner. The probability of accuracy of such data can be increased by having workers know that the lists will be verified by the supervisor, and by drawing on such supplementary sources as time study data already available, work sampling such as that described, job descriptions, flow charts, production control data, and other sources of information concerning how employees spend their time.

One other point worth brief mention is the fact that hours for individual employees may not total forty or whatever the number in the standard week. It is difficult to account for all employee time. Some tasks may be omitted without realizing it, especially where no daily log is kept, but some shortage will occur through delays, rests, and interruptions not accounted for. It is probably best to inform employees that they are not expected to account for all hours—that a margin of ten to fifteen per cent is to be expected.

Preparing the activity list. The activity list is merely a list of the major activities for which a unit is responsible; Figure 5-7 illustrates such a list. It is used in work distribution analysis for purposes of grouping or classifying the individual tasks performed by employees.

[1] A more detailed description of work sampling techniques is presented in Chapter 23.

To determine the major classes of activity in his unit, the supervisor, perhaps with the assistance of an analyst, may refer to the organization manual or to job descriptions if these are available. Completeness of the list can be checked by study of individual task lists and, where necessary, the activity list can be made up entirely from these lists.

Preparing the work distribution chart. The chart itself can then be prepared, preferably with the supervisor doing most of the work but with an analyst available for help when needed. Major classes of activity, taken directly from the activity list, are entered in the left-hand column as shown in Figure 5-4; these may be arranged in descending order by number of hours in the final draft of the chart. Employees' names and job titles are shown in the headings of the vertical columns, in descending order of job rank from left to right. Hour columns are included for each employee's tasks, for totals by tasks, and for totals by activities.

Employee tasks and times are then entered in the body of the chart, under the name of the employee performing them and beside the activity classification they represent.

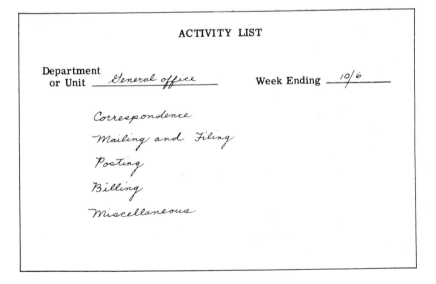

ACTIVITY LIST

Department or Unit _General office_   Week Ending _10/6_

Correspondence

Mailing and Filing

Posting

Billing

Miscellaneous

Figure 5-7. Activity list for a unit

Hour columns may then be totaled. As suggested in connection with task lists, total hours for employees may not be equal to the full work week in all cases. If they fall far under, this may itself suggest the need for realigning some duties among employees, need for better scheduling, or other improvements; but a ten to fifteen per cent margin would

seem reasonable if only because of inconstant work flow, rests, interruptions, etc.

Analyzing the work distribution chart. The chart is now ready for
critical examination by the supervisor. In this examination the assistance
of the analyst may very well be requested, but best results seem likely
when the primary responsibility is left with the supervisor. The degree
of the supervisor's enthusiasm for the project is likely to vary in proportion to his responsibility for it; he knows the details of his work more
thoroughly than anyone else in management; he is the one who must be
able to get his employees to cooperate; he is the one who later must take
any remedial action indicated by the study.

The soundest approach for analysis of the work distribution chart is
probably that of following a prepared list of searching questions which
deal with the most common weaknesses in the distribution of work
within departments and units. Probably the most widely-used list of such
questions is that designed by the U. S. Bureau of the Budget for analyzing
work distribution in government agencies.[2] The questions in the list are
as follows:

1. *What activities take the most time? Should these take the most time?* In
the illustration in Figure 5-4, should the activity of correspondence take more
time than any other? The supervisor who is familiar with the work should be
able to appraise this.

2. *Is there any misdirected effort? Any time being spent on unnecessary tasks?*
In the illustration, perhaps Lucy Kregel would not have to check a "hunt list"
if there were a good system of charging out material from files.

3. *Are skills being used properly?* Marvin Lincoln, the supervisor of the unit
charted, is posting accounts receivable five hours a week. Could he make better use of this time? Melvin Hay, the mail clerk, may be doing a task for which
his skill is inadequate when he reads and routes incoming mail for four hours
a week. Would a switch in duties be desirable?

4. *Are your employees doing too many unrelated tasks?* Probably none of the
employees in the unit charted are performing duties that are too widely varied,
considering that this is a general office unit, although there is opportunity for
greater specialization if desired.

5. *Are tasks spread too thinly?* The fact that three different employees in the
unit are posting accounts receivable might be criticized, as an example.

6. *Is work distributed evenly?* Familiarity with the work involved might reveal that certain of the clerks have to work a great deal harder than others to
carry out their assigned tasks.

---

[2] *Work Simplification as Exemplified by the Work Simplification Program of the
U. S. Bureau of the Budget* (Chicago: Public Administration Service, 1950), p. 22.

The prime advantage of the above checklist is that of simplicity—and this is a feature of key importance when supervisors are to carry most of the program. Some basic types of possible improvement in work distribution are not included, however. For detailed study, a more complete scheme of analysis is presented below, with questions arranged in a logical three-way grouping.

Analysis of the objectives of the unit

1. *What are the basic objectives of the unit—the reasons for its existence?* Are these objectives justifiable? If so, would any other basis for organizing the unit be more effective in attaining them?

The possibilities of eliminating the entire unit, combining it with another, or reorganizing on some completely different basis should not be overlooked.

Analysis of activities

1. *Is any activity—or any task within an activity—of doubtful value?* What, specifically, does each contribute; is this clearly worthwhile? Could the activity or task be eliminated, combined with others, or simplified?

2. *Are time allotments in proportion to relative importance?* Are major activities getting the most time; is this true for major tasks under each? Do any minor activities or tasks seem to be taking up too much time?

3. *Do all activities now being performed in this unit belong there?* There should be basic similarity or logical relationship. Some might more logically be assigned to other units.

4. *Which activities might justify procedural analysis?* Those involving step-by-step sequences and consuming considerable amounts of time should be marked for process charting, forms analysis, and other types of procedural analysis.

Analysis of employee assignments

1. *Is each employee achieving the optimum degree of specialization?*
   a. Are there signs of *overspecialization* (too narrow a range of duties)? Consider the following:
      (1) Is monotony a serious problem on some jobs?
      (2) Does any employee have such a narrow view of overall functioning of the unit that such problems as failure to cooperate and excessive errors due to indifference result?
      (3) Is service slow because so many people handle each order or transaction—with many delays, movements, much familiarization time required?

(4) Are elaborate controls or duplicate checking necessary to insure that the various people involved do their parts satisfactorily?

(5) Do employees lack versatility? Are some unable to shift to other duties during peak loads of work, absences, vacations, or other times?

b. Are there signs of *underspecialization* (too wide a range of duties)? Consider the following:

(1) Is it difficult for an employee to develop adequate skill and dexterity on any specific clerical operation within a reasonable learning period? Does efficiency seem consistently low or turnover high on any job? Do employees on certain jobs always seem to lack confidence?

(2) Are highly-rated or scarce skills poorly utilized?

(3) Does the scattering of work volume for certain operations among different people make it difficult to justify equipment that would increase efficiency greatly? Or does present equipment stand idle for an excessive portion of the time?

(4) Is there a need to place responsibility for certain key operations on one or a few persons?

(5) Is there serious loss of time in changing from one duty to another?

2. *Is the work load distributed evenly and fairly?* Does one employee have too much work while another does not have enough?

Job analysis

The techniques of organizational charting and manual preparation and those of analyzing work distribution have been concerned, respectively, with the structure of the entire organization and the distribution of work to different jobs within a unit.

A third and final level of organizational analysis is that of the job itself. The broader forms of analysis, particularly work distribution analysis, largely prescribe the limits of the individual job if they have been carried out effectively.

Chapter 4 was devoted to basic considerations in deciding the content of the individual job, and these factors have been considered further under work distribution analysis. In Chapter 27, the role of job analysis and job description in personnel programs will be considered.

Analysis of the informal organization

The foregoing tools of analysis are designed to aid in surveying and improving *formal* organization. Formal organization covers all officially-designated lines of authority and responsibility.

As considered in Chapter 2, there are also many unofficial or informal work relationships and lines of communication within an organization.

Techniques of analysis in this field are less easily designed, due to the complexity of factors involved. Perhaps the most commonly-used approach is the *sociogram*—a device employed chiefly by psychologists and sociologists to chart lines of preference. Each employee is asked such questions as "with what person or persons (in the particular group) would you prefer to spend your time?" Answers are indicated by lines connecting the different individuals involved. Formal grouping of persons who have like interests may be found to improve morale and performance. The persons on the receiving end of the most preference lines are considered the natural leaders.

Another useful approach is the *contactual survey*. The actual contacts made among individuals in the process of carrying out a procedure are counted and classified by type such as contacts to obtain information, to work out agreements, or to pass along a rumor. Information is gathered through careful observation and tactful questioning of the employees in a work group.

Research specialists in sociology and psychology are building a large body of knowledge regarding informal organization and the workings of employee groups. It is to be hoped that increased attention will be directed to the development of practical tools of analysis which can be understood and used by office executives and supervisors who do not possess specialized background in these fields.

QUESTIONS FOR STUDY AND DISCUSSION

1. Distinguish between "principles of organization," and "techniques of organizational analysis."
2. Review and state the basic steps of analysis in the general approach to problem solving.
3. Name several basic tools of analysis which can be used in the study of formal organization and indicate briefly the portion of the organization for which each is designed.
4. What does a good organization chart show? What does it fail to show?
5. What are some of the weaknesses in distribution of work among employees which may show up when a work distribution chart is used?
6. Outline the principal steps in preparation and use of a work distribution chart, and indicate who should participate in carrying out each step.
7. What is the usual method of obtaining basic data on tasks performed by employees; the advantages and disadvantages of this method? What are other methods which may supplement or replace the method just described?
8. What is probably the soundest approach to analyzing a work distribution chart?
9. What is informal organization? Describe a technique for analyzing informal organization.

Case 5-1. The Baker Engineering Company

The Baker Engineering Company was founded at about the time of the outbreak of World War II, and it has experienced extremely rapid growth since that time. The morale of the executives and employees is generally high, and the outlook for the future is bright. Several major changes in the organization structure have been necessary during the past few years; most of these have involved setting up new divisions, departments, and units as these seemed warranted.

The management of the company has never attempted to draw up an organization chart or to prepare an organization manual. Mr. J. T. O'Rourke, the president of the company, has a strong conviction that in firms using these techniques, executives become "organization-chart conscious." By this he means that they tend to want to build fences around their departments, to be cautious about offering help to other departments, and to become generally less cooperative.

Certain other high-ranking executives feel that much could be gained from use of organization charts at the present stage of development of the firm. Mr. O'Rourke has consented to place the subject on the agenda for discussion of the next meeting of the executive committee.

Problems and questions:

a. What strengths and what weaknesses can you see in the point of view of the president of the company?

b. What recommendation would you make to the executive committee regarding the matter?

Case 5-2. The Riddell Manufacturing Company

Mr. E. O. Pierce was employed recently by the Riddell Company as organization and methods analyst. He has been assigned no operating responsibilities, and he will be free to devote his full time to assisting executives and departmental supervisors in a staff capacity.

Mr. Pierce believes that the most pressing needs for improvement exist in the management of the office activities of the firm. He hopes to get a work simplification program going which will include procedures and methods improvement, forms design and control, layout improvement, and performance standards. Before undertaking this program, however, he feels that he should initiate study of functions and specific duties for which each department is now responsible. In this way he might be able to improve on the present assignment of work to departments and to individuals within departments, perhaps discovering areas where further development is needed, spotting some types of work that could be omitted without great loss, and promoting more logical groupings of necessary activities.

As a first step, Mr. Pierce has met with the supervisors of the firm and, after considerable discussion, has secured agreement from them to a study of internal assignments of duties within their departments. The following procedure is being carried out in making the studies:

1. Mr. Pierce instructs each supervisor on the purposes and method of preparation of a work distribution chart.

2. The supervisor guides each employee in preparing a task list.

3. The supervisor prepares an activity list for his section.

4. Using the task lists and the activity list, the supervisor prepares a work distribution chart for his section.

5. Mr. Pierce then reviews the chart with the supervisor and helps him to interpret it.

6. Any improvements worked out are noted on a revised work distribution chart which is kept for reference both by the supervisor and by Mr. Pierce.

The supervisor of the supply unit has just secured task lists from all of the six employees in the unit. A summary of information contained in the lists is as follows:

Mr. Smith, supervisor: gives dictation, 8 hours; reviews work of subordinates, 12 hours; meets with subordinates, 1 hour; meets with superiors, 6 hours; gives and directs training, 10 hours; and supervises, 3 hours.

Mary, teleprinter operator: opens communication machines for transmission, 2 hours; keeps records of messages sent and received, 4 hours; distributes company memos, 4 hours; transmits messages via TWX system, 8 hours; handles telegrams called in via telephone, 2 hours; crosstrains, 3 hours; transmits messages via private wire, 6 hours; processes and delivers incoming messages, 5 hours; attends unit meetings, 1 hour; closes communication machines, 1 hour; and types, 2 hours.

Jane, teleprinter operator: processes incoming and outgoing messages, 12 hours; sends opening message and backlog report to home office, 2 hours; files messages, 3 hours; attends unit meetings, 1 hour; closes communication machines, 1 hour; transmits messages on private wire system, 10 hours; types, 2 hours; crosstrains on other jobs, 4 hours; handles telegrams called in via telephone, 1 hour; helps collate company paper, 1 hour; and attends company booster activities, 1 hour.

Carol, supply clerk: operates switchboard, 2 hours; opens and reviews supply mail, 2 hours; types supply requisitions, 11 hours; processes requisitions through post index, 8 hours; handles correspondence regarding supply matters, 5 hours; attends unit meetings, 1 hour; assists walk-in employees with supply problems, 4 hours; makes up sales promotion kits for agents, 2 hours; and files, 3 hours.

Barbara, clerk typist: opens and distributes mail, 4 hours; pays company bills, 8 hours; types correspondence, 4 hours; files, 3 hours; answers telephone, 2 hours; crosstrains on other jobs, 12 hours; attends unit meetings, 1 hour; and handles special surveys and reports, 4 hours.

John, stock clerk: fills requisitions, 22 hours; restocks supply shelves, 4 hours; receives supplies, 6 hours; ships supplies, 5 hours; and attends group meetings, 1 hour.

The supervisor of the supply unit had instructed his staff to estimate the time allocations to duties as just given and he discussed the estimates with each person individually before tasks lists were prepared in final form. In addition to the hours listed above, each employee spends a total of two hours per week on his or her break period.

Problems and questions:

a. Discuss and critically analyze the procedure used by both Mr. Pierce and Mr. Smith in conducting the work distribution study.

b. Prepare a work distribution chart showing the present distribution of tasks by major activities for each individual.

c. Study the work distribution chart and prepare a list of improvements you believe are necessary for more efficient and effective operations of the unit.

d. Prepare a new work distribution chart incorporating your improvements listed above.

Case 5-3. Sunderlin Aviation Corporation

Departments and individual jobs have been specialized to a high degree in this company, where some 20,000 people are employed. The vice-president of manufacturing, with advice from the methods division, recently directed supervisors at all levels to secure task lists for employees supervised. These were to be prepared by each employee from a record or log of activities which the employee was to make up each day for a period of one week. Completed task lists were then to be delivered to the methods division which would arrange tasks in work distribution charts and would then send recommendations back to the individual supervisor as to needed rearrangements.

The chief draftsman instructed his personnel to keep daily records and make up the task lists as directed. Before the week was past, however, he went around to workers individually and suggested that they show fewer hours in certain minor classes of activities and more hours on certain major ones. The reasons he gave were that a heavier load of work was probably coming up in a few more weeks and, besides, some jobs might be eliminated by management if this precaution were not taken.

Problems and questions:

a. Are the special instructions of the chief draftsman likely to increase or to decrease the value of the attempt to analyze work distribution within his department? Discuss briefly.

b. Can you suggest any improvements in the general approach followed by the vice-president of manufacturing and the methods division in trying to improve work distribution? List and justify.

III

SYSTEMS DESIGN

A growing number of management scholars agree that the most significant developments in the practice of management during the next decade may center around the *systems concept*. Previously-existing ideas about the field of usefulness for systems are being expanded greatly. Long regarded as a valuable tool of management in insuring orderly approaches to getting repetitive work accomplished, system is now regarded as having vast potential for coordinating all the activities of an enterprise, for shaping increasingly efficient methods, and for greatly simplifying the work of management.

The *need* for extended use of systems is now accentuated by the existence of larger and more complex organizations, keener competition, and an ever-smaller margin for error in managerial decisions. The *means* for such extension are now being developed to meet the expanded need. Improved understanding of the decision-making process, a broader perspective and sharper tools in systems analysis, and revolutionary developments in data processing methods and other methods of providing information are bringing changes at an accelerated pace.

In Part III, we shall first consider management informational and reporting needs, following the assumption that these must be the "outputs" of systems. Then we shall consider the intriguing possibilities for systems integration which may lead ultimately to the linking of the operations of an enterprise in one coordinated, master system. Different levels of systems will be considered, with special emphasis on procedures—since procedures bring systems down to the level of arrangement of individual operations in logical sequence.

We shall consider both design of procedures and methods, and the expression of procedures in written form for purposes of clarification and communication. We shall study the philosophy and techniques of procedures and methods improvement, both from the view of staff and that of line personnel who may become involved in work simplification efforts. We shall devote special attention to the mechanization trend which is now changing the nature of office operations so drastically, and to policies and techniques of analysis—so valuable to management in harnessing the powerful new tools now becoming available.

6

MANAGEMENT
INFORMATIONAL
AND REPORTING NEEDS

Growing dependence of management upon information • Discipline of information • The basic problem of determining information needed • The management information system • New tools of informational analysis: decision theory, operations research, systems design, data processing • Managerial reporting

More than half a century ago, Frederick W. Taylor defined scientific management as "management by facts and measurement rather than by guesswork." In the interim, scientific management has been widely studied and discussed, but it probably has remained more a dream than a reality. Recent and pending developments, however, are bringing to fruition many of the efforts of the pioneers of scientific management. Probably Mr. Taylor would smile at management's new tools and techniques—although he might frown at approaches sometimes followed in utilizing them.

The acceleration of the scientific management movement is due, on one hand, to growing complexities which face managements and, on the other, to improved means for coping with these complexities. Organizations grow larger and more diversified, product competition grows keener, and the margin for error in managerial decision grows narrower. Management skills, in response, are gradually maturing and management tools are becoming sharper and more versatile.

The evolution of management skills is not yet generally understood, as indicated by the following statement by Professor Alex W. Rathe:

> In the public image, the executive is not yet a man who analyzes a problem carefully and considers all alternatives before making a decision. Rather, he is still the "Daddy Warbucks" type: a man in a black suit who has five telephones on his desk, all of them in constant use. He barks orders into one, crosses up his competition through another, and buys square miles of property in Antarctica through a third—all off the cuff, on the spur of the moment. Absurd as this image may be, the important thing about it is that it in no way suggests or implies the need for information. In the public image of today, the executive does not need information because he has a sixth sense which somehow or other always guides him automatically in the right direction.[1]

The Growing Dependence of Management Upon Information

There has been a widespread notion, shared by persons both inside and outside of management, that executive effectiveness is almost exclusively a *personal* skill, and that a manager endowed with this ability (or who acquires it) will usually be successful and that one who lacks it will be far less effective.

Individuals unquestionably differ greatly in their capacity for leadership. But, one may ask, can the most able top executive decide wisely on whether to offer a new product line if he has no knowledge of market potential, competitor activities, organizational changes involved, or capital required? Can a competent departmental superintendent or branch manager decide upon inventory to be carried without knowledge of sales program requirements, production and shipping schedules, carrying costs, availability prospects, and price trends? Or can a capable first-line supervisor decide how best to assign the day's work volume if he has no knowledge of overall schedules, service standards, nature and volume of current work to be processed, and capabilities of his individual employees and their equipment?

And at either level, even though the manager involved possesses rather complete information—will he be successful in carrying out a plan of action unless he can effectively communicate his ideas to his superiors, asssociates in management, subordinate employees, and outsiders?

There is an old saying that knowledge is power. Management in today's business environment provides ample substantiation for this axiom. The ability to get results depends greatly upon having adequate, accurate, and timely information.

[1] Alex W. Rathe, "The Role of the Office Manager in the Modern Business Enterprise," *The Changing Dimensions of Office Management*, AMA Management Report No. 41 (New York: American Management Association, 1960), p. 14.

The Discipline of Information

Management is expected to make things happen, not wait and hope that desired results will occur and problems disappear. In accomplishing this central task, management must work through people—executives and employees who represent different specialties and who possess varied backgrounds and interests.

There is growing recognition that what an individual will do in an organization and how he will do it depend upon the information that flows to him and that which flows from him. The two-directional characteristic of information flow is a highly significant requirement. The information which flows to the individual is the basis for decisions made and action taken. The information which flows from him is the basis for reporting results achieved and experience accumulated. The return flow is, perhaps, just as important as the initial flow; it is the "feedback" which enables management to adjust plans as needed, and it has an important side-benefit—it goes far in developing a true sense of responsibility in the one who reports on his experience.

It is thus apparent that information exercises a discipline of its own which is quite distinct from personal leadership skills. Under increasingly complex conditions, management must now deliberately design informational systems which will mold individual behavior and coordinate the actions of executives and employees in accordance with a master plan.

Such a discipline of information does not mean "thought control" in an autocratic sense, nor does it mean reduction of personal initiative. On the contrary, it presents management with the challenge of providing information needed by each individual in order to think and act in responsible, self-actuating terms. Indeed, responsibility is impossible without understanding, and understanding is impossible without information. The "molding" of individual behavior, ideally, will be largely a voluntary process if people know what they are doing and why; the coordination will be chiefly self-coordination based upon understanding of the end results desired, the standards which the organization lives by, and the relationships with other persons involved in team effort.

The Basic Problem

An executive who had extensive experience with data processing recently gave a talk in which he described an idyllic picture of the Office of the Future. That night he had a nightmare about an avalanche of data descending upon him, and a thought ran throughout, "Data, data everywhere and not a drop to drink." [2]

Recent advances in data processing technology now offer management a veritable mountain of data. So vast has been the increase that many managements have considered their major challenge to be "slaying the paper monster" which threatens to devour their enterprises by creating higher administrative costs and diverting attention from productive activities. Much attention, consequently, has been directed to "house cleaning" which eliminates unnecessary clerical work, simplifies that which remains, and mechanizes operations wherever greater speed and lower cost may result.

Such efforts have often been successful in achieving immediate objectives. Results are sometimes clouded by experiences where apparent economies have turned out to be false. On the whole, however, many sound economies have been realized from work simplification, performance standards, and related techniques; many more await the management which will make serious efforts to unsnarl red tape and use efficient methods.

But house cleaning efforts focus attention upon information that should *not* be obtained or communicated, and upon methods of doing work that should *not* be continued. Their focus is a negative one which may easily overemphasize economy and underemphasize effectiveness. Their limitations are evident: one does not set up an order-filling system, nor design a form, nor select a particular machine *primarily* to see how economically he can make it operate. Instead, he takes such action to make a positive contribution to the objectives of the enterprise.

The more basic problem, therefore, is determining *what information management does need in order to make sound decisions;* then, and only then, designing reports, systems, procedures, forms, equipment and other means to fill the specific requirements.

Gerald L. Phillippe, President of General Electric Company, recently defined the problem in these terms: "What is needed is a planned system . . . which selects, rejects, edits, and headlines business information— in short, which turns it into *business intelligence.*" [3]

Determining Information Needed

The most fundamental approach in determining the informational requirements of a specific enterprise seems to be in considering the

[2] Owen Smith, "Automating Management's Current Confusion," *Administrative Management,* October, 1961, p. 20.

[3] Gerald L. Phillippe, "What Management Really Wants from Data Processing," *Data Processing Today: A Progress Report,* AMA Management Report No. 46 (New York: American Management Association, 1960), p. 12.

primary phases of the administrative process. If we think of the administrative process as being concerned chiefly with operations, we find two principal types of decisions—*planning* and *control.*

Planning is laying out a course of action for the future. It requires clarification of objectives, development of policies to guide action, design of programs for specific periods, and design of systems and methods.

Controlling is guiding operations in accordance with plans and insuring that desired results are achieved.

It is thus necessary to:

1. Provide each manager with the information needed for *planning* end results and means to be followed to achieve these results.
2. Require from each manager the information needed for *controlling* (measuring and appraising) his accomplishments.

Information needed for planning

General objectives must be set by top management, preferably drawing upon the thinking and experience of others in the organization. Then sub-goals must be set by each responsible member, again taking advantage of the ideas of others.

Business *objectives* are of two broad types: *economic* and *social.* Economic objectives involve decisions on "Who are our customers and who should they be? What are their needs and how are these needs changing? How can we gauge our efficiency, and what return on investment should we aim for?" Social objectives involve decisions on "What are our responsibilities to our employees, the community, and the kind of society we wish to live in?"

Setting objectives requires information from both internal and external sources. Internal experience and capabilities must be known, strengths maximized, and weaknesses corrected or neutralized. But management must also remain informed on general economic conditions, growth trends for the industry, competitor activities, social and political developments, and other external factors. Most managements provide for internal "intelligence" much more systematically than they do for external intelligence.

Then, the *means* by which goals can be obtained (policies, systems, programs, etc.) must be planned, and widespread participation is likely to yield particularly gratifying rewards with this type of planning. Accordingly, information of real significance must be supplied to each manager or employee, enabling him to think in responsible terms. We have noted that management's greatest problem, here, is deciding just what information is needed, and in being selective regarding the vast amount of data now available.

An approach which offers special promise lies in concentrating upon *success factors* found to be especially important to the particular industry and firm. These include key financial variables (such as sales, costs, and prices) which tend to be constant from industry to industry, and key non-financial variables which vary widely and can be discerned only by close analysis. Illustrating the latter are styling and good dealer organization in the automobile industry; innovations in policy coverage, good agency management, and rapid, accurate office support in the insurance industry. Possibly-vital factors can be turned up in consultation with broad-gauge executives of the firm, then correlated with general measures of attainment such as overall earnings and growth, thus establising their validity as key indicators. Once determined, these success factors can be made the focus of information provided *to* individual managers, and of that requested *from* them.

Information provided to each manager should also be linked closely to each program for which he is currently responsible. Ideally, he will have a leading role in planning his own program and setting his own targets, subject to general objectives and policies. The program for a division manager for the coming year may call for a 12% increase in gross volume, a 5% decrease in per-unit administrative costs, and 75% of new personnel to be college graduates. Then specific policies, decision rules, standards, systems, and budgets can be designed, and the organization can be modified if necessary.

Information needed for control

Necessary for this purpose is a reporting system which focuses upon the key variables or critical "success factors" in operating the particular operating unit. Management by objectives, with the individual manager playing a major role in setting his goals and measuring his attainments, can then become a reality. The discipline of measuring and reporting major accomplishments in the areas for which a manager is accountable is usually highly beneficial—developing a keener sense of responsibility than could otherwise be achieved. The best kind of control is self-control, wherever it can be effected.

Because of the immense potential of good reporting systems, the final section of this chapter will be devoted to management reports in relation to management controls over performance, and to provision of information on internal operations necessary in planning.

The Management Information System

The preceding discussion of informational needs for planning and controlling has implications for executive positions of all types and levels. As suggested earlier, it is possible to strongly influence what a manager will do and how he will do it by channeling adequate and timely information to him.

While information is important to an individual manager, its greatest potential lies in the possibility of establishing a flow of information which helps to coordinate and unify the efforts of various individuals and specialized units. In other words, what each individual does within an organization is but a part of a larger scheme or system.

Most organizations make extensive use of functional specialization such as by sales, production, and finance. This is, to a high degree, desirable and inevitable. But as Drucker has noted, the functional specialist's legitimate desire for workmanship becomes, unless counterbalanced, a centrifugal force which tears the enterprise apart and converts it into a loose confederation of functional empires.[4] Other writers have referred to these specialized units as "island kingdoms."

This condition has many implications; probably one of the most significant is the need to interrelate the information which enters and leaves each unit in such a manner that overall objectives will largely control and integrate the activities of all subordinate units.

The most promising solution appears to be an extension of a concept long familiar in business and elsewhere—the *systems concept*. The operation of a business, or any other enterprise, may well be viewed as a single system which is pointed toward achievement of certain objectives.

It is therefore theoretically possible to design an informational system which guides the operating systems mentioned and so influences and shapes them to achieve optimum performance for the enterprise, and to create a whole that is greater than the sum of its parts. Revolutionary developments in data acquisition, processing, and communicating systems are providing great impetus to the development of such master systems. It would be difficult today to find a firm of fair size which is not taking at least some preparatory steps toward developing a master systems plan, aimed at achieving fuller coordination of its operations.

In the following chapter, the potentialities and limitations of systems integration will be considered in more detail. It may be sufficient to suggest here that the concept at this time is more a dream than a reality in most organizations, but that it seems likely to provide the basic model for systems development in years to come.

Who will determine information requirements?

Certain suggestions in the previous section may seem to imply that

---

[4] Peter F. Drucker, *The Practice of Management* (New York: Harper & Row, Publishers, 1954), p. 122.

some all-knowing, master planning and systems group should determine what basic information will be provided to sales, production, and other functional departments or divisions. Such an approach would, of course, be completely unrealistic. The heads and employees of specialized units usually know better than anyone else the types of information needed for planning and controlling their particular operations.

Instead of doing their managing in "splendid isolation," however, functional specialists are now working, increasingly, in *teams*, often with staff help from operations researchers, systems analysts, and data processing specialists. The functional specialists do not relinquish decision-making authority; they are involved, increasingly, in coordinative efforts, and they can often benefit greatly from staff knowledge and analysis. Moreover, a demand seems to be emerging for professional administrators who have both a good grasp of general functional needs and a good understanding of systems and data processing possibilities—who can search out and "sell" possibilities for coordination and for reduced duplication to functional and divisional heads.

The New Tools of Informational Analysis

During the years since World War II, management has developed new approaches and refined certain older ones for determining and satisfying its informational needs. Four such approaches will be considered here: decision theory, operations research, systems design, and data processing. Decision theory and operations research will be described in brief, general terms; selected references will be suggested for persons who desire more complete treatment. Systems design and data processing will merely be introduced at this point, but they will occupy major attention in later sections of this book.

Decision theory places managerial decisions in a spectrum, from complex to routine. At the upper end are decisions regarding the basic objectives and policies of the enterprise. At the lower end are the routine decisions necessary in daily operations. In between are decisions of obtaining manpower, materials, equipment, and other necessary resources; evaluating departmental performance in terms of sales and production goals and other standards; and other decisions chiefly concerned with implementing top-level plans and goals.

Of particular interest is management's ability to program, or prescribe in advance, rules to guide decisions of different levels and types. Thus we find that at the top we deal mainly with "nonprogrammed" decisions; in the middle, with "partially-programmed" decisions; at lower levels, with "highly-programmed" decisions—the latter based mainly upon established procedures and methods for handling routine work.

Alex Simon has compared the decision-making structure of an organization with a three-layer cake.[5] Figure 6-1 represents an adaptation of Simon's ideas in a simple diagram.

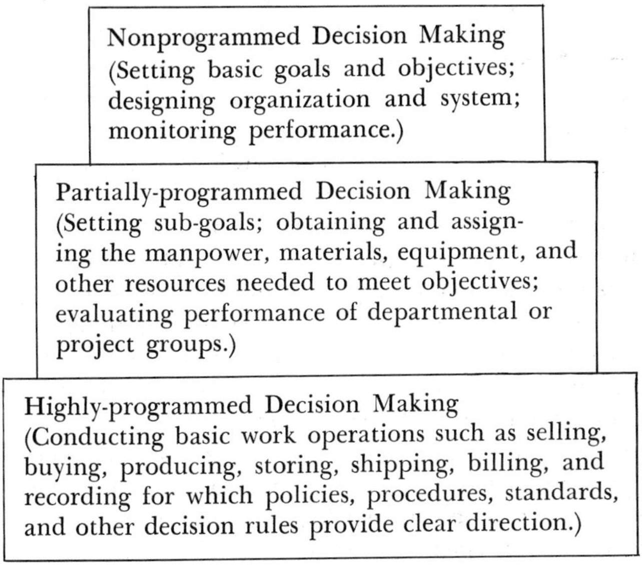

> Nonprogrammed Decision Making
> (Setting basic goals and objectives;
> designing organization and system;
> monitoring performance.)

> Partially-programmed Decision Making
> (Setting sub-goals; obtaining and assigning the manpower, materials, equipment, and other resources needed to meet objectives; evaluating performance of departmental or project groups.)

> Highly-programmed Decision Making
> (Conducting basic work operations such as selling, buying, producing, storing, shipping, billing, and recording for which policies, procedures, standards, and other decision rules provide clear direction.)

Figure 6-1. The decision-making structure of an organization

The "ability to program," in turn, largely determines the potential for mechanization and automation. Routine, operating decisions can be mechanized readily; major portions of middle-management decisions can be programmed and mechanized; top-level decisions can be aided greatly by mechanized information-processing systems even though they are likely to involve many new and intangible factors and to require much human judgment.

Common to all types and levels of decisions is the need for adequate, accurate, and timely information. Even where human judgment is involved to a high degree, better information will contribute to sounder decisions.

Determining specifically what information is pertinent and significant regarding a decision is often an extremely complex undertaking. Presently, much progress has been made in processing operating data, and in analyzing problems which can readily be expressed in mathematical terms. But in the nonprogrammed and "unstructured" areas such as determining objectives, defining problems, and evaluating many kinds of

5 Alex Simon, *The New Science of Management Decision* (New York: Harper & Row, Publishers, 1960), p. 40.

results, the most ardent theorists freely admit that decision-making remains a frontier.

Operations research, as a concept, originated during World War II as an approach in designing complex weapons systems. It involved use of a wide range of scientific and mathematical concepts. It was directed particularly toward designing mathematical models or formulae which could guide actual systems. It normally required a team approach, with specialists from different fields contributing.

Operations research concepts and methods have been adapted to many types of business problems in recent years, after it was realized that such problems can be expressed in quantitative terms. Human judgment continues—and will continue—to play the major and, ordinarily, the final role in most business decisions; but we are finding that judgment can be aided and be made less subjective in an increasing number of business problems. Applications range from determining the optimum number of check-out counters in a supermarket to simulating an entire business operation for a period of years in advance.

Of particular interest to management is the fact that operations research is proving to have great value in analyzing information (what factors bear upon a problem, in what relationship, etc.). For instance, what information is needed in deciding product-mix, the optimum number and location of warehouses, probable results of alternative marketing approaches, and a multitude of other business problems. Factors which lend themselves to mathematical expression are analyzed. Then intangible factors, e.g., many aspects of human behavior, ethical values, and attitudes toward public responsibility are considered subjectively in arriving at final decisions. The team approach is still typical: team members studying a problem such as determining the optimum "mix" of products to be offered might include representatives of marketing, engineering, production, finance, cost accounting, systems design, data processing—and at least one member especially proficient in mathematics.

Systems design, then, concentrates upon *how* to gather, coordinate, and process the information desired by general management and functional specialists. It develops informational systems needed to guide operating systems. In the process, it may stimulate management to define more carefully the information needed and the objectives of the information. When necessary, systems design may cut across functional lines and strive to optimize the overall interests of the organization. Systems design defines techniques to be employed—procedures, equipment, forms, records, types of communication, etc. Fundamentals of systems design will be considered in the following chapter; a major portion of remaining chapters will be devoted to analysis of specific systems and methods.

Data processing involves actual gathering, transmitting, storing, and processing of data as specified in the design of systems. Although constituting only the most impressive methods and tools of systems design, data processing has undergone developments of revolutionary proportions during the past decade; it has given new and vaster dimensions to systems capabilities and to management understanding of information which may be brought to bear upon decisions.

Managerial Reporting and the Information System

As noted in the preceding section, management needs to provide each responsible member of the enterprise with information needed for planning future activities, and to require from him the information needed for controlling his accomplishments. Responsible managements recognize the importance of reports, and recent emphasis has been on improving and streamlining the reporting system. Among the many factors influencing this renewed emphasis on managerial reports, the following three seem to stand out.[6]

1. The long-term growth in size and complexity of many business operations.

2. The growing need for better ways of measuring executive performance.

3. The development of faster, larger-capacity, information producing equipment.

These motivators of management information reporting systems appear to be doing their job almost too effectively. Adrian McDonough, Director of the Taylor Management Laboratory, at the Wharton School of Finance has suggested that "half the cost of running our economy is the cost of information. No other field offers such concentrated room for improvement as does information analysis."[7] Herman Limberg has referred to the increase in management information as a "paper octopus" which, in the span of only half a century has grown to monstrous proportions.[8]

Organizational distance, specialization, and limitations of human comprehension force management to rely heavily upon *reports* in communicating information both downward and upward. Reports are basically summaries of information—at least, they should be.

A system of reporting is vital to any management information system, but especially to a responsible, decentralized management. Decentralization compels delegation of authority and assignment of responsibility

[6] Richard F. Neuschel, *Management by System* (New York: McGraw-Hill Book Company, Inc., 1960), p. 205.

[7] Adrian McDonough, "Today's Office—Room for Improvement," *Dun's Review and Modern Industry*, September, 1958, p. 50.

[8] Herman Limberg, "Management by Objective," *The Office*, April, 1961.

down the organization hierarchy in order to facilitate effective and efficient operations at all points. Consequently, each executive, supervisor, or foreman is a manager—a manager who is accountable for results in his own sphere of operations. It logically follows then, that each manager not only should, but must, report on those operations of the firm for which he has accepted the responsibility and the authority.

The vast amount of detailed information now available from high-speed data processing departments points up, as never before, the need to be *selective* in the types of information disseminated, and to present that information in readily understandable form.

The key or critical *success factors,* financial and non-financial, discussed earlier in this chapter, should be the foundation for selecting that information and data to be reported to top management. Such a data selection process has been referred to as the "dashboard" philosophy of management reporting.[9] This is an analogy of management reports with the concept of the automobile dashboard. The operation of the automobile is governed by a few flash reports such as gas, temperature, and speed. Businesses should be run in much the same way, with the reporting system *selecting the pertinent data* and flashing it to management's attention only when necessary.

Purpose of managerial reports

The general purpose of reports is to communicate information upward and downward in the organization. Reports communicate information upward to facilitate management review and administrations, and downward to inform subordinates and to encourage their interest and sense of responsibility. A manager must report his results to get the support and cooperation of his superiors and employees under his supervision.

A system of managerial reporting thus solves the third problem in determining information needs, as presented earlier in this Chapter— that of requiring from each manager the information needed for measuring and appraising his accomplishments.

In essence, the purpose of managerial reporting is to promote the concept of *management by objectives.* Management in a decentralized organization must operate in relation to objectives, standards, and budgets, not in relation to supervision from above. Management by objectives involves *both* planning reports and control reports. Planning reports establish the basic objectives and goals for a unit; control reports evaluate current progress in relation to the planning reports. These two types of reports will be discussed later in this section.

9 Ralph E. Steere, "Reports and Decision: Russian Roulette?" *Advanced Management-Office Executive,* November, 1962, p. 12.

Management reporting by exception

Reporting by exception is a means of implementing the familiar exception principle—managerial control is facilitated by concentrating attention upon the significant exceptions to planned results. The purpose and objectives of exception reporting are to:

1. Eliminate all unnecessary details from the reports.

2. Inform higher management of deviations or unanticipated trends—then cover these in subsequent reports until corrected.

3. Call attention of higher management to those situations which cannot be remedied at lower levels.

It is apparent that an integrated system of objectives, standards, forecasts, and budgets is necessary to realize effective reporting by exception. Reports are basically summaries—capsules which highlight trends and deviations from planned results, either good or poor. These items, all elements of planning and control, are necessary to allow adequate interpretation of the results, to facilitate comparisons, and to provide a base for future and corrective planning.

Pyramid nature of good reporting

In essence, management by exception and reporting by exception logically result in a "pyramid of reports." That is, reports prepared at the lower levels of management are more numerous and contain considerable detail; as information contained in these reports is transmitted upward through the organization, detail is eliminated, resulting in concise, integrated reports. Higher management is not, and should not, be concerned with the details of the lower level operations *except* where these vary significantly from planned results.

If all details of direct operations were reported to top management, there would probably be little time to perform the necessary company planning, organizing, and general management duties. Therefore, the data contained in various reports are summarized as they move upward in the management hierarchy. The exceptions to standards, budgets, and predetermined plans are the primary interest of middle and top management, while first line management requires the details in order to take the necessary corrective action.

An example of pyramid reporting and reporting by exception is the "report of financial audits" of a prominent insurance company. Three separate reports of the financial audit are prepared before it reaches top management.

The auditing team prepares a *detailed report* which is little more than a compilation of the mass of items appearing on the working papers. The detailed report is submitted to the Vice-President and Controller's office where a *combined summary* is prepared and issued to the Chief Administrative Officer and to the Chief Functional Officer. The combined summary contains considerable detail, but it is more descriptive and reaches some conclusions. The significant elements of the combined summary are then boiled down to a *resumé in memorandum* form which is furnished to the President and the First Vice-President.

Classification of reports

Three basic classifications of managerial reports are by purpose, timing, and style. The purpose is usually for planning or control; timing is periodic or special; style is formal or informal.

PURPOSE: The concepts and factors included in *planning reports* should follow the basic planning process of management. This allows consolidation of the reports as they travel up the chain of command. Such factors include:

1. Appraising the standing of the firm within the industry.
2. Identifying opportunities for improvements.
3. Estimating the effect upon the firm from adopting various alternatives.
4. Identifying the trends in the firm's operations and making comparisons with industry trends and with competitor trends.

By contrast with control reports, planning reports emphasize more historical data in order to develop and analyze trends and performance, and are usually not prepared or reviewed as often. Planning reports are a means by which members of the organization express goals and objectives and indicate the general means by which these goals and objectives are to be reached. Budgets are a typical form of planning reports and usually stem from other forms of planning reports, the sales and economic forecasts.

Control reports follow the channels of the formal organization rather closely and reflect particular areas of responsibility and performance. The specific areas of control may vary among firms, but usually the areas of performance measurement are personnel, productivity, work load (man-hour efficiency), quality, and cost or expense. Control reports measure actual results against what should have occurred—planned events and budgets—and explain any significant variations. Control reports essentially represent that information which is necessary to operate the firm currently, and as a result, they cover a relatively short time—the current month, quarter, and year, to date.

TIMING: *Periodic reports* are scheduled, repetitive reports, usually formally established and controlled within the organization. Normal procedure is to issue these periodic reports on a regular distribution basis to appropriate executives and responsible employees. Periodic reports include both control and planning reports, but because of the frequency of issuance and nature of the information, they are usually control types of reports. Typical periodic reports are the profit and loss statements and balance sheets.

Special reports emphasize certain timely elements and subjects which seem important to management and are needed to plan future action. They are non-repetitive and largely non-predictable. Statistical reports are frequently prepared to analyze, in detail, certain elements of the control reports which have shown that immediate managerial attention is needed. Typical reports of this nature involve such subjects as detailed sales analyses, cost-spread analyses, special audits, and economic trends forecasts.

STYLE: *Formal reporting* is the officially designated method of collecting that information and data needed by management at all levels for proper planning and administration of the organization. Formal reporting is usually recorded, permanent data which follows the formal organizational channels of the organization.

Informal reports do not ordinarily involve official documents. Considerable effort is given to verbal reporting, either in person or by telephone, as well as reporting through the use of notes or memoranda. Informal reporting, like informal communication, often disregards the formal structure of the organization, consisting of superior-subordinate relationships, and patterns itself more to the particular needs at hand.

Major elements of good reports

There are many elements of good reports. Some of the most important include the following:

1. *Accuracy.* Obviously, if a report is worth preparing, the data should be accurate. Frequently, important managerial decisions involving large sums of money are made on the basis of simple reports, and accurate data are a must.

2. *General appearance.* This involves the report format and the style of writing. The arrangement should be attractive, and the writing or presentation should be brief, clear, and complete. Simplicity is a good guide for report preparation.

3. *Relevancy.* Reports should be discontinued when they no longer serve their purpose.

4. *Current application.* Reports should present current data so that timely management decisions may be made and corrective action taken.

The report format

Only certain *fundamental guides* to successful report writing can be considered here. The basic elements of the report format include the following sections.

1. *Summary or memorandum:* Users ordinarily appreciate a condensed summary at the *beginning of the report.* Here, the purpose, objectives, and methodology are briefly outlined, along with the *crux* of the report. Condensed recommendations and conclusions should also be included in the summary. By placing this information at the beginning of the report, busy executives can quickly read the essentials of the report and if necessary or interested, may turn to the body of the report for the detail.

2. *Table of contents:* This facilitates reading by allowing busy executives to get a quick picture of what is in the report and permits them to easily select that portion to be read.

3. *Appendix:* The appendix should be used to keep the technical data and supporting data separated from the body of the report. This shortens and speeds the presentation of the main ideas and allows more emphasis to be placed on those data or charts which rightly belong in the body of the report.

4. *Headings:* Nothing is as dull as solid pages of report text. They are monotonous and discourage the reader from giving adequate attention to the information presented. Headings and subheadings should always be used to break up the text into an easily read format.

5. *Text:* The text should be simply written, in a direct style. Technical language should be avoided when possible and care should be taken not to talk down to the reader. Pictures, charts, and tables should be used to help the text present important comparisons and data, but care should be taken not to overwork these tools. The appendix is the appropriate place for the mass of details.

Reports control

A reports control program is necessary to hold the quantity of reports and the detail included in the reports within manageable proportions. A reports control system will usually improve the quality of the information which management needs for administrative action.

Business data, economic conditions, and organization situations are continuously changing, pointing up the need for continually evaluating the reports system within an organization. Without this continual evaluation, additional reports will gradually be adopted, resulting in an increased cost of report preparation together with a decreased utilization because of the complexity and duplication of various reports.

A *master report control* schedule should be devised, whereby the essential elements of the different reports may be compared and analyzed. Typical elements involved in a control report schedule are: name and brief description of the report, number of copies prepared, where and how prepared, to whom circulated and for what purpose, retention period, frequency of issuance, and cost. In the analysis of this control device, such questions asked are:

1. Is this report necessary?
2. Can it be condensed and combined with other reports?
3. Are all data pertinent and relevant to the report's purpose and use?
4. Can the frequency of issuance be altered?
5. Is the report being successfully used—read, actually referred to, and used in making sounder decisions?

Only through a planned system of report inventory, screening the reports and the data on them, and overall analysis, can a system of reports be maintained at maximum effectiveness. Responsibility for such a program should be that of the administrative manager or some other high-level staff position with sufficient authority to influence organization planning and development, while coordinating information gathered throughout the firm.

Two examples of report systems

Two outstanding examples of reporting systems will help the reader grasp the vastness of this area of management informational requirements. These examples vividly demonstrate that effective and efficient reporting systems are tailor-made for the particular organization. Major factors to look for in these illustrations are the stress on administrative effectiveness and the value of the reports to the various levels of management.

The City of New York [10]

The City of New York created a management reporting system based on the program budget. The program budget sets up goals and objectives against which the performance of the various departments can be measured. The structure of the reporting system is divided into two parts: (1) an annual planning statement for each budgeted program, including objectives and expected results for the coming year and standards by which the results will be evaluated; (2) quarterly reports of accomplishments, in terms of the predetermined standards. It is only logical that a public enterprise such as this base its re-

[10] The data for this case example were summarized from: Herman Limberg, "Management by Objective," *The Office*, April, 1961, pp. 14-25.

porting system on budgets in order to provide both the public and the administration an operational report of the City's operations.

The particular "pattern of reporting" developed by the City of New York is based on the primary elements of the management process: planning, coordinating, and control. In brief summary these elements are:

1. Clarification of mission of each department
2. Review and analysis of the budgeted programs
3. Development of reporting programs objectives
4. Development of standards of performance
5. Establishment of policies regarding administrative reporting
6. Review and evaluation of planning, organizing, and systems and procedures to determine adequacy of meeting program objectives
7. Periodic reporting of accomplishments with respect to objectives
8. Review and analysis of variance from standard performance
9. Follow-up to implement necessary improvements

The objectives of the City of New York's management reporting system were summarized by an executive order issued in July, 1956: "The management reporting system developed by the City Administrator is intended to provide a means by which the Mayor, the City Administrator, and the department heads can, through periodic reports, keep apprised of the accomplishments and program with respect to the Administrative management."

The reporting program of the City of New York has made substantial progress in the inculcation of the practice of management principles. Specifically, such a reporting system has focused on the facilities for compilation and flow of required data, in preventing deviations from planned objectives, in correcting conditions resulting in failures, and has necessitated integrating of systems and planning into the total management process in a continuing cycle rather than on a crash basis, all with respect to pre-planned program budgets.

The Cleveland Electric Illuminating Company [11]

The Cleveland Electric Illuminating Company utilizes a system of management reporting as a *technique to compel performance*. This system is based on the company's philosophy of a decentralized management in which decentralization necessarily involves delegation. It is built around two key elements of management—planning and control.

Planning reports at Cleveland Illuminating are subdivided into three sections: the period 5-10 years in the future, the next five immediate years, and annual budget reports. The first two planning reports are obviously long-run, while the annual budget report is a short-run report. The two long-run planning reports emphasize ideas, opinions, and problems likely to be experienced in the periods in question. The company feels that this type of reporting develops interest at all levels toward thinking in terms of the future. The annual budget report requires that a manager state his plans, objectives, and emphasizes accountability and responsibility to see that events conform to

[11] The data for this case example were summarized from: Charles F. Brunner, "Reporting as a Technique to Compel Performance," in *Organizing for Effective Systems Planning and Control*, AMA Special Report No. 12 (New York: American Management Association, 1956), pp. 161-163.

plans. Annual budget reports are prepared in three sections—progress, planning, and budget support. Budget reports for each division of the firm are consolidated into seven reports to top management, one each from the Vice President in charge of the seven major elements.

Control reports emphasize performance analysis. The Cleveland Illuminating Company feels that control reporting is a solution to the problem of upward communication, in that in a decentralized form of management, reporting is essential for coordination and control.

The particular areas covered by the control reports are workload, productivity, quality, cost and expense, planning, and personnel. Each month managers at all levels submit control reports to their respective supervisors. Ultimately, each of the seven Vice-Presidents prepares an overall report for his major organization element and copies of these seven reports are furnishd to the President and Executive Vice-President.

Cleveland Illuminating Company believes that a system of reporting as established in their company compels a manager to think, that it requires an element of soul searching, and that it compels performance. They believe that with a philosophy of decentralized management, reporting—that is, planned reporting—is essential to the success of the firm.

QUESTIONS FOR STUDY AND DISCUSSION

1. What current practices may indicate an acceleration of the scientific management movement?

2. Does a "born leader" require much if any information in order to make sound decisions or will he make these intuitively? Consider one or more specific examples of problems that often must be decided.

3. Just how would the two-way flow of information provided with regard to a current need for cost reduction have "disciplinary" effects on the individuals involved?

4. Is modern data processing equipment largely solving the management problem of selectivity with regard to data gathered? Is some "house cleaning" needed, also?—Explain. Is anything else needed?

5. Is there a significant difference between "data" and "information"?—Explain.

6. Compare the types of information which might aid a manager in *planning* his future manpower needs with the types which might aid him in *controlling* this important area.

7. Explain the concept of "success factors." What factors would you expect to fit this classification in the men's retail clothing business, in the ready-mix concrete industry, and in the computer manufacturing and distributing industry? How could one best go about trying to determine "success factors" for a given type of enterprise?

8. Describe a management information system. Where, in an organization, should such a system begin? Where should it end? Is there any difference between a management information system and a management reporting system?

9. Who should determine the specific types of information which flow to and from a sales manager (or other executive)?

10. Explain briefly how each of the following tools of informational analysis contributes: decision theory, operations research, systems design, and data proc-

essing. Relate Alex Simon's "three-layer cake" example to each of these tools, with particular reference to management progress in making decisions of different kinds.

11. Why must management now rely heavily upon reports? Explain and illustrate the concepts of reporting by exception and the pyramid nature of good reporting.

12. In what principal ways may reports be classified? What are the most basic requirements of each class of reports?

13. Consider and appraise the general elements suggested as requirements of good reports, and note particularly the basic guides to effective report format.

14. What seem to be the most essential features in effective reports control?

15. Make a critical appraisal of the reporting systems of the City of New York and the Cleveland Electric Illuminating Company, in the light of sound reporting principles.

Case 6-1. Scientific Management and Information Technology

Frederick W. Taylor liked to define scientific management as "knowing exactly what you want men to do, and then seeing that they do it in the best and cheapest way." He set out to develop a science of management which would apply the logic of reflective thinking to determined facts in the solution of management problems. Certain of the most fundamental concepts which Taylor developed are summarized below:

1. An accurate body of knowledge regarding the factors which bear upon managerial problems.

2. Measures of forces which influence attainment of management objectives, and standards of performance and conditions.

3. Principles to guide managerial and operative performance.

4. Preplanning of operations.

5. Definite procedures, specifying effective methods for managerial and operational performance.

Problems and questions:

a. Does modern information technology seem to be related very closely to the scientific management concepts developed more than half a century ago by Taylor and his associates?

b. For each of the concepts summarized, specifically what if any contribution may information technology now be able to make?

Case 6-2. The Lowell Corporation

The reporting system of the Lowell Corporation, a food producing enterprise having some 60 plants in different locations, includes reports from individual plants, reports from each of ten divisions into which the plants are grouped, and consolidated reports from all divisions for top management information. One section of a monthly plant report on manufacturing expenses calls for separate dollar amounts and percentages control, maintenance, housekeeping, material handling-plant, material handling-shipping, carton stripping, bag header work, and overtime premium; and concludes with total actual compensation and total planned compensation.

Problems and questions:

a. How much of the detail in the plant report on manufacturing expenses would you recommend including in the divisional expense report which groups this plant report with those of other plants in the division?

b. How much of the detail would you recommend including in the consolidated report for all divisions which is prepared for top management review?

c. What is the reasoning behind your recommendations?

Case 6-3. Reports Justification

Four executives from different firms were recently discussing the problem of how to be selective in regard to reports prepared, in view of the vast potential of data processing output now available.

One executive described how, before getting a computer into operation in his firm, different department heads and their key people were called together and asked (1) whether they wanted each report formerly prepared, (2) why, (3) what specific use they would make of it, and (4) whether it would be worth the cost estimate of producing it. A sizeable number of reports were voluntarily discontinued, as a result of this effort.

Another executive told how his data processing head had won top management approval for discontinuing release of *all* reports until some person asked for one and explained his need. A substantial reduction of reports followed this approach, also.

A third executive described one accounting report which had seemed to be of doubtful value, even though it had been going to fifteen executives. With approval of higher management, the accounting department discontinued the report. There were no immediate objections, and the accounting head and others concluded, "What a waste that has been." But a certain experience later, where a serious error was made in certain projections needed in inventory planning, indicated that discontinuation of this particular report had "backfired," at least in that instance.

A fourth executive mentioned that one of the members of a study committee which had been established to work on the reports control problem happened to be his company's purchasing agent. The pur-

chasing agent had suggested a close analogy between the problem of
reports justification and that of value analysis in purchasing—which he
defined as balancing what you get against what you pay, and engineering
unnecessary cost factors out of each purchased item. He produced a
checklist of ten "Tests of Value" which had been compiled by General
Electric, and included the following:

Every material, every part, every operation must pass these tests:

1. Does its use contribute value?
2. Is its cost proportionate to its usefulness?
3. Does it need all of its features?
4. Is there anything better for the intended use?
5. Can a usable part be made by a lower cost method?
6. Can a standard product be found which will be usable?
7. Is it made on proper tooling, considering quantities used?
8. Do material, reasonable labor, overhead, and profit total its cost?
9. Will another dependable supplier provide it for less?
10. Is anyone buying it for less?

The fourth executive described how his firm had been able to make
only minor adaptations in the value analysis approach and put it to
excellent use in justifying and screening reports.

Problems and questions:

a. Appraise carefully each of the approaches. What do you consider to be the
strong points and the weak points of each?

b. Is the analogy of reports justification and value analysis in purchasing a
sound one? What modifications in the "Tests of Value" checklist would you need
to make in order to develop a useful set of guides in appraising individual reports?

7

SYSTEMS DESIGN
AND INTEGRATION

The meaning of system · Values and limitations of management systems · Need for systems integration · Means of integrating systems: the master systems plan; the flow of information

---

The Meaning of System

Management's task has been defined as setting objectives for an enterprise, then leading the enterprise in achieving these objectives. This is a task which yearly makes higher demands. Enterprises grow larger and more complex; responsibilities widen; competition toughens; the margin for error in decision narrows.

Confronted by a maze of complex, and often conflicting, elements, management is forced to search for logical relationships and patterns. It must perceive goals clearly, then it must make things simple and orderly through *system.*

The concept of system is a familiar one. Perhaps the term "systematic" has an even sharper connotation. Any undertaking may be approached systematically or haphazardly.

In management, a system may be regarded as a planned approach to activities necessary to attain desired objectives. Consider, for example, a system for approving credit risks in a business firm. The general objective would probably be to screen out the prospective credit buyers who would be unable or unwilling to pay, and to encourage those who would. A sequence of steps is therefore established: taking the application on a specially designed form, interviewing the applicant, checking references, deciding whether to grant credit and if so, how much, and notifying the applicant. This sequence is then followed in essentially the same pattern for each new credit applicant.

Any well-managed enterprise has many such systems. Indeed, any enterprise operates through a network of systems. There is now a strong trend in management circles to view an entire enterprise as one master system, consisting of separate systems for making and completing sales, buying or producing goods, providing personnel, and carrying out other work-sequences. This concept is essentially what is meant by "systems-integration," and we shall explore it further. First, let us consider specific reasons why systems are so widely used in management, and also, certain limitations which should be kept in mind.

Values and Limitations of Management Systems

Systems make the following contributions to management effectiveness:

1. *Focus upon end results.* Purposes must be clearly discerned if systems are to be used effectively. Well-designed systems can go far toward insuring customer satisfaction, reduced costs, higher profits, etc.

2. *Plan of action that is purposeful, orderly, efficient.* Managers and employees are given a track to run on; waste motion, delay, and uncertainty can be minimized; responsibility for specific tasks can be assigned.

3. *Coordination of specialized activities.* The varied and sometimes conflicting interests of functional specialists can be fitted together in an over-all pattern which best serves the entire enterprise.

4. *Basis for control.* Current work can be guided, consistency achieved, results measured against standards, then reported to provide "feedback" necessary either to adjust methods of handling or to modify expectations.

5. *Liberation of management.* Matthies notes that good systems do not restrict, they liberate.[1] They leave the boss free to do what only he can do. He can plan, initiate desirable action, examine the results of that action, evaluate performance, initiate improvement, delegate with confidence—providing he will use systems to do the 90 per cent of the work which does not require his attention.

It is important to recognize *limitations of systems* along with advantages. A system is no better than the planning that goes into it, and weakness in a system will be compounded by repeated usage. A system must be kept up to date, and what was effective when originally designed can easily become obsolete or inadequate for new needs. And no system

[1] Leslie Matthies, "How to Improve Administration: Ten Easy Lessons from a Systems Man," *Shaping a New Concept for Administrative Management,* AMA Management Report No. 56 (New York: American Management Association, 1961), p. 112.

should be so rigid as to preclude flexibility, nor so detailed as to destroy initiative.

In one firm, systems may cover operations like a blanket, laying out virtually all activities in formal detail and leaving little to the discretion of managers and employees; in another, they may be informal, with each employee left mainly to his own devices. Each firm must strive for the happy medium which fits its particular circumstances. A related problem concerns enforcement of systems; better results usually follow from using them as broad guides and "enabling" approaches, rather than as restrictions and rules to be "policed."

The Need for Systems Integration

Lyndall Urwick, the noted British management authority, once said: "An organization is essentially an extremely complicated system of co-operation—in itself a single machine—in which effectiveness is dependent less and less on the quality of the individual efforts and more and more on the logic of the total design, and the provision with which each individual's contribution is geared to a master plan." A growing number of managements seem to be in agreement with this view. Indeed, it is rather difficult today to find a large or medium-sized firm in which some sort of study is not under way to develop a *master systems plan,* and many smaller firms are taking similar action.

The idea of looking at an enterprise as a single, integrated system is surprisingly new and foreign to most administrators and students of management, despite long familiarity with such diverse concepts as solar systems, respiratory systems of the human body, and economic systems of nations and regions.

Traditional approaches to systems design and improvement have concentrated upon relatively short procedural cycles, often limited to "applications" within functional fields such as a payroll application or an inventory control application, which is dealt with as an isolated problem area. In instances where a major procedure or system cuts across a number of departmental lines such as sales, production, and accounting, each specialized group is likely to be concerned primarily with its own goals. Systems analysts, while often simplifying individual systems and reducing duplication of effort, have too seldom had the entire enterprise in perspective.

But as noted earlier, interdepartmental conflicts of immediate interest may take a heavy toll from overall effectiveness. The sales department is likely to want new product designs, extensive finished goods inventories, and prompt deliveries. These understandable desires may conflict with the production department, which likes long, uninterrupted runs of stable designs; with the materials department, which likes to keep inventories low; with the traffic department, which may be inclined to place economy of delivery before promptness. Where a good spirit of cooperation exists, such conflicts can usually be resolved moderately well through special communications effort at the time, although similar problems may continue to crop up, probably causing some loss due to friction, duplication of effort, and lack of overall perspective. In the absence of a healthy state of cooperation, specialized groups may function as "island kingdoms," perceiving only vaguely any mutuality of interests with others.

The challenge to each management, clearly, is to gradually develop a master systems plan which provides "built-in" coordination and subordinates departmental goals to the general goals of the enterprise. Such a "total systems concept" is likely to be merely an arrangement ideal for many years after its inception. Yet, it probably provides the best general model for long-term coordination, operating efficiency, and total optimization of the enterprise objectives. And even though full attainment of the ideal arrangement may not be achieved for some time (indeed, the "ideal" itself may change), current study of any specific system, procedure, or method should be done with an eye to its impact upon the "total system"—moving gradually toward the ideal, being conscious of deviations, and having good reasons for making them.

The river system analogy

Similarity between an enterprise in operation and a river system has often been noted. A river has a destination (or goal) into which it delivers its output. The main stream of the river is fed by major tributaries, and each of these is supplied by minor tributaries which are fed initially by water input (glaciers, snow, current rainfall, underground springs, etc.). Each segment of the river system is thus supplied by input from one or more sources; in turn it produces output which feeds a larger segment.

A man-made enterprise is also a system, although seldom as well-ordered as a natural system. A business enterprise, like a river, has a destination or goal. The mainstream of the business is always *customer service* in some form, and there are usually at least two major tributaries —*creating* a useful product or service and *distributing* it. There are supporting tributaries (or subsystems) for providing manpower, materials, supplies, equipment, etc.; each of these is likely to consist of a small network of procedures and operations.

Another comparison may be pertinent. For persons in sales, production, materials, traffic, manpower, or any other business system to take isolated or uncoordinated action may be as impractical as it would be for a river tributary to attempt to separate itself from the main stream, head for the open plain, or try to run uphill.

Illustrative plans

The Carborundum Company [2]

One of the pioneering efforts in systems integration was carried out by the Carborundum Company. The management of this firm began with the idea that *all* operations in the company stemmed from the customer's order. Further study suggested that all action could be traced to one of five types of original *source data:*

1. Customer order
2. Labor information
3. Materials, supplies, and services
4. Physical assets
5. Master information records

A central data processing unit was then established in Niagara Falls, New York, with teletype transmission facilities for punched paper tape to each of twelve district offices. Four *basic record files* (the master information records mentioned above) were established and stored in the computer at central data processing:

1. Master customer file
2. Master product file
3. Finished goods inventory
4. Orders in process

The receipt of a customer order at one of the district offices begins the operation. A Friden Flexowriter is used to write the sales order and simultaneously prepare a punched paper tape which is transmitted via teletype to the central data processing system.

As the order data are processed in the computer, required data are selected from the stored master files, and the master files are up-dated to represent the current status of customer orders.

An order-action process is initiated by the computer and sent via teletype to the originating office to confirm the status of the customer order. Manufacturing and shipping orders are also written by the computer as a by-product of transmitting the order-action data.

Each warehouse informs the computer via punched paper tape and teletype-writer when the particular order has been shipped, and this information is processed through the computer to clear the order-in-process file and to write the invoice.

A significant by-product of this integrated system is retained data, a history of the complete transaction which is used for periodic processing of sales and inventory reports and analyses. Daily reports on sales are available to management by mid-morning of the day following—a process which formerly took two weeks.

---

[2] Adapted from: "From Customer Order to Annual Report: The Total Systems Approach to EDP" (A Presentation by The Carborundum Company, Niagara Falls, New York), *Techniques of Office Cost Control,* AMA Management Report No. 26 (New York: American Management Association, 1959), pp. 89-110.

The Southland Life Insurance Company

An early approach to systems integration by an insurance company was the Consolidated Functions plan of the Southland Life Insurance Company.

Southland Life consolidated all of its ordinary life policy files into a single magnetic tape policy record which is passed daily through an IBM 650 Tape Ramac system. Punched cards representing policy activity or requested information are fed into the computer during these daily passes of the magnetic tape files. As a result of this simple effort, the computer system performs the following operations:

1. Handles all premium billing, valuation, and commission accounting, file maintenance, and policy dating.
2. Up-dates all policies each day, according to card data input and writes the policy on new reels of tape.
3. Makes contractual changes (changes which are not initiated by punched cards) automatically as needed according to date, premium, and other information stored in the policy file.
4. Makes requested changes in policy status with each daily pass of the file.
5. Furnishes current policy status reports daily, after all up-dating is complete.
6. Furnishes a daily transaction register showing all input, output, and changes to records, serving policy history purposes and providing a basis for detail reports to agents and summary reports to management.
7. Produces quarterly and annual financial reports.

Benefits include more integration or "consolidation" of effort, greater accuracy and speed of operations, daily control, reports and summaries not previously obtainable, and greater ease of conversion to faster and more versatile equipment since the original installation.

The Means of Integrating Systems

A generalized approach to integrating systems has already been indicated. Basically, the approach requires defining the "outputs" or goals desired from the total system, then defining the major "inputs" which influence achievement of these general goals. The same approach then must be extended backward through subsystems and supporting operations. Finally, the different parts must be interrelated.

Two major steps are needed to move toward integration of systems: (1) development of a master plan of systems and subsystems, and (2) development of information flow which guides operative activities involved in the systems.

The master systems plan

A desirable preliminary in developing a master systems plan is recognition of the different levels of systems likely to be found in any enterprise:

1. *The total system* of operations, designed to achieve general enterprise goals

2. *Integrated systems* (or combinations of major, related subsystems) such as the linking of production control with inventory control, or of sales with accounts receivable, or of purchases with accounts payable

3. *Subsystems* such as the entire inventory control system, made up of separate procedures for requisitioning, issuing, reordering, receiving, and up-dating records

4. *Procedures* such as the inventory requisitioning procedure, made up of a series of operations such as checking stock, preparing a materials requisition, securing proper authorization, and transmitting the requisition

5. *Methods* which are simply the means of performing individual operations, such as use of a standard form and a typewriter by a clerk in preparing a materials requisition

An integrated production system (not a total or master system) is sketched in skeleton form in Figure 7-1, extended to the level of procedures. Here, the direct output of the system is the level of production requirements necessary to meet actual and forecasted sales. The production requirements in turn are filled by drawing from finished goods inventory and goods produced currently. Current production requirements dictate materials, labor, equipment, and scheduling needs; each of these calls for further processing. Note that the *output* of each segment serves as the *input* for the next higher segment. Note also the dotted lines which indicate *feedback* of billing and accounts receivable data which will aid in projecting sales for subsequent periods, and of standards and control data which will influence current production plans and requirements.

The flow of information

The successively smaller segments (systems, procedures, methods) of an integrated system are often grouped under the general heading of *subsystems*. The total design must reflect both the input-output chain of each subsystem, and the interrelationships among different subsystems. The output of one subsystem may be the input of one or more other subsystems, or it may be the final output requested by management.

To illustrate the intricate relationships which must be thought out, Figure 7-2 presents the production requirements subsystem, which is only one of the components included in Figure 7-1, and shows its basic inputs and outputs. *Input* data on gross requirements are drawn from the operations subsystem; labor inventory data from the personnel and payroll subsystem; material inventory data from the inventory subsystem; line capacity data from the industrial engineering subsystem; operations progress data from the operations subsystem. At this point, other input

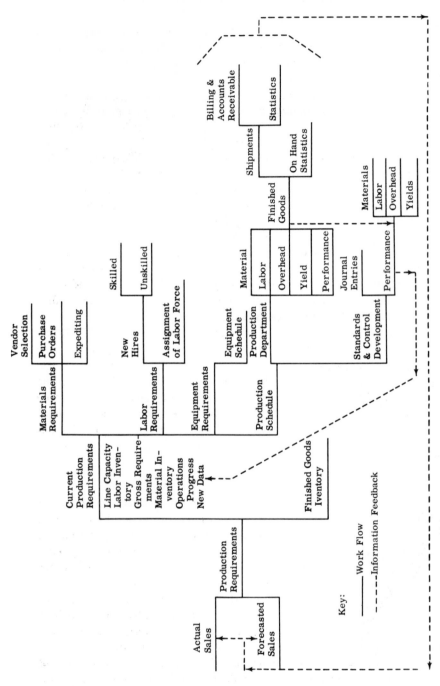

Figure 7-1. Integrated Production Management System Skeleton Flow Chart

data enter in the form of labor standards, labor performance, material performance, and actual yields obtained via feedback for control purposes. The *output* of the current production requirements subsystem includes management reports on material requirements, labor requirements, and equipment schedules to aid planning of the activities of these respective units; production schedule output data become input for the operations subsystem.

While never a simple task, the analysis involved in systems integration is by no means an impossible undertaking. One or more analysts, working with responsible heads of departments and units, make the task manageable by starting with the overall framework, then breaking each system and subsystem down by use of flow charts and other techniques to determine the flow of work and the information needed by people to guide each work step. The value of relating each segment to an over-all pattern, or master systems plan, can not be over-emphasized. Coordination of work flow which frequently crosses departmental lines, and "least cost through least use of data" (making the same data serve as many needs as possible) will require working to a master plan.

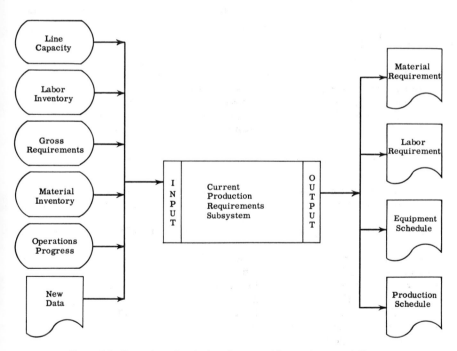

Figure 7-2. Illustration of a single subsystem within an Integrated Master Systems Plan for Production Management

We shall conclude this necessarily brief discussion of systems integration by suggesting certain basic requirements:

1. *A master systems plan is invaluable,* even though rough and still evolving.

2. Management at each level and for each unit must *specify goals and types of information* needed for planning and control. Formidable problems exist in this area, but operations research is throwing more light upon elements which bear upon decisions.

3. Each operating system or subsystem is guided by information and, in turn, produces other information; hence, careful *design of information flow can largely shape and govern actual operations.*

4. Key elements in the design of subsystems are the *input-output chain, interrelationships among subsystems,* and *feedback* of information on results actually experienced.

5. *Data must be increasingly multi-purpose and compatible*—serving as many needs as possible, and expressed in the same units of measurement, time scale, and machine language wherever possible (these requirements will be explained further in the data processing chapters).

While the challenges are great, the potential rewards seem almost limitless. One top executive of a prominent organization recently described them:

> There is every reason to suppose that most corporations will ultimately acquire electronic data processing systems of one kind or another. When this comes about, the competitive edge will go to those organizations which integrate systems and machines within a clearcut pattern of corporate purpose. Here is where administrative management can make its greatest contribution.[3]

QUESTIONS FOR STUDY AND DISCUSSION

1. Define the terms "system" and "systematic" in your own words. Suggest several systems which you normally follow in off-the-job activities—then several work systems that are common to most business enterprises.

2. Are systems finding increased use in businesses and other enterprises? Why or why not?

3. What seem to be the major values of systems?—the major limitations? Try to apply each of these to a system which would link the principal activities in a sales and customer service system for television sets by a department store—including making the sale, obtaining a set from the warehouse or other storage area, delivering the set, installing it, and carrying out any other steps which you may regard as essential to this system.

4. Define "integrated systems" and "total systems." What seem to be the

[3] George W. Chane, "Centralized Administrative Management: The Need, the Promise, and the Challenge," from *Shaping a New Concept of Administrative Management,* AMA Management Report No. 56 (New York: American Management Association, 1961), p. 14.

strongest pressures upon management to move toward more integration of systems? Does the analogy between a river system and the total system of an enterprise seem to be a sound one?—Explain.

5. Describe and appraise the systems integration efforts of the Carborundum Company and the Southland Life Insurance Company.

6. Distinguish as clearly as possible the different levels of system. Note the inventory illustration presented in the text, then suggest another illustration which will make clear the breakdown of a system.

7. Explain the general approach involved in designing the information flow necessary to move toward linking or integrating systems. Make clear, particularly, the input-output relationship, and give one or more illustrations. Do the same for the concept of subsystems.

8. Note and appraise critically each of the basic requirements for systems integration as suggested in the final portion of the chapter. Which of these requirements seem to present the greatest obstacles for management?

9. Are "total systems" already within reach of most enterprises?—why or why not? What are the future prospects for the total systems approach? Where and to what extent does data processing enter the picture of total systems?

10. What general implications does further extension of the systems concept seem to have for (a) management decisions, (b) organization structures, (c) qualifications of managers, and (d) the role of administrative management in the general management scheme?

Case 7-1. Otis Manufacturing Company

In early 1958, the management of Otis Manufacturing Company committed itself to the establishment of a totally integrated electronic data processing system to streamline the means of manufacturing and the design and reporting of managerial information. Elements of this proposed system included parts design, engineering status, purchasing, receiving, warehousing, production planning and control, shipping, billing, direct costing, finished parts inventory, plus other manufacturing and accounting managerial functions.

The master plan received the full support and backing of top management, and current implementation of the plan continues to receive this support. Company personnel and outside observers have noted that this manner of initiating electronic data processing operations represents a direct departure from the customary approach of easing into EDP by planning and implementing only one step at a time, often resulting in a perpetual battle for funds and top management support.

The total system conceived at Otis Manufacturing Company is, in its entirety, an integrated network of sub-systems. Each sub-system has been created to provide input data for other sub-systems and to function as an integrated whole. Typical sub-systems in the total systems plan are: (1) engineering release which begins the data processing cycle with the release of new and revised engineering drawings to manufacturing; (2) requirements explosion based upon material and supplies, and tools necessary to complete the engineering drawings and contract obligations; (3) scheduled net requirements which compares weekly the gross contractual parts and requirements with the current manufacturing status; (4) parts and tools requirements which control the tool status in all stages of development; (5) inventory control designed to provide management with the control of raw materials, parts, and finished goods required to fulfill the necessary contract and spare parts obligations; (6) the procurement sub-system designed to improve the planning and control of the purchased material and parts; and (7) work in process sub-system which maintains a daily current status and accumulates material labor costs on each production order from release to final completion. Other sub-systems are shop scheduling, labor performance, product build up cost, and initial contract forecasts.

As the master plan was originally conceived, it was to be implemented in three phases. The first phase of the EDP total systems plan provided the vital and necessary cornerstone of the integrated program. Phase one included the following:

1. Basic planning of the total system.

2. Definition and establishment of rudimentary files to serve as the basis of phase 2.

3. Development of a material code system for use in manufacturing.

4. Conversion of selected applications to magnetic tape computer processing.

The second phase involved the turning point in the program and produced the first usable, tangible results from the total system. All parts of the manufacturing control system were refined, installed, and operated with current data, directly supporting the planning, operations, and evaluation of current production.

The third and final phase called for expansion into a completely integrated and company-wide information system. Phase three included:

1. The tying in of support functions such as information, personnel and industrial relations, and economic forecasting.

2. Continued improvements and refinements of the work operations adapted in phases one and two.

3. Wide use of simulation, operations research, and other scientific techniques.

4. Refined forecasting and long-range planning.

5. Introduction of real-time electronic data processing.

The management of Otis Manufacturing Company does not expect that it will ever reach a "totally integrated" status since new projects are constantly being created, existing projects demand revision, and new advances in data processing technology present areas of further economy and integration.

The master systems plan has been directly coordinated by the EDP Manager throughout its existence. In many respects the requirements and approval for future expansion, projects for conversion to computer processing, and staff additions were predetermined by the master plan.

The EDP department conducts its own feasibility studies for addition of new equipment. For example, recent decisions have been made to change operations from the IBM 7070 computer to the new IBM 7040 computer, and to exchange an IBM 1401 computer for a new medium size IBM 1460 computer. The EDP management made the studies regarding the exchange of these machines considering monthly rental, speed, storage capacity, expandability of the equipment's system, compatibility with existing computer and data processing equipment, and volume of work to be processed. These studies were then presented to top management to justify the commitment of funds. Subjective considerations regarding the time sequence in which to obtain additions of personnel and equipment in the EDP department are the sole responsibility of the EDP manager and his staff.

The existence of a master systems plan has helped the Otis management in other respects, too. A plan with such company-wide scope has necessarily enlisted the interest, cooperation, and coordination of operating management at all levels and functions within the organization. In fact, operating management are frequently pressuring EDP for early implementation of parts of the master plan that affect them directly. Many of these requests must be denied, however, because the work operations are so closely programmed for conversions to data processing.

The master plan has prepared operating employees for the eventual changes that will occur in their departments and helped insure their cooperation for the new procedures. In particular the total systems plan developed a "questioning attitude" in the minds of all responsible executives regarding future and possible applications for computer processing.

The master plan and the EDP department have taken away a considerable amount of work and responsibility previously held by the Industrial Engineering department, as well as considerable operations and analyses of functional departments. The scope of the EDP department has been increasing, while the scope of other departments has been decreasing.

Problems and questions:

a. This short case illustration indicated mostly advantages for such a preplanned master system. Discuss any disadvantages of such a plan that you see.

b. What, in your opinion, are the basic criteria necessary to the success of a master plan such as this?

c. Is any resentment and professional jealousy likely to be created by such a system? How can this best be controlled or eliminated?

d. Describe the leadership characteristics which you feel the EDP manager in this situation should possess.

8

PROCEDURES MANUALS

Special role of procedures · Procedures manuals and their uses · Responsibility for procedures manuals · Effective presentation of procedures · Maintenance of procedures · Procedures audits

---

The systems concept was introduced in the preceding chapter. A system was defined as a planned approach to carrying out activities needed for achieving objectives. Any enterprise operates through a network of systems. There are systems for sales and receivables; purchases and payables; man-power procurement, development, utilization, and compensation, etc.

Different levels of systems were discussed. These tend to follow a descending scale from the master or total system for the entire enterprise, to combinations of related systems, single systems, procedures, and methods—with the general term "subsystem" often used to indicate further breakdown of any one of the systems levels. The value of developing a master systems plan was stressed. Such a plan is needed to link the various systems and subsystems, and to coordinate the efforts of special units and personnel in a manner that serves overall objectives. It seems probable that the concept of the master or integrated system will serve as the basic model for systems design in the future.

We shall concern ourselves in this chapter mainly with one level of system—that of procedures. In studying procedures, we shall consider the following questions:

1. What special role is filled by procedures in administration?
2. What is a procedures manual, and what needs does it serve?
3. Who prepares procedures manuals, and who receives them?

4. What forms of procedures are most effective?

5. What is involved in maintaining and enforcing procedures?

The Special Role of Procedures

A procedure, as suggested earlier, is a specific work-sequence. It is a series of operations pointed toward achieving a particular objective, such as recording a sales order, hiring an employee, or requisitioning a company car. A procedure thus stands between a system and an operation. A system for completing a sale is made up of a network of procedures, one of which is likely to be that of collection for credit sales; one of the operations in the collection procedure is likely to be that of "aging" accounts receivables to indicate appropriate handling of accounts outstanding for varying periods of time.

Why should we single out procedures for special emphasis and study? The reason is that procedures bring system down to the level of actual work operations and individual responsibilities. A procedure lays out the sequence of steps usually followed in performing a recurring type of work—and most of the work of a typical enterprise *is* recurring or repetitive. If well-designed, a procedure tells *who* does *what* and, in general, *how* and *when*. Thus it specifies work steps necessary, assigns responsibility, and relates what one person does to what others do.

A system, as such, is concerned with broad relationships and will often be expressed in one or more flow charts, accompanied by the group or "bundle" of procedures that make it up. A procedure is the working level of system; it is an actual *guide* to employees on how to proceed each time a particular, recurring type of work is to be performed.

A well-designed procedure serves as:

A standing plan of work
A means of coordinating effort
A tool of communication
A basis for control of performance

These uses of procedure, and certain ideas soon to be considered regarding form of presentation, may be studied by referring to Figure 8-1, which illustrates the form used by one firm for presenting a simple procedure.

Procedures Manuals and Their Uses

Procedures ordinarily must be expressed in written form if they are to serve the needs outlined. Written expression forces *clarification* of ideas, and it facilitates *communication* to all concerned.

		NUMBER 17 - 05	PAGE 1	OF 1

COMPANY PROCEDURE

ELECTRONICS TEMCO & MISSILES COMPANY

TITLE: MILITARY DEFERMENT

ORIGINAL ISSUE | THIS REVISION

SUBJECT

DRAFT DEFERMENT FOR EMPLOYEES IN
CRITICAL JOB CLASSIFICATIONS

APPROVED

Clyde Skeen
Executive Vice President
and General Manager

ORGANIZATIONS AFFECTED: Company General Offices
                           All Divisions

GENERAL:

Jobs essential to the defense of the Nation are designated as critical occupations by the United States Department of Labor. Anyone working in one of these occupations may request deferment from military service by submitting a request via his supervision to Industrial Relations.

PROCEDURE:

I. Employee's Supervision

    A. Receive request for military deferment from the employee.

    B. Notify Industrial Relations of the employee's deferment request and furnish them written information concerning the employee's job classification, responsibilities and contracts on which he is working.

    C. Receive notice of Company and Draft Board's decision.

    D. Notify the employee of the decision.

II. Industrial Relations

    A. Receive the request for deferment and supporting data from the employee's supervision.

    B. Prepare and submit a formal deferment request to the employee's Draft Board.

    C. Receive the Draft Board's decision and appeal a denied deferment as necessary.

    D. Notify the employee's supervision of the decision and/or appeal.

    E. Maintain records of employees on whom deferments have been requested.

YAA:jc   SYSTEMS & PROCEDURES DEPARTMENT

TEMCO FM 304-15

Figure 8-1. Illustration of typical company procedures publication form

There is no better way to clarify thinking than to try to put thoughts into writing. Lawrence Appley has compared the process of shaping thoughts into words with that of an artist painting a picture on canvas.[1] Conscious creating, arranging, establishing, and relating of thoughts is required, whether a manager is attempting to design a procedure (or other plan) alone or soliciting help from others. And the value does not end when the procedure is first reduced to writing. Having it in written form serves as an invitation for others to improve or clarify the procedure (an invitation which, unfortunately, is not always accepted).

Once a procedure is developed and expressed in writing, its chief purpose becomes that of communicating information to each person concerned. Management must decide on who is to receive and use the procedure, who is to prepare and authorize it, what manner of presentation will be most effective, and what efforts are necessary to maintain and enforce it. The remainder of this chapter will be devoted chiefly to considering problems of effective communication through written procedures.

Responsibility for Preparing and Distributing Procedures Manuals

The need for a procedure design or revision may arise from:

A direct request by an executive who becomes aware of a need.
A problem revealed during study of another procedure.
Continuing efforts by systems analysts to search out possible improvements.
A general systems study initiated by top management.
Changes in organization or methods.
Shortcomings in procedures turned up during procedures audits, or other sources.

Whatever the source, information regarding the need for a procedures study usually will be transmitted to the Procedures Department or its equivalent (in a small firm, to the manager or a person designated by him). Investigation is carried out by the procedures analyst working in a staff capacity with the various managers and employees involved in the procedure and, when possible, drawing upon and coordinating their ideas. When the most satisfactory design is worked out, the procedure is written up and is usually signed by an appropriate executive to convey authority. An approved procedure is actually an *order* to perform work in a certain way, although there may be flexibility in application of the procedure. New or revised procedures are then distributed to department heads and others who may need to refer to them.

Below is an outline of a "procedure for handling procedures," intended as an illustration rather than as a model to fit all needs.

[1] Lawrence A. Appley, "Put It in Writing," *Management News,* Vol. 35, No. 5.

1. The head of any department desiring a procedures study or audit shall send to Systems and Procedures two copies of a requisition which contains the following information:
   a. Requesting department
   b. Brief statement of problem
   c. Suggested solution
   d. Other departments affected
   e. Signature of departmental supervisor
2. Systems and Procedures shall:
   a. Prepare and maintain a Company Policy Manual (contents described)
   b. Prepare and maintain a Company Procedure Manual
      (1) Take procedural action on own volition, or by request of affected departments or higher management
      (2) Gather and analyze facts relating to the problem from each affected department
      (3) Prepare copies of proposed procedures and send to the head of each department for approval or request for further study
      (4) Send final draft to affected Vice President(s) for approval
      (5) Have approved procedure printed and distributed to manual holders
   c. Control all business forms
   d. Perform periodic systems analyses
   e. Attempt to mediate any disputes or objections regarding procedures changes; if not successful, make thorough report to appropriate Vice President (s)

The outline presented above is quite typical of the approach followed in firms where a staff department consisting of procedures specialists provides assistance to all other departments. A common variation in large firms is to have a small internal procedures staff within each large department, which assumes responsibility for departmental procedures; and to have Systems and Procedures or a comparable staff department study and issue interdepartmental procedures. Such a combination provides specialized analysis within departments and general coordination where necessary.

Effective Presentation

Procedure manuals were said, earlier, to make two principal contributions: (1) force clarification of ideas, and (2) facilitate communication. Each of these contributions is vitally important, and the two must go together for maximum effectiveness. Care in design of a procedure will be largely wasted unless an equal degree of care in presenting it is exercised.

Since the purpose of a procedure is to instruct employees in what to do and when, there is an obvious challenge to make such instructions clear and precise. The following basic guides are suggested:

1. *Use easy-to-understand wording.* Problems in semantics, or word meanings and interpretations, are difficult enough in face-to-face communication. They are far more difficult in technical writing such as that in manuals and reports, so look for the simple, direct way to express an idea, and avoid technical jargon.

2. *Use action words in a simple, command style.* Leslie Matthies has conducted extensive research in verbs or verb ideas needed to serve procedure requirements, and he found that the following list of fourteen "workhorse" verbs can be made to convey nearly every idea needed in procedures: [2]

Sends	Provides	Decides
Shows	Prepares	Receives
Issues	Uses	Forwards
Obtains	Checks	Requests
Records	Places	

3. *Use a cookbook style in putting words together.* Follow the general pattern of *who-does-what* for most purposes. A procedure is not the place for use of stirring prose nor for legal-style explanations. If the *why* of the procedure needs to be explained, cover it in a brief policy section at the beginning. The primary use of a written procedure is for *reference,* so make it easy to find instructions. Do not *try* to include all the detail needed for *training,* even though the procedural outline may aid in training; specially-prepared training materials are better as learning tools.

4. *Strive for both brevity and completeness.* A tall order, but attainable through the who-does-what formula, and by keeping the user in mind in applying this formula. The "who" may be the holder of a particular job or may be a department; the "what" should leave no doubt regarding specific forms, records, reports, and other instruments essential to the procedure.

5. *Adapt the procedural format to the user.* More specific instructions will be needed in a job outline than in a departmental procedure, and more in a departmental procedure than in a general procedure. The number of people involved, the types of work, the sequence of activities (whether regular and continuous), and the levels of responsibility are factors which may influence the choice of format.[3]

[2] Leslie H. Matthies, *The Playscript Procedure* (New York: Office Publications, Inc., 1961), p. 95.

[3] Clifford I. Haga, in "Report and Procedure Writing: Design It, Don't Write It," *Proceedings of 14th International Systems Meeting,* Systems and Procedures Association, 1962, presents an excellent classification of procedural needs and of layouts particularly appropriate to each.

Among other good sources which treat procedures manuals are Victor Lazzaro, *Systems and Procedures* (Englewood Cliffs, N.J.: Prentice-Hall, Inc., 1959); Richard F. Neuschel, *Management by System* (New York: McGraw-Hill Book Company, Inc., 1960); and the entire book authored by Matthies and cited above.

The guides suggested can be understood and appreciated by considering an ingenious procedural arrangement devised by Matthies, which he terms a "playscript procedure." The playscript approach was developed on the premise that a procedure should be a simple write-up that tells people how to proceed and how to work together. Matthies contrasts a procedure written in a conventional form, presented in Figure 8-2, with the same procedure written in playscript form, as

---

STANDARD PRACTICE INSTRUCTION

Subject: Handling Transfers and Budget Adjustment of Personnel

It shall be company policy and practice to transfer employees from one department to another when the work needs so require such transfers.

Transfers of personnel shall not be made without prior adjustment of the current personnel budgets and work-load records maintained currently in the accounting and finance division, budget and planning section.

The personnel department shall have the authority to secure the receiving department's supervisory signature on all transfers which are to go between over-head and productive departments. Personnel shall set the effective date of transfer, and this shall be added to Form 457, Transfer Request, in the space provided. Copies 2 and 3 shall be sent to department receiving personnel so transferred, while copy number 1 will be filed.

All budget and work-load records shall be adjusted from a copy of Form 457 which shall be sent to the budget and planning section of accounting and finance.

Approval of both the releasing and receiving departments supervisors shall be necessary before the request for a transfer can be effective.

The department personnel records, but not the Personnel Department folder, shall be sent to the receiving department, along with their copy of Form 457. All other affected personnel records shall be posted to reflect the transfer, particularly in the receiving department, as receiving department records must be up to date and each employee shall be currently charged to the correct burden or cost-center account.

It is company policy to keep such employee's record folder in a locked personnel records cabinet. Only supervisors shall have access to, or refer to these records.

Figure 8-2. A procedure written in a conventional style

shown in Figure 8-3.[4] Note how the playscript version makes clear *who-does-what,* and with what ease and speed anyone referring to the procedure could find the information needed.

Here is the playscript version of the procedure just presented.

PROCEDURE

Subject: Personnel Transfers

Responsibility	*Action*
Releasing Supervisor	1. Completes Form 457, "Transfer Request."
	2. Sends both copies to Budgets and Planning.
Budgets and Planning	3. Adjusts budget and workload records.
	4. Sends both copies of Form 457 to Personnel.
Personnel	5. Secures receiving department supervisor's signature.
	6. Adds effective date of transfer to Form 457 and:
	a. Sends copy 2 to receiving department.
	b. Files copy 1.
	7. Notifies releasing department of effective date by telephone.
	8. Places file copy of Form 457 in personnel folder.
Releasing Supervisor	9. Sends department personnel records folder to receiving department.
	10. Posts permanent records to reflect change.
	11. Files employeé records folder in locked personnel records cabinet.

Figure 8-3. Playscript format for procedures writing

Not every type of procedure would lend itself to the playscript format, but the approach is flexible and can be adapted to a wide variety of needs.

Further reference, at this point, to the procedure illustrated in Figure

[4] Matthies, *op. cit.,* pp. 101-103.

8-1 will indicate other desirable elements in format. Note the identifying and indexing information in the top portion, the signature by a high-ranking line executive, the organizations (or, where appropriate, departments affected—at this point, the forms used are also often summarized), the general policy statement, and the system of outlining the procedure. Loose-leaf pages, as used here, are standard practice because of the frequent additions and revisions which are necessary.

Maintenance of Procedures

Two problems with written procedures most frequently mentioned by users are: difficulty in understanding them (the subject of the preceding section) and too infrequent additions and revisions.

To cope with the latter problem, many firms now make periodic analyses of all procedures, checking with persons responsible for each step. Other measures include careful indexing and dating of revisions; notifying the Procedures Department regarding any change in organization or methods which might signal a necessary change in procedure.

Department heads, employees, and other users have responsibilities in this area, also. They should be encouraged to report instances where written procedures are obsolete, not sufficiently flexible to meet operating needs, or unsatisfactory for some other reason. Finally, they have a responsibility to keep their own manuals up to date, inserting newly-written procedures and replacing old ones with revised versions.

Procedures Audits

Procedures are tools of basic importance in both planning and controlling. In order to make certain that procedures are being followed, a great many enterprises conduct *audits* of procedure. These consist of spot-checks of actual work to determine conformance.

Management philosophy differs significantly regarding the proper use of procedures audits. Traditionally, such audits have been handled as a method of checking upon the performance (or conformance) of lower-level operating of staff personnel. They are usually conducted by head-quarters staff personnel, who report their findings to higher management. Audit results are frequently used as a basis for evaluating individual performance. They may influence salary, promotions, and other rewards and penalties.

A shift in thinking regarding effective use of audits now seems to be occurring, at least in a considerable number of enterprises. Where audits have been used as a top-down control device and have served as the basis for rewards and penalties, they have often drawn a disproportionate amount of attention from lower-level personnel—who usually can and will find ways to "audit well" if a great deal depends upon doing so. Service to customers, training of employees, long-range planning, and other necessary managerial functions may suffer.

There is a growing tendency to use procedures audits less as a "policing" device and more as a "learning" device for those audited. The audit team may consist largely of personnel who are usually engaged in the same type of work, in another location. Spot-checks tend to be more general in nature, and the emphasis placed upon constructive suggestions to those audited. A report containing recommendations is left with the persons audited; a copy or summary may go to higher management, but evaluation of performance is done more in terms of actual, measurable results (profits, sales, costs, promptness of service, etc.) than in terms of whether a unit or individual "follows the book" exactly in achieving those results.

Particularly in decentralized organizations, the trends just noted are observable. In the first place, procedural instructions to field divisions or departments are now more often couched in terms of "what is to be accomplished" than in the details of "how." There may of course need to be some standard policies and procedures in order to "present the same face to the public" in terms of service standards and customer expectations. Other standard practices may be required for comparability of basic financial and statistical data, compliance with legal requirements, compatibility of data processing equipment, and for other special reasons. But the procedures themselves are generally less rigid, and any procedural audits conducted are primarily for the purpose of providing help to decentralized units in achieving their objectives. In some cases, very broad policy and procedural statements are issued from headquarters, then field units make up their own detailed statements in order to achieve both the general uniformity needed and adaptation to local conditions and requirements.

QUESTIONS FOR STUDY AND DISCUSSION

1. Why do procedures (among the different levels of systems) warrant special emphasis and study? What purposes do they serve?

2. A bank has a supply room and a clerk who maintains and issues supplies to personnel of different departments when they request them. Certain routine practices are followed by most departments, covering amounts and times of replenishing supplies; but no standard, written procedure has been developed. Can you envision any problems that probably arise under this arrangement? What specific advantage should result from careful preparation of a written procedure to cover replenishment of departmental supplies?

3. What different individuals or groups might participate, or bear some re-

sponsibility, for designing and writing the supplies procedure just described? Why should each participate?

4. Critically appraise the "procedure for handling procedures" which is presented as an illustration in the chapter. What are some variations that might be appropriate under varying circumstances?

5. What seem to be the principal problems which are encountered in procedures writing? Study and appraise each of the basic guides suggested for increasing the effectiveness of written procedures.

6. Describe the "playscript" format for written procedures; single out its most significant advantages as you see them; and try to suggest any types of procedural situations for which this particular format might not be adequate.

7. What problems are frequently encountered in maintenance of procedures? How can these be met?

8. What are procedures audits? What different schools of thought seem to exist with regard to most effective use of audits? With which school are you inclined to agree, and why?

Case 8-1. Noay Manufacturing Company

Procedure 101.6. Master Cycling Requirements for Suppliers

Suppliers of the firm shall be required to set up periodic tool inspection schedules for items fabricated according to the firm's specification and design. The quality control department shall have jurisdiction over the qualification and application of periodic tool inspections at the supplier's premises.

The purchasing department shall be the medium through which initial contact with the supplier is made by the quality control departmental representative.

The suppliers shall receive initial and subsequent instruction regarding the system of requirements for regulation and control of the ensuing periodic tool inspections by the quality control department which in addition must assume the responsibility for assuring that the supplier's gaging and testing devices are checked periodically for accuracy, establish for the supplier a schedule to cover inspection on the basis of a unit or time limit at the appropriate designated intervals, require the supplier to maintain and institute a system to satisfactorily record the necessary operations, maintain resident inspectors where practicable, or itinerant inspectors to be sure that suppliers are complying with firm's specifications, and review and make disposition of waivers of periodic inspections when they are requested by the supplier.

Initial and subsequent coordination with quality control shall be established by the purchasing department concerning any negotiations with the suppliers, which in addition is responsible for the selection of the vendor and forwarding the appropriate information with regard to contractual effectivity and specification to the quality control department and instructing each supplier at the beginning of the contract period that the requirements with regard to the periodic inspections (heretofore mentioned) must be complied with during the life of the existing contractual period and services.

(Signed)   W. W. Blake

Chief, Systems and Procedures

Problems and questions:

 a. Write the above procedure in playscript form.
 b. After completing the revision, consider these questions:
    (1) What difficulties if any were encountered in re-writing the procedure?
    (2) What improvements, if any, do you believe that the playscript version achieved?

9

PROCEDURES AND METHODS IMPROVEMENT

Objectives of procedures and methods improvement · Barriers to improvement · Organization for procedures and methods improvement · A general approach to improvement · Conducting procedures improvement studies · Conducting methods improvement studies

---

Procedures bring system down to the level of actual operations and individual performance. They lay out work steps in sequences which will achieve specific purposes such as processing an insurance claim for property damage.

Careful design of a procedure and expressing it in written form are essential steps in effective use of this basic tool. Putting procedures in written form forces clarification of thought regarding them, and facilitates communication with persons applying them.

The fact that there are written procedures is not an absolute indication of effective operations, however. A written procedure may be merely a record of how work has been done in the past. The changing needs of an enterprise, and the appearance of new methods for meeting these needs, will render most procedures obsolete in time.

There is strong need, therefore, for a continuing program of *improvement* of procedures and methods. Targets include any inefficiencies such as duplication of effort, inadequacies of a procedure or method for meeting new requirements, obsolete equipment, unsatisfactory records and reports, etc. In this chapter, we shall study the requirements of an organized approach to improvement of procedures and methods, considering the following factors:

1. Objectives of procedures and methods improvements
2. Barriers to improvement
3. Organization—who should be responsible and who should participate
4. A general approach to procedures and methods improvement
5. Conducting procedures improvement studies
6. Conducting methods improvement studies

Objectives of Procedures and Methods Improvement

The general objectives of improvement efforts in these fields are greater *effectiveness* and more *economy*.

Improved effectiveness means, most of all, improved service to customers—service that is prompt, as error-free as possible, sufficiently well-rounded, and satisfactory in other respects, depending upon customer needs. Effectiveness also shows itself in employee morale, executive efficiency, coordination of operating units and personnel, and external effects such as those upon community good will and public opinion.

Improved economy means higher productivity at lower costs, good utilization of personnel and equipment, inventories kept at optimum levels, and many other aspects of operation.

The success of an enterprise in today's competitive environment will depend heavily upon continued improvements. A good product and good personnel are not enough. The business (broadly conceived) usually goes to the firm which provides the best combination of quality, service, and price; and these results do not just happen. They are influenced by many philosophies and practices of management, and one of the most important is the general system of operations—which makes it possible to get a reliable product or service out more promptly than other enterprises, at competitive prices.

Social responsibilities are also very much involved, even though we may not often associate procedural efficiency with these. A rising standard of living and a sound economy depend greatly upon the efficiency of individual enterprises. We are seeing that technological improvements in the office field are creating more jobs, rather than fewer, just as technological improvements have done in all other fields. At the same time, there are problems of changing skill requirements, retraining, mobility of employees, etc., which any responsible management must solve to the extent of its ability.

Barriers to Improvement

It is important, when considering approaches to procedures and methods improvements, to be aware of common obstacles. Some are psychological, some economic, and there are others.

In a real sense, a program of improvement in these fields is a war against habit. As organizations are formed, many practices are established not through careful analysis but to meet the needs of the moment. There is often much patterning after practices followed in other enterprises which, of course, may operate under quite different conditions. Once practices are established, employees become accustomed to them and feel secure in their ability to follow them; there is likely to be some resistance to change, as a consequence. There is a hopeful side to the "habit" problem, however. We are now realizing that *improvement can be made a habit,* just as following past practice can be; this characteristic of human behavior will be examined further.

There are other barriers. Individuals, particularly if they are functional specialists, as most employees are, may lack understanding of the role of procedures and broader systems in achieving objectives such as those mentioned in the preceding section. In some enterprises, organizational frictions may result in duplicate efforts and poor coordination. "Alibi systems," such as a costly control procedure to prevent an error from occurring, are frequently set up where top-down control makes strong demands. Even procedures and methods analysts are often limited in perspective, and may go overboard on the most efficient equipment, economy in the records system, tight work standards, and other single areas of improvement without due consideration of how these may influence overall effectiveness and economy.

Each of these barriers is a problem to be reckoned with, but study of each readily indicates that it either can be overcome or adjustment can be made to allow improvement efforts to proceed. Actually, there is no choice but to do so. Innovation is a requirement for survival, in business enterprises, and probably in all others. There is an old saying that "running a business is like riding a bicycle; if you stop, you fall down."

Organization for Procedures and Methods Improvement

Many persons may need to play a variety of roles if improvement efforts are to be effective.

Top management must be convinced of the merit of the improvement program, must initiate it (or give initial authorization) and must lend active, continuing support. Enthusiasm by higher management, when accompanied by good communication and understanding regarding purposes, will quickly find its way through lower levels. Indifference will work in the same way, as systems specialists who have tried to bring programs in "through the back door" have learned.

Outside consultants may play an important but, normally, limited role in the total effort for improvement. If well qualified, they can give a firm the benefit of specialized knowledge, broad experience, and objective viewpoint. They can supply both talent and time when these are not available internally. Cost considerations may dictate that they be used mainly for special projects such as launching a new forms control or work standards program, analyzing a particularly difficult cost problem, or training company personnel in the techniques of work simplification. Too great a reliance upon consultants may slow the development of a true sense of responsibility on the part of company personnel.

Supplier representatives, in such fields as equipment, forms, and supplies, now increasingly compete in terms of service which they can render along with supplying suitable products. They are often trained to conduct thorough studies of a firm's needs in their particular areas, and they bring a background of experience accumulated in other firms. It is probably unwise to rely entirely upon the recommendations of a single sales or service representative; the firm should carry its own analysis to a feasible degree, and it may ask more than one supplier to take a look at the problem area. But this source of help is an increasingly valuable one, and no management should ignore it.

Procedures analysts (who may be called systems analysts, methods analysts, specialists in forms, layout, equipment, standards, or other area) will ordinarily constitute the backbone of the improvement program. This does not mean that they can conduct it by themselves; they bring *specialization and time* required for such improvements, and they can promote a *permanent and continuing program* of improvement.

Procedures analysts ordinarily work in a staff relationship with operating executives and employees. They may take action mainly upon receipt of direct requests for assistance from operating heads; they may be charged by higher management with the responsibility of constantly searching out improvements; they may make periodic systems studies of a general nature; they are likely to rely heavily, at times, on major equipment conversion (such as data processing) or organizational realignment which changes procedural relationships; and they may assist supervisors and employees with improvement efforts made by the latter.

Qualifications needed include an inquiring mind; analytical ability; familiarity with basic techniques in the areas in which they will concentrate (systems charting, forms analysis, layout planning, standards development, etc.); familiarity with the organization and the philosophy of its management; an understanding of human nature, since a great amount of joint effort and communication with others will be required. A person entering the field will need time to become familiar with the organizational and operative requirements of the particular enterprise, and he will benefit immeasurably if he can work for some time with senior analysts in developing and sharpening his technical skills. He may obtain help from analysts in other firms, professional associations, and from special schools and workshops conducted by outside groups and educational institutions.

In an organization too small to justify a full-time analyst, someone who possesses abilities such as those described above may be given part-time responsibility for methods improvements. The important consideration here is that no matter how small the organization, *someone* should be giving continuing attention to methods improvement; whoever this may be, time must be allowed for the work if it is to be carried on effectively.

Supervisors and employees are increasingly being brought into work simplification efforts, with potential values so great that most of the following chapter will be devoted to their contribution. Basic requirements are a demonstrated receptiveness to ideas for improvement on the part of higher management, and an organized approach which will provide constant stimulation, follow-through, and recognition. Limitations of specialized knowledge and of time are obvious; at the same time, familiarity with operating problems and needs, along with motivational benefits because of personal involvement, make this a nearly wide-open field in most enterprises.

A General Approach to Procedures and Methods Improvement

A brief, general approach which will apply to almost any kind of systems improvement problem, one closely related to the scientific method of problem-solving as applied anywhere, will now be presented. We shall then consider how the general approach can be adapted to procedures and methods improvement problems of different types.

The outline presented below is followed widely:

1. Decide on project for study

This step may be thought of as "searching the environment" for possible improvements—and these are usually not hard to find. Unsatisfactory service to customers, high costs, unsatisfactory personnel or equipment utilization, interruptions in work flow, inadequate forms and reports, duplicate effort, and some particular part of the work which is repetitive, high-volume, bottleneck, or monotonous—these are some clues which indicate the need for systems analysis. Conversion to a new data processing system, reorganization, or other new developments may also signal the need for systems changes. A need may be observed and a study initiated by several sources, as noted previously; departments needing help, higher management, the systems staff itself, line personnel who wish to undertake study projects, or others.

2. Describe present system (or procedure or method)

The description may be in narrative form, charts, measurement data, other forms, or a combination. Charting is especially useful, and will be studied further; a well-adapted chart can help the analyst in visualizing relationships and improvement opportunities, and also those who would be affected by any proposed change.

A variety of methods of gathering the information may be employed—study of information available in performance summaries or other documents already available, interview, observation, work sampling, and other means appropriate to the problem. Certain methods will be considered more specifically in the subsequent discussions of procedures and methods studies, and in other chapters.

3. Analyze and improve present system

This important step will first require determination of criteria for appraising the former system and any proposed improvement—maximum volume, time required, quality, costs, crucial features of service in satisfying customer demand, etc.

Then, actual data obtained from the description of the present system must be carefully studied. In addition to direct measures of performance factors, such as those just indicated, checklists of principles regarding factors influencing less-than-satisfactory results are very often helpful. One person or small group may do much of the spade work during this stage, but before its completion the joint thinking of representative persons involved or affected is almost certain to be helpful.

4. Sell and install improved system

Acceptance by persons affected will go far in making any system work successfully, no matter how brilliantly conceived. The best tools for winning acceptance are *communication* and *participation,* in most cases. Particularly valuable in methods and higher-level systems improvements will be participation and personal involvement of persons affected in any proposed change. Thorough, two-way communication is also essential for understanding needs, purposes, effects upon individuals, assurances that personal interests will be protected, and knowledge of how the new plan will operate. Here is one area where recognition of the staff role filled by analysts is particularly important; they must win rather than demand acceptance, and they must be willing to temper their own judgments and recommendations in terms of the reactions of operating personnel who are affected.

Installation of a new procedure or method will often require much care in training personnel in the new approach, making physical changes called for, and following up carefully to see that plans are working out.

5. Maintain and audit the system

Maintenance of written procedures has been discussed previously. Failures or shortcomings in procedures and methods will often come to light in the process of carrying on operations, but this cannot be taken for granted. Periodic analyses of the system and its continued adequacy are generally desirable. Some managements schedule such checks at definite intervals, varying with the nature of the system and the results obtained from it.

Conducting Procedures Improvement Studies

The general approach just presented can be readily applied to procedures improvement studies.

Procedures improvement studies are often initiated by higher management or by the procedures staff, since they often cut across departments, although the need may be suggested by operating personnel involved in a procedure not functioning effectively. Any of the inadequacies suggested in the general approach may suggest the need for such a study.

Major steps in the procedure studied must be broken down and recorded so they can be subjected to careful analysis. The steps may be recorded in various forms, ranging from as simple list to an elaborate chart. Probably the most widely used tool of procedures analysis is a *flow process chart,* as shown in Figure 9-1. In using the process chart, the steps involved in the *present* procedure are first listed in sequence on a chart form; each step is then classified graphically by using the appropriate symbol.

O   A large circle denotes any action or operation taking place.

o   A small circle indicates transportation, as when there is movement from one place to another.

□   A square denotes an inspection, as when something is checked or verified.

D   A D shows delays or storage, as when something remains in one place for awhile, pending further disposition.

FLOW PROCESS CHART

JOB *Process Checks thru Audit + thru Bkpg Dept.*
CHART BEGINS *Front door*
CHART ENDS *Bkpg. File*

Page No. of pp.
Date *4/15*
PREPARED BY *J. R. O'Brien*

CLASSIFICATIONS	DATA

SUMMARY	PRESENT NO.	PRESENT TIME	PROPOSED NO.	PROPOSED TIME	DIFFERENCE NO.	DIFFERENCE TIME
◯ OPERATION	6	15.5	3	13.0	3	2.5
⟂ TRANSPORTATION	9	1.2	5	.5?	4	.6
▢ INSPECTION	4	33.8	4	24.9	0	8.9
D DELAYS	6	26.5	5	21.5	1	5.
TOTAL TRAVEL	336 FT.		165 FT.		171 FT.	

IS THIS PROCESS OR JOB NECESSARY? ☐
OR CAN IT BE ELIMINATED? ☐
CAN IT BE SIMPLIFIED? ☑

OPERATION / TRANSPORTATION / INSPECTION / DELAY / DISTANCE — IN FEET / TIME — IN MINUTES

PRESENT OPERATION OR STEP

1 To Audit Dept.
2 Proved (hand machine)
3 To "coop" sorting rack
4 Wait to be sorted
5 Sorted
6 Wait to be proved
7 To proofing desk
8 Ledger totals run + compared
9 To storage table
10 Sorted in piles
11 Wait for bookkeeper
12 To work place
13 Sorted by account name
14 Ledger File Light Paid
15 Wait for prelist of balances
16 Posted + total proved
17 Wait for processing
18 To machine
19 Microfilmed
20 To cancelling machine
21 Cancelled
22 To bookkeeper
23 Wait to be filed
24 Filed by account name
25 To file
26

PROPOSED OPERATION OR STEP

1 To Audit Dept.
2 Proved (automatic machine)
3 Wait to be proved
4 Totals run + compared
5 Wait to be picked up
6 To bookkeeper
7 Sorted by acct. number
8 Ledger File Light Paid
9 Wait for prelist of balances
10 Posted + total proved
11 Wait for processing
12 To machine
13 Microfilmed + cancelled
14 To bookkeeper
15 Wait to be filed
16 Filed by acct. number
17 To file
18
19
20
21
22
23
24
25
26

UNIVERSITY OF ILLINOIS — COLLEGE OF COMMERCE AND BUSINESS ADMINISTRATION — BUSINESS MANAGEMENT SERVICE

M48

Figure 9-1. A process chart showing present and proposed procedures

The flow process chart also shows the distance in feet whenever transportation is involved, and time required to perform each step; in some instances, only delay steps are timed, to point up opportunities for reducing interruptions in work flow. The time and distance features of a flow process chart are particularly useful in appraising layout of equipment, where rearrangements might cut down on movements and necessary delays; but they also serve other purposes.

Another basic charting tool of the procedures analyst is the *flow dia-*

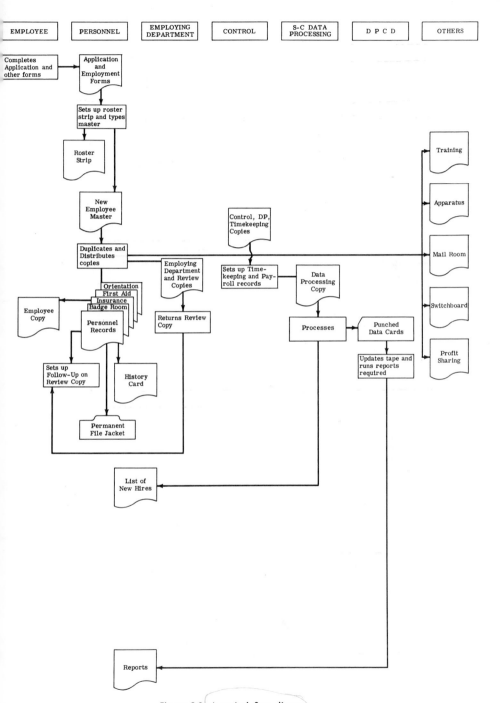

EMPLOYEE	PERSONNEL	EMPLOYING DEPARTMENT	CONTROL	S-C DATA PROCESSING	D P C D	OTHERS

Completes Application and other forms

Application and Employment Forms

Sets up roster strip and types master

Roster Strip

New Employee Master

Duplicates and Distributes copies

Control, DP, Timekeeping Copies

Employing Department and Review Copies

Sets up Timekeeping and Payroll records

Data Processing Copy

Training

Apparatus

Mail Room

Orientation
First Aid
Insurance
Badge Room

Employee Copy

Personnel Records

Returns Review Copy

Processes

Punched Data Cards

Switchboard

Profit Sharing

Sets up Follow-Up on Review Copy

History Card

Updates tape and runs reports required

Permanent File Jacket

List of New Hires

Reports

Figure 9-2. A typical flow diagram

gram. The special value of a flow diagram is its capacity to show a number of flows at the same time, as when a procedure begins with a single action but then branches out into several work flows. Vertical columns may show departments which handle each portion of the procedure. An illustration of a flow diagram is presented in Figure 9-2.

Evaluation of steps and development of an improved approach can then be carried out by studying the charts and other means of recording the present procedure. A general formula, applicable to any form of systems improvement, is: Eliminate—Combine—Rearrange—Simplify. Each step can be studied with these purposes in mind, considered in the sequence suggested—since eliminating a wasteful step is the best kind of improvement, and the others follow a general priority of desirability.

A checklist such as the following will facilitate more thorough analysis:

1. Is each step (or operation) actually necessary?

2. Can certain steps be combined to form a single step?

3. Should any operation be subdivided and the various parts added to another operation?

4. Is the sequence of steps the best possible?

5. Can any operation be done more economically in another department?

6. If an operation is changed, what effect will it have on other operations in the procedure?

7. Can any filing operations be eliminated or changed in sequence?

8. Can any work details be eliminated, shortened, or expedited?

9. Is the operation duplicated at any point in the procedure?

10. What interruptions or delays can be reduced?

11. Are information, facts, and data supplied in suitable condition for use?

12. Can the originator perform additional work or supply more information that would make subsequent operations easier?

13. Can information or forms be sorted into order simultaneously with this operation for use in the next operation?

14. Is the operation a bottleneck in the procedure? If so, can work be scheduled differently?

15. Can any part of the work be performed during waiting time or idle time?

16. Can the vendor or customer be consulted to help make joint operations easier and more economical?

17. Where materials must be checked for accuracy, can calculated risks be taken and spot checks substituted for checks of individual units?

18. Have the employees who carry out the procedure been consulted for their views on changes which might be indicated?

Formulation of an improved version of the procedure under study will gradually emerge from the questioning done by analysts, and from careful clearing with everyone who will use the procedure. Typically, the direct users and their supervisors will spot loopholes and see opportunities for improvement of the tentatively proposed procedure. In any event, they will be much more receptive to the modification if they have been consulted regarding it, and have had the benefit of thorough explanation of advantages. When a "proposed" revision, such as that shown in the right-hand column of Figure 9-1, is finally agreed to by all concerned, the new procedure is written up in complete form, signed by an executive who can convey authority, and distributed for inclusion in manuals held by the persons affected.

Conducting Methods Improvement Studies

Improvements from procedural analysis can be very substantial. Further improvements can usually be realized by going a step beyond and conducting detailed study of the method of performing each individual operation.

Quite clearly, this type of study logically should follow study of an entire procedure. It is wise to go after the big improvements—the big savings—first. Moreover, as a result of procedures simplification, some operations may be eliminated entirely. One operation in a procedure for handling incoming mail, for example, might be that of entering basic data regarding all incoming pieces of first-class mail in a register for control purposes. Procedural analysis might reveal that the values gained do not warrant the effort and cost expended, and that devoting a lot of analysis to such an operation would not be as desirable as eliminating it entirely.

The values of other levels of systems improvement may be derived from methods improvement. Specifically, improvement of individual operations can reduce fatigue, save time, and save cost. Work can be completed and delivered more promptly. A greater volume of work can be done with the same personnel. Revolutionary changes in equipment design offer tremendous potentialities for increasing productivity.

Selecting the project for study

Even a one-time operation may justify some use of "organized common sense," as methods analysis is sometimes called. Benefits expected must be weighed against effort and costs likely to be required. Particularly high returns may result from study of repetitive, high-volume operations because small savings multiplied will add up to substantial amounts. Bottleneck operations may be improved to the point where work flows smoothly and with fewer delays. Monotonous or fatiguing operations may warrant special attention; some methods programs make the reduction of fatigue their primary objective.

Breaking down and recording the present method

At the level of methods analysis, an operation is broken down into elements, and even body motions, in the most detailed type of analysis. The method by which the operation is performed is usually determined through observation, although an unusually high-volume or troublesome operation may justify filming and a close study of the film.

The type of form for recording the breakdown of the operation may range from a simple list of motions to an elaborate chart which records and classifies motions, and invites questioning on a systematic basis. Most widely used among motion charts is the Right- and Left-Hand Chart. This is the workhorse of motion study charts, just as the Flow Process Chart is the device most commonly used in procedures analysis.

The Right- and Left-Hand Chart shows the motions performed by each hand, as the title suggests. It also classifies these motions by certain basic types, using symbols for ready identification and emphasis. The exact symbols used vary, but the following combination has been used widely.

OPERATION O	Used whenever a body member does something at one location such as writing, operating an office machine, or grasping an object.
TRANSPORTATION o	Used whenever a body member moves toward or away from an object.
HOLD ⍵	Used when an object is held in position so something can be done to it. Example: holding a pen in one hand in order to screw the top on.
DELAY D	Used whenever a body member is idle or waiting for other body members.

To illustrate, the original method of typing requisitions in a certain firm is charted in Figure 9-3. A look at the sketch of the work-place at the top shows a secretarial-type desk with typewriter in left pedestal, a calculator, and trays for blank forms, written requisitions, and finished work, all placed as indicated.

The right hand goes to the tray containing blank requisition forms and grasps one; the left hand waits during this time. Both hands move to the typewriter, and both insert the blank form. The right hand then moves to the tray of written requisitions (previously made out in rough form by department heads desiring materials), grasps the next requisition to be typed, moves it to the side of the typewriter, releases the requisition, and moves into position at the typewriter; the left hand again has merely waited during these steps. Both hands type the requisition. Then the right hand moves to the calculator, records the figures and determines the total, and moves back into position at the typewriter; the left hand again has waited. Both hands then type the total on the requisition, and both are involved in removing the requisition from the typewriter. The right hand then takes the finished requisition to the "Finished" box on the desk and releases it, while the left hand waits.

Each of the steps just described is identified on the chart by the appropriate symbol. The summary at the bottom shows that the left hand was involved in four operations while the right hand was involved in nine. The left hand had a part in one movement, while the right hand was involved in eight. The left hand had twelve delays or waits, while the right hand had none. Neither hand had any "holds" in this operation.

Analysis of present method

After the present method has been broken down into steps and charted, the operation as a whole and each individual step involved can be analyzed in the light of established principles of motion economy. The pioneering effort to formulate such principles was that of Frank and Lillian Gilbreth. One of the greatest tributes that could be paid to these pioneers is the fact that the original Gilbreth list of motion principles and techniques of analysis has stood up for almost half a century with only minor changes, despite the fact that many capable people have attempted to improve upon it.

The Gilbreth list of principles was rather lengthy; although having application to all types of work, some of the principles are less directly involved in office operations than in factory operations. Accordingly, a simplified list of principles especially applicable to analysis of office operations is presented here:

1. Question the necessity of each step. *The easiest way to do a job is not to do it.*

2. Place all materials and equipment in definite positions *within the normal working area* (charted in Figure 9-4).

3. Use both hands simultaneously whenever possible and try to keep the amount of work done by each in balance.

4. Use the simplest motions possible—finger motions rather than wrist, wrist rather than arm, arm rather than body, and so forth.

5. Use motions that are smooth, rhythmic, and continuous.

6. Make sure the equipment is suited to the job.

7. Make sure the person performing the job is well fitted to it and is given sufficient training.

OPERATION ANALYSIS CHART

OPERATION ___ Typing requisitions ___

RIGHT AND LEFT HAND CHART

PRESENT METHOD ☒
PROPOSED METHOD ☐

OPERATION ○
TRANSPORTATION ○
HOLD ◠
DELAY D

SKETCH AREA ▶

A—Blank requisition forms
B—Finished work
C—Handwritten requisitions
D—Calculator
E—Typewriter
F—Chair

LEFT HAND	CLASSIFICATION	RIGHT HAND
	○ ○ ◠ ● ○ ● ○ ◠ D	To supply of forms
	○ ○ ◠ ● ● ○ ○ ◠ D	Grasp blank form
To typewriter	○ ● ◠ D ○ ● ○ ◠ D	To typewriter
Insert blank form	● ○ ◠ D ● ○ ○ ◠ D	Insert blank form
	○ ○ ◠ ● ○ ● ○ ◠ D	To written requisition
	○ ○ ◠ ● ● ○ ○ ◠ D	Grasp written requisition
	○ ○ ◠ ● ○ ● ○ ◠ D	To side of typewriter
	○ ○ ◠ ● ● ○ ○ ◠ D	Release requisition
	○ ○ ◠ ● ○ ● ○ ◠ D	To typewriter
Type requisition	● ○ ◠ D ● ○ ○ ◠ D	Type requisition
	○ ○ ◠ ● ○ ● ○ ◠ D	To calculator
	○ ○ ◠ ● ● ○ ○ ◠ D	Record figures and total
	○ ○ ◠ ● ○ ● ○ ◠ D	To typewriter
Type total	● ○ ◠ D ● ○ ○ ◠ D	Type total
Remove paper from typewriter	● ○ ◠ D ● ○ ○ ◠ D	Remove paper from typewriter
	○ ○ ◠ ● ○ ● ○ ◠ D	To "Finished" box on desk
	○ ○ ◠ ● ● ○ ○ ◠ D	Release finished requisition
	○ ○ ◠ D ○ ○ ◠ D	
	○ ○ ◠ D ○ ○ ◠ D	
	○ ○ ◠ D ○ ○ ◠ D	
	○ ○ ◠ D ○ ○ ◠ D	
	○ ○ ◠ D ○ ○ ◠ D	

	TOTALS			TOTALS	

SUMMARY	PRESENT			PROPOSED			SAVING		
	LH	RH	BOTH	LH	RH	BOTH	LH	RH	NET
○	4	9	13						
○	7	8	9						
◠	0	0	0						
D	12	0	12						
TOTAL									

PREPARED BY
Sam Gift

UNIVERSITY OF ILLINOIS — COLLEGE OF COMMERCE AND BUSINESS ADMINISTRATION — BUSINESS MANAGEMENT SERVICE

Figure 9-3. Right- and left-hand chart of present method of typing requisitions

The second principle described above merits special attention. For each arm there is a normal working area, and it is highly desirable that materials and tools be placed within this area so that stretching, bending, and similar efforts can be minimized. The normal working area is charted in Figure 9-4. As shown, there is also a maximum area for the arm extended, and there is an overlapping area in which items should be placed if both hands must work on them at the same time. Any materials and equipment placed outside the normal working area should be viewed critically, particularly if they must be used frequently.

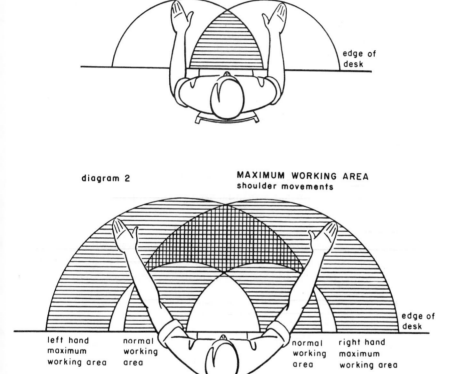

Figure 9-4. Charts showing normal and maximum working areas

To illustrate these principles, refer again to Figure 9-3. It is quickly apparent that several motion principles are violated. One wonders immediately whether all of the delays and movements are necessary. All materials and equipment except the typewriter are located outside the normal working area for the typist as she sits at the typewriter. It is obvious that the right hand is being made to do most of the work while the left hand is used little except in the actual typing. Motions are complex and fatiguing; the typist must make long reaches and must turn completely around to operate the calculator. There seems to be little opportunity for getting rhythm into the work. Possibilities for improved equipment also may suggest themselves.

Development of improved method

These considerations will suggest various specific improvements. Each work step should be examined critically in the light of the different motion principles which may apply to it. The best type of improvement, where justified, is to eliminate a wasteful operation entirely; other general types of improvement may lie in combining, rearranging, or simplifying steps that must be retained.

An improved version of the method of typing requisitions is shown in Figure 9-5. The sketch at the top of the chart suggests a rearrangement of materials and equipment in the workplace. A shelf has been added behind the typewriter, with compartments for the three items of material built into the top of the shelf at a height that just clears the top of the typewriter. The calculator has been placed just to the right of the typist, as indicated.

This arrangement permits the sequence of work steps charted in Figure 9-5. Delays have been reduced greatly; all materials and equipment are now within the normal working area; work for the hands is more nearly equalized; distances travelled are shorter; the entire operation is faster and less fatiguing.

It should be emphasized that the improved method which has been suggested is only one of many possibilities. Perhaps the reader can suggest other solutions that would be even more satisfactory than the one described.

Installation of improved method

After the new method has been planned, actual installation must still be carried out; the success of the proposed method will depend greatly upon how carefully this final phase is approached. The work of installing a new method seems to fall logically into four phases: winning acceptance, making physical changes, training personnel, and following up on results.

The most satisfactory solution to the problem of winning acceptance is likely to be the one suggested earlier—consulting the individuals involved in the methods change as early as possible in the planning of the improvement, and drawing as many as possible of the ideas for the improved method from them. Perhaps ideally, the entire plan should be conceived and worked out by the supervisor and the employee directly involved, aided only by training in work simplification previously acquired. If for some reason most of the work of analysis must be done by a staff analyst, the utmost tact and sales ability will be required; the more

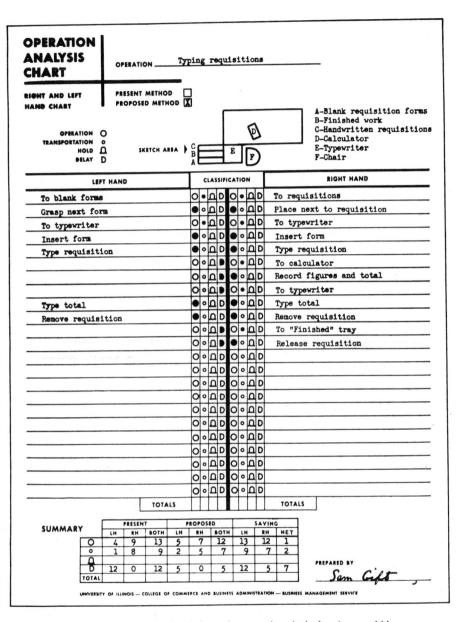

OPERATION ANALYSIS CHART

RIGHT AND LEFT HAND CHART

OPERATION ___ Typing requisitions

PRESENT METHOD ☐
PROPOSED METHOD ☒

OPERATION ○
TRANSPORTATION ○
HOLD ⌂
DELAY D

SKETCH AREA

A–Blank requisition forms
B–Finished work
C–Handwritten requisitions
D–Calculator
E–Typewriter
F–Chair

LEFT HAND	CLASSIFICATION		RIGHT HAND
To blank forms	○ ● ⌂ D	○ ● ⌂ D	To requisitions
Grasp next form	● ○ ⌂ D	● ○ ⌂ D	Place next to requisition
To typewriter	○ ● ⌂ D	○ ● ⌂ D	To typewriter
Insert form	● ○ ⌂ D	● ○ ⌂ D	Insert form
Type requisition	● ○ ⌂ D	● ○ ⌂ D	Type requisition
	○ ○ ⌂ ■	○ ● ⌂ D	To calculator
	○ ○ ⌂ ■	● ○ ⌂ D	Record figures and total
	○ ○ ⌂ ■	○ ● ⌂ D	To typewriter
Type total	● ○ ⌂ D	● ○ ⌂ D	Type total
Remove requisition	● ○ ⌂ D	● ○ ⌂ D	Remove requisition
	○ ○ ⌂ ■	○ ● ⌂ D	To "Finished" tray
	○ ○ ⌂ ■	● ○ ⌂ D	Release requisition
	○ ○ ⌂ D	○ ○ ⌂ D	
	○ ○ ⌂ D	○ ○ ⌂ D	
	○ ○ ⌂ D	○ ○ ⌂ D	
	○ ○ ⌂ D	○ ○ ⌂ D	
	○ ○ ⌂ D	○ ○ ⌂ D	
	○ ○ ⌂ D	○ ○ ⌂ D	
	○ ○ ⌂ D	○ ○ ⌂ D	
	○ ○ ⌂ D	○ ○ ⌂ D	
	○ ○ ⌂ D	○ ○ ⌂ D	
	○ ○ ⌂ D	○ ○ ⌂ D	
	TOTALS		TOTALS

SUMMARY

	PRESENT			PROPOSED			SAVING		
	LH	RH	BOTH	LH	RH	BOTH	LH	RH	NET
○	4	9	13	5	7	12	13	12	1
○	1	8	9	2	5	7	9	7	2
⌂									
D	12	0	12	5	0	5	12	5	7
TOTAL									

PREPARED BY
Sam Gift

UNIVERSITY OF ILLINOIS — COLLEGE OF COMMERCE AND BUSINESS ADMINISTRATION — BUSINESS MANAGEMENT SERVICE

Figure 9-5. Right- and left-hand chart of proposed method of typing requisitions

the analyst consults the persons actually involved in the operation, the better will be the chances of success.

Physical changes in the requisition-typing example were simple and inexpensive. This is probably typical of most methods improvements;

they await only the use of a little of the organized common sense involved in work simplification. In many instances, company personnel can make all physical changes necessary. In other cases, mechanizing an operation previously performed by manual methods may be justified.

Training personnel in new methods will usually involve primarily a change in work habits, although new skills may have to be developed in some instances. Success is likely to depend upon the attitude of the employee—which relates to the first point of winning acceptance—and upon the use of a sound approach to training.

Follow-up on results with a new method should be an integral part of the procedure. What looked like an excellent idea sometimes fails miserably because of failure to analyze the situation accurately, failure to win employee or supervisor, failure to train the individual adequately, or some other short-coming in the approach. The follow-up may well include analysis of costs and savings involved in each methods change. This may serve the dual purpose of checking the soundness of any change being tried and of justifying time allowance for methods work and other forms of work simplification.

Special applications of methods analysis

The above-described approach to analysis of methods is of a general sort, and it can be used or adapted to a wide variety of needs. For particular types of methods, there are more specialized tools of analysis—such as forms spread sheets, equipment utilization charts, time study data sheets, and checklists of principles or points to look for when close study is desired. In some cases, the sort of general approach to methods analysis which has just been considered can be combined with "tailored" techniques of analysis in study of a form, a layout, a desk arrangement, a machine, or another specific method of getting work accomplished.

Throughout our study of procedures and methods analysis, we have noted the importance of the human element in any proposed improvement. We shall explore this concept further in the next chapter.

QUESTIONS FOR STUDY AND DISCUSSION

1. Why—even with a good program of written procedures and manuals—is there need for a continuing program of procedures and methods improvements? What specific factors lead to this need?

2. What are the general objectives of procedures and methods improvement? Does one objective seem most important?—Explain.

3. Are improvements in procedures and methods generally welcomed by the personnel affected by them? Why or why not? What barriers may be encountered, and how may each be surmounted?

4. In general terms, what role in improving procedures and methods can best be filled by each of the following: (a) top management, (b) outside consultants, (c) supplier representatives, (d) procedures analysts, and (e) supervisors and employees? Explain and justify each suggested role.

5. Study carefully the five-step approach suggested for procedures and methods improvement. Does it seem applicable to almost any improvement problem in these areas? Explain the justification, or lack of justification, for each step.

6. What are some of the most common "clues" which may indicate improvement needs? How can each be spotted?

7. What are the special values of charting procedures and methods? Could one not do as well merely by observing operations carefully and thinking critically about them?

8. What seem to be management's best techniques for selling (or winning acceptance of) proposed improvements? Why are these techniques effective?—what assumptions does management follow when it uses each?

9. Which normally should be studied first in the same general area of work—procedures or methods? Why? Might this order need to be reversed in some situations?—Explain.

10. What are the basic differences among the flow process chart, the flow diagram, and the operations analysis chart? When is each appropriate?

Case 9-1. The Harter Paint Company

It was found that in making an across-the-counter sale in this store, the average transaction followed this process: salesman takes can of paint from shelf and carries it ten feet to counter; inserts carbon in sales pad; writes sales slip in duplicate; removes both copies from pad; extracts carbon; replaces carbon in pad; takes customer's money and walks eight feet to cash register; rings up sale; makes change; walks eight feet back to counter; gives first copy of sales slip, change, and paint to customer; takes duplicate sales slip to bookkeeper 15 feet away; bookkeeper inspects slip; sales slip posted to daybook; sales slip posted to cash journal; bookkeeper carries sales slip to file ten feet away; slip is filed numerically in file; slip remains in file until end of month.

After the process was studied in detail by a work simplification specialist, it was proposed that the process be changed so as to reduce the steps to the following: salesman takes can of paint from shelf and carries it ten feet to counter; writes sales slip on a combination invoice and cash register which utilizes one-time carbon paper; makes change; gives customer first copy of sales slip, change, and paint; retains copies of sales slips in register compartment until end of day; bookkeeper picks up sales slips at end of day; bookkeeper carries slips to his desk 15 feet away; bookkeeper inspects sales slips; sales slip totals are posted to cash journal; bookkeeper files duplicate sales slips by number in desk file (to form daybook); slips remain in file until end of month.

Problems and questions:

Using the process chart in Figure 9-1 as a guide, prepare a simple process chart with pen and ink covering the present and proposed steps in this procedure. Indicate the appropriate symbols and distances in feet, based on such information as is provided. Summarize the differences between the present and the proposed procedures.

Case 9-2. The Merrimac National Bank

The management of the Merrimac National Bank recently created the position of methods analyst and hired Mr. H. A. Barker, a recent college graduate. Mr. Barker was introduced to all management personnel at a general meeting, and it was announced that he would be available to help any company official to study methods problems of his department. Mr. Barker could be reached by telephone and would try to schedule requests as promptly as possible.

Several weeks have passed, but Mr. Barker has had only a limited number of requests for his services. The president of the bank is aware of the situation; it is his opinion that the situation can be remedied by the passage of a little more time and by more initiative on Mr. Barker's part in contacting department heads. The president is convinced that most of the selling of the program should be done by Mr. Barker himself.

Mr. Barker feels that top management has let him down somewhat in the introduction of the methods program, and has expected him to "bring the program in the back door" and to do all the selling himself. It has been Mr. Barker's observation that the department heads have been nonprogressive and hard to convince on the several occasions when he has tried to point out weaknesses in present methods. He has just about reached the conclusion that the only way he will ever be able to accomplish much in the new position will be in persuading the president to give him actual authority needed to compel department heads to make changes where they will not cooperate otherwise.

Problems and questions:

a. Do you agree with Mr. Barker's analysis of the situation and with his conclusion?

b. Can you suggest any improvements in either Mr. Barker's approach or in that of higher management?

Case 9-3. Collating Problem

A certain operation involves the arrangement in proper order of six pages of printed material. After the six pages have been collated, they must be stapled together. Two staples must be driven into the collated pages, but the stapler is equipped with two heads. Thus it is only necessary to align the pages in the stapler and actuate the stapler once. Both staples are driven in simultaneously.

As shown in the accompanying sketch of the layout of the workplace, the pages are numbered from one to six. The vertical row on the far left

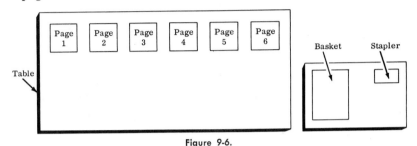

Figure 9-6.

consists of first pages, the next row, second pages, and so on. The pages are placed on the flat surface of the table top. The operator must be particularly careful when performing the collating operation not to get pages into the wrong rows. The stapler is placed on a stand just to the right of the page-six row.

The collating job is now performed as follows. The operator grasps page one with right hand and brings it to the left hand. The right hand moves to page two, grasps it, brings it to the left hand. This sequence is followed for the remaining pages. After page six has been released to the left hand both hands move to the stapler. The six pages are jogged (using both hands). After jogging, the left hand aligns the pages in the stapler, and the right hand moves to the actuating handle. As soon as the pages have been aligned, the right hand actuates the stapler. The stapled pages are then removed with the left hand and dropped in a basket situated alongside the stapler.

Problems and questions:

a. Which principles of motion economy are violated in the present method?
b. Sketch an improved workplace layout which corrects the weaknesses noted in the preceding question.
c. Prepare Right- and Left-Hand Charts of both the present and the proposed methods (*optional with instructor*).

Case 9-4. The Branscome Company

The Branscome Company has an office force of about thirty employees. The company has been in business for many years, and its office procedures, forms, and equipment are clearly in great need of a modernization program.

A new president of the company has just been named, and he has announced that office modernization will be one of his first matters of concern. He has asked for suggestions concerning who should be assigned responsibility for the modernization program. Replies have been varied, but they seem to suggest three principal alternatives:

Hire a full-time methods analyst.

Assign the responsibility to the best qualified of the present executives and relieve him of a portion of his former duties.

Bring in an outside consultant who would launch much-needed improvement projects and train other executives in how to carry on the program after his departure.

Problems and questions:

Appraise each of these possibilities and make a preliminary recommendation.

a. Is more specific information needed before a final decision is made?

b. If so, what types?

Case 9-5. The Lincoln Select-Risk Insurance Company

The manner of processing and closing medical payment claims in this firm has come under management scrutiny. A somewhat abbreviated outline of the present procedure is presented below.

1. Mail Clerk opens and date stamps mail, allows to accumulate for an average of 30 minutes per batch, delivers to X-Card (expiration card) Clerk 75 feet away.

2. X-Card Clerk attaches X-cards to mail, delivers to claim basket 123 feet distant, where there is an average wait of 15 minutes.

3. Claim Representative reviews mail, authorizes payment, attaches numbered claim jacket, makes entries on blank claim mat—and delivers to Draft Typist 102 feet away, where the average wait is about 20 minutes.

4. Draft Typist types payment draft, delivers to Accounting 105 feet distant.

5. Accounting allows batch of drafts to accumulate for about 90 minutes, then signs and returns to Claim Secretary 105 feet away, who mails payment draft, and sends claim file to Claim Mat Typist 102 feet distant.

6. After average 20-minute wait, Claim Mat Typist types claim mat, then sends to Draft Typist who verifies.

7. Draft Typist then delivers claim file and claim mat to multilith, 236 feet away where claim jacket, claim index card, and stat card are run off from mat, with all then delivered 176 feet to Record Control Clerk where 30-minute delay typically occurs.

8. Record Control Clerk sorts and delivers the claim jacket and claim index cards to File unit 100 feet away, and stat card to Accounting 102 feet away.

9. File Clerk pulls permanent file on policyholder and delivers with claim jacket to Underwriting, 120 feet away, for average wait of 25 minutes before processing.

10. Underwriting records basic facts of the claim, then releases all back to File Unit, 120 feet distant.

The most questionable steps of this procedure, in the view of several persons who have studied it, are steps 4, 6, and 8, which many believe could better be handled by a claim secretary or clerk located near the Claim Representative.

Problems and questions:

Prepare a flow process chart of the present procedure, then prepare a chart of the procedure which you would propose to incorporate the improvements suggested and any others which may seem desirable. Make what seem to be reasonable estimates as to the time of delays and distances traveled.

10

WORK SIMPLIFICATION
BY LINE AND STAFF

*The origin of the work simplification concept · Basic approach
to work simplification · One firm's experience · Variations ·
General observations*

Students of management (in and out
of school) have undoubtedly been impressed by certain contrasts in
results attained with particular programs when these are approached
in different ways.

To illustrate, a budget can be a whip if used in one way, or it can be
an opportunity for responsible participation and for understanding the
economic facts of life if used in another.

A procedures audit, as noted in an earlier chapter, can be a policing
action, or it can serve primarily as a learning experience for those
audited, while still giving higher management the facts needed for
control.

A new program of major scope such as addition of a new product line
or expansion into a new territory may generate great enthusiasm among
members of top management. By the time the word reaches the supervisory and employee levels, the new program may sound like just more
work to do and, possibly, some uncertainty regarding one's own security
in the new scheme of things.

Almost any change, even growth itself, can be a threat or it can be a
challenge. It is not surprising, then, that one of the most vivid contrasts
lies in the area of methods improvement, because methods improvement
by definition is a constant process of change.

No one questions the necessity of methods improvement, yet in some situations it can be a serious morale depressant. In other cases, it proves to be one of the finest of morale builders. There are, of course, many degrees in between—such as grudging compliance or acceptance without enthusiasm.

The Origin of the Work Simplification Concept

In the early 1930's, an industrial engineer named Allen Mogenson, who had been working primarily in factories, made a profound yet simple discovery. Mogenson had very often had the experience of coming into a line department and attempting to suggest improvements, establish time standards, or encourage other changes which seemed to be needed. He was impressed by how often his efforts were met with resistance. Persons involved, foremen as well as employees, often seemed to feel that there was an implied criticism of them, and they were not sure what might develop if the proposed changes were put into effect.

So Mogenson decided to follow the old adage, "If you can't lick them, join them." He decided to try to bring line personnel in on the act and to get them involved directly in planning and methods improvements which affected them.

After a considerable amount of study and experimentation, Mogenson established a school on work simplification in Lake Placid, New York, which is still in operation and has had many hundreds of graduates. Essentially, the plan of the course is to bring representatives of different companies to the school for six weeks of intensive training, after which they return to their organizations to conduct work simplification training and follow-up programs for their own supervisors and employees.

A great many other consultants, professors, company training directors, and industrial engineers have come around to a similar way of thinking. There are now other work simplification schools and conferences in a number of locations. Many articles and several books have been written on the subject of line participation in methods improvements.

The term "work simplification," while still often used in a general sense in referring to any type of work improvement, is now used increasingly by systems analysts and industrial engineers to indicate programs which involve line participation.

Such programs are now in operation in thousands of prominent and diversified companies, including International Business Machines, Eastman-Kodak, Marshall Field, Sears, Prudential Insurance, Maytag, and the U. S. Department of State. The *Wall Street Journal* carried a feature article in the December 8, 1959, issue, with the caption "Work Simplification—Firms Use Employees' Common Sense to Cut Costs, Boost Profits," which described several successful programs then in operation; and many other firms have introduced similar programs in more recent years.

Basic Approach to Work Simplification

Essential elements of a work simplification program, as here defined, are *development of a questioning attitude* toward the way things are done, and *provision of an organized approach* for thinking out and suggesting improvements.

A training program, while not absolutely essential, is likely to greatly increase the probability of successful results. Such a training program attempts to bring many of the same principles and tools of methods improvement, long used by staff specialists, down to the level of supervisors and employees, and to influence them to actively participate in improvements in their own work, with which they are familiar.

A typical class in work simplification includes about six to ten sessions. Efforts are made, first, to develop a questioning attitude, making it possible to spot improvement needs such as bottlenecks, high-cost operations, errors, and excessive movement or delay. A common, and very useful, suggestion is to develop the habit of seeing every job in three parts: (1) make-ready, (2) do, and (3) put away—to visualize possibilities for reducing non-productive activities.

Then, a series of training sessions will be devoted to equipping participants with certain tools of analysis such as simple flow charts, layout charts, work distribution charts, and check lists on forms design.

Finally, most such programs devote the closing portion of the training to actual working out, usually in small teams, of actual improvement projects, with the assistance of the training leader and other staff specialists when necessary.

Vitally important before-and-after steps are strong support by higher management before launching such a program, and provision for follow-up and continued interest afterward.

One Firm's Experience

To provide clearer understanding of the operation of a work simplification program, certain highlights of the program of Texas Instruments, Inc., will be described.

Several years ago, the top management of this organization became convinced of the value of getting more of their people involved in methods improvement, even though at the time they already had a competent industrial engineering department, a systems department, and a suggestion system. They sent a representative to a school in work simplification; this man then returned and guided the establishment of a work simplification training program. First, the top and middle levels of management were given an abbreviated version of the training program, for their information and to win their support.

During the intervening years, Texas Instruments has run most of their first-line supervisors and foremen, many professional and technical employees, and many operative employees through the program. They estimate that they are currently saving more than one million dollars a year *directly* from projects worked upon by participants in the training program. Their top executives believe that morale benefits have been far greater.

One of the first steps taken was dispensing with their suggestion system. They said to their employees, in effect: "We don't want just your occasional brilliant idea; we want your best thinking all of the time, and we will recognize and reward you for it." The reward system now consists of publicity and recognition for useful suggestions submitted, consideration in merit increases and promotions, and a profit sharing plan. Each employee is encouraged to contribute the best of his constructive thinking, thus providing an outlet for any creative ability he may possess.

The diversity in types of work performed by the groups being trained in work simplification has led Texas Instruments to modify the program somewhat for *five* different groups: production hourly employees, production supervisors, administrative personnel, secretary-clerical personnel, and engineering personnel.

The outline of the training conferences for the Administrative group is presented below.

Work Simplification Program

Administrative Conferences

Conference #1—The Work Simplification Concept

> Philosophy of work simplification
> History of program
> Objectives and needs
> The consultative approach
> Movie "Cavalcade of Office Work Simplification"

Conference #2—The Organized Approach

> Getting the green light on
> Law of intelligent action
> Five-step improvement pattern
> Movie "5 Steps to Office Work Simplification"

Conference #3—The Present Method

> Observation
> The questioning attitude
> Introduction to charting
> The flow process chart

Chart form X
Movie "How to Make a Flow Process Chart"

Conference #4—The Improved Method

Developing the improved method
Evaluating the improved method
Presenting the improved method
Participation in form "X"
Movie "Selling America"

Conference #5—Systems Analysis—Motion Planning

Procedure flow charting
Analyzing the system
Office motion planning
Motion planning principles
Motion planning demonstrations
Movie "Don't Be Left Behind"

Conference #6—Records Management

Controlling records
Handling records
Filing and storing
Retention and destruction
Correspondence

Conference #7—Forms Design and Control

Key to office activity
Forms control
Forms design
Forms cost
Forms reproduction

Conference #8—Survey of Other Important Tools

Work sampling
Work distribution chart
Multiple activity charting
RH-LH charting
Brainstorming
The camera
Movie "Work Sampling"

Conference #9—Improvement Communications

Communications in improvement
Problem-solving conference techniques
Managing our time
Movie "Production 5118"

Conference #10—Summary

Review of conference material
Individual project presentation
Planning continued work simplification use
Movie "1104 Sutton Place"

An example of a flow process chart actually developed by a participant in this work simplification training program is presented in Figures 10-1 and 10-2, in before-and-after versions. A report form which is used for evaluation of improvement projects is shown in Figure 10-3.

The success of the Texas Instruments program in work simplification speaks for itself. Employees and managers at different levels express strong enthusiasm for the program, and give it much credit for contributing to productivity and morale.

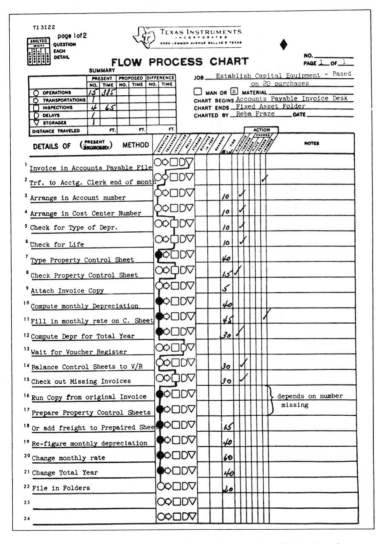

Figure 10-1. Flow process chart for work operations "before" work simplification project

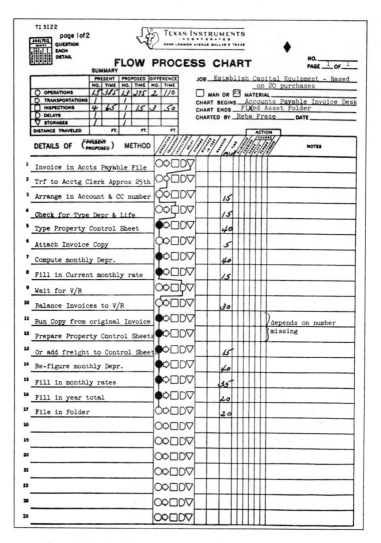

Figure 10-2. Flow process chart for work operations "after" work simplification project

Some variations in other enterprises

The Maytag Company has both a work simplification program and a suggestion system. They now have an 80% acceptance rate on suggestions, because employees screen out the poor ones before submitting them. They know better what to look for and how to present their recommendations.

WORK SIMPLIFICATION PROJECT EVALUATION REPORT

TI 3110 6/60 — TEXAS INSTRUMENTS INCORPORATED — SEMICONDUCTOR-COMPONENTS DIVISION

SUBMITTED BY: Reba Fraze		WORK ASSIGNMENT:		
SUPERVISOR: Richard McCarter	DEPT.: Staff Accounting	W/S ENGINEER: Don Webb	DATE OF REPORT:	DATE INSTALLED:

OPERATION, PROCESS, OR PROCEDURE AFFECTED: Establishing Capital Equipment

DESCRIPTION OF IMPROVED METHOD: Receive invoices earlier in month to improve flow of work. Eliminated writing in monthly depreciation and total year twice. Combined several operations to save time.

CHECK ITEMS OF IMPROVEMENT
QUALITY ____ LABOR X MATERIAL ____ YIELD ____ SAFETY ____ SPACE ____ MORALE ____
CUSTOMER SERVICE ____ PROCESS FLOW X EQUIP. UTIL. ____ INVENTORY ____ OTHER ____

OTHER AREAS WHERE THIS IMPROVEMENT WOULD BE POSSIBLE, IF KNOWN: — EXPECTED LONGEVITY: MOS.

SUMMARY OF ANNUAL SAVINGS BASED ON

		PRESENT		PROPOSED	
LABOR	1. MAN HOURS PER (~~1000~~ 20 UNITS) (~~DAYS~~) month ( )	7.5 MH		4 5/6 MH	
	2. ANNUAL PRODUCTION IN (1000 UNITS) (DAYS) ( )				
	3. TOTAL MAN HOURS PER YEAR	90 MH/YR		58 MH/YR	
	4. LABOR COST PER HOUR	$ 2.00		$ 2.00	
	5. TOTAL ANNUAL LABOR COST		$ 180.00		$ 116.00
O.H.	6. 50% OF TOTAL ANNUAL LABOR COST		$ 90.00		$ 58.00
OTHER	7. MATERIALS, SUPPLIES, ETC. (LIST ITEMS)				
	8. COST PER	$		$	
	9. USAGE PER YEAR				
	10. TOTAL ANNUAL COST OF MATERIALS, SUPPLIES, ETC.		$		$
	11. TOTAL ANNUAL COST		$ 270.00		$ 174.00

TOTAL GROSS SAVINGS: $ 96.00	INSTALLATION COST: $	FOR	RETURN ON INVESTMENT: TO 1

REVIEW: This proposal will save time during the peak work load period of monthly closings. It is being installed immediately.

BY Richard L. McCarter

BY

BY

ATTACH CHARTS, SKETCHES, GRAPHS, DETAILED SAVINGS COMPUTATIONS, ETC.

Figure 10-3. Work simplification project evaluation report

Sears, Roebuck, and Company provides for follow-up after training by encouraging any person who has completed the study program to sit in with a project study team for one hour a week.

In a certain large DuPont plant, a special effort is made to encourage every person to come through with one suggestion that can be accepted. They feel that this will make a "believer" of him for life.

The IBM Data Processing Division regularly issues to all branch offices a bulletin which passes along tips for improvement worked out in other branch offices throughout the country.

At Prudential Insurance, material in what was formerly a work simplification course is now merged with human relations and other material in their basic supervisory course for all supervisors, in the belief that it is difficult, if not impossible, to separate considerations involving people and work.

General observations

Where does a work simplification program leave the Systems and Procedures group? The answer is—busier than ever. Typically, they *conduct* the training or assist materially with it. They are called upon for technical assistance by line people working on projects. They, of course, still handle the more difficult problems themselves, particularly those cutting across departmental lines; or they work with project study teams which include representatives of these departments. Generally, they like work simplification training better than anyone else because they find that after training, employees are more improvement-conscious than ever.

There are many problems associated with an effective work simplification program that involves line personnel—support by top management and all other levels of management, persuading supervisors to make time in work schedules for such training (especially in early stages), finding suitable projects for study, providing opportunities for adequate follow-up, and resolving the issue of how best to reward personnel for usable improvement proposals.

But the key to the success of such programs, where carefully administered and adequately supported, lies perhaps in the personal involvement and the opportunity for self-expression provided. Those who praise "employee-centered" supervision and condemn "work-centered" supervision may find fault with such an approach—but it is probably true that the highest type of employee-centered supervision is that which provides employees with opportunities to accomplish useful work while using their creative abilities to the fullest degree.

QUESTIONS FOR STUDY AND DISCUSSION

1. Does the manner in which management approaches personnel in introducing particular programs seem to have much bearing upon success of the programs?

Consider contrasting approaches and results likely in the case of budgets, pro-cedures audits, a program to increase sales, a program to reduce costs, and a program to improve the effectiveness of performance appraisal (or merit rating). Does the field of methods improvement offer a particularly striking contrast of the sort considered?—why or why not? Can you suggest other common problem areas in management where similar contrasts might appear?

2. What person is credited with doing most to pioneer work simplification by line personnel? Why did he become interested? How have he and other leaders in this field gone about providing guidance to individual enterprises?

3. Why are both a questioning attitude and an organized approach necessary to success in work simplification?

4. Describe basic elements in a typical training program for work simplifica-tion. What before-and-after steps seem necessary, and why?

5. The outline of a work simplification training program used by Texas In-struments, Inc., for administrative personnel (mainly office supervisors and de-partment heads) was presented. Consider possible adaptations in such a training program which make it more effective for secretary-clerical personnel.

6. What suggestions can you offer for solving each of the following problems which may be met in making work simplification programs fully effective: (a) gaining active support from top management, (b) persuading supervisors to allow time away from regular operations, (c) finding suitable projects for study, (d) providing opportunities for adequate follow-up?

7. Practice varies on the issue of whether to have both a suggestion system with rewards and a work simplification program such as those described in this chap-ter. Present reasons supporting each side of this issue, then state and justify your own conclusions.

8. Could friction arise between persons in charge of a work simplification pro-gram for line personnel and those in charge of staff programs of systems and procedures analysis? If such friction might arise, how could it be minimized or overcome?

Case 10-1. Hall Electronics, Inc.

Shortly after the end of World War II a small group of men who, during the War, had acquired experience of varied types in the fast developing field of electronics, founded Barstow Enterprises—described in some of its early advertising as "the small firm which specializes in doing big jobs." The founders were fortunate in possessing an unusual combina-tion of engineering skill, production experience, and managerial ability. Despite limited capital at the beginning, they were able to secure govern-ment contracts for several types of electronic controls systems and to expand rapidly. By 1952, about five years after the firm's origin, annual sales had passed $10,000,000.

Growth brought problems, particularly in the area of cost reduction; and since a fairly large number of similar firms had been formed at about the same time, competition grew keen. In an effort to maintain the firm's position, its management decided in late 1952 to establish a work simplification program which would involve as many as possible of its line supervisors and employees in methods improvement and cost reduction efforts. A consultant was brought in to help in planning the program and to conduct a brief, initial training program for all management personnel in work simplification philosophy and techniques. Then an industrial engineer, with special help from the consultant, continued the program. Results surpassed all expectations; direct savings from improvement projects initiated by line personnel amounted to more than $150,000 during the first full year of the program. Unreported savings from improvements made after completion of the program were thought to be even greater; and the management was of the belief that benefits in the form of improved morale were greater still than the cost savings.

Barstow Enterprises continued to grow; and in 1955 a subsidiary known as Hall Electronics, Inc., was established. The parent firm had confined its operations largely to producing complex, electronic systems on a custom (almost job-shop) basis under government contracts. Hall Electronics, in contrast, mass-produced a line of standard electronic components which were to be marketed both to governmental users and private industry, for assembly with other parts into products of different types. Most of key positions in Hall Electronics were filled by personnel from the parent company. Woman employees were hired to fill most of the operative jobs, one reason being the manual nature of the operations and the dexterity with which women could perform these operations. Production lines were laid out with about twelve to eighteen women to a line. Each line was supervised by a group leader.

The new firm experienced even more rapid growth than its parent organization. It began to pull ahead of competitors in product design and sales volume, and it had to add many employees and work much overtime to meet the demand. Working conditions were good; wages and salaries were above prevailing levels; and morale was very high among most employees and management personnel. Very rapid promotions were required; this need, combined with the need to add large numbers of operative personnel, created a tremendous training problem at all levels.

The nature of the operations and the amount of training required seemed to present an even more fertile field for a work simplification program, with widespread line participation, than that which had existed in Barstow Enterprises. Such a program, accordingly, was launched with great care; and a long-range plan was laid for taking all supervisors and most operative personnel through work simplification training. Two types of classes were designed—one for hourly employees, the other for supervisory and technical employees in combination. The classes for hourly employees consisted of a two-hour session each week for eight weeks; those for supervisory-technical employees lasted twelve weeks. Subject matter was basically similar. With each group, efforts were made to develop the questioning attitude toward existing work methods, an organized approach for improving these methods, and actual application of improvement techniques to a project in the participant's own department. The supervisory-technical groups received somewhat more intensive training, were taught certain added techniques such as those involved in communications and conference leadership, and were encouraged to tackle somewhat more ambitious projects.

The program was well received from the beginning; cost reductions were substantial and they soon mounted to impressive figures. Personnel completing the courses and participating in improvement projects seemed to derive much satisfaction from the experience. Each department was allowed a quota of class members who could be accommodated, and there was a waiting list of persons for each class.

The management of Hall Electronics had instituted a profit-sharing plan early in the firm's existence, and it was quite easy for leaders and participants in the work simplification program to relate improvements made to shares of profit which would be returned to each employee. Publicity, recognition dinners, and other means of showing appreciation were employed; there were no cash awards, but employee interest remained high.

The Work Simplification Section was placed organizationally under a Chief Industrial Engineer, along with other industrial engineering and systems improvement units. So effective was the work simplification program in improving work methods on the job that, for a considerable period, virtually all methods improvement efforts were left to this program, with other industrial engineering personnel devoting most of their attention to building construction, major equipment requirements, layout, work standards, and other problems.

Continued rapid growth led to the bringing in from the outside of an increasing number of management personnel, both administrative and staff. Lack of background in work simplification by most of these individuals was reflected in a somewhat lesser degree of support for the program from them; most agreed to the program in principle but did not give it active support, and some showed reluctance to release employees to participate in the program. Top management, still strongly sold on the program, became aware of the situation and initiated a three-day conference of all management personnel above the supervisory level. During the conference, the same consulting group which had guided the original installation of the program presented a program designed to increase understanding, interest, and support on the part of all management. The conference was highly effective; results showed immediately in a higher level of cooperation from those department heads who had not had earlier exposure to work simplification training and in renewed interest on the part of some who had experienced the training some years earlier.

Only a few months after this conference, however, a very strong company-wide movement was begun to mechanize operations wherever possible, in order to meet competitive pressures and to take advantage of technological advances. In office as well as factory operations, many tasks formerly performed manually were mechanized; office machines and related equipment were automated where possible; many office applications were converted to computer processing; systems and forms were planned carefully by technical experts; and numerous other methods improvements were assigned to staff specialists newly-employed.

The cumulative effects of the efforts of specialized staff personnel to mechanize operations and to make other improvements, while beneficial from cost and efficiency standpoints in most cases, dealt the work simplification program a severe blow. Increasingly, participants in training classes would ask such questions as:

—"With all the engineers and other specialists we have now, how can I, Joe Doakes, hope to improve a process?"
—"This looks like it might be an improvement but surely not, because someone else would already have thought of it."
—"How could I ever hope to sell this improvement to my boss and to the staff people who would come swarming all over the place?"

The work simplification training leaders attempted to counter such doubts and to combat what seemed to be growing inertia on the part of line people in suggesting improvements, by such reasoning as the following: The design or selection of new equipment is always necessarily "rough," hence numerous opportunities exist for debugging and refining the equipment to make it more effective in actual operation. Mechanization, in fact, depends heavily upon the concept of work simplification, since someone must always first spot a need for improvement —and who is better qualified than the person now doing the job? In working methods improvements, engineers, systems analysts, and other staff specialists can learn much from employees presently doing the work. And continuing needs will always exist for further improvement and for adapting methods to changing work needs.

Much emphasis from the beginning had been placed upon the development of individual improvement projects which required each participant to apply principles and techniques to an actual problem in his department. Illustrative of individual projects was one which replaced lengthy pricing and extending of physical inventory sheets by determination of average unit prices and multiplying total number of units in process by the average; another resulted in moving a special customer file section from central files to the unit which used the files regularly. Direct savings from each project were determined carefully and accumulated.

Cost savings reported from improvement projects developed during the classes continued to be very substantial. There were indications that provision for follow-up and continued encouragement of work simplification efforts varied greatly from department to department and even unit to unit, however. Requests began to come from department heads to play down the *projects* as part of the classes, and to place more emphasis on the psychological aspects of individual response to rapidly-changing work situations. Projects seemed to become harder to find. To meet this problem, work simplification personnel started going into departments and helping class members spot possible improvement projects—always discussing such possibilities with supervisors involved, although a great many of the supervisors had not had the training themselves. Many department heads became reluctant to release personnel from their regular duties for participation in the classes; this problem was met by securing approval of top management (still thoroughly sold on the program) of a budget large enough so employee time in class or working on projects could be charged against the Work Simplification Section Budget rather than against the budget of the supervisor releasing the employee.

Most of the department heads appeared to welcome the change in budget arrangement, but some continued to show reluctance to release employees for the training, raising questions as to whether benefits gained offset problems created when employees are away from the job. One head of a major department requested and obtained approval from top management to have his personnel excluded from the program, with the explanation that they were needed so greatly for current work requirements. Other department heads continued to question the "project" emphasis in the training, in view of strong staff units now available to render expert guidance in virtually every problem area; most of these favored continuing the work simplification program but with more of a "concept" approach, emphasizing the philosophy of work simplification, the need for acceptance of methods improvement and innovation, and other aspects of human response to the work situation.

A recent reorganization has moved Work Simplification out of Industrial Engineering and placed it under the Training Section of the Personnel Department, which is headed by a Vice-President. Training in work simplification now emphasizes the human relations aspects of adapting to change, cooperation with one's supervisor and with staff specialists in the design and installation of improvements. The use of individual improvement projects has been reduced substantially. With groups where possibilities for savings seem great, such as engineering groups, projects are still an integral part of the training. There continues to be quite strong employee interest in gaining admission to the program each time a new class is announced.

Problems and questions:

a. Appraise the experience of Hall Electronics with work simplification. Does it seem to you that results achieved have approached the maximum or optimum attainable?

b. What principal problems were faced along the way?—what do you think of the manner in which each was met?

c. Suggest any improvements in the general approach, or any part of it, which you believe might have resulted in still greater benefits than those achieved.

d. Does it seem likely that a work simplification program of the sort involved here may have a "life cycle"—with different contributions possible at different stages of the growth of a firm? Would an effective work simplification program eventually "work itself out of a job" in some situations?

Case 10-2. The Warren National Bank

The president of the Warren National Bank was recently approached by his personnel manager with a tentative job evaluation plan. The president had approved the idea of a program of this sort, the main purpose being to establish a more equitable salary arrangement and one which could be explained to employees.

The rating scale for comparing jobs included eight factors, among which were knowledge, relationships, and certain others. As the president studied the plan, he raised an interesting question: "Why don't we include as a factor on every job description the responsibility to search constantly for better methods of doing the job? I believe that every person working for this bank knows more about something than anyone else, and that if we are wise and skillful enough, we should be able to use his ability both to his betterment and that of the company. And, of course, the 'one best way' today is not likely to be the 'one best way' tomorrow."

The personnel manager took the project with him for further study.

Problems and questions:

a. How do you react to the president's suggestion, especially to the philosophy expressed?

b. Would the new "factor" which he suggested be a compensable one, one that could be measured and rewarded in varying degrees for different jobs?

11

MECHANIZATION
IN ADMINISTRATIVE
PROCESSES

Policies guiding mechanization · Maintenance of office equipment · Classification of office equipment · Basic, general-purpose equipment · New developments in integrating office machines

---

Office machines have come a long way since Queen Anne granted a patent for a "writing machine" in 1714, and since Christopher Sholes presented the world with the first practical typewriter in 1873.

Today, administrators are faced with a bewildering array of machines which have been devised for virtually all types of operations. Mechanization, coming first to factory processes because of obvious value in aiding physical operations directly involved in production, is now moving into office and administrative processes at a pace which seems likely to surpass its progress in the factory.

The reasons for accelerated mechanization in administrative processes are apparent. The relatively slow beginning left a long way to go, and at least part of the movement must be regarded as a catching-up process. Basic changes in the nature of enterprises and the operations involved are having profound effects; one indication is the fact that the number of "white-collar" workers exceeded "blue-collar" workers for the first time in 1956, and are now rapidly increasing their lead.

Businesses, growing in size and complexity, and ever-keener competition are influencing management to look for sharper tools not only in *physical* production but in *mental* work as well, such as that involved in problem-recognition, analysis, memory, and communication to achieve understanding. Technological advances in office machines and related equipment to meet administrative needs are now progressing with amazing speed. For the past twenty years, the office equipment industry has been one of the leading growth industries. Developments are now so rapid that managers find it difficult to remain informed on new equipment available. This difficulty is perhaps best illustrated by the appearance of a new "growth industry"—special service organizations which help users select equipment from the many different types available.

Policies Guiding Mechanization

General criteria for design or choice of methods for performing operations can be summarized under the headings of *effectiveness, economy,* and *impact on employees.* These criteria apply directly to problems of mechanization. A set of guides for applying them to specific problems such as matching needs and equipment will be presented in this section.

A logical beginning in any situation when purchase of an office machine is being considered is to pose the following questions:

1. Is a machine really needed?
2. If a machine is needed, which one should be selected?

Establishing the need

For an increasing number of office operations, the answer to the first question is in the affirmative. But the need for a machine, even when available commercially, should never be taken for granted.

Alternatives should be considered first. Is it possible that the work itself could be eliminated, simplified, rescheduled, or altered in such a way as to eliminate the necessity for mechanization? The management of one firm was considering the expansion of its data processing installation to take care of a heavy weekly peak load, until it discovered that by better scheduling and fuller utilization of present equipment the problem could be solved without the expansion.

What are the possibilities for "sub-contracting" the work under study to outside service agencies? As noted in the introductory chapter, a remarkable development of service agencies is now occurring; no alert management will overlook the possibility that a service agency might perform many types of work more effectively and more economically.

If the work clearly is necessary, does it really require a machine, or is it possible that the work could be done by a simple, non-mechanical means? One device that could be used far more is the prepared table of values, such as rates, prices, products of numbers commonly multiplied, and many other applications. Another practical device is the slide rule, which is rapid, inexpensive, and sufficiently accurate for many purposes.

Making the selection

In a great many cases a machine will be justified; the problem then becomes one of choice or, in some cases, one of special design.

A wide range of types of machines is available. There are a great many competitive models in most types, and each is likely to provide optional or special features which should be considered by the buyer. Moreover, an investment in the typical office machine requires a considerable outlay of money; the possibility of obsolescence causes a machine to be a somewhat unstable asset. These considerations suggest the need for objective study of any proposed purchase of an office machine.

An analysis in three stages usually will be justified, following the sequence below.

1. *What are the requirements of the operation which may be met through mechanization?*

What goals are sought in mechanization?—prompter customer service, reduced administrative cost, facilitation of other internal operations, fewer errors, less monotonous work for employees, solution to labor shortage? Then—what specific processes are involved, what are their volume and speed requirements, how highly standardized are they, and what are the prospects as to future demands for this operation (permanent or temporary, growing or declining, etc.)?

Both the precise nature of goals sought and the nature of the specific processes involved are necessary in establishing the need. If competitive success in the industry depends heavily upon prompt service, this consideration may outweigh all others, for example. If the enterprise is caught in a "cost squeeze," getting the work done more economically may be the dominant consideration. Or the optimum combination of these and other goals may be sought, with some of major and some of minor concern.

The nature of the process involved, the capacity and speed requirements, the degree of standardization, and other considerations will narrow the field to certain types of equipment, which will be more appropriate —*special-purpose* equipment to do only this operation but do it well, or *general-purpose* equipment which will perform this and other operations under widely varying conditions? Illustrative of a special-purpose machine is a check-writing machine; a desk calculator or typewriter would come nearer to being general-purpose, although the difference is one of degree—for example, one calculator may be much more versatile than another.

2. *Which machines, among competitive types and makes available, appear to have the capacity, speed, and special features needed in the operation?*

The rapid growth of the office equipment industry has attracted many competitors, and there are few if any machine needs which would now not have a rather large number of prospective suppliers. And office machines, like automobiles, are now available in wide varieties of "horsepower," size, speed, and special features. It is important, therefore, to ascertain which suppliers have equipment which may seem to fit the needs of a given operation; leads are, of course, available through advertisements in trade publications, machines exhibitions, reputable suppliers, recommendations by consultants, etc.

Evaluating the available features of a supplier's equipment will justify close study and comparison; although a supplier may offer a considerable variety of features, it is likely that his equipment will excel in certain aspects, be somewhat less satisfactory in others. One make of copying machines may produce clearer copies but at higher costs; the buyer must decide which is more important for his need.

There is also much variation in speed and capacity. It is usually possible to find pretty nearly the optimum characteristics if one searches carefully—so, why pay for a labeling machine capable of affixing labels to various materials at 12,000 an hour if the need is for labeling only one type of material and the volume is 12,000 a week?

Or, why get the automatic division feature on a desk calculator unless the operation requires enough of this work to make it worthwhile? On the other hand, if there is a recurring need to rush blueprints to distant units of a firm, facsimile reproduction and transmission may be a wiser approach than a slower and less costly method of providing the blueprints. As obvious as such precautions may appear, it is likely that *most* machine selections are somewhat less than the best currently available for the uses intended. And there is, of course, the continuing problem of remaining informed on new developments which might show a particular choice in an entirely different light.

3. *Which of the machines that appear to "qualify" for the operation should offer the best overall solution to the specific needs of the enterprise?*

In general, one might be justified in saying—"the simplest, least-expensive machine to do the job"—but a set of more specific questions should usually be considered. With the preceding discussion as background, a checklist of pertinent questions follows.

a. Is the output of a particular machine suitable to needs in terms of accuracy, neatness, and other quality factors?

b. Is speed of service adequate for meeting customer needs and/or for facilitating other internal operations which may depend upon this one?

c. Is cost justified by benefits gained, either in direct dollar savings or in indirect benefits such as competitive advantage through prompter service, or better information for long-range plans? Even though not an easy undertaking, efforts ordinarily should be made to assess the value of such intangible benefits as the last mentioned. The alternatives may be a penny-wise, pound-foolish approach, or a tendency to commit the firm to luxuries which may be impressive but impractical. The large investment involved in many modern data processing installations makes a combination of open-mindedness and prudence particularly appropriate in this area.

  (1) Does the obsolescence factor warrant special consideration for the equipment under study? Many firms have policies requiring that machines of certain types pay for themselves in a specified number of years, or perhaps in one-fourth of their useful life. Such policies have merit under the current rapid rate of obsolescence of many machines; but if used, they should reflect varying rates of obsolescence, and due allowance should be made for intangible benefits such as those discussed above.

  (2) Does the outlook for the operation under study justify special consideration? Is the need likely to continue, or may it be uncertain because of the changing nature or volume of work, the prospect of major overhauling of systems, or other reasons?

d. Does the equipment offer the necessary flexibility and adaptability? Consider not only variations in the given operation but other operations which might employ the equipment as well.

e. Is leasing possible? If so, would leasing be preferable to purchase? This important alternative will be considered in a brief, separate section.

f. Could maintenance needs be met effectively and economically? Key factors in maintenance decisions will also be treated in a separate section.

g. Could the very important problems of employee adjustment be solved—acceptance of change, adequate supply of potentially able employees, training needs, reduction of such problems as drudgery and excessive errors where present?

Before the final choice is made, actual tryout of one or more of the "most likely" machines can be vitally beneficial. Arrangements can usually be made to bring smaller machines to the firm for a short trial on the work to be processed. Larger equipment often can be tried out, with a reasonable degree of satisfaction, in the premises of the supplier.

Purchase versus lease

Leasing as a means of financing office equipment is now in extensive and growing use. Primary reasons include the following:

1. *Reduced capital outlay for equipment.* Funds may be limited. Even if this is not the case, more profitable uses of funds may exist, such as in programs calling for more aggressive research or sales promotion involving addition of skilled personnel; or inventory which can be turned quickly; or general expansion.

2. *Up-to-date equipment without permanent commitment of funds.* The obsolescence danger can be minimized for many types of equipment by leasing recent models, with the opportunity to retain the equipment or change to still newer models when the lease period expires.

3. *Temporary or fill-in needs.* Short-term needs, for special or temporary programs and for filling in during peak loads of work volume, may be met more wisely by leasing than outright purchase.

4. *Trial use.* Suppliers may offer free trial of certain types of equipment for short periods. For equipment not available for trial, or for equipment justifying longer and more intensive trial before purchase, leasing arrangements are often available.

5. *Servicing provided.* Leasing arrangements usually provide for servicing the equipment leased.

Each benefit of leasing has its price, of course. Firms having heavy, continuing need for equipment, or having no better alternatives in use of funds, or lacking the opportunity to lease even when wishing to do so, will usually continue to purchase office equipment. It appears to be true, however, that alternative uses of funds are being scrutinized much more closely than in earlier years, and that accelerated obsolescence is causing many managements to take a harder look at buying than formerly.

Maintenance of Office Equipment

When a machine breaks down or functions improperly, much valuable time can be lost, other operations are interrupted, costly errors occur, and other damages result. Hence, adequate provision for maintenance may, in some cases, be almost as important as selecting the equipment.

Alternative arrangements include: combining rental and maintenance services in lease agreements (just discussed); service contracts, either with the supplier or with independent agencies; on-call service by supplier or independent agency on special request; and providing own maintenance personnel and facilities.

In most firms, outside service is ordinarily used. Larger firms may have the resources to service certain types of office equipment but are likely to be forced to rely upon outside specialists for most maintenance requirements.

The choice between service contracts or on-call service is somewhat controversial, even among firms which make use of both. Service contracts specify a fixed fee (which may be considered an advantage by some firms) for providing preventive maintenance through regular checkup and servicing, along with prompt service when breakdowns occur; the fees may be considered expensive, particularly where equipment is not heavily utilized. On-call service may be considered advantageous where equipment utilization is not extremely heavy, where maintenance service is available on short notice, where trade-ins of certain equipment (such as typewriters) are made frequently enough to minimize maintenance requirements, and where cost comparisons show savings without serious interruption of normal operations.

Responsibility for equipment selection and maintenance

Factors considered in the preceding discussion indicate that several persons or groups normally should participate in office equipment selection decisions.

Basically, equipment selection is an important part of the overall problem of systems design. Hence, systems analysts or, in the smaller firm, an office manager who does systems and methods analysis along with other duties, have the necessary special qualifications. They can aid in establishing the need, evaluating past experience as revealed by equipment records, insuring conformance to overall standardization programs, and determining and evaluating alternative types of equipment available.

Operators of the equipment and their supervisors should, of course, contribute their ideas regarding experience with equipment in the past and prospective needs; their recommendations should weigh heavily in decisions, but in coordinating other operations and systems requirements may sometimes require a broader view. Ideally, most decisions will be made by a team of users, systems analysts, and sometimes cost analysts and other specialists.

Valuable outside help can be secured from sales representatives of equipment suppliers, who have acquired much knowledge and experience in working with other enterprises. One of the most notable trends in office equipment and supplies competition is the provision of more and better systems help, even to the point of doing much of the basic systems design, training the user's personnel, and following up at intervals to insure proper usage. Particularly striking are the current efforts of computer manufacturers to design programs (or software) to fit the particular systems requirements of certain industries and even individual enterprises which use their equipment. The need to maintain an objective attitude toward the offerings and avowed advantages of different suppliers is important; reputable suppliers attempt (not always with complete success) to train and supervise their representatives to insure customer satisfaction to a degree where they will recommend other prospective buyers, and encourage repeat business. Trying out the offerings of two or more suppliers is of obvious value.

The services of independent consultants will not often be required in office equipment selection, although in advising in complex systems problems, they often strongly influence specific choices of equipment. Direct assistance with comparative cost analysis and other dimensions of the problem is available if desired. And, as mentioned earlier, a new type of consulting service is now developing—that of conducting impartial analysis of needs and equipment available, and making specific recommendations to users.

Classification of Office Equipment

There is no easy way to classify office equipment. One can list many types—some having uses that are quite specialized, others serving such a variety of operations that they cannot be tied down to any one.

For the sake of continuity, we shall relate classes of equipment to the basic categories of methods by which office operations are carried out: assembling, processing, communicating, and recording. The sequence suggested is followed in only a very general way. Virtually all office processes do fall into one or the other of the categories.

Equipment for assembling data

"Data collecting" may be a more descriptive term for this category of operations. There are few data-collecting machines as such.

Most original data come into the enterprise either as oral or written messages in conducting primary activities, such as purchasing and sales. Other data arise from subsequent activities such as production; provision of manpower, materials, and equipment; and accounting. "Feedback" data for control purposes are developed continuously from work in process. All such data may be entered manually or mechanically on forms, reports, and other documents. Oral communications also play a vital role in assembling information.

Certain highly promising developments are occurring in the field of source-data automation. Among these are optical scanning devices, magnetic ink readers, and voice-to-written message translation. These devices will be treated in the section of data processing which deals with data acquisition, since they enter directly into processing sequences.

Equipment for processing data

Data processing involves actually changing data into a more refined and useful form, either as a part of current operations or from specific planning or control usage. Machine methods are in particularly heavy use for processing data. Among principal processing machines are:

Adding machines
Calculating machines
Punched card machines
Computers

Equipment for recording data

A broad definition of recording equipment also takes in many types of machines, including those for initial recording, reproduction, and retention. Prominent among the recording machines are:

Typewriters
Copying machines (for few copies)
Duplicating machines (for many copies)
Microfilming equipment

Filing and other records storage equipment serve the primary functions of retention and retrieval; an increasing portion of records storage is being done in computer storage equipment and various kinds of motorized files.

Forms, reports, and other documents are other important recording methods. Of course, the most basic method for original entry of data is still handwriting.

Equipment for communicating data

Rapid and significant advances in communications "gear" of many types have been made. Major groupings include:

Mailroom equipment (mailing, addressing, labeling, etc.)
Dictating and transcribing equipment
Intercommunications equipment
External transmission equipment

Having particular promise is equipment for transmitting data from machine to machine.

Most types of equipment mentioned thus far are best understood and appreciated when considered in relation to the basic processes with which they are associated. External message transmission equipment, the teletypewriter, for example, can be appraised most effectively by considering the general function, processes, and requirements of communication. For this reason, the above-listed types of equipment will be considered in later chapters which deal with basic categories of office methods and services. The only exceptions to this approach are certain machines which are "general purpose" and do not fall neatly into later treatments of process categories. These include typewriters; adding, calculating, and accounting machines; punched card machines; and miscellaneous machines and other equipment; they will now be given brief treatment. Of special consideration is the fact that basic equipment of the first three types just mentioned, while performing primary functions, now frequently produce by-products such as paper tape, magnetic tape, or punched cards, which serve as *input* to computers and other machines. This feature is a key to *integrated data processing,* to be considered in a later chapter.

Basic General-Purpose Equipment

Detailed descriptions of the many types of equipment available are neither possible nor appropriate in this book. Moreover, new and improved models of many types of equipment are appearing at such a rapid pace that nearly any model pictured or described might soon be obsolete. Individuals desiring specific descriptions can easily obtain them by communicating directly with supplier representatives; referring to advertisements in trade and professional publications; attending equipment exhibitions; following up on leads furnished by business associates; and by utilizing other sources of information. A valuable service is now provided by many periodicals in the form of a reply card inserted in each issue, keyed by number to supplier advertisements and offering to send descriptive materials and/or have representatives call.

Typewriters

Still the most widely used office machine, the modern typewriter is definitely "not what it used to be." The standard typewriter continues to be the workhorse in most offices. Electric models are rapidly gaining in popularity, however, and currently account for more than one-third of typewriter sales volume.

The mounting popularity of electric typewriters arises from their ability to produce uniform print, a cleaner "write," more carbon copies, and greater output with less operator fatigue. New features include proportional spacing, paper injector-ejectors, and tabulating mechanisms which sense metallic ink printed into business forms. One model, the IBM Selectric, has no key bars; characters appear on a golf-ball size printing head, easily interchangeable for other type-styles, thus offering versatility, no key-jams, easy cleaning, and requiring less desk-space, since only the printing head moves back and forth across the carriage.

Other important typewriter variations are: the automatic typewriter, which operates either from a punched tape as described above or from a perforated record roll and produces individually typed letters at speeds in the order of 175 words a minute; the composing typewriter, which features interchangeable type-styles for setting up master copy with varied headings and even margins; and the teletypewriter which transmits messages over telephone circuits. The teletypewriter is now being put to such varied and significant uses that it will be considered further in sections on communications and data processing.

Figure 11-1. *Left:* The Smith-Corona electric portable typewriter; *below:* the new IBM Selectric typewriter.

Smith-Corona Marchant, Inc.

International Business Machines Corp.

Adding, calculating, and accounting machines

Standard office equipment concerned with "arithmetic" operations include adding, calculating, and accounting machines. Even with the advent of high-powered electronic devices, these machines seem likely to remain as old stand-bys. One reason for this is that, although efficient programming is prevalent today, tasks of an exceptional nature still arise. Also, many offices are not yet utilizing IDP equipment.

This being true, manufacturers of such standard equipment and machinery continue to improve it. The speed of these machines will probably not be increased greatly, but more and more operations can be performed automatically.

Adding machines: Adding machines are limited to addition and subtraction, in most cases. They may be used for multiplication and division but their speed and capacity in this work is not as great as other types

Figure 11-1 (cont.). *Right:* The Friden automatic calculator; *below:* the National Class 33 Accounting machine. Note the typewriter keyboard for alphabetical posting.

Friden, Inc.

National Cash Register Company

of machines. Most adding machines employ automatic printing devices which print both the factors and the results, and are available in either electric or manual models with a choice of a full keyboard or a ten key arrangement.

Calculating machines: Calculating machines are used primarily for multiplication and division, accomplishing these functions by repetitive, high-speed addition and subtraction. Calculating machines are, then, highly developed adding machines and can be used for simple addition and subtraction operations. Most standard calculating machines are non-listing and have a full keyboard, showing the answer in a dial on the machine.

There are two types of calculating machines, rotary and key-driven. Depression of a key causes a key-driven machine to operate where rotary calculators require that an activating bar be depressed.

Calculators have their widest uses in statistical work where a large number of percentages and ratios are determined, and in invoice or payroll work that requires extensive multiplication operations.

Accounting machines: "Accounting machine" is a broad classification used to include bookkeeping, billing, and posting machines, as well as the specific accounting machines. Accounting machines have several accumulators or registers whereby totals from several classifications of data may be obtained. Accounting machines perform accounting work in the literal sense of the word, their basic purpose being to prepare accounting documents and to totalize accumulated sums. The primary factor which distinguishes bookkeeping and accounting machines from other office machines is their ability to enter descriptive information such as simple numerical codes or complete alphabetical descriptions. Some of the larger accounting machines will, for example, type the customer's name together with a brief description of the sale and the unit cost and then compute the discount, compute the total amount, pick up the previous balance, and print the new balance.

Typical applications of accounting machines involve accounts payable, customer billing, and preparing depositor's ledger and statement for bank operations.

Punched card machines

Punched card equipment is recognized to be the most economical means of entry to automatic data processing. However, much of the punched card equipment in the nation is found in installations that not only do not have a computer system, but have no plans for employing one because of the limited size of the company or because of the prohibitive cost involved.

Virtually every commercial processing system, including tape-oriented systems, use punched cards as one means of input or output. It is not unusual to find smaller configurations of electronic computer systems in which punched cards are a principal input-output medium.

Punched card machines utilize standard size cards into which small holes are punched. The holes are coded to represent numerical or alphabetical information. The most commonly used cards have a maximum capacity of eighty (IBM) or ninety (Remington Rand) columns, thus permitting a maximum of eighty or ninety numbers or letters per card. When a punched card is processed through a machine, an electrical or mechanical impulse through the small holes causes the mechanism to operate and the data which the holes represent are then counted, sorted, listed, printed, or computed, depending upon the type of machine used and the results desired.

While punched card machines come in hundreds of different models, sizes, and types, there are essentially eight basic functional punched card machines. These are:

1. Card punch—Punches holes in the cards from a keyboard which resembles a standard typewriter keyboard.

2. Card punch verifier—A similar machine to the card punch, except that punching is exchanged for an electric impulse to verify that the proper data has been punched.

3. Interpreter—Interprets the punched holes in the cards and prints the information on the card.

4. Sorter—Arranges the punched cards in a desired sequence, or selects predetermined cards depending on the punched holes.

5. Collator—Selects predetermined classes of cards, interfiles or matches two related groups of cards which have been sorted into parallel sequences.

6. Reproducer—Punches data from one set of punched cards into another set of cards, or punches data from one master card into a group of following cards.

7. Calculator—Performs arithmetic and logic operations from data in punched cards.

8. Tabulator—Reads, summarizes, and prints information from data in punched cards.

The significance of punched card machines lies in the common language provided by the punched card. The punched card is an important element in the concept of integrated data processing discussed in a later chapter. Once the data is punched in the cards, the cards can be summarized, sorted, and processed in an almost unlimited variety of operations as required by management or by the nature of the operations.

Applications of punched cards are constantly being multiplied as new uses for them continue to be found. The new teleprocessing devices—

equipment that transmits machine information over long distances—are an example of the major role played by the punched card. The IBM data transceiver, equipped with the digital subset feature, transmits and receives punched card data over conventional dial telephone lines at regular message rates, or over new high-speed telegraph circuits. The long-distance transmission of data is one of the fastest growing areas in the field of data processing.[1] And it does not depend on the presence of a computer in the integrated system.

Another example of a relatively new application for the punched card

1 Data transmission is covered in detail in Chapter 13.

Figure 11-2. *Left:* The IBM electric card punch, featuring the movable keyboard; *below:* the IBM 84 Sorter is a highly versatile machine which sorts cards by photoelectrically sensing holes punched in selected card columns.

International Business Machines Corp.

is the data collection system—a system that permits work-in-progress reports to be flashed by means of a punched card from remote stations to a central processing location.

Punched card machines or "systems" have their widest use in performing such operations as analyzing, correlating, and summarizing operating data; handling customer billing and accounts receivable; handling accounts payable; preparing payrolls and distributing labor costs; and maintaining inventory control records.

There are only two American manufacturers of powered punched card machines: International Business Machines and Remington Rand Divi-

Figure 11-2 (cont.). *Left:* The IBM 88 Collator is a high speed card-selecting and filing machine; *below:* the IBM 407 Accounting Machine prepares reports and records from punched IBM cards.

International Business Machines Corp.

sion of Sperry Rand Corporation. The basic machines manufactured by these companies are similar but not compatible, and both IBM and Remington Rand machines may be either rented or purchased. The Underwood Samas line of punched card machines manufactured in England, is also well known in this country.

Miscellaneous office machines

A miscellaneous category of office machines includes those machines which, because of their price, size, or function, seem insignificant. The proper use of many of these miscellaneous machines will, however, greatly facilitate the accuracy, volume, and ease with which many office tasks are performed.

Counters: These machines are used to count units of work for production and control purposes. Typical counting devices can be attached to typewriters to record the number of key strokes.

Staplers: Electric staplers are used primarily as an auxiliary to paper collating machines, permitting rapid and easier stapling of booklets or other large groups of papers.

Letter openers: These machines speed up the letter-opening operation considerably and reduce the possibility of mutilating the contents of the envelopes. Letter openers utilize a guarded cutting edge which snips a hairline edge off envelopes as fast as they can be fed into the machines.

Numbering machines: These machines or devices are used in placing numbers in chronological order on papers, such as numbering incoming orders as a means of controlling the priority assignment.

Daters and time stamps: These devices are used in affixing the exact time of receipt of a document, particularly in dating incoming correspondence.

New Developments in Integrating Office Machines

Of special importance to the development of a "common language" for sequential processing of the data on an integrated basis are the tape-punch attachments which produce punched tape as a by-product of the regular operations. Punched paper tape attachments or features are quite common on such standard office machines as typewriters, adding, calculating, and accounting machines. These features allow a tape to be punched of the essential data generated from operating the office machine—totals, summaries, or even the complete data itself. The punched tape output is compatible with standard tabulating or electronic data processing equipment and is a direct input source for computer systems or for other machines which have tape-read devices attached and are capable of automatic operation. These paper punch features allow isolated, small firms to prepare their basic records in their usual way, but to simultaneously prepare a punched tape that is processed by service bureaus in preparing consolidated reports billing, and similar routine office reports or summaries.

Figure 11-3 shows the paper punch feature on a typewriter, the widely used Flexowriter, and on an adding machine, the Synchro.

QUESTIONS FOR STUDY AND DISCUSSION

1. Why was mechanization much slower in coming to office and administrative processes than to factory processes? Why is there now such an acceleration in office mechanization? What does the future appear to hold?

2. The management of a firm has decided to embark upon an expanded program of sales promotion which looks as if it may require greatly increased volume in the clerical operations of typing, addressing, and preparation of outgoing mail. Acquisition of a substantial number of office machines of different types is being considered. Would you recommend that they consider certain alternatives before buying much additional equipment?—if so, what alternatives and why should each be considered?

3. Study carefully and critically the three steps or stages of analysis suggested for making a selection of a specific machine or other piece of equipment. If a small group of department heads held a discussion of the new demands posed by the expanded sales promotion program described in question two, then proposed the immediate purchase of ten electric typewriters of a certain make, an addressing machine advertised in the current issue of a trade magazine, and a mailing machine of a type that they know another firm to be using currently—what are several important factors that might be overlooked?

4. Suggest several specific conditions which might make leasing preferable to purchase of office equipment. Why does the alternative of leasing seem to be receiving more attention than formerly?

5. What factors warrant chief consideration in the decision of whether to use service contracts, on-call outside service, or own maintainence personnel and facilities in servicing office equipment?

6. A decision is soon to be made in a certain firm regarding the possibility of acquiring dictating and recording equipment, and regarding choice of the specific make and type if the decision is in favor of acquiring such equipment. What different persons or groups might well share in the responsibility of making these decisions, and what might each contribute?

7. Note the basic categories suggested for office equipment. Suggest illustrative machines which cut across these categories to such an extent that they are difficult to classify. What are "general-purpose" machines? What, then, would you regard as "special purpose" machines, and when would the latter be justified?

8. Study the descriptions of basic, general-purpose office machines, noting particularly any significant trends in recent models. How many of these seem likely to be made "extinct" by computers and other powerful new equipment? What, particularly, seems to be the outlook for continued use of punched card machines?—will punched tape and other developments reduce the need for such equipment?

9. What are the best sources through which anyone interested may stay in-

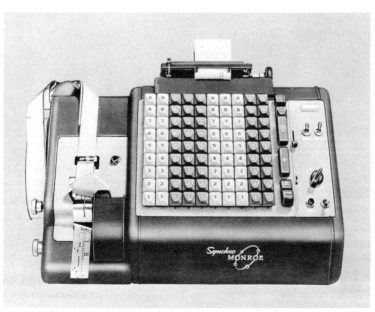

Figure 11-3. *Above:* the Friden Flexowriter; *below:* the Synchro-Monroe adding machine.

formed on new and improved models of office equipment? What are the advantages and limitations of each power?

Case 11-1. Lion Tire Company

The office manager of the Lion Tire Company is considering the purchase of a copying machine. Current practice requires a clerk-typist to retype the desired information, but this has not been too satisfactory because of the time involved.

The February, 1962, issue of *The Office* included a formula which had been converted into a table indicating under what cost, salary, and time saved conditions certain purchases of office machines would be justified. This table is reproduced below. The office manager was very much interested in this method and he decided to apply the table to the decision to purchase an office copying machine.

The office copier being considered sells for $2500. The office manager expects that the net employee time saved will be 35-40 minutes per day and the salary of the clerk-typist who would operate the office machine is $3500 per annum.

Problems and questions:

a. Should the office manager purchase the copying machine which costs $2500? Why?

b. What other considerations are involved in such a decision, if any? How should these be evaluated?

Case 11-2. Mechanization and Employment

The general relationship between factory mechanization and the number of jobs in existence is quite generally understood. At least, there is a rather high degree of agreement regarding it among management scholars, of whatever calling.

The usual explanation, in a highly simplified form, is that improved technology in factory operations has led to lower costs of production, enabling firms to price their products and services for less and to bring them within reach of more and more consumers. Items which formerly were within the buying power of only a few have been brought within reach of more and more people, while quality has improved at the same time. Expanding markets have led to increased production, distribution, finance, and service industries of many types. New types of jobs in large numbers have come into being. Many more jobs have been created by technological advances than have been displaced.

Daily Time Saving Needed to Justify Equipment Cost									
WEEKLY SALARY ➜	$58	$68	$77	$87	$96	$106	$115	$135	$154
ANNUAL SALARY ➜	$3000	$3500	$4000	$4500	$5000	$5500	$6000	$7000	$8000
EQUIPMENT COST ↓	NECESSARY MINUTES PER DAY SAVING TO JUSTIFY EXPENSE								
$100	2	1	1	1	1	1	1	1	1
$200	3	3	2	2	2	2	1	1	1
$300	5	4	4	3	3	3	2	2	2
$400	6	6	5	4	4	4	3	3	2
$500	8	7	6	5	5	4	4	3	3
$600	10	8	7	6	6	5	5	4	4
$700	11	10	8	8	7	6	5	5	4
$800	13	11	10	9	8	7	6	6	5
$900	14	12	11	10	9	8	7	6	5
$1000	16	14	12	11	10	9	8	7	6
$1100	18	15	13	12	11	10	9	7	7
$1200	19	16	14	13	12	11	9	8	7
$1300	21	18	16	14	13	11	10	9	8
$1400	22	19	17	15	14	12	11	10	8
$1500	24	21	18	16	14	13	12	10	9
$1600	26	22	19	17	15	14	13	11	10
$1700	27	23	20	18	16	15	13	12	10
$1800	29	25	22	19	17	16	14	12	11
$1900	30	26	23	20	18	17	15	13	11
$2000	32	27	24	21	19	18	16	14	12
$3000	48	42	36	32	28	26	24	21	18

BASIS OF COMPUTATIONS: 2000 hours per year, 250 eight-hour days, 10% per year for depreciation of equipment (no allowance for tax portion of cost).

Source: *The Office*—February, 1962.

Problems and questions:

a. Do the same relationships hold in regard to office mechanization and "information technology"? Does the same explanation fit, or must it be modified?

b. In the office as in the factory, many skills are being made obsolete by the upsurge of mechanization. What are the obligations of (1) management, (2) the employee, (3) unions, and (4) government, in minimizing hardship and facilitating adjustment to the new working environment?

IV

DATA COLLECTION
AND PROCESSING METHODS

Office operations have been previously classified as being concerned with assembling, processing, communicating, and recording information. Each operation is performed by a *method* of some sort, hence, a great deal is at stake in methods design and selection. Parts IV, V, and VI will be devoted to different groupings of methods, with emphasis upon basic descriptions needed to understand what is available, policies to guide in selecting appropriate methods, and techniques of analysis which guide selection and use. General criteria in appraising methods are *effectiveness and economy;* specific criteria, based upon these, will be developed for each of the classes of methods.

In Part IV, we shall concentrate attention upon the electronic computer and auxiliary equipment and methods which it has made possible. The computer itself is but a method. But it is so powerful and versatile a method or tool that its impact is not limited to the speed and capacity of processing given data. The computer is expanding to such a degree man's ability to marshal and utilize information that it is producing a revolution in the performance of mental work which may be of even greater significance than the Industrial Revolution, which brought so many changes to manual work operations.

The organization structure of an enterprise may be altered substantially. The computer is the "prime mover" for implementing the systems concept, considered in Part III. So far-reaching are the implications of electronic data processing that every person in management needs basic familiarity with the computer and its capabilities, so he may be an intelligent user of its services, even though he may have only limited technical skill in computer programming and administration.

The basic nature of computers; illustrative applications; special adaptations for integrated data processing, data acquisition, data transmission, and information retrieval; and problems in administering a data processing installation, will be considered in the chapters in Part IV.

12

COMPUTER FUNCTIONS
AND APPLICATIONS

*History of mechanization · Need for familiarity with com-
puter systems · Basic components of computer systems · Computer configurations · Computer programming · Software for
computer systems · Common language for computers · Trends
in electronic computer systems*

The electronic computer is a tech-
nological breakthrough which has few parallels. Debate centers on the
question of "revolution—or evolution?" when the electronic computer is
discussed.

A Short History

Those who consider the computer as but one additional step in the
long evolutionary process of mechanization can point to the general accumulation of human knowledge regarding machines and tools. They
note such forerunners as the abacus which was developed many centuries
ago, Pascal's calculator in 1642, Babbage's differential analyzer in the
1860's, and Hollerith's punched card equipment in 1889.

But the electronic computer represents a tremendous leap forward and
brings changes in the conduct of human affairs which may be unprecedented. Consider the vastly intricate calculations of an aerospace
project; the classification, storage, and retrieval of a substantial portion
of the accumulated knowledge in a field such as medicine, law, or
political science; the simulation and choice from alternate courses of

future action for a business or other enterprise; the coordination of the current operations of a complex enterprise into an integrated or total system.

Many persons have observed that the Industrial Revolution brought sweeping changes in manual operations, where the electronic computer ushers in a revolution in mental activities—greatly extending man's power to understand and control the forces which shape his destiny.

Certainly the suddenness of the advent and the development of the modern electronic computer seems to be a revolutionary characteristic. The first true electronic computer is generally acknowledged to be the ENIAC developed at the University of Pennsylvania in 1946 for use by the Navy in solving complex ballistic firing problems. Significant refinements followed soon afterward, the most notable being the stored program feature which made it possible to feed both the instructions needed and the raw data to be processed into a computer.

Potentialities for computer usage in administrative and other fields quickly became apparent. Applications of the computer systems to governmental operations other than scientific came with the installation of the Univac I for the Bureau of the Census in 1951. The first installation of an electronic computer system for daily cyclical business operations was a Remington Rand Univac computer installed in August of 1953 for the General Electric Company at Appliance Park, Kentucky.[1] Early business and governmental usage of computer systems was quite limited in scope, in part due to: (1) scientifically oriented equipment design, (2) limited understanding of computers by persons outside the physical sciences, and (3) limited comprehension of the management decision-making process and of information which could contribute, if available, to sound managerial decisions.

Since manufacturers recognized and responded to the immense potential of computers for data processing in business and governmental operations by designing equipment to fit these needs, and as managerial knowledge accumulated, the number of computers utilized for data processing far surpassed the number used for scientific research and problem-solving. From a handful in 1956, the number of such computers reached approximately 6,000 in 1960, and is expected to exceed 45,000 by 1965.

There seems to be little doubt that business applications of electronic computers will continue to increase in the next several decades. Certain important developments are now appearing, however, which are altering the basic elements in the race for leadership in the computer field. These developments include manufacturer redirection of emphasis from designing more powerful hardware to concentrating upon improving customer

[1] Franklin Life Insurance Company ordered a Univac in June, 1952, for insurance applications.

service through providing software items such as programmed applications, common language programs, and other services. There is a noticeable increase in the effort to provide the customer with computer systems planned for his particular needs. These developments will be discussed more fully later in this chapter.

Need for Familiarity with Computer Systems

Many functional specialists, while impressed with accomplishments of computers, have asked, "Why should a sales manager, operating division manager, accountant, personnel manager, or other specialist be concerned with even the most rudimentary features of computers? Why not leave all such problems to the computer and systems people?"

Perhaps the best reply is that basic familiarity with the capabilities and requirements of computer equipment will: (1) increase awareness of possible uses, (2) improve the ability of functional specialists to define problems in terms which facilitate computer utilization, and (3) improve ability to communicate with systems and computer specialists with regard to informational needs and problems requiring solutions.

Also involved in the degree and nature of potential utilization of any proposed installation is the need for great care in feasibility studies and thorough preparation before computer systems are installed. The potential utilization of computer systems by a business depends not merely upon the work of computer specialists, but to a great extent upon the general cognizance of the applications of electronic processing held by the entire work force and especially by the management at all levels and locations. The full potential of a computer system can only be realized by using it throughout the organization. This requires understanding, acceptance, and the willing cooperation of each responsible employee.

At the same time, the need for technical assistance from systems and data processing specialists grows as uses expand and more complex problems are undertaken. The result is many attractive career opportunities for persons who have special interests in systems design and analysis, computer programming, and allied operations.

Indeed, it is striking how rapidly knowledge and sophisticated usage of a computer installation can penetrate all parts of an organization, and how specialists come to think increasingly in terms of clear definition of problems, information needed for decisions, and the best means of gathering and processing this information.

Range of applications

The several examples of business applications below indicate the versatility of computer systems in business and governmental procedures and underscore the need for general familiarity.

Computer applications have been developed to appraise investment portfolio selection. This particular financial application uses statistical variables to measure risk. A wide range of answers is offered, showing the expected return and the degree of risk associated with *each combination* of stocks in the portfolio. Individual stocks are not evaluated.

Computer systems are now giving stock quotations. One such computer is called the Ultronic Stockmaster and will furnish the last sale price, bid, asked, daily high and low, volume traded, yesterday's close, last four quarter earnings, indicated dividend rate, and the time of the last sale. Central computers located strategically in the financial centers around the United States store information, and brokerage firms communicate with the computer via individual desk sets. Another computer, the Telifile, uses voice stored replies to quote the stock, bid, offer, open, high, low, last prices, and current volume. Stock data are stored on a magnetic drum, and the voice message is stored and read off an audio drum. Incoming calls (over regular telephone network) are connected to a high speed multiplexor, which has the capacity to give over 1,000 quotations per minute. The voice message is read directly off the vocabulary drum and transmitted with the requested stock information directly to the broker.

Computers have been used in real-time (concurrent) applications to control a steel company's hot strip mill. Three different computers—Westinghouse, Daystrom, and General Electric—are used in this operation. These computers receive data on: 113 temperatures, 4 ratios of fuel to air, 63 pressures, 40 position reports, 12 speeds, 4 product dimensions, and 1 weight. After real-time analysis, corrections are made for speed, screw-down settings, alarm signaled if predetermined limits are exceeded, and the necessary accounting and payroll data accumulated.

Production applications have made extensive use of computer capabilities. Computers are used to analyze large engineering and construction projects by comparing all related variables and determining which job elements need to be expedited for any given change in total time at a given related cost structure. This type of computer application was first developed to plan and control production of the Navy's first atomic submarine, the Nautilus.

Computer applications have also been directed toward the marketing function. A typical marketing operation is to predict how various combinations of marketing mix (sales promotion, research and development, price, etc.) would affect expansion and share-of-the-market strategies. Another is to control inventories and hold investment to a minimum while improving customer service through speedier delivery from warehouses.

Computers are used quite extensively in business simulation exercises, both by business firms and by educational institutions. Carnegie Institute of Technology bases several of its Graduate Industrial Administration courses around an extremely complex business simulation exercise. The American Management Association was among the first industrial users of business simulation exercises through the application of electronic computers with its "Top Management Decision Simulation" in 1957.

Not all computer applications deal with planning and control. On the contrary, most users try to justify such installations through "bread-and-butter" applications in processing current orders, accounting, billing, payroll, and other applications which may hardly be glamorous but are highly significant to effective and economical operations.

Possibly the largest single application of electronic data processing equipment is the automation of the Internal Revenue Service (IRS). The tax returns for some 78 million taxpayers will be processed by computers in 1966. The basic records of each taxpayer such as personal data and *all* reportable income for the current year will be stored in the computer's memory and automatically compared with individual returns. The system will automatically analyze the tax records and files indicating those individuals who failed to make returns, filed duplicate claims for refunds, owe a balance, or those individual returns which show unusual characteristics. The government expects the system to pay for itself in one year, bringing in some 200 million of heretofore unreported and uncollected tax revenue.

Basic Components of a Computer System

There are two general types of computer systems—digital and analog. An analog computer represents a number by some analogous physical quantity. In an analog computer, the analog of a number is generally a voltage, a resistance, or some other variable physical quantity; and computations are performed by combining these quantities. Analog computers measure one physical system against another and establish controls within pre-set limits (such as metal expansion against temperature, in a thermostat). Analog computers are normally best suited for scientific and research applications because of their capacity to quickly calculate large, complicated, scientific and mathematical problems, and they have rather limited storage facilities and input-output devices so often needed for administrative uses.

In electronic data processing for business and administration, we are chiefly concerned with digital computers, for they deal directly with the numbers involved in processing data or in analyzing problems.

General purpose digital computer systems are better suited for business application since their computational speed (although fast, is slower than analog computers) is of no particular problem in that most business applications require simple arithmetic operations. Typical business computer applications of billing, inventory control, and payroll require storage capacities that are extremely large and flexible and highly flexible input-output devices.

A digital computer is basically a calculating machine with extraordinary capabilities. It can perform the basic *arithmetic* functions at very high speeds. It can also compare numbers as to size, and as to whether minus, plus, or zero; it can then make additional calculations and comparisons as called for in solving a problem or processing a standard routine. This latter feature is often referred to as the computer's *logical capability*.

All digital computers consist of four major sections: (1) *input-output,* for transferring information into and out of the computer, (2) *storage or memory,* where data and other information can be stored, (3) *processing or arithmetic,* in which operations are performed on the stored data, and (4) *control,* for coordinating the other units so that the desired sequence of operations is performed. Figure 12-1 shows these four basic computer components in their normal sequential relationship. Figure 12-2 shows an IBM 1401 computer installation with each of the components designated. A brief description of the functions of each of the four basic components, the alternate means of providing for it, and trends now appearing in the design of each will be presented in the ensuing section.

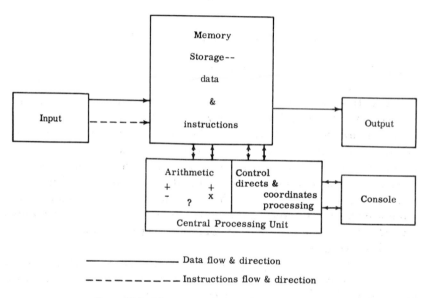

Figure 12-1. Schematic Illustration of Computer System

Input-output

An input device, working from punched cards, punched paper tape, magnetic tape, magnetic ink characters, printed documents, or other media, feeds both the processing instructions and the data to be processed into the storage unit.

Involved in input, therefore, are the important functions of *data acquisition* and *data transmission.* Obtaining needed facts in a "machine-sensible" form which can be read directly into the computer is one of the greatest challenges to business today. At stake are speed, cost, and accuracy of transmission. Where data must be transferred manually or by relatively crude mechanical means from one source to another, added

International Business Machines Corp.

Figure 12-2. Photo of IBM 1410 General Purpose Digital Computer System

time and effort are required, and the possibility of errors is obviously increased.

The output system prints out results at the conclusion of processing. Direct printing output is by mechanical means in systems devised thus far; while mechanical printers have been devised which can print up to 1,000 lines per minute, this speed is still far less than that of the internal electronic circuitry of the computer. One widely used method of coping with limited speed output is to print out on magnetic tape, which can be done much more rapidly, then do actual printing of reports from magnetic tape as a separate operation, not typing up valuable computer time.

Input has been regarded, traditionally, as the weakest link in computer systems—with output a close second. The input medium most commonly used has been the punched card, primarily because punched card systems were already in wide use and are still highly suitable for many routine processing tasks. Accordingly, widely used are card readers which feed cards into a computer at a pace much slower than its internal capabilities.

Advances in input-output: Significant advances in input devices have been made through the use of punched paper tape, magnetic tape, buffers, and new devices for data acquisition and data transmission. The preparation of punched paper tape with the Friden Flexowriter was discussed in a previous chapter. Magnetic tape has the advantage of a much more rapid input and of storing the same quantity of data much more compactly than either punched cards or punched paper tape. Data acquisition involves preparing the data for computer application at the earliest possible point in the work flow. More particularly, it involves such developments as "source data automation," and will be discussed more fully in the following chapter.

New methods of *data transmission* in sending and receiving data direct from machine to machine are also very useful and have great potential as input devices. Data transmission will also be discussed in some detail in the following chapter. Particularly significant is the development of teleprocessing, which provides for transmission of data over regular long-distance telephone circuits.

An impressive indication of the potentialities of data transmission development was a recent estimate by top executives of the American Telephone and Telegraph Company. By 1970, they expect as much as one-half of their *total revenue* to come from data transmission as distinguished from voice communication.

"Buffers" for both the input and output of data allow the overlapping of computer operations. Data can be read into storage *from buffers* or out of storage *into buffers* in only a small fraction of the time ordinarily taken for the input-output operations. That is, the computer may process data from one operation simultaneously while output data of the previous problem is being read out from an output buffer *and* while the data for the next operation is being read into an input buffer. Through the use of several buffers for input and output functions, reading, writing, and computer computations can occur simultaneously at processing speeds which are near the actual speed of the computer's circuitry.

Storage

Computer storage is equivalent to an electronic filing cabinet, completely indexed and, in some cases, instantaneously accessible to the computer. All data must be read into main storage from an input unit where it is then stored for future use in either internal or external storage, or held in main storage for processing. Each location, position, or section of storage is numbered so the stored data can be readily located by the computer as needed. The size or capacity of the storage units in a given electronic data processing system determines the amount of information that can be processed at one time.

Storage can consist of either internal (primary) storage which is an integral part of the processing unit of the computer, or external (secondary) storage, which is usually provided by auxiliary or peripheral equipment. Most business data processing systems demand both types of storage to provide the extensive filing capacity needed for normal business record keeping.

The most frequently used types of internal storage are magnetic cores, magnetic drum, and magnetic disks, although other forms exist for specialized systems. Magnetic core storage is currently the most popular method in use because it provides the fastest access to the information in storage. It is, however, also the most expensive common storage device in terms of cost per storage location. The cores are a series of tiny rings of ferromagnetic material, a few hundredths of an inch in diameter, which can be individually magnetized in a few millionths of a second. Usually a series of seven cores is needed to record a given digit, letter, or character of information.

Magnetic drum storage is second in terms of access speed and is considerably lower in cost per storage location than core storage. As the name indicates, this type of storage is located on a drum, on the surface of which are many magnetized spots or cells. This drum is rotated at very high speeds so that a "head" or reading device can scan the surface of the drum for the information desired from the magnetized spots in a given location on the drum.

Magnetic disk storage frequently appears as an external or auxiliary piece of equipment because of its physical design. The unit itself may actually resemble the familiar juke box, as it is often a cabinet containing a set of stacked disks that resemble phonograph records. These records have, on both front and back surfaces, a series of concentric rings which are in reality a series of magnetized spots in which information may be stored until needed for processing. The records revolve at a very high speed and the information contained in the magnetized spots is "read" by a reading head (or heads) which moves up and down on an access arm to any given data address or location requested. Most magnetic disk type storage devices have even slower accessibility than drum type storage, but have a compensating advantage in a capacity that extends into millions of digits.

The three types of primary storage described above can also be classified as auxiliary storage when the storage units are not a part of the processing unit. External storage may also be in the form of files of punched cards or rolls of punched tape and would contain information which has already been processed or is waiting to be processed by the computer. Normally, this last type of storage would not be considered a part of the computer system.

A special field which may be regarded as an offshoot of computer and auxiliary storage applications is that of *information retrieval*. This involves the storage and rapid retrieval of specialized types of information desired for reference. So significant is this field becoming that it will be given separate attention in the following chapter.

Control

A control unit analyzes the stored program of instructions and informs the machine what is required and in what sequence. This is the "directing brain" of the computer.

Necessary control is ordinarily exercised by the internal circuitry of the computer. Following the program of instruction, it will call data from the buffer or storage, process it, return it to storage, and call on the printer to print out the final results.

The console provides for a means for the operator to communicate with and manually control certain functions of the digital computer system. The operator can start or stop the machine, regulate the input and output devices, and control other functions of the system. Lights on the console signal errors, visually display data in the system, or permit the operator to manually check out new programs.

Arithmetic

An arithmetic unit performs computations at tremendous speeds, as ordered by the control unit. The time required for electronic switching is usually quoted in microseconds (millionths of seconds). For example, an IBM 7070 computer can add or subtract 17,000 five-digit numbers per second.

Basic operations are addition and subtraction (which become multiplication and division when repeated) and certain logical comparisons. These operations are carried on through use of electronic switches, counters, gates, and other circuitry, which need not be of concern to the user.

Digital computer code: Digital computers perform their arithmetic functions by means of an electronic switching device through a system of numbers that can be completely determined by either an "on" or "off" position. The binary number system is a two-digit system which is compatible with the two electrical states, "on-off," of digital computers. The binary system uses two symbols, zero and one, in varying combinations. The value of the decimal depends upon the position of the digit "1" in the binary system. Figure 12-3 illustrates the respective decimal values assigned to the first five binary positions.

By following a logical pattern, any decimal value may be represented in pure binary form. Each "place" in the binary code has a corresponding decimal value. That is, in Figure 12-3, the decimal 22 is represented in its pure binary equivalent as a "one" in positions 2, 3, and 5, whose total

	Pure Binary Equivalent				
	5	4	3	2	1	Binary Position
Decimal	16	8	4	2	1	Value of Binary Position
1	0	0	0	0	1
2	0	0	0	1	0
3	0	0	0	1	1
20	1	0	1	0	0
22	1	0	1	1	0

Figure 12-3. Illustration of Binary Decimal System

value is equal to 22. Beginning at the right, or low order position, and working left, the decimal values of the binary position double each time; therefore, the binary decimal system is said to be a base 2 system, while the regular decimal system is a base 10 system.

Because of the unlimited number of binary positions which would be required to express *any* number in the pure binary form, most computers use a *code variation* of the binary system. One of the most common variations is the "binary-coded" system. This involves only the first four binary positions and their respective *values* of 1, 2, 4, and 8. Any decimal digit (0-9) can be represented by a combination of these four binary values. In the binary-coded system there is a *separate binary equivalent* for each digit of the decimal number in question, as shown in Figure 12-4 below.

Decimal	Binary-coded equivalent		
0			1010
6			0110
9			1001
10		0001	1010
18		0001	1000
37		0011	0111
256	0010	0101	0110
729	0111	0011	1001

Figure 12-4. Illustration of Binary-coded System

The binary symbols 0 and 1 are commonly called bits. Subsequent chapters in this part of the text will frequently refer to the speed of computers or data transmission equipment as "so many bits per second." A "no-bit" is usually a zero, while the term "bit" itself is usually meant to be the "1" in a binary position.

The method or system used by electronic computers to represent data is known as a code. In the computer the code relates data to a fixed number of binary symbols. By the proper arrangement of the binary symbols (bit, no-bit) all characters, both alpha and numeric, can be represented by a different combination of bits, as shown in Figure 12-5.

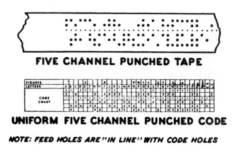

FIVE CHANNEL PUNCHED TAPE

UNIFORM FIVE CHANNEL PUNCHED CODE

NOTE: *FEED HOLES ARE "IN LINE" WITH CODE HOLES*

Figure 12-5. A punched paper tape code

Computer Configurations

Digital computers come in almost any size and combination of component functions to meet customer needs. A general classification of computer systems, other than the digital and analog mentioned previously, is according to size—small, medium, and large. This classification of size is usually based on two factors, cost (either purchase or rental) and storage capacity. It is readily apparent, however, that to a large degree, cost is a direct result of capacity; consequently, some computer systems can be found in both the medium and large size classifications. For example, the basic Honeywell 400 computer is a medium size computer, but with a full complement of component memory units and accessory equipment, it becomes classed as a large computer system.

Analog computers are rather limited in their configurations, not having the capacity for external storage units or flexible input-output devices. On the other hand, the flexible configurations of digital computers is what makes them highly adaptable to business use. For example, the IBM 705 computer system will operate with up to 100 tape units on line. Most computer systems will operate from a wide variety of input-output features including punched cards, punched paper tape, magnetic tape, console typewriter, teletypewriter, and special data transmission terminal units. In addition, high speed printers may be used as output devices. The significant aspect regarding computer configuration is that most any need can be provided for, and the "expandability" of additional storage or input-output units allows sufficient room to extend the scope and size of the computer applications.

Configurations of computer systems can be classified, according to their application, into four general types:

1. *In-line* application is also commonly referred to as on-line, and indicates that the related computer equipment (usually referring to input or output) is directly connected to and operates under the control of the computer.

2. *Off-line* application involves computer applications where the related equipment (again usually input or output) is detached from and operated independently of the computer.

3. *Real-time* application requires processing data involved in an operation fast enough so that the processed results can be re-entered into the operation and used to control the remaining parts of the operation. Rocket and missile control by computer is an example of real-time computer application.

4. *Delayed-time* application is commonly referred to as "batching" because the data is processed after it has been made a matter of record.

Small-sized computer systems usually rent from $750 to $4,000 per month and sell for below $50,000. Medium-sized computer systems usually rent for between $4,000 and $15,000 per month and sell for between $50,000 and $500,000. Large-sized computers have an outright sale price of above $500,000, and a rental price of above $15,000 per month. Brief examples of large, medium, and small computer systems are given in Figure 12-6. The particular computers chosen are for illustrative purposes only, and it is certainly not the intention of the authors to exclude other highly satisfactory and successful manufacturers.

Computer Programming

Computer programming is the technique of expressing, in a logical sequence, a series of commands or instructions which will serve to direct the computer to perform a given operation. These must be written in a language that is acceptable to the computer and, as each type of computer system usually has its own language, the programmer must be trained in the techniques of programming for each particular computer system to be used.

Programmer training, studies involving the methods and procedures to be followed, development of flow charts and diagrams which can be translated to computer language by programming, and the many hours involved in the actual writing of the thousands of instructions that make up the programs, all result in what is often an enormous financial outlay. In many instances, this nearly equals the actual cost of the computer equipment itself. The actual time spent in this programming period may also be of great importance in the operation and management of the business involved. The initial time to train a programmer usually requires only a few weeks of concentrated study, but the development of a

COMPUTER SYSTEM AND SIZE	GENERAL FEATURES	INPUT-OUTPUT METHODS Input	Output	STORAGE	SOFTWARE	NORMAL APPLICATIONS AND GENERAL COMMENTS
Small System IBM 1440	Avg. rental $2,600 mo. Avg. purch. price $200,000 Magnetic disk storage packs	PC, MT, TW, MICR	PC, Pr, MT, TW	Random Access Magnetic Tape Disks, 3 million characters each, with up to 5 in operation at one time	Autocoder, SORT	MICR processing of bank checks Inventory management Scheduling and purchasing
Medium System IBM 1401	Avg. rental $6,500 mo. Avg. purch. $310,000 Solid State transistorized	PC, PT, MT, TW, TTW, MICR, & data transmission devices	PC, TTW, PT MT, TW & data transmission devices High-Speed printer	Core storage 14,000-16,000 alphanumerical characters External storage Magnetic tape disk	COBOL, SPS, Autocoder FORTRAN	Utilities billing Inventory simulation Operates as peripheral equipment for layer computer systems
Large System Univac 1107	Avg. rental $50,000 mo. Avg. purch. $2,500,000	PC, PT MT, TW TTW, & data transmission devices	PC, TTW, PT, MT, TW, & data transmission devices High-speed printer	Thin-film memory cores. 16,384-65,536 words External storage Magnetic tape disk	COBOL FORTRAN SPS ALGOL	Information retrieval Utilities billing

Key: PC-punched card PT-punched paper tape MT-magnetic tape TW-typewriter TTW-teletypewriter
Pr-Printer MICR-Magnetic Ink Character Recognition

Figure 12-6. Illustration of key features of small-, medium- and large-scale electronic computer systems

competent, accurate, and relatively efficient programmer may involve additional months of actual practice in his new technical profession.

Techniques of programming

Techniques of programming vary. In essence, however, the work of programming begins with considering the nature of the solution or end results desired, then tracing in specific detail (each small step) the processing steps needed to produce the desired results, and finally expressing the program in a language that can be understood and followed by the particular computer to be used.

Principal programming steps may thus include:

1. Developing a general flow chart which indicates the input-output expected from the program.

2. Developing a detailed flow chart—a "block diagram"—of the functions the components must perform to obtain the desired results. A block diagram is a graphic representation of the procedures by which data are processed within a system.

3. Preparing the program of instructions in a form and sequence usable by the computer.

A general flow chart shows what jobs are to be done and a block diagram shows how the jobs are done. Flow charts are frequently composed solely of symbols representing the form in which data appear at various stages in the process. The actual operations that must be performed are only indicated. Figure 12-7 illustrates a flow chart for a payroll operation.

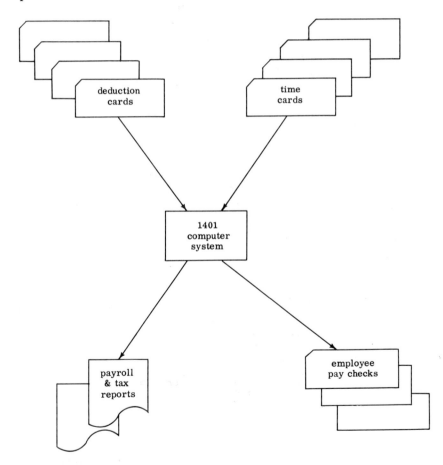

Figure 12-7. Flow diagram for payroll operation

Block diagrams are important in programming computer operations because they give the programmer a means of visualizing the sequences in the operation, where the arithmetic and logic operations occur, and the relationship existing between various portions of the program. Figure 12-8 illustrates a block diagram for reconciliation of daily cash report.

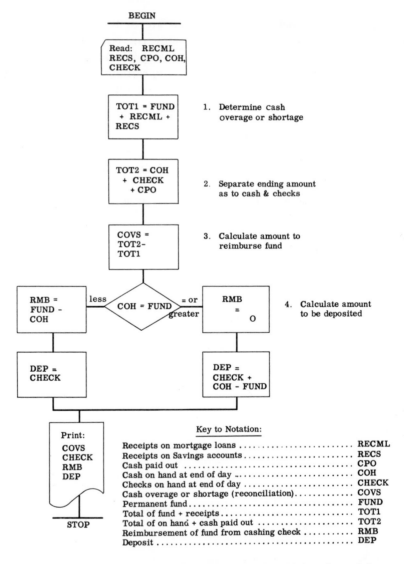

Figure 12-8. Illustration of simple block diagram (or detailed flow diagram) for reconciliation of daily cash report. The key to the notation will help interpret the FORTRAN language used in the diagram.

The basic problem of programming is to write the composite instructions (called coding) in the machine language or in a language usable by the machine. Two problems or obstacles arise when coding a program:

1. Instructions must be written in exact sequence as they are to be executed.
2. The full burden of logic is placed on the programmer.

Many of the problems of writing programs have been overcome to some extent or simplified considerably by more advanced systems of program generation. A program system consists of two basic parts—a language and a processor. A programmer writes a program of instructions for an operation that is in a language form convenient and practical for human manipulation, but with standard rules for punctuation, symbols, abbreviations, and language. The processor is a pre-established stored program that converts the written program into machine language (object program). The object program is then used by the computer to actually perform the job operation.

Computer Software

As discussed previously, systems analysis and programming computer applications are extremely expensive operations which are usually equal to the cost of the computer system. Many users have been extremely disappointed at the time and expense required to program a computer system after delivery. Consequently, computer customers are demanding that computer systems fit their particular needs and that the manufacturers accept considerable responsibility for furnishing the necessary programs. This seems to have been the turning point in the race for computer hardware, i.e., the complexity, speed, size, and storage capacity of computer systems, and the redirection of attention and efforts toward *customer service.*

Computer manufacturers are taking a second look at their computer systems and are concentrating their attention on preparing programs according to the customer's needs, to facilitate use of the computer system. An important element in this emphasis on customer service is the manufacturer's effort to develop computer "software" packages to help sell their systems. This is done through "program libraries" available to the customer or computer-user association. It places considerable emphasis on "job-lot" programming for particular customer applications.

Computer-user associations, specialized consultants, and computer manufacturers have accumulated large investments in the development of standard programs and systems with the object of simplifying computer applications so that the computer systems may be quickly put to work on the operations they are designed for, without undue cost or time for the user. Consequently, the "software" packages included with computer systems have become a significant competitive item.

This is evidenced by the fact that the computer manufacturers' programming departments are rapidly expanding and producing standard programs, as well as developing new applications and programs to increase the use of computers, which in turn increases the potential computer market. For example, IBM has approximately 6,000 programs in its library, and Minneapolis-Honeywell has given program development equal status with the engineering, sales, and production divisions.

Manufacturers are realizing, however, that producing programs for common applications is not sufficient, from the viewpoint of the customer. Manufacturers are now attempting to develop software packages (computer systems and applications) for particular industries in an effort to show these industries the economies and advantages of using computer systems.

IBM has developed several standard programs for common computer applications in particular industries. Examples are the SURE program for utility billing using the IBM 7070 or 7074 computer systems. The SURE program will process about 95 per cent of any utility company's billing operation. MOS (Management Operating Systems) is another type of industrial program developed by IBM for individual industries. For example, an MOS program has been developed for the textile industry, which is essentially six separate basic programs for:

1. Forecasting production requirements.
2. Scheduling production as to looms and machines.
3. Determining raw material requirements.
4. Producing daily production orders.
5. Controlling production flow through manufacturing stages.
6. Compiling management reports on each machine and each line of product.

Software packages and customer services also include significant advances in programming requirements for the computer systems. Program compilers and common languages for the various computer systems have been developed to simplify the job of writing the program. They are discussed in more detail later in this chapter.

Common Language for Computers

Computer software has solved many problems for both users and manufacturers. But the problem of economical, universal programming has still not been solved. Developers and researchers have long been searching for a way to make the computer itself a programmer. To a large extent, this has been accomplished, first, through mnemonic systems called "assemblers," and second, through "compilers." A mnemonic program is written in shorthand English using cartications of commands like add, subtract, multiply, etc. The processor translates this mnemonic language to computer language as appropriate in generating the object deck.

For example, a part of the mnemonic language for the 1401 computer is illustrated as follows:

Computer Operation	Mnemonic Symbol	Computer Language Code
Multiply	M	@
Clear Word Mark	CW	⊠
Divide	D	%

Compilers are master programs by which a computer is able to write its own program from rather general instructions written in either English or a form of algebraic symbols. Of particular significance to the development of common language systems for computers are the concepts of general automatic programming computer systems. These "packaged logic" or software language systems represent a major achievement in computer programming. Some of the names of the more general language systems are:

ALGO (Universal algebraic language compiler)
ALGOL (International algebraic compiler)
COBOL (Common business oriented language)
FORTRAN (Formula translating language for scientific computations)

FORTRAN and COBOL are the programming languages with the most extensive use. COBOL is an English language program capable of being implemented in a wide variety of digital computers for use in the solution of business data processing problems. The need for a COBOL language program system was first conceived in 1959 by the Assistant Secretary of Defense. The COBOL language system as used today is the result of a group effort composed of several manufacturers' representatives and governmental agencies. COBOL is a programming system which all computers must have to be eligible for government purchase or rental. Consequently, every computer manufacturer is hurrying to perfect a COBOL compiler for their particular series of computers.

FORTRAN is an automatic coding system which closely resembles the ordinary language of mathematics, and although it was developed primarily by IBM for IBM computers, it has been adapted to other computer systems such as the Control Data Corporation's 160, 160A, and 1604 computers and the RCA 601 computer. The FORTRAN language is intended to be capable of expressing any numerical computation problem, dealing with particular problems containing large sets of formulae and many variables.

Figure 12-9 shows a comparison between COBOL, FORTRAN, symbolic (or mnemonic) and the machine language itself. The situation programmed is outlined below.

PROBLEM: Assume two values are in storage in the computer—
1. The year-to-date earnings (YTDE)
2. The current month's earnings (EARN)

REQUIRED: Instruct the computer to up-date the yearly earnings to date by adding to it the current month's earnings.

Type of instruction language	Computer Instruction
Machine language	21 01000 02000
SPS-symbolic	A YTDE EARN
FORTRAN	YTDE = YTDE + EARN
COBOL	ADD EARN TO YTDE

Figure 12-9. Illustrative Program-Compiler Languages

In the machine language the code 21 instructs the computer to add the quantities (data) stored in location 01000 to the data stored in location 02000. As such, the programmer must keep careful track of the storage location of the various data which will be processed by the computer, and where the answer will be, so that the data can be "read out" of storage and printed.

The symbolic language uses the mnemonic code "A" to instruct the computer to add; the code words YTDE and EARN tell the computer what to add.

FORTRAN instructions are quite similar to COBOL, particularly in the case of this highly simplified example. The FORTRAN instruction tells the computer that YTDE should be equal to YTDE plus whatever amount is in current earnings (EARN). The computer will then execute the necessary addition to up-date yearly earnings.

COBOL is the simplest instruction of all. It closely resembles a common English statement. The instruction is self-explanatory in that the computer is simply told to add current earnings to yearly earnings to date.

Trends in Electronic Computer Systems

The application of computer systems in industry reached the turning point in 1960-61. After several years of experimenting with computer systems applications, industry seemed to adopt a "settled down" approach to the implementation of computer systems in a calculated, business-like manner. The general profit squeeze of industry around 1957-60, together with the sudden realization that the computer system itself constituted only about half of the expense of computer system application, led the business firms to demand more in the way of programming, systems services, and special equipment. Increased competition was also being experienced by the manufacturers in the computer field. With the hardware race somewhat neutralized, manufacturers turned their attention to specialized computer markets, applications, and customer requirements. Several of the more significant trends in computer systems technology and administration are briefly discussed in the following section.

Improved memory storage: Random access storage devices of magnetic disks and magnetic tape paved the way for real-time computer applications, but it was not very long before these storage media became outdated by more rapid storage devices, the ferrite-core storage and, more recently, thin-film memory.

Thin-film storage devices were perfected to give electronic computers a smaller size and more rapid access to internal memory. Although present storage speeds are measured in microseconds (millionths), thin-film storage speeds are measured in "nanoseconds" or in terms of *billionths* of a second. Thin-film operations are more than twice as fast as the ferrite-core storage computers. Core storage cycle time (time required to read and write data) is 1.5 microseconds, while thin-film storage cycle time is .6 microseconds.

Thin-film memory computers are built with non-destructive readout properties which make computers more reliable than they have been to date, since the memory cannot be destroyed or affected by use. When thin magnetic film begins to be used for performing logic as well as for memory functions, computers will have even greater capabilities and will be well on their way to self-adaptive functions, i.e., organizing themselves to do a job in the best possible way, and even to program themselves completely.

Speedier output for computers: As discussed previously in this chapter, input and output speeds are the main drawbacks to efficient computer systems. In part, this problem was eliminated with the development of buffers allowing overlapping of computer operations. But the problem of filing, storing, and handling bulky print out still remained and usually required several steps to record it on microfilm for permanent storage. This process of converting computer machine language read out on magnetic tape to human language on microfilm at speeds comparable to the computer's operations has been solved with DACOM (Datascope Computer Output Microfilmer).

In operation, DACOM can record a page of 64 lines of 126 characters in the almost incredibly brief period of approximately one-half a second. Further, peripheral equipment, due to be operational in the very near future, includes devices for on-the-spot, high-speed processing for continuous or selective production of "hard copies" from the film. Through a special optical system, the computer output data can be photographed with the desired background format (a statement or a bill, for example) producing an optically combinated microfilm image. This makes it quite practical to record large quantities of information or to prepare customer statements as they are processed by the computer system equipment.

Miniaturization: The number of component parts in an electronic computer system has increased from around 100 to over 200,000, and the end does not seem to be in sight. Technology advancement has been the only factor which has made the increase in parts either feasible or practical. Thin-film, discussed above, represents an effort to solve some of the problems forced on the industry for smaller, lighter, and speedier electronic computers.

A more recent development in miniature electronic computers is the integrated semi-conductor modular circuit or unit. One model of this functional semi-conductor contains *eight transistors and twelve resistors,* but is only about the size of a small transistor. Individual components —transistors, resistors, coils, etc.—are being replaced by semi-conductors that are functional packages within themselves. As a single unit, a semi-conductor handles such sub-activities of electronics as amplification, frequency conversions, and electronic switching.

The pressure for miniaturization of component parts came not only as a result of the need for smaller or faster computers, but also from the need to develop circuitry components that require less maintenance and that will perform more functions within themselves. The need is to design components or "modules of circuits" that can be repaired in the field, i.e., that can be interchanged by simply plugging in a new module-component. This need is particularly evident in the military and space age applications of electronic computer systems, where delays are unusually expensive.

Improved input devices: Improved data input for computers has been one of the primary goals of computer system researchers for quite some time. Considerable time and expense are incurred in preparing data for computer use. The repetitive manual tasks of preparing input data also increase the chance of errors in the data. Possibly the most significant new input feature to date is optical scanning. This involves converting printed or typed data from regular business documents into magnetic tape data at extremely fast speeds. A second significant implementation in input data research is Magnetic Ink Character Recognition, known as MICR. MICR is usually associated with bank check processing, but it has other business uses such as identifying customer account numbers and employee payroll numbers. The more advanced systems of data transmission devices also reflect input efforts; data can now be transmitted long distance directly between the magnetic cores of two computer systems. Data input will be covered more fully in the following chapter under Data Acquisition.

Specialized services: This includes not only the software packages discussed previously, but such services as specially designed computer systems for particular applications (for example, the IBM 7090 computer for airlines reservation application), the establishment of computer service bureaus to serve small business computer needs and overflow requirements of the larger computer systems, and the development of systems, procedures, and programs for computer systems for particular industries (for example, the IBM "MOS" programs as discussed previously). The development of common language compilers and the inclusion of several compilers with each computer system greatly simplifies the programming job and makes it considerably more flexible.

Administrative adaptation: There have also been significant advances in the administrative adaptations of computer systems for business application. These trends are identified by computer concepts such as integrated data processing, data acquisition, data transmission, and information retrieval. These concepts are so important and so significant to administrative management that they receive more detailed attention in the next chapter.

QUESTIONS FOR STUDY AND DISCUSSION

1. Does the development of the electronic computer constitute a revolution, or is it but one important step in the long evolution of mechanization? Evaluate each point of view.

2. What is the basic purpose of a data processing system in administration? What are the secondary purposes?

3. Does a person whose primary interests are in marketing, production, finance, or some other specialized field need some familiarity with computers? If so, why, and how much familiarity?

4. Several applications of computer systems were presented in this chapter to illustrate their versatility. Suggest several other applications, or fields for present or potential use.

5. Briefly describe the basic components of a computer system and the functions of each component. What variations in the makeup of each of the components are now available?

6. Explain the rudiments of binary coding and justify its usage in digital computers.

7. Until rather recently, most business applications of computer systems involved the "batching" process. Recently, however, there has been considerable use of "real-time" computer applications in business. How can you explain this shift in emphasis? What are its advantages, if any? What are its limitations, and what new requirements are imposed?

8. The results of a recent independent study of the present use and current innovations in computer systems in business indicated that in the future, "software" would be the primary factor in competition among computer manufacturers, and in success of the computer systems, in individual firms. Differentiate between computer software and hardware and comment on this conclusion. What do you predict for the future? Why?

Case 12-1. Joint Use of an Electronic Computer

Four insurance companies with homes offices in a medium-sized city are conducting a joint study of the feasibility of securing an electronic computer and adapting it to their operations. They have found that the initial price of the computer would be slightly more than one million dollars.

The price seems too great for individual purchase and installation by any of the firms, and they are considering various alternatives—forming a new company which would operate the computer and make the service available on a fee basis to each of the four interested companies, each of which would own one-fourth of the stock in the new company; attempting to persuade one of the manufacturers of the large computers to set up a service bureau in the city which could take care of the individual needs of the four companies; and trying to get by individually with smaller electronic computers which are less costly and more readily available, though offering fewer features desired for certain applications in each company.

Problems and questions:

a. What types of information would you suggest that the companies secure in attempting to reach the best solution?

b. Give a preliminary appraisal of each of the possibilities—recognizing, of course, that more specific information would be needed before a final decision.

Case 12-2. Personnel Problems in Introduction of an Electronic Computer

After a thorough and detailed study of company needs, a committee of management personnel in the Mid-States Utility Company recently made a recommendation that a large electronic computer be installed, and that many of the data-processing operations in company offices be carried out through use of the computer.

An office union represents most of the office employees of the company. When learning of the development, local union officials called a meeting of all members and raised certain questions. What would the installation mean in terms of the numbers of clerical employees needed? Would the company be likely to want to re-classify many jobs and employees?—and would such changes include any probable downgrading? These were only a few of the questions that were raised.

After considerable discussion, the members of the union agreed that they would take no stand of outright opposition to the installation, but that their leaders would draft a list of recommendations and that they would present these to the management of the company during preliminary negotiations about to begin on the new contract.

Problems and questions:

Prepare the set of recommendations you would have for dealing with this situation.

13

SPECIALIZED COMPUTER CONCEPTS

Integrated data processing · Data acquisition · Data transmission · Information retrieval · Summary

Certain offshoots of data processing technology have developed to the point where they may rival the electronic computer in potential impact. Included are data processing, data acquisition, data transmission, and information retrieval. Basic concepts and illustrations needed for understanding these developing fields will be considered in this chapter.

Integrated Data Processing

The most significant characteristics of the electronic computer are probably those of *speed* and *integration* of processing. The integration feature is apparent when it is recognized that a computer system is made up of a series of interconnected units of equipment which can process long sequences of work steps at high speeds.

But the principle of integration did not originate with the electronic computer, and integrated data application is by no means confined to computer systems. Punched card systems which utilize the same cards for a series of processing steps, such as preparing sales orders, invoices, shipping forms, inventory control records, and statistical reports, were in use for decades before the advent of the computer. And standard or conventional office machines can now be linked together—with or without a computer included in the sequence—so they form integrated systems.

True "integrated data processing" or IDP, as the concept is now usually abbreviated, did not come until the development of a code or "common language" which could activate different machines, and a medium such as a punched tape which could transmit information from machine to machine.

IDP is the first building block for the "total systems" concept discussed in Chapter 7. It is too much to expect the "total system" concept to completely permeate a complex enterprise today. Much planning is required first; computer systems, upon which total systems must depend, are still in their infancy. Most total systems (so called because the "total" concept is the ultimate goal of the users) involve only one, or two at the most, major phases of an organization's functions. Building a total system is not accomplished overnight, nor is it ever really accomplished, for new and changing information requirements are always occurring.

The essential difference between the IDP and total systems concepts is that a total system necessarily involves IDP for each of the organization's systems. With all organizational systems united through IDP, the concept of a total system is possible, and all that remains is to summarize and analyze the data and to prepare management information reports.

A totally integrated data processing system, whether it be punched tape or electronic computer, must consider complete managerial information requirements for each function and at each level in the organization. IDP systems should provide for the sequential processing of information beginning with detailed operating data at the lowest level and ending with summary information of key importance for top management.

IDP concepts and illustrations

The United States Steel Corporation: [1] The pioneering, large-scale application of integrated data processing was developed in the United States Steel Corporation and was first demonstrated at a special conference of the American Management Association in February, 1954. The common language used was the uniform five-channel punched tape already in wide use in the communications field. As described by officials, the concept underlying the United States Steel system included two basic steps.

1. Record data at the point of origin on office machines (adding machines, typewriters, or others) which create punched tapes or cards as the automatic by-product of the recording operation.
2. Process original and subsequent data on office machines which read and punch tapes or cards, so all data are self-perpetuating.

To illustrate, an ordinary adding machine may be used to record and total an original series of numbers. At the same time this is being done by the operator, a tape punch which has been connected with the machine will punch a code into a tape. Then, the punched tape produced on the adding machine

[1] Adapted from: "U.S. Steel Sets Up Automatic Office," *Office Management*, March, 1954.

feeds into an automatic bookkeeping machine which performs its function on the data and at the same time produces another punched tape with essential data to be carried forward to the next machine. The information may then be channeled to other automatic machines and, if desired, may ultimately be converted to magnetic tape and may enter into the calculations of an electronic computer.

The American Bosch Arma Corporation: [2] The American Bosch Arma Corporation of Springfield, Massachusetts has recently incorporated a "total system" concept in its management information system. This IDP system is based upon what American Bosch Arma's management calls the forward look which emphasizes the ultimate goals of information systems, the modular approach to information processing which divides the requirements into logical and manageable units, and assembly line or "continuous flow" processing of the information within the total system.

For example, as each shipping ticket is received, it is posted to the following master accounts in the computer's memory storage:

1. Detail by sales branch and product class
2. Summary by sales branch
3. Summary by product class
4. Grand total of sales
5. Cost of goods sold by branch
6. Cost of goods sold by product class
7. Total cost of goods sold
8. Inventories by product class
9. Inventory totals

American Bosch Arma's IDP system provides computer sorting or processing of all data collected, smooth handling of peak, end-of-period work loads, and the preparation of reports and summaries of activity for management upon demand. Management reports and operating results are prepared when requested by simply reading out the current balances in the master and sub-accounts stored in the computer's memory. The immediate availability of managerial reports greatly facilitates the management decision and control functions, and provides more pertinent information for decentralized operations.

The Shell Oil Company: [3] Shell Oil has installed an integrated data processing system in its collection and revenue functions and is continuing with plans to establish all company transactions on an integrated basis. The initial phase of the IDP system at Shell Oil was installed to provide for the automatic handling and processing of collection data at the point of sale to final consolidation at the Shell data processing center in New York City. The system is designed to accumulate transaction data at the source and to process it quickly through the necessary accounting and analysis functions.

[2] Adapted from: John Field, "Total Systems: A Definition and A Case History," *Advances in EDP and Information Systems*, AMA Management Report No. 62 (New York: American Management Association, 1961), pp. 151-168.
[3] *Ibid.*

Small-size computers at each of the shipping stations around the United States, and related office equipment at installations that do not qualify for a computer, are all integrated into and compatible with computer equipment in the central data processing office. Through the continuous and immediate processing of source data, end-of-period operating reports are immediately available for any management level.

For example, the local computers in the selected sales offices will, from a simple, universal stored program, perform the following functions:

1. Write all transaction documents automatically.
2. Compute, punch, and store all required totals.
3. Recognize special billing requirements when writing customer invoices.
4. Select, punch and communicate transaction details and summary data for regional or central processing, and for sales and statistical reports.
5. Produce sales and stock control reports.

With the automatic processing of all local transactions on an integrated data processing basis, Shell Oil produces consolidated managerial reports as a by-product of normal everyday operations involving detailed plant invoice documents.

Current applications of IDP follow the same basic concepts that were pioneered by U. S. Steel, as illustrated above. As the other illustrations indicated, common language media have been refined and usage has been extended to virtually all types of office machines—including electronic data computers.

It should be repeated that IDP applications are not dependent upon computer systems, however. Opportunities of carrying out the process of integration with machines of different types, thereby automating entire procedures, seem almost limitless. Illustrative of possibilities is the experience of a book club which tied an addressing machine in with a sorting machine and a punching machine to handle monthly transactions with over two million members. Savings were more than 10,000 work hours per month.[4]

Benefits of IDP

Present and potential benefits offered by IDP include:

1. *Major contribution to systems integration.* The value of viewing the work of any enterprise as a network of serialized processes, each guided by appropriate information, was considered in Chapter 7. Close linkage of the different parts of the master system is needed to keep all activity directed toward over-all objectives and to coordinate specialized activities whose immediate objectives may often conflict with each other. The common language of IDP makes possible, and requires,

4 Ralph W. Fairbanks, "Electronics Moves Into The Office," *Office Management,* June, 1953.

interdepartmental standardization and systemization of informational needs. Where an electronic computer is used, IDP can provide standardized input data at high speeds.

2. *Greater speed.* The fast transmission of data from one step to the next can result in cutting customer delivery time from days to hours, keep inventory records more current, and provide management with timely information for planning and control.

3. *Reduced costs.* The expression "least cost through most use of data" conveys the idea of capturing basic data at its inception, then making the same data serve as many needs as possible—with obvious reductions of duplication and timing of clerical costs.

4. *Greater accuracy.* A large portion of clerical errors commonly experienced are human errors in transferring data from one document to another. Since data transmission is largely done mechanically under IDP, errors can be reduced essentially to those made in original recording of data and those made in programming interrelated operations in sequence.

Limitations of IDP

The benefits suggested above do not come easily. Most difficult to achieve is likely to be the "total system" orientation necessary for maximum effectiveness, since most systems cut across departmental lines and require adaptation and standardization of many types of information. Other problems arise in determining whether volume justifies a proposed conversion, in insuring compatibility, and in providing for balanced capacity of different units of equipment. Solutions of these and other problems met in developing an effective IDP system are certain to require the most careful preparation. Potential benefits, however, appear to have tremendous significance.

Data Acquisition

Data acquisition is concerned with planning the information to be used in the computer system and the subsequent conversion of this information into machine-usable form. Planning for information requirements was discussed in Chapter 6. It is quite clear that definite planning and programs are necessary to assure that each manager furnishes the proper data, as well as receives the appropriate reports.

As already noted, input is the weakest link in a computer system. Converting the data for input provides a real bottleneck and problem area for data acquisition. The "technical" problem of input devices has been resolved somewhat through the use of magnetic tape, direct computer-to-computer data transmission, and through the use of input buffers. But data acquisition—obtaining necessary facts in a machine-sensible form which can be read directly into the computer—remains one of the greatest challenges to business management today. At stake are speed, cost, and accuracy. Where data must be transferred manually or by relatively crude mechanical means from one source to another, added time and effort are required, and the possibility of error is obviously increased.

Two very significant concepts in data acquisition are *integrated data processing* and *source data automation*. IDP has been discussed previously in this chapter and its importance to data acquisition stems from the *common language* used in an integrated system. IDP provides for serialized processing of information data, results in greater speed and reduced costs and, since a common language is utilized throughout the processing, greater accuracy of the input data is realized.

Source data automation is closely related to an IDP system as discussed above and earlier in this chapter. Any fully integrated data processing system logically includes source data automation. Source data automation, as the title aptly implies, involves interception of the data at its origin in the organization and immediately reducing it to a machine-usable form—a common language. Some of the most expensive processes of IDP, and of data processing in general, involve preparing the data for computer use.

This "input bottleneck" of computer systems stems from the fact that even the most sophisticated electronic computers have always required human help to function efficiently and effectively. With the capacity of computers to memorize and analyze millions of facts and figures at rapid speed, the material fed into them had first to be digested and put in a form the machines could comprehend. For economical employment of an expensive electronic computer, this required platoons of trained personnel to code the data for machine use. This work is tedious, and the rate of turnover among such employees is usually high. Consequently, huge savings are possible in time, effort, personnel, and cost, if the data to be processed can be reduced to machine-usable form at its *source*.

New developments in source data automation

The paper punch machines referred to previously are very popular as reliable methods of source data automation. They have one drawback —that of a rather slow input speed. More recent innovations in the field of source data automation are *optical scanning* and *magnetic ink character recognition*.

Optical scanning. Optical scanners have the ability to read pages of ordinary business documents and to translate the information into a punched paper tape code at very fast reading rates. One manufacturer has recently announced an optical reader which can be used as a *direct input device* for a computer system. Optical scanners can be controlled either to read the entire page of data, or to be selective and scan the documents for key words or isolated data.

> *Applications in billing procedures:* Optical scanners are performing a variety of tasks for business today. For example, optical scanners are used by the gasoline and oil industry to improve the efficiency of their credit card billing systems. These optical scanners read the account numbers on customer invoices and convert the invoices into punched cards for further processing. Common use of optical scanning equipment is found in the telephone industry and the general utility field, in the automatic handling of customer bill stubs which return to the company's accounting department with payments rendered.
>
> *A transportation application:* [5] Ryder Truck Lines, Incorporated processes some 12,000 way bills per hour by optically reading the typed data, transferring it to a computer system, and sorting and stacking the bills as designated.

Magnetic ink character recognition: MICR is commonly associated with the "coded characters" on the bottom of bank checks, although this is not the only application of MICR. MICR was initiated by the American Bankers Association (ABA) in an effort to reduce the clerical handling of the millions of checks which are processed each year, and in anticipation of an increased volume of check processing in the future.

MICR consists of coding each check with the home bank's identification numbers and other related data, at a specific location on the check. A specific location was assigned so that the characters could be read from checks of all sizes.

The MICR sorter-reader reads the characters (senses the amount of iron oxide in each character) and sorts the checks in much the same way as punched cards are sorted. Reading and sorting speeds for check processing range up to 57,000 checks per hour, including transferring data into compatible computer systems.

> *A banking application:* [6] Such a MICR system of processing magnetic ink coded paper checks has allowed the Manufacturers National Bank of Detroit to sort its returned checks while simultaneously posting the transaction and up-dating the customer account records. Each day the Manufacturers National Bank's MICR system posts approximately 160,000 transactions and handles 500 to 900 customer account inquiries. Maximum utilization of the investment funds can be realized with the immediate knowledge of deposit and saving balances and current trends furnished by the MICR system.

[5] Adapted from: W. B. Hamilton, Jr., "Optical Character Recognition System," *Data Processing*, July, 1962, pp. 22-26.

[6] Adapted from: John C. Calhoun, "Bank Aims For A Total System," *Data Processing*, June, 1962, pp. 38-42.

Data Transmission

The remarkable developments in data processing during the past decade have been matched, probably through necessity, by developments in data transmission—commonly defined as "machines talking to machines." All methods of transmitting source data to the point of processing, then transmitting results back, create time lags which may erase any gains in processing efficiency.

The basic impetus for rapid improvement of data transmission stems from basic changes in the modern enterprise. Multi-plant and multi-divisional organizations are becoming more common with expansion, diversification of products and services, and geographic dispersion. Competitive success often hinges upon cutting the time between sale and delivery; upon efficiently utilizing production, storage, and delivery capacity; upon coordinating and minimizing inventories held in different locations; and upon other factors which depend heavily upon effective communication and coordination. Only through an effective combination of data processing and data transmission can a management develop the informational network it requires.

The resources of the communication industry applied to such needs are extremely encouraging; perhaps no other industry is now in a more dynamic state. Mr. Frederick R. Kappel, President of the American Telephone and Telegraph Company, has predicted that by 1970 at least half of his firm's volume will be in a form other than voice communication. Data transmission in earlier years was limited to the use of telegraph-grade circuits mainly used by Western Union and by American Telephone and Telegraph for their teletype and related services, and by other telephone companies. Paper tape equipment was usually used and continues to be widely used. While satisfactory for limited message service, the traditional equipment had to be supplemented by equipment offering much greater speed and capacity to meet present-day data communication requirements.

Accordingly, we have seen successive development of voice-grade circuits, microwave (ultra high-frequency radio), and space satellites. The possibilities of further developments defy the layman's imagination.

Of particularly widespread interest has been the Data-Phone developed by Bell Telephone Laboratories, which can transmit data in machine language over regular or leased telephone circuits, thus providing great flexibility at relatively low costs. One Data-Phone unit receives data in the form of electrical pulses or bits from any one of several types of office machines that utilize punched cards, punched tape, or magnetic tape, and converts these into a tone suitable for transmission. A Data-

Phone unit at the receiving end reconverts the tone into electrical bits that may be fed into a computer or into a variety of other business machines. Connections are made as regular telephone calls and charges are at the same rate; a relatively low monthly rental covers the cost of the Data-Phone equipment itself.

> A large, pioneering installation of the Data-Phone was that by the Hardware Mutuals-Sentry Life Insurance Group in 1961. This installation linked an IBM 7070 computer system in the home office in Stevens Point, Wisconsin, with thirty-two branch offices throughout the nation. Using punched cards, a transceiver, and a Data-Phone, an operator in any branch office puts through a long-distance call to the data processing center and then transmits operating data on all personal insurance lines on a daily basis—normally following a schedule which has each branch transmit data at a certain time of day for maximum equipment utilization. New policies, transfers, cancellations, premium payments, and other items are processed almost immediately; central records are up-dated and summary information is sent back to the branch. Accuracy is higher, and operating costs are substantially lower than before introduction of the system.

The potentialities of the Data-Phone system and other still more powerful systems now being developed, with their capacity for accepting punched cards, punched tape, and magnetic tape, are obviously great. Firms with multi-plant or multi-divisional operations can have direct, rapid communications between branch and headquarters and among branches, as well as with outside firms.

Microwave provides even greater capacity and speed for firms needing it. Both American Telephone and Telegraph and several private (unregulated) manufacturers are developing broadband microwave systems with tremendous capacities. Thus far, normal commercial needs have not required the more powerful systems; the general feeling seems to be that voice circuits, such as those supplied for Data-Phone installations and high grade teletype circuits, will suffice for most data transmission needs. One firm, however, North American Aviation, Inc., now links two computer centers by microwave system; others are likely to follow to provide communication between large computer centers, as additional systems are developed and refined.

For the future, satellite relays offer almost unlimited possibilities for long-distance communication of nearly all types. Research in this field, combined with many challenges for improving shorter-range service, seem certain to make data transmission technology one of the most dynamic of all fields for many years to come.

Data transmission concepts and illustrations

Because of the technical complexity of the many developments in data transmission techniques and devices, and the speed of change currently in progress, nothing more than a very brief description and certain illustrations is appropriate here.

Magnetic tape data transmission devices provide for transmission of databits at rates of 150 to 300 characters per second. The data is modulated for transmission and demodulated at the receiving end to provide the necessary checks for character validity. With the proper terminal devices, data can be transmitted directly between core storage of two or more computer systems.

Data collection systems provide for a flexible number of input stations connected through a control unit to a modified card punch. Instead of accumulating paper or card documents at the originating departments (such as employee time cards) data is entered directly into the input station and transmitted to the central computer system as the transactions occur. Information from all locations is immediately available for processing in punch card form at a central processing point.

Initial experiments in data transmission have been successfully conducted using the space satellite "Telstar." [7] An experimental message was transmitted at a rate of 2,000 words per minute via Telstar between Paoli, Pennsylvania and Detroit, Michigan. Possibilities for data transmission via satellites open completely new horizons and appear to offer nearly limitless opportunities.

One of the more common and flexible types of data transmission devices uses punched paper tape. The Data-Phone system discussed previously can transmit punched paper tape data, as well as data from punched cards. Speed of punched paper tape data transmitting devices ranges up to 1,200 bits per second. Punched paper tape data transmitting devices also use a modulating or parity checking feature to assure accuracy of transmission.

A brief review of several data transmission systems now in operation provides an indication of the vastness and potential impact of this area of data processing upon the operations and structure of modern business organizations. These brief illustrations have been selected merely to indicate the variety of data transmission systems as used in modern, progressive businesses and to illustrate how these organizations solved their particular problems of efficient computer applications.

A centralized computing center: [8] Douglas Aircraft linked its Charlotte, North Carolina plant to its data processing center in Santa Monica, California (2,200 miles) by using the Collins Kineplex equipment. The North Carolina plant has direct access to the computer system in California for solving complex technical problems. The company estimates that the work is accomplished for one-third of what it would cost to install a computer system in Charlotte, North Carolina.

A marketing distribution system: [9] Westinghouse Corporation has integrated all its sales offices and field and factory warehouses for industrial products

---

[7] "Data Transmission Via Space," *Data Processing*, November, 1962.

[8] Adapted from: Norman J. Ream, "Advances in Data Communications (Transmission and Reception)," *Advances in EDP and Information Systems*, AMA Management Report 62 (New York: American Management Association, 1961), p. 46.

[9] For a detailed account of this integrated system, see: Carl Rieser, "The Distribution Upheaval IV: The Short-Order Economy," *Fortune*, August, 1962, pp. 91-93.

with a centralized electronic computer system in Pittsburgh, Pennsylvania.

Customer order data are teletyped to the computer center from various offices throughout the United States. With a minimum of manual effort and handling of the data, the electronic computer system is programmed to perform such operations as: re-order from the supplier or manufacturer if the inventory falls below predetermined minimums; prepare the customer's invoice, taking into account complicated discount structures and shipping costs; select and notify the warehouse with the ordered item in stock which is closest to the customer's receiving location to make the necessary shipments.

This computerized marketing distribution system processes over 1,500 orders each day, and future plans call for installing a larger, real-time computer system capable of handling some 15,000 orders and inquiries daily.

Benefits from this system include a substantial reduction in inventory of industrial products, increased flow of cash, and greatly improved customer service—a very important consideration in today's highly competitive economy.

An airlines reservation system: [10] When the American Airlines "Sabre" reservation system became operational in 1963, it was one of the most advanced data transmission systems in service. The American Airlines "Sabre" data transmission system was developed specifically for airline reservation problems and related functions, and provides direct transmission of ticket agent's input to the storage and memory facilities of the computer system. Specially designed agent consoles in various offices throughout the U. S. were directly linked with an IBM 7090 computer system in New York City. The unique feature of this system is that the agent can communicate back and forth with the computer in New York City in much the same way as a telephone conversation might be handled. The computer system performs the following functions relative to airline reservation and passenger service, and operational functions:

1. Provides up to date seat inventory status for each flight.
2. Maintains a complete record of passengers' names and addresses and special requests, such as a rental car.
3. Transmits teletype messages to other airlines requesting space and answers their requests for space.
4. Supplies flight number, departure time, and arrival time.
5. Notifies agency to take special action, e.g., flight changes, delays, etc.
6. Maintains aircraft log and engine maintenance records, as well as cost and revenue data for each flight and aircraft.

The computer completely rechecks each transaction to assure that all data have been received and recorded by the computer. An "OK" is signaled by the computer at the completion of each transaction.

A brokerage operation: [11] The brokerage firm of Merrill, Lynch, Pierce, Fenner, and Smith linked each of its 130 offices to a central computing center by teletype so that bills may be issued directly to the offices involved. The computer system processes approximately 16,000 daily transactions and then

[10] Adapted from: James D. Gallagher, *Management Information Systems and the Computer*, AMA Research Study Series No. 51 (New York: American Management Association, 1961), pp. 150-176.

[11] *Ibid.*, p. 47.

directly bills the respective brokerage office via teletype local billing tape. Management estimated that it has saved $82,000 per year with this data transmission system.

Information Retrieval

One of the newest and most promising areas in computer application is information retrieval. Several large computer manufacturers forecast a huge market for computers specially designed for information retrieval applications. The reasons for such optimism are indicated by a *Business Week* estimate in 1961, that one and one-half billion dollars a year, or about 12 per cent of the nation's annual research expenditures were for "information services or searching the literature." [12] Experience has indicated that from 25 to 75 per cent of these information research expenses may have been wasted through duplication of effort because the researchers did not know what had been accomplished previously in the particular areas of study.

Because of the increasingly technical nature of competition in many fields, and because of the increasing volume of technical publications of all types, new methods of searching our vast storehouses of technical knowledge and achievements are vitally needed to assure efficient and economical application of future research funds and effort.

There are essentially three types of individual effort in the classification and retrieval of information. These are: (1) the author of the data, (2) the indexer, who determines how the information is to be coded, sorted, and stored, and in what categories, and (3) the searcher for the information, who needs to locate data of a particular nature. Basically, information retrieved involves storing vast amounts of data, both alphabetic and numeric, in electronic computers and providing a means by which any part of that information can be located almost instantly and reconverted to its original form.

Information retrieval (IR) represents a major breakthrough in computer technology and application. EDP systems are now not limited simply to replacing manual work operations. The increased storage capacity combined with the improved ability to utilize computer systems in managerial situations has provided a whole new area for computer applications. The concept of IR makes it possible for management to store its basic master accounts (records) in the computer's memory, update these accounts on a daily basis, and call forth at any time, all or any combination of the account balances. This application of IR was mentioned in the case examples of the Shell Oil and American Bosch Arma companies earlier in this chapter, where daily profit and loss statements

---

12 "Machines Take Toil Out of Searching Files," *Business Week,* July 8, 1961.

and balance sheets were available to management by simply "reading out" the stored information.

For example, customer accounts for billing can now be stored in the computer systems, and managerial analyses, such as balances over a certain amount, date of last payment, average order size, etc., can be performed almost immediately. These analyses were previously impractical because of the limitations of time and accessibility to the data. The application and scope of IR systems to business situations are limited only to the imagination and ingenuity of the management, researcher, and the EDP specialist.

Information retrieval concepts and illustrations

Not all information retrieval systems depend solely on a complicated coding or indexing system. New developments in microfilm techniques, together with allied developments in the microfilm window punched card and the storage and reproduction of tangible film strips, are changing the original concepts of information retrieval. A new development in microdocument storage and retrieval by one manufacturer represents a reduction ratio in size of 40,000:1.[13] With such a reduction ratio, a 300 page book could be recorded completely on a *square inch of film*. Regular microfilm copies are used as the input data for the new microfilm process. The new technique is not yet fully developed for commercial, mass production application, but its potential impact on information retrieval will probably be astonishing.

The Central Intelligence Agency's information retrieval system discussed below is an illustration of a microfilm storage and retrieval system. Not only is the information stored and coded through a system of indexing, but the selected document can be obtained immediately via the microfilm window of a punched card.

Information retrieval systems are in their infancy, however, but the two examples below of rather new and experimental applications will indicate the scope and potential for this area of electronic computer applications.[14]

> *Technical literature:* One of the first IR systems to be established was Western Reserve's Documentation Center for the American Society for Metals. Western Reserve personnel abstract, catalog, and code about 36,000 pages on metallurgy a year and store the data in a General Electric 225 computer system. As researchers, scientists, or educators raise a question on a particular aspect of metallurgy, an indexer prepares the inquiry for the computer through

[13] A. S. Tauber and W. C. Myers, "Photochromic Micro-images," *Data Processing,* November, 1962, p. 36.

[14] Adapted from: "Machines Take Toil Out of Searching Files," *Business Week,* July 8, 1961, pp. 45-46.

a system of codes. The result is a list of all publications which may be relevant to the subject of the question.

Government intelligence data: Possibly one of the largest and most intricate IR systems is the "Walnut" system of the Central Intelligence Agency. The CIA's Walnut system combines an IBM 1401 computer system with a microfilm memory index to store and index the many security reports received each day. A document to be stored is first reduced to ordinary microfilm and then reduced again on Kalfax (a miniature film) to the size of a pinhead. Fifty strips of Kalfax, each holding 99 document pages, hang in a rectangular plastic box called a "cell." Two-hundred cells form a circular module storing 990,000 document pages. The computer is programmed to read key words in the request for information and to print out related titles and punch a card for each title. The searcher reviews the title list and inserts the corresponding card into an "image file." The selected strips from the cells are then exposed onto a small microfilm window of a punched card. Almost immediately the card is flipped out of the machine and the requested document can be read by use of a special viewer.

Information retrieval is not without its disadvantages, however. It is extremely difficult to place a value on an IR system, because the real value of information must be considered in view of the cost of not having the information when it is needed. The Western Reserve Documentation Center estimates that it costs about $6.49 to process a single document for storage in the electronic computer.[15] Although this is a direct cost, it is relatively cheap when one considers the many hours of research time and the millions of dollars which are invested for research.

Indexing is another problem in IR. To store factual data in a computer's memory, the data must be "coded or labeled" to identify their content in such a way that their relevancy can be recognized by different people in the future. In other words, the searcher must think like the indexer, and the indexer must think as the writer thought and as the searchers *will think* in the future. Indexing must, therefore, be both specific and broad in order to anticipate the many varied requests for related information. E. I. du Pont Company's research staff maintains a relatively small IR center for the company's technological and scientific needs. Du Pont believes that an article is not properly indexed unless it is indexed under approximately 50 titles. This detailed indexing of technical documents is what du Pont refers to as "deep indexing." [16]

Semantics is another problem area frequently encountered in information retrieval applications. Semantics is a generic term which describes the differences of meanings that words may have for different people. These differences may come from viewpoints of the different people,

---

[15] *Ibid.,* p. 55.
[16] B. E. Holm, "Improved Information Storage and Retrieval Systems in Industry," *Advances in EDP and Information Systems,* AMA Management Report No. 62 (New York: American Management Association, 1961), p. 68.

the variety of meanings that the words may correctly have, or from the use of the word in combinations with other words and phrases. These three factors combine to create a problem situation in indexing information to be stored in computer memories and even a greater problem when searching for data. The deep indexing mentioned above is one method of dealing with the semantic problems.

Information retrieval applications

Some possible future applications of information retrieval theory to practical everyday affairs are discussed below. These are not futuristic dreams, but practical IR applications which, in most cases, have already received considerable attention and research.

Medical data: The physician in the future will, as a matter of routine, enter both personal history and diagnostic data regarding his patient to the electronic memory of a computer and have immediate access to a vast "consultative network." Such a system furnishes the physician with key facts related with his particular case—the equivalent of many time-consuming and expensive consultations with other physicians. The computer's memory (storage) is continually expanded as more cases are processed and coded for storage, much like the "experience" the physician gains from his practice.

In fact, experiments on diagnosing with computers have been done by Dr. Keeve Broadman, New York Hospital-Cornell University Medical College.[17] Dr. Broadman used an electronic computer to analyze data which patients supplied by answering questionnaires. In a series of tests, the machine's ability to diagnose the condition of 350 patients was compared with that of a physician who had made preliminary diagnoses from the same information as that given to the machine. On diseases not involving psychoneurosis, the computer scored 48% and the MD 43%. When emotional illness was involved, however, the MD identified 81% while the computer scored only 42%.

Scientific data: An area of particular significance for IR application is an information center for technical literature. This is not a small task. Each year technical writers all over the world produce about 60,000 books, 100,000 research reports, and over a million articles. If researchers and scientists are to keep pace with today's dynamic economy, this vast material and knowledge should be readily accessible.

Legal data: Another application of IR which seems to have great merit is the classification, coding, and storage of legal data in the memory units of computer systems. Considerable portions of any lawyer's time and effort are spent in searching the law for precedents, for proof, and for tangible evidence which would support his particular case. The storage of the legal data for ready accessibility to any lawyer, would enable the lawyer to practice more of his profession in the real sense of the word. The Health Law Center of the University of Pittsburgh is currently doing research in searching legal data without indexing by looking for pertinent, significant key words in the full text of the laws.

[17] American Medical Association, "Electronic Diagnosis: Computers, Medicine Join Forces," *The AMA News,* November 16, 1959, p. 2.

Business data: IR systems are also becoming established in business operations. Through random access and real-time computers, business firms now have immediate access to all of their stored data. This development paved the way for "assembly line" posting of individual documents to the master accounts (as discussed in the American Bosch Arma IDP example). Major oil companies with several million credit accounts now have access to any account directly without having to scan the entire file until the desired account is located. This permits more diligent credit control and economical customer service in answering customers' inquiries. The American Airlines "Sabre" system, Westinghouse's market distribution application, Shell Oil's and American Bosch Arma's IDP applications all involved the concept of information retrieval.

Summary

IDP, data acquisition, data transmission, and IR are all closely interrelated concepts of computer applications which have their essence in facilitating modern, efficient, aggressive management of business organizations.

Each of these concepts is concerned with information—information needed to intelligently manage a competitive business. True integrated data processing, or a "total information system," cannot be achieved in a decentralized organization without careful planning and without effective data acquisition and data transmission. The concept of information retrieval is directly applicable to the problem of "real-time" computer applications, because to have effective IDP and data transmission, the data being integrated must be immediately available—either from transmission or from updating through current posting of operating results. The fact that a computer is capable of going *directly* to a particular customer's records and billing information is very much a function of information retrieval. Data acquisition embraces aspects of all concepts of computer applications; the data must first be acquired and prepared for input into the computer system. Preferably, data acquisition should include source data automation and integrated data processing to realize the full efficiencies of computer processing.

IDP, data acquisition, data transmission, and IR are not, then, isolated computer applications of the future. They are tangible, useful applications of today. In order to achieve effective and efficient computer system operations, management should review its entire informational requirements, procedures, and systems design. One of management's initial responsibilities is to set forth the information requirements which are needed in each functional area and at each level within the organization. Delegation of authority and assignment of responsibilities must be more explicit so that proper *blocks of information* can be established to assist responsible individuals in making better decisions. Above all, management should realize that IDP and data transmission information systems know no boundaries—they are organizational, wide in scope and application. Particularly significant overall benefits which may be realized from these computer system applications are:

1. Such applications are the most efficient and economical because they furnish the company with the required information at the lowest cost.

2. Data are collected at their source and as it originates—providing for practical and feasible decentralized operations through data transmission to centralized computer systems.

3. One piece of information can serve all functions and levels of the business, through integrated transmission and timely retrieval.

4. Such applications permit an immediate, day-to-day analysis of the operating results and allow controls to be instigated much sooner than ordinarily.

Regardless of the capabilities and/or possibilities of IDP, data acquisition, data transmission and information retrieval systems with respect to business organizations, the end results can be no better than the *design of the total system of information and reports* as planned and conceived by top management.

QUESTIONS FOR STUDY AND DISCUSSION

1. Define and clearly differentiate the four major computer concepts considered in this chapter; then point out any significant relationships that seem to exist among them. What do you see as the future potentialities for each—in business applications and in other fields where you believe they may find use?

2. What is source data automation? What are its implications for business applications of electronic data processing systems? Is it possible that the absence of source data automation was a primary factor in the dissatisfaction of computer users in the middle and late 1950's? Is it still a primary factor in determining the effectiveness of computer systems for business?—Explain. Two examples of optical scanning as used in source data automation were given in this chapter. Suggest other possible applications of this concept in business.

3. In its simplest form, data transmission is the sending and receiving of machine data over long-distance wires. Is it conceivable that a basically technical process such as this could affect the whole philosophy of management with respect to centralization and decentralization? Consider specifically such well-known decentralized companies as General Motors and General Electric.

4. The American Telephone and Telegraph Company (AT&T) is expecting one-half of its total revenue in 1970 to stem from data transmission services. How can you account for and justify such an estimate?

5. The computer concepts as presented in this chapter all had their beginnings in types of installations other than business. All of them have been proven as contributors to more effective management, but only after a considerable time lag. Comment on the reluctance of business to recognize the benefits from such concepts and to pioneer research and development in their implementation.

6. The concept of information retrieval has thus far been applied primarily to

scientific purposes and other highly specialized fields of knowledge. Discuss this concept in relation to its value and potential for business applications.

7. Despite the lag in computer applications for business and industry as indicated in the previous question, recent trends illustrate conclusively that the computer has now been widely accepted in business. Among other effects caused by the computer, what principal changes in organizational structure appear to be most likely to occur? What changes are likely as a result of integrated data processing?

Case 13-1. Applications of Computer Concepts for Business

Illustrative applications of information retrieval techniques presented in this chapter were the Walnut System of the Central Intelligence Agency and the Western Reserve Documentation Center. The Walnut System handles hundreds of intelligence reports daily, storing them in an electronic computer system. The Western Reserve Center abstracts some 36,000 papers each year on the subject of metallurgy and enters this data in computer storage.

Data acquisition concepts involved the Ryder Truck Lines billing and invoicing system, and magnetic ink character recognition for banking systems.

The Hardware Mutuals-Sentry Life Insurance Data-Phone system, the Westinghouse marketing distribution problem, and the American Airlines "Sabre" country-wide reservation system all presented illustrative applications of various data transmission concepts.

Integrated data-processing concepts were demonstrated by the examples from Shell Oil, American Bosch Arma, and U. S. Steel. These companies used a common language of either punched paper tape or magnetic tape to integrate entire series of operations, sometimes located in different sections of the country.

Problems and questions:

a. Review these illustrative applications of computer concepts, and recall any other applications with which you may be familiar.

b. Suggest and discuss an actual or potential example of a business application for each of these concepts.

c. Discuss the present and potential impact of these computer concepts upon the organization of the business firm.

d. How are these concepts interrelated, if at all?

e. Which of these computer concepts has been the slowest to develop in business applications? Why? What are your recommendations for management in this area?

f. Outline your recommendations for management to prepare for the future use of these and other computer concepts. Support your recommendations.

14

ADMINISTRATION
OF DATA PROCESSING

Need for critical viewpoint and broad perspectives · Feasibility of computer usage · Organization of the data processing function · Preparing personnel for conversion to EDP · Managing data processing operations · Computer service bureaus and small business usage · Management adaptations and challenges

---

The chapters just preceding have dealt mainly with *technical* aspects of data processing and with illustrative applications. Full realization of the technical potentialities of the new tools will depend heavily upon the *administrative* perception and skill exercised in putting them to most effective use in specific situations. Attention will therefore now be directed to the following pertinent areas.

1. Need for a critical viewpoint and a broad perspective.
2. Studying the feasibility of computer usage.
3. Organizing the data processing function.
4. Preparing personnel for conversion to electronic data processing systems.
5. Administering data processing operations.
6. Management adaptations and challenges.

Need for Critical Viewpoint and Broad Perspective

Early experiences with large-scale data processing systems, particularly computers, were very often disappointing. A feature article in the *Busi-*

ness Week issue of June 21, 1958 (following what might be termed the first wave of first-generation computers) noted that the electronic computer revolution in business was then in a stage of uncertainty because complex electronic computers had been adopted by industry almost with a religious fervor, but users were frequently unsure of what to do with the computers once they had obtained them. There were frequent complaints regarding experience with the "electronic marvels." Costs were higher than estimated, and the heavy burden of programming and planning for full or efficient utilization had not been anticipated; consequently, results frequently fell short of expectations. In one survey, some 40% of the computer users were somewhat disillusioned.[1]

Not many firms returned computers to manufacturers. In 1958, there were approximately 1,800 computers in use and 3,000 on order. In 1962, there were over 7,000 computers in service and there were orders for over 8,000 additional computers of all sizes and models. Included were 5,200 orders for IBM's 1401 model—a medium-size general-purpose digital computer.[2]

It is now evident that the electronic computer is a vital and necessary part of the modern business organization. Computers cannot be ignored, or relegated to the minor roles of replacing simple manual tasks. There is a dual challenge for managers to increase their efforts to utilize computers effectively, and for manufacturers to fit designs and services more carefully to needs. Efforts such as these require highly critical analysis of current systems, procedures, and operations, and a broad perspective regarding future applications of the electronic computer.

Today, while experience has taught many lessons, it is probable that the typical installation is not accomplishing all it might. A study committee of a prominent banking management association compared the present stage of the computer industry with that of the automobile industry when people first made up their minds that the automobile was here to stay.

Much of the explanation for early disappointments lies in superficial planning, unwillingness to make major changes in established systems and organization, and absence of a perspective which takes in the *whole* organization rather than focusing on one or a few specialized applications.

Neuschel makes one of his typically penetrating observations in noting that:

> . . . there is no quick, easy path to achieving *optimum* use of a computer in business operations. Nor will the mere acquisition of a computer enable

---

[1] "Business Week Reports to Readers on: Computers," *Business Week,* June 21, 1958, p. 70.

[2] "A Census of Computers," *The Office,* March, 1962, pp. 140-141.

management to avoid any difficult problems that it was not willing to face squarely in the past. Clearly, those who profit most—or indeed at all—from electronic data processing will be those who have the courage to apply an exacting, fundamental point of view to the question of whether or not to use such equipment. Only through its willingness to apply this kind of discipline will a company force itself to learn how to use this new tool at anywhere near the limit of its capacity of versatility.[3]

Studying the Feasibility of Computer Usage

Basic steps in a systematic approach to studying computer feasibility include (1) the initial size-up, and (2) the detailed feasibility study.[4]

Initial size-up

A detailed feasibility study is time-consuming and costly. At stake may be not only the investment in the equipment and the extensive preparations required before installation, but sweeping changes in decision-making, organization structure and qualifications of personnel as well. Viewed from the opposite direction, however, the problems created by indecision or inactivity—if real need should be found to exist—may exact an even higher price in terms of missed opportunities, competitor advantages, and other losses or costs.

The first need, therefore, is that of "studying the feasibility of a feasibility study"—in other words, of determining whether potential benefits through use of electronic equipment seem great enough to justify study in depth.

Where a computer installation is being considered, a top-management group—often the executive committee itself—should examine critically the needs of the enterprise which might be served more effectively than by present methods. The top-management group may well begin by asking such questions as the following:

1. Do problems such as the following exist?
   a. generally high and rising administrative costs
   b. one or more particularly high-volume clerical routines
   c. difficulty in providing customer service of the type desired
   d. difficulty in scheduling production
   e. heavy inventory costs

[3] Richard F. Neuschel, *Management by System* (New York: McGraw-Hill Book Company, Inc., 1960), p. 272.

[4] More detailed treatments of feasibility study approaches are available from many sources. Among good treatments are the National Industrial Conference Board's Reports No. 92, *Management's Role in Electronic Data Processing*, and No. 98, *Administration of Electronic Data Processing;* Ralph Weindling, H. W. Matthews, and P. T. Bridgeman, *A Management Guide to Computer Feasibility* (Detroit: American Data Processing, Inc., 1962); and Richard F. Neuschel, *op. cit.*

  f. quality control difficulties

  g. involved problems in analyzing market needs

 2. If these or comparable problems do exist, how serious are they?

 3. Does it seem probable that data processing equipment now available could help in solving these problems; if so, would benefits gained justify the cost and effort required in change over?

The executive committee, or other top-level group which makes the initial size-up, is likely to have only limited familiarity with the capabilities of available equipment. For this reason, they probably will need to draw in systems analysts, outside consulting help, or equipment supplier representatives when preliminary study reaches the point that some significant areas of potential usage of new equipment have been defined. But it is extremely important that early attention be directed to exploring the need for more detailed study—rather than to attempt to make final or even tentative decisions justifying installation.

If further study then seems justified, the next step usually will be the appointment of a study team to carry out detailed analysis. Ideally, such a group should report to the top executive and have its work reviewed by the executive committee. The detail study group should be given complete backing by top management, as much investigatory power as may be needed, and sufficient relief from other duties to devote a substantial amount of time and effort likely to be required. The study group should include representatives from departments which seem likely to be the heaviest potential users, also, at least one person experienced in systems analysis and one thoroughly familiar with computers—even if the latter requirement necessitates bringing in a consultant. The group should be headed by a person who is systems-oriented, thorough, and diplomatic in relations with others; he may be a good prospect to head up the installation, if it is made, although this may not be a dominant consideration.

Detailed feasibility study

The detailed study group will first wish to clarify its objectives. Normally, these will include the following:

 1. To determine whether electronic data processing would increase the overall efficiency of the enterprise.

 2. To determine most promising areas of application, and to determine broad systems requirements in these areas.

 3. To survey available equipment in terms of suitability and costs, and to develop a recommendation as to size and make most appropriate.

 4. To compare costs of present systems and proposed systems.

5. To appraise intangible benefits and problems.

6. To recommend, if justified, the projected system and equipment, and to recommend a schedule of conversion to the new system, including training of personnel.

In a given situation, the study group may need to be particularly sure of higher management expectations (which the group itself may influence) such as whether direct savings in clerical costs are expected to pay for the equipment. Also, how carefully factors such as better customer service, improved planning and control, etc., are to be appraised. Of particular interest will be the question of how far management will be willing to go in adjusting systems, organization, personnel, and other factors involved.

The mission of the study group (and its specific objectives as just considered) should be announced by top management. The study group will probably then wish to have exploratory meetings with department heads and reach an understanding of their objectives and the help they will need.

Once objectives are clarified and understood, their attainment is most likely to reach fruition if the members of the study team take a broad systems approach. Certain major areas of application may stand out almost immediately; other areas may show little, if any, potential use of electronic equipment. But some time and effort should be devoted to tracing and studying the over-all systems network. Here a master systems plan, such as considered in Chapter 7, is of tremendous value. The different systems can be scrutinized more carefully for potential areas of application; their interrelationships can be studied with a view to integrating data, files, and processing steps where possible.

For each system, it may then be well to flow chart or block diagram the present approach—showing outputs (orders filled, reports for control purposes, net income determination, etc.), the inputs (forms, records, etc.), and the intermediate processing steps. Volume, time, and cost data should also be secured.

Critical study should then be directed to the present system of operations. Executives most concerned should be queried as to what they would like to have from the system, whether they are getting what they want, and what improvements in results they may wish to suggest. Volume, time, and cost data can usually be developed from already-prepared statistical and accounting records, although considerable effort may be required to combine it into a form which embraces the entire system involved.

Next, the design of the new system should be carried out—focusing upon outputs desired, upon efficiency in each stage of processing, upon possibilities for integration among systems, and upon adaptability to computer handling. The feasibility study group probably should carry the new systems design to the point of flow charting or block diagramming the basic steps; and of defining outputs, inputs, volume, and time requirements. More detailed analysis would, of course, be required later in the programming stage.

When the principal systems having greatest potential computer usage have thus been designed, particular attention should be given to possibilities of integration. Throughout the process, continuous communication with key people involved is highly desirable, so that *their* needs and suggestions can be considered, thereby winning the highest possible degree of acceptance.

A summary of total data processing requirements, with some allowance for growth, should then be prepared and made the basis for evaluating different sizes and makes of equipment available. With the requirements of the systems design firmly resolved, the detail study group should then turn itself to an appraisal of the computer equipment available to meet the needs of the new systems design. Factors usually considered in such an analysis are:

1. Computer capabilities
   a. Internal storage capacities and external storage possibilities.
   b. Computation speed.
   c. Types of input-output media and speed of each.
   d. Additional features which may be acquired at a later date.
   e. Type and ease of programming.
2. Manufacturer services
   a. Software packages provided with the computers.
   b. Maintenance services.
   c. Programming assistance.
   d. Reputation of manufacturer.
3. Reliability of equipment and special requirements
   a. Expected down-time as experienced by other users.
   b. Maintenance time as required by other users.
   c. Power requirement and air conditioning.
   d. Structural requirements of floor.
4. Personnel requirements and flexibility of system
   a. Number of people required to operate proposed system.
   b. Amount of unused capacity in the original equipment available for expansion.
   c. Compatibility of equipment for future expansion.
5. Estimated cost of each of the above items

It logically follows that the next step in the feasibility study is to compare costs of the present and proposed system of operation. To a large extent the cost of the computer system can be obtained from the manufacturer and verified from discussions with other firms with similar installations.

It is extremely important to establish accurate and detailed costs for the *present* system of operations. This involves the detailed study of the present system and procedures discussed previously. Neuschel provides an excellent checklist of facts to be obtained in this part of the survey, slightly altered here.[5]

1. Function preferred—What work is performed when and in what sequence, by whom, how and why.

2. Quantitative and qualitative data—Volume of work and the man hours required, including how well—accuracy, timeliness, etc.—the functions are performed.

3. Flow of work—Direction, distance, method of communicating, frequency, and degree of stability of the volume.

One word of caution. In studying and costing the present system, the costs previously experienced should be adjusted for the possible efficiencies and other cost saving operations which have become apparent during the study. Ordinarily, there are improvements to be found in any system, and deducting the possible savings from existing costs is vital to the justification of a computer system.

> For example, one large eastern firm conducted a feasibility study and determined that the proposed computer system would result in a net savings to the firm of about $270,000 per year. When an outside consultant was asked to verify the findings, some $305,000 in possible net savings per year were discovered through economies of the *present* system, resulting in a *net deficit* of $25,000 per year which would result if the computer were installed and the existing system left basically unchanged except for faster processing.

Equally important in comparing costs of the present and proposed systems is the need to include all relevant costs associated with the computer installation. Frequently, many of those costs are overlooked or ignored, resulting in inefficient and uneconomical operations and dissatisfied managements. The list below provides a good indication of the various costs associated with computer installations. No dollar figures are furnished, since actual costs vary considerably with the circumstances of each system.

1. Operating Costs
    a. Computer rental and associated equipment. Rental prices for second-

[5] Richard F. Neuschel, *op. cit.*, p. 143.

and third-shift operations should also be obtained to plan for future expanded operations.

b. Minimum computer staff needs—full time operators, programmers, and systems analysts.

c. Associated peripheral equipment necessary to prepare the original data.

d. Clerical force to operate the associated equipment.

e. Power requirements and air conditioning.

f. Continuing programming and research costs.

g. Miscellaneous supplies, magnetic tape, punched cards, etc.—an important item.

2. Start-Up Costs

a. Installation—air conditioning, moisture control, reinforcing floors.

b. Programming and converting original data into machine language.

c. Feasibility studies.

d. Training.

e. Duplicate operations of present and proposed systems during initial stages of operations.

f. "Purifying" files prior to use by computer.

g. Rearranging organizational structure and system to accommodate new computer department. This often results in inefficiencies for a short time in all departments.

One of management's most difficult and challenging tasks regarding feasibility studies is to appraise the subjective and intangible benefits accruing from the adoption of a computer installation. Possibly, the executive decision to install a computer system will override the cost study of computer versus present operations because there are many benefits of computer applications for which dollar evaluation cannot be made. It is not uncommon for computer systems to appear to operate at a loss when only the manual operations they replaced are considered.

For example, one company was operating a computer system at a net loss set at approximately $500,000 until management assigned a value of over $700,000 per year to the improved managerial information system.

It is difficult for a firm to realistically appraise the value of electronic computer applications. At best, it is only an educated estimate, but who is in a better position to make such an estimate than the company management? Among intangible benefits which may justify consideration are:

1. *Improved customer service.* With cost and profit advantages often almost neutralized through keen competition, *service to the customer* is becoming an important item in the fight for the market share. Computers enable a firm to analyze situations more quickly and make better decisions, as well as provide

the customer with better service through order processing, inventory control, billing, and the like.

2. *Improved management information systems.* Evaluations in this area depend upon such factors as "How much more effective will the organization be, as a whole, with the informational capabilities of the computers?" "Can better management planning, direction, and control be achieved through use of a computer and if so, what is the value to the firm?"

3. *Company prestige and status.* Many firms believe that having a computer system is good for public relations and their management attaches a value to this service. A firm may have a reputation of being a leader in the industry, and may feel that electronic data process provides evidence necessary to demonstrate that it is maintaining its place of leadership in the industry. Disadvantages in weighing this factor too heavily are readily seen, yet it is often an important consideration.

4. *Impetus for change.* New computer systems not only require changes in the particular operation being replaced but also provide the impetus for other changes within the organization. For many reasons, changes in manual operations are difficult to achieve unless there is some compelling, significant force such as computer conversion to provide the motivation.

5. *Other intangibles.* Other intangible factors management must appraise when concluding computer feasibility studies are: the willingness of the company to alter its present system and organization in order to fit the needs of the electronic program; the availability of competent, trained employees capable of carrying out the proposed computer system; the success of other companies with similar programs. Although experience has shown that computer success in one company is no guarantee, it does provide support and confidence, and helps in avoiding problem areas.

Less than optimum utilization is possibly the most difficult factor to contend with in these intangible, subjective appraisals of computer feasibility. As mentioned previously in this chapter, when computers were in their infancy, many companies installed systems with much enthusiasm and fanfare, only to realize later that the computer did not accomplish all it was supposed to at the anticipated costs. Computers often sat idle because necessary systems design and programming had not been completed beforehand. It appeared that many firms wanted to "keep up with the Joneses." Executive desire is a powerful motive—more powerful than some firms would like to admit—and management must have a good reason to believe that satisfactory cost savings will result, or that some *other significant benefits* will be realized, before authorizing detailed computer studies and ultimate installation.

Organization of the Data Processing Function

The organization of the data processing function should be based upon one primary criterion—that of service to the other elements of the organization. This is particularly evident when considering the major roles computers play in processing management information. Obviously, the particular uses that a company makes of its computer facilities will influence the organizational arrangements, as will the emphasis that is accorded the ultimate potential of computer systems.

The data processing department traditionally has been a part of the controller's organization—a major segment of that important staff unit. This is in keeping with the specialized service rendered by the data processing unit and its close relationship to other services provided by the controller's department. Then, too, most data processing systems are initiated in the controller's organization where they can be applied to clerical tasks that lend themselves to mechanization such as inventory control, customer billing, and payroll.

There now seems to be a trend, already noted in Chapter 3, for the data processing department (including computers and peripheral equipment) to be headed by a top-ranking staff executive who has a title such as "Vice-President, Administrative Services," or "Vice-President, Management Information," who may also be in charge of informational analysis, systems analysis, and administrative services of other types. This means that management provision of information service can make a greater contribution to corporate planning and control, and can serve all functional departments since it is not subordinate to any single department. Equal voice with key departments such as production, engineering, and sales may assist vitally in coordinating all specialized functions in the accomplishment of the general objectives of the enterprise. A few large companies (usually insurance companies) have established the electronic data processing as a separate staff unit. Obviously, the size and importance of the unit varies in different firms and will influence the status and position of the unit within the organization structure.

Time only will tell what the ultimate organizational position will be for computer systems and management information services. Considerable variation from firm to firm seems likely and appropriate. Whatever the arrangement, it appears certain that management information services will become increasingly important and will play a larger role in the organization of top management activities.

The internal organization of an EDP department depends quite heavily upon the quantity of peripheral machines and the size of the electronic computers. Operations of an extremely large EDP system can usually be organized into the following separate, but closely related, units which require their own specialized activities:

1. System study
2. Programming
3. Computer operations

A typical EDP organization chart may look something like the illustration in Figure 14-1, below.

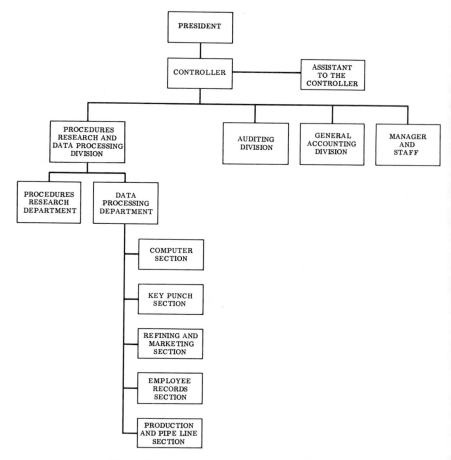

Figure 14-1. Typical organization of a large EDP unit

An alternative arrangement, dependent upon the emphasis necessary to perform the EDP function, may have systems study a separate unit, with programming and computer operations combined. Other combinations of the EDP unit are also possible, as long as they serve the needs of the organization. Ordinarily, punched card equipment is not merged or included as a part of large computer units except as necessary input-output equipment. In small or medium computer installations, date tabulators and computer operations are usually combined.

Preparing Personnel for Conversion to EDP

Ralph Cordiner, Chairman of the Board, General Electric Company, has said: "Good planning for automation includes planning for the all-important human problems as well as mechanical and financial problems."

Normally, people resist changes of any kind, probably because of fear of the unknown. In the case of a major change in the organizational arrangement and systems flow, the employee's fear is increased because his job, security, and future are directly involved.

Preparing the employees and developing favorable attitudes to the conversion of electronic data processing are necessary to the success of the program. Some of the reasons for this are: [6]

1. An EDP program usually cuts across and largely ignores departmental lines, even while requiring interdepartmental support.

2. The development of an EDP program which will benefit the entire organization requires access to the data of other departments and an understanding of each department's systems and procedures.

3. Frank, timely discussions of the facts regarding the conversion to EDP eliminates uncertainty and unrest.

4. By discussing the conversion well ahead of the actual installation, employees have an opportunity to discuss it among themselves and become accustomed to the idea.

5. An EDP program is company-wide, involving many people who do not come under the supervision of the manager of the EDP program. Consequently, considerable emphasis is placed upon the procedure to inform employees in other departments and to win their support.

Management's failure to prepare the employees for conversion to EDP can seriously hinder the electronic computer program. Antagonism, resistance, or reluctance on the part of the employees—all employees, but especially those involved with the computer program—can seriously hinder the program's chances of success.

An employee's primary interest during a conversion to EDP is likely

[6] Adapted from: Carl G. Baumes, *Administration of Electronic Data Processing*, N.I.C.B. Studies in Business Policy, No. 98 (New York: National Industrial Conference Board, Inc., 1961), p. 105.

to be his security—particularly job security. Typical questions asked by employees in these situations are:

Will my present job be changed?
Will some of us be fired?
Will I be able to keep my present job?
Will my salary be reduced?
Will I have to work in the EDP unit?
Will I be able to use my present training, or will I have to learn new, more difficult skills?

Such questions reflect employee fears and must be treated with utmost seriousness. The general objectives and subject matter of an effective employee communication program probably should contain, as a minimum, information on:

Job security
Importance of employees in EDP installations
New opportunities provided by EDP systems

Job security. Although few companies have a formal, guaranteed job policy, almost all companies issue some type of assurance to the employees stating that their jobs will not be downgraded, nor their pay reduced. The statement below from a president of an insurance company is typical of the employee assurances regarding job security: [7]

> I want to assure all of you who are now on the staff of the company that although the changes in our work which will result from using this modern equipment may affect the work which you are now doing, it will not result in the down-grading of any individual or the release from our services of any individual.

Such reassurances will have a solid basis in fact, in most instances. Normal attrition through voluntary turnover of employees usually provides much of the cushion needed for gradual EDP conversion. New job opportunities, discussed later, will usually provide even more flexibility.

Importance of people. Employees, when not adequately informed, may get the impression that EDP systems replace people almost overnight. Management must make a special effort to quell the fears of the employees and to reassure them that people are important and needed in electronic computer work. Typical statements issued by management regarding the importance of people in EDP conversions and operations are: [8]

[7] *Ibid.*, p. 107.
[8] *Ibid.*, p. 107.

. . . I believe that in due course this (conversion to EDP) is going to result in the up-grading of many posts held by our employees. These jobs will become broader in concept and in the responsibility carried. In due course many of you will be given the opportunity of qualifying for needed jobs.

. . . the electronic computer isn't the threshold to a manless era with giant mechanical geniuses doing all the work. Don't forget, a person must tell it (the computer) what to do.

New job opportunities. It is very desirable that management point out the many new job opportunities which will be available because of the electronic computer installation. The emphasis here should be on the need for new and critical skills to operate the computer systems and the related peripheral equipment.

There are many ways of informing the employees and of winning their support for the EDP conversion and operations. These can be combined in an effective, sincere program of employee communication. Methods of communicating with employees regarding EDP conversions include special pamphlets, open-house visits, group meetings, and personal letters sent to the employee's homes.

Of special value in winning employee support will be provision for extensive participation by subordinates throughout the preparatory stages. Leo Moore has made an illuminating statement which is especially pertinent here.

Contrary to the common management assumption, it can be demonstrated that people really like change and do not mind criticism if they make the changes and criticisms themselves. Subordinates resist the new ideas of managers, and line men resist the ideas of staff experts, because of the positions they are maneuvered into. If people down the line are to contribute new ideas and support change, then they must have the feeling that time spent on improvement is time well spent.[9]

A basic challenge to management thus exists in winning the cooperation and support of the employees in EDP installations. Their resistance to major changes can be both frustrating and uneconomical. Their understanding and support can go far toward ensuring ultimate success.

Managing Data Processing Operations

Most of the literature regarding EDP has been concerned with the technical aspects of computers, their uses and applications. This is easily understandable, in a new, highly-complicated, and dynamic field. The technical capabilities and achievements of electronic computers are

[9] Leo Moore, "Too Much Management, Too Little Change," *Harvard Business Review*, Vol. 34 (Jan.-Feb., 1956), 41.

colorful and exciting. However, one must not overlook the *administrative* responsibility of putting these highly expensive and complicated computers to work in practical situations so that there is a net advantage to the organization. John Sinclair, President of the National Industrial Conference Board, has made a pertinent observation:

> In short, the very characteristics that make electronic data processing so attractive impose upon the company the need for rigorous planning and intelligent administration. Without good planning, sound organization, efficient systems, and the active cooperation of affected personnel, the equipment's power is frustrated.[10]

Administrative planning of EDP refers to the feasibility study, the job of preparing the employees for conversion, and the organizational adjustments—all discussed previously. Other important elements of EDP are discussed below. These include staffing with key personnel, training, control, and maximum utilization of the equipment.

One of the foremost aspects of managing data processing operations involves staffing the department with qualified individuals. Admittedly, selection of personnel for EDP operations to date has been partly trial-and-error, with some aid from aptitude testing and experimentation. But increased experience, improved college training programs, and the general emphasis now placed on EDP work have all added greatly to the supply of trained computer specialists.

Most individual companies are doing their own training for computer programmers and systems analysts, recognizing that trained and experienced employees are in high demand and difficult to acquire. An important element of staffing the EDP department is defining key jobs and establishing job descriptions. All too often these basic procedures are overlooked because of the newness of the EDP work operations, the degree of technical skill required for EDP operations, and the highly dynamic nature of EDP job descriptions. These factors emphasize the need for management to express, in writing, the job descriptions and specifications of the key jobs. Such pre-planning greatly facilitates the already difficult job of staffing EDP departments.

Another basic function of administrative EDP involves evaluating performance and progress. It is essential to understand that the machines themselves are evaluated, as well as the employees. One-shift rental costs of large-scale computer systems average from $2,000-$3,000 per day. Obviously, management is extremely interested in obtaining full utilization of the computer equipment in order to approach profit-

---

[10] John Sinclair, "Foreword," to Carl G. Baumes, *Administration of Electronic Data Processing, op. cit.*

able operations. In this respect, the information listed below is typical of EDP evaluations performed in experienced companies.

1. The number and percentage of available computer hours which have been used productively.

2. The number and percentage of computer hours lost through mechanical failure or maintenance.

3. Manpower requirements—direct hours—associated with the EDP department.

4. Operating cost of the EDP units—salaries, rental, and supplies.

Other EDP administrative functions relate briefly to the continuing programs for systems study and revisions, the use of second and third shifts, and renting unused or idle equipment to other organizations. A continuing effort must be made to maintain efficiency and coordination of operations through systems review and implementation, if the firm is to take immediate advantage of newly discovered improvements. Systems review also keeps the idea and problem of constant improvement before the employees, encourages suggestions, and reduces resistance to the changes when they become necessary.

Rental prices for second and third shifts are significantly lower than for first-shift operations. There are considerable advantages to be gained from having a smaller configuration of equipment and using it on a second- and, possibly a third-shift basis. Extra shifts also provide the opportunity to do special work, test new programs, and to refine existing programs and procedures. It should be recognized, however, that the use of second and third shifts depends upon the availability of data for processing. The use of multi-shift computer operations may not be feasible for those firms that do not regularly operate multi-shift operations.

Renting unused computer equipment time to other users is a popular procedure for optimizing equipment costs. It has the advantage of flexibility: rental hours can be varied, dependent upon the time available and the need. It also has considerable advantages for both parties because cost of idle equipment is recovered and many small businesses can fill their needs by renting idle computer time from companies with computer systems. In large metropolitan areas with a concentration of computer systems operating, it is not uncommon for small firms to have a flexible arrangement for rented computer time with several firms in order to improve the possibility of locating available capacity when the need arises. Larger firms frequently develop mutual arrangements whereby peak loads and rush jobs can be handled on a loan (no charge) basis.

One example of a rental agreement is between an insurance company and an oil company. The oil firm subleases an eight-hour shift per day from the insurance firm located in the same building. The oil firm pays a slightly higher cost than the cost of the second-shift rental for the insurance firm and a slightly lower cost than the one-shift rental that the oil firm would have to pay the equipment manufacturer. The oil firm pays for and furnishes all supplies and employees to operate the system during its shift; the insurance company furnishes the necessary facilities such as heat, light, air conditioning, and the computer. In this agreement both firms and the equipment manufacturer benefit.

Computer Service Bureaus and Small Business Usage

The slowdown in the computer hardware race, the change in emphasis from hardware to software, and the increased trend for computer manufacturers to provide computer facilities and systems for particular firms, industries, and applications, have all led to an increase in the general awareness of the potential for computer systems in enterprises of all types and sizes. Manufacturers have realized that specialized computer systems are uneconomical for many smaller firms to own or rent, and have attempted to meet this need through computer service bureaus.

Computer service bureaus are one good answer to the integrated information system needs of small businesses. Through the application of common language and source data automation, small businesses can gain greater benefits from computer service centers, because of reduced computer time, more adequate reports, and faster service. The automatic punched tape attachments for standard office machines such as billing, accounting, adding, and typewriters, provide the ready-made punched tape inputs for electronic computer systems.

The problem of collecting data for input into the computers is greatly simplified, since it takes no more of the small firm's time to prepare punched tape as a by-product of normal operations. The variety and detail of reports possible through common language systems are virtually unlimited. Service bureaus thus provide the small business with data and information that was formerly the sole province of much larger organizations.

Some computer service bureaus maintain complete staffs of economists and mathematicians, as well as programming specialists to serve the small firm, as the following illustration indicates.

General Electric has recently opened a new computer center in Dallas, Texas, serving the southwestern region. This is the third computer center of the kind opened by GE (six are planned) and it will have an investment in equipment alone of over $500,000. The center will be equipped with the GE 225 general-purpose computer, high-speed document handlers, and related

supporting equipment. GE's Dallas computer center was the first in its area
to offer MICR for use by banks. The computer center will offer programming
and systems services in addition to selling computer time.

An interesting variation of service bureau operation is presented
below:

> There is a west coast, privately operated computer service bureau that pro-
> vides "do-it-yourself" computer operations. Under this arrangement, custom-
> ers provide programs, supplies, and everything but the computer. The cost is
> considerably lower, and the individual firms have the opportunity to "get into
> the computer operations" on a gradual basis.

By making use of computer service organization, small business can
take advantage of the most powerful electronic data processing machines
available without any capital investment, and without hiring additional
personnel. The cost is only for the computer time used ($500-$700 per
hour of running time) plus a small charge of $8-$10 per hour for programming if a standard program is not available.

Typical business problems of the small firm which are highly adaptable
to computer service center applications are:

> 1. Lengthy data processing problems. Electronic processing makes possible
> the rapid processing of a great amount of clerical data such as payroll, billing,
> and sales analysis.
> 2. Engineering problems. Through access to computer systems, small manu-
> facturers can enter new fields which were closed to them because of technical
> engineering requirements. Typical complicated, engineering applications in-
> clude heat and stress analysis and vibration analysis.
> 3. Transportation and distribution problems. Typical operations of this
> nature include most economic route and load designs. Such factors included
> in transportation problems are mileage, traffic congestion, toll roads, and load
> capacities. In one such case, an electronic computer analyzed some 10 million
> possible routes in just a few hours—a job that would have taken several years
> to solve manually.
> 4. Management analysis. Principal applications here for small businesses
> are determining where to locate new business by collectively evaluating such
> factors as customer demand, transportation, traffic, utilities, rent, and patterns
> of growth. A particularly significant and popular service offered by computer
> bureaus is forecasting sales and demand—performing market research by de-
> termining sales probabilities in different geographical areas for different
> products.

Computer service bureaus are by no means limited to serving small
businesses, however. During peak loads or rush periods, they provide
"overflow service" for larger firms with computer systems of their own.
One common use of service centers by larger firms is that of placing
smaller computational operations on the service bureau's systems so as

not to tie up the firm's own large computer with simple short run operations. The major problem in large firm usage often involves the compatibility of the computer systems—whether the same input can be accepted by both computers, and whether the service center's computer can be programmed for the same operations. Increasing problems of compatibility are being solved through common language systems.

Management Adaptations and Challenges

Business organization is at the door of a new era that will result in unprecedented advances of office mechanization and an evolution in methods of managerial operations and control of enterprises. Probably there has been no era, other than the Industrial Revolution, in which management has faced a comparable challenge. The possibilities and capabilities of computer applications are limited only by the imagination and capital of the researchers, manufacturers, and users of the equipment.

At the present time, a large majority of electronic computer applications throughout the country are nothing more than the mechanization of the manual operations of the past. The greater challenge to management is to adapt its entire philosophy and mode of operation to the new horizons opened by computer technology, and to integrate electronic data processing applications with the managerial decision-making activity of the enterprise.

Thus, *management* adaptation is not a process of revolution, but a *project of evolution*—a natural, common occurrence in business procedures, but one of unparalleled potential.

The concepts of Data Transmission, Integrated Data Processing, and Information Retrieval (considered in Chapter 13) are areas of computer applications which will alter concepts of organization theory and managerial decision-making, and will create completely new systems and procedures. Management must be ready—and willing—to accept the challenge and to implement those new processes not only in the operations of the firm but, more particularly, in the *management of the firm.*

One significant need in the new technology is clear management *perspective.* Admiral Lewis L. Strauss has made this point in a particularly challenging statement:

> And now we are told that automation is at the threshold of a new era in which men will be relieved of the necessity for decision—relieved of the responsibility, too. Great computers composed of circuits as yet uninvented and nameless will be fed the elements of our problems and, in a twinkling, on the basis of a multitude of facts and assumptions previously memorized, produce an answer like the weighing machines at county fairs, counseling us to stand

firm or retreat, to love or to fear. No man is to bear any responsibility for these decisions, all of them as coldly impersonal as the diodes and transistors and other components of the devices themselves.

May that day be far distant. For though machines may show us the preferred ways to goals, the goals themselves will continue to be set by men with their eyes on the stars. And what machine can ever supply the elements of justice and compassion which, as man's awareness of his common brotherhood expands, must enter more and more often into the decisions which man must make for his brothers and for himself.[11]

QUESTIONS FOR STUDY AND DISCUSSION

1. The idea is often expressed that automation is the cause of a large part of our unemployment problems in this country. Until the late 1950's this problem was primarily that of the plant or production worker. What will the development of computer for business systems applications do to the office labor force? What specific effects seem likely in terms of total jobs available, type of jobs, and types of skills needed?

2. Business research has indicated that one reason why management has sometimes been disappointed with computer installations is that the cost has been considerably larger than anticipated. A primary contributor appears to be "get-ready" costs which are frequently overlooked by management. Suggest reasons for omission of such costs from consideration. List and discuss the get-ready costs that you feel all organizations should consider when planning for computer applications and operations.

3. The end result of a computer feasibility study often is a subjective decision of management to install the computer system. Does this seem to void the expense and time spent in making the feasibility study? What can you suggest that management do to improve the feasibility study with respect to installing computer systems?

4. How does managerial decision making seem likely to change with the availability of high-speed, integrated data processing systems?

5. Many business articles have noted considerable dissatisfaction from the installation of computer systems. In spite of these observations, the use of computers is increasing beyond all expectations. How can you account for this seeming paradox?

6. It was pointed out in this chapter that the change to computer applications or to data processing systems often provides the impetus for other changes in organization and operations. Comment on this conclusion. Do you agree? Why or why not?

7. An authority in the field of electronic data processing and systems analysis has said that the "market for computer systems has changed from that of a seller's market to that of a buyer's market." Do you agree? If so, how can you explain such a shift, and what influences may it have upon user demands and upon supplier efforts to appeal to users?

8. Small firms have been by-passed and somewhat ignored in the computer market until rather recently. Electronic computer systems have traditionally been considered a big business innovation. Is the situation now changing?—if so, what

---

[11] Lewis L. Strauss, *Men and Decisions*, Copyright 1962 by Lewis L. Strauss and the Lewis L. Strauss Literary Trust. Reprinted by permission of Doubleday & Company, Inc.

factors are bringing about change? What do you predict for the future regarding small-firm usage of data processing systems and methods?

9. How do you explain the statement by Leo Moore to the effect that people really like change and do not mind criticism, if they do it themselves? What are the implications for top management?

10. One electronic data processing service corporation now provides services in the complete processing of commercial and scientific applications of computer systems, hourly rental of small, medium-, and large-size computer time, and the complete data processing management services. This firm is less than a year old, and its services are in considerable demand. From a business viewpoint, how can you justify the existence of such a service? Do you feel that there is a real need for this type of service in view of the services rendered by the computer manufacturers? What do you expect for the future for independent computer service corporations?

Case 14-1. Midwest Sports Incorporated

Midwest Sports Incorporated is a relatively small manufacturer and distributor of a wide variety of sporting goods. It is located in a large midwestern city, enjoys a good source of labor, and is centrally located to its customers. Midwest Sports sells to both retailers and wholesalers, and has been enjoying considerable success in recent years with the advent of more leisure time for the average worker together with proportionate increases in disposable income.

In order to economically increase the size and scope of the firm's activities, management decided in early 1962 to initiate computer processing of its inventory and sales distribution work, with long-range plans to integrate other management functions as soon as procedures and systems could be worked out. Therefore, a data processing department was established and the position of Director of Data Processing was created. To assure that this new job received the full support of top management, it was originally structured to report directly to the Executive Vice-President of the firm. The Director of Data Processing had complete authority and responsibility for all data processing operations and was instructed to proceed as rapidly as possible toward the accomplishment of the department's objectives and goals.

Work operations were built around the "whole job" concept, that is the procedures specialists were to have complete authority to conduct the necessary studies, work out the new procedures and systems, and to implement these systems into the operations of the firm. While certain initial misgivings were expressed by other management members and workers of the firm regarding the scope of the systems specialists, this did not last long for top management was quick to point out the necessity for one individual to have complete responsibility for designing any given data processing system in order to achieve the maximum degree of coordination among specialists in the varying functional fields involved. Then, too, these systems specialists enjoyed the benefits of representing, on paper at least, the Executive Vice-President of the firm.

In 1963 the top-management structure of Midwest Sports was rearranged. A new position of Vice-President of Finance was created and staffed from outside the firm. Responsibility for the data processing department was changed from the Executive Vice-President to the new Vice-President of Finance. Other duties placed under the new Vice-President were accounting, governmental reporting, internal auditing, systems and procedures, and administrative services. The Executive Vice-President retained direct responsibility for manufacturing and sales.

The reasoning given by top management for such a move was to better realign the duties and responsibilities of its top level executives.

Problems and questions:

a. Discuss the advantages and disadvantages of each of these types of organizational arrangements from the viewpoint of the effectiveness of the EDP department.

b. Since the EDP department still reports to an executive at the Vice-President level, is there likely to be any change in the influence and authority exercised by the EDP function?

c. Does it seem possible that the top management had other and more specific reasons for changing the organizational location of the Director of Data Processing? Explain.

d. Comment on the reasoning given by management for the establishment of the "whole job concept" for the systems specialists. What alternatives did management have and what are the advantages and disadvantages of these alternatives?

Case 14-2. Sunrise Dairies, Incorporated

Assume that you are the Vice-President, Administrative Services, for Sunrise Dairies and have been appointed by the president to head a committee to investigate the feasibility of data processing equipment for the firm's accounting system. The following facts and information have been gathered and briefly summarized for your consideration.

The present accounting procedures are based upon route driver prepared records. Route drivers are responsible for keeping daily records of their customer activity, pricing these records at the end of the month, and mailing the daily record to the customer as a monthly bill. The company feels that this detail contributes to a high turnover rate among the route driver-salesmen since many are either unwilling or unable to keep the required accurate records. Maintenance of the daily records also leaves the route drivers little time for special promotion and sales activity. Customer satisfaction and service has not been acceptable lately, due partly to the frequent billing errors and handwritten statements. Since the customer records are forwarded to the customer as the monthly bill, the firm is left with no detail records for statistical analysis and control. Gross volume is about all that can be evaluated, and because of the large areas covered by some routes, this data is not always very useful.

The feasibility study revealed that 13 jobs could be eliminated by the establishment of a data processing department—seven comptometer clerks, three accounting clearks, a posting machine operator, a payroll clerk, and a part-time clerk. Total monthly salaries of these employees amounts to $3481. Payroll costs, taxes, benefits, etc., for these employees are estimated to be $150 per month.

To offset this reduction in employees, the data processing department would require four additional employees—a data processing supervisor and three data processing operators—at a total salary of $1350 per month.

After careful appraisal of data processing equipment available, the feasibility committee chose a particular manufacturer on the basis of adaptability, and expandability of equipment, and for the customer services by the manufacturer provided. A minimum, beginning complement of machines, recommended by the manufacturer, would amount to $2000 monthly rental or $99,260 if purchased outright. Maintenance is included in the monthly rental cost, but if the machines are purchased a monthly maintenance contract would cost $293. The dairy's policy is to write off all machines over a five-year period.

The feasibility committee, after consultation with the representatives of the manufacturers, propose that the following operations be processed by data processing department:

1. Retail route accounting.
2. Daily load and driver settlement accounting.
3. Wholesale accounting records.
4. Payroll—salary and commission.
5. Vehicle expense records.
6. Plant production accounting and control—producers report, butterfat analysis, and storage reconciliation.

Certain other costs will be incurred, however, if the data processing system is adopted. These miscellaneous charges are for such items as freight, control panels, wires, initial card design, and initial card expense. The total amount is estimated to be $1671. These expenses are offset somewhat by reducing the depreciation and maintenance on several office machines which will not be needed with the data processing system. This amounts to $124.

Once the data processing system becomes fully operational, it would be capable of handling an increasing volume of work without increased costs—either in personnel or in equipment. Machine accuracy would reduce time-consuming and expensive errors. Important sales and operative information such as accounts receivable aging and valuable statistical analyses would be available at no extra cost.

Problems and questions:

a. As chairman of the feasibility committee, sift through the facts presented above and prepare a report for top management presenting the significant data found in this case.

b. Outline your specific recommendations to management regarding the implementation of data processing for Sunrise Dairies, Incorporated, including a suggested time table of major operations.

c. Evaluate the lease versus purchase alternative for the proposed data processing equipment.

d. What other information, if any, do you feel that you need in order to prepare a complete and accurate feasibility report for top management's consideration?

Case 14-3. Data Processing Management Services, Inc.

This firm was organized in 1961 to provide consulting and managerial services for private firms. Services offered fall into three principal areas, normally combined in a single package:

1. Consulting services on all phases of data processing—studies of feasibility, installation, operation, utilization, staffing, and other areas.

2. Actual processing of work at all stages—systems design, programming, testing, and operation.

3. Sub-leasing of computer time (made possible by their own leasing of surplus time from other firms).

The guiding philosophy behind the services offered by DPMS (to use their abbreviation) is the belief that many firms will find it both more effective and less expensive to contract for these specialized services than to provide them independently. They advance the following reasons to support this view:

1. The problem of providing competent personnel is assumed by the consulting firm.

2. Training requirements of client firm personnel are reduced greatly and spread out over a period sufficient to permit gradual assimilation of knowledge and skills needed.

3. Operating problems are reduced significantly through use of well-trained personnel.

4. Time from inception to production is often reduced by as much as two-thirds.

In order to render the services advertised with greatest effectiveness and to allow client firms gradually to become self-sufficient in their own operations, DPMS insists upon long-term contracts, typically three to five years in duration.

Early experiences have been quite encouraging. Several client firms report a high degree of satisfaction with the competence of the specialists which DPMS has assembled, much time saved in converting to data processing equipment, and more expertly written programs than they would have been able to produce with their own personnel.

In one firm using the services, an interesting contrast in viewpoints among certain personnel exists. The Controller, under whom the data processing function is located, believes that the very substantial reduction in time required to convert, coupled with greater assurance of competent programming and general management of the installation, clearly justifies the arrangement. The Systems Manager, under the Controller, recognizes the advantages just stated but believes that a great deal may have been sacrificed by not having the full experience of working out the problems of studying feasibility, staffing, control, etc. He wonders whether the outside group will be sufficiently flexible in their thinking and will make needed adaptations, or whether they may apply concepts developed elsewhere without enough modification to fit his firm's unique needs. He is unsure about the more or less automatic learning that his personnel and other personnel within the firm will do while the contract is in effect, with DPMS carrying the responsibility for results. He feels that the major challenge of the future lies in systems integration, and he wonders whether this may not require greater depth of understanding of company operations than any outside group can bring. He has observed that most other firms have been able to work directly with supplier representatives and have developed personnel of their own who know or learn their own business operations intimately and acquire needed technical skills in data processing.

Problems and questions:

a. Is there a real field of need—a gap between what the machine supplier and the firm installing EDP can do jointly—that seems likely to lead to establishment of a rather large number of consulting firms of this special type?

b. What do you think about the combination of services offered by DPMS? The advantages claimed? The long-term contract sought?

c. How valid and how significant are the views of (a) the Controller, and (b) the Systems Manager, of the client firm cited: Are their respective points of view partly understandable from consideration of the positions they hold? Which way would you, as a detached observer, lean in this controversy, and why would you feel as you do?

V

COMMUNICATIONS AND RECORDS MANAGEMENT

Communications management, from an administration viewpoint, includes the entire field of message composition and transmission. Records management includes the recording, preserving, and retrieving, when necessary, of virtually every type of information. The vital importance of these services, and of the effectiveness and economy with which they are performed, justify careful analysis by any person having responsibility in the administrative management field.

In Part V, we shall consider principles in composing letters and other messages, and approaches to improvement; dictation and transcription; transmission of messages. We shall study forms—vitally influential means of both recording and communicating information. We shall study office reproduction services—particularly use of copying and duplicating equipment. Finally, we shall study filing, records, retention, and microfilming.

Each of these services is of critical importance in the administration of any enterprise. *Every* person who has, or may have, managerial responsibility will need to be familiar with them, partly because of direct involvement, partly because he must know enough about them to insure adequate services.

15

COMMUNICATION MANAGEMENT

Challenge of communication · Key principles in composing messages · Letter writing principles · Dictation and transcription · Reception service · Methods of transmitting internal and external messages

Challenge of Communications

"Communication" is the process of conveying messages. In order that communication may occur, messages must be composed, transmitted, and understood.

The potentialities of communication as a management tool are so great that it is difficult to recognize them, easy to under-rate them. Effectiveness in dealing with customers and others outside the enterprise, and effectiveness in dealing with personnel employed by the enterprise and, presumably, engaged in joint efforts to achieve its objectives, is greatly dependent upon communication.

Every idea, fact, or opinion is in a dormant state until transmitted and understood. And, if "the road to Hell is paved with good intentions," then the road to failure in management is surely paved with good ideas, poorly communication. However sound, ideas merely conceived will have little impact until they are communicated to persons whose needs they fill or who, in turn, may implement or develop them further.

The number of messages communicated at approximate maximum effectiveness is undoubtedly far lower than the number which lose much of their impact because they are vague, incomplete, confusing, poorly adapted to the recipient, curt, late, or deficient in some other important aspect.

The challenge to students (in and out of school) has been well put by Drucker:

> The manager has a specific tool: information. He does not "handle" people; he motivates, guides, organizes people to do their own work. His tool —his only tool—to do all this is the spoken or written word or the language of numbers. No matter whether the manager's job is engineering, accounting, or selling, his effectiveness depends on his ability to listen and to read, on his ability to speak and to write. He needs skill in getting his thinking across to other people as well as skill in finding out what other people are after . . . Of all the skills he needs, today's manager possesses least those of reading, writing, speaking, and figuring.[1]

Thus the importance of communication in both the information system of the enterprise, and in the personal career of the manager or employee, warrant careful attention.

We shall consider two major areas of communications activity: (1) composing messages, and (2) transmitting messages. Treatment will necessarily be brief and focused upon administrative requirements.

Prime objectives of communication, from the administrative view, are *effectiveness* and *economy*—with priority following the sequence presented. Effectiveness, or success in getting needed information across, is of course most basic; upon this depends the justification for placing a telephone call, writing a letter, or engaging in any other communications activity.

Economy, however, is significant when we consider such current estimates as half the cost of doing business made up by handling information, three-fourths of executive time being devoted to communication in one form or another, and an average cost of two dollars for each letter written. Such considerations challenge one to look for all legitimate economies—without paying the price in reduced effectiveness, which may be greater than the result of any given economy measure.

Composing Letters and Other Messages

Effective composition of messages is partly a matter of attitude, partly a matter of technique. The "sender" must know what he wants to communicate, and he must have a real desire to get his message across and to convey a feeling of helpfulness and goodwill at the same time. He must practice empathy (placing himself in the recipient's shoes), a concept aptly described as the "you-attitude." Techniques, then, can be adapted

---

[1] Peter F. Drucker, *The Practice of Management* (New York: Harper & Row, Publishers, 1954), p. 346.

to purposes and attitudes which bear upon effectiveness, and at the same time foster economy.

A brief presentation of principles of message composition appears below, framed primarily in terms of letters but generally applicable to other messages. For persons who desire more information on both the psychological aspects of communication and the techniques, there is a wealth of information available in other sources.

Key principles in composing messages

1. Determine the purposes of the message. Usually there will be a central purpose of conveying certain information, and an important secondary purpose of conveying a feeling of helpfulness and goodwill.

2. Plan the message. Know the ideas that you want to put across, and arrange them in a logical sequence before you begin the communication.

3. Use a conversational, natural language. Aim for directness and simplicity.

4. Be complete and clear. Try to make one message do the job.

5. Be brief—but not *too* brief. Be selective in using detail.

6. Be courteous, *always.* Being clear, complete, yet concise, are long steps toward being courteous. Keep in mind the simple, basic concept of the "you-attitude"; be considerate, friendly, and helpful.

Correspondence improvement programs

Particularly significant in the communications of most enterprises is written correspondence, both external and internal. Much is at stake, and there is almost always room for improvement.

Accordingly, correspondence improvement is a matter of major concern to managers. Such improvement does not come easily. There are barriers such as deeply-rooted language habits and traditional writing styles. Almost everyone is likely to be somewhat sensitive about his writing inadequacies, and resentful about suggested improvements.

Even so, encouraging results have been achieved in many organizations. Prerequisites for effective improvement programs seem to include top-management support, specialized guidance (by competent training specialist, consultant, and/or committee), and a planned approach which provides systematic study of writing principles, individualized counseling, and ample provision for follow-up time.

Illustrative approaches

One company's program includes instruction by a professor from a local university in twelve two-hour weekly sessions. Constructive criticism of each writer's individual efforts, carried out in personal counseling sessions, supplements group study, as does a monthly bulletin containing helpful hints.

Another program provides for sending a "correspondence problem" once a month to each correspondent in the numerous branch offices of a large firm. The correspondent prepares the letter he would have sent and submits it to a committee in the home office. The members of the committee write comments on each letter, select the three best letters from those submitted, and send the marked letter submitted by each correspondent and the three winning letters to each participant each month.

The program of a large insurance company begins with a ten-hour classroom course in basic principles. Specialists then review carbon copies of ten letters actually written by each participant and conduct personal counseling sessions, repeating the review procedure each six months, and conducting follow-up classroom sessions at regular intervals.

In the offices of a well-known department store, the improvement program is started with only one carefully-conducted classroom session. Then the specialist in charge, a professor, collects five random samples of actual letters each three weeks, marks suggested improvements, has a counseling session with each individual, and repeats the three-week cycle until letters of suitable quality are being written—for some persons, the study period may thus be as short as three weeks; for others, it may continue for several months or even longer. The professor makes a photocopy of each marked letter for his own file; the marked original is returned to the participant for his guidance and continued study.

The central idea of the correspondence training program for a large bank is that "it is the writer's responsibility to be understood." Writing consultants helped plan and launch the program; continuing staff help is provided by members of the training staff. Four 1½-hour class meetings, normally one week apart, are conducted; audio-visual aids are used extensively; and informal group participation is encouraged. Following the class sessions each participant receives at least one hour of individual consultation. Bulletins outlining common correspondence problems provide follow-up and are combined into a manual by each participant.

Correspondence manuals and bulletins

Bulletins are widely used for improvement and control of correspondence manuals. A good illustration is provided by the Prudential Insurance Company of America in the form of a manual entitled "Effective Writing," which contains a portion of the study material for a basic training course and follows the outline below:

Public Relations in Our Letters
   I. Purpose of Course
   II. Filmstrip, "One Out of Every Six"—Humanics and Mechanics of Effective Writing
   III. Public Relations Aspect of Letter Writing
      A. Opinion Survey
      B. The Way to Good Public Relations
   IV. The Other Side of Letter Writing
      A. Mechanics
      B. The Five C's—clear, complete, concise, correct, courteous

The Language and Purpose of a Business Letter
    I. Aims of a Business Letter
   II. Ways to Achieve These Aims and to Avoid Pitfalls
      A. Be courteous and friendly
      B. Include or ask for all the facts
      C. Relax, be natural, just talk
      D. Use talk language

Planning a Letter
    I. Goozling
   II. Grammar
  III. Five Steps in Planning a Letter
      A. Know your purpose
      B. Get all the facts
      C. Visualize your reader
      D. Determine what to say—find the soft spot
      E. Decide on the sequence of what you say—Letter Carpentry

Letter Formulas
    I. The Star, the Chain, and the Hook
      A. Star—get attention
      B. Chain—the Why of the Letter
      C. Hook—get action
   II. Headline and Narrative
      A. Headline method—when we can say *yes*
      B. Narrative method—when we have to say *no*
  III. Punctuation

A Review of Letter Writing Principles
    I. Review
   II. A word about Dictating Practices
      A. Responsibilities of a dictator
      B. Responsibilities of a transcriber

Some correspondence manuals include "guide letters" which stress form or content or both. Some present model letters for a wide variety of recurring situations. These can be varied to fit individual cases.

To sustain interest and foster learning, bulletins released at rather frequent intervals are helpful. Each may emphasize a principle or a problem area, and may include "horrible examples," prize-winning letters, problem situations, and other material.

Form letters and paragraphs are an extension of the "guide letter" principle mentioned above. These widely-used tools are a practical necessity in mass mailings. They are usually quite satisfactory in routine correspondence where the need is for transmission of *factual information.* Use of automatic typewriters and improved duplicating equipment can, of course, give a "personal" look to a form letter, often improving its effectiveness; there is, however, a proper place and situation for both form letters and personally dictated letters. Form paragraphs, of course, offer more flexibility for combinations of personally dictated paragraphs and form paragraphs; they often result in real economies—for example, in the answering of inquiries.

The NOMA simplified letter

The National Office Management Association has been active in promoting interest in the Simplified Letter, and a considerable number of organizations have adopted the simplified format for all company correspondence. The differences between the Simplified Letter and the conventional letter are demonstrated in the sample letter shown in Figure 15-1 and in the table shown in Figure 15-2.

It is apparent that the simplified letter is actually simpler to write, and is closer to conversational communication than the conventional letter. A basic motion unit analysis of the typing alone on a ninety-six-word letter proves a saving with the Simplified Letter of ten and seven-tenths per cent. This results from a reduction in key-strokes and a reduction in motion for positioning the typewriter carriage.

The slogan of Simplified Letter advocates is "There's more to a truly Simplified Letter than simply dropping 'Dear' and 'Yours truly.'" Simplified format is important but more important is the improvement in the content of the letter itself. It is suggested that in writing a Simplified Letter the dictator follow this procedure:

1. At the start, instead of fumbling around trying to decide whether to begin "Dear Sir, Dear Mr. X, Dear Bob, or Esteemed Sir," you forget it altogether.

2. Then comes the subject. In ordinary letters this may not be stated until you have consumed several paragraphs. State the problem or the point of the letter at the outset.

3. Then your first sentence, all-important in getting your reader to read. The first line of your letter, like the first handshake, is your introduction to your reader. Make it firm and convincing. Make it different, not stereotyped. Make it pertinent.

4. Plan your letters. Organize your facts in logical order. Follow your logic. When you've spoken your piece, break it off not by a fatuous "Yours truly," but by a little reminder that YOU'RE YOU.

5. Be concise, clear, and courteous. Usually the fewer paragraphs the better. Be friendly and warm. Adjust your faucet to the reader. Don't scald him, but don't give him goose pimples either.

Officers of the National Office Management Association report a gradual

NATIONAL OFFICE MANAGEMENT ASSOCIATION
122 WEST CHELTEN AVENUE
PHILADELPHIA 44, PA.

Dated Today

this is a
SIMPLIFIED
letter

Ms. Office Secretary
Better Business Letters, Inc.
1 Main Street
Busytown, U. S. A.

SIMPLIFIED LETTER (subject)

There's a new movement under way to take some of the monotony out of letters given you to type, Ms. Secretary. The movement is symbolized by the Simplified Letter being sponsored by NOMA.

What is it? You're reading a sample.

Notice the left block format and the general positioning of the letter. We didn't write "Dear Miss -----," nor will we write "Yours truly" or "Sincerely yours." Are they really important? We feel just as friendly toward you without them.

Notice the following points:

1. Date location
2. The address
3. The subject
4. The name of the writer

Now take a look at the Suggestions prepared for you. Talk them over with your boss. But don't form a final opinion until you've really tried out The Letter. That's what our secretary did. As a matter of fact, she finally wrote most of the Suggestions herself.

She says she's sold -- and hopes you'll have good luck with better (Simplified) letters.

Arthur H. Gager

there is more to a truly
SIMPLIFIED LETTER
than simply dropping
dear and yours truly

Arthur H. Gager - Staff Director, Technical Division

cc: R. P. Brecht, W. H. Evans, H F Grebe

Figure 15-1. A simplified letter

increase in use of the Simplified Letter. Many business executives are reluctant to adopt correspondence styles which differ markedly from traditional forms. Some say, "I like it—but how can I know whether the man on the other end will like it." A number go further and express the belief that something is sacrificed in the way of dignity, and some continue to feel that "Dear Mr. _____" and "Cordially yours" add a personal touch which they prefer not to give up. The fact that each year a great number of firms are changing to the form, seems to indicate changes in views which may eventually lead to widespread adoption of the Simplified Letter.

THE CONVENTIONAL LETTER	THE SIMPLIFIED LETTER
1. The date is at the far right. Why?	1. The date is at the left—you're starting where the typewriter starts.
2. The address shifts to the far left. All's well.	2. The full address is at the left—ready for a window envelope and as permanent reference on the letter itself. Think of the keystrokes saved by not having to retype the address on the envelope.
3. The meaningless salutation stays put but is waste since it's not you, but form that dictates it.	
4. To be fancy, the paragraphs are indented five spaces. This job is multiplied by the number of paragraphs.	3. Next the subject—at the left. A provocative opening and filing clue.
5. Back to the left margin for the body of the letter.	4. No indentation—paragraph starts without tabular delay.
6. Zoom! Over to the right again for the "complimentary" close.	5. The typewritten signature again at the left. No matter how weirdly the letter is signed . . . the reader still knows who wrote it.

The Conventional Letter (continued):

7. The company name picks another spot —why use it when it's shown in the letterhead?

8. A final zig to the left to put in the dictator's initials (why?) and the typist's to the right.

The Simplified Letter (continued):

Every important feature of this letter is on a flagpole. In a pile of papers, by lifting the left edge of the covering page a little, *all* the reference information springs into view. Try that with a conventional form!

Figure 15-2. A comparison of the conventional and the simplified letter

Dictation and Transcription

A little time and effort devoted to improvement of one's dictating techniques can pay off in better messages requiring less time. And developments in dictating and transcribing equipment have been so rapid during recent years that much presently-owned equipment is obsolete.

Recommended dictation techniques

1. *Prepare for dictation before you begin.* Plan message content if needed; make notes or outlines where helpful. Arrange to have all matching correspondence, supporting documents, and other necessary data on hand. Schedule most dictation for regular time periods each day, and avoid interruptions if possible.

2. *Learn to think in sentences and paragraphs.* Word-or-phrase-at-a-time dic-

tating compares with hunt-and-peck typing; actually, it is worse because it slows down the flow of thought.

3. *Speak distinctly at a normal, even rate.* Enunciate clearly; avoid mumbling; avoid telescoping two or more words together.

4. *Dictate paragraphs and unusual marks of punctuation.* Dictating *all* punctuation will aid clear thinking, if you possess this ability or are willing to develop it.

5. *Indicate corrections orally.* Mark the indicator slip if using recording equipment.

6. *Give full instructions regarding work requirements.* Give time needs, special handling, number and distribution of copies, etc.

Equipment for dictating and transcribing

The "high cost of words" in today's managerial environment has been noted earlier. One result has been pressure to mechanize the dictating and recording of messages, and manufacturers have responded with developments which rival those in any other field of office operations.

New equipment design has resulted in great improvement in the fidelity of voice reproduction, and a host of new features have been added which make for greater convenience. In many cases, costs have been cut, as well.

Making rapid gains have been magnetic recording media—high-fidelity, re-usable, easily erased, available in large-capacity tape as well as disc or belt. Plastic belts and discs continue to be popular; though not usually re-usable, they are inexpensive and can be mailed or disposed of when desired.

Still widely used is the full complement of equipment, including a microphone, recording machine, transcribing unit and recording medium. Two new developments, rapidly gaining favor, are network systems which alter the usual equipment combination, and portable units.

The network system employs remote dictating stations (usually ordinary telephone handsets or intercoms), centralized recording machines, and a pool of typists. Its greatest advantage is the manner in which a minimum number of transcribing personnel can do the work of many dictators. Generally, a number of central recording machines are employed, with the use of relay and switching facilities; if one recording machine is busy, the dictator will automatically be switched to an unoccupied machine. The disc, belt, or tape is then placed in a transcribing machine and typed by one of the pool members. Work can be done under skilled supervision, the load evenly distributed, and high standards of quality maintained. Equipment costs are estimated to run less than half of those for separate dictating machines. For example, one large bank has a network in which 1,300 executives are served by 41 recording machines.

Portability as a feature in dictating machines is hardly new, and nearly all such equipment is becoming lighter and more compact. In recent years, demand for portable units has increased significantly. The earlier appeal of such equipment was mainly to traveling salesmen. Many other users are now becoming convinced that executives should have portable dictating units nearby, night and day, to record "bright ideas" whenever they strike; it is also convenient to have the equipment available for catching up on dictation at odd hours.

Representative models of dictating equipment are illustrated in Figure 15-3.

Receptionist Service

One communications service not yet considered involves neither message composition nor message transmission but is an important factor in the success of any enterprise. This is the service of reception—receiving persons who visit the firm on an endless variety of missions.

The often-repeated statement that "first impressions are lasting impressions" applies with special weight to the work of the receptionist. Visitors form impressions quickly regarding the type of treatment they receive, and they tend to judge the entire organization and its management on the basis of their initial reception.

Two factors seem to stand out in determining whether reception service is effective: *efficiency* and *courtesy*.

Efficiency in reception service means prompt greeting of the visitor, intelligent discussion with him of the company representative who should serve his needs, prompt arrangement with this representative for conferring with the visitor, and efficient handling of the introduction of the visitor to the company representative.

Courtesy is given a good start when efficiency is present; in other words, since the visitor had a purpose in coming to the firm, prompt and satisfying arrangements for him to present his ideas are themselves a genuine courtesy. The good impression formed by efficient reception can be greatly reinforced, however, by carrying out the arrangements in a pleasant and friendly manner. Sincere interest in providing for his needs and in making him comfortable during any waiting period is an attitude that the visitor can quickly detect.

The physical arrangements are important, also; the modern reception room provides an atmosphere of comfort—with good interior decoration, good lighting, comfortable seating, well-chosen reading material, rest room facilities, telephone for outside use, and an efficient internal communications system.

It is apparent that the position of receptionist is one of key importance.

Dictaphone Corporation

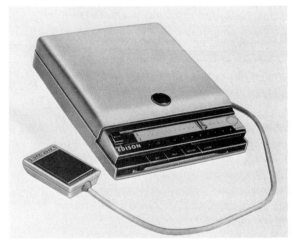

Figure 15-3. *Above:* The Dictaphone transistor-line telecord dictation system; *left:* the Edison Escort, a battery-powered portable dictating machine; *below:* the new IBM "Executary" dictation unit.

McGraw-Edison Company

International Business Machines Corp.

A combination of intelligence, neat appearance, poise, courtesy, and warmth of personality is much to be desired. Special grooming and training, not only in reception technique but in company background and operations, are of obvious value. Some companies try to fill such openings with personnel who already have considerable background and familiarity with company operations, and who have the personal traits noted.

Transmitting Messages

The degree of success achieved in communication has been shown in the preceding section to depend greatly upon effectiveness in *composing messages* that convey the meaning intended and promote good will.

We shall now be concerned with methods of transmitting messages with appropriate *speed, accuracy,* and *economy.* Truly remarkable advances have occurred during recent years in "communications gear" of a great many types; managerial effectiveness may often depend heavily upon installation of systems well-fitted to needs.

Messages may be classified as either internal or external, and as oral or written. The ensuing discussion will utilize these classifications.

Internal transmission—oral

Within an enterprise, oral communication, other than face-to-face contact is accomplished chiefly through interphone systems and inter-communications (intercom) systems.

Interphone systems utilize dial handsets and automatic switchboards, making them small-scale telephone systems installed on the premises. The PAX (Private Automatic Exchange) is the nerve center of the system and translates all commands received. The PAX is built on the modular principle and can be expanded to accommodate many hundreds of telephones if needed. Among significant, recent developments are: (1) direct-call push buttons to reach frequently-called personnel, eliminating the need for dialing, (2) loudspeaker attachments which permit hands-free operation, (3) devices for automatic hunting of free lines, (4) devices for automatic holding of a busy station, (5) direct connection with centralized dictation centers, and (6) conference call devices which permit group discussion. A modern push-button telephone is illustrated in Figure 15-4.

Intercom systems are now chiefly of the amplifier-speaker type; they now offer high-fidelity sound transmission and are much more attractive than early models. Master stations, which can call all other stations, and sub-stations, which can call only master stations, are available and include: (1) handset attachment to permit semi-private conversation, (2) lights or chimes which announce calls, (3) signals to indicate when other stations are in use, (4) executive override to permit breaking into a station when necessary, (5) plug-in connections to permit portability, and (6) conference call capabilities. A versatile intercom system is illustrated in Figure 15-5.

Internal transmission—written

For delivery of internal memoranda, letters, and other written messages, a wide range of equipment is available. Continuing to supplement and, in many cases, to eliminate the need for equipment, is messenger service. It is usually provided from a centralized mailroom in the larger organization, and follows an established route and time schedule for

American Telephone and Telegraph

Figure 15-4. The call director—a large capacity push-button telephone

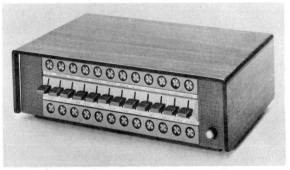

Dictograph Products, Inc.

Figure 15-5. An amplifier-speaker intercommunication unit. This fully transistorized system has a newly developed "magic eye" which indicates who is calling and automatically leaves a message if the executive is away from his desk.

pickup and delivery. Selected types of equipment will now be considered very briefly.

Mechanized delivery systems are rapidly increasing in use, including pneumatic tube systems and conveyor systems. These systems are most suitable when standard-sized messages need to be delivered over fixed paths at high rates of speed. Large volume and rather great distances also influence justification.

Pneumatic tube systems are used for carrying inter-office mail, telegrams, punched cards, office supplies, drugs, currency, test ingots, and a wide variety of other items. Carriers of various sizes and shapes are available; a typical carrier is illustrated in Figure 15-6, and a receiving and sending station is shown in Figure 15-7. The most automatic systems provide direct, point-to-point service without the necessity of a relay station.

Conveyors, long relegated to the factory and warehouse, are now finding uses in moving paper where volume and speed justify, and where layout and materials handled are readily adapted. Examples of applications of pneumatic tubes and conveyors follow:

A meat packaging firm uses air tubes to handle all types of paper work such as correspondence, time cards, instruction sheets, shipping schedules, re-

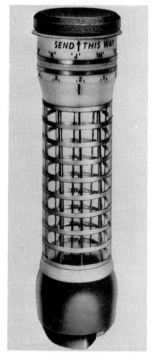

Lamson Corporation

Figure 15-6. A pneumatic tube carrier

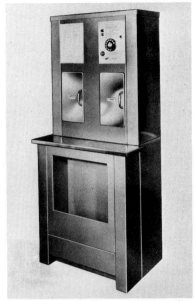

Lamson Corporation

Figure 15-7. A pneumatic tube system sending and receiving station

ceiving slips, memoranda, and requisitions. It also sends small samples, tools, and parts at high speed between departments.

Use of an air tube system which connects a group of motor banks with a large central bank has been interpreted to qualify the motor banks as parts of the central bank, rather than as branches which are not allowed under the banking law of the state. Five-pound-capacity carriers containing coin, currency, checks, and correspondence flow between the main bank and the motor banks, a distance of 612 feet in 20 seconds.

The New York office of Dun & Bradstreet uses a ticket system for handling telephone inquiries. Twenty-eight telephone operators jot down the name of the individual or firm on a slip and drop it on a conveyor belt which carries it to a dispatching clerk. He folds it at one end, drops it into one of the 32 tube lines corresponding to each file station, and presses a button to build pressure in the tube. Within a few seconds, a file clerk receives the slip, checks it against information in the files, and returns the slip to the telephone operator by a multi-channel conveyor belt. A similar paper conveyor belt is shown in Figure 15-8. Because of the speed of the system, even those calls involving several listings can be answered while the customer is on the phone, thus avoiding time-consuming and expensive call-backs.

Wire communication systems are now coming into very wide use for internal as well as external transmission. *Facsimile* systems permit the transmission of exact duplicates between two points; they include scanners, which convert light and dark areas into corresponding impulses

Union Carbide Corporation

Figure 15-8. A 16-channel paper conveyor system

and "burn" the image on a special paper at the receiving end; electric longhand systems which transmit handwritten messages and reproduce them instantly on continuous forms at receiving units. These offer many uses in banks, hotels, railroads, retail credit organizations, and firms of all types where certain departments must do extensive communicating with each other. A significant development is a longhand system which transmits handwriting over ordinary telephone circuits; transmitting and receiving units of this system are presented in Figure 15-9. *Teletypewriters* will be considered as external transmission equipment, although they are now finding many internal uses as well. *Closed circuit television,* commonly used in airline ticket offices and brokerage houses, is now being used for other purposes—as in a certain large savings and loan association, where tellers call a clerk in the records room and have a necessary signature card or record placed under a TV camera which transmits the image to the teller desiring it, thus improving service, reducing errors, and saving time and cost.

External transmission—oral

Despite the many advances in other types of transmission equipment, the telephone remains the workhorse in external oral communication. Contributing factors are its speed, the personalized nature of the communication, and the fact that it can be used by anyone. Design trends include "hands off" equipment which permits the user to talk while consulting files or doing something else, automatic dialing by pressing

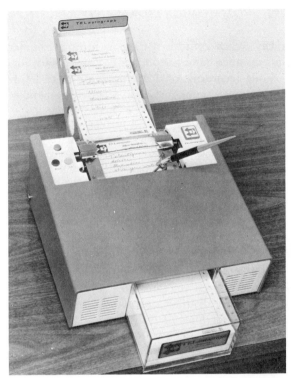

Figure 15-9. Phonewriter transmitter and receiver

a key which controls a memory unit accommodating up to 850 names and numbers, and telephones equipped with loudspeakers.

Voice-recording (or dictating) equipment has been considered earlier in the composition of messages. Such equipment is now finding other uses.

> A large wholesale company experienced an excessive number of errors in an order entry system which required each salesman to give details to one of four order-takers over the telephone. Conversion to a new system allows one person to monitor four voice-recording machines, with telephone attachments. When a salesman calls in, he is immediately switched to a machine which records his order. The recorded discs are played back, and clerks select prepunched order cards for processing on tabulating equipment. Errors have been reduced, delivery speeded up, and substantial clerical savings realized.

External transmission—written

The field of external transmission of written messages is so broad that only the briefest reference to principal methods can be given here. Persons desiring detailed, current information will find many sources available. The methods of transmission which will be noted briefly include: (1) Mail service, (2) wire communications—including facsimile, telegraph, teletypewriter, and data transmission, and (3) microwave.

Mail service

Perhaps the best way to appreciate the value of mail service and the postal system is to try to imagine operating without them. Currently, business firms alone are sending some 25 billion pieces annually, and the volume is increasing steadily. To meet the growing volume problems, management is seeking to cut costs and increase efficiency.

Mailroom and related functions are taking on a new look with greatly increased mechanization and improved controls. The standardized nature and the volume of mailroom operations make them a "natural" for mechanization; new, faster, and more efficient machinery is being made available for addressing, collating, folding, inserting, sorting, stacking, tying, sealing, weighing, stamping (now metering, almost universally), and conveying operations. Centralized mailroom operations are usually a "must"—for skilled supervision, justification of equipment, improved service to departments, control of postage, and specialized personnel.

Special care in design of mailing procedures is justified because of the dependence of primary operations upon efficient mail service and because of the substantial costs involved. The procedure for handling incoming mail will normally include:

1. Mail pickup at the post office before working hours and at intervals during the day dependent upon train and plane schedules

2. Opening (all but "Personal"), time-stamping, sorting, and distributing to handling departments early enough to minimize delay, with matching correspondence attached where justified

3. Special handling of "money mail"—remittance amounts and names of senders recorded on a daily record sheet

4. Daily reports of the volume of mail received, remittances, times of distributions, and other information desired for control purposes

The procedure for handling outgoing mail will usually include, as a minimum:

1. Collection of mail by messengers from outbaskets on desks in different departments, following a regular schedule (unless conveyors are used for this purpose)

2. Sorting by class of mail and by destination; some firms find it desirable for mailroom personnel to verify addresses on letters against envelopes

3. Mechanical addressing and labeling where volume justifies and mailing lists can be used

4. Folding, inserting, sealing, and stamping; mailing machines now perform all of these operations in sequence, with close meter control over postage

5. Dispatching of outgoing mail at the post office where volume justifies, at times coordinated closely with train and plane schedules

Wire communications

Telegraph services are, of course, very widely used and well-adapted to situations in which speed must be combined with a relatively brief written message. Messages may be given to the telegraph company over the telephone, transmitted by a teleprinter, or sent through use of a scanning-type facsimile machine. Standard, day letter, night letter, and serial service is available, at varying costs; hence, careful weighing of needs and costs is highly desirable.

Teletypewriter equipment has been mentioned earlier. For external use, the teletype circuits are interconnected by Teletypewriter Exchange Service (TWX) of the American Telephone and Telegraph Company. TWX's 60,000-plus subscribers can now communicate with each other through direct dialing in most instances; telephone operators are available in regional centers to assist with calls that require special handling. Equipment is leased, and toll charges amount to approximately half the cost of regular long-distance telephone calls, while providing two-way communication and a written record. Teletypewriter usage for internal purposes is also increasing rapidly—as in a certain printing firm, where copies of the operations sheet for each order are sent simultaneously to each department which will be involved so all get the information accurately and with ample time to do necessary planning. Increasing use of teletypewriters to provide input data for computer centers has been discussed previously. The first crude model of a teletypewriter was put in operation in 1849. Long a valued type of equipment, it seems that only in recent years has the versatility of the teletypewriter been generally appreciated. A recent model is pictured in Figure 15-10.

Teletype Corporation

Figure 15-10. Teletype Model 28 automatic send-receive set. A complete station in a compact console with facilities for sending and receiving on message paper or sprocket-fed business forms. Tape may be manually prepared for automatic transmission or produced automatically as a by-product of send-receive operations.

Data transmission systems were discussed at length in Chapter 13. The potential impact of "machines talking to machines" is obviously vast. The impressive progress being made by organizations in this fast-developing field is illustrated by Western Union's Tele-Card system, which operates with specially equipped key punch machines, converting punched cards to standard teleprinter signals over leased wire systems. There is the IBM 1001 Data Transmission system which transmits data in punched card form from remote locations to a central data processing department, linked either by leased or regular telephone lines. There is the Autofax system which transmits data over regular telephone lines using conventional telephone handsets. There is Bell Data-Speed punched tape transmission equipment capable of handling over 1,000 words a minute. Before this book comes off the press, there will be models of even greater capabilities.

Microwave is a means of radio communications which utilizes ultra-high frequencies to carry data in the form of electrical impulses. Data currently can be transmitted at 62,000 characters a second. As mentioned in the data transmission section, microwave and satellite transmission represent exciting frontiers. One current business use of microwave is Speed Mail messages (International Telephone and Telegraph Corporation), prepared on accordion-folded, gum-sealed paper, electronically read and transmitted by microwave with exact reproductions received, sealed, and delivered. Another is the Videograph (A. B. Dick) in which the transmitting unit converts source material into television-like signals which are sent by microwave to the printer, which reproduces an exact copy, all in a matter of seconds.

QUESTIONS FOR STUDY AND DISCUSSION

1. What is at stake in good communication? Are the full potentialities of communication frequently overlooked?—if so, how can this be explained? Appraise Drucker's challenge to managers and to students in general regarding development of communications skills.

2. Do you agree that *effectiveness* and *economy* are prime objectives of communication, from the administrative point of view? How do you feel about priority between these two criteria?—Explain. Would it be possible to go overboard on either, to the neglect of the other?

3. Study carefully the brief list of principles suggested for composing messages. Which seem most significant to you? Which seems more important in message composition—attitude or technique?

4. Why is correspondence improvement often a difficult undertaking? What prerequisites seem necessary? Compare the alternative approaches to improvement which are described in the text; which seem particularly promising? Can you suggest other approaches which might yield satisfactory results?

5. Describe the purposes and typical format of correspondence manuals. What do you see as the proper roles for guide letters, form letters, and form paragraphs?

6. What are the distinctive features of the NOMA Simplified Letter? Do you feel that this form, or one similar, will eventually be accepted in business usage generally?—why or why not? What efforts would be required to gain more widespread acceptance, as you see the problem?

7. One executive finds it very difficult to dictate a letter or memorandum; he prefers to write the message out first, believing that not only does he produce a better letter but that he actually saves time through not having to re-do so many letters which come out poorly when he tries to dictate. How do you feel about this person's experience and the conclusions he has reached? Could he learn and

apply techniques such as those recommended for dictating, in the text, and change his approach to good advantage?

8. What principal types of dictating equipment are now available, and what seem to be the most significant trends in design and use of such equipment? Do you feel that there will continue to be a demand for shorthand skills?—Explain.

9. Outline what seem to you to be the main requirements for good reception service.

10. What are the primary criteria to be considered in choosing from alternative means of transmitting messages? In view of dependence of managerial effectiveness upon careful choice of transmission methods, and in view of rapid technological advancements in this field, study closely the descriptions of equipment now available and the conditions pointing toward use of each type. Even with the impressive developments in other forms of transmission, does mail service seem likely to continue as the "workhorse" method of transmitting messages?—if so, what special attention does it warrant?

11. Mentioned in the long-range plans of one of the telephone companies is the possibility of establishing a flat rate for monthly telephone service, for which a customer would be allowed to make an unlimited number of calls anywhere within the United States at no additional cost. If this proposed service materializes, how do you expect it to affect the entire communications function?

Case 15-1. The Alliance Chemical Company

The Alliance Chemical Company found recently that complaints were mounting—both inside and outside the office—about the company's telephone communications.

In order to learn whether the fault rested in the switchboard operator, the telephone equipment, or in some other area, the office manager called in representatives of the telephone company to study the situation.

The telephone personnel found that some of the difficulty was due to inexperience of the switchboard operator, but they found that at least as important a reason for trouble was the unnecessary demands on her time made by Alliance officials who were not using their telephones properly.

The worst features were:

Failure of company executives to notify the operator of their whereabouts after having placed a long-distance call.

Placing a long-distance call and then hanging up before the operator could learn which official was placing the call.

The telephone company secured management approval of a four-day monitoring, or listening in, period in order to determine other common errors made by the company personnel in use of the telephone. A training program was then carried out, based upon the company's own needs and incorporating the best techniques of telephone usage. Results have been highly satisfactory.

Problems and questions:

a. Would a program such as this be feasible for the typical firm?

b. Why should such a program as this be necessary in any firm for an operation so common and so familiar as use of the telephone?

Case 15-2. Tobin Drug Stores, Inc.

During a period of extremely competitive conditions, the top management of the company decided upon an ambitious and far-reaching program, designed to capture a larger share of the market. New and higher sales goals were set, an aggressive advertising campaign was launched, and a plan of special incentives for sales representatives was initiated.

Much time was devoted in top-management committees to discussion of the new program. It was decided that division heads would discuss the program with their superintendents, superintendents would then hold similar discussions with their supervisors, and supervisors in turn would present the plans in meetings with their employees. There would be follow-ups through company publications, but the word-of-mouth discussions would be the principal means of communication.

Responses to the discussions were interesting and varied. Top executives saw the program as having tremendous potential consequences for the future of the company, and they were highly enthusiastic regarding it. Middle-management personnel also were strongly impressed; they tended to accept at face value the optimistic predictions of higher management regarding the program.

At the level of first-line supervisors, the announcement met with a lukewarm response; the supervisors were only mildly enthusiastic at best, and some expressed opinions that about the only effect on them would likely be more work expected. At the employee level, the new program seemed to make little if any impression. Some supervisors never got around to any sort of discussion of the new program with their employees. In units where the subject was discussed, employees generally seemed to feel that the program would have little effect on them personally.

Problems and questions:

a. How can the variation in responses be explained?

b. Can you suggest any steps which might have improved the reception of the new program at the supervisory and worker levels?

c. What do you recommend to management now? Why?

Case 15-3. Planning for Dictation

Three executives who are employed by the same firm find it necessary to dictate a great many letters. Their approaches to composing letters provide interesting contrasts.

One of the men jots down a topical outline of what he intends to say.

The second has prepared checklists of what seem to be the key points to consider in dealing with the principal types of situation encountered, from time to time, and he makes quick reference to these to the appropriate checklist when composing a letter.

The third begins dictating immediately after reading a letter which he is to answer or after checking facts needed where he initiates correspondence, feeling that he has written so many letters that no special preparation is needed, also that his letters are more natural and informal as a result.

Problems and questions:

Appraise each of the approaches. Does one seem clearly superior to the others? Might each be appropriate under some circumstances?—if so, what?

Case 15-4. Galbraith Jobbing Company

Mr. A. Q. Blankenship, the president of the Galbraith Jobbing Company, recently attended a conference for executives at which he heard a highly effective talk on the subject of good letter writing. He came home so enthusiastic about the subject that he resolved to take immediate steps to correct what he now regarded as a woefully unsatisfactory situation.

Mr. Blankenship's first impression was that the soundest approach to the problem would lie in reorganizing the work and employing a small staff of professional correspondents. When letters would need to be written on any special topic, such as on a sales or purchasing matter, the executive wishing to write the letter would supply basic data to one of the special correspondents. The correspondent would then compose the letter, using the most effective techniques, and the letter would then be returned to the executive for approval and signature.

Problems and questions:

a. What advantages and disadvantages can you see in Mr. Blankenship's plan?

b. Do you think he should consider other solutions to the problem of unsatisfactory correspondence in his company? If so, what other methods would you recommend that he consider?

Case 15-5. Key Considerations in Letter Writing

One office executive suggests that the most important factor in good letter writing is to develop good technique. He believes the key considerations in technique include taking the "you-attitude," writing in a friendly rather than argumentative manner, focusing on a central selling point, and being clear, concise, and complete.

A fellow executive disagrees. He maintains that technique is less important than the writer's attitude. If the writer is convinced that his position is fair and if his letter breathes a spirit of genuine good will, the second executive feels that technique will pretty well take care of itself.

Problems and questions:

a. What are the merits of each point of view?

b. Do you feel that one of the points of view is sounder than the other? If so, give principal reasons.

Case 15-6. Insurance Communications Network

The Southwest Region of the National Insurance Company has been experiencing increasing costs in its inter-office and interregional communication network. Each major claims service office (CSO) in the Southwest Region has a teletypewriter for communicating with its regional office and other regional offices throughout the country. An investigation of this situation revealed the following facts.

1. The Company presently uses leased teletypewriter wires (or private wires) between regional offices. The cost per message, depending upon volume, is approximately one-fifth of the regular teletypewriter message.

2. The teletypewriter rate from each CSO in the Southwest Region to any other foreign regional office is greater than the combined rate to its home regional office and leased wire rate to the foreign home office.

Problems and questions:

a. Based upon supplied data, what would be your recommendations to management? Discuss the reasoning behind your recommendation.

b. What factors did you consider in reaching your recommendation?

c. What other facts do you need in this case, if any?

16

FORMS DESIGN
AND CONTROL

*The nature of forms · Forms design · Forms control · Forms-
handling equipment · Reproduction of forms*

The Nature of Forms

For an introduction to the subject
of forms, please examine briefly the blank check presented below.

Then consider these questions. Is this actually a form? Why or why
not? What "fixed data" are pre-printed on the check? How does the
bank management know the items to pre-print? What "variable data"
are *not* printed on the check but must be filled in by the person who
draws the check? What results would be likely to occur if a bank did

no pre-printing of checks but left entirely to each depositor the manner in which he wrote out checks on his account?

Study of a blank check, simple and familiar though it is, can provide a rather good orientation to the nature and use of forms. A form may be defined as a piece of paper bearing fixed data and providing spaces for variable data. Thus the information that is constant or known in advance can be made a standard part of the form. It is then necessary to fill in only the information that varies, or may vary, with each transaction; this information is called for specifically; and a standard position on the form is established for each item, thus reducing uncertainty and saving time.

Our analysis would be much the same if we were considering an invoice, a purchase order, or an employment application form. It would be basically the same if we were examining an insurance policy, although we might be impressed by the large portion of fixed data and the small portion of variable data—made possible by special design of one policy form for automobile coverage, another for accident and health coverage, and so forth.

Forms may be unobtrusive, unimpressive, unglamorous, and even dull. Yet, as someone has observed, we depend upon forms from birth to death, for they supply the very proof and span of our existence.

Purposes of forms

We can summarize the purposes served by forms as follows:

1. They make clear *what information* must be gathered and communicated.

2. They provide a *specific location* for each item of information needed, thus facilitating data entry, processing, and reference.

3. They eliminate the need for recopying standard or *repetitive information.*

4. They facilitate use of *multiple copies,* often greatly simplifying procedures as a result.

5. They *identify records* and facilitate filing and future reference.

Forms function both as *procedural instruments* and as *instructions* to individual employees and managers. In a purchasing procedure, forms gather information on items desired, quantity, price, shipping instructions, and other elements of information; they communicate the information to the seller, buyer, receiving department, accounting department, and others who must make decisions and take action to consummate the purchase. At the same time, each person who is involved in the procedure is guided in the performance of certain operations. He is given a "road map" to follow.

The general criteria for appraising forms are the same as those suggested for appraising other methods—*effectiveness* and *economy*. Factors in effectiveness have just been considered; a good form will aid greatly in assembling, processing, communicating, and recording information.

The factor of economy justifies special attention. Study of a blank check or any other well-designed form will indicate that it represents a money-saving way to gather and provide information. Yet cost, in this instance, can be deceptive. For every dollar spent in producing forms (designing and reproducing copies), an average of about seventeen dollars is likely to be spent for clerical labor in doing the work called for on the forms.

Even greater may be the cost of *not* gathering information actually needed. If the purchasing procedures mentioned above were carried out entirely by means of oral communication and memory, one may be sure that the price of this approach would be far greater than that necessary for the most elaborate set of forms.

Carefully-planned programs for the *design* and the *control* of forms are clearly needed. We shall now consider: (1) forms design, (2) forms control, (3) forms-handling equipment, and (4) reproduction of forms.

Forms Design

The potentialities of forms in making *positive* contributions to management have been suggested, along with the possibility of unrealized benefits and less-than-ideal design.

Experiences in many enterprises have demonstrated that highly significant improvements can be realized through well-conceived programs of forms design and control.

> One firm retained a forms consultant to guide them in establishing a forms control program. One of the consultant's first questions was, "Approximately how many forms do you now have?" The answer, "probably between 300 and 400," was badly in error, as revealed when the consultant rounded up 2,400 forms in two weeks. Fortunately, he was then able to guide the management in a gradual reduction to about half the original number of forms.

Types of forms

Forms have been designed for a wide range of uses. Among the many types are cut forms (single sheet), continuous forms, card record forms, tag forms, stock forms, pegboard forms, and forms for special functions such as sales books, machine accounting forms, check forms, and numerous others.[1]

[1] Many comprehensive descriptions of forms are available. Among the better ones are Ray Marien, *Marien On Forms Control* (Englewood Cliffs, N.J.: Prentice-Hall, Inc., 1963); Frank M. Knox, *Design and Control of Business Forms* (New York: McGraw-

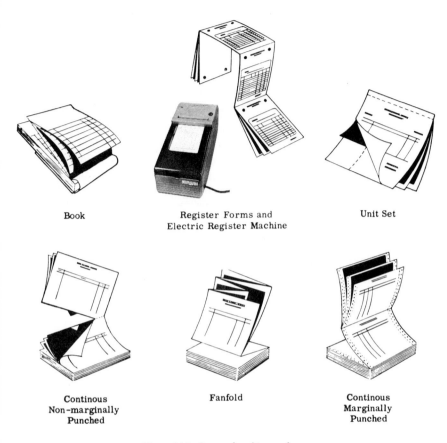

Figure 16-1. Types of multi-copy forms

Multi-copy forms justify special consideration because of tremendous time-saving potentialities. Figure 16-1 illustrates basic types of forms which are adapted to multiple-copy arrangements. Included are hand-written books in which file copies can be retained; register forms, also handwritten, but in continuous, perforated sets, with a carbon roll contained in the machine; unit sets with one-time carbon and perforated stub easily removed; fanfold, continuous forms that are perforated and in accordion-like folds; continuous, non-marginally punched forms used in machines; continuous, marginally punched forms used on machines equipped with forms-feeding devices. Forms of the last-mentioned category are engaged by tractor pins in the marginal punching, thus insuring

Hill Book Company, Inc., 1952); and Wallace B. Sadauskas, *Manual of Business Forms* (New York: Office Publications, Inc., 1961). Good current materials appear frequently in professional journals such as *The Office Executive, The Office,* and *Administrative Management.*

accurate alignment from part to part and set to set; they are now used on typewriters, billing machines, addressing machines, teletypewriters, tabulators, and high-speed printers of output from computers.

A tool of analysis that has special value in considering possibilities for combining separate forms into a multiple set is the "Forms Spread Sheet" or "Recurring Data Chart" such as that illustrated in Figure 16-2. The feasibility of alterations, combinations, and use of multi-copy sets, are suggested through use of such a chart.

A development of particular significance in forms design has been Magnetic Ink Character Recognition (MICR), a process used chiefly by banks thus far in printing data in magnetic ink in certain reserved spaces

FORMS ANALYSIS CHART OF RECURRING DATA	FORM TITLE →	Job Ticket	Prod'n Order	Ship. Inst.	Office Memo				TOTAL
DATE OF ANALYSIS Nov. 16, '60 PAGE 1 OF PAGES 1									
ACTIVITY Distribution									
ANALYST JJD									
ITEMIZED DATA		FORM NO. 166	FORM NO. 114	FORM NO. 216	FORM NO. 091	FORM NO.	FORM NO.	
1. Item Description		X	X	X	X				
2. Quantity				X					
3. Invoice No.		X	X	X	X				
4. Marking Description				X					
5. Production Cont'l No.		X	X						
6. Consignee				X	X				
7.									
8.									
9.									
10.									
11.									
12.									
13.									
14.									
15.									
16.									
17.									
18.									
19.									
20.									
21.									
22.									
23.									
24.									
25.									
TOTAL ☐ CARRIED FORWARD ☐									

Figure 16-2. Recurring data chart

at the bottom of checks. Note the MICR characters printed on the check shown in Figure 16-3. Data printed are usually those needed by the bank to clear checks promptly—the routing symbol, transit number, customer code number, and consecutive check number. The characters can be read by both sorter-reader machines and by humans. When desired, data can be read by the sorter-reader, compared with account balances stored in a computer, customers' accounts can be updated, and statements printed. While used chiefly, thus far, by banks for processing checks, uses of MICR are now being extended, as noted in Chapter 13.

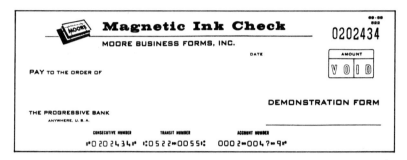

Figure 16-3. Magnetic ink characters used in bank check processing

Principles of forms design

Basic requirements in forms design are that forms be easy to write, easy to read, and pleasing in appearance. The following checklist of specific principles is offered for consideration in design of all types of forms.

1. Give the form a name that is sufficiently descriptive to indicate its function.

2. Provide a form number for specific identification.

3. Use a box design, with captions printed in small but distinct type in upper left corners of sections; this provides added space for entries and keeps captions visible to the operator while entering the variable data.

4. Arrange items so writing proceeds from left to right and from top to bottom, and as far as possible, note usage—from items used all the time to those having minimum use.

5. Group related information; have all shipping information in the same general area, for example.

6. Try to have the sequence of items agree with the sequence of the same items on any form or worksheet from which the data are transcribed.

7. Lay out forms to correspond to formats of tabulating cards when to serve as source documents; this facilitates key punching and reduces error.

8. Use boxes for entries when possible. (See Figure 16-4b.)

9. Allow sufficient space for entering data. Consider the exact horizontal and vertical spacing of the machine to be used in completing the form (if a machine is used) and the maximum number of characters that will be entered in each box. Hand-filled forms are normally provided with ¼" vertical spacing and ⅛" horizontal spacing for each character. Forms layout charts are frequently helpful in drawing copy according to spacing required.

10. Take full advantage of tab stops and other time saving features, in designing the form. Electronic tab stops on some machines call for printing of vertical rules in electrically conductive ink, which are read by the machine.

11. Design forms which will contain mailing addresses to fit window envelopes, usually using fold marks.

12. Place filing information, such as by production number, on the form according to how the document will be filed—if loose in vertical file, number in upper right.

13. Place simple instructions directly on the form, preceding sections to which they apply. Use an accompanying procedure or directive if detailed and complex instructions are required.

14. Consider colored ink for captions, or constant data, if variable data should stand out for readability. Use recessive colors such as brown or green.

15. Incorporate routing instructions for each copy in the margin, and use a different color paper for quick identification.

16. Consider limitations in color of the ink which can be reproduced by copying machines to be used.

17. Use various type faces, heavy rules, and shaded areas to highlight certain areas or to guide completion of the form.

18. Make type faces legible but not so dominant that they detract from filled-in data.

19. Provide for any data to be omitted from one or more internal parts of a multiple-part form by such means as printed "block-outs," carbon with uncoated areas, or perforations so undesired information may be torn off.

20. Use standard sizes when possible, for filing in standardized equipment and for economy in printing.

Figures 16-4a and 16-4b present before and after versions of a form for reporting errors. The improved draft applies many of the principles just suggested and may justify careful study.

Paper specified for a form should be dictated by *use factors,* including: (1) appearance, (2) amount of handling likely, (3) number of copies to be produced in one writing, (4) length of time to be retained, (5) specific use of form. In general, mechanical wood pulps (newspaper grade), although inexpensive, should not be used if forms are to be retained for a long period of time. Sulphite paper, also derived from wood, is avail-

ANALYSIS OF CUSTOMER DISSATISFACTION

DATE _____

CUSTOMER _____

ADDRESS _____

DEALER _____

PRODUCT _____ ORDER NO. _____

LOSS CHARGED TO _____ DEPARTMENT _____

SUPERVISOR _____ EMPLOYEE _____

ADJUSTMENT MADE _____

DETAILS OF ERROR _____

EXPLANATION OF EMPLOYEE RESPONSIBLE

HOW CAN THIS DISSATISFACTION BE PREVENTED FROM HAPPENING AGAIN?

(Use back of this sheet if more space is needed)

EMPLOYEE'S SIGNATURE _____

SUPERVISOR'S SIGNATURE _____

REVIEWED BY _____

Figure 16-4a. Form for reporting errors—*before revision*

able in different grades and is the type usually used for forms. Rag content papers are needed when appearance, permanency, or durability are dominant considerations. Carbon paper is available in different weights, colors, and sensitivity; advance tests of suitability are very often advisable. NCR paper (no carbon required) has chemical coating which produces an impression and eliminates the carbon disposal problem; it is more expensive and not always flexible enough, but is gaining in use because of labor saving and convenience.

Forms Control

As noted earlier, cost of the processing of forms may average seventeen times the cost of producing and filing the forms. Forms control, therefore, is also a means of exercising management control over work. Specific purposes of forms control include:

D11 9 63

FACTORY ERROR REPORT

CUSTOMER NAME		DATE	ORDER NO.
STREET ADDRESS		DEALER NAME	
CITY & STATE		PRODUCT	

ADJUSTMENT	LOSS CHARGED TO	DEPT. A	B	C	D	E	OTHER

DETAILS OF ERROR

EMPLOYEE EXPLANATION

WHAT CAN BE DONE TO PREVENT RECURRENCE

EMPLOYEE NAME	EMP. INITIALS	SUPERVISOR NAME	SUPV.INITIALS	REVIEWED BY (INITIALS)
				PRODUCTION MGR.

Advantages of redesign:
(1) Wasted space vertically and at margins has been eliminated resulting in a smaller, more economical form.
(2) The arrows in the stub represent a form of instructions as they indicate the margin and tab settings.
(3) Every machine writing position except for (Dept. B, C, D and other; initials will be hand written) can be reached by either a carriage return or tab. Horizontal spacing held to a minimum and manual hand positioning entirely eliminated.
(4) Box headings were used to permit more writing space.
(5) The proper space for each entry has been provided as a result of an analysis of complete forms (previous versions).
(6) Boxes for simple X entry provided where possible.
(7) The filing reference , order number, was placed in proper position.
(8) Form is set on double spacing the entire form length.
(9) Marginal words (Production Mgr. on Copy# 1) provided to facilitate distribution (a form of the printed instruction).
(10)A more descriptive form name has been given.
(11)A form number has been provided so that the form may be specifically identified.

Figure 16-4b. Form for reporting errors—*after revision*

1. Proper design of forms which will insure maximum clerical efficiency.

2. Elimination of obsolete forms.

3. Consolidation of forms to minimize duplicate effort.

4. Minimization of printing costs.

Responsibility for forms control

Forms control is normally *group* control, with the forms control group usually including representatives from different departments. At least one specialist in forms design should be included. The specialist is likely to be a systems and procedures department member who has special training, experience, and interest in forms; his influence will usually be great. Members of the group probably will meet frequently during early stages of a forms control program; later, they may meet at scheduled intervals or may be on call when their services are needed.

Typically, the forms control group will function as follows:

1. Assemble and classify samples of all forms in use.

2. Establish and maintain a master file, with an indexing system which makes it easy to determine what forms are already in use and available, and the relationships among forms.

3. Receive requisitions for new forms or redesigns of existing forms; these requests may originate from the user or as a result of a general systems study.

4. Provide for maintenance of accurate inventory records of all forms, and for consideration of redesign when supplies reach minimum quantities, with the user notified at that time.

5. Decide upon reproduction processes to be used and, usually, whether printing will be done with inside or outside facilities.

6. Study and recommend forms-handling equipment which may facilitate use of forms for different purposes.

Forms file

It is common practice to have two types of forms files. The first is a *numerical file,* which files all forms by identifying numbers on forms, and includes a sample of the form, specifications, and changes which may affect the design or quantity to be ordered at the next printing. The second is a *functional file,* in which forms are filed by the function which they serve. The latter file uses classifications: which group forms contain similar data (this is often by subject, operation, and function served). This is an excellent tool for indicating the possibility for eliminating or consolidating forms.

Procedure in forms requisitioning and reordering

Requisitions for new form designs, redesigns of existing forms, and replenishment of stock of existing forms should be submitted to the forms specialist—who may be a member of the forms control committee. He must also coordinate the program and carry most investigations through at least the preliminary stages and often, to the point where the committee members will merely need to agree or disagree with proposed action. A forms requisition sheet is illustrated in Figure 16-5.

The forms specialist or coordinator should then:

1. Check to see if there are other forms in use which serve essentially the same purpose; if so, study these to ascertain if all are necessary or if it is possible to combine certain forms. The value of complete forms indexes and files becomes obvious at this point.

2. Study any proposed new design or redesign in the light of sound principles, such as those previously outlined; then, if needed, assist the person requesting the form in completing the design and the specifications.

Form 428
Rev. 1/4/56

REQUISITION FOR ORDERING FORMS

TO THE FORMS SUPERVISOR: DATE _____

( ) 1. *Reprint* attached form on same size, color, and quality of paper.
    (a) Quantity to be printed   _____
    (b) Quantity used monthly   _____
    (c) Quantity now on hand   _____
        ( ) Print   ( ) Mimeo   ( ) Offset

( ) 2. Reprint attached form *with revisions* as noted below and on attached.
    (a) Quantity to be printed   _____
    (b) Quantity used monthly   _____
    (c) Quantity now on hand   _____
    (d) Purpose of revision   _____

    (e) Paper color   _____
    (f) Paper weight   _____
    (g) Ink color   _____
        ( ) Print   ( ) Mimeo   ( ) Offset

( ) 3. Print new form as shown in attached sample.
    (a) Quantity to be printed   _____
    (b) Quantity to be used monthly   _____
    (c) Purpose of form   _____

    (d) Paper color   _____
    (e) Paper weight   _____
    (f) Ink color   _____
        ( ) Print   ( ) Mimeo   ( ) Offset

Name of requesting officer	Department	Division
Date on which forms are required	Dept'l approval	Div'l approval

Figure 16-5. A forms design and approval request sheet which may be used in ordering new or revised forms

3. Consider inventory status and pending systems changes which may alter the need for the form in the future.

4. Present the proposal to the forms control committee, along with any supporting information and recommendations which may be of value to them in evaluating the proposal.

5. Follow up on decisions by the control committee in taking action indicated and doing further work with the person requesting the form.

Forms-Handling Equipment

Along with the machines which literally turn out tons of forms in a sizable organization each day, there are several highly useful types of auxiliary equipment which many managements overlook. Among these are *detachers* which separate continuous forms into sets or single sheets for subsequent handling operations; some models also imprint information such as signatures on payroll checks, some count forms, and some slit forms in any vertical position. Detachers can be obtained with form feeding speeds up to approximately 250 feet a minute. Some high-speed detachers are linked with conveyor belts which carry forms to a back stop where they are stacked in a semi-vertical position.

Decollators and deleavers are other types of equipment which aid modern forms handling. Figure 16-6 shows a detacher with a forms stacker, and a waterfall decollator.

Reproduction of Forms

Decisions must be made on whether to print forms on internal duplicating equipment or obtain them from outside suppliers. Ordinarily, only simple, single cut forms are printed internally, unless volume is heavy. Multiple-copy forms are usually obtained from either local printers or national manufacturers of forms because of the complex nature of both the rotary press equipment used and the manufacturing processes.

Two primary means of printing are used in reproducing forms: letterpress, which applies ink to a raised image as it passes under an inking roller and then transfers ink to paper; and offset printing or lithography, which involves "burning" the image on a metal plate used on a rotary press, and using a rubber blanket cylinder to transfer the impression to paper. The advantages of the latter are superior quality and ability to print screened art effects.

Careful analysis of quality, volume, and costs should be carried out before deciding on internal or external printing, and in choosing printing methods.

Figure 16-6. *Right:* A Moore Business Forms waterfall decollator used for separating multi-copy carbon f i l l e d forms; *below:* A Moore Business Forms detacher with a forms stacker used to separate continuous forms.

Moore Business Forms, Inc.

The services of reputable forms manufacturers can be of tremendous value. Such firms have systems specialists and service representatives who usually will be able to bring much past experience to bear upon the forms design and printing problems of a particular enterprise. At the same time, it is ordinarily too much to expect that they will have the perspective and time to comprehend whole systems; they concentrate mainly upon particular applications.

QUESTIONS FOR STUDY AND DISCUSSION

1. Does it seem probable that most persons, in and out of business, underrate the impact of printed forms? If you belive so, what explanations can you offer for this situation?

2. What is the function of "fixed data" on forms and what is the function of "variable data"? Is there a challenge to use more of one type and less of the other?—Explain.

3. Study carefully the purposes and functions of forms. Does each seem accurate and significant? Compare in importance the use of forms as procedural instruments and as instructions to individual employees and managers. Do forms constitute a special type of communications?

4. Can the factor of *economy* in forms be deceptive? Explain carefully.

5. Note the principal types of forms which have been devised for different uses. Why do multi-copy forms offer special promise? Can they, at the same time, lead to waste? Study the forms spread sheet and suggest principal uses.

6. What is MICR; what are its chief uses at present; and what do you see as potential uses for the future?

7. Distinguish between "forms design" and "forms control," and explain the need for each. Study carefully the list of principles of forms design; does each seem justified? How can such a list best be used?

8. What are the purposes of forms control?

9. In one firm, forms have been controlled by a committee which includes a forms analyst and representatives from the accounting, production, and sales departments. The committee has the authority to approve requests for new forms and to reprint forms already in use. The forms analyst has recently asked the controller, who is his superior, to dissolve the committee and make him alone responsible, saying that the committee members routinely approve virtually every request that comes to them. If you were the controller, what questions would you wish to ask before approving or disapproving this request?

10. If you were given the assignment of appraising and improving the forms system of a grocery chain, where would you start and what later steps would you follow? Why?

11. What kinds of master files may be desirable in forms control? Justify each type suggested.

12. Study critically the procedure suggested for forms requisitioning and reordering.

13. What principal types of forms handling equipment are now in wide use? Is there a relationship between increased use of such equipment and rapid increase of data processing equipment? In what other ways may modern data processing influence forms design, control, and handling?

Case 16-1. Blair Wholesale Grocers

Blair Wholesale Grocers paid a typist, Miss Carroll, $1.50 per hour to type sales orders. On an average, her output was 100 orders per day. The forms (unit sets) cost $33.20 per M. Miss Carroll normally worked 40 hours per week, but, due to sales growth, she was now regularly working 5 hours per week overtime at time and a half.

The Systems Analyst at Blair had recommended to the Office Manager that continuous marginally punched sales orders be used. Although they cost more than the unit sets, $38.72 per M, and a forms feeding device for Miss Carroll's typewriter would have to be purchased at a cost of $75.00, the Systems Analyst estimated that the typing effort would be approximately 15 per cent more efficient.

The Office Manager had never used continuous forms before and hesitated in making his decision to change.

Problems and questions:

    a. What would your decision be if you were office manager? Why?
    b. What effect would this change have on Miss Carroll? Why?

Case 16-2. Blough Pharmaceutical Company

The invoicing procedure followed in the Blough Pharmaceutical Company involves the typing of two forms: (1) a shipping label and (2) a 5-part invoice form. The label contains the following data (maximum number of characters in parenthesis): Order number (6) and ship to address (3 lines at 30 each). The invoice, in addition to the above information, requires: Sold to address (3 lines at 30 each), customer's purchase order number (8), sales representatives name (17), invoice date (8), and date shipped (8).

The invoice is filed by order number. Since both forms are typed for each order and both contain common information, consideration should be given to combining the two.

Problem:

Prepare a drawing of part 1 of the invoice and part 6, which will be the label. (Note: The machine used in the above case spaces 10 characters to the inch horizontally and 6 lines to the inch vertically.)

17

OFFICE REPRODUCTION SERVICES

Growth and functions of office reproduction services · Determining the need · Organization of office reproduction services · Basic reproduction processes · The problem of choice · Illustrative applications · Managing office reproduction services

---

Since paper work plays a vital role in communications and because wide distribution of information is required, reproduction equipment is indispensable to an efficient office. Modern businesses are inundated with paper work. Increased office activities, improved services to the customer, governmental controls and regulations, and the increased need for management to have more and better information faster, have all been instrumental in the mounting volume of paper work. Obviously, office costs are increasing too, partly as the result of this increased paper work. Company office reproduction or duplication of the many tasks requiring special copies, file copies, or "for your information" copies of business data are significant factors in the never-ending fight to control increasing office costs, while simultaneously attempting to improve the information service to management and to the organization.

Growth of Office Reproduction Services

Every business firm has a need for office reproduction services. Prior to the recent developments in office reproduction methods, most firms either relied upon outside print shops, which were costly in both time and money, or upon methods dependent upon typists, which were equally expensive. Actually, reproduction services started as a part-time activity in such functions as engineering design and production photographic services. Reproduction services grew at a tremendous rate during the war, and have continued to grow as management has recognized their potential and as administrative problems have increased and become more complex, making existing practices impractical. Office reproduction has become an integral part of the information system of many progressive businesses and has become a necessary part of managerial activities.

Such growth of office reproduction services created a new organizational entity—that of an office reproduction functional service unit. *Dun's Review and Modern Industry* reports that sales of office reproduction equipment have passed the sales of more publicized dictating equipment, and that in 1961, total sales of copier machines reached $300 million—an increase of some 20 per cent over the previous year.[1] Another authoritative source reports that more than two billion dollars are spent annually to provide the multiple as well as facsimile copies of administrative and technical material needed by businesses and industry, and estimates that dollar volume spent on reproduction services will double by 1975.[2]

Advantages of Office Reproduction Services

Reproduction equipment provides a means for eliminating repetition when it becomes necessary to reproduce office paper work. Dependent upon the complexity of the material to be produced, a great deal of time can be saved. For example, a letter that might require 20 minutes to retype can be produced on a copying machine in a matter of seconds. If a hundred copies of the same letter are required and, say, ten carbon copies can be made at a time, it would take $3\frac{1}{3}$ hours to type. Using an office copier to make an offset master and then running the master off on an offset duplicator would take but a few minutes.

Obviously, the particular advantages realized by any one firm from installing reproduction service depends upon the type of equipment selected, and the manner in which it is used. Listed below are a few of the more common advantages most firms may reasonably expect from office reproduction devices.

[1] "Hardware for the Future," *Dun's Review and Modern Industry*, September, 1962, added supplement, *Special Report on the Office*, p. S 126.

[2] Albert Prioletta, "Business and Industry Reproduction Services," *The Office*, January, 1961, p. 119.

1. Reproduction machines are highly flexible, accepting a wide variety of letters, reports, diagrams, notes, and in some cases, colors.

2. Office reproduction services eliminate bottlenecks in the flow of information by quickly reproducing desired data and passing the original data on to interested executives.

3. Office reproduction may often be less expensive than use of outside services or the clerical time required internally for manual retype or reproduction of the documents.

4. A better informed and better coordinated management team results since many executives do not hesitate to ask for "information copies" provided by reproduction methods.

Determining the Need for Office Reproduction Services

The need for office reproduction services frequently may be quite evident to management from a reproduction survey. But the solution which first offers itself is not always the one which can yield the greatest returns in time, cost, effectiveness, and efficiency. A firm contemplating any type of office reproduction equipment should survey and analyze the job operations to determine where, why, how much, and what type of reproduction equipment is needed. Following is a simple office reproduction survey checklist to assist in making such a survey and analysis.

1. *Analyze the flow of work and office practices.* Particular attention should be paid to the distribution of reports—the number of copies, to whom sent, and the use made of them. The type of original data, quality of paper, bound reports, color, etc., should be noted, as these affect the type of reproduction equipment selected. Special requests by management for certain types of data should be studied also, along with the time element of reproducing the data, for rush requests are frequently received for particular types of data and copy requirements.

2. *Streamline the number and flow of reports.* Eliminate or combine as many reports as possible, and dependent upon the analysis in No. 1, above, eliminate duplicate copies, if at all possible.

3. *Survey reproduction equipment available.* Much assistance can be gained here from manufacturers' representatives of the various types of reproduction equipment. While initial cost of the equipment is certainly a consideration, operating costs—the cost per sheet reproduced—are more important. Involved in per-sheet costs are such items as the time required to operate the equipment, multiple copies available from one master, use of fluid machines which require frequent changes, and speed. Many firms find a need for two types or styles of reproduction equipment, one for small, short-run reproduction tasks and one for large, long-run reproduction tasks.

Organization of Office Reproduction Services

The services provided by an office reproduction department can or-dinarily be more efficient in a centralized operation. The supervisor of this function usually reports to the office or administrative services man-ager. Centralized office reproduction services provide many advantages for a firm, including:

1. Centralized office reproduction services allow specialization and higher qual-ity output.
2. Centralization minimizes investment and maximizes utilization of equip-ment and employee time.
3. Centralization results in considerable flexibility and variety of reproduction methods allowing several methods to be combined to obtain maximum efficiency.
4. Centralized reproduction services provide better management control and fix responsibility.
5. Centralized reproduction services facilitate equipment servicing and put the work in the hands of experienced and skilled operators.

A contrasting trend is the decentralization of the small, inexpensive, easy-to-use reproduction machines. These machines usually operate from a direct-copy process and are located throughout the organization where they can provide the necessary copies in a hurry, and where they are most convenient to the people who use them.

Because reproduction services have such potential and are directly involved with the increasingly important area of management informa-tion systems, many firms are giving their office reproduction unit depart-mental status. The reproduction manager functions as a staff consultant on all reproduction service needs, frequently crossing departmental lines. In the fall of 1960, the American Management Association held a three-day conference to discuss the scope and future of this new concept of office reproduction services. It was concluded that a responsible executive is necessary to adequately supervise such a service, and that he must be capable of planning, organizing, and establishing policy for the total office reproduction function in order to assure the improved efficiency and productivity now demanded.

Basic Reproduction Processes

As already implied, reproduction involves two basically different proc-esses—copying and duplicating. Copying equipment is used to make rela-tively few copies of existing material without the use of a master or stencil. Duplicating equipment, which requires either a master, stencil, or set type, is used to produce a great number of copies and at low cost per copy.

The copying process

Copying equipment is being used more in combination with duplicators. Most copying machines have the ability to make masters for at least one of the duplicating processes. The advantages of reproduction equipment are multiplied when applications for such uses exist.

Many copying machines cost less than $100. Since they are easy to use and since the cost is not prohibitive, they can be strategically located in the organization. A particular advantage for using copying machines is that the original itself is the master. Consequently, the reproduction is as nearly an exact copy of the original as can be expected.

But the economies in the quantities of copies which can be produced by a copying machine are quite limited. Since most copying processes require that an operator use the original copy for each copy desired, long-run reproduction operations would become slow and expensive. Figure 17-1 provides a comparison of the basic copying processes and includes brief mention of the characteristics of each process.

Process	Speed* (Copies Per Minute)	Length of Run for Which Best Suited**	Copying Processes Which Can Prepare Masters or Stencils	Characteristics of the Process
Gelatin	10-75	10-100	Facsimile	Prints on paper with glossy finish. Best copies from purple carbon, but other colors can be used and can be run simultaneously. Copies become fainter as run continues.
Spirit	40-120	10-400	Facsimile; Xerography	Prints on paper with glossy finish. Variety of colors possible, but purple gives best results. Numerous colors can be run simultaneously. Copies become fainter as run continues.
Special Liquid (AZOGRAPH; CHEMOGRAPH; COLUMBIA TRANSFER)	40-120	10-125	None at present	These three processes perform like the spirit process, but feature "cleanliness"—printing dyes are not formed until paper enters machine, to avoid stain hazard. Printing color is approximately blue-black, varying with the process. Copies become fainter as run continues. Some machines can handle spirit process as well.
Stencil	40-200	10 to 10,000	Facsimile (special units)	Copies are possible in any color ink on any color paper. Quick-drying inks permit use of bond and similar papers; other inks require rough paper. Some machines print more than one color simultaneously.
Offset	75-150	10 to many thousands	Diazo; Facsimile; Verifax; Xerography	Copies are of high quality. Ink and paper color can be varied; one ink run at a time. Equipment requires reasonably experienced operator.
Relief	40-100	300 to 100,000	None—type must be set	Copies resemble typing or printing, depending on whether ribbon is used. Process often used for "fill-in" items and work with changing copy, since type can be changed during run. Prints one color at a time on any color paper.

* Speed figures are estimates for letter-size copies, and allow for differences between manual and electric operation, as well as for machine differences. As circumstances vary, figures above or below those listed may be obtained.

** These figures do not represent machine limitations but are based on "practical" considerations such as cost, speed, method of operation, and other factors.

Administrative Management

Figure 17-1. Comparison of office copying processes

The duplicating processes

Duplicating processes are intended to make multiple copies at high speeds and are used in situations requiring many copies and where the economies of long-run reproduction can be realized. Duplicating equipment is used, too, in systems where repetitive information, once typed, is used to prepare the required forms involved in the same transaction, e.g., a work order, bill of lading, and invoice. Information not required on one form may easily be "blocked out." This amounts to an integrated data processing system in one of its more simple forms.

Most stencils for duplicating processes can be prepared by typewriter, an advantage which allows the requisitioning department to prepare and be responsible for its own stencils. Several of the duplicating processes produce professional copies which are more than adequate for use as business forms, information letters to the employees, reports, and working papers, to name just a few. Costs per copy vary considerably with the length of the run and the quality of the materials used. As a general rule, the cost per sheet of a run of more than just a few copies is a fraction of a cent. Figure 17-2 provides a comparison of the duplicating processes available for office reproduction work. Because of the wide variations with each process, no attempt is made to provide illustrative costs. Note that Figure 17-1 for the comparison of copying methods and Figure 17-2 are closely related; the copying equipment which can prepare masters of stencils for duplicating work is identified. The length of the run, shown in the comparison of duplicating equipment, provides some

Process	Speed*	Cost Per Copy*	Can Process Enlarge or Reduce?	Duplicating Processes for Which Stencils or Masters Can Be Prepared	Characteristics of the Process
Diffusion Transfer	1 copy in 15 seconds to 1 minute	4-9 cents	Most cannot	Offset; Stencil (in special units)	Copies are positives on white or colored coated paper; some units make negatives. Sensitive to wide range of colors. Can make translucencies for diazo process. Some units can make several prints from one negative, and a number of companies now offer single-sheet multiple-copy processes, which utilize the original negative as master.
Dye Transfer	1 copy in 50 seconds; 5 in 1 minute	9-10 cents (single); (1 cent for extras)	No	Offset	Copies are positives on bond or similar non-sensitized paper. Several prints can be made from one matrix. Process is otherwise similar to photocopying.
Thermography	1 copy in 4 seconds	4½-5 cents	No	None	Copies are positives on buff or colored paper which can be reinforced with heavier backing. Process less sensitive to some kinds of ink. Papers easily laminated in these machines.
Xerography	1 copy in 3 minutes	5 cents	Yes	Offset; Spirit	Copies are positives on various kinds of paper or film. Process is widely used to make offset masters. It is sensitive to wide range of colors. Can make translucencies for diazo process.
Diazo	200-800 copies per hour	about 1 cent	No	Offset	Copies are positives, in various possible colors. Translucent, one-sided originals required, or translucency must be made first Process sensitive to most colors, less so to purples.
Stabilization	4 copies per minute	5 cents	No	Offset	Sensitive to wide range of tone. Copies almost any color without need of filters.
Facsimile	1 copy in 3 minutes	5 cents	No	Offset; Stencil; Gelatin; Spirit	Copies are positives on specially treated paper. Process is used widely for wire communications, is getting increased use for stencil cutting.

* Speed and copy costs are estimates for letter-size copies using materials of average quality and runs of average length. As circumstances vary, figures above or below those listed may be obtained. Speed figures allow not only for machine differences but for differences between manual and power operation.

Administrative Management

Figure 17-2. Comparison of office duplicating processes

idea of the economies or the break-even point for the economies of long-run reproduction tasks.

The Problem of Choice

The potential output by reproducing equipment is staggering. Therefore, extreme care must be taken to insure that meaningless paper work is not reproduced and distributed. The cost of this practice is not so much in the reproduction itself, but rather in the time required to convey, read, and file the material. However, Administrative Management reports in a memo to its readers that wasted photocopier paper and developer cost American business and industry more than 20 million dollars annually. Some of this waste is necessary, but the report goes on to say that even small firms often waste enough copy paper in one year to pay for the cost of the machine.[3]

As illustrated in the previous two sections, there are a number of processes for copying and duplicating. No one process is best for every need. Each seems to have certain advantages and, invariably, shortcomings. The particular needs of the organization should determine which equipment will serve the best. Equipment is available for virtually every need, and because of strong competition between the manufacturers in this field, better equipment to serve the various needs is constantly being developed and introduced.

Some of the criteria which may be used to compare different processes are quality, cost, speed, and number of copies. High-quality reproduction can be acquired if the cost is of no particular consequence. Many copying machines produce copies that are clear with respect to the data reproduced, but because of the particular process, the background of the copy is cloudy, dingy looking, or considered untidy, by some standards. However, there are copy processes which produce almost perfect black on white copies that closely resemble the original. Quality is a definite criterion when one considers the user of the copy, but for ordinary in-company use, most copy machines are quite satisfactory.

Speed and cost are considered simultaneously when considering the length of the reproduction run. Obviously, for the longer run, duplicating equipment provides the most economical operations. However, some copying machines will produce up to five copies from a negative, and frequently, experienced operators can obtain up to eight copies from one negative. The firm should closely analyze the average number of copies required when choosing reproduction equipment. As mentioned previously, in most cases a combination of copying and duplicating equip-

[3] "A Memo—Beware of Photocopying Wastes," *Administrative Management,* April, 1962, p. 88.

ment provides the best service to the firm, particularly if the copying machine can prepare stencils or masters for the duplicating process. The problem of choice is greatly simplified if the overall results are considered, and if the integration of the two reproduction processes is achieved through compatibility of the equipment.

Representative copying and duplicating machines are shown in Figure 17-3.

Illustrative Applications of Reproducing Processes

The following examples illustrate the versatility of copying and duplicating machines and provide an indication of their potential for business applications. Because of the economies of long runs, duplicating equipment is most popular for reproducing company forms, reports, etc., while the copying equipment has a definite niche in the short-run reproduction tasks of correspondence, medical billing, and "for your information" copies.

Reproduction of company paper materials: [4] One company now uses the offset process to print its own company materials such as forms, letterheads, bulletins, pages of books, promotional literature, price lists, etc., rather than using outside printing sources. Through the use of offset equipment, 2,000 or more copies can be delivered to the requesting department in about 20 minutes, where time involved through using outside printers could run into days. Because of the speed with which forms and other material for special use can be reproduced, space normally used for storing forms can be used for other purposes. Waste through forms obsolescence is eliminated.

Reproduction in production scheduling: [5] A shirt manufacturing company is using photocopy equipment to meet the increasing pressure on the reproduction department. To meet market deadlines, each department must carry out its specified operation in a rapid assembly line fashion. About 50 production order forms must be combined with costing forms and reproduced every day; these combined forms are distributed to some 20 key points throughout the company and are subject to correction and change at any time.

As each order is received, the merchandising department initiates a 16" x 10" preprinted form on which penciled instructions are given to various other departments. A cutting order, giving cutters instructions to go to work on the lot, is attached to the production order with transparent tape, and the orders are reproduced for distribution.

With the former system, the reproduction order was an original paper master. Merchandising used a special pencil to fill in production information before sending the production order to the reproduction department for duplication. Separate forms were used for the cutting order and for costing.

---

[4] Bernard Heinrich, "How Three Techniques Helped Admiral Sales Corporation Increase Printing Capacity 50%," *The Office*, March, 1961, p. 108.

[5] "Photocopying Is Data Processing Too," *Administrative Management*, June, 1961, pp. 26-28.

Figure 17-3. *Above:* The popular Thermo-Fax copying machine; *left:* the Xerox 914 office copier; *below:* Tandem model 1275 offset duplicator. The operating speed ranges up to 6,000 sheets per hour.

Every time there was a production change, a new master had to be used, new information entered, and old information transcribed. With the photocopy method, changes are handled by crossing out the old data, entering new figures, and sending the form back for a new master, reproduction, and redistribution. Only the corrected figures have to be transcribed and not the entire form, as in the case of the former method.

The purchasing agent for this company estimates that the full time of two clerical employees has been saved; clerical retranscribing has been practically eliminated; the simple copying techniques permit employees to use the equipment with a minimum of instruction.

Reproduction in educational research: [6] A 30 per cent increase in operating efficiency at no increase in cost has been achieved by Encyclopedia Britannica's library research department, Chicago, through the use of copying machines. Each owner of an Encyclopedia Britannica is allowed to submit 50 questions within a ten-year period, and in 1959, 110,000 questions were answered. With the use of a copying machine, only an original report and one carbon copy are typed in reply to a question. The carbon copy is mailed to the first person requesting the report, and the original is filed. Each time an additional request is received for the same report, a copy is made in seconds on the copying machine and sent to the subscriber. Since only one copy of each report is now retained, this is a saving in files—an important benefit with 200,000 reports on file, with thousands more being accumulated every year.

One of the most recent applications of company copying equipment is in correspondence services. Although not recent in design, it is rather recent in general acceptance. The method described below is one way busy executives can save their time as well as the time of the secretaries in the mounting communication requirements of modern business.

Reproduction of business correspondence: [7] A copying machine can reduce at least 50 per cent of the time required to reply to a letter. Through this method, the incoming letter is read, reply is handwritten on a margin of the letter, the letter is run through a copying machine and mailed, while the original is filed.

Contrasted with the conventional way of replying to correspondence, this method eliminates dictating, typing, proofreading, and correcting, as well as saving in filing space when only one sheet, instead of the usual two, needs to be filed. The filing space saving is advantageous where correspondence is microfilmed. For the originator of the letter, the machine copying method makes it unnecessary for him to remove the filed copy of his letter when he receives the reply.

Administration of Office Reproduction Services

Effective reproduction services require effective administration. Responsibility must be determined and sufficient authority granted to integrate

[6] "Copying Machines Save Retyping at Encyclopaedia Britannica," *The Office,* April, 1960, p. 268.

[7] "How a Copying Machine Aids Letter Answering," *The Office,* October, 1959, p. 264.

this function with other functions of the firm. Large reproduction tasks of a recurring nature should be assigned definite schedules so that other reproduction work can be arranged accordingly. Requirements should also be established as to the requisitioning procedures for reproduction work. A simple form showing the responsible individual, account code to be charged, number of copies, date material is required, type of method desired (this may not necessarily be at the discretion of the requisitioning individual), and special instructions should be used. A typical reproduction requisition slip is shown in Figure 17-4.

XYZ COMPANY

ANYTOWN, U.S.A.

REPRODUCTION ORDER

Department to be charged _____ Account code _____

Stencil furnished _____ Reproduction authorized by _____

Date _____ Title _____

Type of Reproduction	No. of Copies	Return Stencil	Date Needed	for office use only	
				Operator	Total Hours

When ready: Deliver to _____

Call _____

Signed _____

Title _____

Figure 17-4. Reproduction order for inter-office use

The reproduction service should also prepare end-of-the-period reports for managerial control. Dependent upon the size of the service, standards may be set, or simple ratios of employee hours to the number of copies prepared may be used. In any event, certain standards, goals, or objectives of performance, including quality, should be established to provide some incentive for the employees engaged in the reproduction function. Records should also be maintained to indicate the departments which are making most use of the reproduction services. Such an analysis often points out economies and advantages to management and to the departments which are not using the reproduction facilities. A centralized reproduction service can best serve the organization if all departments use the reproduction facilities to the maximum extent justified.

Following are some procedural guides which should be considered in operating a reproduction department—including both duplicating and copying machines.[8]

1. Furnish stenographers with *short-run* masters rather than medium-run plates if they need less than 100 copies. This saves five cents per master and will provide up to 100 good copies.

2. Use plain sheets for second and third copies of correspondence instead of printed onionskin. Save the cost of that printing since 99 per cent of those copies go into the file.

3. Use plain sulphite instead of rag content tissue sheets for carbon copies. They get very little handling and most are retained only a few years.

4. Limit the operation of copying machines to skilled persons. The contents of the wastebaskets around copying machines operated by the unskilled are frequently full of "practice" copies.

5. If a large volume of one-time carbon forms are used, use the decollated carbons for typewriter carbons. Even if it serves for only one or two letters, it is cheaper than typewriter carbons. Some big insurance companies follow this procedure.

6. Remember that *one* kind of copying machine does not do the best job for all kinds of copies. There is no universal copier. All four basic processes may be needed, and this means different equipment for different needs: silver transfer, diazo, thermograph, and chemical transfer.

QUESTIONS FOR STUDY AND DISCUSSION

1. How can the tremendous growth in use of office reproduction services be explained? What possible advantages are suggested?—what disadvantages?

2. Does control of office reproduction seem to offer possibilities for controlling, or influencing, other activities which are carried on in an organization?—Explain.

3. For what reasons are centralized reproduction services ordinarily more efficient? Under what circumstances might decentralized arrangements be more suitable?

4. Distinguish "copying machines" from "duplicating machines." Compare the principal copying and duplicating devices now available, as summarized in the chapter. With so many types of equipment to choose from, how can one be sure of making the best choice for a given need? Are there certain general criteria which may aid in making the choice?

5. Examine the several illustrations of use of reproducing processes for different purposes. Are any conclusions warranted?

6. Consider the suggestions for improved administration of office reproduction services. Which seem to offer the most potential for improvement? Can you add other suggestions?

[8] Adapted from: "57 Ways to Save Money," *The Office*, November, 1961, pp. 149-50, 262.

7. A recent article in a business journal contained an estimate that some two billion dollars are being spent annually in business alone for office reproduction services. Another article estimates that this dollar volume will double by the year 1975. What challenges are suggested for management?

Case 17-1. The Mountain States Life Insurance Company

The office services manager is currently facing the problem of determining copy cost on Xerox 914 contrasted to an offset printing process operated in the company reproduction department. A heavy volume of requests is received by the office manager for varying number of copies of different documents. A majority of these requests are from the policy-writing division and are involved in the preparation of policies and related records.

A study was made to determine at what point the costs of copies from the Xerox 914 would compare with the offset printing process. Copy costs will vary according to whether they are made directly from the Xerox 914, typed originally on a duplimat, retyped from the original to a duplimat, or copied from the original to the duplimat on the Xerox 914. The cost to produce 10 copies in the examples shown below includes the supplies actually used in the operation and an hourly salary rate which includes all overhead expenses.

A. Copies prepared on the Xerox 914 are approximately 6¢ each. The cost for each copy remains the same regardless of volume.

B. Copies made on the offset press where original typing is on a duplimat cost approximately 5¢ each. The cost per copy will be considerably less as the volume increases.

C. If the original is retyped on the duplimat and copies are made from the offset press, each copy will cost approximately 8¢. The cost per copy will be considerably less as the volume increases.

D. If the duplimat is made from the Xerox 914 and the copies are run on the offset press in the Reproduction Department, the cost for each copy is approximately 5½¢. The cost per copy will be considerably less as the volume increases.

Problems and questions:

a. Discuss the general advantages of each of the four alternative duplicating processes.

b. What factors should be considered in choosing from among the alternatives, and how would you weight these factors to indicate their importance?

c. What action do you recommend that the office services manager now take?

18

FILING, RECORDS RETENTION, AND MICROFILMING

Dependence of management on files and records · Basic purposes and requirements for sound program · Objectives and policies · Organization for records management and filing · Filing systems, equipment, and supplies · Records retention · Transfer and destruction · Microfilming and information retrieval

---

Earlier chapters have dealt with management informational needs for making and carrying out decisions, and with the organization, systems, procedures, and methods required to fill these needs. A substantial section has been devoted to methods of collecting, processing, and communicating data. These methods both *create and use records* of wide variety and immense volume; in a broad sense, all of them can be regarded as falling within the realm of records management. They have not been specifically treated in this manner in this book because of the need for emphasis upon the positive contribution each makes to the informational needs of management and to the role played by each method in filling these needs.

Dependence of Management on Files and Records Storage

It is now essential to consider the vital dependence of all other data-handling methods upon the office "memory"—commonly referred to as its system of files and records storage. A small amount of reflection will indicate that, actually, each of the other methods constantly dips into this reservoir. Filing is treated last only because the completion of virtually every transaction is the act of storing information regarding it—information which may be used repeatedly, or which may never again see the light of day. (The term "never" is used advisedly; there is an element of permanence in the ceremony with which much material is deposited in file cabinets, one closely akin to that involved in burial rites.)

Filing and records systems, like other data handling methods and services, should be subjects of interest to everyone within an organization. Non-specialists as well as specialists should be concerned. They are the users of stored information, and should be generally familiar with problems and remedies involved—if only to be aware of needs, to seek the help of specialists when required, and to know where and how to get stored information when needed.

One of the best ways to appreciate the contribution made by the filing and records storage program is to attempt to conceive of a situation where *no* such program would exist. If no records were maintained of sales, purchases, credit, employee work history, equipment and other company assets, plans for products and services, or a multitude of other items, the situation would be chaotic, considering the limits of the human memory.

Almost as bad is a *poor* filing program—folders and file drawers bulging with mainly unused material, free access by anyone to the files, no control over material out of files, etc. Under such circumstances, locating a necessary item comes near to being an accident.

Basic Purposes

In contrast to examples such as those cited above, a good filing and records control program is one that stores, preserves, and provides, promptly, the documents actually needed by management and employees. Current transactions are adequately recorded; past experience is at management's fingertips.

Specifically, the basic purposes of such a program are those of *use* (present and future) and *protection* (chiefly legal). Both are important, but factors of use greatly outweigh legal considerations for the great majority of records; legal protection alone would probably justify only an extremely small portion of the records now maintained in the typical firm.

Another factor to be considered is the possibility of reducing costs in the filing and records control programs. E. J. Leahy, President of the National Records Management Council (an independent, non-profit organization) recently estimated that obsolete records, alone, are costing business firms in this country more than $300,000,000 annually.

Requirements for Sound Program

Key requirements for an effective and economical filing and records control program include the following:

1. Objectives and policies carefully formulated and clearly understood.
2. Organization suitable to needs, with responsibility clearly defined.
3. Filing systems, equipment, and supplies designed to meet needs.
4. Retention system which provides and applies a time-table to all documents, insuring that they will be retained while justified, and destroyed when no longer worth the cost in facilities and effort.

Special elements involved in the above basic requirements, but warranting separate consideration, are computer storage of information and microfilming.

Remaining sections of this chapter will be devoted to consideration of these topics.

Objectives and Policies

There is a special need for a clear statement of objectives and policies in the records management area because of the general use of records and files throughout an organization. There is also a need for central control and efficient administration.

To meet this need, many firms have prepared *records manuals* which lay out:

1. Basic purposes to be served by files and records storage.
2. Policies which apply to all files.
3. Responsibility for systems design and for actual administration.
4. Master index of all items stored, where they are kept, and by what methods they are indexed and filed.
5. Procedure for users to obtain and return materials.
6. Standards guiding selection of filing equipment and supplies.
7. Records retention program.

The general purposes of use and protection have already been discussed briefly. A given management should be as specific as possible in making clear the objectives sought and the relative importance attached to such elements as ready reference; legal proof of transactions, assets, liabilities, etc.; summarization and analysis of operating experience to guide future plans and decisions; retention of records for only as long as is fully justified for purposes of use and protection. Policy statements, then, will set forth positive rules of action which expand upon the objectives and provide guides for their implementation.

Organization for Records Management and Filing

Certain key organizational questions demand answers in any enterprise: Who should design filing systems? Who should administer actual files? Who should design and administer the records retention program? How can the desired level of coordination and standardization among departments be achieved?

Organizational arrangements to satisfy these requirements vary greatly from company to company. According to a survey conducted by the National Office Management Association, practices in 1300 companies vary, as follows:

> 39 per cent of the companies have formal records control programs; 51 per cent have informal programs; 10 per cent have no such programs at all.
>
> 35 per cent of those companies having formal programs have them administered by department heads, separately; 34 per cent have one executive in charge; 18 per cent have an executive group or committee in charge; 3 per cent use other officials; and 10 per cent did not report.[1]

Despite the wide variation in practice and the large portion of firms which have either informal programs or no programs at all, there seem to be compelling reasons for some degree of centralized control over records. The exact arrangement apparently does, and should, vary substantially from company to company.

In Chapter 3, the subject of *physical centralization* of files (actual storage in a central location) was considered, along with centralization of other office services. Advantages and disadvantages were noted, and the suggestion was made that the management of any given firm would be wise to consider those applicable to its own situation and determine what it wants most to accomplish. It was suggested, also, that almost never would a central file contain all of the stored documents of a firm; some would be retained in separate departments, often for valid reasons.

The key consideration here lies in the distinction between physical centralization and centralized control. Whether physical centralization of files is carried out to a high degree, or to a limited degree, or not at

---

[1] Charles E. Ginder, "Records Administration: A Report on a NOMA Survey," *The Office Executive*, March, 1961.

all, some measure of *central control of decentralized records* is likely to be necessary.

Many firms have established a position of *Records Administrator,* who usually reports to a top-ranking executive such as Administrative Vice-President or Controller; his responsibility is providing help to departmental executives in designing records systems and equipment, coordinating departmental records programs, minimizing duplication of records, maintaining a master index, and coordinating the records retention program. Some firms have given such an executive functional authority over some or all of these functions.

With or without the position of Records Administrator, a *Records Control Committee* is quite helpful. Such a committee usually consists of representatives of various departments who can bring their unique needs to the attention of the committee, facilitate coordination, and contribute to policy formulation. In a relatively small firm, they may handle the entire program. When volume and diversity of records seem to justify it, the committee plan seems to work better in conjunction with a full-time administrator who knows systems and equipment. The administrator should also be one who can take a general view of departmental requirements, be a "watchdog" with regard to duplicate records and inefficient methods, and take the lead in administering the retention program.

Filing Systems, Equipment, and Supplies

Much of the success of filing installations will depend upon the care with which systems and equipment are fitted to needs. A very brief description and analysis of these important tools will now be presented; excellent, detailed treatments are available elsewhere, if needed.[2] Four principal headings will be considered:

1. Methods of indexing
2. Supplies and equipment
3. Filing procedures
4. Systems design

Methods of indexing

Indexing refers to the manner of classifying items. In filing, the indexing scheme must be built into the original design of the system,

[2] An authoritative treatment from the management point of view is Harry Wylie, ed., *The Office Management Handbook* (New York: The Ronald Press Company, 1958). A more complete treatment of rules for filing is shown in M. K. Odell and E. P. Strong, *Records Management and Filing Operations* (New York: McGraw-Hill Book Company, Inc., 1947), pp. 133-172. Much excellent material on specific systems can be obtained from manufacturers of filing equipment and supplies.

then it must be applied currently in deciding where to file particular
documents.

There are two basic indexing methods (in terms of captions): *alphabetical* and *numerical.* Each has many variations, and it is common
experience to find different forms of both methods being used for varying
needs in the same firm. Figure 18-1 presents a summary of basic methods
and some of the more widely-used adaptations as discussed below.

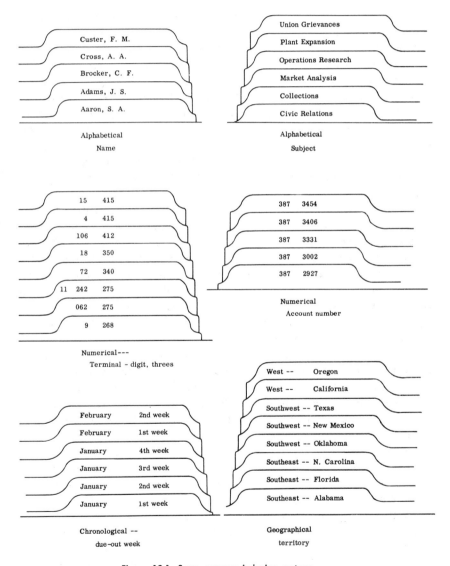

Figure 18-1. Some common indexing systems

Alphabetical filing is the most widely used method. File drawers or other containers are divided into alphabetical subdivisions, with guide cards or markers indicating the proper location for any given item to be filed or removed from the file. Arrangement may be by *name* of individual or organization, or by *subject*. Cross-indexing, with an item filed by one caption but cross-referenced by another, can be used where reference by either name or subject may be made frequently enough to justify this.

Numerical filing, in various forms, is also very widely used. In its "pure" form, numerical filing is most often used for materials which are numbered serially, such as orders, invoices, and checks; file guides or markers are arranged by numerical groupings, and individual items are filed in numerical sequence. The method is also widely used in assigning code numbers to customer accounts, insurance policies, or other subjects; basic filing is done according to these numbers, and alphabetical or another form of cross-referencing (usually card), is maintained where needed.

Adaptations and combinations of alphabetic and numeric methods are numerous and often ingenious. Alphabetic arrangements may start with a territorial breakdown of geographic regions—states and districts; then individual customer accounts are placed within the proper districts, either by name, subject, or code number. Numerical arrangements may involve *significant numbering* resembling the familiar Dewey Decimal system used in libraries, government agencies, and some business firms. *Mnemonic* arrangements include combinations of letters and numbers which will aid memory or association—such as PT-124 for a certain plastic tube carried in stock. *Phonetic* arrangements group names that sound alike but are spelled differently, through use of numerical coding; this method has proved useful where extensive name files are maintained and problems of definite identification may arise. The Social Security Administration is, undoubtedly, the largest single user of this system.

One adaptation of numerical filing that has special value for many purposes is *chronological* filing. Guides are arranged by days of the month, or other time series arrangement, and items are filed first by the date or time designation, then by either alphabetic or numerical classification. Chronological filing is useful in situations where material should be given attention on certain dates, such as follow-up on sales approaches, credit due dates, etc. An apt name often applied to this method is "tickler file."

Another significant adaptation of numerical filing is terminal digit filing. Terminal digit filing has been found especially useful in insurance companies, but has been used in motor vehicle registration and driver license files as well. With this method, numbers are read from *right to left,* and file groupings are by *pairs* of numbers. A battery of filing cabinets (any number) is arranged with outside captions on file drawers. These range from 00 for the first drawer to 99 for the last. Within each drawer, secondary guides are used; if the first drawer (or group of drawers) is designated 00, it would contain secondary guides, again ranging from 00 to 99. Then, if an item numbered 5 27 00 is to be filed, it would go to drawer 00, behind guide 27 within that drawer, either in consecutive order behind that guide or placed in the front of that group, depending upon whether volume and frequency of reference would justify the time necessary to place it in exact order.

Although at first slightly bewildering to one accustomed to thinking in terms of consecutive numbering, this approach is soon mastered and can produce highly beneficial results. Where new items are numbered serially, the terminal digit method spreads file items over the entire battery of files for each 100 new items, rather than having all new items congested at the end of the files. This spreads work evenly, making it possible to assign each clerk responsibility for a section of the files (if there are five clerks, the first may handle all items with terminal digits 00 through 19, for example). Thus, the work load will be well balanced and clerks will not be in each other's way. Other proven advantages are increased speed, fewer misfiles, simpler sorting, greater flexibility, and unlimited expansion.

The diversity of indexing methods and the physical dispersion of files throughout an organization point strongly to the need for a *master index.* Such an index shows where all documents are stored and how they are indexed; thus, it serves as an inventory of all files maintained, and as a control medium helpful in reducing duplication of filed material. It is frequently expanded to include retention schedules for material of different types (to be discussed shortly). It is comparable to a library card catalog, except that it usually shows only types of classifications of material, not specific captions. Maintenance of a master index may be one of the major responsibilities of—and justifications for—a Records Administrator within the organization structure.

Supplies and equipment

Of vital importance in effective filing and records management are supplies and equipment. These will now be considered very briefly; the general references on filing cited earlier contain detailed descriptions, and many other sources of specific information are available.

Filing supplies include cards, folders, guides, labels, and a large variety of other items. *Cards* used in filing are actually printed forms, in most cases, with material condensed and adapted to the card format. Personnel, inventory, sales, vendor, and credit records, as well as many other types of basic information, have been successfully adapted to cards. In some cases, these make use of visible indexing; in others, they are indexed by use of standard guides.

Folders are justified when original correspondence or other documents are to be retained—either for future reference requirements or to avoid the step of summarizing and transferring to card forms. Folders are available in a wide variety of styles and materials—with tabs in different positions, triple-scoring at the bottom for expansion, provision for adjustable signals attached to tabs for spotlighting significant information, folders suspended on metal frames to keep papers neat and orderly, and many other features designed to fill special needs.

Guides are of particular importance for guiding the eye in finding and filing papers. They also support folders and facilitate orderliness of files. Guides are available in all standard drawer sizes; in manila stock, pressboard, and even heavier materials; in series consisting of primary, secondary, and further breakdowns of material; with tabs in different positions, either vertical or slanted; with a wide array of other features which adapt them to unique needs. Closely related are *labels* which identify individual guides, folders, and drawers; these are obtainable in printed or blank form, gummed or plain, fixed or movable, and in various colors for indicating specific classifications, thus facilitating speed and accuracy.

Equipment for filing includes cabinets, trays, shelves, stools, stands, sorter equipment, and other items—available in a wide range of types and sizes to accommodate virtually every filing need. Only a brief treatment of some of the more important types will be attempted here.

Vertical-file cabinets are the most widely-used containers of office records. They are available in different sizes and combinations, notably letter-size and legal-size in width, and single-drawer to six-drawer in depth (with four drawers still most common). The standard drawer in a four-drawer cabinet holds about 5,000 sheets of paper, 300 medium-weight folders, and 25 guides. With space at a premium, many firms are changing to five-drawer cabinets which are no larger than standard four-drawer cabinets. Metal cabinets are now greatly in the majority for active files; light metal, fiberboard, or other inexpensive material are frequently used for transfer files.

Open-shelf files are growing in popularity for filing both active and inactive records. Their major advantage is that of economy of space; savings of up to 50 per cent of floor space are common since space needed for opening file drawers is eliminated and shelves may be extended vertically to as many as eight or more. Open-shelf arrangements for active files are limited chiefly to those away from public view; they are especially well adapted to inactive files. Special guides and folders with adaptations of most of the tab and label arrangements common in cabinet filing are available. As the "fight for inner space" mounts in intensity, there seems little doubt that open-shelf filing will continue to be increasingly in demand.

Visible-index files warrant special consideration by alert management. Visible strips or tabs with small signals attached (usually plastic or celluloid) can display surprisingly large amounts of information, speed location of material, and spotlight items needing attention. Signals are made to represent classifications, dates, and other significant information, through both color and position. Most common is the horizontal-tray type, illustrated in Figure 18-2, containing card records to which postings

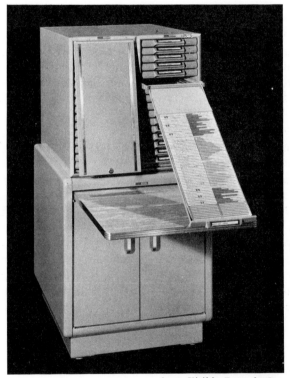

Acme Visible Records, Inc.

Figure 18-2. Acme horizontal-tray type visible-record file

or other entries can be made without removing the card. Other types merely present indexing information in a form for quick reference, and include panel boards, stands, and racks.

Other types of files are highly useful for special needs. Motorized card files which may store many thousands of cards, any one of which can be brought into view almost instantaneously by means of an electrical control; rotary (or wheel-type) files for card records needed for frequent reference; reciprocating files which slide backward and forward for an operator who works from a seated position—are only a few of the special designs. Special-purpose equipment such as the types just mentioned may yield highly rewarding results when fulfilling specific needs.

Basic filing procedure

The effectiveness of actual file operations depends greatly upon having a carefully worked-out procedure for processing current records. The basic procedure usually consists of the following steps:

1. Read the record over quickly to determine the proper filing classification.

2. Mark the record according to its classification. This may be done by using a colored pencil and encircling certain key words or numbers on the record, or by stamping or writing an appropriate notation on the record. At this point, a cross-reference sheet should be prepared, if considered necessary. Also, if the record will require follow-up on a later date, a follow-up slip should be made out and filed by date in a tickler file.

3. Sort the records into various classifications to facilitate filing.

4. File the records under the proper classification. The newest addition to the file should always be placed on top or at the front of other papers in a file.

5. Make a record of withdrawals from the file by inserting in place of the withdrawal record an "out card," which bears a notation concerning the date of the withdrawal and the name of the person who has the record.

The final step mentioned—that of recording withdrawals and controlling material out of files—may justify special attention in some situations, dependent upon the need to know where particular material is and to insure its prompt return. Specific requisitioning of material, formal charge-out, follow-up through use of a tickler file or by a color system for "out guides," and other steps may be justified to meet special needs.

Systems design

It should be clear at this point that a filing system consists of many seemingly "little" things which in combination make a highly significant contribution to managerial and operating efficiency. Since files are the "memory" of the firm, it is obviously important that this reservoir of information be capable of preserving necessary information and of producing it accurately and quickly when required.

The design of a particular filing system is usually a joint effort of qualified company personnel (often including methods or systems analysts) and representatives of firms which offer supplies and equipment. When a problem of major importance justifies, independent consulting service may be used.

As indicated in earlier sections, the chief elements of the systems to be designed for specific needs include (1) the method or combination of methods of indexing, (2) suitable equipment and supplies, chosen from the wide range of types available, and (3) the basic procedure for filing and finding material.

Records Retention

Previous sections have emphasized the role of files as the "office memory" and the need for systematic storage of records. The basic purposes of the records management program were stated as those of *use* and *protection* of necessary records. The positive contribution which good records can make will be the first and most important consideration in any sound program.

Yet the mounting tide of paper work, or the "paper octopus" (as some have referred to it), confronts management with serious challenges. One of the most important challenges is the need for establishing a records retention program which applies a *timetable* to all documents; this would insure that they will be retained while justified and destroyed when no longer worth their cost in human effort and physical facilities.

Of most pressing concern is the factor of *costs*. Other problems are interference with rapid location of needed records (clerks having to search through a lot of inactive or dead items to find those they need); unjustified demands upon clerical help in the face of growing shortages; the use of large amounts of space which become scarcer and more costly each year.

The retention schedule

The heart of an effective records retention program is a suitable retention schedule, tailored to the needs of the firm. Such a schedule will specify for each class of document the following minimum items of information:

1. Its *active* life, during which it should be readily accessible in original form.

2. Its *inactive* life, during which it should be retained but probably *transferred* to less costly space and equipment, or *microfilmed*.

3. Its *destruction,* when further retention is justified neither by use nor law.

Studies of the National Records Management Council have indicated that, for a typical business, less than 10 per cent of records must be kept permanently; about 20 per cent must be retained currently and automatically retired when no longer current; approximately 30 per cent should be stored in inactive, less costly areas; from 35 to 40 per cent should be destroyed.

Many routine items, obviously, should not be filed at all. Many others should be retained only for very short periods, such as much of the supporting detail for basic records that will be retained. Other material may be justified for somewhat longer periods but may not justify choice space. With other material, legal considerations may govern—for example, records involving accounts receivable, accounts payable and notes. Contracts may be kept inactive for a relatively short period after the transaction is completed, then kept in storage files until requirements of the Statutes of Limitations have been met.

Striking developments in microfilming equipment are revolutionizing many techniques of records storage and information retrieval, and they alone would probably justify a fresh look at the entire records program within many firms. Certain of these developments will be considered in a separate section.

The work of developing a retention schedule should usually begin with a complete *inventory* of records. Then should come the development of a *schedule of suggested retention periods* which specifies for each class of documents the active life, inactive life, microfilming where desirable, and time for destruction. Where filed materials are segregated in a manner which allows them to be treated as a group, special notations on items themselves are not likely to be needed; otherwise, records employees may be instructed to stamp or mark a permanent record with a *P*, a record of current but not permanent value with a *C,* and a record of only temporary value with a *T*. Or, a system of notations that is even more specific as to time for retention may be used. A record retention schedule of a large insurance company is shown in Figure 18-3. Note that this retention schedule indicates the method of disposal in addition to the other information.

Transfer and Destruction

Closely related to the retention schedule is the need for an effective plan for transfer of materials when they reach the inactive stage, and a plan for destruction when they reach the point where they can be "purged" without incurring loss that is greater than the cost of retaining them.

The principal methods of transfer are:

(1) *Periodic*—which requires movement of materials from active files to in-

May 7, 1963

SECTION – RECORDS AND REPORTS
SUBJECT – RECORD RETENTION SCHEDULE –
ADMINISTRATIVE SERVICES

This procedure indicates the required retention period for the records created and accumulated by Administrative Services. The Superintendent of Administrative Services is responsible for the execution of the Administrative Services records program.

Since Administrative Services seeks the cooperation of other departments in the destruction of obsolete and unnecessary records, it is essential that we conduct our records management program efficiently.

Listed below is the information necessary to implement a records management program for those records maintained by the Administrative Services Department.

FORM NUMBER	TITLE OF RECORD	RETENTION PERIOD	METHOD OF DISPOSAL	DESTROY
G 133	Purchase Order	Current Yr.+ 2 Yrs.	Complete*	Yearly
G 4266	Requisition	Current Yr.+ 2 Yrs.	Intact**	Yearly
G 4324	Weekly Automobile Operating Report and Expense Statement	Current Yr.+ 2 Yrs. After Disposal of Car	Intact	Yearly
G 4724	Shipping Requisition	Current Yr.+ 2 Yrs.	Intact	Yearly
G 4726	Postage Survey Slips	6 Months	Intact	Semi–Annually
G 4747	Automobile Registration Card	Permanent		
G 4758	Company Car Memo	Current Yr.+ 2 Yrs. After Disposal of Car	Intact	Yearly
G 4766	Weekly Report of Misdirected Mail	1 Year	Intact	Yearly
G 4787	Receiving Register	1 Year	Intact	Yearly
G 4958	Low Stock Notice	Current Yr.+ 1 Yr.	Intact	Yearly
G 4979	Detail Budget Estimate Report 4th Qt.	Permanent		
	Detail Budget Estimate Report 1st, 2nd and 3rd Quarter	3 Months	Complete	Quarterly
	Budget Notes and Work Papers	Current Yr.+ 5 Yrs.	Complete	Yearly
G 4987	Post Index Cover Card	Current Yr.+ 5 Yrs.	Intact	Yearly
G 4988	Post Index Insert Sheet	Current Yr.+ 5 Yrs.	Intact	Yearly
G 5002	Maintenance Call Slips	Current Yr.+ 1 Yr.	Intact	Yearly
G 5012	Requisition for Material from Storage Files	Current Yr.+ 1 Yr.	Intact	Yearly
G 5201	Housekeeping Inspection Report	Current Yr.+ 1 Yr.	Intact	Yearly
G 5215	Request for Quotation	Current Yr.+ 5 Yrs.	Complete	Yearly
G 5217	Annual Request Form (Consolidated Purchase)	Current Yr.+ 1 Yr.	Intact	Yearly
G 5219	Housekeeping Frequency Record	Current Yr.+ 2 Yrs.	Intact	Yearly
G 5260	Preventive Maintenance Post Index Cover Card	Until Item or Major Parts Replaced	Intact	When Obsolete
G 5261	Preventive Manintenance Post Index Inspection Card	Unitl Item or Major Parts Replaced	Intact	When Obsolete

* "Complete" indicates that the item is to be destroyed completely by shredding or burning.
** "Intact" indicates that the item is to be discarded as waste.

Recordak Corporation

Figure 18-3. Illustration of records retention schedule used by one large insurance firm. Only partial schedule is shown.

active files at specific intervals (once or twice a year, or other). At the established interval, either *all* material is moved to inactive files (which will usually need to be nearby for reference to the more recent items), or *all material older* than an established age or date will be thus transferred.

(2) *Perpetual*—which usually involves movement of records of particular cases, projects, or jobs from active to inactive files when the cases are completed; thus, some transferring is going on nearly all the time.

COMMUNICATIONS AND RECORDS MANAGEMENT

Transfer equipment, as discussed previously, can consist of light-weight, inexpensive containers or open shelves. Fewer guides are needed; if reference is extremely infrequent, folders may be dispensed with to save space. Low-value storage areas in the same building may be used, or less costly storage space in a location some distance away may be used—the need for access, the availability of space, and the cost of space in alternative locations are usually the chief determinants.

Destruction or culling of dead records should then follow on schedule. It is interesting to note that some managements define a "dead record" *not* as one that is completely valueless, but rather as one that no longer has enough value to justify retaining it. They are willing to take a calculated risk that there will be calls for some of the material. Unless legally required to keep particular material, they may dispose of it, expecting that savings will out-weigh potential losses.

> When first instituting systematic records management programs, firms often find that they have accumulated vast stores of unneeded records. One prominent firm destroyed 120 carloads of miscellaneous records, and transferred 300 carloads to a five-story archives building. Another found that its accumulation of old papers would make a stack fifty-one times as high as the Empire State Building. Still another threw out over half its files, sold about one hundred tons of waste paper, and estimated an annual savings of $26,000 from reclaimed office space and equipment.

While great savings may result from culling and disposing of unnecessary records, it is important to note that far greater savings can be achieved where the culling is done *before* the material is filed in the first place. The most appropriate depository for a large portion of material continues to be a circular receptacle commonly known as "File 13."

Microfilming and Information Retrieval

The dual process of placing records in storage and retrieving information from stored records has been altered greatly by the development of microfilming. This process, under which records are photographed at high speed on narrow safety film, permits records to be reduced so that they require little space, and to be retained indefinitely. When someone wishes to see a record that has been microfilmed, it is necessary only to pull the film reel on which the document appears, place the film on a "reader," and then, following the microfilm code system, locate the record on the film. If a copy of the record is needed, a photographic device on the reader will permit a copy to be made.

Basic equipment includes cameras (available for film sizes from 8 mm. to 70 mm.), readers for projecting images, photoprinting attachments, and cabinets for storing film. Cameras and readers are available which offer a wide range of capacities and special features (such as copy material accommodated, film width, reduction ratio, size and clarity of image, photocopy attachments available, and others). Cameras are either *rotary*, reproducing single-sheet material at high speeds, or *planetary*, usually slower but more versatile. Readers are either *opaque* (projecting the image on an opaque surface which reflects it), or *translucent* (projecting onto a mirror and through a translucent screen). Prices of both cameras and readers vary with capabilities desired, ranging from small, portable units to high-capacity units which combine virtually all microfilming functions. There is a distinct trend toward more compactness in design.

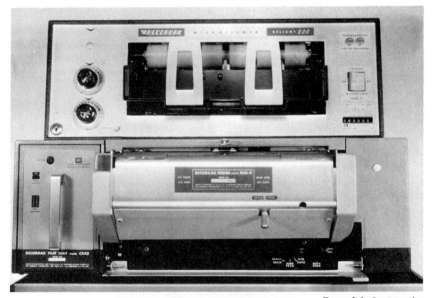

Recordak Corporation

Figure 18-4. A highly versatile Recordak microfilmer camera

Figure 18-4 shows a camera unit which provides speed, versatility, and compactness. Figure 18-5 shows a reader-printer which projects an 11″ by 11″ image and produces a facsimile print quickly and economically.

Microfilming offers many advantages; these can be grouped into the categories of records storage and information retrieval.

Records storage can be aided in the following principal ways:

1. Space-saving. This is the greatest single advantage. Microfilming permits more than 99 per cent saving in space. Documents may be reduced in size as much as 40 to 1; as many as 5,000 letters of standard size may be placed upon a 100-foot roll of 16 mm film; and as many as 600 rolls of film may be filed in

a cabinet 3 feet high. Such savings in space mean direct cost reduction of substantial proportions, and they free space for more productive use.

2. Legal protection. Filmed records are admissible in most law courts as primary evidence.

3. Records preservation and safety. The passage of time causes less deterioration of film than would occur with original paper documents. Copies of important records can be made and stored in a small space away from the original location to protect against fire, loss, theft, and bombings. Some late models do double filming, making one copy for active use and one for security.

Information retrieval is the area of most rapid advancement in microfilming today, despite the substantial advantages in records storage cited above. The increasingly close relationship of data processing and microfilming has been considered briefly in the chapters on data processing. These developments and other new uses being found for microfilming promise a bright future for the technique.

Some present and prospective uses of microfilming in the information retrieval field are:

1. Rapid "look-up." Even with present-day equipment of standard designs, a large volume of information, stored on as many rolls of film as are needed, is accessible to the extent that an individual item of information (document or

Figure 18-5. A Recordak microfilm reader-printer. In addition to reading the microfilm, hard-copy prints can be made by simply pressing a button.

other) may be projected in a matter of seconds. As microfilming systems are developed to the point of linkage with high-speed data processing machines, through photomemory and random access to millions of miniaturized images, one of the most significant breakthroughs in automation and systems will be achieved.

2. Duplication. Rapid, exact printing can be done from film with existing equipment. Prints are not yet quite as legible as originals, and some colored papers are rather difficult to reproduce; but usable copies can nearly always be obtained and improvements are coming rapidly. Checks, sales slips, stock catalog items, library materials, and many other items are currently being copied from microfilm.

3. Communication. Wartime V-mail was an example of the use of microfilm for low-cost, rapid transportation of information in quantity. A typical current use is transmission of branch office reports on film to the home office. With further development of microfilm-data processing combinations, and with rapid extension of long-range data transmission systems, the use of mail, telegraph, teletype, and other traditional means of communication seem likely to be increasingly limited in scope.

The potentialities of microfilm-data handling combinations in the years ahead are so tremendous that they defy the imagination. As of this writing, IBM is developing an information retrieval system for the Central Intelligence Agency which is expected to retrieve any one of 99 million documents from a storage center in five seconds; many businesses, having much less complex problems of information retrieval, are utilizing smaller microfilm systems for business records, but the principles are the same.[3] Research of virtually all types, both pure and applied—scientific, medical, legal, economic, social, educational, business, and other—seems likely to be revolutionized by developments just over the horizon.

QUESTIONS FOR STUDY AND DISCUSSION

1. Just what purposes are served by files in an enterprise? In the light of these purposes, who should participate in the design of filing systems? Should the same person or persons administer current filing operations?

2. Suppose that you have just been appointed chief administrative officer to establish and maintain a company filing and records retention system for a small independent chain of grocery stores. Discuss the major steps and operations you would consider in establishing such a system.

3. "The actual operation of filing in business is fairly simple and straightforward. For example, you just put the B's behind the A's, then the C's behind the B's, and so on. But the design and management of a filing system are quite complicated and are neglected." Appraise this statement carefully.

4. Describe the basic indexing methods and indicate when each is likely to be

[3] "The Decision That Can't Wait," *Dun's Review and Modern Industry*, September, 1961.

appropriate. What trends are apparent in filing supplies and equipment and for what reasons are they developing?

5. Explain the concept of terminal digit filing. What are its special advantages? Its limitations?

6. Relate a records retention program to the concept of information retrieval as discussed in Chapter 13. What advantages do you see in establishing extensive information retrieval programs to store business records? What disadvantages?

7. In actual practice a records retention program is often administered separately from a filing system, records retention being sometimes referred to as the company "archives." Suggest probable reasons for such separation of managerial control. How can it be justified?

8. Two opposing points of view may be stated as follows:

"A good reason for maintaining large files of records is that the value of information is not determinable until the information is needed and is not available." In contrast, "Hanging on to a record because somebody may need it someday simply loads the files with papers that will probably never be looked at. In records retention as in other areas of business, a calculated risk must be taken." Which of these concepts do you support? Why?

9. The use of microfilm for records retention has been, so far at least, a tremendous aid for overloaded files and crowded storage rooms. Discuss the long-range effects of microfilm techniques on records retention and information retrieval concepts in general. What limitations do you see, if any?

10. Do you feel that a college course should be offered in the area of records management for those students who are majoring in administrative or office management? Why? If not, suggest several methods by which this information and knowledge could be best obtained.

Case 18-1. Some Variations in Filing Practice

One prominent firm for many years has followed the practice of returning nearly all letters received, along with its replies to them. It retains items that are pending, places these in "suspense" files, and disposes of these just as soon as they can be settled, rather than filing them permanently. It also retains unusually important items, but holds these to a very small portion of total items received. The management justifies these practices on the basis that the savings thus realized far more than offset costs which may result from occasional items which may come up again in the future—and it follows a very liberal policy in adjusting most items of the latter sort.

Another firm, which receives a great many inquiries, follows the practice of having the proper person reply by making marginal notations directly on the inquiry, then returning a photocopy of the letter thus "answered" to the inquirer and filing the original.

Problems and questions:

Appraise the effects of each of these practices upon (a) the firm, and (b) the customers or patrons of the firm. Under what conditions, if any, do you believe that either practice could be justified?

Case 18-2. The Safeway Fire Insurance Company

Until recently, the policy records of this company were filed in folders arranged alphabetically by the name of the agent servicing the territory involved, then numerically within the folder for the agent. A 4 x 6 card file for all policies served as a numerical cross index so any policy could be located if the agent's name was not known.

This system made it possible for an underwriter or other person needing access to a particular agent's file to find the folder quickly in the alphabetical arrangement, although he then had to thumb through all policies within the agent's folder to find the name of the desired policyholder. This process became increasingly cumbersome as the number of policies increased, and the process of refiling likewise became more time-consuming.

The following changes were made: The card index was rearranged to provide a grouping first by agent in alphabetical order, then by policy number under each agent—so underwriters and others could quickly find any given policy number, cards being easier to manipulate than folders. A terminal digit system was then set up for storage of the basic policy records. To the present, only the last four numbers are considered in grouping policies into folders; thus all ending in the number 9362 would be placed in the same folder, and those ending in 9363 would be in the following folder. No effort is made to keep preceding digits in strict numerical order; seldom are more than fifteen or twenty policies in the same folder, and the exact policy number (from among those ending in 9362 or any other set of terminal digits) can be spotted quickly.

Each clerk is assigned a certain number of file cabinets, and the number series are arranged horizontally (the parallel drawer in the cabinet to the right containing terminal numbers immediately following those to the left).

A comparison of results obtained with the terminal digit system and the former system indicated that basic policy records could be filed (or refiled) in about one-eighth the time required in the former alphabetic-numeric combination file.

Problems and questions:

a. What advantages other than the saving of time in filing basic policy records should result through use of the terminal digit system?

b. What problems, or possible problems, can you envision with the new system, and how serious are they? Does the change in systems seem to be clearly justified?

Case 18-3. A Filing Problem

A certain large insurance company does no charging out of records taken from files, on the premise that any given item (whether a new policy application, a transfer or reinstatement, a request for change in coverage, an inquiry, or other item) is likely to pass through the hands of a fairly large number of people while it is being processed, and that maintaining an up-to-date follow-up of every item would be impossible. Instead, they prepare a "hunt list" which includes every item asked for by anyone during a twenty-four hour period ending at noon each day; and immediately after noon, one or more file clerks make the rounds of the office and attempt to find all such items.

Problems and questions:

What do you think of the "hunt list" approach in this situation?—in other types of situations? Can you suggest possible means of making a charge-out system work here? Can you suggest ways of getting best results from the "hunt list" if this procedure is to be continued?

VI

PHYSICAL FACILITIES

All of the physical facilities of an enterprise (other than equipment directly used) are *methods* for accomplishing work.

At stake here, as with other methods, are effectiveness and economy. The tremendous expansion of enterprises has created problems in securing sufficient space, desirable space, and space that can be justified financially. Challenging problems arise in deciding whether to build or lease, in the selection and maintenance of building services, in planning layout of equipment for available floor space, and related problems. The general working environment for employees will have substantial influence upon morale and productivity.

We shall, therefore, now consider office layout and space management, the working environment (lighting, air conditioning, sound conditioning, and color design), and the office location and building.

19

OFFICE LAYOUT
AND SPACE MANAGEMENT

---

*Objectives and principles of office layout · Tools for planning
the office layout · Steps in laying out the office · Maximum
utilization of space · Moving the office · New developments
in layout*

The "fight for inner space" being waged by managements almost everywhere was mentioned briefly in the introduction to Part VI. The high cost of space, demands for more desirable space, rapid growth of enterprises, and frequent adjustments required, cause layout and space management to become high-priority factors for most managements—critical factors for many.

Office layout may be defined as the *arrangement of equipment within available floor space.* Space management may be thought of as *providing space which will yield maximum productivity and effectiveness at minimum cost.*

Office layout is important because of its effects on work flow, on economy of floor space and equipment, on employee comfort and satisfaction, and on impressions given to visitors. Layout planning can be carried out most effectively if incorporated in the planning of a new building. Opportunities are provided at such a time for careful study of space requirements. Close cooperation between the building architect and the executives of the firm can insure the availability of space in types and amounts that will facilitate performance of the work of the organization.

The more common problem, however, is that of having to lay out office facilities in a building which was not tailored to fit the needs of the particular firm. Space is often limited, and units must be fitted into such space as is available.

In both situations, the basic approach to planning layout is much the same. It is wise to begin with a clear picture of objectives, to refer freely to the general principles of layout planning available, to consider carefully the particular space needs of the firm, and to follow a sound step-by-step approach in actually planning the layout. These phases will now be considered in the sequence presented.

Objectives of Office Layout

The general objectives of office layout include:

1. Effective work flow.
2. Space that is ample and well-utilized.
3. Employee comfort and satisfaction.
4. Ease of supervision.
5. Favorable impression on customers and visitors.
6. Ample flexibility for varying needs.
7. Balanced capacity of equipment and personnel at each stage in work flow.

The management of a given firm must determine which of these objectives, or others, is most important to the success of the operation. Each of the objectives mentioned will now be discussed briefly.

Of special importance is the objective of good work flow. Equipment should be arranged so that work follows a straight line flow as nearly as possible, so that delays are held to a minimum. In the absence of a planned work flow it is not unusual to find work flowing in all directions —forward, backward, and criss-crossing previous routes—with the result that papers are handled excessively and that personnel must engage in needless travel. A typical example is in the handling of orders. If the work flow is effective, the order will originate in the mail room and will then flow directly to the inventory control office, the pricing unit, the order typing department, and to such other units as must deal with the order before it is completed. If the work flow is ineffective, the order may travel unnecessarily great distances, retrace its path, criss-cross previous routes, and be interrupted at various points. Such a contrast is afforded by Figure 19-1.

Certain tests of work flow have been found effective:

1. Check backtracking and criss-crossing by charting layout and tracing work flow.

2. Make process charts of dominant procedures involved in the floor area

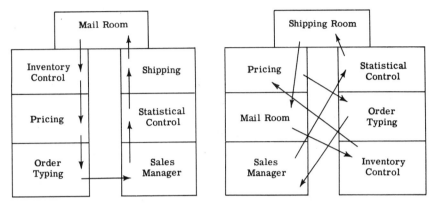

Figure 19-1. (Left), an office layout in which a straight line flow is utilized. This arrangement permits the work order to follow a direct and orderly route through the office. (Right), an ineffective office layout in which the work order does not follow an orderly pattern of flow. As a result, the possibility of delay and confusion is increased

under study, checking particularly the distances traveled and the time of delays between operations. An alternative approach may be timing an entire procedure, then timing productive steps in the procedure (necessary operations and checking steps) and finding the difference.

3. Check bottlenecks by measuring total productive capacity of workers and equipment assigned to each operation in a procedure, then compare. A simple "neck chart," such as that presented below for an invoicing procedure, can show out-of-balance conditions, and demonstrate that overall speed is limited by the operation allotted the smallest capacity.

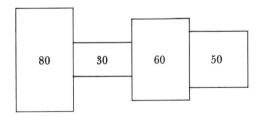

Typing:	Extending:	Checking:	Mailing:
80 units	30 units	60 units	50 units
(4 clerks,	(2 clerks,	(3 clerks,	(2 clerks,
20 units ea.)	15 units ea.)	20 units ea.)	25 units ea.)

4. Observe whether some workers are constantly pressed while others frequently run out of work.

5. Observe whether a very large percentage of workers are constantly on their

feet. An average of ten per cent is considered a suitable maximum for efficiency in many offices.

Space should be adequate and well-suited to job and employee needs. Cost and work flow considerations dictate that available space should also be well-utilized. Standards recommended for different classifications of employees will be presented in a later section of this chapter.

Employee comfort and satisfaction may be strongly influenced by layout. Uncrowded conditions, convenience to employee service facilities, and suitable location with reference to light sources are some of the needs in this category.

Ease of supervision may be affected by the placement of the supervisor with reference to employees, by the concentration or dispersion of the employees, by accessibility to related departments, and by other layout factors.

A favorable impression on customers and visitors is of extreme importance where outsiders see part or all of the office area. Note in Figure 19-2 how much more efficient and attractive an office is made by an improved layout and use of more modern equipment.

Flexibility should be sufficient to permit readily altering the layout when justified by work needs. Fluctuations in volume, changes in emphasis in customer service, and normal growth are some of the reasons why flexibility is needed.

Principles of Office Layout

By striving to achieve the basic objectives that have just been discussed, office executives can make a major contribution to operating efficiency. Of much help may be more detailed statements of layout principles; these sum up the experiences of many firms and provide specific guides for the layout planner. The chief value of such a statement of principles lies in its use as a checklist in connection with an actual situation. A statement of selected principles follows.

1. Work should flow continuously forward, as nearly as possible in a straight line.

2. Departments and divisions which have similar and related functions should be placed near each other to reduce travel time.

3. Central service groups, such as stenographic pools, file rooms, and tabulating units should be conveniently located near the departments and the employees who use them.

4. Furniture and equipment should be arranged in straight line symmetry, with any angular placement of desks and chairs reserved for supervisory personnel.

5. Space allowances should be adequate for work needs and employee comfort.

6. Furniture and equipment of uniform size make for greater flexibility and more uniform appearance.

7. Aisles should be wide enough so that persons walking will not brush against the desks of employees. There should be an unobstructed aisle from the desk area to the drinking fountain, rest rooms, etc. Clear access to exits and fire escapes should be provided for safety reasons.

8. Employees ordinarily should face in the same direction, with supervisors placed to the rear of work groups.

9. Desks should be arranged so that no employee is compelled to face an objectionable light source. Where possible, illumination should strike the employee's work area from above and slightly behind the employee.

10. Units which utilize noisy equipment, such as tabulating machines, may need to be partitioned off to avoid disturbing other units.

11. Employees whose work requires close concentration may justify partial or full-length partitions.

12. Units which have much contact with the public should be so located as to be easily accessible to the public without disturbing other departments.

13. Large, rectangular blocks of space facilitate work flow and provide greater flexibility.

14. Keep from public view departments in which work is necessarily untidy.

15. Provide suitable light and air conditioning for all employees.

16. Locate necessary private offices where they interfere least.

17. Consider personnel and equipment needs, both present and future.

Laying Out the Office—Who and When

Who should handle the work of laying out the office? If the firm has an office manager, he will probably coordinate layout plans for the organization and he may do a large part of the detailed planning. If there is a planning or methods department, the detailed work of layout planning will probably be delegated to one or more staff specialists who are available to help general executives and department heads when needed. If there are no specialists in office management, then the work of layout planning may be delegated to some person who has the necessary interest and time for doing justice to this important undertaking. In any event, it is a good idea to discuss present and proposed plans with department heads and employees involved. This may produce some excellent suggestions, and it is almost certain to result in a higher degree of cooperation than would be attainable otherwise.

When should the layout of the office be studied? Whenever a situation is seen which calls for a change in layout. Specifically, the layout plan should be studied when there are changes in procedures, increases or

General American Life Insurance Company

Figure 19-2. The office in the upper photograph presents a somewhat cluttered, poorly arranged appearance. The same office in the lower photograph appears attractive and efficient as a result of an improved layout and the use of more modern equipment.

decreases in the number of personnel required, or inadequacies in current space.

Changes in procedure are a signal to review the office layout because of the interdependence of procedures and office arrangement. For example, if it is decided to install an accounting machine which will change various billing and posting procedures in the office, it will be necessary to rearrange the office to locate the machine properly and to take care of the changes in work assignment of the employees affected by the installation of the machine.

Increases and decreases in personnel in given units are a signal to review the office layout, since the plan of layout is largely governed by the number of personnel in the office. For example, if it is decided to transfer office reproduction functions to a central organization it will be necessary to rearrange the office to absorb space formerly occupied by the reproduction equipment and personnel.

Inadequacy of current space is also a cue to review the office layout. It may be found that the inadequacy stems from a poor arrangement which can be easily changed, or it may be found that there is simply insufficient space provided for the office and that a request for additional space should be made to management.

In addition, every office should follow a plan of reviewing the layout of the office periodically. This review, which should be made *every two or three years,* is important. As a matter of fact, it is a widely-held belief that an office layout that has not been reviewed for three years is probably wrong. The office is a dynamic and changing entity; the progressive office makes changes periodically and as they are needed in order to meet changing requirements.

Checking with top management

Before undertaking a major layout program, the office manager should consult with top management and reach an agreement on standards to be observed in allocating space to different levels of employees. Such standards will prove to be a useful guide in planning, and will provide a basis for uniformity in space assignments throughout the organization.

It is also a good idea to learn from top management what plans exist for expanding or contracting the size of the office. For example, it is well to know if there is any plan under consideration to decentralize any of the current functions of the office or to transfer to the office from elsewhere any new functions not now being performed. In addition, it is well to find out as much as can be learned concerning the volume of anticipated sales and service operations, since the volume of work will determine the number of employees needed and the size of the space required. If, for example, a firm is undertaking a vigorous advertising campaign which is expected to increase sales by one-third, an attempt should be made to convert anticipated sales into equivalent space requirements for the new personnel who will be needed to handle these orders.

An agreement should also be reached concerning such matters as desk sizes to be provided employees; types and sizes of file cabinets; whether partial, movable partitions should be used instead of full, permanent partitions in setting up corridors and private offices; and whether modular and sectional furniture should be used instead of standard styles of office furniture.

Tools for Planning the Office Layout

In many organizations, the chief layout tool is a rough sketch showing the shape and size of floor space available. While the rough sketch may be sufficient in some cases, additional tools will permit more precise planning of the layout. In many cases it will be useful to have a blueprint of the available area, a drawing of the floor space made to scale, and templates or models of such physical properties as desks, chairs, and files. These tools for planning the office layout are discussed briefly in the following paragraphs.

A blueprint of the available area

This will be useful in providing accurate measurements and in determining the exact location of facilities in the space under consideration. The blueprint will also provide information which will be needed relating to the location of electrical outlets and electrical and telephone wiring.

A drawing of the floor space, made to scale

The layout should be plotted on this drawing, preferably on the basis of one-quarter inch to the foot. In addition, the location of rest rooms, stairways, halls, windows, electrical outlets, door swings, heating units, and all permanent partitions should be shown. Reference should be made to the blueprint to insure accuracy in all measurements. This drawing provides a graphic view of the office area and its facilities and permits as effective a study of the entire areas as if one were to walk through the space itself. See Figure 19-3 for a scale drawing of an office layout.

Templates or models of physical items to be used in the space

Templates are paper shapes, cut to scale size, which represent the space required by each item of furniture and equipment in the office. Templates can be purchased in packets or can be made by hand. Models are simply three-dimensional figures of wood or plastic which represent desks, files,

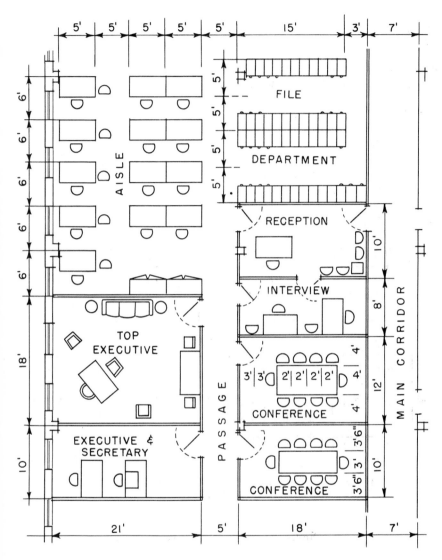

Figure 19-3. A typical scale drawing of an office layout

and other pieces of equipment. These models, which may be purchased in sizes to scale, are valuable in expediting the planning of the layout. The use of models and templates makes it possible to envision exactly how a given plan of office layout will appear. A sheet of office layout templates drawn to scale for different-sized desks and file cabinets is shown in Figure 19-4.

Flow process charts

Flow process charts were treated in some detail in Chapter 9. They are extremely helpful in layout planning, especially in focusing attention on distance traveled and time of delays.

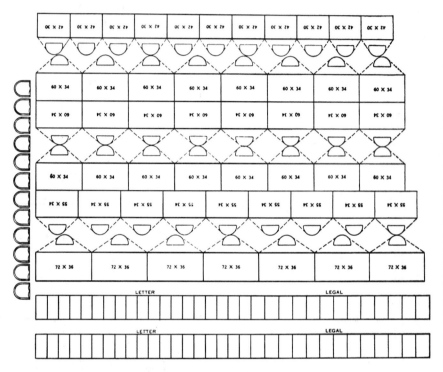

Figure 19-4. A sheet of office layout templates drawn to scale for different-sized desks and file cabinets

Steps in Laying Out the Office

It is important that the person designated to handle the laying out of an office familiarize himself with the plan of organization and the principal procedures. He should also make certain that work simplification possibilities have been explored so that current procedures are as well planned and as efficient as possible. Thereafter, he will assemble the necessary layout tools and will follow these steps in planning the office layout:

1. Discuss with each supervisor and department head present and future space needs, and the direction and plan of work flow on all operations in the

office. This is important not only to provide the individual with a closer view of work operations but also to fulfill the requirement that supervisors and managerial personnel be consulted whenever changes or innovations are contemplated.

2. Refer to the blueprint, and then prepare a drawing to scale of the space under consideration, showing the location of such items as windows, doors, and columns.

3. Formulate a tentative plan of office layout by arranging templates or models on the scale drawing which has been made. Observe the principles of good layout (see earlier section on principles of office layout). Any compromising on certain principles should be dependent on the relative importance to the firm of different objectives. It may take a considerable amount of ingenuity and time to arrange and rearrange the templates or models until the right plan of layout is found. Get final approval from all personnel directly affected.

4. Identify all items of equipment on the layout plan, then label pieces of equipment to correspond, and make the actual move at a time when confusion will be minimized.

Space requirements in office layout

Standards as to space needs have been mentioned repeatedly in earlier sections of this chapter, and they will now be considered in more specific terms. Space requirements vary considerably, depending on such factors as the size of furniture and equipment items to be used in the space, the shape of the floor space available, and the location of permanent facilities such as elevators, stairways, windows, rest rooms, and exits. The following list of suggested space allowances will be found helpful in most situations:

> 75-85 square feet for a clerical worker
> 75 square feet for a chief clerk
> 100 square feet for a supervisor
> 130 square feet for a junior executive
> 200 square feet for a first-level executive
> 310 square feet for a department head
> 400 square feet for a top executive
> 5-foot width for main aisles
> 4-foot width for secondary aisles

The amount of space allocated to employees under a schedule of this kind may be broken down in this manner:

> 75 square feet for a clerical worker
> 54 in. desk and chair (54 × 70 in.) = 26.25 sq. ft.
> Aisle (18 × 70 in.)   8.75 sq. ft.
> Additional space for files
>   and related items   40.00 sq. ft.
> Total   75.00 sq. ft.

These figures, of course, are merely guides; what will be best for any given office will depend on the circumstances. As is apparent, an important factor in any program of space utilization concerns the size of desks which are used, and the way in which desks and files are arranged.

Desks come in many different sizes. For the most part, desks 54 by 32 inches are provided for clerical workers, desks 60 by 34 inches are provided for higher-level employees, and desks 66 by 36 inches and 76 by 36 inches are provided for top-level executives. It is essential in planning a new office to make a decision concerning the desk sizes which will be used throughout the organization for different levels of employees.

Desk arrangement is an important factor in computing space requirements. As shown in Figure 19-5, considerably more space is required if each desk is centered and surrounded by aisle space than if desks are grouped end to end in units of two and three desks.

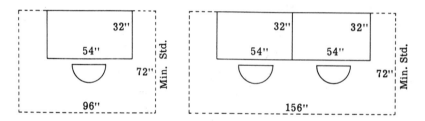

Figure 19-5. Note in the figure at the left that the clerical desk arranged singly requires forty-eight square feet of space. However, as shown in the figure to the right, two clerical desks of the same size arranged end to end require only seventy-eight square feet of space—which is about twenty per cent less space than would be required by two desks arranged singly.

Private offices

The extent to which private offices are provided to employees will depend on the wishes and judgment of management. Each case may have to be dealt with separately. In some organizations, a degree of privacy is created by giving managerial personnel a low railing around their desks. However, such an arrangement does not provide the individual with the freedom from distraction and noise which is a chief objective of a private office. Among the questions which may be asked in deciding whether or not to give an employee a private office are the following:

1. Does he have a position of sufficient prestige to justify his having a private office?

2. Does his work require a level of concentration which can best be provided by a private office?

3. Would his work interfere with the work of others?

4. Does his work involve activities of a confidential nature or does he frequently confer with others on matters which can best be handled in the privacy of a private office?

There seems little question that private offices should be provided for most top-level executives. However, it is well to weigh carefully the disadvantages of private offices:

1. Supervisory personnel do not have the close contact that is possible in an open area.

2. More floor space is consumed.

3. Smooth and uninterrupted work flow is harder to achieve.

4. Problems of air conditioning and lighting are complicated.

5. Private offices are more expensive to build and maintain.

For such reasons as these, there is a widespread trend to provide large, open areas for office operations, and to place first-line supervisors—and sometimes higher-level executives such as superintendents and department heads—with the employees supervised. Occasional need for complete privacy can be met satisfactorily through provision of one or more conference rooms. A trend toward smaller private offices is also evident.

Where limited privacy is desired for supervisory personnel or for employees whose work requires close concentration, dwarfed partitions or modular units can do an excellent job of combining privacy with economy of space. Equipment of this type will be described in the following section.

Maximum Utilization of Space

Maximum utilization of office space has become an increasingly important criterion for management, in view of rising costs of office space. Increased clerical production partly compensates for increased clerical costs; thus, any contribution which better space management can make to clerical productivity will be reflected directly.

The average rental rates for office space have been rising about 5% each year for the past several years. Factors affecting these increased costs are improved working conditions—lighting, air conditioning, and decorating—and increased construction costs. Increased structural costs are necessitated in part by the larger and heavier machines used in many offices today. Most data processing installations require specially reinforced flooring, as well as special air conditioning and conduits for cables.

As a general rule of thumb, office layout planning is half simple arithmetic and half judgment on the part of management. The arithmetic portion comes from multiplying the suggested space allowances (see Space Requirements in Office Layout on page 351) times the number of people in each category. Judgment comes in the physical arrangement of fixtures and furniture, and in designing the environment of the office layout. J. J. Murphy has developed five basic principles for maximum utilization of office space to guide the judgment portion of office layout design. These principles are combined below with some principles developed by Duffy, Inc., a New York space planning and designing organization.[1]

1. Provide adequate lighting. Fifty to eighty footcandles of illumination are suggested to reduce the premium placed on space adjacent to windows. The Illuminating Engineering Society is advocating more light all around in the office, averaging about three times as much as present acceptable standards. The Society contends that the increased illumination significantly reduces employee fatigue.

2. Provide acoustical soundproofing. This is essential to keep the noise level within acceptable limits, particularly in view of the increased usage of office machines. A large insurance company installed acoustical materials in its main office and the noise level dropped about 15%. There were resulting decreases in the number of typing errors and in turnover and absenteeism.

3. Provide adequate ventilation. Too often air conditioning and air treatment become inadequate as the size of the work force grows. Special efforts are necessary to maintain sufficient air treatment for maximum employee efficiency.

4. Make minimum use of permanent and semi-permanent partitions. This permits maximum flexibility in design, does not take up so much floor space, and does not hinder lighting and air conditioning design. In fact, as many walls and doors as possible should be eliminated, for a door utilizes about 18 square feet of office space, and a wall occupies about six inches of office space.

5. Maximize the use of modular units of furniture. This helps to minimize aisle and work space and simultaneously provides privacy for many employees. Modular units are discussed later in this chapter.

6. Utilize the "upper space." This involves using the areas above file cabinets for storage shelves. This space can, in many cases, eliminate one or more private rooms which are used for storage and miscellaneous activities. Some estimates show that over $1,000 per year are saved in rental alone for a private office 12 x 15 feet.

7. Utilize space near the elevators and entrances for reception and display. Reception service can be just as effective if established adjacent to the entrance rather than back within the working area of the office.

8. Eliminate private rooms for secretaries. Secretaries can conveniently and

---

[1] J. J. Murphy, "How Much Space and Where?" *Office Executive*, October, 1961, p. 19; and "More Space in the Same Space," *Office Executive*, October, 1961, p. 26.

comfortably be placed, either individually or in small groups, in foyers or corridors outside executive offices, with substantial savings in floor space.

9. Send dead or inactive files to a private warehouse for storage. Company-owned and operated warehouses are quite expensive, averaging over $5 per square foot.

10. Emphasize flexibility. Perhaps the most important factor in utilizing office space is flexibility. The changing nature and structure of the office—its enlarged staff, its increased business activities—plus continuing developments in automation and electronics, and a rise in the number of long-term leases all have required flexible facilities that can be adapted to these changes. New modular designs allow almost infinite layout changes by merely shifting a partition—dwarfed or full size. Flexibility can also be achieved through renting office space with provisions for growth or decrease, as the need may be.

There are no panaceas for office layout. Consideration of the simple guides mentioned above, however, should provide maximum productivity with existing office space. One never knows until the necessary changes and revised layouts are attempted—but in view of the increasing space costs, the need for attention to space efficiency is greatly emphasized. A considerable amount of simple judgment is necessary to achieve effective and maximum use of office space.

Moving the Office

Most office organizations move at some time during their existence. This can be a painful and disturbing experience—but it need not be if planned correctly. A well planned office move has several significant elements. These are briefly discussed below.

1. Inform the employees and customers well in advance of the move. Employees naturally resist change and they are particularly inclined to be dubious about moving to a new location. Questions which need answering are: what floor will they be working on; what type of decorating and furnishings; whether there are windows in the new location; what sort of eating facilities, parking for private cars and public transportation; where other departments will be located in the new layout (so that they can keep up with friends), and many others. The employees should be made as familiar as possible with the new location prior to the move. Small group meetings are excellent means for executives to answer such questions and to personally explain the move. The employee's interests regarding the move should be developed and maintained through effective use of company publications and personnel letters. Customers should also be included in the education program and invited to visit the new facilities. Some confusion will reign during

the move, but adequate informational efforts will minimize this confusion.

2. The details of the new layout should be studied carefully. Departmental assignments should be firmly established, as well as unit locations, individual desks, and miscellaneous equipment. The layout principles and layout tools discussed previously in this chapter are essential for proper layout planning. If possible, the employees should be shown the new layout, with all individual locations indicated. Detail plans should include the location of telephone and electrical needs. Allowance should be made for future space requirements—15 per cent is a generally accepted guide. In layout planning, place the heavy equipment and files along outside walls or over structural cross-members to avoid overloading the floor.

3. Schedule the move over a weekend or during some slack period in the work volume. Productivity will be low for a short time after the move while the employees become adjusted to their new surroundings and to the new requirements of work flow imposed by the new and different arrangements of organizational units, but it will improve as employees become adjusted to the more modern or spacious environment.

4. Tag and number all items of furniture, fixtures, and equipment. Each piece of property should be tagged to identify the unit and department to which it belongs and its exact location in the new layout. Different colored tags can be used for each room, department, or floor. The schedule of the move can then be planned around the identification tags, i.e., first to be moved is department A 1, red tags, floor __, room __, going to the __ floor, room __. This allows an orderly move in a planned, controlled sequence. The equipment going to the most distant corner should be moved first, and that going next to the entrance, last.

5. Certain employees should be selected, made familiar with the details of the move, and assigned definite responsibilities at both the old and new locations. These employees can provide valuable assistance in coordinating the move, helping to direct the traffic, and answering numerous questions.

6. Obtain the necessary support and help from the local traffic department to facilitate loading and unloading of the trucks.

New Developments in Layout

Movable partitions

Many modern office buildings use movable partitions almost exclusively in setting up private offices. These partitions—made of metal, wood, plastic, or glass—provide attractive separations between offices and give executives the prestige and privacy they require. These partitions can be easily and inexpensively moved as required. Movable partitions can be obtained which are sound-conditioned and which provide the occupants complete privacy. The cost is much less than that of the usual permanent partitions.

Dwarfed partitions

Movable, dwarfed partitions, from 4 to 6 feet and higher in height, provide employees with most of the benefits of privacy and prestige without the attendant disadvantages of complete partitions. When low partitions are used the offices can be heated, ventilated, and lighted using the standard equipment; separate lighting fixtures and heating ducts are unnecessary. Dwarfed partitions often have a glass railing at the top. See Figure 19-6 for diagrams showing different basic arrangements of movable, free-standing partitions in private and semi-private offices.

Modular units

One of the most significant recent developments in the field of office layout is that of modular units. These units ordinarily consist of a combined desk and file cabinet with a working surface on top of each, and dwarfed, movable partitions. These units effectively combine privacy, easy access to working materials, and economy of space. See Figure 19-7 for an example of a modular office unit. Figure 19-8 shows how modular units can actually provide greater working area and a more efficient arrangement for the employee.

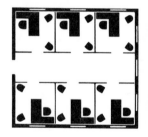 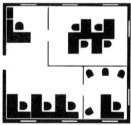 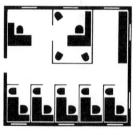

Globe-Wernicke Company

(A)	(B)	(C)
In this arrangement six private executive offices are made possible by the use of free-standing partitions	This layout shows how an executive office and a four-station clerical group can be separated from other departments by means of free-standing partitions	Free-standing partition panels held in position by floor connectors make possible a series of five private offices and an executive office

Figure 19-6. Illustrations demonstrating the use of free-standing, movable partitions

Globe-Wernicke Company

Figure 19-7. This shows an all-steel modular office unit, which provides a larger working area for each employee, and also provides an element of privacy between desks

Unitizing is also a popular new device for saving space and at the same time providing employees an element of privacy. This represents merely an extension of the principle of the modular unit, as shown in Figure 19-9.

Mistakes in Layout

Certain types of errors in office layout seem to be so common that they justify special mention:

1. There is a tendency to venerate the original layout. Even though work requirements may change drastically and even where the office may have moved to entirely new quarters, the old plan of layout may be continued simply because of precedent.

2. There is still a tendency to plan offices in more or less permanent form, segregating the various offices and corridors with heavy, built-in partitions. As

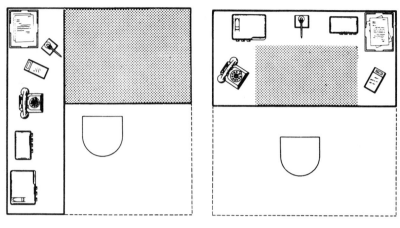

Globe-Wernicke Company

Figure 19-8. The dark areas shown in these two drawings represent the amount of work area provided by the conventional and the modular desk plans. (Left), with the conventional desk, regardless of how large the top may be, the greater portion is taken up by the necessary desk top working accessories—desk tray, dictating machine, calendar pad, desk set, telephone, and intercom. What remains is the desk top working surface—a small area. This lack of adequate working surface causes papers to pile up and results in inefficiency, a disorderly desk top, and insufficient space to arrange work or hold conferences. (Right), the modular plan eliminates this condition. All the necessary working accessories are placed on the auxiliary surface, leaving the desk top a clear, free-working area that is 100 per cent usable.

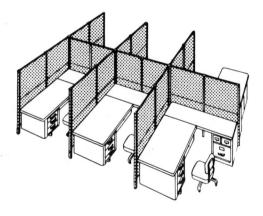

Figure 19-9. This illustration shows the unitizing of six desks in such a way as to conserve space and provide employees with an element of privacy.

a consequence it is difficult and expensive to make changes even if management wants to make them.

3. There is a tendency for the more vocal executives to be given more space for their departments and employees than is given other departments. Final decisions concerning allocations of space and layout should be made by someone having an overall viewpoint and having sufficient authority to insure fair and equitable allocations of space.

QUESTIONS FOR STUDY AND DISCUSSION

1. Have you ever worked or visited in an office where everything was badly congested, desks and other equipment jammed up, barely enough aisle space for people to pass, material stacked on top of file cabinets, etc.? If so, what were your impressions regarding productivity and morale? Do people become accustomed to such conditions to the point where they have little if any influence?

2. Office layout and effective management of space are receiving much more attention from management than in former years. Suggest major reasons for this trend. What do you predict for the future?

3. Which of the basic objectives of layout seem *most* important? Justify your answer.

4. At what times or on what occasions should office layout be studied? Why?

5. What is a "neck chart"? How may it be used in testing work flow? What other tests of work flow may be helpful, and how may each contribute? If flow process charts are used, what aspects of work flow may they point up for special study?

6. The prevailing school of thought with reference to space allowances has been to follow a scale which consistently allows more space in proportion to higher job class—ranging from clerical worker to top executive. Some persons have recently suggested that there should be only a very general relationship of this sort, and that a sounder basis is that of determining the actual space required for efficient performance on each job whatever the level. Evaluate each of these points of view. Do you see any merit in the latter?—any difficulties in putting it into practice?

7. Based upon study of layout principles and of recent developments in equipment and building design, suggest what seem to you to be management's best means of coping with each of the following problems:

    a. Prestige of employees and executives

    b. Privacy needed

    c. Flexibility in layout

    d. Maximum utilization of office space

8. If given an assignment of planning an office layout (or participating in such a project), what steps in sequence would you follow?

9. Moving an office is a costly and time-consuming process. Most firms experience one or more moves, however. Outline a plan for such a move which would minimize confusion and interruption of regular operations.

Case 19-1. Appraisal of a General Layout Pattern

Study the layout pattern that is sketched in Fig. 19-10, and answer the questions which follow it:

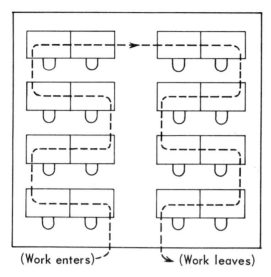

(Work enters) ↗   ↘ (Work leaves)

Figure 19-10.

Problems and questions:

In the light of layout principles studied and other considerations which you believe to be pertinent:

a. What probable advantages would be realized by this arrangement?

b. What probable disadvantages can you see in the arrangement indicated?

c. What kinds of work (general) might best lend themselves to such an arrangement, and what problems if any would have to be worked out in order to achieve successful results?

Case 19-2. Grayson Sales Corporation

The Grayson Sales Corporation employs over 600 salesmen throughout the country. Each month these salesmen send in their expense vouchers, together with related reports for their sales activity for that week. The payment section of the accounting department in the home office in Chicago has the responsibility of checking and verifying the pay and voucher data, writing the checks, and sending them to the salesmen. Since a payroll procedure is involved, the company is interested in providing as efficient service as possible so as not to delay the issuance of pay drafts to the salesmen. The following operations, in sequence, are currently handled by the payment section.

1. Incoming mail from all salesmen is sorted in the mail room and all salesmen's travel vouchers for the week are sent to the voucher clerk.

2. The voucher clerk checks the figures turned in by each salesman against the sales record that has been obtained from another section.

It is the responsibility of the voucher clerk to determine that all of the data are correct. If duplicate copies of the material are needed, the material is sent to the duplicating clerk.

3. The duplication clerk makes all requested duplicates and forwards all material to the pay records clerk.

4. The pay records clerk takes from the file the pay record of each salesman due payment at this time, attaches the salesman's expense account ledger, and forwards the material to the check writing clerk.

5. The check writing clerk verifies that all figures are correct and then prepares a company payroll check.

6. These checks together with all materials are forwarded to the itinerary clerk who checks to see that there are sufficient copies of travel forms. If duplicates are needed, all material is sent back to the duplication clerk and the requested copies are made.

7. All material is then forwarded to the payment chief who makes a final verification of all figures and signs the checks. The payment checks are then forwarded to the mail room and the pay records to the posting department, to be returned later for filing.

8. The mail room encloses the pay draft and the proper related data in an envelope and mails it to the salesman.

Problems and questions:

a. The office layout of the payment section is presented in Figure 19-11. Make a rough sketch of the present layout and trace the work flow using a dotted or colored line.

b. Prepare a list of improvements which should be incorporated to provide better work operations.

c. Draw a scaled revision of this layout incorporating any suggestions that you feel will improve the efficiency of the office.

Case 19-3. Pennsylvania Roadways Bureau

This bureau, located in a space 24 by 40 feet, is concerned with checking and keeping up to date all official road maps in the state. The work comes to the bureau in the form of reports from county and district road supervisors advising the bureau of road changes which are planned, in progress, or completed. To date, no one had ever taken the time to study the arrangement of the bureau and to determine a better plan of layout. Recently, the chief asked the head of the planning department to design a more efficient layout of the offices. See Fig. 19-12 for present layout.

The work in the bureau follows this pattern. Incoming mail enters the mail room where it is opened and time-stamped and then taken to the

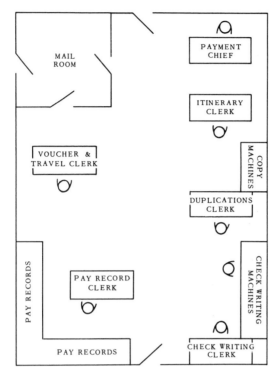

Figure 19-11. Diagram showing layout of the Payments Section of the Accounting
Department of a sales concern

secretary of the assistant chief. She makes two basic sorts: all proposals for
road changes go to the planning department, and all mail covering road
changes which have been completed go to the secretary of the chief. All
other mail goes to the assistant chief.

When the secretary of the chief receives the mail covering completed
road changes, she goes to the records office where she pulls the file on each
case. Then she gives this mail and the corresponding files to the chief for
review and final approval. After approval, the chief's secretary takes this
mail to the art department where actual drawings of completed road
changes are made on maps. The art department then gives completed
drawings to the mail room for wrapping and mailing to the printer.

Problem:

The only partitions which are permanent are those around the mail room and
the records office. Place a thin piece of paper over the drawing of the office and
trace the outline of the bureau and of the two permanent offices. Then, using a
ruler, change the plan of layout for the bureau so that there will be a straight
line flow of work based on the information provided. The only procedural

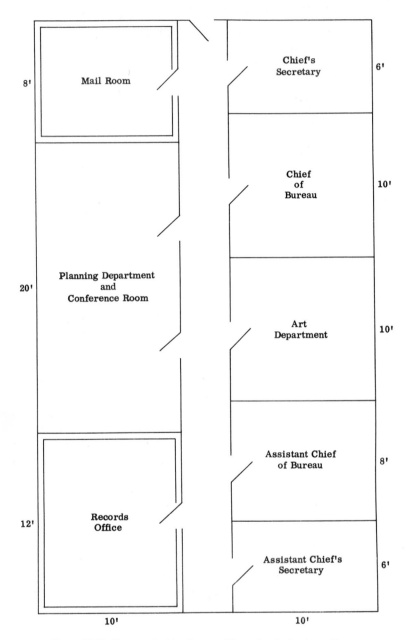

Figure 19-12. Diagram showing layout of Pennsylvania Roadways Bureau

change to be made concerns the secretary of the assistant chief, who has been given responsibility for the records office and will hereafter be the only person who will be permitted to take records from the office. Each office in the revised plan should have the same amount of space it had in the original drawing, except for the planning department which is being reduced in length from twenty feet to fourteen feet, and the assistant chief who, since he sees so many callers, is having his office enlarged in length from eight feet to fourteen feet.

After preparing your revised layout, write a brief paragraph supporting the revision you have made.

Case 19-4. Ed Billings

Ed Billings is superintendent of an office department which employs some 35 people. Ed has been with the firm for about 20 years, and he is respected for his technical knowledge. He expects a high level of performance from his people, and he is frank in letting them know this.

Ed has had his desk placed directly in the front and center of the general office in which all of the 35 employees are located; and he says that he prefers to have it this way because he can keep an eye on operations and always know what is going on, also that it discourages excessive talking and moving about. His employees, particularly the newer ones, frequently talk among themselves about how Ed's "glaring at them" makes them nervous and keeps them on edge.

Problems and questions:

Appraise the pros and cons of the layout arrangement involved here, considering any factors which may be involved in addition to those mentioned. Do you feel that the advantages achieved by Ed Billings by this arrangement probably outweigh the disadvantages?

20

THE WORKING
ENVIRONMENT

---

*Office lighting · Color conditioning · Air conditioning · Sound
conditioning · Music conditioning · Office furnishings*

The developments in technology
which have been given so much stress in earlier chapters have been
matched by improvements in the working environment in which today's
office worker and executive spend most of their waking hours. Just as
there has been a revolution in much of the equipment available for administrative use during the past decade, there has been a revolution in
both the *interiors* and the *exteriors* of office buildings.

The design of the office building itself is shaped largely by the work
that goes on inside it, and by consideration for the people who will work
or visit there. Physical factors which determine human comfort and convenience include:

> Lighting
> Color conditioning
> Air conditioning
> Sound conditioning
> Furnishings

These factors will be considered briefly before specific study of building design and location.

Office Lighting

Probably the best way to grasp the importance of lighting to office
management is to realize that virtually every office task is a *seeing* task.

The role of office activity in supplying information needed by management is carried out mainly through the preparation, storage, and use of records. Visual needs in working with records are greater than those in any other general class of work.

Specific values or benefits of good lighting in the office include:

1. Increased productivity (although it is difficult to measure exactly how much)
2. Better work quality
3. Reduction in eyestrain and mental fatigue
4. Better employee morale
5. Higher prestige for the firm

Lighting is measured in footcandles. One footcandle is the amount of direct light which is found one foot distant from a standard candle.

Increased productivity

A change from poor lighting conditions to good is almost certain to result in some increase in the rate of work output.

The Public Buildings Service of the federal government has conducted some interesting tests in an office of the Bureau of the Census. From a 30 footcandle, indirect incandescent installation, a change was made to a 50 footcandle, fluorescent installation with light and colorful finishes for ceiling and walls. Even though conditions had been better than those existing in many offices before the change, an increase of 3.5 per cent in productivity was then noted. In a Bureau of Internal Revenue office, an increase in illumination from 10 footcandles of poor light to 50 footcandles of good light, combined with new, light-colored wall finishes, was found to produce a 5.5 per cent increase in over-all production.[1]

Just how much of the improvement may be attributed to lighting in such situations is never easy to determine because so many other factors can influence output at the same time as the lighting. Changes in the state of morale of employees may alter output, and morale obviously is affected by a great many factors.[2] The gaining of additional experience by given personnel, changes in the nature of work being processed or of methods used, and variations in work load are other factors that may be

[1] R. L. Oetting, "Surveys Show Better Lighting Raises Office Output," *American Business,* January, 1953.

[2] A portion of the famed Hawthorne experiments involved varying the lighting intensity and then checking the production which resulted from the different intensities. It was concluded that employee attitude and interest have such a strong influence on productivity that these factors may largely offset the effects of changes in lighting or in other environmental factors.

hard to control in any comparison of *before* and *after* lighting installations.

But even though precise effects of lighting on productivity are difficult to determine, the experimental data available, the laboratory research of lighting equipment manufacturers and engineering societies, and the experiences of thousands of firms with productivity after modernization of lighting add up to very convincing evidence that a real relationship exists.

Improved quality of work

Accuracy and neatness of office work can be improved appreciably by bringing light up to accepted standards. Where visual needs are not met, errors are more frequent—probably due in part to inability to see with sufficient exactness in inferior light and in part to eyestrain and fatigue which hamper normal seeing ability.

Reduction in eyestrain and mental fatigue

Working at office tasks for prolonged periods under poor light causes eyestrain and may cause eyesight defects to develop or to be aggravated. More energy must be expended, also, and this leads to increased fatigue.

Better employee morale

Improved morale will result when employees feel that management is interested in their well-being, and when the working atmosphere is pleasant. Good lighting and good use of color which must accompany good lighting will do much toward creating such an atmosphere.

Good employee morale, in turn, has many advantages—higher productivity, reduced turnover, and lowered absenteeism are especially notable. *Also,* higher-grade applicants can be attracted.

Higher company prestige

An attractive and efficient lighting installation makes a favorable impression on visitors of all types who call at the firm. It adds to the general reputation of the firm for progressiveness and efficiency of operation.

Factors to be controlled

The factors which must be controlled if the values of good lighting just discussed are to be realized may be considered broadly under two headings: *quantity* and *quality.* A background in the field of illuminating engineering would be required for complete technical understanding of these factors. While the typical office executive neither possesses nor needs any such degree of understanding, he should have at least a

measure of familiarity with principal problems met and sources of help
available in meeting them.

The *quantity,* or intensity, of light is perhaps its most familiar characteristic. Having sufficient light is of tremendous importance in all
seeing tasks. Some tasks obviously require much more light than others.

Differences in vision requirements and differences in amounts actually
being provided should be measured rather than ignored or estimated.
The practical approach to the problem of determining lighting needs
is that of measuring the amount of light being provided through use of
a light meter and comparing this amount with the standard amount
recommended by one of the associations that have devoted a great
amount of research to lighting needs. The number of footcandles being
provided in a certain spot in the office may be read directly from the dial
of the meter. Such a meter (see Figure 20-1) can be purchased inexpensively; the local power company will usually furnish without charge a
representative who will check the quantity of light currently being
provided.

General Electric Company

**Figure 20-1. A pocket-size light meter, which will measure a range of from one
to one hundred footcandles**

The two associations that have done the most with establishing and
publicizing recommended standards are the *Illuminating Engineering
Society* and the *American Standards Association.* The general summary
of recommended values of illumination which is published by the Illuminating Engineering Society is reproduced in Figure 20-2. It should
be emphasized that these are minimum standards and that they are
based upon the assumption of good cleaning and maintenance which
will sustain intensity at the levels suggested. These standards have increased greatly over the recommendations of the Society made just a
few years earlier. This increase is probably attributable in part to improved control of quality of light (reduction of glare, etc.) which makes

more quantity usable. Many installations are now using 150-300 foot-candles. This tremendous lighting level produces a great deal of heat, which is now being utilized in heating the buildings in winter, resulting in lower heating costs. During the winter, the heat from the lights can be redistributed through the ventilating system. During the summer months, the heat is vented outside either through the use of water circulating through the luminaires or by using the ventilating system. Waste air is circulated around and past the fixtures. This procedure eliminates heat, resulting in increased economy of the air conditioning system. Luminous ceilings provide maximum effectiveness of these procedures.

Significant research on intensity and other lighting features is being carried on constantly by leading manufacturers of lighting equipment, and lighting consultants from these firms are available for help with unusual problems. Most ordinary lighting situations can be handled adequately by a reputable local supplier.

Just as important a factor as quantity of light is that of *quality*. More employee complaints probably are caused by defective quality than quantity; many complaints of insufficient light can be traced to quality deficiencies.[3]

Good-quality light is light that is relatively free from glare and that is diffused evenly about the seeing area. Brightness should be relatively uniform rather than varying greatly in different portions of the area. Shadows should be minimized, although it is impossible to eliminate them entirely.

Glare is of two types—direct and reflected. Direct glare is that produced directly by a sharply-contrasting light source, either natural (sunlight) or artificial, within the field of vision. Direct glare from the sun can be minimized by placing little if any dependence upon sunlight, and either reducing window space, using a type of glass that will deflect the rays of the sun, or using Venetian blinds or screens. Direct glare from artificial light sources can be minimized by avoidance of fixtures that are too bright, too numerous, or too low, and by avoidance of dark backgrounds which accentuate the brightness of the light fixtures. Certain comfort controls that can give further help are shields or louvers which remove the light source from the employee's view, or use of a secondary surface to transmit the light—such as the ceiling in indirect systems or the transmitting panels in luminous ceilings. Continuous-row fixtures, such as those frequently used with fluorescent units, are effective in avoiding the clutter of many individual units.[4]

Reflected glare occurs when light strikes a bright or a polished reflect-

[3] R. L. Oetting, "How You Can Eliminate Lighting Complaints," *American Business*, November, 1952.
[4] *Ibid.*

Recommended Illumination Levels	
Type of Office or Work	Footcandles on Task *
Cartography, designing, detailed drafting	200
Accounting, auditing, tabulating, bookkeeping business machine operation, reading poor reproductions, rough layout drafting	150
Regular office work, reading good reproductions, reading or transcribing handwriting in hard pencil or on poor paper. Active filing, index references, mail sorting, critical visual tasks in conference rooms	100
Reading or transcribing handwriting in ink or medium pencil on good quality paper, intermittent filing	70
Reading high contrast or well-printed material, tasks and areas not involving critical or prolonged seeing such as conferring, interviewing, inactive files and washrooms	30
Corridors, elevators, escalators, stairways	20 **

* Minimum on task at any time.
** Or not less than ⅕ the level in adjacent areas.

Illuminating Engineering Society, New York

Figure 20-2. A summary of recommended standards for office illumination

ing surface—walls, desk tops, machines, or others. The reflection factor, or reflecting capacity, of any surface depends upon its color and finish. Walls and furnishings, according to a noted color consultant, should have a reflection factor of between 40 and 60 per cent, ceilings 75 to 80 per cent.[5] This means use of one or a combination of light colors for walls and furnishings such as light shades of green, blue, gray, tan, cream, or yellow. Ceilings can be white with a dull finish or they may have a light color tint. For office machines and other equipment, the lighter shades of gray, green, and tan are rapidly replacing the old olive green and black colors; they reflect more light and blend into their surroundings. Shiny metal trim is being eliminated, and dull-finish keys on office machines are becoming common.

The choice and planning of lighting installations

Lighting may be direct or semi-direct, with all or most of the light coming directly from the light source to objects in the lighted area.

[5] Fabor Birren, quoted in "Light and Color Control," *The Integrated Office,* Management Magazines, Inc., 141 E. 44th St., New York 17, N.Y.

Or it may be indirect or semi-indirect, with all or most of the light reflected from the ceiling and diffused evenly about the room.

Sources are chiefly either incandescent or fluorescent. A large majority of new installations are fluorescent; chief advantages are less glare, less heat, lower current consumption, and chance for choice of colors. Figure 20-3 illustrates a modern, well-illuminated office area.

Union Carbide Corporation

Figure 20-3. A modern office illustrating recessed, diffused fluorescent lighting

Most office lighting in the newer installations is provided in uniform amounts throughout a given room or work area. In special cases, local lighting for a job that has special visual requirements may be justified, but in such cases the general lighting in the background should be sufficient to avoid glare.

The choice of the best general system and the selection and placement of lighting fixtures are jobs for experts. Suitable help may usually be secured from suppliers of lighting equipment. For special lighting problems, or for working out the master plan of a large installation, consulting engineers who specialize in the lighting field are available.

Lighting maintenance

An increasingly common practice in offices and other work areas is that of group replacement of light bulbs on a regularly-scheduled basis.

This is wise. Lamps usually lose 10 to 25 per cent of their efficiency before they go out, and the resulting dimness can cause the amount provided to fall below recommended standards. The labor of replacing bulbs is greatly reduced when all in a work area can be replaced at one time, or when alternate bulbs are replaced on separate schedules to keep intensity more uniform. The inconvenience to employees can be minimized since the work can be done after working hours.

Cleaning of light fixtures needs to be done according to a suitable schedule, also, since both the efficiency and appearance of fixtures are influenced greatly. The same is true for office windows, which are a source for a large percentage of the daytime illumination in many organizations.

Color Conditioning

The technique of color dynamics is one which interests most of us. Human beings are fascinated by color. This is because there is a dynamic quality in color which activates and stimulates the emotions. Further, the use of color opens many possibilities for making offices pleasing and attractive to the eye. As with lighting and other factors in the working environment, it is not possible to attribute specific production gains to the use of color in offices; yet there are evidences that the effective use of color can enhance the work environment and have at least an indirect effect on employee productivity.

It is generally believed that the following colors, various shades of which are often found in modern offices, convey the indicated feelings:

> red—heat, action, excitement
> orange—warmth
> yellow—warmth
> brown—warmth
> blue—coolness
> green—coolness
> purple—dignity

Most color experts suggest that offices which receive predominantly northern light (which has a bluish tinge) utilize a blend of warm colors. Offices which receive predominantly southern light (which has a yellowish tinge) should utilize a blend of cooler colors.

Different color combinations, schemes, and variety may be used to break the monotony of bare walls in the office. Neutral colors, too, are frequently used in modern offices and the possibility of monotony is offset by ingenious use of color—often in modern paintings or in the carpeting or draperies. Soft, pastel colors which have a feminine quality and bold, bright colors which have a masculine flavor may be used respectively in lounge areas used exclusively by women or men.

The role of color in determining the lighting reflection factor of walls, ceilings, floors, and furnishings has already been discussed. The color of the light source itself may also be controlled; both fluorescent and incandescent lamps are now available in a variety of shades.

The use of light and color is perhaps the subtlest means of creating positive working conditions. By using touches of stimulating colors, the eye can be refreshed or stimulated according to the color used and the effect desired. Really strong colors are best reserved for accessories such as draperies, chair coverings and wall decorations. Wood, though expensive, makes a luxurious background, rich in color and attractive in grain and texture. Beautiful colors are even more attractive against a backdrop of natural wood.

Color and lighting can also be used to provide some degree of individuality; each section may be given its own color scheme or varying intensities of lighting if the general area is divided into several distinct departments. In summary, the best use of color and light is one which achieves its purpose without calling undue attention to itself. There's a fine line between attraction and distraction, but the consequences can be overwhelming.[6]

Air Conditioning

Another phase of working conditions and the work environment relates to the conditioning of air.

Most of the same values can be realized—higher productivity, better quality of work, improved employee comfort and health, higher morale, and a more favorable impression on visitors. An additional benefit with systems which filter the air is the resulting decrease in cleaning and decorating costs.

At the Interstate Securities Company in Kansas City, Missouri, employee efficiency was reported up 20 per cent after air conditioning was installed.[7] Other reports of from 10 per cent to 50 per cent improvement in performance have been made so commonly that the beneficial effects of air conditioning on productivity cannot be doubted. As is true of other factors in the working environment, such specific amounts of improvement or quality of work from air conditioning are difficult to

[6] Lawrence Victor, "Office Design—The General Area," *Administrative Management,* September, 1961, pp. 26-32.

[7] Wells, Norris, "Is Investment in Air Conditioning Sure to Pay Off?" *American Business,* April, 1954.

measure with exactness because of the many other factors which may influence these improvements at the same time.

Air conditioning may be used to control one or more of the following factors of air as indicated:

1. Circulation—movement and changing of air for freshness.

2. Purity—filtering out objectionable particles such as dust, smoke, fumes.

3. Humidity—maintaining proper relationships between moisture content of the air and the temperature.

4. Temperature—maintaining comfortable heat levels.

Complete air conditioning will control all four of these factors. Whether all are provided usually will depend upon the system considered most feasible in view of atmospheric conditions in the geographic location involved, the characteristics of the building and the sections of the space to be air-conditioned, and the costs of alternative systems.

Air conditioning systems fall into two principal categories—central and package. Central systems service entire buildings; they usually include a large central refrigeration unit, a series of conditioning or fan units, and a system of ducts and vents. Package units include both refrigeration and conditioning equipment within a single case or "package." Most large office buildings now being erected provide central units, but package units are finding wide acceptance in servicing small areas and old buildings. The smaller units have certain special advantages including ease of installation, ease of moving when floor plans are changed, and independent temperature and humidity controls on each unit.

The choice of system and the planning of the air-conditioning installations often present complex problems. In many cases the assistance of a competent air-conditioning engineer should be secured.

Sound Conditioning

Noise and the office executive are enemies of long standing. Noise is known to have detrimental effects on health and on the physical, mental, and nervous mechanisms of individuals. Effects on performance include difficulty of concentration, hence reduced output, higher error rates, difficulty in use of the telephone, and higher absenteeism. Increased fatigue and lowered morale of employees are other effects.

Today, few types of excessive office noise need be tolerated because solutions are available. These solutions usually involve one or a combination of the three approaches listed below:

1. Attack noise at its source.

Common solutions of this type include use of quieter machines, noiseless type-writers, hoods for equipment, sound-absorbent cushions, and maintenance to keep machines in good working order.

2. Soundproof room interiors.

Walls, ceilings, and floors can be covered with sound-conditioning materials which will absorb rather than reflect noise (see Figure 20-4 for examples of sound-conditioning materials). Sound-absorbing. rugs, carpets, and drapes may also be used.

3. Isolate the noisy equipment.

Some equipment, such as tabulating and accounting machines, may need to be separated and partitioned with sound-absorbent materials.

Sound, which is measured in decibels (a unit designating the smallest change in sound which it is possible for the ear to detect), can be controlled. The wise office executive is always on the alert for ways and means of reducing and controlling the noise level in offices.

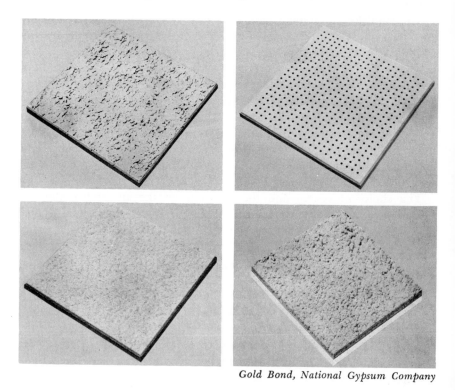

Gold Bond, National Gypsum Company

Figure 20-4. Examples of different sound-absorbent materials that may be used in sound-conditioning the walls and ceilings of business offices

Music Conditioning

Music in offices is now widespread and there is little indication that its use is declining in popularity. Music while we work tends to relieve tensions and tendencies to boredom. It also has a stimulating effect. Music may be brought into an office by wire from a central transmitting organization, such as Muzak, which provides planned programs of daily music, or it may be provided internally by a phonograph manned by the office receptionist or telephone operator. It goes without saying that music in offices should be played very softly, should be of a type which is not distracting, and should be played at intervals during the day rather than continuously.

Industrial music transmitting firms take considerable care in choosing programs of music. In their planning they ordinarily utilize the standard employee energy curve which indicates that at mid-morning and at mid-afternoon there is a low ebb of energy among employees. To meet these low ebbs of energy it is customary to provide music of a more stimulating nature than is otherwise played.

Of the many studies which have been reported on the use of music in offices, actual production gains have been noted in some offices of from 4 to 20 per cent. Surveys conducted among employees in offices where programs of planned music are provided indicate that employees on the whole favor the use of music. However, it must be pointed out that this feeling is by no means universal. Some employees object strenuously to music in the office on the grounds that it interferes with concentration and promotes such undesirable by-products as whistling, humming, and foot-tapping among employees.

Office Furnishings

When we speak of office furnishings, we usually think of the following basic items:

Desks
Chairs
File cabinets and other filing equipment
Miscellaneous furniture—tables, shelves, safes and related items

It is difficult to determine how greatly the quality of office furniture and equipment contributes to the efficiency of employees. Examples can be cited of firms with outstanding records of employee productivity in which the furniture and equipment used, as well as other environmental factors, have left much to be desired. Similarly, many well-furnished and equipped offices with exemplary working conditions house employees whose productivity is poor. In the final analysis, it is probably the individual or human element that is most important in determining office productivity.

Notwithstanding the importance of the individual, it is widely believed that well-designed and effective office furniture and a favorable working environment have a beneficial effect on employee productivity and serve as a physical means of assisting employees in performing their tasks more efficiently. The use of well-selected furnishings and an effective work atmosphere may also serve as a source of incentive by stimulating employees to do better work and by improving their morale and their attitudes toward their jobs.

Desks

Probably the most important working tool of the office employee is his desk. The desk is the employee's base of operations. Nearly all of his working hours are spent there. These considerations suggest the need for great care in the selection of desks.

The principal factors to be considered in choice of desks include *functional aspects, prestige factors, costs,* and *possibilities for standardization.*

Functional considerations include all features which directly influence performance of the work. A smooth working surface should be provided. Size and height should be adequate for the requirements of the work and should be adapted to the normal working area, or normal reach, of the employee. Storage space within the desk should be ample and well-organized. Special features which facilitate performance of the work may be justified. For example, there are desks with a recessed center section for use in typewriter operation; there are desks with a recessed side section for use in computing machine operation; there are secretarial desks which provide for a typewriter in one of the pedestals; there are desks which are triangular in shape; and there are conference-type desks with oversize tops and a deep overhang which permit a number of persons to sit in comfort around the desk.

Prestige factors are involved chiefly in selection of desks for executives. The importance of decisions made by executives may justify special facilities, as may the impression made upon visitors. Partially offsetting these considerations is the tendency toward fewer private offices and more large, general offices; in the latter, desks for supervisors, superintendents, and any other executives placed with the employees may be very similar to the employee desks except for being placed at an angle or for being somewhat larger.

Cost considerations suggest the folly of hunting for bargains in buying desks. For illustration, let us assume a difference of $75 in purchase price between the least-expensive clerical desk available and one that is attractive, sturdy, well-designed, and specially adapted to the work; the actual difference would often be even less than this figure. If we assume that the active life of the desk is fifteen years, the portion of the purchase price to be charged off each year amounts to $5. At the same time, the annual salary of the clerk who uses the desk is likely to be $3000 or more. Based upon these figures alone, it becomes clear that an improvement in productive efficiency of only one-sixth of one per cent ($5 as a percentage of $3000) would justify the better desk.

Standardization of desks has a number of values. If standardization is followed such advantages accrue as uniformity in appearance and layout, economy of floor space, simpler maintenance, and quantity discounts in initial purchase. Figure 20-5 illustrates a modern functional desk, designed for modular application.

While desks come in a wide variety of colors and finishes, the sizes have become pretty well standardized. Desk height is usually fixed at thirty and one-half inches, although some modern executive desks are built lower and range in height from twenty-eight to twenty-nine inches. Many desks have adjustable legs which permit the height to be regulated. Desk dimensions have been generally standardized into the following size groups:

Top executive	76 × 36
Executive	66 × 36
Junior executive	60 × 34
Clerical	54 × 32
Junior clerical	42 × 30

Chairs

The desk may be the most important working tool of the office employee, as suggested in the preceding section, but the piece of equipment which plays the greatest role in adding to or minimizing physical fatigue is the chair. Since most office work is performed in a seated position there is a natural relationship between the work efficiency of the employee and the kind of chair which he uses.

It appears that the three most important requirements for an office chair are that it should provide support to the back and encourage good posture, that it should be adjustable so as to fit the user properly, and that the seat should be comfortable.

Many so-called posture chairs do little to foster good posture on the part of the user, since they do not provide sufficiently firm support to

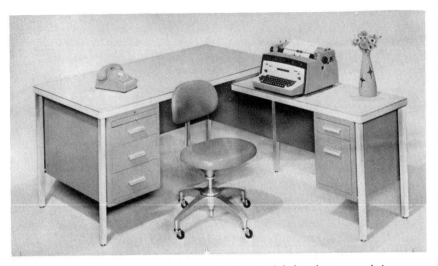

Figure 20-5. A modular arrangement of a functional desk and a posture chair

the back or because they are so difficult to adjust that employees simply do not make the necessary adjustments. Figure 20-5 illustrates a modern office chair designed for maximum employee comfort.

The fact that a good chair is provided is no guarantee that the employee will use it properly. In many cases the user will need to be reminded to sit erectly so that the back can be supported by the back rest of the chair. The user may also need to be assisted in adjusting the chair so that the seat height is correct, the back-rest height is correct, and the horizontal position of the back rest is correct.

Files and miscellaneous furniture

Along with desks and chairs, files and a wide assortment of other items of furniture are needed in the effective and efficient design of office layout. Filing equipment, in the form of cabinets and other containers, comes in hundreds of different sizes and types designed to take care of virtually every filing need. Files and filing methods were discussed under Records Management in Chapter 18. The miscellaneous category includes tables, cabinets, shelves, racks, safes, vaults, stands, etc. Because these items are so diverse and because individual needs and preferences will so largely determine choices, no attempt will be made to discuss these items individually.

QUESTIONS FOR STUDY AND DISCUSSION

1. A statement was made in the chapter that there has been a revolution in both the interiors and the exteriors of office buildings. Does this statement seem

to exaggerate the significance of the changes which have occurred? What specific developments may be suggested to support the statement?

2. What does management have at stake in modernizing and otherwise improving the working environment?

3. Compare the importance of lighting in offices with its importance in factories and retail stores. What specific values may be expected from good lighting? What are the principal factors of lighting which must be controlled, and how may each be brought under control?

4. How would you go about determining whether sufficient lighting intensity is being provided for a specific operation such as looking up shipping rates in a prepared table and entering them on worksheets?

5. A new list of recommended standards for different seeing tasks is published every few years by the Illuminating Engineering Society and by the American Standards Association. To the present, *every* set of intensity standards has placed recommendations at higher levels. How can this be explained? Where will the trend end? What do you predict for the future and why?

6. What is involved in "color conditioning"? Is expert guidance justified in this area?

7. What factors or properties of air may be controlled by air conditioning? Are air-conditioning demands affected by any other office developments of recent years?

8. Name, explain, and illustrate uses of the principal approaches to controlling noise.

9. What seem to be the chief benefits of music in an office environment?—the chief problems?

10. How important is it to have a suitable office desk?—what various advantages may be realized? By what principal factors may the suitability of a desk be evaluated? Is the office desk a good item on which to economize in the original purchase price? Explain. Apply the same questions to providing a suitable office chair.

Case 20-1. Effects of a New Lighting Installation

The voucher unit of the Municipal Utility Company has for several years used a work standard of 15 vouchers typed per hour. The actual production rate varies considerably because of variation in incoming work load, variation in difficulty of work, changes in personnel, and other factors.

Recently, the semi-direct incandescent lighting system which had been in use was replaced by a fluorescent installation, after careful study of needs by the lighting equipment distributor. General lighting intensity was stepped up from an average of 20 foot candles to an average of 45 footcandles.

Production during the first three weeks after the change averaged approximately 21 vouchers typed per hour.

Problems and questions:

a. Would management be justified in attributing the production increase to the improvement in lighting? Discuss carefully.

b. If you were setting up a controlled experiment to determine the relationship between good lighting and production output, would you handle any factors differently from the way they were handled here? If so, explain.

Case 20-2. Investment in Air Conditioning

A study of the feasibility of air conditioning a certain office department revealed the information presented below:

Average hourly wage rate	$1.50
Average loss of time daily due to heat	1 hour
Number of employees	20
Number of working days requiring air conditioning	110
Operating cost per day	$4.00
Initial investment	$5200.00

Problems and questions:

a. Based upon the data shown, how quickly would the installation pay for itself?

b. Do you feel that the plan of analysis followed is sound?

Case 20-3. The Maxey Real Estate Company

This firm, located in the Chicago Loop, has 41 full-time employees. While the office is well located and the plan of layout is satisfactory, it does not present a favorable impression. In analyzing the factors contributing to this poor appearance, the office manager decided that part of the reason lay in the fact that all desks and chairs were of wood and had been in use for 24 years. All filing equipment, however, was of steel and was new. The reason that the filing equipment was new was that it had recently been acquired when a mortgage had been foreclosed on the property of a files manufacturer, and the real estate firm had been able to acquire this equipment at a fraction of its retail cost.

When the office manager proposed that all desks and chairs be replaced with new, steel furniture which would match the filing equipment, the vice-president said that he had considered doing this but, since it would cost $5000, he felt the firm could not afford it. The office manager, however, said that if they kept the new desks and chairs as long as the present desks and chairs had been kept, the cost could be amortized at the rate of only $5 per year per employee. The vice-president immediately challenged the office manager's figures.

Problems and questions:

Was the office manager correct in his statement? Do you think the expenditure is justified? Why?

21

THE OFFICE LOCATION
AND BUILDING

---

*Controlling influence of general objectives · Location of firm
as a whole · The decentralization trend · Special considerations in locating office departments · Objectives of office space
· Alternative solutions to problems of space · Technical considerations in building design · Participation in building
planning*

Decisions regarding location and
buildings are not made frequently by any given firm; when they are
made, they have far-reaching importance. Sometimes they make the
difference between success and failure for the business. In any case, they
greatly influence the degree of success.

During the years since World War II, business has undergone vast
expansion. Decisions regarding location, buildings, and equipment have
been necessary in a great many firms—probably most of them.

The primary concern here is with office problems which arise in connection with location and building.

Controlling Influence of General Objectives of the Firm

Where should an office be located? The service role of office activity
furnishes the general answer to this question. Office work is found in
every department and in every unit of a firm, as emphasized in preceding
chapters. It is a part of all other functions; there is good reason for considering it merely as a process involved in carrying out functions of
any sort.

Office activity, then, needs to be provided where it can best serve the objectives of the organization as a whole and the requirements of sales, production, and other primary departments, since such service is the reason for its existence.

It is apparent, therefore, that office location is directly dependent upon the broader problem of location of the firm as a whole. A detailed general discussion of the location of business firms would be outside the scope of this book, but brief attention to the nature of the problem should help in pointing up areas where office needs may require consideration.

Choice of Location of the Firm as a Whole

The decision on locating the firm ordinarily must be based upon a wide range of factors. These are likely to include markets, raw material, transportation, labor supply, power, taxes, state and local laws, trends in regional and local development, living conditions and commuting problems for employees, availability of suitable local sites, optimum size for each plant or division, and often many others.

Such factors must be considered painstakingly to insure that no significant ones are overlooked. Equally important—and sometimes more difficult—is the weighing of these factors for relative importance. Alternative locations must then be appraised in terms of each of the significant factors.

Probably the soundest approach in evaluating each of a number of possible locations is to make a cost analysis for each alternative location. Then, measurements other than cost may be appropriate, such as traffic count for a retail establishment. Finally, careful judgment, based on the best information available, will be necessary. This general approach can be followed in making decisions first, regarding the general region or area, next, regarding the community, and finally, regarding the specific site.

The Decentralization Trend

The most notable trend in business location today is the tendency to decentralize—to get away from original concentration in one location or under one management. This trend has taken many forms.

Since World War II, industry, with many types of business following, has been developing at a rapid rate in many areas which formerly had little industry. The South, long asleep as far as industrial potential is concerned, is stirring. The Pacific Coastal area has undergone tremendous industrial expension. The North Central, Atlantic Coastal, Mid-

western, and Rocky Mountain states are making important gains, particularly in favored areas. The industrial Northeast and the Great Lakes
region continue to hold their own as the most important areas indus-
trially and to register gains. The trend in geographic decentralization
has been aptly described as a leveling-up rather than a leveling-down
movement.

Large concerns which had traditionally operated from a single central
location have more and more followed the pattern of setting up branches
in different parts of the country. They have done so to take advantage
of regional markets, raw material, transportation economies, labor supply, greater protection from enemy attack in case of war, and other
factors of special importance in individual cases. Some have been concerned with keeping each plant small enough for convenient administration and for close labor-management relationships.

The move to the suburbs

A highly interesting phase of the decentralization trend at the local
level is the tendency to locate new facilities in suburban locations, small
cities, and towns. Suburbs, particularly, have been popular. They can
often combine most of the advantages of the large city—accessibility to
customers and other business associates, nearness to main transportation
arteries—with the conveniences of the small city or town. Among the
latter are space that is less costly and ample for future expansion, less-
congested traffic and easier parking, and greater ease of modernization
and landscaping.

A decision to move to a suburb often means trading a leasing arrangement in a skyscraper-type building for an ownership arrangement in a
one-story building which is designed to fit the processes of the particular
firm, improve morale and productivity of employees, and make a more
favorable impression upon customers and the general public.

Of particular interest has been the movement, or planned movement,
of the offices of several prominent New York firms to the Westchester
County area just north of the city. The main offices of the *Reader's
Digest* have always been located there; they are now being joined, or
may soon be joined, by important office units of General Foods, New York
Central, Standard Vacuum Oil Company, General Electric, and others.[1]
The same sort of development is taking place on a smaller scale in many
other parts of the country. To some extent it seems to be related to the
trend toward the community shopping center. A major suburban shopping center in Dallas, Texas, for example, includes not only the usual
commercial establishments but a general office building and a large

[1] Robert M. Smith, "Office in the Suburbs: Foresight or Fallacy?" *Office Management and Equipment,* January, 1954.

branch office of an insurance company, with a number of small, modern factories close by.

For any suburban area, there is, of course, a saturation point beyond which the original advantages may begin to disappear; this is a consideration that should be kept in mind in appraising a possible location in a suburb. It is probably well to add that such a move means trading one set of problems for a new set. It is still too early to appraise the long-range potentialities of the trend, but there seems little basis for any longer denying its existence as a trend.

Special Considerations in Locating Office Departments and Services

The need to fit office activities and facilities in with the general organizational scheme of the firm has already been emphasized. In most cases this means placing offices right in departments needing them or locating them as near to these departments as possible, although rapid improvements in communication methods promise to make this less of a requirement. Where plant noise is a problem, or where no portion of a plant building can be adapted readily to office needs, a separate office building adjacent to the other may be erected. It is very common to have sales and buying offices in cities some distance away from the home facilities of a firm; the determining considerations here, however, are the requirements of the sales and buying functions, and not the office activities as such.

The general office building which has space to lease plays a highly important role in the office space field. Single offices, suites, and entire floors are leased to a variety of different business firms, including insurance companies, sales organizations, and professional practitioners. Most of these buildings are multi-story, and most are located in downtown areas. Firms having only limited needs for space or desiring the downtown location make up most of the tenants of such buildings, although in some cases a large firm will occupy several floors or even the entire building. Further discussion of leasing will follow in a later section.

Tied very closely to the problem of location is that of securing suitable building space. Building needs may limit choice of location; location requirements, in turn, may limit the possible variations in building design. Often a compromise between ideal location and ideal building design is necessary.

The tremendous development of new business firms since World War II has been noted. Each new firm or new branch has had to plan and secure suitable building space. Older firms also have faced the space problem, since nearly all have expanded.

Office building needs depend upon the general objectives and the primary types of work involved in carrying on a firm's business, just as do location requirements. Office work can be made much more efficient by specially-designed facilities, however; regardless of location, there is now a strong trend to modernize the office environment. The modern office is a far cry from the gas-lighted, high-ceilinged, roll-top-desk version of only a few decades ago.

Two contrasting types of office buildings are pictured in Figure 21-1. The Pan Am Building with some 2.4 million square feet of rentable floor space is the world's largest commercial office building. It is located in the heart of Manhattan Island and represents revolutionary concepts of design and building construction. Since the building is atop Grand Central Station, all utilities and services are located above ground. The E. I. du Pont de Nemours Building illustrates design features characteristic of suburban construction. Having strong appeal to employees are the wooded countryside and the large parking lots adjacent to the building.

Objectives with Regard to Office Space

Specific problems related to building space requirements of office work can be analyzed carefully only in the light of objectives with regard to such space. The principal objectives for office building space include:

Facilitation of working processes
Provision for employee comfort and health
Favorable impression on visitors and general public
Flexibility needed for growth and for varying needs
Costs proportionate to values gained

Each objective will now be examined briefly.

Facilitation of working processes

There is a growing tendency in management planning to consider the building as just another piece of production equipment—the most important piece, to be sure, but one rendering a contribution comparable in type to that of any single machine or tool, and one that should be integrated along with other equipment into the overall system of operations. This line of thinking has resulted in a great increase in functional buildings—buildings tailored to fit the processes that are to be carried on inside of them.

Relatively few buildings were erected from the beginning of the depression of the 1930's until after World War II except for those

Figure 21-1. Contrasting modern buildings in urban and suburban locations: Pan Am, New York City, and E. I. du Pont de Nemours & Co., Newark, Delaware.

needed directly in war production. Most of the buildings erected before that period were designed to be structurally sound and to withstand physical forces on the outside. There was relatively little concern with what went on in the inside.

The modern office building (or the office portion of a larger building) is designed to facilitate the work and at the same time to meet other needs which will be considered. Before the architect starts to work on building plans, he is fully informed regarding the nature and size of organizational units to be housed, the procedural and work flow needs, the expectations as to future growth, and other basic information needed for a tailor-made design. From such data, he—working closely with company personnel—can work out the amount and types of space needed, floor loads, lighting installations, air conditioning, noise control, mechanical delivery systems, and other special installations.

Provision for employee comfort and health

An office building should facilitate the performance of work. It should also provide a favorable environment for the employee. Effects on comfort, health, and morale can be far-reaching; these in turn influence productivity, low turnover, low absenteeism, ease of attracting applicants for positions, and other desired results.

The modern office is indeed a pleasant place in which to work. In appearance it can be a showplace, whether viewed from the exterior or the interior. From a utility standpoint, the well-designed building makes it possible to get work done with more efficiency and less fatigue. Good lighting, air conditioning, and noise control are important safeguards to health.

Favorable impression on visitors and general public

The public relations value of good building design and maintenance is undoubtedly very great. An attractive, modern building adds tremendous local prestige, and it contributes to a generally favorable impression upon customers, business associates, suppliers' representatives, applicants for positions, and others who call at the place of business.

The field of industrial and office landscaping is rapidly gaining recognition and patronage. By taking such measures as planning the entire exterior layout to fit in with the neighborhood, screening unsightly areas, and providing good upkeep for lawns and shrubs, a firm takes an important step toward becoming a good business citizen.

Flexibility needed for growth and for varying needs

A building represents a long-term commitment, and one on which fixed charges must be met in bad times as well as good. This suggests the need for careful projection of the rate of growth of the firm for as many years ahead as possible. The management of the firm should either make advance provision for probable space requirements in the foreseeable future, or it should at least make tentative plans as to how these needs can be met when they arise.

Possible changes in amounts of space should be anticipated, as should changes in the proportioning of space for different purposes, and changes in lighting, air conditioning, noise control requirements, and other building services. Among desirable provisions will be those for emphasizing large general offices rather than having space cut up by permanent partitions. Adequate electrical outlets, ducts and vents, and general soundproofing are other desirable provisions. Space likely to be needed in future years may be leased to desirable tenants on a short-term arrangement. Possibilities for expanding the building either vertically or horizontally should be considered from the beginning, and either the building structure strengthened accordingly or plans made for securing additional ground space when needed.

Costs proportionate to values gained

Not only does a building need to serve each of the purposes previously considered, but it must do so economically. Depreciation charges, maintenance costs, insurance, and taxes—whether paid by an owner-occupant or included in the rental paid by a tenant—all need to be evaluated in terms of value received and then compared with competitors' costs. Costs such as these can usually be determined with considerable accuracy. Not so easy to determine, even though of obvious significance, is the influence of the building on labor stability and productivity.

Maximum usable square footage of floor space needs to be sought, and dead space should be held to a minimum. Uses for the less desirable space should also be found; if the building design has been planned with care there should be little space which is undesirable.

On a rental basis, good, air-conditioned office space may range anywhere from about $6 to $10 per square foot, depending on condition and location.

Alternative Solutions to Problems in Obtaining Needed Space

Meeting a space problem by erecting a building may, at first thought, seem to be the ideal solution. Actually, it may be far wiser to regard this as the last resort rather than the first.

When an existing firm finds space inadequate, the first possibility to consider probably should be that of *making better use of present space.* Some possible approaches include improving the layout of equipment, mechanizing where one person might do the work of several, cutting out wasted steps and motions from procedures, transferring inactive files to storage, and using modular furniture—such as the L-shaped desk with partition attached, which can be placed back-to-back with other desks. Controlling production to more effectively utilize personnel and equipment is another basic approach to better use of space.

The second possibility in logical sequence for the existing firm—and first for the new firm—probably should be that of *leasing* space. Leasing may be preferable when space requirements are very limited in amount, or where the need is either temporary or uncertain, where capital limitations require it, or where the trend in building costs is expected to go down sharply later. Much may also depend upon the location desired; leasing may be the only method by which space may be secured in the exact area needed, particularly if this is a downtown area. Some firms prefer leasing because they can pass most of the headaches of building management back to the owners. The possibility of leasing more space than needed originally and of subleasing some space on a short-term basis gives a desirable element of flexibility.

Buying a building that is already erected is probably next in the logical sequence of considerations, although this is a less likely possibility in most cases. Buying may be justified in order to get into a specific location where all building space is already occupied and where a suitable building can be secured. Or it may be justified in order to save time required for construction, or where economic conditions make buying preferable to building. The possibility deserves some consideration in any case.

Finally, *erecting a building* may be fully justified and highly advantageous under the right circumstances. In the case of an established firm with demand for its products or services relatively stable and permanent, the erection of its own building will make it possible to tailor the building to fit the specific processes of the firm and, usually, to place it in an advantageous location. Company prestige with employees, visitors, and the general public may be enhanced by an attractive building. A carefully-selected fixed asset may be added to the capital structure of the firm. New problems are taken on, also. For one, a long-term financial obligation is assumed that must be met in times of low volume and economic depression, just as under favorable conditions. Also, there is less flexibility than when space is leased, and it becomes doubly important that future space needs be accurately estimated. These may or may not constitute serious problems for a firm.

Technical Considerations in Building Design

Whatever the arrangement decided upon for obtaining the space needed, there will be certain technical requirements that must be met in view of the circumstances of the particular firm. Most of these will require the help of the architect and some will require other specialists; but any office executive needs some familiarity with them if only to know when to call upon specialists for help.

Space allocations, ideally, will be worked out on a systematic basis before a building is erected. The best way to do this is to classify office space needs by type of position and to establish standard allowances for each class. Space standards are given detailed discussion in the chapter on office layout.

Reference was made earlier to the need for considering general *patterns of work flow* and for fitting the building and the building services around these. This phase of the analysis may be aided greatly by layout charts and process charts, both of which will be discussed in later chapters. Floor traffic count in different sections of former quarters, study of buildings of similar firms, and similar techniques may also be helpful.

Very thorough plans for lighting, air conditioning, and noise control need to be made from the outset. Artificial light is being depended upon more and more; this means lower ceilings and, where desired, a reduction in window space—with completely windowless buildings becoming quite common. Glass block may be used to admit natural light in addition to that coming through windows, if desired.

Electrical fixtures and air-conditioning vents can be coordinated with column widths and window modules so that partitions can be moved easily and office layouts changed quickly. Hung ceilings in corridors can provide the required drop or ceiling space needed for main air conditioning ducts; others can be placed under floors. Such installations as these are much more easily made in new buildings, but most old buildings provide sufficient space for adding them.[2]

Adequate transportation facilities also need to be incorporated into the building design from the outset. Elevators, escalators, and mechanical delivery systems may justify consideration; the specific requirements will depend upon transportation needs and the size and height of the building.

The foundation and the structural framework then need to be planned and considered in terms of the other requirements mentioned. The specifications for the foundation will be determined largely by the number of stories and the nature of soil underneath, but it needs strength to

2 *Ibid.*

spare. The possibility of adding one or more floors to meet expansion needs will often be a factor of vital importance, particularly where it is impossible to add space horizontally.

The structural framework of newer buildings is most often either steel frame or reinforced concrete, both of which ordinarily have all the weight of the building borne by the framework. Since walls are of the curtain rather than bearing type, modification is simpler and the entire structure is stronger. Walls are most commonly of brick, but they may be of masonry, glass, aluminum, or other material. Floor load or capacity of from seventy-five to one hundred pounds per square foot of floor space is considered adequate for most office needs.

For a considerable period, the trend has been toward greater use of general offices; these call for large, rectangular areas of space. Private offices are more and more limited to high-ranking executives and persons who perform duties requiring privacy. Partitions are held to a minimum; where needed they are now more often the readily-movable type. Shoulder-height partitions and desk partitions in modular units are also increasingly depended upon to cover limited needs for privacy. These developments were considered in Chapter 19, the chapter on office layout.

Building maintenance problems also justify careful attention in original building design. Window, wall, ceiling, and floor surfaces present major housekeeping problems which can be simplified by foresight in choice of materials and design. The servicing of building installations for lighting, air conditioning, and transportation can also be made much easier when planned carefully in advance.

Who Should Participate in Building Planning?

The specialist in the building planning field is, of course, the architect. Traditionally, the responsibility of the architect was considered to be that of designing a structurally-sound building, guided by information furnished him by the owners with regard to space and cost specifications.

In recent years, the trend has been to place more emphasis on the functional design of buildings—upon tailoring them to fit the processes involved. The other objectives discussed in this chapter—employee comfort and health, favorable impression on visitors and general public, flexibility as needed, and reasonable costs—also have entered the design picture chiefly in the post-World War II period.

Most architects have been very alert to these developments. One result is that company personnel are being allowed a much more active part in building planning at all stages, with special attention to design phases that may be expected to influence employee satisfaction. Department heads and supervisors, staff personnel who have special responsibilities (such as procedures, cost accounting, personnel, and purchasing), and employees themselves are being consulted on details affecting their own particular phases of work.

Increased use is also being made of outside specialists other than, or in addition to, the architect. These include consultants in office procedures and layout, specialists in color and interior decoration, representatives of suppliers of the various building installations, and sometimes others.

One special planning group in the building design field deserves mention because of the value and the uniqueness of its services. The Building Planning Service Council of the National Association of Building Owners and Managers serves in an advisory capacity to architects and building owners in the planning stages of new buildings. The council functions through appointing a committee of company executives who have had experience in planning and erecting a building similar to one about to be designed. This committee looks particularly for features that will affect the economical operation of the building throughout its life; they endeavor to give the firm erecting the building the benefit of their experience and to make the building "depression-proof."

QUESTIONS FOR STUDY AND DISCUSSION

1. What basic, general factors should determine where offices and office activities are located? Does your answer seem merely to state the obvious?—if so, why do most managers view this problem as a difficult one?

2. What sort of general approach would you recommend that a firm follow in determining the best area in which to locate? The particular community? The specific site?

3. Contrast a typical office building in an urban area with one in a suburban location. Why have many businesses moved to the suburbs? Why have a substantial number moved back to urban locations? What do you predict for the next decade?

4. Distinguish geographic decentralization from managerial decentralization. Then relate the two concepts—do they tend to go together? Explain. What do you expect to develop in both areas in the years ahead?

5. How will data processing, information systems, and integrated data processing affect the location of office buildings? The location of branch offices throughout the country?

6. What types of needs are served by the general office building that has space to lease?

7. The concept of "functional" office buildings has gained rapidly in acceptance. Just what is included in this concept, and why has it gained popularity?

8. In what ways are the interests of employees, visitors, and the general public provided for in modern building design? Is the *corporate image* influenced significantly by both building exteriors and interiors? Explain.

9. In view of the rapid growth which characterizes so many enterprises today, what appear to be the most effective means of providing for flexibility and ex-

pansion to meet future needs? How far ahead do you believe a management should attempt to look?

10. What alternative solutions may a firm have in obtaining building space; in what sequence should they be considered; and what conditions may justify each?

11. Who should participate in building planning, and what should be the contribution of each?

Case 21-1. International Distributing Company

A regional office of the International Distributing Company was set up in leased quarters. The quarters were located in a relatively new building which was quite well lighted and had central air conditioning. For about two years, the space seemed quite adequate.

Continued growth gradually resulted in a crowding of desks, files, and other equipment. The stage was reached where a layout pattern was necessitated which consisted of five desks, side by side, separated from a similar group by an aisle barely wide enough for two people to pass. The work required telephones on many desks, and a large number of typewriters, dictating, and transcribing equipment, calculators, and special equipment of various types. The noise level was high and distractions were numerous.

Three months ago, the regional office was moved into a new building constructed by International and designed especially for the operations required. Space is more than ample for present needs and no desks adjoin; the layout was planned with careful attention to work flow; and lighting, color design, air conditioning, and sound conditioning all meet high standards.

Productivity has risen noticeably since the move as measured by total clerical-minutes-per-order; and employee turnover has been reduced by more than one-third.

Problems and questions:

a. In this situation, does it appear that International was, in effect, paying for the new building for some time before actually constructing it? Discuss.

b. Does it seem probable that the improvements in productivity and reduced turnover will continue, or is it likely that after "the new wears off," productivity and turnover will return to former levels? What factors may influence the results?

Case 21-2. The Move to the Suburbs

A writer in one of the leading magazines in the field of office management recently suggested that the office "trek to the suburbs" may be waning.

He noted the following problems in any office move to a suburban area:

1. Employees ordinarily are forced to live in the same suburb because of transportation limitations.

2. Proximity to downtown concentrations of related businesses is sacrificed.

3. Opportunities for leasing are limited; the firm may have to construct its own building.

4. The younger and more promising executives may fear that by isolating themselves in a suburb they are tying their future to their present company.

5. No population center, even a small one, is safe from atomic attack by an enemy force.

6. Office mechanization makes large numbers of personnel less necessary, hence removing much of the premium on space which is one of the suburb's greatest assets.

7. Lower-echelon personnel may be unable or unwilling to buy homes in wealthy suburban areas.

8. Zoning difficulties in small communities may be troublesome.

There are some offsetting advantages to moving to the suburbs which this author failed to note, but some of the objections which he raises can obviously be very real.

Problems and questions:

a. Consider each of the problems noted and try to decide just how serious an obstacle each would be to a move to the suburbs.

b. Summarize the key advantages of such a move.

Case 21-3. Planning a New Building

Before the Womack Company had an architect start plans for a new building, department heads, supervisors, and employees were asked to contribute their ideas. What features did they want in the new building? What didn't they like about the old?

Not all of the ideas could be used, but most of them turned out to be good ones. The suggestions were summarized and turned over to the architect, who was able to incorporate most of them in the final building plan.

Problems and questions:

a. Do you suppose there were many suggestions that would have been overlooked by the architects if this approach had not been followed? Discuss.

b. Was the approach really justified, or is it possible that there may be more disadvantages than advantages involved?

VII

PERFORMANCE STANDARDS AND CONTROL

Control of performance has been defined previously as insuring that work proceeds according to plan and that desired results are achieved. The close relationship between control and planning is readily apparent; in a real sense, control is the "other half" of planning. Goals and courses of action are laid out in planning; achievement of these and other planning elements is the concern of control.

The process of control requires: (1) setting standards of performance; (2) measuring current performance; (3) comparing current results with planned results; and (4) taking corrective action where needed.

A prerequisite to the setting of performance standards is the standardization of *methods*. Methods should first be improved where possible, then they must be standardized to a considerable degree before any level of accomplishment can be predicted with confidence.

Following standardization of methods, performance standards can be established. The primary factors in performance which can be measured and standardized include *time, quantity, quality,* and *cost.* Confident expectations and uniformly high performance will vary with the care devoted to setting and applying standards in these basic areas. Accordingly, the next series of chapters will be devoted to the process of controlling office operations, including the factors just outlined.

A consideration of key significance in the design and application of controls is that of human response. Control in an authoritarian sense is being replaced by concepts such as over-all review and evaluation accompanied by a high degree of delegation and of self-control wherever possible. We shall be particularly mindful of human reactions to controls, since the effectiveness of such controls is likely to depend heavily upon the degree of understanding and acceptance on the part of persons who will be affected.

22

METHODS
STANDARDIZATION

---

*Nature of standards and standardization · Methods stand-
ards—types and benefits · Approaches to standardization*

Methods have been treated in this
book as *means* of performing operations. Study of management informational needs for planning and control decisions led us into systems design
which, in turn, led to study of methods of assembling, processing, communicating, and recording data, and of the building and working environment, which are also methods of performing work, in a broad sense.

Anyone involved in management has a large stake in methods—perhaps
best pointed up by the annual cost of some $40 billion dollars for clerical
salaries. Persons concentrating upon administrative management must
be even more greatly concerned, for their recommendations will largely
determine methods design. Accordingly, we have attempted to develop
an awareness of different methods available for accomplishing various
tasks, and to suggest techniques of analysis, selection, and improvement of
methods which will result in greater *effectiveness* and *economy*. At various
points, we have also made note of the importance of *standardization* of
methods, but we now need to give specific consideration to this area.

Standardization and the use of standards provide the link between
planning and control. Standards are themselves plans; at the same time,
standards are the yardsticks essential to control.

Nature of Standards and Standardization

The word *standardization* is usually used to suggest achievement of
uniformity; for example, a firm may standardize on an approach to
pricing its products, or investigating credit applications, or on use of a

standard letter form for all general correspondence. The word *standards*, on the other hand, is most often used to mean output goals, such as typing 20 invoices an hour. Leffingwell resolved this seeming inconsistency in this statement: "In management practice, 'setting standards' means the determining of levels of accomplishment, *after* all factors which affect accomplishment have been standardized." [1]

Standards may be developed for use in a single enterprise, or they may be developed to apply generally to firms in the entire industry or even in all industries. Long recognized as important in product design, standards of this type include many hundreds of items such as nuts and bolts, light sockets, milk bottles, automobile tires and bumper heights—all having obvious benefits to consumer, distributor, and producer.

Administrative tools and practices which can be standardized form a long list. Most, however, can be grouped under two broad headings: (1) *methods standards,* and (2) *performance standards.* We shall consider methods standards in this chapter, performance standards and their uses in succeeding chapters.

Methods Standards—Types and Benefits

Some appreciation of the potential contribution of methods standardization can be gained from considering the long experience of one prominent organization.

The Western Electric Company, since 1907, has maintained record retention schedules, and since 1928, has provided a catalog which includes specifications for equipment for the guidance of managers. Results have included substantial economies, interchangeability of equipment throughout the company, and greatly facilitated purchasing activities. In their recently-constructed building in downtown New York, use of modular desks 30 inches in depth, rather than the customary 34 inches, resulted in better utilization of high-priced general office desk space.

The following classification of areas in which standardization of office methods can be particularly useful will be considered:

> Human activities
> Machines
> Furniture
> Forms and records
> Supplies
> Space allotments
> Working environment

[1] William H. Leffingwell and Edwin M. Robinson, *Textbook of Office Management* (New York: McGraw-Hill Book Company, Inc., 1950).

Human activities

Both the manual and mental activities involved in carrying out an operation will lend themselves to standardization in varying degrees. We have dealt with the concept of "programmed" decisions earlier; we have also considered policies and procedures, which are sometimes called *standing plans* for dealing with recurring situations. Study of techniques of analysis of the motions involved in performing operations suggested the existence of numerous possibilities for improvement. It is appropriate to mention here the logical sequence involved in *simplifying first, then standardizing*—whether human activities are involved or methods of other sorts. Find the best way to do a job; then try to make this the standard way, but allow for the possibility of individual differences in ability to apply the standard approach, and for the probability that new and better approaches will evolve with the passing of time.

Machines

Standardization of machines is usually in terms of basic features and brands. To illustrate, one company management decided to use dictating equipment rather than shorthand stenography, and then standardized on one vendor's machine, permitting discs and belts to be interchangeable.

Furniture

Standardization of furniture takes into account several features: dimensions of desks, material from which desks and other furniture are made (steel, wood, or other), posture chair types and adjustability, heights of tables and cabinets, etc. At stake are suitability for tasks, interchangeability, economy in purchase and maintenance, and effective layout arrangements.

Forms and records

Particularly important here is design of standard forms to serve recurring needs, thus cutting down on numerous forms which differ only slightly in design, and facilitating multiple-copy, one-writing forms; also standardizing paper stock, carbon paper, and equipment to be used in completing. Of great significance, also, is classification and retention of records, providing standard time periods for keeping various documents in active and inactive storage, for microfilming when appropriate, and for eventual destruction of most records. Firms embarking upon projects of forms standardization or records retention scheduling for the first time usually come up with surprising results—as did the medium-sized manufacturing firm which destroyed the equivalent of 2.5 million pieces of paper contained in 150 letter-size file cabinets.

Supplies

Here are found a lot of "little" things which add up to large expenditures and to substantial influence upon effective results—such as standard types of paper most suitable for different uses; also carbon paper, erasers, clips, inks, pencils, ribbons, staples, stencils, file folders, guides, etc.

Space allotments

Costly, and often scarce, office space has led to much greater concern for standardization of space requirements for different uses. Both job *types* and job *levels* are considered in space allotments; former square-footage allowances tended to follow job level in most cases, but now work requirements and equipment needed to perform the job most effectively are increasingly being considered in space allowances.

Working environment

Recommendations for higher standards of lighting intensity for work having different visual requirements have been considered earlier, along with features to insure the desired quality of light. Standards are also needed to cover maximum noise levels, temperature, humidity, circulation, and purity of air. Colors of furnishings, covering for walls and floors, and other characteristics of office interiors and exteriors are now being carefully designed, then standardized.

The *general benefits* which may be realized from standardization of office methods will now be more easily appreciated:

1. *Greater assurance of suitability to tasks.* Here it should be emphasized that standardization is in no sense synonymous with perfection. Blue Goose No. 174 carbon paper may be an inexpensive, low-grade paper, but may fill a need for rough carbon copies to be retained for reference purposes only; thus, it may be specified as standard for that usage, at substantial economy but no loss of effectiveness.

2. *Greater economy.* Methods that will do the job, yet possess no great amount of unneeded capacity, extras, or frills, can produce real savings. Interchangeability, quantity buying, and better and more economical maintenance can produce economies. It should be emphasized, however, that doing without necessary features will produce false, rather than genuine, economies.

3. *Simplified administration.* Standards are, in fact, standing plans which cover recurring problems. Thus, assuming a careful study is made before establishment of a standard practice, management will be freed from having to make a great number of comparatively routine decisions, yet have confidence that good practice will be followed consistently.

4. *Greater compatibility of methods.* Increased emphasis upon automated processes, added to normal needs for interchangeability, make it highly desirable that "common languages" be developed for computers and peripheral equipment. Currently, the problem of making equipment, forms, and even personnel compatible in integrated systems is one of the greatest challenges to management.

5. *Performance standards and control made possible.* Just as Frederick W. Taylor learned that work standards could not be set and followed until methods (such as the best method of loading pig iron onto freight cars, and the most suitable size and type of shovel for certain materials) were standardized, we must recognize that control of the quantity, quality, time, and cost of performing office tasks will depend upon standardization of methods used. This relationship will become increasingly apparent in the succeeding chapters.

Approaches to Standardization

Standardization, as noted previously, may be applied to methods used for the same or similar tasks throughout an enterprise. It may be extended, in some instances, to all firms in an industry or to industry generally, or to all agencies in a department of government or all departments. Thus, we have what are commonly referred to as *company* (or enterprise) standards and *general* standards.

Company standardization programs

Responsibility for providing a continuing program of encouragement and help to company standardization efforts is usually assigned to the Systems Department (or Procedures, Methods, Planning, or whatever this department may be called). The justification for this arrangement seems to be in the close relationship between the design and simplification of systems and systems elements, on one hand, and standardization of what are currently the best practices, on the other.

In practice, office operating methods used are so varied that it is customary to make much use of committees. Some firms establish Standards Committees which are standing committees to promote and coordinate standardization efforts in areas where methods are involved. In others, special committees are charged with the responsibility for studying and standardizing in particular methods areas, such as a Forms Control Committee or a Computer Study Committee. On either standing or special committees, a systems department representative will usually be found, in order to provide specialized staff assistance.

The procedures followed also necessarily vary with different methods areas, but since the concept of standardization presupposes that a number of alternative methods for performing a task may exist, the basic approach usually follows a sequence much like the one outlined below:

1. *Determine the purpose of the operation and the needs to be met.*

2. *Determine the alternative methods* of performing the operation; for example, a certain communications need might conceivably be met by mail service, telegraph, teletypewriter, and other means. For some methods, classification may be necessary, if not already done—as with forms which serve similar uses or contain similar information.

3. *Compare the alternative methods* in terms of factors of crucial importance to the satisfaction of the purpose of the operation (accuracy, promptness, economy, etc.), recognizing limits such as cost, or other.

4. *Select the best method or methods* on the basis of comparison of alternatives.

5. *Standardize and prepare written specifications*—to crystallize thinking and to place the decision on record so it can be communicated and used as a guide to future decisions. Standard items which can be requisitioned are often incorporated into standard stock catalogs.

General standardization programs

Many office operating methods are common to different business firms, governmental agencies, and other organizations. A large number of these appear to be ripe for *general standardization*—with benefits comparable to those attained through industrial standardization efforts, such as reducing the varieties of milk bottles from 49 to 4.

An illustration of what can be done in the office standards field is the standard for desk and table dimensions presented in Figure 22-1. This standard, sponsored by the National Office Management Association and accepted and published by the American Standards Association, encourages uniformity while permitting all flexibility necessary for normal requirements. Its effect was to reduce the number of desk and table sizes from 101 to a more practical 48, thus benefiting producer and distributor through lower production costs and lower inventories; the user benefited through quantity purchases, interchangeability, symmetrical layout arrangements, and other advantages.

The leading national association in the general standards field is the American Standards Association, a federation of 121 professional societies and trade associations and more than 20,000 company members who provide most of the support for the association. Long active in the industrial standards field, ASA has accepted and published more than 1,800 standards. The lag in office standards is indicated by the fact that only about 20 of these are in the office field. The first office standard, inciden-

DIVISION 1
OFFICE FURNITURE

NOMA
N1.1-1951
•
ASA
X2.1.1-1951

NOMA
OFFICE STANDARD

Dimensions of Desks and Tables for General Office Use

1. Scope and Purpose

1.1 This standard provides a range of over-all dimensions for desks and tables for general office use. All dimensions are not included, but conformance to those given will permit uniformity in arrangement while allowing for variations to meet functional requirements or special features required by some purchasers.

2. Definitions

For the purpose of this standard, the following definitions are used to clarify terminology.

2.1 General Office Desks and Tables. General office desks and tables are limited to desks and tables of 60-in. width and less and do not include the larger executive sizes.

2.2 Single-Pedestal Desks. Single-pedestal desks have a drawer or compartment arrangement at only one side of the user's position.

2.3 Double-Pedestal Desks. Double-pedestal desks have drawer or compartment arrangements at both sides of the user's position.

2.4 Width. The width is the long dimension measured from edge to edge of the desk or table top.

2.5 Depth. The depth is the short dimension measured from front to back edges of the desk or table top.

2.6 Height. The height is the distance of the extreme upper working surface of the desk top or table top from the floor.

2.7 Front. The front of the desk is that part at which the user normally sits.

2.8 Right and Left Designations. The right portion or pedestal of the desk or table is that part to the right of the user seated at the front of the desk or table, the left is that part to the left of the user.

3. Over-all Dimensions of Desk and Table Tops

3.1 The over-all dimensions of desk and table tops shall conform to those listed in Table I.

3.2 A tolerance of plus or minus ¼ in. shall be permitted on the over-all top dimensions specified in Table I.

TABLE I

General Classification	Over-All Top Dimensions (Inches)			
	Metal		Wood	
	Width	Depth	Width	Depth
Double Pedestal	50	30	50	32
	55	30	52	32
	60	30	58	32
	60	34	60	34
Single Pedestal	40	30	42	32
	45	30	44	32
	45*	34*		
Tables	45	30	42	32
	50	30	44	32
	55	30	50	32
	60	30	52	32
	60	34	58	32
			60	34

*Flat top or fixed bed metal typewriter desks only.

4. Height

4.1 The height of the desk or table shall be either 29 in. or 30¼ in. if fixed, or adjustable between these levels.

4.2 A tolerance of plus or minus ¼ in. shall be permitted in the height of the desk or table.

- Approved as American Standard by the American Standards Association, Incorporated—May 23, 1951
- Sponsor: National Office Management Association

NATIONAL OFFICE MANAGEMENT ASSOCIATION
132 WEST CHELTEN AVENUE, PHILADELPHIA 44, PA.

Figure 22-1. Standard for dimensions of desks and tables, sponsored by the National Office Management Association and accepted by the American Standards Association

tally, was the standard for desk and table dimensions mentioned above.[2]

Because of the potentialities and challenges which now seem to exist in the office standards field, the principal approaches by which an ASA standard may be developed will be presented briefly:

1. The sectional committee method, wherein an interested association normally submits a project for study and lends administrative and technical support; an ASA sectional committee representing other interested organizations studies the project, agrees on a proposal, determines whether consensus favoring the proposed standard exists among the different groups principally affected, then accepts and publishes the standard, if satisfied with results.

2. The existing standards method, in which a standard already recognized in one trade or professional group may be submitted to ASA, which in turn conducts a mail canvass of other associations concerned to establish consensus.

3. The general acceptance method, under which a simple standard can be accepted at a general conference attended by all interested groups.

The American Standards Association has a Sectional Committee X2 on Office Standards, with five separate sub-committees: (1) office furniture, (2) paper, (3) forms, records, and procedures, (4) consumable office supplies, and (5) machines. Sponsoring groups which have promoted particular standards have included the National Office Management Association, the Systems and Procedures Association of America, the Office Equipment Manufacturers' Institute, and others. Currently, there is great need for organizations to sponsor standards studies for continued progress in this important field.[3]

The challenges are great. The recent technological advances and almost overwhelming array of equipment and supplies now appearing on the market may lend a sense of urgency to the standardization movement. It is particularly desirable for new equipment to be standardized early in its development. The classic example is, of course, the typewriter, developed almost a century ago. The keyboard was based upon a modification of a printer's type case, except that keys were rearranged so they would not jam; the left hand did 56 per cent of the work, and the weaker fingers a large share of that percentage.

Special challenges now exist in the data processing field, where compatibility is required to facilitate data communication and to simplify

[2] An up-to-date listing of office standards, as well as detailed write-ups, may be obtained at nominal charges from American Standards Association, 70 East 45th St., New York 17, N. Y. A similar listing of standards sponsored by the National Office Management Association may be obtained by addressing the latter association at 1927 Old York Road, Willow Grove, Pa.

[3] See A. R. Hutchison, "Will You Help Sponsor Some Standards for Offices?" *The Office,* October, 1959; and Merrill R. Tabor, "Life Insurance Officers Seek Standardization," *The Office,* January, 1961.

conversion of data from one machine to another. Encouraging progress has been made, but a great deal of additional work remains to be done.

QUESTIONS FOR STUDY AND DISCUSSION

1. In what way does *control* depend upon standards? Why are *methods standards* desirable prerequisites to performance standards? Study carefully the introduction to Part VII and try to develop a good general grasp of the concept of control; do you question any of the basic relationships suggested?

2. For review, explain the relationship of methods to procedures and systems.

3. Differentiate between standardization and standards. In practical usage, which must come first, and why?

4. Does the classification of office methods which is suggested in the chapter seem to be all-inclusive, or can you think of important methods areas which are omitted? What principal values seem to be attainable through standardization of each of the classes of methods, considered separately? Then what general benefits may be expected from standardization wherever applied?

5. One of the suggested classes of methods is that of human activities. In view of the temperamental, emotional, and unpredictable behavior of most individuals, is it possible that we may create more problems than we will solve, through efforts at standardization in this area? At what point would standardization be carried too far?

6. Distinguish *company* (or other enterprise) standards and *general* standards.

7. Assume that dictating equipment of several types is currently in use in different departments in your organization, with each user having been allowed a high degree of freedom to requisition the specific type which appeals to him. You have been asked to head up a study to explore the possibilities of standardizing one or a few types and makes of this equipment. How would you proceed?

8. The American Standards Association has been very active and influential in promoting general standards. How can you account for the fact that of some 1800 such standards in general industrial usage, only slightly more than 20 are in the office field? Is there anywhere nearly as great a need in the office area as in the other areas? What approach is usually followed in getting general standards adopted? When such standards are adopted, are they compulsory for all users?—do you feel that they should be?

9. How, in your opinion, will the extremely rapid growth of data processing affect and be affected by standardization? Can you identify some elements of standardization that are already present in the data processing field?

10. What are the different factors, or dimensions, of *performance* which may often justify measures and standards, following methods standardization? (Review the introduction to Part VII; then apply and relate these factors in study of Chapters 23, 24, and 25.)

Case 22-1. Standardization of Typewriter Keyboard

The arrangement of keys on a standard typewriter keyboard developed from efforts to avoid the jamming of keys while adapting a printer's type case. The resulting combination forces fingers of the left hand to do about 56 per cent of the work, and forces the weaker fingers to do a large share of the work of each hand.

Many individuals have been concerned with this problem and have studied possibilities of improved arrangement. Some 30 years ago, a man worked out an arrangement of keys that would shift slightly more than half of the work to the right hand and would have the stronger fingers perform a larger share than the weaker ones. The quality of his work was widely recognized; numerous experiments demonstrated its superiority over the existing arrangement; and he even succeeded in persuading the Department of the Navy to modify the keyboards of a group of machines and conduct special training with a sizeable number of persons, with highly encouraging results. He, and other persons interested, tried for several years to interest typewriter manufacturers in changing to the improved arrangement. But we continue to use essentially the same keyboard that was worked out with virtually no planning when the typewriter was first invented almost a century ago.

Problems and questions:

a. Suggest reasons for continued use of the unplanned, admittedly inefficient keyboard.

b. Will the present keyboard arrangement *ever* be changed, in your opinion? Explain your views on the subject.

c. What approach would you recommend as offering the greatest promise in bringing about eventual improvement of the existing keyboard arrangement? Outline basic steps which you would recommend.

Case 22-2. Fidelity Bank and Trust Company

In this organization a supplies supervisor is in charge of all receipts, storage, and issuance of office supplies used in the firm. Much difficulty has been encountered in rendering smooth, efficient service to operating departments. Most of the problems have occurred in connection with issuing supplies. The rate of usage of many important types of supplies has been going up faster than either the rate of increase in business volume or the rate of increase in the number of office employees. An effort is made to have each department draw its supplies on a particular afternoon of each week, but several of the department heads pay little attention to this. Employees frequently come to the supply room and request small quantities of supplies without bringing a properly signed requisition from their department heads. Some departments seem to do a conscientious job of planning and controlling supplies needs; others seem to think there should be no limit to the amount of supplies they are allowed to use or as to the time when they should be able to get these supplies.

The supplies supervisor has come up with this plan: why not have a standard arrangement of individual supplies in one or two drawers of each clerk's desk, and a standard arrangement for general or reserve supplies for each department in a supply cabinet for the department? A standard amount of each item for a week's usage also would be determined. Then, after working hours, have a stockroom attendant take a cart that is loaded with all basic supply items used by a department and make the rounds of each desk and supply cabinet, adding supplies as required, and charging the supplies to each individual and department as he goes along. Emergency needs through the week could still be taken care of, although the supplies supervisor believes these would be greatly reduced.

Problems and questions:

a. Appraise the advantages and disadvantages of the proposed plan. Do you think it would be worth a try?

b. If the decision were made to try the plan, what suggestions would you make regarding the approach which the supplies supervisor might use in attempting to win the acceptance and cooperation of the department heads?

23

TIME STANDARDS;
WORK MEASUREMENT

---

*Uses of time standards · Special characteristics of office work ·
Approaches to setting standards · Work measurement*

Some seventy-five years ago, Frederick W. Taylor observed widespread conflict between management and working men. He reached the conclusion that much of this conflict could be resolved if management could only determine "what is a fair day's work" and then provide a "fair day's pay" in return.

Taylor's interest in a "fair day's pay for a fair day's work" led him into pioneering work in the time study field. He quickly learned that before he could set time standards and thus determine a fair day's work, he had to standardize and bring under control the methods of doing the job, the equipment, the materials, and even the qualifications sought in men for doing particular work.

With the benefit of hindsight, and in the light of technological and social changes since Taylor's pioneering efforts, scholars of today can find some limitations in the "fair day's pay for a fair day's work" concept as a solution to many management problems. But the value to management of knowing *how long a work assignment should take* is probably even greater now than in Taylor's day.

Uses of Time Standards

Time standards aid management in both *planning* and *controlling*. They are actually plans of a special sort; they are standing plans as to how long any given work, or phase of work, should take. Thus, they can serve a number of specific planning needs of management, which we shall examine. At the same time, time standards are the "yardsticks" needed to assess current results actually achieved, take corrective action, and bring work "under control."

Among specific applications in *planning*, management can use time standards for the following purposes:

1. (*Plan and schedule operations.*) If a customer desires delivery on an order within three days, for example, a schedule will be made up by working back from the deadline in terms of time known to be required for delivery, packaging, order-filling from stock, preparation of order forms, and other required steps, then arranging to have personnel, equipment, and other resources available to meet the schedule. Fluctuations in volume, such as peak loads, can be anticipated and prepared for.

2. (*Determine workforce and equipment needs.*) If a billing department uses a cycle billing approach to level work load and averages sending out 400 invoices a day, and if one employee can process 10 invoices an hour or 80 a day as an average, it becomes apparent that 5 billing clerks are needed and that each will need equipment for carrying out his function.

3. (*Provide a basis for determining cost standards.*) Human and machine time are major determinants of both direct costs and overhead. Conversion of expected time needs into probable costs will make it possible to budget, compare alternative methods for getting a job done, quote prices and bids, determine funds to be needed, and utilize cost standards for other planning needs.

4. (*Set goals for employees* and utilize these goals in motivation, training, compensation, and other supervisory responsibilities. Performance generally improves greatly when people have work goals. High standards, fairly administered, have been found to increase morale. Human reactions to work standards are both significant and complex; they will be considered further in a later section.

Time standards then become a primary basis for *control* of current performance. Specifically, they make possible:

1. *Production control.* Coordinating current work so that the needed quantity of work is completed within desired *time* limits depends upon having standards for reference.

2. *Evaluation of current performance* by comparing measured results with standards, then taking constructive action where needed.

3. *Modification of plans* such as programs and schedules, workforce and equipment, costs, and performance goals—through feedback of information on actual accomplishments.

Special Characteristics of Office Work

Slowness in setting and utilizing time standards has often been attributed to special characteristics of office work such as:

- More mental work usually required—more "hard-to-measure" tasks
- Greater variability of work from case to case
- Numerous small, low-volume tasks not thought to justify standards
- Irregularity in work flow of much office work

Inspection of these characteristics suggests that the difficulties of measuring and standardizing office work frequently are either exaggerated or can be overcome without great difficulty. There is a certain amount of truly creative work for which time requirements may be unpredictable. There is other work in which judgment enters to such an extent that it is difficult to establish standard times for cases or transactions, yet usable standards can be set by averaging times required over a long enough period to take in normal variations. There are unquestionably some tasks which are too inconsequential in time and cost to justify much effort toward time standardization. Despite such considerations, it seems probable that more than three-fourths of all office work is subject to measurement and standardization and would yield good returns for such efforts.

Traditionally, management saw little prospect of significant return from office work standardization. Production and other primary operative work were more inviting. Today, with clerical workers and costs burgeoning, management interest in standards is mounting rapidly. Rapid mechanization, much of it very costly, is bringing concern for high utilization—if a computer is costing $100 an hour whether in use or not, there is an obvious challenge not only to keep it in operation most of the time but to keep it occupied with worthwhile tasks. An increasing number of office operations are now machine-paced; thus, much attention is shifting to machine speeds and capacities.

Approaches to Setting Standards

Certain preliminary steps are of prime importance. *Methods simplification and standardization* logically should precede the setting of a time standard, then the rate of output expected should not be changed frequently or arbitrarily.

Key *checkpoints* should be found which will serve overall control needs —types of work which are measurable, important to objectives, and representative of broader segments of work. Examples may include percentage of orders issued within a certain time period, percentage of accuracy, unit costs, and share of the market. Departmental control may also be selective; certain chief indicators of volume, promptness, quality, costs, employee productivity, and employee turnover can usually be found. A single operation requires determining a unit of measurement which covers or reflects the principal product (or result) of the operation, one which usually requires about the same amount of time (or averages out), and is easily counted. The customer order or its equivalent can often be used; on individual, specialized jobs some more specific unit may be necessary, such as cards posted, letters typed, work-sheets coded, etc.

Basic approaches to setting time standards include (1) production records, (2) work sampling, (3) time study data, and (4) standard time data. A fifth approach, use of "subjective standards," is sometimes included—but it is doubtful that results of this approach should be called standards, because they are merely estimates based upon supervisory observation; it is easy to be misled concerning the productivity of individuals when judging by appearances, and by work variations which may show up only over a period of time.

Production records

Most widely used among the approaches to setting office time standards (if we exclude "subjective" observations and estimates) is that of maintaining records of production over a period, then averaging the results—with certain possible refinements, as we shall note. These are often called historical standards.

The period should be long enough so that all normal variations in the nature of work coming through, and variations in individual performance of employees, will be reflected. Often, much of the necessary information will have already been gathered for other purposes, such as production and sales statistics, cost data, or individual performance evaluation. Where this is not the case, or where past performance data are inadequate, a systematic approach to maintaining production records can be initiated and continued until sufficient information is gathered to support standards which will be reliable.

A form for employee use in keeping a current record of production is illustrated in Figure 23-1. Such a record would usually be turned in daily or weekly to each supervisor for summarization, with key items reported to higher management.

The production records approach is easy to explain and administer. Employees generally are stimulated to higher performance by knowing that some effort is being made to "keep score," and seldom will they resent this approach if they are given adequate explanation of purposes —and if management then exercises good judgment in utilizing the in-

Anderson Printing Co., Inc.
Chicago, Illinois

Date ——————————————

Name ——————————————

Title ——————————————

WORK PRODUCTION REPORT

Please make a brief notation covering what you do during each half-hour period during the day. Be as specific as possible. If you work with people, please list their last names. If you prepare reports, letters, or statements, please state how many you prepare during each period.

8:00-8:30 ———————————   12:30-1:00 ———————————

————————————————   ————————————————

8:30-9:00 ———————————   1:00-1:30 ———————————

————————————————   ————————————————

9:00-9:30 ———————————   1:30-2:00 ———————————

————————————————   ————————————————

9:30-10:00 ———————————   2:00-2:30 ———————————

————————————————   ————————————————

10:00-10:30 ———————————   2:30-3:00 ———————————

————————————————   ————————————————

10:30-11:00 ———————————   3:00-3:30 ———————————

————————————————   ————————————————

11:00-11:30 ———————————   3:30-4:00 ———————————

————————————————   ————————————————

11:30-12:00 ———————————   4:00-4:30 ———————————

————————————————   ————————————————

12:00-12:30 ———————————   4:30-5:00 ———————————

————————————————   ————————————————

Signed ————————————————

Figure 23-1. A production-record form on which employees record their production for each half-hour period of the day

414

formation obtained. Significant advantages of this approach are its comparative ease and the likelihood of favorable employee response. Many managements may feel little need to look for more sophisticated methods.

Critics point out that the production-records approach may be useful and even necessary for current measurement of output, but that standards set by averaging past performance merely tell you what has been done, not what could be done. Such criticism can be valid and can justify a more systematic approach. It should be noted, however, that even past performance data can be refined. By relying more upon performance achieved by selected, fully-trained employees than upon performance of averages, all doing similar work, by adjusting average figures before setting standards (where a justifiable basis may exist), and by maintaining records of production experience and methods changes, through which higher standards might later be justified.

> One approach which illustrates possible refinements in standards based upon production records will be described. Repetitive tasks that do not take much time for completion are sought—card punching, order checking, and filing are examples. A competent, well-trained employee is selected, and assigned a representative variety of the items or cases to be processed (some easy, some complex, some in between), and instructed to work at a normal pace for a period of one hour. During this time, the supervisor observes to satisfy himself that the employee is working at a normal pace. The same sort of test is repeated, with the same employee, for a number of days and the results are averaged. More than one employee can be used if there is any reason to believe that the one selected may not be performing at a desirable rate for a well-placed, well-trained employee. Then allowances for fatigue, delay, and personal needs are made—usually in the proximity of 10%, added to the average time required during the test period. No attempt is made to apply a leveling factor for skill and effort (although this could be done), since selection, observation, and repeated timings of the employee are intended to serve this need.

Such an approach may not result in quite so high a degree of precision as a more scientific approach, yet it holds judgment to a minimum and has the special advantage of greater ease in winning employee understanding and acceptance.

Work sampling

One potentially valuable and, as yet, little-used approach to determining time standards is that of work sampling—mentioned briefly earlier in relation to work distribution analysis. It is actually capable of serving a wide variety of management needs.

Work sampling, in essence, is spot checking and drawing conclusions regarding the full range of possible items on the basis of percentages established from the spot check. If time standards are being developed, work sampling may be used as a refined approach to developing and interpreting production records.

Maurice A. Murray, of the American Insurance Company, provides a simple illustration of the use of work sampling in establishing a time standard for a filing operation. The file operator is observed at work a pre-determined number of times during the day. For purposes of simplicity, let us say one-hundred observations; the number may need to be larger and may need to be extended over a longer period, but the distribution of activities observed, as shown below, will indicate the nature of the basic approach. At the end of the day, the record of the one hundred observations might read:

Task	Observations	% of Total
Filing	25	25
Sorting	20	20
Telephone	5	5
Pulling	35	35
Personal	15	15
	100	100

We know the number of minutes in the working day, 450 in this case, so we can readily determine how much time is consumed on each task.

Task	% of total		Min. in day		Time on each task
Filing	25	×	450	=	112.5 min.

At the same time, if we have kept a record of the production for the day on each task and have determined that the clerk filed 450 cards, we can determine the unit time:

Task	Time on each task		Production		Time per unit
Filing	112.5 min.	÷	450 cards	=	0.25 min/card

The key to accuracy of sampling is in the number of observations made and how they are made. Generally, the larger the number of observations, the more accurate the results. A practical balance of accuracy and expense can be attained by deciding upon a suitable degree of reliability for the intended use, then determining the sample size needed to produce this result.[1] Then, a person with only limited training can make ob-

[1] Sampling tables can be found in most statistics books, in the treatment of probability. One excellent source which describes work sampling in detail and presents sampling tables as well is Bertrand L. Hansen, *Work Sampling* (Englewood Cliffs, N.J.: Prentice-Hall, Inc., 1960). Certain useful rule-of-thumb sample sizes for different purposes include: (1) Locating a trouble area, 400 observations; (2) Isolating elements of overhead, 1,000 observations; (3) Machine and personnel utilization, 4,000 observations; and (4) Establishing standards, 10,000 observations.

servations at random intervals. The American Insurance Company records the observations by use of mark sensing on punched cards; results are verified later by more highly skilled analysts who spot-check them by use of time study or standard time data, and they do any adjusting and levelling believed necessary.

Time study

Time study by stopwatch is not as widely used as the production records and averaging approach but, in skilled hands, can probably result in somewhat greater precision in results.

Study of the time data sheet in Figure 23-2 will indicate the basic ap-

TIME STUDY DATA SHEET																							
Operation: Order Processing										Operator's Name: Barbara Miller													
Observer: J.T. Powell										Date of Study: 11-15													
Element	1		2		3		4		5		6		7		8		9		10		Selected Average	Rating	Base Time
	T	R	T	R	T	R	T	R	T	R	T	R	T	R	T	R	T	R	T	R			
Edit Order	33	00 33	31	38	29	42	31	51	Ⓐ28	449 484	43	99	32	95	29	97	28	95	30	84	0.301	1.10	0.331
Pull Customer Card	20	53	19	57	21	63	18	69	19	503	16	615	20	715	22	819	19	914	18	1002	0.182	1.10	0.200
Post Order	25	78	26	83	25	88	23	92	24	27	22	37	24	39	21	40	22	36	25	27	0.237	1.10	0.261
Check for Accuracy	29	107	30	213	32	320	29	421	29	56	26	63	29	68	27	67	18	54	29	56	0.289	1.10	0.318
TOTAL BASE TIME																					XXX	XXX	

Allowance for Fatigue and Delay __12__ %   0.132 minutes

Standard Time per Unit (Base Time plus Allowance)   1.242 minutes

Standard Output in Units per Hour   48.309 units/hour

Notes (interruptions, irregularities, other comments):

Ⓐ Asked supervisor about possible price discrepancy, from 4.49 to 4.84 minutes

Figure 23-2. Time study data sheet for order processing operation

proach. In this illustration, an order processing operation is broken down into four principal elements: editing customer orders for conformance to company policy and price; pulling the customer's card from the file; posting the order; checking for accuracy. A stopwatch is started at the beginning of the first element and allowed to run continuously, with a reading made at the end of each element and recorded under the "R" column. The watch continues to run as the operator goes through successive cycles of the same four elements, each cycle being the processing of a different customer order. Then the observer, or analyst, goes back and computes the differences between cumulative times in the "R" column to arrive at individual element times which he enters in the "T" column. Ten cycles of the operation are shown in this illustration; this will often be a sufficient number, but the need is to include enough cycles to indicate a cluster of element times, with most being nearly equal.

A selected average is then computed by throwing out any times which are extreme or greatly separated from what seems to be the cluster, then averaging the remainder. Note that times obtained for the editing element of the sixth cycle and the checking element of the ninth cycle were excluded, on the premise that something of an unusual nature happened in each instance which could throw the average off too greatly if included. An interruption occurred in the editing step of the fifth trip through the operation; as indicated, the time involved was omitted. Adjustments of the selected average times then were made in the form of a rating factor of 1.10 (which means simply that the typical worker can be expected to require 10% more time for the operation than this one did) and an allowance for fatigue and delay of 12% in addition, to arrive at a rate which an operator could be expected to sustain throughout the day.

Essential preliminaries are standardization of methods and conditions under which the work will be performed, and selection of a competent, conscientious employee who is given a thorough explanation of the purpose of the study.

Stopwatch timing obviously requires the use of well-trained analysts, particularly if adjustments such as rating for skill and effort and other judgments are to be made. Experienced analysts usually agree on such adjustments, however.

While stopwatch timing is regarded by many persons as the most scientific approach to the setting of time standards, there is also widespread agreement that it is the weakest from a psychological standpoint. Insecurity, defensiveness, fear of personal criticism, and other hostilities are common results of stopwatch timing; employees may try to "out guess" the analyst and pace themselves at rates which they can live with comfortably in the future; the analyst, in turn, must try to make adjustments and allowances—and the whole process may require more subjectivity in judgment before it is completed than would a straightforward treatment of past accomplishments. This is not to suggest that stopwatch timing has no place in office standards; it is merely to emphasize the need for well-trained analysts, objectives which protect worker interests, and painstaking efforts to communicate the objectives and the necessity for the program.

Standard time data

Standard time data have been developed for a wide variety of basic motions common to many tasks. The best known pioneering work in this field was probably that called MTM (Methods-Time-Measurement), a system developed by Maynard, Stegemerten, and Schwab in the 1940's for factory work. Further refinement has been carried out in the intervening years, and the basic approach has now been extended to office tasks, and is gaining quite rapidly in acceptance. Much of the work of developing time data for standard motions and elements has been done by consulting firms, who can justify the extensive laboratory work necessary in preparing standard time values. Some use is made of time study by stopwatch; a great amount of use is also made of photographing operations to permit detailed motion analysis in order to determine the most efficient motions and to develop standard times for the separate elements. The work culminates in development of a catalog of standard motions, with time assigned to each. Any user can then break down the motions in a given operation, look them up in the catalog of standards, and put together an overall time standard for the operation.

A recent adaptation of MTM to clerical operations has been developed by Serge A. Birn and associates and named Master Clerical Data. Clerical work is classified into thirteen categories of *elements* (not bodily motions), thus greatly simplifying application to clerical tasks. Most routine clerical tasks can be described in terms of a few steps, and it is only necessary to see what general actions are involved in a task, select the appropriate time value worked out in Master Clerical Data for each action and arrive at a total time span for performing the entire task.[2] This approach holds much promise and is already being used by a rather large number of prominent firms.

Work Measurement

In considering time standards for office work, we have made frequent reference to work measurement. This is inevitable, for the two go hand in hand. Work measurement is necessary to *establish* standards (measurement in the form of production records, work sampling, time study, standard time data, or other means); it is then necessary to *apply* standards in evaluating current work.

[2] For a full description of the Master Clerical Data concept and approach, see Serge A. Birn, R. M. Crossman, and Ralph W. Eastwood, *Measurement and Control of Office Costs* (New York: McGraw-Hill Book Company, Inc., 1961).

Work measurement is principally a control tool, and can serve a number of highly important uses, as described in the beginning portion of this chapter. Work measurement, guided by time standards, will make possible the control of current work to be processed, the provision of workforce and equipment actually needed, the determination and evaluation of costs incurred, the evaluation of employee performance in terms of goals set by use of standards, and the modification of plans of many types through "feedback" of information on actual accomplishments.

The unit of measurement, as mentioned briefly in discussing the preliminary work necessary in setting time standards, should reflect key accomplishment, be relatively uniform, and readily counted.

The customer's *order,* or its equivalent, is the most common overall unit of measurement. Managements commonly set general standards in terms of "one-day service," or "90% policy issuance within three days of receipt of the application," or "clerical minutes per order," or "machine time per order."

For direct measurement of performance of the work in a unit or on a single operation, a more specific unit is likely to be needed—such as invoices typed, cards addressed, and envelopes addressed. Items that vary considerably, such as invoices, will usually average out over a reasonable time period in terms of time requirements; this will serve most planning and control needs.

There are many "short-cut" means of measurement which should be utilized whenever possible. Many items are serially numbered; hence, the difference between the first number assigned during a period and the last will measure the work in process. It is possible to weigh mail of a certain class and convert to number of pieces per pound, use dollar volume of postage as a rough guide, measure inches of cards and convert to numbers, count reams of paper used in reproduction work, and measure typewritten work by key strokes, lines, square inches, letters, and discs or belts transcribed. Many machines now are equipped with counters which measure output automatically.

Forms for keeping current records of production have been mentioned in relation to setting time standards; such a form was illustrated in Figure 23-1. Employees maintain these records currently and turn them in daily or weekly to supervisors who summarize them, use them for planning and control needs, and report general results to higher management, as called for.

Work measurement and motivation

One might expect widespread employee resentment to work standards and measurement. It is true that there have been numerous instances when work measures have been used as a means of steadily increasing pressure upon employees for higher and higher production—called the "speed-up" by union members and others. Workers have often responded by pacing their rates of production at levels they can maintain comfortably, and by deliberately restricting output in some cases.

But there is nothing about work measurement, per se, which should produce such negative results. Properly used, they can motivate positively, for they can provide goals which are needed and actually desired by most persons.

Work standards and attainments can serve as effective communications tools; supervisors have many opportunities to discuss with each employee such facts as costs, effectiveness of methods and equipment, fluctuations in work volume, and individual progress. Many problems and suggestions will come to light if the supervisor demonstrates real interest and concern for the mutual interests of the employee and the enterprise.

Some firms, notably the International Business Machines Corporation, have long used variable norms for different employees doing the same work—standards that challenge the individual, whatever his background of experience. Their experience bears out the findings of research—that persons respond favorably to high standards, fairly administered.

Increased awareness of the values of *self-control* are bringing another shift in application of standards and measures. Rather than provide the results of measurement primarily to superiors for top-down control (even though some of this may be necessary), many managements are increasingly feeding information on results obtained, trends, comparisons, and the like directly to the individual responsible for doing the work, for his own evaluation and adjustment. Such an approach appears to be essential for development of a genuine sense of responsibility.

QUESTIONS FOR STUDY AND DISCUSSION

1. What preliminary work did Frederick W. Taylor find that he had to do before he could establish the "fair day's pay for a fair day's work" concept to which he dedicated much of his effort? Can you see certain limitations in use of this concept today, even if a fair day's work is determined for a given operation and is then rewarded by a fair day's pay?

2. Explain and illustrate the different purposes for which management can use time standards in *planning* and in *controlling*. In a general way, try to show how each of these purposes could be furthered by time standards in the operations of a bank—particularly in the deposit, loan, and loan-collection functions.

3. Office work is often said to have special characteristics which complicate the work of setting time standards. What are several possible characteristics of this sort, and how valid does each of them seem to be? Do they suggest that time standards are impractical for office work?

4. Explain the use of key checkpoints and of units of measurement in setting time standards; offer illustrations to fit varying operations.

5. Describe, compare, and evaluate the use of each of the following approaches

in setting office time standards: (a) production records, (b) work sampling, (c) time study data, and (d) standard time data. In what circumstances would each be particularly appropriate?

6. Does work sampling seem to justify much wider usage than it has found thus far? Does it have certain features which make it particularly adaptable to office tasks?

7. Appraise this statement: "While stopwatch timing is regarded by many persons as the most scientific approach to the setting of time standards, there is also widespread agreement that it is the weakest from a psychological standpoint."

8. Is work measurement involved in *setting* time standards or in *applying* these to current output? Lay out what seem to be the key requirements for a suitable *unit of measurement;* suggest illustrations of general or overall units of measurement and of specific units of measurement for single operations. Is it ever wise to resort to "short-cut" means of measurement?

9. Do employees tend to respond positively when they have production (or output) goals and measurement of work produced, or do they respond negatively? What factors may influence the results obtained through goal-setting and work measurement? In what way is the concept of self-control related? Do you see much potential in the latter concept for management in the future?

Case 23-1. Stopwatch Timing of a Duplicating Operation

The principal steps in operating a spirit duplicating machine on a production (or continuous) basis may be summarized as (1) Placing paper supply in machine, (2) Setting controls, (3) Placing master in clamp, (4) Operating machine, and (5) Removing master and finished work.

In the order-writing department of a firm in which this process is used regularly, an average of 12 copies are made in each run. The first step mentioned above, loading paper into the machine, has to be done only about once every ten runs or cycles; this step takes approximately 0.50 minutes each time it is done, or an average of 0.05 per cycle.

Using the above information and following the general approach described in Chapter 23, set up a time study sheet in which you include the following cycle times, assuming that the watch runs continuously.

	0.00					
Setting controls	.10	.84	.52	.19	.83	.90
Placing master	.23	.96	.66	.35	3.42	4.04
Operating machine	.52	1.24	.96	.62	.70	.30
Removing material	..69	.40	2.11	.76	.83	.55

In the fifth cycle, the master required reinforcement with Scotch tape to close a lining tear, using up 0.50 minutes.

Problem:

Using the data supplied, find the selected average; then apply an over-all rating factor of 1.10 and an allowance for fatigue and delay of an additional

10 per cent and arrive at a standard time for the operation. Do you feel that you have information on a large enough number of cycles to produce a reliable standard? How could you be reasonably sure?

Case 23-2. The Madison National Automobile Insurance Company

The Madison National is a mutual company which concentrates on careful selection of risks to be insured and upon efficient operation. Since its founding in 1924, it has pioneered a rather large number of features of insurance coverage which have had wide appeal and which have been imitated by other companies. Careful selection and training of agents are emphasized, as is fair and prompt settlement of claims. The company has enjoyed a steady and rapid growth, and it is now one of the largest in its field.

The top management organization of the company consists of a Board of Directors, President, Executive Vice-President, Vice-President of Operations who has line authority over all field operations, and staff Vice-Presidents over Agency, Claims, Underwriting, Finance, Planning and Research, Administrative Services, Personnel, Public Relations, and Investments.

The field organization includes some sixty territorial divisions, each of which serves a geographical concentration of approximately 100,000 policy-holders. The divisions are grouped into regions, with a regional office established to serve a group of three divisions, ordinarily. Each regional office typically includes line management for the three divisions, and staff departments in Personnel, Administrative Services, Accounting, and Data Processing. Each operating division is made up of separate sections in Underwriting, Claims, and Service, each headed by a superintendent, and each in turn including two or more units headed by supervisors. The function of Agency is organized under an Agency Director for each division, who in turn supervises District Managers, each over a group of agents. At the top of the regional office organization, there are a Regional Vice-President, a Deputy Vice-President of Operations, and a Deputy Vice-President of Agency.

In 1946, the company instituted a performance control program for the joint purpose of measuring the efficiency of the operating divisions and of serving as a basis for a bonus program for executives down to the level of superintendent. Bonuses were very substantial, amounting to as much as one-third of base salary for top achievement. The bonus system was applied only to operating executives; agency executives and personnel were covered by a separate compensation program.

Three principal factors were considered in determining whether an operating executive qualified for a bonus and if so, what amount:

(1) Issuance of at least 80 per cent of policies within seven calendar days from the time applications were received in the office.

(2) Attainment of a performance "factor" or standard which was actually a ratio of the number of policies in force to the number of employees in the division; for example, 11,485 policies per employee.

(3) A satisfactory showing on an audit of conformance to procedures and policies within each section conducted annually by an audit team normally headed by a representative of the home office staff department specializing in the function primarily involved. An unsatisfactory showing on an audit might prevent the superintendent heading the section involved from getting a bonus, but it would not directly affect bonuses earned by heads of other sections in the division.

Most company personnel seemed to agree that the performance control program served as a strong stimulus to operating executives to try to meet the standards set for them. Much attention would be given, for example, to the priority of policies received and issued and to trying to meet or surpass the seven-day standard for promptness.

Presence of the performance "factor" or standard caused division managers and superintendents to limit personnel additions very carefully and to keep employees occupied with productive work as much of the time as possible. The factor was revised for each division every six months, largely on the basis of experience of the division during the period just passed although with any anticipated changes or contingencies presumably taken into account.

The program of annual audits encouraged close attention to conformance to procedure and led to frequent "self-audits," particularly a short while before the annual audit was expected. At these times, much attention was given to getting everything in the best possible shape for the audit.

Unit supervisors were not included in the bonus program. The top management of the firm held the belief that to include them would be to tempt them to place too much pressure upon employees in their individual units and cause them to lose sight of general objectives; also, it seemed necessary to cut off the program at some point and this seemed the logical stopping place.

Supervisors frequently expressed discontent with the program. Not only were they left out with regard to bonuses, but they often felt that their superiors were constantly putting pressure on them so that the superiors, in turn, could qualify for the bonus. They noted that such practices as the following often tended to be encouraged in order to meet the seven-day policy issuance standard: they were sometimes told to look for easy or routine policies in sufficient numbers to push through and reach the desired percentage. The performance factor forced them many times, in their view, to operate with fewer personnel than were really needed for certain operations, to neglect training toward the end of the year when cumulative production would be compared with the factor for bonus determination, and often to ignore policyholder needs or at least place these secondary to the performance program. The audits led to much stress on procedural detail, to "following the book," and to undertaking special efforts for having everything in "clean" shape for the audits. And supervisors often felt that their own promotions and pay increases were influenced greatly by how well their units did in contributing to the performance program.

Neither supervisors nor their immediate superiors ever quite understood just how the performance factor was determined. They wondered whether the home office staff people who arrived at it were sufficiently familiar with local problems, peculiarities in service requirements, state insurance laws, and similar considerations to take these adequately into account in setting the factor. They felt that the practice of basing the new factor, released each six months, on experience during the previous period, too often meant a lag in the number of personnel allowed, particularly since fairly rapid growth was taking place almost constantly.

By 1957, top management had become increasingly aware of some of the problems just mentioned, and it took action in the form of "folding" most of the bonuses of operating executives directly into their salaries, and of providing bonuses only up to about five per cent of base salaries. They also ceased to use the term "audit," and substituted the term "survey," and changed the nature of this device somewhat—doing only spot checking rather than detailed checking as had been carried out before, discussing results at the time of the survey with supervisors and superintendents involved and emphasizing value of the survey as a learning experience, but continuing to evaluate each unit surveyed, with this evaluation continuing to be one of the considerations in bonus determination.

These changes have unquestionably reduced the pressure upon operating executives and personnel. Yet most of the criticisms mentioned above are still heard, and the opinions of personnel toward the performance control program vary from those which would like to see the entire program thrown out to those which would leave the program as it is with only minor changes.

Problems and questions:

a. What central problem or problems are posed here?

b. How well do the three measuring criteria seem to be related to overall objectives of the company, and how satisfactorily do they appear to cover the most important factors of performance needed to achieve objectives in the insurance business?

c. How satisfactory was the "performance factor"—both in terms of how it was determined and how it was applied?

d. Would inclusion of supervisors in the bonus program seem likely to remedy or eliminate most of the undesirable results which they have attributed to the program?

e. Can personnel usually figure out ways to "beat" just about any control system if they wish to? What lessons may be indicated for management generally?

f. Was the "folding in" of the bonus amounts justified?—was it effective? Were the changes in the audit procedure desirable ones?—appraise reasons for the changes and responses which might be expected to follow.

g. What should now be done? Consider alternative courses of action, factors bearing upon each, and the specific action that you would now recommend and why you recommend it.

24

PRODUCTION CONTROL; CONTROLLING VOLUME FLUCTUATIONS

Basic nature of production control · Control procedure: routing, scheduling, dispatching, follow-up · Human aspects of controls · Work volume fluctuations · Costs involved · Recommended general approach · Alternative methods of handling

---

Plans with regard to office work are not self-executing. Management must take steps to insure that they are carried out. Several factors must be controlled if objectives are to be attained, among these are quality, quantity, time, and cost of the work performed.

Basic Nature of Production Control

The factors of *quantity* and of *time required* in performing work are the ones dealt with in production control. Quality control and cost control are usually handled as separate and distinct areas of specialization; they will be considered in later chapters of this book.

Production control is concerned particularly with *coordination* of the current performance of work by the different departments, units, and employees. Steps are taken to insure that each does its part at the right time so that orders or quotas of production are completed when needed. This is a tremendously important contribution to good management. Customer satisfaction and good utilization of both personnel and equipment are directly at stake. Employee satisfaction also may be affected greatly by the types of controls exercised.

Controls over production may be simple or elaborate. Figure 24-1 illustrates a record kept by a supervisor in one firm for his own use in insuring prompt handling of incoming mail.

INCOMING MAIL REGISTER				
Writer and Company	Date of Material	Person Handling	Date Assigned	Date to Complete
J. B. Armstrong, Continental Lines	3/22	LCS	3/24	3/24
Mack S. Conrad, Lowell Mfg. Co.	3/23	JRT	3/24	3/25

Figure 24-1. Control record for incoming mail

Through this simple form, each piece of incoming mail is assigned to an employee in the department and a completion time suggested. While work is in progress, the supervisor knows exactly where each item may be found, the time when the item should be disposed of, and the work load assigned to each employee. Carbon copies of replies are then turned in, and the supervisor merely draws a line through the appropriate entries. Such an approach would hardly be adequate or suitable for some control purposes, but it serves to indicate the basic nature of production control and to show that even a simple system can bring reasonable assurance of satisfactory performance.

The work of production control includes four primary functions. These are routing, scheduling, dispatching, and follow-up. Much of the discussion to follow will center around these functions. First, some brief definitions:

Routing is determining the route or path that any current project of work is to follow. This usually involves specifying operations in proper sequence; it may also name specific departments, equipment, and personnel where these need to be indicated.

Scheduling is working out a time table for the different operations on a project. The usual approach is to work back from the desired completion date and to allow for the time required by each work phase. The starting and finishing times for each phase of work can thus be determined.

Dispatching is releasing orders and instructions—giving the go-ahead sign for actual execution. This is usually done just far enough in advance so that each unit or employee involved can make needed preparations, although more advance notice can be given when needed.

Follow-up is checking on the progress being made. It consists of recording output, comparing actual with scheduled output, and reporting the status of work produced. The status of all current production may be summarized if desired, or only serious delays or interferences may be reported where executive time is to be conserved.

Factors Determining Control Procedure

The exact procedure that a given firm will follow in performing the four control functions usually should depend upon whether work is done under conditions of mass production, job order production, or lot production. Most office work is processed in lots or batches; the term "block control" is sometimes used to indicate the type of control most often appropriate. Large office departments often have flow of work planned on a production-line basis, with work narrowly subdivided, much as in factory mass production. Even in such cases, however, work is usually assigned in blocks or batches and controlled accordingly. Variations in control procedure to cover different production situations will be considered in later discussion of specific techniques.

Comparison with Production Control in Factories

The similarity of many control problems in office and factory work may be noted in passing. The same basic control functions are involved in coordinating both types of work, and many of the techniques are similar. Office work has certain peculiarities—it is usually more variable, it often requires greater mental effort, it involves much detail, and time standards are often not available. Nevertheless, it has much in common with factory work. Factory managers have been aware of the need for production control for a long time; most office executives can learn much in this area from their factory counterparts. Some adaptations of factory control techniques to office situations will be noted in the following sections.

Specialization of the production control function has been carried much further in factories than in offices. The typical factory has a central department which clears and coordinates all production orders or quotas; this department is usually called either the production control department or the planning department. Few office organizations have gone so far. Indeed, the service emphasis and the all-pervasive nature of office work would limit the possibilities of centralization of control in most cases. But some top executives and operating division heads do exercise overall control with regard to major office work units—such as clerical-minutes-per-order and rate of policy issuance within a standard time period—often delegating the detailed work of such controls to a staff assistant. Most controls over office production, however, are on a departmental, rather than central, basis.

Techniques involved in carrying out the basic control functions for office work will now be considered.

Routing

The most basic tool in office routing is the *procedure*. As suggested previously, a procedure is the sequence of steps involved in carrying out a given type of work.

Even though details vary, the major steps followed in performing most types of office work can be virtually the same each time the work is performed. This enables management to establish procedures, and to route current work through the appropriate procedures. Thus, all incoming mail may go through the same basic steps of opening, time stamping, sorting by class, sorting by handling department, and delivery to handling department.

The original planning of procedures may be done with the help of procedure analysts or, if these are not available, by operating executives and employees. At least the more important procedures ordinarily should be expressed in written form; as pointed out earlier, this facilitates understanding and insures uniform handling by a carefully-thought-out approach. The result will be an information source of great value for training and reference.

In relation to production control, the procedure manual serves as a master routing guide, quite comparable to the factory master plan of work which serves as a permanent record of the standard routing required to make a product or part.

New work (orders, inquiries, etc.) comes in by some means of communication—mail, telephone, telegraph, personal call, or otherwise. If the work poses no special problems, it may be possible to run it through the standard procedure without any use of special routing forms or devices.

Closer control may be provided by use of a *route sheet* which lays out the successive steps. Special justification for a route sheet may exist when unusual features in the work require that a special sequence of steps must be followed, when the work must pass through the hands of a large number of employees, when new employees may be unfamiliar with procedure, when the scheduled or actual time of performance are to be recorded, or in other situations calling for a formal routing. Even with a well-understood procedure, there is always the problem of routing to specific individuals and machines within a department, and the use of route sheets may save time and confusion.

A simple illustration of an office route sheet is given in Figure 24-2.

ROUTE SHEET								
Procedure Order				Date to start 2/1/62				
Items Customer Orders 2411-2420				Routed by ANH				
Number of items 10								
Operation	Department	Equipment	Std. Min. pc	Schedule		Actual	
				Start	Finish	Start	Finish
Orders received, checked	Sales	Compt.	7	8:05	9:15	8:03	9:10
Credit approved	Credit		6	9:30	10:30	9:32	10:30
Work orders, invoices prepared	Order	Typ. Ditto	12	10:45	1:45	10:46	1:41
Orders filled	Stock		15	2:00	4:30	2:07	4:53

Figure 24-2. Combined route sheet and progress control record

A route sheet of this general type may be made up in duplicate with one copy to travel with the work and the other to be retained by the executive or control clerk. Or, where special preparations are required before certain steps can be completed, separate copies of the route sheet may be prepared and dispatched in advance of delivery of the work to each department involved. The information in the heading of the route sheet illustrated, as well as the information in the first three columns, would be entered as a part of the routing process, being determined either by the executive's familiarity with the operations required or by reference to written procedures where necessary and available. Origin and use of the information in the other columns will be considered in the discussion of subsequent control steps.

A problem of special importance in routing may be the decision as to size of batch to be assigned at a time and controlled as a unit. No single standard can be set here, but certain factors worthy of consideration will be mentioned. Employees can experience a feeling of greater accomplishment if the individual batches of work assigned are small enough for completion in a relatively short time, perhaps in an hour or less, when possible. The executive in charge can stay better informed about each employee's progress if the batch is kept reasonably small. Delay in passing work on and in getting later steps started and finished can be held to a minimum. The requirements of the work itself may sometimes justify smaller or larger batches of work, however, as may the experience and ability of the employees involved.

Scheduling

In order to set up a time table for accomplishing office work, certain requirements must be met. Most important are knowledge of the desired completion time, and of standard times required to perform successive phases of the work. With this information, it is possible to work back from the desired completion time and to determine the time at which each earlier phase should be started and finished, informing personnel accordingly. Often there may be no specific calendar deadline; in such cases, such a policy as "three-day service" or "as promptly as possible" may set a working deadline.

The dependence of scheduling upon time standards is apparent. As mentioned in the chapter on standards, time standards may be set through use of time study or through other less precise means. In any case, an approximation of time requirements should be obtainable for most types of work.

There are many devices for recording and utilizing schedules. The route sheet in Figure 24-2 illustrates such a device. The starting and finishing times in the schedule column are determined on the basis of time requirements for the number of items to be processed, plus allowance for delivery time, and they were entered as a part of the scheduling operation. Both the executive in control and the personnel involved in carrying out the operations specified are informed about time expectations.

Other scheduling devices are many and varied. One of the most widely-used is the Gantt Chart. Named for its developer, Henry Lawrence Gantt, one of the pioneers in the scientific management movement, this type of chart can be adapted to a wide variety of uses in production control. The basic pattern is always the same, however; it shows action taking place as time passes. An illustration of the use of such a chart for controlling work in a transcription department is shown in Figure 24-3. Based upon a time standard of forty-five minutes per cylinder transcribed, the supervisor assigns work to available transcribers, indicating work scheduled by the light lines enclosed by brackets and indicating work accomplished by the heavy lines just above.

Such a chart enables the supervisor to utilize employees fully and to plan work ahead for each, while providing for any preferences of dictators and any priority needs at the same time. He can stay informed on the status of each dictation job, these being identified by the initials of the personnel dictating them. In the illustration, the supervisor has checked progress at 9 o'clock as indicated by the *V* mark; she has found Smith running approximately fifteen minutes behind with cylinders dictated by *LS*, Rogers right on schedule with her assignments, and Miller about ten minutes ahead of schedule. The chart illustrated serves not only as a scheduling device but as a basis for dispatching and follow-up, soon to be discussed. So versatile is the Gantt Chart that it can be adapted to

WORK SCHEDULE										
Department Transcription **Work Unit** Cylinder										
Supervisor Sarah Landy **Time/Unit** 45 min.										
Employee	**Hour**									
	8	9	10	11	1	2	3	4		
Smith	*LS*	*V*	*TM*	*AR*						
Rogers										
Miller										

Figure 24-3. Gantt Progress Chart showing work scheduled and work completed

serve any or all of the basic functions of control when desired. This type of chart is also simple to understand and to use.

Most of the other types of scheduling devices are based on either the tabular approach of the route sheet or the graphic approach of the Gantt Chart. They include visible index cards, tape boards, hook boards, clip boards, and others which contain essentially the same information but portray it more visibly, more graphically, or more simply.

If a schedule is to be attainable, certain requirements in addition to knowledge of deadlines and time standards must be met. Personnel and equipment must both be available in sufficient quantities at successive work stations, and capacity should be kept as nearly as possible in balance; in other words, there should be no bottlenecks. The number of personnel assigned to each type of job and to each unit needs to be decided in terms of time requirements of work to be performed.

Load charts in scheduling

Equipment that is costly or that requires scarce skills may often justify the use of load charts for effective and efficient utilization. Load charts are particularly appropriate for data processing equipment because of the extremely high cost and the demands for full and efficient utilization.

The scheduling of data processing operations requires coordination of machines, operators, and work volume.

Use of load charts for scheduling data processing offers the following specific advantages:

1. Anticipates requirements of operators and equipment.

2. Reduces conflicts by sequentially assigning job operations to various machines and operators.

3. Holds overtime requirements to a minimum.

4. Levels peak loads, thereby keeping operators and equipment at a minimum level for satisfactory operations.

5. Establishes firm times for receipt of raw data and output of the desired reports, information analyses, and other work.

6. Establishes records of data processing operations so that continual evaluations may be made and improvements implemented.

Load charts may be as elaborate as desired by the firm, or may be quite simple as long as the essential purpose is served. Possibly the most common type of load chart is the bar chart, resembling the Gantt Chart discussed previously. There are many variations of this type of chart, limited only by the ingenuity of the individual. A variation of a load chart is presented in Figure 24-4. Available hours per week for each individual machine in a data processing department are first shown;

SOUTHWEST DISTRIBUTING COMPANY

Machine Load and Performance Record

Week _____ Oct. 15 _____

Machine	Available Hours (1)	Scheduled Hours (2)	Actual Hours (3)	Percentage of Utilization (3) ÷ (1)	Percentage of Standard Performance (2) ÷ (3)	Comments
Card Punch 1	40	36	40	100	90	
Card Punch 2	40	38	38	95	100	
Card Punch 3	40	32	31	78	103	Maint. 1 hrs.
Total Punch	120	106	109	91	97	
Sorter	40	28	31	78	90	Repair 4 hrs.
Collator	40	35	35	88	100	
407 Tab	40	40	43	107	93	O.T. Oct. 16
Reproducer						
Totals	240	209	218	91	96	

Figure 24-4. Machine load and analysis work sheet

these represent the base or 100% of capacity. Against this maximum, jobs are scheduled for completion during the week; then actual hours used are shown and the utilization percentage determined for each machine. Finally, the percentage of standard, or scheduled, hours represented by actual hours required, is included to measure performance.

Load charts are designed primarily for the efficient scheduling of machines, but they are also quite useful in scheduling operator assignments to the various machines and job operations to be performed. Little use can be made of load charts unless operators are scheduled to be available at the time the work is scheduled. In many cases this problem can be met by simply assigning certain operators to the different types of machines, but in larger installations with several tabulating or computer operators, it becomes necessary to schedule the operators as the machines are scheduled.

Scheduling the processing and completion of reports is as equally an important need as scheduling equipment, machines, and workers. Again, the nature of the particular operations will determine the make-up of the schedule, but it should contain at least the following details:

1. Report name and number.
2. Due-in time of the detail data.
3. Due-out time of the complete report.
4. Recording of actual times for the above operations for evaluation and follow-up purposes.

The use of such load charts allows the total available hours ahead for each machine to be apportioned in advance to specific jobs or batches of work, thus assuring full utilization and making possible advance checking on the feasibility of schedules.

A special problem in scheduling is encountered when work loads fluctuate greatly. This is a very common situation and one that challenges the most able management. So important, and so commonly neglected is this problem that it is treated in the final section of this chapter.

Dispatching

The release of office work to employees and the giving of needed instructions are activities usually carried out by the immediate supervisor. As mentioned in connection with routing, there may be psychological and other advantages in favor of releasing relatively small batches of work at a time. There may be similar advantage in releasing work shortly before it is to be started, allowing only the time needed for preparation.

The scheduling forms and devices previously discussed can be used to signal the time for dispatching, or the receipt of work itself, after completion at earlier stages, may be used.

Follow-up

To assure that work actually stays "under control," methods must be developed to determine whether work actually progresses according to schedule. Control of the production process and, particularly, control of a data processing system has one primary objective—that of improvement through evaluation and follow-up.

We have recognized that control of production requires that management:

1. Specify clearly the work and volume to be done.
2. Determine work loads for equipment and for employees.
3. Schedule the operations to be performed.

Essentially, the follow-up process is a simple arithmetic problem. With the above three factors in mind, follow-up involves maintaining close control of the volume of work that enters the unit, the volume of work that has left the unit, and the stage of completion of the work that still remains in the unit. As the work is received in the unit, it should be entered in some sort of log to indicate that it has been received and is available for processing. The work-received log facilitates scheduling; if a bottleneck should occur, a quick look at the log indicates the work that has been received and that is available for re-scheduling in order to maintain full utilization of the machines and workers.

Current production follow-up is primarily concerned with the control of the *work* as it is in process, but another significant aspect of follow-up is the evaluation of the progress of the *unit* in meeting the schedules established and in evaluating the efficiency with which this is done. That is, management must determine what caused the bottlenecks, why a particular operation was behind schedule, and what can be done to improve the utilization of the machines and employees in the future. Evaluation is particularly important in a data processing department for maintaining efficient percentages of machine utilization in view of the large expense involved.

When operating data and other facts have been collected, classified, and summarized, it is possible to evaluate volume, time, cost, errors, overtime, maintenance, and other critical factors for each of the machines, workers, and job operations. Comparisons and evaluations such as these point out weak spots in the operation, and only through such follow-up and evaluation can intelligent decisions be made for subsequent improvement.

Basically, two types of evaluation reports are most significant—machine usage and job performance. These evaluations stem from the scheduling and load charts discussed previously. It is important to evaluate the machine effectiveness and efficiency with respect to schedule and other criteria, but it is also quite important to evaluate the results of processing the individual job operations to facilitate future scheduling and control planning when the job is next processed. Examples of machine and job summaries are shown in Figure 24-5 and Figure 24-6. Figure 24-5 is an illustration of State Farm Mutual Automobile Insurance Company's machine utilization and machine and salary cost report prepared at the end of each period. This report is used primarily to evaluate the utilization and cost of the data processing operations as related to a fixed base of the number of policies in force. It illustrates a generally applicable principle—the value of selecting some fixed, dominant basis and relating the efficiency of an expensive operation for evaluation purposes. This report is designed to give the user a general, over-all picture of the equipment status, usage, and rental costs. Other detailed reports supplement this general report.

Human Relations Aspects of Controls

A consideration of great importance in the design and administration of controls is that of the reactions of personnel to them.

There are instances when controls are used in a way that creates extreme tension and pressure on employees. Supervisors, wanting to make a good showing for higher management, may do a lot of "whip-cracking." Employees may see no personal benefit whatsoever in controls, and they often may be critical of the fairness of the work standards involved in controls. Whether intentional or not, the administration of controls more often seems to be attended by negative than by positive discipline—by pressure and threats rather than by satisfaction of employee desires.

The fundamental soundness of the concept of control cannot be doubted. The success of an organization in achieving its objectives depends directly upon keeping the quantity, quality, time, and cost of necessary work "under control" as measured by reasonable standards of performance.

The way in which employees will react to controls probably depends upon whether they have a general understanding of the controls exercised and of the uses to which they are put, whether they feel that work load is fair, and whether they see little threat to their own personal security.

What seems to be greatly needed is better explanation of controls by

STATE FARM MUTUAL AUTOMOBILE INSURANCE COMPANY
DATA PROCESSING DEPARTMENT
MACHINE UTILIZATION AND MACHINE AND SALARY COST PER POLICY

OFFICE _____ DATE _____

DESCRIPTION	TYPE	NO. OF MACH-INES	SHIFT NUMBER	HOURS UTILIZED REGULAR DOWNTIME, INS. TIME	AVAILABLE REGULAR HOURS	UTILIZATION % RATIO	NON PRODUCTIVE HOURS	OVER TIME HOURS	MACHINE RENTAL OWNED AND LEASED	RENTAL COST PER 100,000 POLICIES IN FORCE
COLLATORS	077		1							
	085									
	088		2							
SORTERS	080		1							
	082		2							
	083									
TABULATORS	407		1							
			2							
	402		1							
	403									
	416		2							
	419									
REPRODUCING AND SUMMARY PUNCH	513		1							
	514									
	519		2							
	523									
INTERPRETER	548		1							
	552		2							
	557									
CALCULATORS	604		1							
	650		2							
KEY PUNCH	016									
	024									
EQUIPMENT	026									
	031									
	056									

PRIMARY SHIFT:
SECOND SHIFT:

TOTAL

RENT COST PER POLICY
SALARY COST PER POLICY
RENT AND SALARY COST PER POLICY

Figure 24-5. Machine utilization report

438

SOUTHERN UTILITIES INC.

Job Performance Record

Week _____

Job Operation	Schedule Hours	Actual Hours	Performance Std %	Comments
Payroll–monthly	23	22	105	
Mo. Report 589	16	18	89	new clerk--
Mo. Report # 1	11			
Totals	39	40	98	

Figure 24-6. Record of progress on individual jobs

management—their nature and uses and the employee's stake in them. Communication in the other direction should be provided, also; employees ordinarily should be given greater opportunity to participate in the planning stages with regard to controls, and at all times management should be receptive to worker suggestions regarding current experience with controls.

Work Volume Fluctuations

A significant problem area in the management of most offices is coping with the problem of work load fluctuations. Office work loads have a way of accumulating. This is a characteristic known only too well by any office supervisor or clerk. In an insurance home office, the Monday load of policy applications is often about double the Friday load. Figure 24-7 illustrates the daily fluctuations of policy applications received for a typical insurance firm. In a bank, more volume often is handled on Saturday morning than on any other full day. There probably are few business establishments of any type that do not have similar patterns of fluctuations—if not by weekdays, then by hours of the day, certain times of the month, one or more seasons, and on such special occasions as inventory, annual report, and income tax time.

This experience is so common, in fact, that in many firms it is not regarded as a problem at all. It is accepted as merely a way of life in the office.

The literature on office management offers little help. During the ten

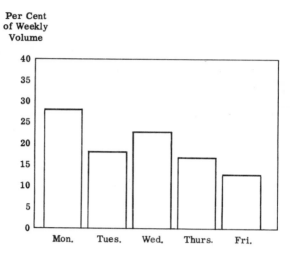

Figure 24-7. Policy applications received by an insurance company on different weekdays

years just past, a bare half-dozen articles in the leading business magazines have dealt with the problem of peak loads. This might be interpreted as an indication that the problem actually is one of little significance. A more plausible explanation is that absence of work measurement and standards in most offices has held back recognition of the problem; that in offices that have done something with work measurement and have obtained a fairly clear picture of fluctuations in volume, uncertainty exists as to how to bring them under effective control.

Costs Involved

What, if any, added costs result from the peak load tendency? There are many of them and some are highly elusive.

A study of clerical errors in the order department of a manufacturing concern showed that on their heaviest weekday, the error percentage was about fifty per cent higher than the rate on the day considered to be normal in volume. In a wholesale drug firm, an invariable breakdown in promptness of service to customers was found to follow the heaviest weekday.

In studies of employee morale—whether conducted through surveys, termination interviews, suggestion systems, turnover and absenteeism analysis, or other means—a very common employee gripe concerns the pressure that is put on during peak periods in work volume, and the boredom that follows during slack periods.

But the most conspicuous, and probably the greatest dollar costs, are likely to be those directly related to poor use of employee time and to poor utilization of equipment and space. During shortages of qualified office personnel, this phase of the problem is particularly significant.

Common Methods of Handling

As is true with almost any other commonly encountered problem, peak loads have been approached in a variety of ways. All too often, the solution attempted is the first one that offers itself; seldom is the approach in any way scientific.

Probably the most common approach is that of carrying a reserve of personnel all the time to meet peak loads when they occur. Not many department heads would admit that they are guilty of this practice, but a careful look at variations in worker output at different times and a little attention to work standards will usually reveal some degree of overstaffing in anticipation of recurring peak loads. It is an expensive luxury, at best.

Very commonly used, also, is overtime. Sometimes this may be the only way out, but unit costs during overtime are usually found in production studies to be just about double their amount during regular time. This suggests rather forcefully that *overtime should be the last instead of the first resort.*

Reduction or elimination of overtime should not, however, be considered a panacea. The total picture of optimum performance for the organization as a whole must always be retained. In this respect, planned and controlled overtime in some minor departments may be quite economical to avoid delays and idle time in a major department later in the production process. This is a very common managerial practice in firms using expensive data processing equipment, and it requires extraordinary scheduling skill. Often net costs can be reduced if one or more minor departments operate on a *controlled overtime* basis to prepare data for processing in order to eliminate costly delays and idle time in the computer department.

Other methods used include cycle billing, temporary help, utility clerks, preparatory steps done in anticipation of heavy loads and many more.

But seldom, indeed, can a firm be found in which the problem has been subjected to careful analysis. Most heads of office departments, while knowing that they are intermittently snowed under and relatively idle, have never tried to get a clear picture of the usual size and timing of even their most troublesome peak loads. Few have analyzed carefully the causes of their heavy loads and the factors that limit the choice of methods in handling them.

What seems to be needed is an economical plan that will insure thorough consideration of the alternative methods by which any given peak load might be handled. Here is a sample of such a plan.

Recommended General Approach

1. Make a preliminary appraisal to spot types of work that occur in troublesome peak loads.

Work types known to fluctuate violently, to affect large portions of the organization, or to constitute bottleneck steps in procedures may yield the greatest improvements; any fluctuating work load may justify study.

2. Determine the usual pattern of variation in work load for any specific type of work selected for analysis.

A count of incoming volume and a simple chart will reveal a surprisingly uniform pattern in most cases. If a more accurate determination is desired, percentages or index numbers of loads received in the different time phases of a period may be established.

3. Try to explain fluctuations in the work load; determine principal causes.

4. Determine whether performance must be started and finished within rigid deadlines or whether some flexibility in scheduling may exist.

5. Consider possible improvements in work methods and equipment that might reduce the impact of the peak load.

Work simplification and mechanization can often take much of the pressure out of peak loads; these always warrant careful consideration. But even when only the necessary work is performed and when most efficient methods are used, work volume will still fluctuate. Computer systems can go a long way in absorbing peak loads; the problem here is one of how to utilize the systems fully during normal periods of the production cycle. Overcapacity can sometimes be solved by leasing time to other users; undercapacity may be relieved by leasing time from other firms or from service bureaus. A small amount of overtime in a computer department, if properly utilized, can produce a considerable amount of work. But to be most effective and economical, such operations should be deliberately planned and controlled. The problem of peak loads cannot be eliminated through improved methods and equipment, but it can be reduced considerably—more so in computerized operations than in other systems.

6. Consider the alternative methods by which the peak load might be handled, and get facts needed in deciding on the method or the combination best suited.

A list of principal methods with key requirements of each will be presented in the concluding section of this chapter.

7. Apply method or methods apparently most suitable and evaluate results.

Alternative Methods

Step number six in this list is important enough to warrant special attention. In meeting a given peak load problem, the various alternatives available should be studied carefully, in preference to taking the first method that offers itself. There are many avenues open. Some of the more promising of these will now be considered briefly.

For economy of effort, the methods suggested might be considered roughly in the sequence presented. Conditions that seem to point to use of each of the methods will be considered in each case.

All of the methods presented, and probably any others that might be added to the list, have one common characteristic—that of finding and taking advantage of flexibility in some form. When a peak load hits, something has to give.

Flexible schedule

1. Where it might be feasible to smooth out the irregularity in work volume before it hits the office:

    a. Consider varying or retiming sales efforts where losses in volume or in quality of service would not be prohibitive.

    b. Consider securing advance orders, producing more stock, or in other ways trying to stabilize the pattern of incoming volume.

Each of these efforts would involve modifying sales or production efforts in some way, and is likely to result in loud outcries that the tail is trying to wag the dog. It is, of course, the height of foolishness to let office convenience dictate sales and production policies. But it may be almost equally foolish to ignore office convenience and costs; they deserve consideration at least at their face value.

An interesting example of failure to do this was provided by an insurance company which for many years had a sales contest during one week of the year, with attractive (and expensive) prizes to winners. Dissatisfaction from various sources finally led to an investigation which indicated strongly that total annual volume was being increased very little by the contest, since sales lagged greatly before and after the contest period. Further, the home office marked time during the period just before the contest, then worked under a terrific strain while the contest was in progress, and had a period of relative idleness afterward, since sales representatives had squeezed prospect lists dry—and, incidentally, had taken some policy applications that did not fit individual needs very well, as indicated by higher incidence of lapses. The contest has since been abandoned, to the apparent regret of no one.

2. When promptness of service (either to customers, others outside the firm, or to your own departments that depend on office service) does not require rigid deadlines or exact completion dates:

    a. Consider maintaining a controlled backlog of incoming work and feeding it through evenly.

There are very few types of work for which performance cannot be postponed, slightly moved up, or retimed in some other way. And even a small amount of flexibility in scheduling often can make it possible to level down troublesome peaks in volume. One of the best possibilities, where even a limited amount of flexibility exists, is that of maintaining a controlled backlog of work.

One organization, also an insurance company, found that on Monday it ordinarily receives about twenty-five per cent of its policy applications for the entire week, on Tuesday twenty-one per cent, on Wednesday twenty-two per cent, on Thursday seventeen per cent, and on Friday fifteen per cent. It now holds over about one-fifth of the Monday load for processing early Tuesday morning, and similarly adjusts the carry-over on other days in order to handle about twenty per cent of the weekly volume each day. Adjustments occasionally must be made for unusual variations, but the process comes close to making every day an average day. Overtime is negligible, employees appreciate the even load, and promptness of service seems, actually, to be greater as a result of the slight postponement involved.

    b. Consider doing cycle billing; or staggering due dates for reports, payrolls and other work involving deadlines.

This may be considered merely a special version of the controlled backlog plan. Long used in utility company billing, the method has proved itself useful for many other purposes in recent years. It seems particularly well suited for any type of work that occurs in heavy concentrations at relatively long intervals and that offers some flexibility in time of performance. A worthwhile caution, however, is that any flexibility presumed for this purpose should not entail undue sacrifice by customers or others affected by the office service involved.

    c. Consider dovetailing low-priority work with high-priority work.

Every office has such routine work as bringing records up to date, getting data in shape for control reports, going over files, and checking and replenishing supplies. Such activities have low time priority. Just about any slack time not required for these or other types of work can be devoted to training activities, which ordinarily permit flexible scheduling. All such tasks should be kept out of the way during heavy loads and should be planned systematically for slack periods.

3. Where some of the steps of work involved in a heavy load do not have to be performed in a continuous sequence after the load hits:

    a. Consider doing preparatory steps before, and less urgent steps after, the peak in volume.

Most work can be divided into make-ready, do, and clean-up phases. A type of flexibility may be found in the possibility of getting preliminary information together, keeping cumulative totals, heading up forms and doing other similar steps of a preparatory nature before an expected peak hits. Less urgent steps such as summarizing, filing, and preparing control reports can often be postponed. Limiting factors, here, are the possibilities of extra familiarization time, handling, and storage, since material may be processed in two or more stages. These may be negligible in given situations, and the method often can afford real relief.

Probably most types of office work that occur in peak loads will be found to permit some flexibility in completion time and exact schedules of performance. If one or a combination of the foregoing methods is found suitable, the solution is likely to be quite simple and painless, since it will merely involve some manipulation of performance schedules. Some types of work, however, permit no adjustment of schedules, or at least not enough for a satisfactory solution through one of the methods already considered. In such cases it is necessary to look for flexibility in the personnel assigned to the work involved.

Rigid schedule

1. Where work involves some duties not requiring regularly assigned personnel:

    a. Could temporary relief be had from within the present organization?

        (1) Where different activities within the specific department occur in peak loads at different times, and where several jobs can be mastered by one person.

            (a) Cross-train one or more employees who can be shifted about as needed.

This method can go far toward solving not only peak load problems of an interdepartmental nature, but problems of filling in during absences and vacations, as well. Some firms use the "utility" type of job quite extensively; this can be either a highly-rated or beginner-rated job. The use of a highly-rated utility job usually will provide more flexibility in performing various tasks and provide valuable background for promotions, plus being a high-prestige, sought-after job. Supervisors like cross-training and utility job arrangements because they can handle their own fluctuations in work load without asking for outside assistance.

        (2) Where work load in different departments occurs in peaks

at different times, and where some jobs or duties in each can be learned readily by people outside the department.

    (a) Consider shifting personnel from slack to busy departments.

It is a common experience to find one department snowed under at the same time another is having a light load, and to find the situation reversed the following day. The possibility of shifting some workers who could help at least with routine details of work in the heavily-loaded department warrants consideration in such cases. Interdepartmental cooperation is often a problem here, but special attention in merit rating, assurances to departmental supervisors regarding ampleness of budgets in the future, encouragement of informal supervisory contacts, profit-sharing and other similar means may go a long way toward overcoming resistance. Centralized coordination in some form is an absolute requirement.

    (b) Consider having an unassigned, utility group that could fill in for various departments as needed.

This extends the utility clerk approach to interdepartmental variations in work load. It is closely related to the familiar "flying squadron" method of training, wherein trainees are given a broad base of experience in a limited time period. Here, however, the emphasis is on the utility value of an unassigned group that can be called upon for help during peak loads, vacations, absences and other short-term needs for personnel. With some care in planning individual assignments, much training value may be realized even with the utility emphasis. Staggered times of work concentrations in separate departments, duties that can be performed readily by utility personnel brought in during peaks, and central coordination are important requirements.

    (c) Consider having a central service department or pool— especially if a large part of the work involved in peak loads in different departments calls for basic activities such as typing, transcribing, computing, filing, and so forth.

One of the strongest justifications for providing central office services may be that of more economical handling of peak loads. If heavy demands for office services come at different times in separate departments, a central service department may make it possible to get by with a smaller total clerical force through fuller utilization.

    b. Could temporary relief be had from outside the organization?

      (1) Where some of the duties could be handled by outsiders

        (a) Consider hiring temporary or part-time workers.

Very often, some of the duties involved in peak loads will permit temporary relief from outside an organization; this is a possibility seldom appreciated fully. There are a great many people in the "temporary working force," such as married women formerly employed who would welcome an opportunity to work for limited periods or on a part-time basis. Other important sources are students, retired employees, and individuals employed elsewhere who would like supplemental, part-time employment. Best use of the method calls for careful differentiation of duties, condensed training techniques, and standard practice instructions to guide performance.

> (b) Consider "farming out" part of the overload to service agencies.

One of the most significant developments in extending office production capacities during the past decade has been the tremendous expansion of service agencies. These agencies now provide a wide range of services and supply both personnel and equipment to meet overflow or irregular needs of client firms. Among services commonly available are data processing centers, stenographic and clerical, accounting, duplicating, and nearly any of the other basic office services.

Such agencies are founded upon the very sound principle of matching the overloads of business firms, on one hand, with the desires of many people for temporary or supplemental work, on the other. Most of the employees in the office-type service agencies are married women who do not desire permanent or full-time employment, persons holding other jobs and desiring to supplement their incomes, and students. The typical firm will either send relief personnel to a client or perform work with their own facilities. Careful scheduling of client requirements is obviously necessary. Fees charged are usually slightly higher than the going hourly rate for any given skill, but there is still an obvious saving for many firms which would have to resort to carrying excess personnel, working much overtime, and in some cases investing in equipment which they use only occasionally.

One might expect that the principal users would be small firms. Such firms do utilize the service establishments extensively, but the managements of many large firms have learned that it is more economical for them to have certain types of work done for them than to try to do it themselves.

This important type of service is actually but one of several forms of "sub-contracting" which are now growing rapidly in use. Other forms will be considered in the chapter dealing with cost control.

2. Where work requires special skills and background of regularly assigned personnel:

> a. Could any substantial relief be had through having personnel most directly involved work regularly eight and one-half hours on the day known to be heavy, seven and one-half hours on the day known to be light, or some similar adjustment?

b. Could relief be had through having certain workers or departments work regularly on a special schedule as to time of day—coming earlier, taking more time off at noon and making up later, and so forth?

c. Could relief be had by scheduling vacations during slack seasons?

Methods *a*, *b* and *c* merely involve taking full advantage of possibilities for varying exact time worked by regularly assigned personnel. They provide a highly useful form of flexibility which is used considerably but seldom fully exploited. On most types of work, there are no legal obstacles or other obstacles that cannot be overcome in using them. The most notable exception is probably the requirement in the Walsh-Healey Act of overtime pay after eight hours in any one day for work on contracts with the federal government.

If all other possibilities fail, or cost more than about double the normal unit costs for the work involved in a peak load, then—and only then—use overtime.

QUESTIONS FOR STUDY AND DISCUSSION

1. In what principal ways are the following concepts related: standardization, standards, work measurement, planning, and controlling?

2. What basic factors or aspects of production are dealt with in production control? Is coordination a vital part of production control?—Explain. In what ways may effective production control contribute to customer satisfaction and to employee satisfaction?

3. Name and define the primary functions of production control.

4. Compare the provisions usually made for production control in offices with those usually found in factories, and try to explain any striking similarities or differences.

5. What is the most basic tool of office routing? When may an office route sheet be justified? Why is office work usually assigned and controlled in batches rather than single pieces of paper? What principal factors seem to justify consideration in determining the best size for each batch under varying conditions?

6. What must you know before you can prepare a work schedule? Describe several scheduling devices or instruments which may be helpful in scheduling office work. Explain the Gantt Chart concept as applied to scheduling uses. Does it seem that the Gantt Chart could be adapted to other uses?

7. What is the role of load charts in scheduling? Are load charts now finding increased usage in office work scheduling? What do you predict as to their future usage?

8. What is usually involved in dispatching office work, and what practices may increase the efficiency of this function?

9. Does follow-up, as a control function in office production, seem to justify more attention than at earlier times? Why? or why not?

10. Is machine utilization related to follow-up? What types of control information would you wish to obtain if you were responsible for a costly data processing installation?

11. What considerations seem to determine how employees will react to controls over production?

12. Compare the types of work load fluctuations found in office work with those in business volume generally. What seem to be the principal reasons for office load peaks and valleys? Are certain significant costs incurred because of office work load fluctuations?—if so, what types and do any of these seem controllable?

13. "Low-cost departments should be encouraged to use overtime where the result may be to facilitate operations or reduce overtime in high-cost departments." Comment on this statement and on overtime as a general approach for coping with peak loads of office work volume.

14. To what extent can electronic data processing eliminate or simplify the problem of office load fluctuation? Consider carefully. Is there any need to consider other approaches to coping with such fluctuations since we now have such powerful equipment?

15. Outline steps in a general approach to the handling of office peak loads. What seems to be the key characteristic which must be considered in any problem of choice among methods of handling peak loads?

16. What are several methods by which peak loads may be handled when the work schedule contains flexibility in some form?—when the schedule is rigid? Under what conditions may each be especially suitable? Do you see much significance in the suggestion that there may be a logical sequence in which these alternative methods should be considered? Explain.

Case 24-1. The Martin Mutual Insurance Company

New policy applications ordinarily follow a standard procedure consisting of about 18 principal operations. The clerks know the steps before and after their own, and they send work along to the next step as soon as their own work on a batch of applications is completed.

The applications usually are grouped into batches involving about one hour's work at each operation, and no particular plan is followed in the grouping—each batch is merely an accumulation of about one hour's work.

Some policy applications require considerable variation from the basic procedure, however; and when an employee hits one of these, he is sometimes quite uncertain as to how to handle it and where to take it when he is finished with it. Quite often, policy applications having special features and requiring individual treatment are misplaced and their issuance to the policyholder delayed.

Problems and questions:

a. Can you suggest any improvement in the plan by which work is grouped into batches?

b. Can you suggest any control device which would provide closer control over the processing of the policy applications which have special or unusual features?

Case 24-2. Use of a Gantt Chart

Mr. E. G. Wilson is the head of the billing department of the Mulligan Steel Company. He likes to schedule work carefully in order to get invoices out promptly, utilize the time of clerks fully, and distribute the work load fairly.

He wishes to design a Gantt Chart on which he can assign customer's accounts in batches which will usually require anywhere from one hour to two hours per batch for the clerk doing each. He knows that the average invoice takes about 12 minutes to prepare, and by making allowance for unusual jobs, he can estimate time requirements accordingly.

To test the suitability of the Gantt Chart for this purpose, Mr. Wilson would like to enter the following information on a trial form. Starting at 8 AM, customer accounts 2001-2005 (estimated one hour's work) were assigned to Johnson; accounts 2006-2015 (two hours) to Jones; and accounts 2016-2027 (two and one-fourth hours) to Long. Mr. Wilson would also like to know how he could show a check-up at 9 o'clock which revealed that Johnson was about 80 per cent finished with his work, Jones about 75 per cent through with his entire job, and Long about half through with his assignment.

Problems and questions:

a. Prepare a Gantt Chart of a type that would give Mr. Wilson the information he wishes.

b. What does the chart show regarding current progress with the three work assignments?

c. Appraise the merits of the Gantt Chart for use in this type of control situation.

Case 24-3. Reaction to Controls

In the Carter Engineering Company, each supervisor is expected to fill out a status report at the end of each working day which shows the number of units of each type of work which are on hand and still to be processed in the unit.

These reports are used by their immediate superiors, the superintendents of the company, in a ten-minute discussion session held at the start of each day.

The superintendents consider the status reports and meetings to be highly valuable in helping them to plan and coordinate their work, since they can learn how much work is ahead for other departments and units which perform earlier or later operations in the overall procedure.

The supervisors who prepare the reports are generally quite resentful about them, however. Some of them feel that this method of checking up on them indicates lack of confidence in them by higher management. There is often a scramble just before closing time to "unload" as much work as possible on the next departments ahead in the procedures.

Problems and questions:

a. Appraise the merits of this type of control report.

b. Do you feel that any improvement is needed in the approach to gathering and using the status reports? Explain.

Case 24-4. Varying Problems with Peak Loads

Below are described a number of different types of problems which arise from variations in work load.

A cheese company in Wisconsin prepares various assortments of cheeses in colorful Christmas packages. During the peak season, in November and December, they must process a tremendous number of orders.

For many years, one of the major mail order and retailing firms has had a terrific monthly peak which has resulted from the need to produce accounting and merchandising figures for each of its many mail order houses, catalogue order offices, and retail stores. The overload commences about the fourth day of each month with receipt of individual branch data and lasts through the middle of the month.

The Pacific States National Bank finds that its volume of postings to customers' accounts has followed this pattern, based on averages for the past year: Monday, 19 per cent of weekly volume; Tuesday, 13 per cent; Wednesday, 18 per cent; Thursday, 14 per cent; Friday, 15 per cent; and Saturday morning, 21 per cent. The management of the bank has been expecting a business recession, and an effort has been made to keep personnel at levels capable of handling the load for the lighter days, while making extensive use of overtime on other days. Employees appreciate the premium pay for overtime; but there is occasionally some objection to the long hours, especially on Saturday afternoons. The state in which the bank is located recently passed a "delayed posting" law which permits one day's delay in posting current debits and credits to patrons' accounts.

In the filing department of the Belton Investment Company there is a constant problem of keeping work load in balance. At one time of the week, the clerk in charge of the section of the files for the home state will be rushed; the next day, the one handling nearby states will get the heavy load; the next day, the clerk handling more distant states is the busy one.

As these locations suggest, a large part of the explanation lies in the time required for mail to reach the home office from the different territories served. There are also other variations, some harder to explain. The nature of the work is such that a considerable amount of cross-training would be required if there were to be much shifting of clerks about to help each other out. The supervisor has preferred to leave things as they are, fearing resistance from employees if they were asked to do much cross-training. To a recent question about the situation, the supervisor replied, "Why, they don't mind—as long as they see that the others catch their share of heavy loads on other days."

Problems and questions:

a. For each of these situations, note the principal difficulties which are created by fluctuations in volume.

b. Appraise the present manner of coping with problems met, and suggest one or more approaches which should result in improvements. Support your recommendations.

Case 24-5. Boise Statistical Service Company

The entire unit, consisting of nine female employees, was not performing as well as possible. A check of personnel records revealed that all were average or above average employees. Experience among the employees in general was of sufficient quantity to warrant better work. Mail coming into the unit was not being distributed rapidly. Some individuals would be observed doing nothing, while others had more work than they could accomplish. This inactivity fluctuated from one portion of the unit to another and did not occur on the part of any particular employee or group of employees.

Closer investigation revealed a degree of animosity among the employees. There was subtle bickering which was not apparent on the surface. The difficulty in distributing mail was found to be that if one employee did it, she felt she was doing more work than her share. The inactivity was caused by work piling up at one station, then, as that station would process the work, it would pile up somewhere else and the previous station would go into inactivity. Also contributing to this was the fact that one would not assist the other with the work and would sit idle while waiting for the work. The station that had the work would not release the work as they did it, because by holding it until they had completed all of the work, they would then have a lax period and it would also be a measure of retaliation in that the next station would be swamped.

Problems and questions:

   a. What tools of management would be appropriate here?
   b. How would you, as supervisor, go about finding the cause for the problem?
   c. What possible causes would you suspect?
   d. What solutions might you, as a consultant, recommend to management?

25

QUALITY CONTROL
AND COST CONTROL

Quality control · Quality control and improvement programs · Cost reduction and control · Office budgets

---

Quality Control

A factor of dominant importance in the successful accomplishment of office work is satisfactory quality of work.

A sales ticket which contains a serious error may result in the permanent loss of a very important customer; a tactless letter may likewise have a strongly negative effect. On the other hand, office work which clearly has had the benefit of good judgment and which is accurate and neat will influence favorably the customers, suppliers, and other business associates who may be affected. Good quality work can also be an effective basis for employee pride in work and confidence in management.

Just as a factory must take steps to insure that actual quality of the product is on a par with planned quality, so should an office take steps to insure that the quality of its services is maintained at a satisfactory level.

Office quality factors

Certain quality factors have just been indicated. The primary factor in office quality is *accuracy,* or fewness of errors. Errors may occur either in the making of decisions or in the detailed work of carrying out decisions.

The other principal quality factor is that of *effectiveness* in the manner in which work is carried out. The question here is not whether something is right or wrong, but whether work is performed neatly, tactfully, courteously, or in some other positive manner as called for by the situation. These conditions are more intangible and less subject to precise control than the factor of accuracy; yet their importance in satisfaction and good will is readily apparent.

Standards of quality

As with other factors in performance, standards are needed to prescribe desired levels of quality and to gauge results obtained. Do ninety-nine correctly filed index cards out of one hundred constitute suitable performance, for example? One hundred per cent accuracy may be the ideal, but experience usually shows this to be unattainable, and a more realistic quality goal may need to be set. This is just another way of saying that quality must nearly always be expressed in degrees; with most types of work there is a point of diminishing returns beyond which further efforts to raise quality levels are hard to justify.

Very often, however, it is possible to come much closer to the illusory goal of perfection than past performance has indicated. *Quality improvement* should always be a major consideration, often the dominant one, in a quality control program.

Quality Control and Improvement Programs

Occasional isolated efforts by certain quality-conscious individuals in an organization are likely to have only limited value. What is needed is a continuing program which enlists the interest and the participation of all employees. Although details differ, major steps of such a program include:

1. Determine quality standards.
2. Check actual quality of current work.
3. Record errors and compare to standards.
4. Correct defective work.
5. Analyze and improve quality.

Determine quality standards. There probably is no way to predetermine with mathematical exactness the exact level that office quality should meet. The accuracy actually obtained in any given situation is likely to depend upon the training given the clerical force, the checks and inspections made, and the attitude of the section head and his superiors toward quality.[1]

---

[1] Bennet B. Murdock, "Prudential's Program for Clerical Quality Control," *Office Executive,* January, 1953.

Perhaps the most practical approach to determining attainable standards is to record and to study experience with quality and at the same time to take constructive steps to improve quality.[2] By then determining the level at which actual quality seems to level off, a standard that represents good practice and is at the same time attainable can be found. For example, past records may show ninety-eight per cent accuracy to have been the quality level actually realized in a registering operation. If an improvement program is instituted and a period of improvement follows during which quality results are checked and found to get better and better until they finally seem to level off at about ninety-nine and one-half per cent accuracy, the latter percentage may be regarded as a useful working standard.

The illustration just cited also indicates what is ordinarily the most suitable mode of expressing quality standards; that is, in percentages. For most purposes, the number of cases completed satisfactorily need to be expressed as a percentage of the total cases handled. If mere numbers of correct cases were noted and compared with results obtained by other employees, or with those obtained by the same employees during other periods, differences in volume of work handled would be ignored. For example, one employee might have averaged only three errors a week and another five a week; if the second has turned out twice the work volume of the first, the superior rate of accuracy of the second employee shows up only when expressed in percentage form.

Check actual quality of current work. The checking or inspection step in controlling office quality may be done either by the same people who do the work or by separate checkers. If accuracy is of considerable importance, some form of separate or independent checking usually will be considered desirable.

Checking often does not need to be done on a one hundred per cent basis, however. Not only is one hundred per cent checking a costly process; it tends to cause those doing work to depend excessively upon the checkers and, in spite of the best of checking, some errors are still likely to get by.

Checking on a sampling basis is probably adequate for most types of office work. Those doing the work feel a greater sense of responsibility for quality since they know greater dependence is placed upon them; reasonable assurance of adherence to quality standards can be provided; and the cost of checking can sometimes be cut greatly. Each checking step should justify its cost; special care should be taken to avoid the duplicate checking so commonly found when two or more departments handle successive steps of work.

2 *Ibid.*

If technical staff help is available, the size of a statistically-adequate sample can be determined for each type of work, considering the total volume of cases of the type involved and the level of accuracy sought. If not, arbitrary sample percentages can be used which range from perhaps ten per cent on work when accuracy is not of vital importance to one hundred per cent in the case of items of great monetary value or of key importance for other reasons.[3] Assistance can be obtained in establishing sample tables from which appropriate sample sizes can be determined without having to repeat calculations.

The most common application is the method of *acceptance sampling.* A sample of work is checked—say ten per cent of a batch of invoices—and if the percentage of those accurate in the sample is up to the standard, the entire group is accepted. If the cases in the sample are substandard, however, a larger sample is taken (determinable by reference to a sampling table); if continued below-standard results are found, successively larger samples will be checked until 100% of the cases are verified if necessary. Experience with a given operator's work might then indicate the need for relatively large samples until quality improves sufficiently to go back to the minimum sample size.

Record errors and compare to standard. Some form of error-recording and error-reporting system is a desirable part of a quality control program. As cases are checked, each one that is defective may be described on a form such as that illustrated in Figure 25-1.

ERROR REPORT

Material involved (form, order no., etc.)	Nature of error
Person making error	Date of error
Reason for error (given by person making)	

Figure 25-1.

It is usually a wise policy to return each error to the supervisor or section head of the person who made the error, and through him to the employee. The employee who made the error is then expected to correct

[3] See Alex L. Hart, "Clerical Quality Has Two Dimensions," *Office Executive,* July, 1953, for a discussion of lot-dollar sampling which takes value as well as number of correct cases into account.

it, and he may be asked to give an explanation regarding the cause. Further attention will be given to the constructive handling of errors with employees making them.

A comparison of accuracy achieved to the standard of accuracy expected should be made on a continuing basis, and it needs to be simple and clear so that employees and supervisors can understand it. The best answer is usually a *control chart*. There are several types, but the one best adapted for most purposes of controlling office work is probably the per-cent-defective chart. Such a chart is illustrated in Figure 25-2, based

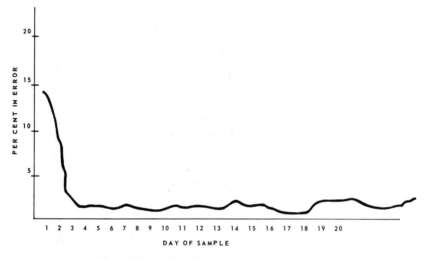

Figure 25-2. Control chart for correspondence errors

upon errors made in transcription of correspondence.

In this chart, letters containing errors are shown to have constituted about thirteen per cent of total letters transcribed on the first day checked but, through improvement efforts and perhaps due partly to the motivation of merely having such a control record, the percentage was reduced until it leveled out at about two per cent defective. If desired, a base line could now be drawn across at the two per cent level to indicate the accepted standard; or for psychological reasons management may choose to regard zero errors as the goal and to show no official acceptance of any higher error rate.

A control chart is probably most often used for an entire unit or department and posted conspicuously for all to see. It may be used on an individual basis, however, as where new employees are being developed, where certain older employees consistently make excessive errors, or where the motivation provided by individual comparisons is believed desirable.

A particularly helpful feature of a quality control chart such as that illustrated is its value in showing quality trends, good or bad, as soon as these begin to develop. Without such a chart, a situation can get badly out of control before anyone becomes aware of it. The chart also serves as a sensitive indicator of the results of efforts to improve quality at any point.

Correct defective work. As already suggested, errors caught by checkers, by persons performing later steps in procedure, or by customers or other outsiders who report them back—all are generally best handled by returning to the person making them for correction and explanation. This requires that the person involved complete the performance of his responsibility; it enables him to save face; it lays the basis for constructive efforts.

Analyze and improve quality. The current trend in progressive organizations is to institute long-range quality improvement programs rather than to rely upon spasmodic "shot in the arm" approaches which have only temporary value. Emphasis is being increasingly devoted to prevention of errors rather than merely to detection and correction of errors already made.

Errors arise from many causes, but they can be dealt with more intelligently if they are classified into categories which will throw light on the best manner of handling them. The following is a usable classification:

1. Errors due primarily to job conditions.
2. Errors due primarily to improper placement of employees involved.
3. Errors due primarily to improper training and supervision.

Any given error may arise from a combination of causes; if these can be understood, treatment can be adapted accordingly.

Many errors may be attributed in large part to job conditions. Inadequate provision for lighting, air conditioning, or noise control may have significant bearing. There may be excessive dependence upon manual operation in situations which could be mechanized readily with reduction in the possibility of human error. Procedures may need overhauling. Job specialization may not be carried far enough, or it may be carried too far with monotony and narrow perspective resulting. Peak work loads and heavy pressure for quantity may cause clerks to neglect quality. If the explanation of a given error or pattern of errors lies in one or more job conditions such as these, a remedy is likely to be indicated in each case; at least management is in a position to make due allowance for the condition.

Poor placement of employees may be the cause of many errors. If a job demands either too much or too little intelligence of an employee, the result may be either strain or monotony, and errors will be more likely to occur. Some people have much higher clerical aptitude than others. Vision, endurance, and other physical limitations may be exceeded in some cases. Some individuals seem to be error prone because of nervous disorders or various conditions of personal maladjustment; many such cases may benefit from proper supervision, but placement may take on special importance. Testing, interviewing, and other selection techniques are now available which can increase the likelihood of careful fitting of employees to jobs, either in initial employment or in evaluating a possible transfer to another job.

A substantial portion of errors must also be attributed to faulty training and supervision. The person handling training often finds it hard to put himself in the place of the learner, and he takes far too much for granted regarding the learner's background and his readiness to learn. The training given is too often merely in terms of *how* and not enough in terms of *why*.

Some of the most rewarding efforts in developing quality-consciousness have been in firms which have encouraged the employees to think in broad terms regarding customer service, the roles of different departments and jobs in serving the customer, and the necessity for teamwork.

Cost Reduction and Control

The increasingly larger role assigned to office work in business firms has been noted at many points in this book. In an effort to manage the various functions of an organization more logically, leadership is turning more to facts—to information needed for logical decisions. The result has been a vast expansion in paper work.

The basic soundness of this emphasis upon more and better office services to sharpen management effectiveness can hardly be disputed. Accordingly, proportions of clerical employees to total employees and proportions of clerical costs to total costs have climbed rapidly.

So great has the clerical segment of activity become that managements are more often beginning to look critically toward this area as one offering a big margin for possible savings. In many organizations there can be little doubt that the office area constitutes the greatest frontier for economy.

In attempting to achieve office economies, however, there are dangers as well as opportunities. The greatest of these dangers probably lies in cost-cutting of an arbitrary or hit-or-miss sort.

What makes this problem a particularly difficult one is the fact that office activity is *service* activity—a means to an end in the organizational scheme of things. The justification for office work is its value in facilitating the primary work of production, sales, finance, and other functions basic to the enterprise. This means that any proposed change in an office service should be considered in terms of what it will do for the primary work being served, and not merely in terms of the office activity itself.

A "penny-wise, pound-foolish" attitude toward office activities is the approach that must be avoided. A sweeping order from top management to reduce clerical staff in all departments by one-fourth, for example, may be very short-sighted. The need, instead, may be for more and better inventory control records, for more rather than fewer sales letters, and for stronger office services of other types. A miserly attitude toward office equipment is likely to result in higher overall costs, poorer service, and lower employee morale than an enlightened approach which gives adequate attention to obsolescence and depreciation. "The things a business needs, it pays for—whether it buys them or not."

Following the same line of reasoning, it is doubtful that one hundred per cent utilization of office personnel and equipment should ever be seriously expected. The service role of most office jobs is such that there needs to be some margin in the ability to adjust to the needs of primary departments being served. Except in degree, the role is not unlike that of a city fire department which must be on call and must have sufficient personnel and equipment to meet varying demands.

While these considerations suggest the need for viewing office services as a part of the overall picture, they should not in any way be interpreted as a justification for waste, extravagance, and other forms of inefficiency in the performance of office work.

Areas of opportunity for office economies

There are many areas of opportunity for sound, legitimate economies in the office field. These have been explored in all major sections of this book. To pull some of these together for illustrative purposes, the following list includes suggestive areas.

1. Better organization and better assignment of responsibilities to departments and to individual jobs.

2. Better design and control of procedures, equipment, layout, forms, and supplies.

3. Better planning and maintenance of building, building services, and other physical facilities.

4. Better standards of quantity, quality, time, and cost of performance.

5. Better administration of personnel—selection, training, compensation, supervision, and other phases.

6. Sub-contracting of office functions and equipment. This method of con-

trolling office costs is becoming so popular that it is given brief mention in the following section.

The sub-contracting trend

With profits getting slimmer, competition for investment funds growing keener, and the general competition for a firm's survival becoming tougher, flexibility is recognized increasingly as a key consideration in corporate strategy.

A primary method of obtaining necessary flexibility is *sub-contracting*. Sub-contracting has long been practiced in the production function of manufacturing and in the general contracting business, and it has been used considerably in certain phases of the marketing function. But only recently has sub-contracting been considered by the office function to have particular use and merit. Leasing is a special form of sub-contracting gaining rapidly in popularity as a method of remaining flexible and reducing capital investment.

A number of areas in which sub-contracting of office services and functions are commonly practiced have been noted earlier. Certain areas which seem to offer particularly attractive economies are briefly discussed below.

a. Temporary office clerical help can be acquired from several national firms such as Kelly Girls, Inc., and Manpower, Inc. The use of temporary clerical help reduces the requirements of permanent employees, or the expensive overtime necessary to cope with peak and seasonal demands. In 1956, Manpower, Inc. had 75 offices throughout the U. S. Today, the same organization has some 250 offices and new ones are being opened at the rate of several per month. Total temporary help registered with Manpower, Inc. is 130,000 and total firms regularly provided with temporary help number about 75,000, including many of the nation's largest corporations.[4]

b. Private, public accounting offices provide specialized accounting services, or if the client chooses, complete accounting and bookkeeping facilities. Many small firms now sub-contract all of their accounting and bookkeeping operations, and many larger firms use the public accounting firms for such operations as audits, special tax problems, complicated financial ventures, and federal income tax returns.

c. Service bureaus, discussed previously in Chapter 14, provide a comparable sub-contracting facility for work adaptable to mechanization. The development of common languages has allowed individual firms to prepare the detailed data as a by-product of normal operations and to contract with a service bureau for analysis of the data and the prepara-

[4] "The Challenge on Costs," *Dun's Review and Modern Industry,* September, 1962, pp. S155-169.

tion of statistical summaries and reports. Large firms also contract considerable work with service bureaus to provide for peak loads, special computational problems, and certain minor operations.

d. Warehousing and storage is another operation many firms are subcontracting for records storage as well as other items. Costs for company owned and operated storage warehouses are approximately twice that of privately operated storage warehouses. Then, too, better service is available from firms that specialize in the storage business.

e. A variation of sub-contracting for office services is leasing of office equipment and machines. Leasing is possibly best known in connection with data processing equipment. More recently, however, many firms are leasing all furniture and fixtures necessary to operate an office, including such items as staplers, clocks, pictures, rugs, desks, chairs, and equipment of many other types. In the long run, leasing of furniture and fixtures is likely to be more expensive than outright purchase, but as with other forms of sub-contracting, it has the primary advantages of flexibility and reduced demands on capital credit which may be better used for other purposes.

> The Radio Corporation of America has outfitted its defense production plant in Camden, New Jersey, by leasing everything from the production line machinery to the office furniture, fixtures, and machines. A particular advantage for flexibility occurs here since the entire plant depends upon highly dynamic and susceptible defense contracts.[5]

Programs of Cost Reduction

Sensing the tremendous possibilities for office economies which exist, progressive managements have undertaken programs to prune waste wherever it can be found. Key features of the more successful programs are large-scale participation by first-line supervisors and employees, continuing efforts, and good sense of proportion in various cost-serving areas.

Particularly successful have been programs in work simplification which have secured maximum participation of supervisors and employees in cutting waste in work methods. Such programs undertake to stimulate cost-consciousness, to develop a questioning attitude, and to furnish helpful tools of analysis such as flow process charts, left- and right-hand charts, forms spread sheets, and others. Generally, these programs reward constructive thinking in some manner—through a suggestion system, through merit rating which takes individual contributions into account, or through some other means. Some programs have as their focal point the use of problem-solving group meetings wherein the members of a unit

5 *Ibid.*

gather on a weekly or other basis and examine critically each phase of work of the unit.

The reason for the need for a continuing program, rather than an economy campaign, is that waste-reduction needs to be made a habit in the thought-pattern of each individual. As one authority has expressed it, an economy wave soon passes, as all waves must, and the organization resumes its old wasteful habits until the next economy wave comes along.[6]

The better programs also attempt to maintain a sense of proportion—emphasizing the service role of office activities, putting first things first, and avoiding the types of economies that backfire through sacrificing something actually needed. The development of such a sense of proportion, or scale of values, requires that management emphasize not only *how* things are done but *why* they are done, and that good communication and consultation with employees be practiced constantly in the making of plans and decisions.

Use of Office Budgets

A budget is a plan of financial requirements during a given time period. It necessarily is based upon analysis of the situation which faces the enterprise (in other words, upon a forecast of needs), and it develops a course of action to be followed. The general uses of any budget are those of planning financial needs in advance and providing a basis for controlling current expenditures.

A complete discussion of budgets would be beyond the scope of this book, but a brief presentation of usual steps will point up applications to office cost control.

The basic steps of budgeting usually include:

1. *Sales forecasting.*

A budget committee representing sales, production, finance, and perhaps other divisions agrees on the forecast, broken down by individual products or services. Market potential, production potential, and overall financial limitations are reconciled.

2. *Preparation of overall financial estimates.*

Cost of the volume-of-sales forecast and gross expected profit may then be determined with accounting help, as may reasonable levels of operating expenses (including office expense) and estimated operating profits. Tentative, overall plans are approved by the executive committee or other top-manage-

----

6 William H. Leffingwell and Edwin M. Robinson, *Textbook in Office Management,* 3rd ed. (New York: McGraw-Hill Book Company, Inc.).

ment body exercising overall control of the budget. In some cases a variable budget may be justified, with four or five sets of budgeted figures prepared for different possible volume levels.

3. *Preparation of departmental budgets.*

Each department head then prepares and proposes a detailed budget estimate for his own department, based upon the volume forecast; this budget request is then fit into the overall financial plan described above, with adjustment possible either in the departmental budget or in the overall allowance, where necessary. Approval by the executive committee then authorizes the use of the budget as a plan or standard.

4. *Enforcement of the budget.*

At the end of each month, a statement of actual expenditures of each department is prepared by accounting and sent to the head of the department involved. Budgeted figures are shown on the same statement, and deviations of actual from budgeted accounts must be explained by the department head. Plans for correcting the deviations may also be called for.

Office expenses will usually be budgeted as a part of the operating expenses of each department using them, but general groupings of office expense items, for example, office supplies expense, may be made for all departments to facilitate overall comparisons.

Viewed as a whole, budgeting requires that management chart a course and stick to it. Maintaining a balance among the different special units is facilitated greatly, for each department head must justify his budget requests to the satisfaction of the other departmental heads. A better overall picture and greater appreciation of the contributions of other departments are other important benefits. The morale of individual department heads is also likely to be increased, particularly if they are given a large part in budget preparation and after they gain experience with the program.

QUESTIONS FOR STUDY AND DISCUSSION

1. Define "quality" as applied to office work. What is at stake in high-quality office work?—what desired results may depend upon this factor?

2. Is a standard of one hundred per cent accuracy feasible and realistic in most office operations? What controls the level of feasible or attainable accuracy? Suggest a practical approach to determining the highest level of accuracy that is feasible for any given operation.

3. In what terms may a standard of accuracy for office work be most suitably expressed? Do sampling techniques seem to hold much promise in office quality control applications?—if so, what techniques and procedures may be worthy of special consideration?

4. One large mail order house for many years has maintained a large quality

control chart which is placed on one of the walls of the room housing its billing department. The chart shows the percentage of invoices which are found to contain errors, posted on a daily basis. Evaluate this approach as a control device.

5. If you were a supervisor, how would you attempt to identify and deal with each of the following types of situations: (1) pattern errors, those that are made time after time at the same point in the work or that take the same basic form repeatedly, and (2) error proneness of a certain clerk? Is there really such a thing as error proneness?

6. Distinguish quality improvement from quality control. Outline major steps that you would recommend for a quality improvement program in a unit that has been making what seem to be an excessive number of errors.

7. There is a delicate balance between quality control and cost control. Attempts to make improvements in one area have often been at the expense of the other. Cite one or more illustrations of how this can happen.

8. Comment on this statement: "The things a business needs, it pays for— whether it buys them or not."

9. Does greatly expanded mechanization reduce sharply the possibilities for economy in performance of office operations? What are some of the most promising areas of opportunity for office economies at present, as you see them?

10. What do you see as the potential for "sub-contracting" in the office field in the years ahead? Explain. Suggest what seem to be several of the most promising areas in which this concept can be applied.

11. Many firms are currently attempting to carry out cost-reduction programs. What seem to be the key features of the more successful programs of this type? Of the less successful ones?

12. Outline principal steps of a typical well-conceived budgeting system. Appraise this statement by one executive: "Extension of budget planning and control down to the level of unit supervisors in my company had the effect of changing the supervisors from leadmen to real managers." Do you believe this executive may have been overenthusiastic in his statement? What sort of changes in the behavior of the supervisors may have caused him to reach this conclusion?

Case 25-1. A Quality-Improvement Campaign

Clerical errors had been a growing problem in the Ajax Milling Company. A concentration of costly and troublesome errors in handling the details of customers orders caused the controller, Mr. H. A. Jordan, to initiate a quality-improvement campaign. For two weeks he tried every quality-improvement device he could think of—a contest, posters stressing quality, articles in the company's house organ, and group meetings in which higher management's concern with the problem was expressed.

The results were satisfactory for a time, but after a period of about a month had passed, the error rate had climbed back to its former level.

Problems and questions:

a. What possible explanations can you offer for the return to excessive error rates?

b. What positive steps can you recommend which might bring about permanent, rather than temporary, clerical quality improvement in the Ajax Company?

Case 25-2. Use of a Quality-Control Chart

Mr. Lyn Bell, supervisor of the order department of the Leighton Printing Company, recently called his employees together to talk about the quality of work being turned out by the department. He was careful not to seem critical of anyone, and he talked briefly about the general importance of quality. He commented that the quality record for the department had been quite good, and he asked whether the members of the group might like to try to do even better.

An interesting discussion followed, and the group decided that they would like to get their quality level still higher. They expressed interest in knowing just what their error rate was and in keeping some type of record which would indicate whether they were making any improvement.

Mr. Bell, accordingly, began to keep a record of errors and to compute the percentage of total orders handled which contained errors of any kind, as checked against the customer's instructions. At the same time he began to post the error percentages on a large quality control chart on a bulletin board near the entrance to the department.

Error rates for the first ten days were as follows: first day, 11 per cent, second—nine per cent, third—six per cent, fourth—four per cent, fifth—three per cent, sixth—two per cent, seventh—three per cent, eighth—three per cent, ninth—two per cent, tenth—three per cent.

Problems and questions:

a. Prepare a quality control chart for the error rates given.
b. Interpret the results of the chart. What happened at each stage of the ten-day period?
c. Appraise the general approach followed by Mr. Bell in introducing the subject of quality to his employees.

Case 25-3. Manner of Reporting Errors

In the Mountain States Casualty Company, errors made in the rate unit are usually caught in the bookkeeping or correspondence units. The problem of just how best to bring these errors to the attention of the people who made them, and to get them corrected, is a rather delicate one. Both the question of who should notify whom, and that of finding the least offensive and the most constructive manner of doing the notifying are troublesome.

Problems and questions:

    a. What different possible solutions exist?

    b. Which of these would seem likely to be effective?

Case 25-4. Errors and Attitude

Janice Buck had been employed with the company three years as a combination clerk-stenographer. She had a quick mind and her physical motions likewise were very rapid. Her typing speed was very high, but her typing errors were also very high. She had the mistaken idea that production and quantity took precedence over quality.

In consultation, Janice was told that she could have an outstanding record as a typist if she could eliminate the errors. She was also told that she could be promoted to much better jobs if it were not for the typing errors.

This seemed to make no impression on her. When she was asked to retype letters because of errors, she considered it an insult and became very obstinate. Whenever possible, she sent out the letters without correcting the errors. She seemed to feel no pride in putting out perfect work.

Problems and questions:

    a. What additional methods of motivation might be tried in such a case?

    b. How thoroughly did supervisor explain consequences of errors?

    c. How much follow-through, inspection of work, expression of interest and of confidence was there?

VIII

MOTIVATION OF OFFICE PERSONNEL

Earlier sections have focused upon the systems concept in administration, in order to provide a unified framework and to promote coordination of specialized functions and units in the current operations of an enterprise. The human element of systems has been recognized at numerous points. In the formulation of plans with regard to systems, procedures, and methods, the value of participation in producing improved ideas and in winning acceptance has been recognized, as has the need for care in communication regarding changes, reasons why programs are being instituted, and other matters which commonly arise in administration.

The emphasis in earlier sections has been upon the "logic of efficiency," however. We have been predominantly concerned with *work systems.* It is now necessary to pull together and consider briefly, but specifically, certain fundamental concepts involved in the *social systems* (or human relationships) upon which work systems depend heavily for their success.

Accordingly, we shall now consider leadership and motivation, selection and placement, appraisal and training, compensation, unionization, personnel administration, and personnel research.

26

LEADERSHIP
AND MOTIVATION

The priority of human needs · The challenge to management · The pattern for leadership · Basic requirements in leadership

---

Management views toward the influences which determine an employee's will to work are now undergoing changes that are substantial and long overdue.

Traditionally, management of governmental, military, religious, and early business organizations assumed that the "prime mover" in motivating people to perform could only be *authority*. Leaders, it was assumed, should make all significant decisions as to what should be done and how. They should have authority to command action of others and to administer rewards and penalties in relation to performance. The source of authority was considered to be the church, the state, the rights of private ownership where existent, or some other source.

Slowly, and of such recent origin that its life span amounts to little more than a tick of the clock in human history, a very different philosophy of motivation has evolved. Although not yet universally accepted, the pattern of thought recognizes serious limitations in top-down, authoritarian leadership. Employee resentment against authoritarian control has been observed to build up as standards of living have risen and as individuals have become less and less dependent upon an employer for their subsistence. Of perhaps equal significance, rising levels of education have caused many persons to raise their levels of aspiration, to wish to make more of their lives than they formerly thought possible.

The American Dream of equal opportunity, freedom, and justice

471

(which some critics denounce as a fiction, but which most observers see as one of the most powerful forces ever to move a group of people) undoubtedly has brought gradual change in beliefs regarding leadership *within* single enterprises, just as it has had profound influence upon leadership in societies generally. The privileges accorded a citizen in a political democracy have encouraged a critical look at treatment of employees as "hired hands" where they have been thus treated in private enterprise. The concept of citizenship within an enterprise, as well as outside, is seen to invite new and higher levels of individual responsibility and involvement, even though important limitations must often be recognized.

In addition to subtle influences which may have penetrated management thought as living standards and educational levels have risen, there have been significant research contributions in the social sciences which have had parallel effects. Elton Mayo headed a team of researchers in conducting the famed Hawthorne Experiments (so named because carried on in the Hawthorne plant of Western Electric) during the late 1920's, which first stirred management thought with this finding: the most influential factor in determining employee performance is the general set of *attitudes* which employees have toward their work, associates, and management. Further research by psychologists, sociologists, anthropologists, and other social scientists has thrown additional light upon the forces which stimulate people to perform effectively while at work. Much research of this type is now in progress.

The Priority of Human Needs

One of the most widely-accepted conceptual frameworks for current theories regarding motivation centers about recognition of the existence of a *priority* in human needs.[1] According to this general theory, human needs tend to follow the pattern below, presented in the sequence in which individuals usually become concerned with them:

1. Physiological needs—for survival, food, clothing, shelter, air to breathe, rest to overcome fatigue, and the like.

2. Safety and security—for protection against danger and deprivation.

3. Social needs—for association with other persons, acceptance, belonging.

4. Egoistic needs—for self-esteem and for a good reputation in the eyes of others.

[1] Most of the developing thought in this area is credited to A. H. Maslow. For a brief discussion of these basic human needs, see the article by A. H. Maslow, in *Psychological Review*, V. 50, 1943, 370-396. For a detailed elaboration of the application of these basic needs to business, see Douglas McGregor, *The Human Side of Enterprise* (New York: McGraw-Hill Book Company, Inc., 1960).

5. Self-fulfillment—for realizing one's potentialities, finding expression for one's creative abilities.

In a society which enjoys a generally high standard of living and a high and rising educational level, such as that in the United States, the first two levels are already reasonably well met for most, although not all, people. Consequently, appeals by management, union, or any other group which are directed primarily toward satisfying these lower-level needs will tend to have only limited effects. Pay, fringe benefits, and job security are no longer powerful motivators, except to the extent that they influence status in the eyes of oneself and others. (It may be noted that persons living in countries where living standards and educational levels remain low tend to be receptive to nearly any source of help, political or other, which offers relief.)

With regard to the higher levels of human needs, especially the egoistic and self-fulfillment needs, a very different situation exists for the typical employee. Most employees in the United States are now predominantly concerned with filling social needs, both on and off the job, and with egoistic needs. They seek acceptance, sense of belonging, status, and recognition in a wide variety of forms. The highest of the needs listed, self-fulfillment (or self-realization, self-actualization, or self-expression), is attained by only a comparative few. In order to achieve it in any large measure, an individual usually must be successful in activity which is meaningful, useful, and creative to the extent of his abilities. He will need opportunity to use his mental as well as his physical talents, in most cases.

Certain management challenges are therefore indicated. The higher-level needs are probably achieved to a high degree by a fairly large proportion of professional people, managers, and performers in special fields such as music and art. They undoubtedly are realized by many individuals in seemingly routine endeavors who see meaning and value in what they are doing.

But for the majority of employees, the egoistic and self-fulfillment needs are largely unfilled. One reason is the close relationship to the *work* each person does, and the usual shortage of opportunities for him, to *think* and use his *creative abilities* in his work.

The Challenge to Management

In the most direct and simple terms, the challenge may be expressed as that of striving to make each employee a *responsible, participating* member of the organization. Achieving this goal requires creating conditions in which he can use his abilities, mental as well as physical, and in which he can see a close relationship between organizational success and his own personal success.

If an environment of this sort can be established, it is realistic to expect a much higher degree of dedication or commitment by an employee to his work and his organization. Self-development, high standards of performance, and a high measure of self-expression in one's work, become goals sought voluntarily rather than demands imposed by an authoritarian source.

Critics of this point of view often note that there are many people who do not want more responsibility and who prefer, instead, to feel a minimum of pressure or tension while at work, preferring outside activities for their satisfactions. There is not the slightest doubt that this is true. People differ greatly in career aspirations—as, for example, a married woman who devotes her primary interests to her family and works only through necessity. Many other persons are quite indifferent, even antagonistic, toward their jobs and employers. But the best answer is a question—were they "born indifferent" or have they become so as a result of years of close, top-down supervision and little opportunity to use decision-making and creative abilities of their own? If one admits that most have had their attitudes shaped largely by their environment, both on and off the job, the possibility of improving attitudes and performance through improving the environment logically follows. Experience supports this view; there are innumerable instances in which an employee, under a supervisor who has encouraged and inspired him, has raised his level of aspiration. There is growing evidence that a stair-step pattern of levels of aspiration, or ambition, parallels closely the priority of human needs which we have considered, and may actually be a part of the same pattern.

At various points in this book we have considered specific practices which encourage improved placement, communication, participation, goal-setting, broader jobs and responsibilities for a larger segment of employees, and other practices consistent with management's developing awareness of previously untapped human resources and enthusiasm. The years to come will, no doubt, see greater progress. There is widespread agreement that we now, at least, have a general model and a foundation upon which to build.

The Pattern of Leadership

While giving increased attention to previously unrecognized needs of employees, management must obviously continue to think about the needs of the organization—about success in meeting its objectives, stability, and growth. Otherwise, there will be little opportunity to serve personal needs such as those just considered; an enterprise must successfully fulfill its primary mission if it is ever to provide employment opportunities.

What is needed, then, is an *integration of interests,* and *leadership* capable of meeting the needs of the organization, its employees, its owners, other special groups, and the general public.

We shall, therefore, now consider briefly certain basic leadership practices which serve general interests. In this chapter we shall consider:

Goal-setting
Designing jobs
Working with superiors
Working with associates
Working with subordinates
Communication
Participation
General leadership requirements

Other, more specialized practices will be treated briefly as sections of later chapters. These include:

Selection and placement
Training and performance appraisal
Compensation
Relations with unions
Personnel administration
Personnel research

Goal-setting

One of the distinctive and necessary marks of an effective leader is his inclination to think and work in terms of goals. Once the goal is clear, he dedicates himself to attaining it and in general follows a philosophy of "results—not excuses." There is a close relationship between being goal-oriented and action-oriented—being determined to make things happen rather than sit back and hope that they will happen or assume that they inevitably will do so.

Goals are familiar to all of us, in relation to work and in relation to personal activities of all sorts. A goal provides a sense of purpose and direction; it provides challenge; it serves as a measure of actual attainment. Goals are powerful motivational influences. A person may go for a walk and wander aimlessly until he decides that he needs an item from a corner drug store; then he quickens his pace and follows the most direct route to that destination.

Work goals must be developed in a logical sequence—starting first with the general objectives of the enterprise, then deriving current goals for each successively smaller organizational unit down to the individual job. At the job level, goals need to be as specific and definite as possible— such as perform work at an average rate of 50 units a day, hold errors to 1% or less, solve a problem of excessive verbiage in letter writing within the next month, become thoroughly cross-trained on another job in the unit within the next two months, etc.

Many managers have found that allowing and encouraging an employee, or group, to participate in setting goals will have highly beneficial effects. If they are provided information regarding general needs, measures by which to gauge performance, and a general atmosphere in which merit is recognized and rewarded, they usually will set higher goals for themselves than management would think of setting, and they probably will achieve them. This experience has been repeated with many types of achievement—quantity, quality, promptness, costs, getting to work on time, etc.

Designing jobs

Chapter 4 dealt entirely with the design of jobs, and little will be repeated here except the emphasis upon the close relationship between job design and motivation.

A meaningful, challenging job can be a powerful source of motivation; it may go far toward providing the means needed for the highest of human needs—self-fulfillment. If a person has opportunity to use his abilities in doing work which seems worthwhile and serious, and particularly if he is allowed some latitude for making decisions that affect his work; he is likely to become so absorbed in it that he does not devote a great amount of time to looking for objectionable features in the working situation.

Required are improved organizational planning at the work level, and careful placement of individuals on jobs which their abilities and interests match.

Working with superiors

Any person who is employed in an organization probably will, and should, direct much of his attention to what his superior expects. One reason why this should be the case is the fact that his work and efforts in performing it should contribute to the goals of the larger unit, of which it is a part. Another reason is the common desire to please the boss and to say and do the things most likely to achieve these ends.

One of the best bits of advice to anyone in an organization, particularly to a relatively new person, is to try to understand and adapt to his boss. He can contribute most and enjoy more personal success by trying to understand and adjust to his boss—support him where he needs help rather than second-guess him, and try to make his plans work rather than search for reasons why they are unsound and cannot work. This does not mean being a "yes-man"; it simply means not being a "no-man"—one's "yes" or "no" or "might this be worth considering?" should be as honest and straightforward an expression of one's true beliefs as circumstances permit.

More than personal relationships is, of course, involved. Understanding one's superior will enhance one's knowledge of the enterprise as a whole—its objectives, general managerial philosophy, the organization structure, the work of other departments, the systems of operation, etc.

Working with associates

As with one's boss, efforts to understand and work effectively with one's associates is of crucial importance.

Of particular significance, here, are needs to be "company-minded rather than merely departmental-minded or job-minded"—in other words, to try to resolve most questions and conflicts of immediate interest by considering what action would serve the best interests of the enterprise as a whole. A good piece of philosophy is the often repeated suggestion that "what we want is one big team, not a lot of little teams."

Worthy of special effort may be concentration upon points where friction frequently arises—such as in release of work in a manner that is convenient for the next unit, and handling errors made in another unit in a manner that will not ruffle feelings.

Important, also, are specific efforts to cooperate, such as lending personnel to units temporarily overloaded, agreeing readily to release of an individual who has been offered a promotion in another unit (or just as soon as conditions will permit), and willingness to listen to anyone and learn from anyone.

Working with subordinates

Much of the remaining material in this chapter and the following chapters deals with leading, or supervising the work of, subordinates. Only certain points of emphasis will be mentioned here.

The role of supervisor is by no means a standard one; in some organizations, he may perform functions which would cause the title "manager" to be more descriptive of his position—he may be responsible for a major unit or department, have a rather large number of subordinates, and even have staff assistants for training, records and reports. In other organizations, he may be more nearly a "lead worker," devoting a large part of his time to actual operations, but having certain responsibilities for supervision of a small group, training employees, handling problems and questions that arise, and similar duties. There is often a real need for a lead worker, but seldom can a lead worker be expected to do justice to both supervision and a substantial amount of operative work; in such instances, operative work has a way of crowding out supervision.

Ideally, a supervisor *will devote most of his time to real supervision*—including planning and assigning current work and following up on it, training, or seeing that training is done properly, taking personal interest in each employee and always "being available," planning improvements, working closely with his superior and fellow supervisors, and other non-routine duties. Under ordinary conditions, he does not perform much operative work himself, although he may pitch in and help during emergencies. It is obvious that a close relationship exists between this type of supervision and good delegation. Delegating, or assigning operative work is a necessity if a supervisor is to have time for such activities.

At the same time, evidence mounts that *general, rather than close, supervision* ordinarily produces better results. Situations obviously vary, but a supervisor will achieve higher productivity and better employee morale if he will let his people know what he expects, train them thoroughly, be careful to insure that current instructions are understood, and be certain to incorporate their ideas into the working plan when feasible. But he then trusts them and encourages a high degree of initiative, rather than "breathing down their necks."

Much of the best thinking and experience in leadership can be summed up in three words: *train—then trust.*

Communication

We have recognized the need for good communication at a large number of points in administrative management and have implied that *two-way* communication is necessary for best results. Emphasis was given to the need for a flow of information to each person who must make decisions, so he will be able to think in responsible terms. Thorough explanation of new plans, programs, systems, and methods is a constant need. Solicitation of employee reactions, questions, and suggestions in virtually every situation where there is some latitude in decision, has been recommended repeatedly. The immediate supervisor plays a key role in both communicating downward and communicating upward; he must also be an effective communicator in his continuing relationships with other supervisors and staff personnel.

A skilled supervisor senses the desires of his employees to know about developments which may affect them—whether these are company-wide in scope, departmental, or individual. People seek such information, and if they do not get it through their supervisor or other formal channels (such as standard forms and reports, memoranda, bulletins, house organs, or general meetings), they will turn to the grapevine for answers to questions or other information of interest. The grapevine is an inevitable part of the communications network of any enterprise; it would be impossible to eliminate it and unwise to try. Management's challenge is to provide a good formal communications program which supplies significant and timely information, and minimizes the dependence by employees upon the grapevine for information vital to their interests and those of the organization. The idea is often summed up in the statement that "the best medicine for rumors is facts."

Most enterprises are more careful with downward communication than with upward. Encouraging a good upward flow of questions, suggestions, and information of other sorts is an undertaking that requires constant vigilance and special effort. As has been frequently observed, an employee tends to tell his boss what he thinks his boss wishes to hear. When the employee learns through experience that the superior is truly receptive to ideas, considers them seriously, and takes them into account, only then will he open up.

Certain prerequisites to effective two-way communication can be noted. Empathy (placing oneself in another's shoes and sensing how he will react), skill in listening and observing, and special effort to get to know one's employees and take personal interest in each of them, are of basic importance if real communication is to occur. Commending good work is a powerful motivator—one widely advocated but not so widely practiced. Communicating with "problem employees" is a special challenge to exhaust constructive efforts to aid such an employee to overcome his problem; if all constructive efforts fail to produce results, then decisive steps must be taken. Finally, the "actions speak louder than words" axiom certainly applies in communication. For example, assigning a challenging task to an employee or asking for his ideas on how to cope with a problem will convey a feeling of confidence and trust, just as over-supervision will convey a feeling of absence of confidence and trust.

Participation

The value of employee ideas in setting goals, formulating plans, improving methods, and controlling one's own performance, has been emphasized throughout our study of administrative management. Many sound ideas come to light which would be ignored otherwise. Morale improves, particularly where a reasonable portion of suggestions are acted upon. Individuals who think creatively develop themselves for higher responsibility.

In practice, participation ranges in degree from complete delegation of a responsibility to consultation on major aspects of a problem or proposal, or on minor details of how to apply a plan already decided upon, or on employee reaction to a predetermined plan. In some cases, there may be no direct participation. These variations are inevitable; some decisions permit a much higher degree of participation than others.

A good general rule, however, is that cited in relation to delegation in Chapter 2: decisions ordinarily should be made at the lowest level where people are capable of making them, consistent with overall coordination. Where delegation is not feasible, the alternative should be to consult persons affected and to incorporate their ideas in the final plan, to the extent possible.

The direct relationship to human needs is again apparent. Participation in numerous forms offers many opportunities for ego-satisfaction and self-fulfillment.

General Requirements in Leadership

Implicit in the preceding discussion of leadership practices, and in those to be considered in later chapters, are fundamental requirements which may be regarded as "common denominators." While specific techniques must be adapted to the leader, the people led, and the situation, we can single out certain attitudes and skills which will increase effectiveness in most situations.

Empathy in communications and in other contacts with people will nearly always lead to better results. A feeling for people and an understanding of a particular person's emotional reactions will enable any leader to adapt his approach to achieve a more favorable response; it is important, however, that the leader attempt to remain objective so that sentiment does not blind him to other requirements.

A *genuine respect for people,* coupled with deliberate effort to bring out the best in each person rather than to focus upon his weaknesses, will show itself in countless relationships, and will encourage people to grow and to live up to the confidence placed in them. Again, *train-then-trust* is recommended as a philosophy to guide much leadership behavior.

Integrity—basic honesty and fairness, acting from conviction as to what is right rather than who is right, and setting high standards for oneself as well as for others—is perhaps the most essential of all leadership qualities. At the same time, integrity must be combined with patience and understanding; people often require time to learn and adjust, and they may have differing values and personal needs. A manager must be a realist; he will need a combination of integrity, tolerance, patience, and a good sense of timing.

We close with the suggestion that *determination to get results* very often proves to be the real measure of difference between highly successful leaders and those less successful. Excuses are on every hand, if one is looking for them. But with a philosophy of "results—not excuses," a leader can nearly always find ways to achieve results; such a philosophy in no way requires that a person be ruthless, unscrupulous, or inconsiderate of others. It suggests, instead, that if his first approach to a problem fails, he will try another approach, and he will use ingenuity and persistence until he finds an approach that leads to the desired ends.

QUESTIONS FOR STUDY AND DISCUSSION

1. The president of a small manufacturing company wanted his firm to grow and prosper. He worked night after night, putting in many long hours developing his plans. He was very enthusiastic about his plans and his company, but the organization never quite shared his enthusiasm. His subordinates agreed that growth was desirable, but they never caught the spirit and fire needed for a winning team. What basic error does it appear that the president committed? What would you have done differently, if you had been president? Why? What do you now recommend that the president do? Why?

2. Comment on the statement "leadership is the motivation of human effort." Would this statement hold true for all types of leadership—military, production, and office situations? Why? How would you change this statement to make it more realistic?

3. The best means of achieving knowledge of work operations is to acquire experience in the work itself. Knowing this to be the case, management often fills supervisory positions by promoting the more productive employees from the work groups. Comment on this method of developing leaders for office-type work units. What are the advantages and the disadvantages? How might the disadvantages be overcome to make this procedure highly effective? Can you suggest an approach that should generally be more effective?

4. Relate the two concepts of communication and participation to leadership.

5. Maintaining the morale of the work group is a definite responsibility of the leader. However, there are many off-the-job factors which directly affect the morale of the employees while on the job. How far should the leader go, and what moral and legal right does he have, in influencing these off-the-job factors in order to create good morale and congenial attitudes of his employees while on the job? What do you recommend in situations such as these? Why?

6. What traits or characteristics do you think are necessary and important for a leader of an office-type organization? Why? Would these be different from a leader in a factory? Why?

7. Assuming that leadership is the motivation of people, the five basic human needs presented in this chapter would be the motivators utilized by the leader. Would you, as a leader, expect to find the same hierarchical arrangement of needs in each of your subordinates? Why?

8. One theory of leadership is the situationist theory, that is, the type of leadership needed depends upon the situation. Does this theory have any application

and relationship to the type of leadership usually found in office organizations? Suggest possible applications.

9. Systems concepts were discussed in earlier chapters of this book and generally dealt with such factors as information systems, procedures systems, and total sub-systems. Relate the general systems concept to leadership. How are these similar? Dissimilar?

10. Differentiate between empathy and sympathy and comment on their application in a leadership role. Which would be more appropriate to office leadership? Why?

Case 26-1. John Morton

John Morton is a supervisor who is considered to be highly proficient in the technical aspects of his work, and he is especially well informed on procedures and operating details.

During one morning recently, however, John did the following things:

1. Took an error back to the supervisor of the unit in which the error was made, threw the case down on his desk, and in an exasperated tone said, "When are your people going to stop doing this?"

2. Started a new employee to work without introducing him to anyone around him.

3. Told one employee of a salary raise that had come through for him but did so in a rather grudging manner, implying doubt as to whether employee really had it coming.

4. Strongly reprimanded a woman employee who came in five minutes late even though this was the first time the woman had been late in two years and car trouble had been the cause.

5. Failed to give any hint of appreciation or commendation to his employees, even though this morning marked the end of an audit during which they all had had to do a lot of extra work.

Problems and questions:

a. What particular shortcoming on John's part seems to have been present in all of these situations?

b. Can this type of shortcoming be remedied? Or do you feel that a person who does such things is hopelessly out of place in a supervisory position?

c. If you feel that John might be able to solve his problem, how would you suggest that he go about doing so?

Case 26-2. The Case of the Ambitious Supervisor

Gerald Prochnow had been employed by the company for four years. During this time he had held a variety of clerical jobs, and his performance on nearly all of these jobs had been superior.

A position as supervisor opened up and Gerald was promoted. Gerald was highly pleased, and he was determined to make good on the new assignment. He hit upon a plan which he believed would go a long way toward insuring success in his first supervisory effort.

Gerald's plan was to impress each employee with how much he (Gerald) already knew about the employee's job. During the first few days Gerald spent approximately two or three hours with each employee in the unit. He devoted this time mainly to performing the job himself, and he worked very rapidly and efficiently while the employee watched.

Several weeks later, while participating in a supervisory training course, Gerald told a group of supervisors what he had done. When asked how the plan seemed to work out, Gerald said he still believed that particular plan to be a good one, but that he happened to have a group of employees who couldn't seem to do anything on their own. They would come to him constantly with questions on problems that they should be able to solve easily by themselves.

Problems and questions:

a. Appraise the probable effects of Gerald's approach to his employees during his first days as a supervisor.

b. Is this an approach that should be recommended to new supervisors generally?

Case 26-3. Frank Young

Frank Young is 20 years old. He has been working for Art Long since the time of his employment one year ago.

He started working with a group of people. For the first three months his work was satisfactory. At that time, he was given a very good appraisal by Art.

After he had been employed for four months, Frank was put on a job which required him to work jointly with one other employee. For a few months his work was fine. Suddenly his attitude toward the company changed, his work slacked off, and he tended to push all the hard tasks on his co-worker. Frank seemed to have the attitude that he was running that section of the unit, and that he was too good to do any hard work. Art talked to him quite frequently about this matter, but it never seemed to affect him to any great extent.

At the time of Frank's yearly appraisal, Art had no choice but to give him a very low score. The problem seemed solved because Frank's work became much better and his attitude toward the company greatly improved.

Later Frank was put on a higher class job which he now holds. However, no formal promotion has yet been made. For the first few weeks, he worked fine, but soon his work started to slow up again. He was not producing what he should have, and he did a lot of unnecessary talking and time-wasting. By this time, Art was very much provoked and had quite a lengthy discussion with Frank, talking very strongly about probations and termination. This discussion, as before, made a great deal of improvement in Frank. Art does not wish to take any drastic steps unless it is absolutely necessary since Frank has the ability to handle any job and could be a definite asset to the company if he would only try.

Problems and questions:

a. What should Art do if Frank does not continue to improve, goes back to his poor working habits, or starts showing improper attitude toward the company?

b. What appear to be the reasons for Frank's behavior?

c. What could the company and Art have done to prevent such a situation from developing?

Case 26-4. The Case of Eugenia

Eugenia holds a position as policy typist. She has been with the company about two years. She is 22 years old and is not married. Her disposition is pleasant, but she is rather slow and careless about her work. During recent months her absences have been excessive.

Today, her supervisor asked her to go to another unit to get some information urgently needed for a report upon which the whole unit was working. He watched her walk slowly out of her own unit and into the ladies' rest room. In about ten minutes, she emerged and walked slowly toward the other section.

In route, she stopped several times to talk with other employees. She then went into the other unit, got the necessary records, and visited for a short while before leaving that unit. She made a trip to the drinking fountain on the way back to her own unit.

By this time, two other employees had had to stop their work on the report and wait for Eugenia to return with the material.

Unknown to either Eugenia or the supervisor, the entire procedure was witnessed by the superintendent of the department.

Problems and questions:

a. If you were the supervisor, what would you do?

b. If you were the superintendent, what would you do?

c. What additional information would be helpful before answering either of these questions? Why?

d. Where do you place the blame for such a situation? Why?

Case 26-5. The Case of Flo

This case study concerns a policy typist, Flo Wilson, a young girl of 17. Her test scores in her personnel shield were excellent, especially her typing. She was one of the fastest typists ever seen in the company, and her work was neat and accurate.

The problem with Flo was that she only worked about half of the time. The rest of the day she would spend talking and running around the building. The supervisor's problem was to try to convince Flo that she should use her great ability and speed to benefit herself and the company.

One point in her favor, as far as she was concerned, was that she easily made production every day. She knew what the standard was for her job and also knew she was 10 to 15 points over standard production.

Hardly a week passed that the supervisor didn't talk to Flo in private and explain that she was wasting half her time and that she was going to have to improve. The supervisor would explain to her that in order to get ahead she was going to have to "stick" to her work and that if she could learn to do this, she would get promoted to a better job because of her great ability.

Flo was finally placed on probation for two months and told that if no improvement was made at the end of the two months, she would be released. At the end of the probation period, she had improved some and was taken off probation, with the understanding that she was to continue to improve on her work habits. This worked fine for a month; after this time the problem was as bad as ever.

Problems and questions:

a. Would you fire the employee, find another job for her with more responsibility, make it so difficult for her she would quit on her own, or take other action?

b. How could management have prevented such a situation?

Case 26-6. A Study of Employee Characteristics

Ronald Wilburn is a supervisor of an office unit in the Harrison Metal Products Company. He recently resolved to spend some time every day in just getting to know his employees better. Below are some of the impressions gained during the next few days.

Louella is about 40 years old and unmarried. She seems to do more than her share of gossiping and spreading rumors. Ronald suspects that she has sometimes criticized him to other employees.

Mabel is a divorcée who has a child to support. She is quite moody and often gets "down on the world." She often seems to feel that she doesn't get a square deal on work assignments, pay raises, and other matters.

Marvin has been an outstanding employee; his production and quality have been high and he has fit in nicely with other employees. Recently, however, he has become very indifferent; and both his work and his interest in getting along with others have suffered as a result.

George is an intelligent person and a good worker. He seems to be somewhat antagonistic, however, and he often says something in a rather critical vein.

Tillie has generally turned in an average performance in regard to both quality and quantity of work, but in one day recently she produced more than double her usual amount of work and there were few errors.

Henry has just been transferred from another department. Ronald has been told that he didn't get along very well there and has been warned that he might cause trouble.

Bill is a very cocky fellow who seems to believe he knows all the answers and is very free in giving them out. He is inclined to use sarcasm and to belittle the ideas of others.

Mary is a conscientious employee and a good producer who ordinarily gets to work promptly in the morning. Recently she has been late to work several times and she has given no explanation.

Dale, a new employee, is a very quiet and reserved person. He seldom says anything unless someone speaks to him first. He has lunch alone and does little visiting with others during break periods.

One group of four employees always band together during lunch and break periods and pay little attention to other employees. Their performance on the job has been satisfactory thus far, however.

Problems and questions:

a. Would the typical department or unit be likely to have this many differences in individual personalities?

b. Based upon the limited amount of information given, what special treatment of each employee described would you recommend for Ronald?

c. Do these findings suggest that Ronald was wise in his resolve to spend some time every day in just getting to know his employees better?

d. What specific techniques should be most useful to Ronald, or any other supervisor, in really getting to know his employees?

27

SELECTION AND PLACEMENT

Objectives of the personnel function · Notice of vacancy ·
Job description and specification · Recruiting · Screening ·
Testing · Interviewing · Selection and placement · Orienta-
tion · Follow-up

In modern business organizations
the personnel function has grown in importance until it now commands
considerable respect. The personnel officer bears equal status with other
major administrative officers of the organization. In addition, the personnel concept has broadened until today it embraces not only the function of employing personnel through the use of scientific selection techniques, but also the function of promoting harmonious relations and improved productivity among workers. Today many alert young men and
women aspire to careers in personnel management.

Each year new knowledge about the aptitudes and motivations of
people is brought to light. With this new knowledge the trained employment technician becomes better equipped to evaluate prospective
employees, to place them, and to indoctrinate and train them on the
job. As research in human abilities continues, and as more is learned
about the essential elements of human productivity and stability, the
employment function will become an increasingly important part of the
scientific management process.

The tremendous growth in the office and kindred worker class, discussed in Chapter 1, has led to even more emphasis being placed upon
the personnel functions of selection and placement of office workers.
The increasing trend of the office worker group is toward demanding
a better qualified employee. Office jobs of today require more skill and
more education, in part because of the impact of electronic data

processing and because of increased complexity of management in all types of enterprises. Selection and placement are vital functions of personnel management in the staffing of modern office organizations.

Objectives of the Personnel Function

Basically there are two objectives of a personnel function which deserve mention here. These are:

1. Develop and stimulate continuing awareness of human relations aspects of virtually every managerial decision and action. This objective supplements the major objectives of the firm and of higher management, and serves to coordinate the personnel activities of line managers throughout the organization.

2. Perform certain personnel services which require technical background, special facilities, and time. This objective is the basis of this chapter; selection and placement services are discussed in detail. The selection and placement of personnel, while but one responsibility of the modern personnel manager, is a most important function. This chapter will present a summary of current thinking with reference to the selection and placement of office personnel in business organizations today.

There are several elements in the modern selection process. These elements and their components will be quite familiar to experienced personnel officers; they should also be familiar to supervisory and executive personnel throughout the organization so that the selection process may be meaningful to those directly concerned with the utilization of the end product: the new employee. These elements are:

1. Notice of vacancy
2. Job description and specification
3. Recruiting
4. Screening
5. Testing
6. Interviewing
7. Selection and placement
8. Orientation
9. Follow-up

Each of these elements in the selection and placement process will now be discussed separately.

Notice of Vacancy or Employee Requisition

While many managers and personnel specialists may not consider this a formal part of selection and placement, it is, nevertheless, the beginning of these procedures. Employee requisitions are extremely important, particularly in large organizations; this notifies the personnel department that an employee is needed or will soon be needed in a particular job classification. Receipt of this employee requisition is the official authorization to the personnel department to initiate the selection and placement procedures.

Where personnel policies and job specifications are relatively complete, requisitions may be quite simple, including merely job title and number and starting date. In other cases, special information may need to be included, such as special qualifications desired, special working conditions, pay level willing to offer, etc.

Job Specification

Job specifications and job descriptions are essential parts of a selection and placement program. These devices provide the personnel function with a clear picture of the job to be filled and the qualifications of the employee to fill it. The job description summarizes the purpose, principal duties, and responsibilities of the job; the job specification describes the minimum, and sometimes the maximum, qualifications of the employee for a particular job. Such information is essential if the selection and placement function is to operate with goals and objectives, and if it is to provide acceptable employees for various vacancies.

Recruiting

Recruiting to fill vacancies which occur in the organization should be from as wide an area as practicable, since the greater the choices, the more likelihood of finding capable personnel for the organization. Recruiting sources may be internal, external, or both.

Internal

Internal recruiting, it has been argued, helps the morale of employees in general and induces present workers to prepare themselves for promotions. It has also been argued that when opportunities for present workers are provided within the organization, a better quality of external applicant is attracted. Further, it is claimed that the employer is in a better position to evaluate those who have worked for him than the candidates who present themselves from the outside—this goes on the assumption that a work test is the best test of an employee's capacities and abilities.

But there are objections to internal recruiting. Among these are the dangers of "in-breeding" and the inadequacies of supply. In-breeding means that the employee tends to demonstrate on the job only what he has learned in the organization, and thus tends to be less productive of new ideas than a newcomer to the firm. While originality does not play a major role in the performance of most office tasks, it may be essential in some. The other objection, inadequacy of supply, refers to the narrow choice which may be faced, particularly in smaller organizations.

External

External recruiting presents many opportunities for a progressive personnel program. The standard sources include the following:

Employment agencies, both public and private. The agency is useful to the employer by serving as a central clearing house in a locality for those who want employees and those who want employment. Some employment agencies have become so proficient in the task of recruiting qualified personnel that they have literally taken over the employment functions for business firms. Private agencies, which charge fees based on the salary of the position into which the applicant is placed, usually specialize in handling specific types of personnel. Public agencies, most of which are operated by the states, charge no fees and usually handle all levels of personnel. Employment agencies, with their broad contacts and experience, represent a recruiting source which should not be overlooked.

Advertising. Newspaper advertising is usually an effective means of securing applicants on short notice, although newspaper ads generally draw a large number of unqualified applicants. To minimize the number of unsuitable applicants, the advertisement should be specific and include sufficient detail. (See Figure 27-1.) Where specialized personnel are required, advertising in trade and professional journals is sometimes quite effective.

In addition to the use of help-wanted ads in recruiting, the organization should not overlook situations-wanted ads in locating possible candidates for vacancies which occur.

Employee referrals. In recent years, the technique of encouraging employees to recommend friends and acquaintances for work in the organization has flourished. Employees frequently like to recommend their friends for employment, particularly if they themselves are happy and satisfied with the firm. Experience indicates that a good employee will usually recommend well-qualified workers. In many organizations, em-

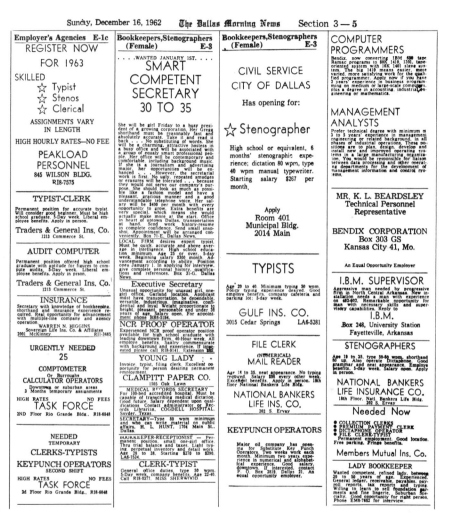

Figure 27-1. Some typical help-wanted ads from the classified section of a newspaper

ployees are periodically furnished with introduction cards which they are asked to give to friends who might wish to apply for employment.

Unsolicited applications. While conditions vary for different types of employment, it is generally unwise to rely on casual labor to meet employment needs. Well-qualified and experienced workers, as well as young people just out of school, may make the rounds of employment offices and should receive the serious consideration of the employment manager. But if an organization depends solely on casual labor the opportunities for selection will be greatly restricted.

Direct recruiting at schools and colleges. This is perhaps the most effective technique of all in recruiting new workers. The schools provide selectivity; a student's progress in school is one index of his probable success on the job. Also, opinions of teachers concerning the abilities, personality, and character of students are available. It is surprising to find that many important business firms with hundreds of openings annually never conduct direct recruiting at schools and colleges, even though it would appear these would be their most effective sources. It is not unusual to hear employment managers state that they haven't any contacts in the schools and have, therefore, waited for the graduates to come to them.

Nearly all schools and colleges today, and particularly business and trade schools, have placement offices which will be glad to arrange a time for employment managers to visit their schools and interview students about to graduate. The schools are usually eager to cooperate with the employment managers because placements arranged through a school enhance the school's reputation. Every organization requiring new employees annually should cultivate a relationship with schools in the area which offer courses providing training in the skills being sought.

Screening

The screening interview is a free exchange of information between the interviewer and the applicant. The interviewer seeks to obtain enough information to determine whether minimum qualifications are met and to give the applicant information about the company and about the job. The applicant can ask questions and make clear his needs and ambitions. Thus, both parties exchange information and data and decide whether to continue the selection process any further.

A person with a broad knowledge of the various positions for which applicants are employed should be designated to do the screening interviewing. Much of this information is readily obtained from job specifications and job descriptions, although direct communication and association with supervisors can provide added insights.

All interviews should be conducted in well-lighted, attractive offices which present the applicant with a favorable impression of the organization. Applicants, however unsuitable they may appear to be, must always be treated with courtesy and respect.

There should be no attempt in the screening interview at detailed analysis of the individual. The interviewer, however, should be sufficiently capable as an evaluator to make a preliminary appraisal of the applicant in a few minute's time. The length of the screening interview should be governed by the time necessary to arrive at a sound decision concerning the applicant's qualification. Care should be taken to avoid arriving at snap decisions based on insufficient data, but the interview should not be prolonged unduly if the applicant is not suitable for employment.

If the applicant appears to be unsuitable for consideration or if it appears that there will be no openings for persons of his qualifications in the near future, it is preferable to explain the situation to the applicant frankly and courteously. Obtaining application forms from all who apply and maintaining extensive files of forms which will probably never be used is wasteful of both time and space. There are, however, situations where possibilities for future needs may exist; then it may be both wise and advantageous (from a public relations standpoint) to encourage the filing of selected applications.

It is important in the screening interview to guard against *stereotyped thinking*. Stereotypes can never be completely erased from attitudes and judgments, but if the tendency toward stereotypes is understood it is possible to be more objective in one's thinking. Stereotyped thinking is a lazy habit into which interviewers fall; it's easier to assume that someone who *looks* like a salesman wouldn't make a good accountant rather than to probe further and make a more valid evaluation. In line with stereotyped thinking is the tendency to pigeonhole a person based on his prior occupation. The mere fact that a person has worked as a retail store clerk or a filling station attendant should not disqualify him for consideration for an office position—if he has the requisite interest and skill.

Through the years the general request for references has elicited from applicants the names of ministers, bankers, and friends of the family— all of whom could be counted on to give a very fine recommendation. While references are still important, the modern application form is more specific and asks for names of supervisors or teachers of business courses under whom the individual has actually worked. Personnel managers are urged to make a common sense appraisal of their application forms and to redesign them, if necessary, in order to include only such items as are needed in order to permit an evaluation of the applicant. Many firms use the same application form in employing messengers as they use in employing top executives. The fallacy of this procedure is apparent when it is considered that information essential in the one case is not essential in the other.

When possible, reference checks with previous employers should be made by telephone. The telephone provides the quickest and most effective means of checking references supplied by the applicant. It is a good

UARCO *INCORPORATED*

APPLICATION FOR EMPLOYMENT

Date _____ 19____

All employment is on a probationary basis for a three month period. Please print all entries. If employed, this application becomes a part of your permanent record. Fill it out completly and accurately.

Name in full _____ Address _____ Telephone No. _____

Date of birth _____ Height _____ Weight _____ Marital Status _____ Social Security No. _____

What are your living accommodations? Own home? _____ Rent? _____ Board? _____ Live with family or relatives? _____

Number of children under 18 _____ Other Dependants _____ Relationship to you _____

Did you ever work for this company before? _____ If so, where? _____

Do you know any present or former employee of this company? _____ If so, whom? _____ From _____ To _____

Are you related to any present or former employee of this company? _____ If so, whom? _____ Relationship _____

Describe any physical defects _____

How many days have you lost because of illness or accident during the past three years? _____

If employed in a department where shift work is available, are you willing to take your turn on the night shift? _____

Are you willing to work over-time if and when necessary? _____

Whom to notify in case of emergency: Name _____ Address _____ Tel. No. _____

EDUCATION

KIND OF SCHOOL	NAME OF SCHOOL	NUMBER OF YEARS ACTUAL CREDIT	COURSE OR MAJOR SUBJECT	AVERAGE GRADE
Grammar school				
High school				
Trade school				
Correspondence				
College				
Other				

Are you now enrolled in any school? _____ Name of school _____

If so, what courses are you taking? _____

Figure 27-2a. A brief employment application form, page 1

494

PREVIOUS EXPERIENCE

Show your last place of employment first

COMPANY	ADDRESS	DURATION (MONTH-YEAR)	KIND OF WORK	SALARY OR WAGES	REASON FOR LEAVING
1.		From / To			
2.		From / To			
3.		From / To			
4.		From / To			
5.		From / To			
6.		From / To			

MILITARY SERVICE

BRANCH	DURATION (MONTH-YEAR)	RANK ATTAINED	GENERAL DUTIES	REASON FOR DISCHARGE
	From / To			

Give the names of your supervisors in company 1., 2., and 3.

1. _____ 2. _____ 3. _____

If now employed, how much advance notice would you give before leaving? _____

What production machinery or office business machines can you operate? _____

Signed _____

DO NOT WRITE BELOW THIS LINE

Employed-to start _____ Position _____ Dept. _____ Rate of Pay _____

Employee No. _____ Clock No. _____ B-U _____

Personnel Department

Figure 27-2b. A brief employment application form, page 2

495

idea to use a telephone questionnaire form so that responses can be recorded and all pertinent facts obtained. An effort should be made to verify statements shown on the application form, to obtain the individual's estimates of the applicant's strong and weak points, and to obtain impressions which will serve as the basis for questions and inquiries during the interview with the applicant.

Testing

Personnel tests are used as an aid in selecting the best qualified applicants, in placing both new applicants and present employees in positions that best match their qualifications, and in selecting employees for promotion. Tests are valuable because they yield information which cannot be obtained, at least with accuracy, through other means. Tests can measure certain abilities, aptitudes and skills which provide objective information on how well the applicant can be expected to perform on the job. But, since the applicant's performance is dependent on many other factors, test information must be used as a supplement to facts gained through other steps in the selection process. Tests can be classified into five broad categories:

1. Mental ability (general intelligence). Measures the ability to learn and to analyze.
2. Aptitude. Measures capacity to learn certain skills, such as clerical or mathematical.
3. Skill. Measures level of ability to perform particular functions, such as shorthand, programming, or welding.
4. Temperamental (personality). Measures behavior tendencies.
5. Interest (preference). Measures interest in or preference for certain activities.

Determining whether tests will be used and which tests to use is usually a matter of personnel policy, although the decision may be left to the personnel executive. Since tests are merely an aid in helping management decide on the selection and placement of the applicant, there may be instances when test administration will be unnecessary, i.e., when acute labor shortages exist and persons of minimum qualifications must be employed quickly. Figure 27-3 illustrates examples of employment tests.

The inadequacies of tests stem from the fact that while tests can indicate what a person is capable of doing, they cannot indicate *what the individual will actually do or how he will actually perform on the job.*

CLERICAL TEST B-2
E. R. Knob Company
Dallas, Texas

(A)

Name ———————————— Date ————————————

READ CAREFULLY: This will test your ability to detect differences

between pairs of names and pairs of numbers. If the two numbers

or names are alike in every respect, insert a check mark (✓) in the

space between. If, however, they are different, insert a zero (0).

The first two problems are correctly marked.

Johnson and Johnson __0__ Johnson & Johnson

Harvey C. Scheutz __✓__ Harvey C. Scheutz

42-192-321-1 _____ 42-191-322-1

Joseph R. Mayer Co. _____ Joseph R. Meyer Co.

81346-BC-876 _____ 81346-BC-876

CLERICAL TEST OF PROBLEM SOLVING ABILITY
Gordon Jones & Associates

(B)

Name ——————————— Date ———————————

INSTRUCTIONS: In the space at the right, insert the number of the
word which correctly answers the question. The first two questions
are answered correctly.
WAIT FOR THE SIGNAL BEFORE BEGINNING.

Good is the opposite of 1--bad, 2--pernicious, 3--haste, 4--love __1__

Valley is the opposite of 1--prairie, 2--hill, 3--river, 4--stream __2__

Intelligent is most nearly like 1--alert, 2--beautiful, 3--wise _____

Success is most nearly like 1--luck, 2--achievement, 3--progress _____

All people have 1--perseverance, 2--integrity, 3--brains, 4--hope _____

Figure 27-3. Examples (A) and (B) show questions, taken from actual employment tests, which are representative of the types of problems frequently found in tests of clerical ability

We should bear in mind that relatively few employees fail on the job because of a lack of skill or ability to do the job. Surveys show that most employees who turn out poorly and whose services must be terminated have lacked incentive or have failed in their relationships with others.

Although employment testing is still in its infancy, it is doubtful if tests will ever provide accurate measures of motivation, perseverance, and the ability to deal effectively with others, inasmuch as these qualities depend almost entirely on the will and personality rather than the ability of the individual. From this it is clear that tests cannot do a complete job of selection or placement and do not deserve the reverence accorded them by some organizations seeking a quick, mechanical means of selecting office employees.

There are four terms in the testing field with which one should be generally familiar: *standardization* means that a test, through a process of experimentation, has been found to have both validity and reliability; *validity* refers to the relationship between the test score and production on the job; *reliability* refers to the consistency in yielding similar results when administered on different occasions; while *norms* are tables of performance scores covering large numbers of personnel who have taken a test. Although standard norms are supplied with the purchase of ready-made tests, users should maintain tables of scores made by local persons who are tested in order that local norms based on the local labor supply may be determined.

Many personnel officers have found straight proficiency tests to be most important in selecting office workers. These tests, which measure the applicant's actual ability and skill in such office tasks as filing, typing, arithmetic, and bookkeeping, may be developed within the organization and may serve very well in indicating the level of the applicant's accomplishment. In preparing these tests it is simply necessary to assemble test materials which, in the estimate of the supervisors involved, indicate knowledge and competence in the various subjects. Tests should then be tried out on employees in the organization. Based on experiences in administering the tests, scores can be rated and norms established which will serve as guides in selecting new employees. Many companies prefer to prepare their own tests of skill and proficiency on the basis that they are in the best position to know what they want and expect of new employees.

There are many personnel tests on the market today, most of which provide norm scores for use in selecting office employees. Several organizations which specialize in developing and distributing personnel tests are: Psychological Corporation, 522 Fifth Avenue, New York; Science Research Associates, 57 W. Grand Avenue, Chicago 10; E. F. Wonderlic, Northfield, Illinois; and World Book Company, Tarrytown, New York.

It is difficult to make a generalization as to which tests and how many should be administered to an applicant. If a typist is being sought and qualifications other than typing skill are not very important, it may be sufficient to administer a single test in typewriting. But as more skills are required, there should be less reliance on single test scores and more reliance on the overall picture resulting from administration of several tests. It is almost essential that the assistance of a trained test specialist be secured in setting up effective batteries of tests to be used in selecting employees.

Interviewing

As the selection process continues for those applicants who appear to be good prospects, additional interviews are held by the person doing the screening interview or by the person responsible for the final employment decision. Although these interviews should usually be more detailed, they should be conducted in the same manner as the initial interview.

It is generally agreed that the interview is the most important element in the selection and placement process. Therefore, special efforts should be made to improve the interview process through continual study and evaluation. Following are some techniques which have been found helpful in conducting an effective and efficient interview.

1. Plan for the interview. The job specification and job description should be reviewed thoroughly to determine the qualifications necessary of the applicant. The application and screening interview record should also be studied to become familiar with the applicant.

2. Provide proper surroundings, as already suggested for the screening interview.

3. Insure adequate time. An interview should never be hurried. Allow plenty of time for the applicant to tell his story. A hurried interview will usually yield poor results and will often antagonize the applicant.

4. Put the applicant at ease. Spend the first few minutes in casual conversation on some topic of common interest, such as home town, weather, or hobby.

5. State questions clearly and avoid leading questions. Satisfactory answers cannot be obtained if the applicant cannot understand the questions. If the questions suggest an answer, the applicant is likely to reply in the manner suggested. Leading questions give the applicant an answer and reveal nothing of real value.

6. Ask personal questions naturally. Personal affairs have a definite bearing on job success and must be covered in the interview. If the personal questions are asked in a normal manner, proper and beneficial answers will usually be received.

7. Let the applicant do most of the talking. The primary purpose of the interview is to get information on which to base an objective evaluation. This can be obtained only if the applicant is allowed to talk.

8. Get answers to all questions. If the applicant avoids answering a

question, there is usually a reason. Probe tactfully for the whole truth.

9. Get exact dates and check inconsistencies. It is essential that the applicant account for all of his time. If there are gaps, these should be investigated thoroughly. And, if contradictory information is given, determine why. It may be an honest mistake, but he should be given a chance to explain.

10. Make the necessary notations immediately. Pertinent information should be recorded either during the interview or immediately following, so that no important details will be forgotten.

11. Conclude the interview tactfully.

Considerable attention has been directed in recent years to the planned or patterned interview in which the interviewer quietly follows a form designed to assure that all pertinent factors relating to the applicant's qualifications will be discussed. Patterned interview forms, such as those available through the Dartnell Corporation, have much to recommend them, for they assist the interviewer in conducting searching and comprehensive interviews. Personnel officers tend to prefer the patterned or direct interview over the non-directive form of interview in the selection process. The non-directive interview, which may be defined as the process of active listening, is generally felt to have real value in counseling employees, but is not sufficiently direct as a selection tool to permit the interviewer to obtain necessary factual information from the applicant.

In the interviewing process there is one technique often overlooked. This is the multiple interview, in which the applicant is interviewed for five or ten minutes by each of several different persons, each of whom fills out a rating form after the interview. These should be planned interviews. The rating forms provided by the personnel office should provide spaces to record observations concerning all important aspects of the prospect's suitability for employment.

Department heads and supervisors, because of their familiarity with office needs, are in an excellent position to contribute an evaluation of the prospect. In most cases, these people like being included in the multiple-interview program, if they are not asked too often; such interviews provide a sense of recognition and offer an occasional respite from established routines. The evaluations presented by different supervisory personnel provide the interviewer with opinions which he may check against his own.

The impressions the applicant receives of the organization during the interviewing and selection process are often lasting. Even though the applicant may not be considered for employment beyond the interview, he should always be treated with friendliness, courtesy, and respect. It should be the aim of the interviewer and others to present the best possible picture of the organization to all who apply for employment.

Selection and Placement

There are few rules that can be laid down for making selection and placement decisions. With present day personnel shortages, selection and placement of clerical workers has become largely a matter of assigning applicants who meet minimum requirements to the department which has been waiting longest for that particular class of worker.

There should, however, be a careful evaluation of accumulated data concerning the applicant, and this should be integrated with the interviewer's knowledge of work requirements. The applicant's qualifications on each of the following elements should be carefully weighed and evaluated:

> Character and motivation
> Work experience
> Academic achievements
> Ability to get along with others
> Performance on personnel tests

There is often a tendency among employment managers to give undue weight to certain of these factors. For example, an applicant who shows outstanding academic achievements may so impress the interviewer that he will fail to evaluate as carefully as he should the applicant's other qualifications. The question is often asked: which of the above elements, if any, should receive the most weight in the selection process? It appears to be the consensus that in selecting an employee for a specific position, successful work experience in similar work is the most important criterion. If the individual has no previous experience, the most important criteria appear to be satisfactory academic achievements and test results, coupled with an indicated ability to get along well with others.

In most firms the supervisor of the department in which the vacancy exists will make the final decision as to whether or not the applicant should be selected. In these cases, the applicant should be escorted to the supervisor, and the supervisor should be provided with a folder containing the applicant's application, reports on references which have been checked, the profile of test results, and the recommendation of the interviewer.

In all cases of selection and placement, it must be remembered that the personnel function is a staff function assisting the line organization.

In this respect the personnel department should not, if circumstances permit, make the final decision to hire an applicant. This should be the responsibility and right of the immediate supervisor of the new employee. An interview with the potential supervisor and, possibly, a short visit to the actual work place should be arranged by the personnel department; the understanding should be: "Here is an applicant that we think may be O.K. See what your reactions are and let us know whether to hire him or not."

The supervisor is in the best position to know the current needs in his unit, the characteristics of other employees, and the particular qualifications of the new employee which would provide balanced strength. Based upon his experience, he may be able to spot certain characteristics which would be of key significance in the employee's success in the job and unit. Finally, the making of the final decision by the supervisor establishes a desirable relationship with the personnel department for mutual cooperation in the future.

When it has been determined that the applicant is both qualified and suitable for a specific position open, and upon the approval of the supervisor of the department in which the applicant will work, the applicant should be notified that he is being accepted for employment. The title and salary of the position should be made clear to him, and he should be told when and where to report for work.

Orientation

Getting new employees off to a good start on their job is of vital importance. Although a sound orientation program takes considerable time and effort, it will probably take more time to answer the questions and handle the problems of the person who has not been properly oriented. Some of the benefits that accrue from an effective orientation program are:

Creates a favorable attitude. First impressions are quite significant and have a definite bearing on an employee's attitudes toward his job, the company and his supervisors. These will affect his morale and performance for quite some time.

Gives accurate information. If information is not given to the applicant by the proper persons, he will have to get it from other sources. These sources will give inadequate information at best, and may present a false picture, particularly if the source happens to be an unhappy employee.

Aids learning and saves time and trouble. A good orientation program gives the employee information that he needs, and helps him to know what to expect on the job. As a result, he is less apt to bother his supervisor and fellow workers with excessive questions and is less likely to make mistakes. Since he knows what is expected of him, grievances caused by misunderstandings are less likely to occur. In general, the new employee should be more satisfied and more productive because of a good start on his job.

Although the orientation process will differ in various firms, the supervisor should always be responsible for discussing job duties with new employees and explaining what is expected of them on the job.

Orientation is a proper and important phase of the selection and placement program. The applicant will have been given some general information about the company and about the job, but he needs additional information, of course. The orientation program is designed to provide this information *gradually* as the new employee needs it, and in quantities that he can absorb it.

Ordinarily, much of the initial day on the job will be spent in getting acquainted with the physical and social surroundings. Typical first day uncertainties and some possible procedures for handling them are outlined below in Figure 27-4. A frequently needed note of caution: postpone detailed explanations, tours, introductions, and the like, until the employee is ready for the information. This calls for careful *timing* and *extending* of the orientation program so that the employee can relate experiences to information.

Many progressive companies have devised comprehensive indoctrination programs for new employees, designed to give new recruits a broad

UNCERTAIN ABOUT	MIGHT BE HANDLED BY

Supervisor and company
  whether made right decision
  whether he can achieve his
    goals
  whether can get along
	Get-acquainted visit initiated by supervisor and frequent follow-ups during the day, with expression of sincere interest.

Fellow employees
  whether he will be accepted
  whether they will like him
	Introduce those employees who will be closely associated with the new employee, *but not* a great many more. Let the new employee meet other employees through his associates.

The job
  whether he can handle it
  whether he will enjoy it
	Assign easy tasks first with frequent follow-ups and encouragement. This allows a good start.

Figure 27-4. Typical first day reactions of new employees and suggested methods
of handling

picture of the entire organization, its history, its present operations, and its plans for the future. Visual aids can be readily adapted for programs of this type. It is also well for the organization to have an illustrated booklet about the organization for distribution to new employees. In planning the orientation program, bear in mind that new employees want to know about the organization for which they work, they want to answer questions their friends may have about it, and they want to feel a part of it.

A good orientation program includes a check back by a personnel representative a week or so after the new employee has begun work to insure that the employee has familiarized himself with the organization and to answer any questions concerning regulations and procedures that may still be unanswered in the employee's mind.

Follow-up

Although a good orientation program will get a new employee off to a good start, this does not assure us that he will adjust to all problems he will meet on his new job. Unless a special effort is made to spot these problems, they may not come to light until serious trouble has developed. Follow-up procedures can detect turnover in the making. As a consequence, opportunities are provided for reducing turnover costs, usually estimated to be at least one hundred dollars per clerical employee who leaves his position, and may in some cases be far higher.

To determine how the employee is adjusting to his job, a *planned follow-up* should be conducted by the supervisor during the first few months of employment. The employee should be assured of the willingness of the supervisor to discuss any questions or problems that might arise. The receipt of the first pay check provides a good opportunity for the supervisor to talk with the employee about how the pay is computed and what the various deductions means. Misunderstandings about the pay received can be a critical factor.

The supervisor will have informal contacts with the employee during each working day and problems should be discussed as they occur. Since new employees usually are on a trial or probationary basis during the first few months of employment, their performance should be critically evaluated during this period. If the performance is not satisfactory, the reasons should be discussed with them, and a written record of these discussions should be made. The supervisor and the employee should determine how his performance can be improved and should set a definite time for accomplishing these improvements.

A common practice in many organizations today is to have a personnel department representative visit with the new employee after about thirty days or six weeks. This allows the employee to become adjusted to his job and to determine what he thinks of his new job. If at all possible, the personnel department employee who did the original interviewing and selection should make the follow-up interview in order to appraise his own efforts in selection and placement.

Another common practice in many firms is a formal appraisal program. Appraisal programs require periodic review and evaluation of employee's performance and consultations with the employee regarding the appraisal. Ordinarily, appraisals are made each three or six months during the first year or two of employment, and annually thereafter. Employee appraisal will be considered more fully in the next chapter.

QUESTIONS FOR STUDY AND DISCUSSION

1. Sometimes impressions are very difficult to control objectively. This results in "stereotyping" the applicants as they apply for employment and as they are processed through the screening process. What methods do you suggest for the personnel employees to be as objective as possible in the selection process? Would you want to be completely objective? Why?

2. In some organizations, which have had difficulty in recruiting, employees are given a bonus award for each person whom they can recruit to work for the organization. An insurance firm in Chicago gives employees $25 for each person whom they can recruit, plus $25 additional if the recruit stays three months. Comment on this method of recruitment. Do you approve? Why? What alternatives do you suggest?

3. Suppose that you are the new vice-president of personnel and the president directs you to establish an employment testing program. Describe the program that you would recommend. What kind of timetable could you expect to give to the president regarding the establishment of a testing program? What would determine this timetable?

4. Discuss the role and place of the personnel department in today's business organization—specifically in relation to the other key departments, and in the development of a proper atmosphere within the firm.

5. One student commented that he did not think personnel tests were particularly necessary since he could recognize strengths and weaknesses in persons within about 15 minutes of discussion. Do you agree with this student? Why? How long do you think that it would take you to recognize the qualities in an applicant?

6. Discuss the relationship of a job description and specification for an office or clerical job to a firm's personnel program. Why are job specifications and descriptions still not used in many office-type organizations?

7. Discuss the purposes of the interview in the selection and placement procedure. With all of the other refinements in the personnel program such as testing and improved applications blanks, do you feel that interviews are really necessary? Why?

8. The use of testing in the personnel program has been generally accepted throughout industry, but little attention has been given to the use of testing programs in the promotion of employees within the organization. Comment on the

use of personnel testing in selecting employees for promotion. Do you approve? Why?

9. Mary was hired as a file clerk, although she had typing skill also. She enjoyed the filing work very much and was doing a satisfactory piece of work. However, when given the opportunity to take a typing job, she accepted. But Mary was unable to keep up with the workload at her new typing job. Some of her inability was due to talking and wasting time and part was just inability to type well enough. Her attitude began to change, becoming, "I don't like the work," or "I can't do all of that," and "I didn't want this job anyway." What factors likely lead to such a situation? Could this situation have been prevented in the selection and placement process? What should the supervisor and management do now?

Case 27-1. Mid States Utility

An opening for a Senior Service Order Clerk has developed. Three people in the Accounts Section are eligible for consideration for promotion to this position.

Mary has been with the company for 13 months. She began as a File Clerk and was promoted to Mail Clerk five months ago. She is doing an excellent job, has a good attendance record, is married, and it looks as though she will be with us for some time. Moving her from the Mail & File Unit at this time would present difficulties because of turnover and promotions in the Unit recently.

Jane has been with the company for 19 months, all of this time being spent in the Accounts Posting Unit. She has adequately performed all jobs in the Unit and is currently doing a good job as Cash Posting Clerk. She is married and her husband is in the service and is currently overseas. Recently she became involved in an intra-unit feud, in which the supervisor had considerable difficulty in settling once and for all who was running the unit. Jane became involved by taking sides and generally helping to keep things stirred up. Although she personally had no problem, she let herself become involved and later had to be criticized for her actions. Her conduct has become known throughout the section.

Jack has been with the company for seven months as a multilith operator. He is single, but contemplating marriage soon. He has a high school education and had no related job experience before coming here. He has been cross-trained on all jobs in the Reproduction Unit. He has done some production scheduling, but not enough to reach any conclusion as to his abilities along that line. However, his learning ability on all the other jobs in the unit was good and he was able to produce fairly quickly. Jack likes the company and has career ideas. He would like to work toward Data Processing. His work habits and attendance have been good.

Problems and questions:

Which one of these people should be promoted to Service Order Clerk? Why?

Case 27-2. Use of Clerical Aptitude Tests in Selection

Several clerical aptitude tests are of the name-comparison and number-comparison variety. Typically, they include columns of paired names such as: Johnson___Johnston, and Brown___Browne; and columns of paired numbers such as 14562___14652 and 83919___83991. Names or numbers which match are to be checked, others left blank; and a time limit is set which presses most persons to complete the test.

Problems and questions:

Does it seem to you that such a test might be a valid indicator of aptitude for some office jobs?—if so, what types of jobs in particular? How would you go about determining whether a given test of the type described is a valid and reliable predictor of success for certain jobs within an enterprise?

Case 27-3. Employment Standards for Beginning Employees

In the United National Insurance Company, the starting position for a majority of employees is that of application file clerk. The work involves mainly the filing of folders which are made up for each new policyholder, pulling these from the files on request, and refiling them. Five-drawer file cabinets are used, arranged in long rows separated by operating divisions. Clerks are on their feet nearly all the time, although limited use can be made of file stools.

File Supervisors have tended to prefer the hiring of young men for these jobs. Since the work is quite fatiguing, the cabinets rather high for most women, and men somewhat easier to supervise than women—according to these supervisors, who are mainly young men themselves—they agree generally that five men can do the work of six women on these particular jobs.

Recently, however, there have been discussions as to the wisdom of the practice of assigning men to the filing jobs. Since the salary is at the minimum level for the company, the typical man hired is an 18-to-20-year-old high school graduate with little if any prior work experience. He may do quite satisfactory work and be well satisfied for a period of time. Frequently, however, he marries within a year or two, begins to have children, incurs financial obligations, and begins to feel the pressure for more income. His opportunities for promotion are limited; a fair number move into positions such as that of rate clerk two grades higher and a few move up into supervisory and specialist positions. Such a man sees persons with more education being started in higher positions and promoted more rapidly, and this may plant seeds of resentment that will grow with the passing of time. He may decide, after a time, that he would be better off in some other type of work, and he may leave the company. If he does so, his training and experience are lost. If he stays with the company, yet cannot move or progress, his supervisors are hard put to explain his limited pay increases and being by-passed for promotions— or after a time, some may yield to the pressure and put him on a job on which they have serious doubts as to his qualifications. Problems are serious enough with such a man within three or four years from the time he is hired; by eight or ten years, they are likely to be critical if he is still around.

Women employees have rather well defined lines of progression into jobs as typist, secretary, correspondent, supervisor, and other responsible jobs. Most can satisfy their career aspirations and meet their economic needs.

As noted earlier, however, women typically are less well fitted for the rather strenuous work of filing as presently carried on. A further consideration is pressure by higher management to reduce administrative costs and to operate as economically as possible in all units. Supervisors continue to requisition men from the Personnel Department. To date, the desires of individual supervisors have generally been followed.

Problems and questions:

a. Is there a need for a more definite statement of policy and standards regarding hiring standards for the jobs involved? If so, what should the policy be? Support your recommendations carefully.

b. Does it seem possible that certain changes in methods or organization could alleviate the problem? If so, what changes might warrant consideration?

28

TRAINING AND RETRAINING EMPLOYEES

Performance appraisal · Nature of learning · What training is · Need for training · Types of employee training · Supervisory training and development · Programmed training for industry · Retraining

---

In the important areas of supervisory and employee development, there are two opposing alternatives for management. The first alternative is to plunge personnel directly into the work and permit them to make errors, learn by their mistakes, and absorb what they can as they go along. The other alternative is to organize a program of training designed to develop the knowledge and skills of personnel.

Training is synonymous with planned development. In training it is the goal of management to develop supervisors and employees in such a way that they will become more capable and productive in their work. C. R. Dooley has adequately described the training concept as:

> Training is not something that is done once to new employees—it is used continuously in every well-run establishment. Every time you get someone to do work the way you want it done, you are training. Every time you give directions or discuss a procedure, you are training.[1]

In this chapter on appraisal and training we shall first discuss performance appraisal. Performance appraisals logically determine what is

[1] C. R. Dooley, "Training Within Industry in the United States," *International Labour Review*, Vol. 54, Nos. 3-4, Sept.-Oct., 1946, 161.

needed in employee training to improve both the individual and the productivity. We shall then discuss the relationship between learning and training, what training is, the need for training, the types of training particularly applicable to office needs today, the current importance of retraining, the new developments in programmed instruction for industry, and supervisory and executive training and development.

Performance Appraisal

Appraisal of employee performance is both an important and an inescapable duty of any manager. Several managerial functions may be served; these include:

1. Guiding employee development.

2. Aiding in decisions with regard to salary increases, promotion, demotion, and discharge.

3. Aiding in assessing present personnel strength and in planning manpower needs for the future.

Traditional approaches have often been directed at serving all of these needs, and sometimes others as well, by a single, top-down rating of employee performance in terms of factors such as the following:

> Accuracy
> Judgment
> Dependability
> Cooperativeness
> Creative ability
> Loyalty
> Ability to deal effectively with others
> Resourcefulness
> Productiveness

Various rating methods have been employed—man-to-man comparisons, rating scales, rating lists, and others. Most widely used is probably the rating scale, made up of factors deemed to be most significant in performance on the job. See Figure 28-1 for a good example of a rating scale which defines each factor briefly and outlines principal degrees of performance on each factor. In many cases, a weight is assigned to each of the degrees, and a total point weighting is arrived at as an evaluation.

The immediate supervisor usually makes the rating without help, although some plans now require him to explain and justify his rating to his superior or, in some cases, to a small committee of other persons familiar with the performance of the employee. The latter course un-

ALDENS

PERSONNEL RATING
for
SECRETARIES, STAFF WORKERS, AND
OTHERS CHARGED WITH SUPERVISION

Name of executive rater_____ Name of employe rated_____

Position_____

Section and Unit_____

Name of reviewing rater_____ Length of service_____On this job since_____

CONSIDER QUALITIES:	(Exceptionally high) 10	(Excellent) 8	REPORT (Good) 6	(Fair) 4	(Poor) 2	POINTS
1. Worker's knowledge of his job refers to: familiarity with various procedures of the work.	Exceptional mastery.	Thorough.	Adequate.	Insufficient knowledge of some phases of job.	Inadequate comprehension.	
2. Worker's work experience refers to: skill and practical wisdom gained by personal knowledge.	Excellent background and training for job.	Comprehensive.	Adequate.	Limited.	Inadequate.	
3. Worker's educational background refers to: amount of formal academic training related to job.	Superior academic training.	Good.	Adequate.	Limited.	Inadequate.	
4. Worker's knowledge of functions related to his job refers to: well-defined understanding of his authority and scope of his job.	Complete.	Well informed.	Adequate.	Insufficient.	Inadequate.	
5. Worker's accuracy refers to: a high percentage of freedom from mistakes.	Extremely accurate.	Very careful.	No more than reasonable time required for revision.	Careless.	Practically worthless work.	
6. Worker's promptness with which he completes his work refers to: ability to perform, execute and achieve an assigned task within an alloted time.	Greatest possible rapidity.	Very rapid.	Good speed.	Slow.	Extremely slow.	
7. Worker's success in following through with a task refers to: necessity of having to have details constantly repeated.	Highly efficient.	Resourceful.	Efficient.	Needs constant supervision.	Lazy.	
8. Worker's ease in learning new methods and following instructions refers to: ability to accept change and work under various conditions.	Excellent under difficult conditions.	Excellent under normal conditions.	Average.	Unsatisfactory.	Dull.	
9. Worker's loyalty to company and eagerness to promote its welfare refers o: being faithful and showing enthusiasm towards the company and its policies.	Extremely loyal.	Loyal.	Passive.	Critical.	Disloyal.	
10. Worker's general company information refers to: knowledge of major and minor policies of all Divisions.	Extremely well informed.	Well informed.	Adequate.	Limited.	Inadequate.	
11. Worker's cooperativeness refers to: an appreciation of collective action for mutual profit or common benefit.	Greatest possible cooperativeness.	Very cooperative.	Cooperative.	Difficult to handle.	Obstructive.	
12. Worker's acceptance of responsibility refers to: willingness to assume duties.	Greatest possible sense of responsibility.	Very willing.	Accepts but does not seek responsibility.	Does assigned tasks reluctantly.	Irresponsible.	
13. Worker's judgment refers to: ability to grasp a situation and draw conclusions.	Superior ability to think and use sound judgment.	Excellent judgment.	Good common sense.	Poor judgment.	Neglects and misinterprets facts.	

Figure 28-1. An example of a rating scale. Note that for each quality being rated there is a weighted scale on which the rater may evaluate the degree of competence which the employe has shown.

questionably results in greater care in making and justifying ratings, if conscientiously administered.

Following the rating, the supervisor is usually (although not always) expected to have one or more counseling sessions with the employee, in which both the favorable aspects of performance (strengths, progress, etc.) and areas of necessary improvement (the terms "weaknesses" or "shortcomings" are now often avoided) are discussed with the employee. Such an approach *can* be quite effective; whether it actually is may often depend upon the previous relationship between supervisor and employee, the time and effort expended by the supervisor to arrive at fair and constructive appraisals, and the thoroughness of counseling discussions of development plans and follow-up efforts.

Perhaps the most significant and promising trend at present is the practice of having the person being rated take a more active and responsible role in the entire process. Rather than depend upon a top-down rating, many plans now have the employee do careful self-appraisal and, in some cases, lay out goals and plans for his own development during the period ahead. A typical approach, subject to numerous variations, is use of a form consisting of such headings as the following, with ample space under each heading:

Breadth of knowledge
What I hope to accomplish during the coming year
How I plan to go about it (specific steps)
How higher management might help

While the employee is thinking through the self-appraisal and development-planning appraisal, his supervisor may go through much the same process. Then the two discuss the appraisal together and reach a "meeting of the minds"—but with the employee assuming primary responsibility. He should be encouraged to think about the needs of the job and his own goals, which can best be met through contributing more to the organization.

This sort of approach to appraisal—concentrating upon development of the individual—seems to work best if separated entirely from salary consideration, which is therefore carried out at a different time. Otherwise, preoccupation with salaries is likely to mean loss of much of the value of constructive appraisal and planning for development.

Key reasons why many appraisal plans are being slanted in the direction just indicated are: the more favorable psychological climate created; the constructive, forward-looking nature of the process; the greater probability of agreement and genuine commitment by the employee to carrying out development plans he has helped to evolve.

The close relationship between performance appraisal and training, at all employee and manager levels, is apparent. An effective appraisal program provides a "built-in" approach to *planning for training and development,* since it can focus upon individual needs, aspirations and plans, while contributing to effective performance of work essential to achieving the objectives of the organization.

The Nature of Learning

For practical purposes, learning may be defined as the acquisition of new habits and the modification of old habits. The human animal learns habits and nothing but habits. Learning is not complete until a habit has been formed. The multiplication table has not been learned until the learner automatically, with little conscious thought, can run through it rapidly or can come up with the answer forty-nine whenever he is confronted with seven times seven. The driver of an automobile has not learned to drive until his feet automatically find the right pedals at the right time and apply the right pressure.

Instructing an employee is the act of helping or coaching the employee to learn the specific desirable habits necessary for the performance of his task. This may involve the modification of old habits that are undesirable on the new job. It takes at least as long to "unlearn" a habit as to acquire a new habit. Replacing a bad habit with a good habit requires more time and effort than merely learning a good habit. This is why we occasionally hear a supervisor say he would prefer an inexperienced person for a certain job "so he can be trained correctly from the beginning."

How habits are formed

Habits result from practice. The habit of spelling the word cat *c-a-t,* or of computing a coefficient of correlation, is the result of long practice. Only by repetitive action by the learner will a habit be acquired. This is true of both mental habits and manual skill habits.

The old adage "practice makes perfect" is only partially true. That *correct* practice makes perfect would be a better statement. This is evidenced by thousands of golfers who are still duffers after many years of incorrect practice. Correct or desirable habits will result only from the practice of the correct procedure. For efficient training the learner should start with the correct method and practice it without deviation until he has formed a strong habit. It is the instructor's job to see that the learner's first—and all subsequent—practices are correct. The learner should be supervised to prevent any departure from the correct procedure during his learning period.

If the learner's first and subsequent practice is to be correct, he must have a clear understanding before he starts practicing the thing he is to do or the act he is to perform. Unless he has a clear mental picture of what he is to try to do, he will be unable to practice correctly, will waste much time in trial and error, and will partially learn some bad habits which he will have to overcome before he can acquire the correct habits.

Whoever is responsible for instructing the learner must be able to get across to the learner a clear understanding of what he is expected to do and how he is to do it. This is usually best accomplished by a combination of telling and showing—in other words, by a demonstration. The new billing clerk, for example, must be told and shown just how and where to get the data, how to operate the billing machine, and what to do with the finished forms. She must be shown how the work is done step by step, each step being explained and demonstrated.

Learning is a natural process

Learning, the acquisition of habits, is a natural process for the normal human being. It is as normal a process as breathing. Individuals naturally acquire habits, good or bad. Through observation, imitation, and trial and error they acquire various habits in their efforts to do the things they want to do and to avoid those things they dislike. Not all of these habits will be desirable, and the rate of learning will not always be as rapid as it would be with help or coaching. Nevertheless, they will learn. The learning of the young sandlot ball players, the ham radio station operators, and the acquired knowledge of Thomas Edison are examples of the learning which takes place with very little if any coaching or assistance.

Children learn a great deal in the first six years of life. They receive much help in the form of personalized, friendly encouragement and example from parents, relatives, and neighbors. Adults learn in much the same way. They respond to personalized, friendly assistance. They tend to resent formality even more than children do. They appreciate help and are willing to be shown how, but they do not like to be ordered to do things.

Those responsible for breaking in new employees will be most effective if their attitude is one of neighborly, helpful friendliness and sincere interest in the progress of the individual. The less they appear cold, disinterested taskmasters or superiors, the better. They should be as naturally, informally helpful as one housewife showing another how to turn the heel on a knitted sock.

Since humans have such a great capacity for learning, provided conditions are favorable, management should make greater use of this capacity. We must remember that any normal person will learn if given a chance, and that the more the individual is helped the faster he will learn.

What Training Is

Planty, McCord and Efferson in *Training Employees and Managers* [2] provide one of the best definitions of training found anywhere. It is as follows:

> Training is the continuous, systematic development among all levels of employees of that knowledge and those skills and attitudes which contribute to their welfare and that of the company.

This definition emphasizes *all* dimensions of training. Learning is a continuous process throughout the life of each individual; therefore, training, or the direction of this learning, must also be continuous. To be effective and accomplish the desired results efficiently, training must be planned systematically. Procedures must be established to overcome the natural, human barriers to learning. In addition, training would be useless if it were aimed at only one level of the employees. Effective training is vital to all levels of employees to form interacting, interlocking work units united in achieving the common objectives of the enterprise and its employees. The last phrase of the above definition—"contributing to welfare"—is particularly important. This implies directly that training's ultimate goal is for the benefit of the company, *but* this benefit will not be realized unless the employees of the firm also receive benefits and rewards from such a program. Thus, a firm can realize the advantages of training only indirectly through improvements in the work force. In essence, training must be a planned, systematic, continuous process providing the proper atmosphere conducive to effective learning. It must be aimed at *all* employees of the firm; the firm realizes the benefits and advantages from training only if the employees also realize benefits and advantages from such a program.

The Need for Training

As already suggested, the need for training is a "constant" in the managerial process. From an individual standpoint, learning goes on continuously throughout life; training is the direction and guidance of this perpetual learning process. Moreover, a well-trained person is likely to be a more secure and confident person, one more likely to adjust successfully to off-the-job problems as well as to those on the job.

From an organizational standpoint, effective training can develop an

[2] Earl Planty, William McCord, and Carlos Efferson, *Training Employees and Managers* (New York: The Ronald Press Company, 1948), p. 24.

employee to a productive level in a minimum of time. The collective influence of a group of well-trained employees can largely determine the success of the enterprise. Higher productivity, lower costs, and lower employee turnover rates are some of the direct benefits.

Training now takes on special importance and urgency because of rapidly-changing technological needs, the growth and complexity of present-day enterprises, generally rising educational levels and new educational processes, and changes in our social system and cultural patterns. Our free enterprise system may depend to a high degree upon how well our separate organizations develop the skills and other attributes requisite to self-direction within a democratic environment.

Types of Employee Training

Orientation and Induction Programs. First impressions of new employees are particularly significant and long lasting. An orientation and induction program is a continuance of the recruitment and selection program, but the importance of a planned guidance program for an employee's first few days on the job dictates that these functions also be considered as training functions. Proper induction and orientation are, therefore, an integral part of the training process. Generally, orientation and induction programs have at least three objectives:

1. Define the terms of employment (new employees).
2. Acquaint the employee in detail with the requirements of his new job.
3. Acquaint the employee with his new surroundings—physical facilities and co-workers.

The length of the breaking-in, or induction and orientation period and the overall cost will vary according to:

1. The nature of the job or assignment (the total knowledge and skill required for the effective performance of the task).
2. The character of the employee's past experience (the amount of knowledge and skill he already has).
3. The employee's ability to learn those things he must learn to become reasonably proficient on the job.
4. The conditions under which the employee must learn.

In a majority of medium-sized and small firms the induction and orientation of new employees is an informal, unplanned process. The new employee simply arrives, the supervisor greets him and introduces him to a few employees, he is given some work, and is told to ask questions if any arise. This is often as far as it goes.

There are some differences of opinions among management specialists concerning the importance of the orientation or induction period. Some believe that this period is vitally important and that the impressions formed by the employee during his first two or three days on the job can have a profound influence on his future productivity. Others feel that the way an individual is treated after he becomes familiar with his new environment is much more important to his morale and his productivity. It stands to reason, however, that a planned program of induction helps insure that new employees receive both basic information about the company and a good initial impression. Some larger firms maintain comprehensive orientation programs in which new employees are brought together in groups, for a single session or for several sessions. At these sessions films may be shown describing the history and scope of the company and its products, lectures may be given to describe the company and its personnel policies, and company officers may be introduced.

Actually, it is not difficult to induct new employees in an effective manner. It is simply necessary that we treat the new employee as we ourselves would like to be treated in similar circumstances. The induction and orientation program should be directed toward giving the new employee the information he needs at a rate he can be expected to absorb it and providing a sense of belonging to his new job assignment. The success and ease of subsequent employee training is greatly influenced by a good induction and orientation program.

On-the-job Training of Employees. Most training is necessarily done "on the job." Relatively few organizations have training departments which assume the task of developing the knowledges and skills of employees. Management should encourage supervisors to devote a portion of their time to training responsibilities, and supervisors must recognize that training of subordinates is one of the most important functions.

On-the-job training involves instruction from several sources and from several types of programs. Training may be done by (1) an experienced employee, (2) the immediate supervisor, (3) a training assistant, or a combination of such individuals. Whoever does the training should have *time, interest,* and *ability to teach.*

For most office needs, a combination of training efforts by experienced employees, the supervisor, and in certain situations, a training assistant, will prove most effective. A common type of training arrangement in a clerical situation is for one particular clerk, usually an older person with considerable skill and experience, to be designated a "coach" or "trainer." This individual receives a slightly larger salary to reflect the added responsibility and is charged with the initial training and orientation of new employees. Another rather common training situation for clerical work operations is for the new worker to understudy the job for sufficient time to learn the fundamentals. Problems with the understudy arrangement are: the employee being replaced may not always be around long enough to sufficiently train the new worker; because the employee is leaving, the attitude for training may not be completely desirable.

Common sense, the circumstances of the situation, and the qualification of the work force will usually dictate the actual training requirements. The important point is that management should recognize that there is or will be a need for training, should plan for a program in terms of the particular requirements, and should *make time* available for carrying out the program.

Necessary conditions for training

The conditions under which the employee must learn will affect the length of the training period, but these conditions can be partially controlled by the employer. The cost of the training period and its effectiveness will depend upon the degree to which these conditions are properly controlled, and the manner in which the employee applies himself to the training situation.

Three basic principles are involved in controlling the conditions necessary for effective training:

1. *Training is most effective when the learning experiences occur under conditions identical with those the trainee will encounter on the job.* The easiest way to apply this principle is to train the employee on his job at his work place. This will make it possible for the employee to learn by working with the actual processes, materials, and equipment he will use as an experienced worker. It will also help him adjust to the environment in which he will work and to his co-workers.

For the great majority of employees in the office, shop, warehouse, or salesroom, on-the-job training is the most effective method to use. For jobs that involve much technical information it may be desirable to provide some training experiences away from the job as a supplement to the experiences provided on the job. Such off-the-job supplementary experiences may consist of special instruction in accounting practices or advanced typewriting. Few jobs in the office are so complicated that they require supplementary off-the-job training. In most cases the individual brings with him the basic knowledge and skills necessary to the performance of his job.

Sometimes, particularly in industry, a "vestibule school" or special training room is set up to provide specialized training. In such cases there is a complete duplication of the machines and work arrangement which will be provided the employee on the job. This form of training, however, has little application in office management.

2. *Training is most effective when some individual in the organization is held responsible for the progress of the learner.* It is necessary that the responsibility for breaking in each new employee be specifically assigned to some member of the management staff. The most logical assignment is to make the employee's immediate supervisor responsible for the employee's progress. The supervisor knows, or should know, exactly what the learner was employed to do and how the various jobs should be performed.

As has been stated, the number of persons assigned to a supervisor should not be so great as to make it impossible for him to devote adequate time to the training of new personnel. If the supervisor has more than twelve or fourteen employees, his other responsibilities will be so great that he will be unable to devote the necessary time to the training of new employees. If it is necessary for the supervisor to have charge of a larger group he should have a qualified assistant to help him in the training of new workers. This arrangement, however, is generally undesirable unless the supervisor maintains very close personal touch with the training activities of his assistant.

3. *Training is most effective if the learner is given helpful, friendly, personal instruction.* Instruction is the act of helping another to learn. Probably the most effective type of instruction is friendly, helpful coaching. This type of instruction involves a minimum of formality, an absence of any teacher-student relationship, and a maximum of helpfulness and cooperation. Coaching is probably the most efficient procedure for expediting learning and reducing the learning period. Instruction may be of any degree of effectiveness—it is measured by the degree to which real help is given, and the extent to which learning is facilitated and the learning period reduced.

It seldom happens that no attempt is made to instruct a new employee. However, the new employee often gets so little real help that his breaking-in period is unduly long and costly both to the employer and the employee, and ultimately to the consumer, who pays for the organization's product or service.

Too often the new employee is put to work with merely a few sketchy directions from his supervisor. The supervisor's statements may be only partially understood and remembered by the employee. The trainee may learn mostly by trial and error, with possibly a bit of help from a neighboring employee. Under such circumstances the cost of training may be higher than it should be.

Perhaps the best technique for general instruction is one which has been widely used for more than thirty-five years. It is sometimes called the "TWI technique" because it was used by the Training Within Industry section of the War Production Board during World War II. The technique is usually described as having four steps:

STEP	PURPOSE OR OBJECTIVE OF THE STEP
Preparation	To create in the learner, or to make sure that he has, a desire to learn the specific task, habit, or habits.
Presentation	To set a clear pattern for the learner to follow, giving him a clear understanding of the task to be done.
Application	To provide an opportunity for the learner to practice the "work pattern" under the supervision of an instructor and thus develop proper work habits.
Test	To make a more or less formal checkup of the learner's ability to perform.

This technique should be used in connection with each task to be learned; that is, each task is considered a separate learning operation which progresses through the various steps. It will be noted that steps one and four are not learning steps. Step one is a preliminary step that the instructor may take to prepare the employee to learn. During this step he learns nothing. The instructor should make sure, however, that the learner really has an interest or desire to learn the task. Similarly, step four is a checkup step in which the instructor, by observation or test, assures himself that the learner has learned and has acquired the habits required by the task being learned. Step four is usually more or less automatic since close supervision given by the instructor during the third step enables him to know when the learner has mastered the task and acquired the necessary *strong* habits. Steps two and three are the real learning steps and are time-consuming. It is in these steps that habits are born and grow to maturity. In step two the instructor, by demonstrating, telling, and questioning gets the learner to understand exactly what is to be done and how it is to be done. An accurate, detailed pattern or mental picture is established in the mind of the learner. This pattern guides all the learner's practice efforts.

Analyzing tasks for training purposes

The instructor cannot set an adequately detailed pattern unless he has analyzed the task and broken it down into its elements. It is often difficult for a highly-skilled individual to analyze a job he can do almost automatically. His habits have become so strong that he acts with little conscious effort. It is difficult for him to realize how much is involved, how many things he does, and how many judgments he makes in doing a simple task. For example, it is difficult for the ordinary individual to make an analysis of what he does in putting on his coat or tying his necktie. His habits are so strong that he performs all the operations without conscious mental effort. The muscular controls and finger and arm motions have become automatic.

Management personnel and even skilled operators are seldom conscious of all the specific knowledge, judgments, and skills employed in the tasks they supervise or perform. They are able to perform each task automatically, just as a good driver uses his hands and feet in driving a car with little or no conscious mental direction. This situation exists with regard to any skillful performance—packing candy, grinding a tool, operating an adding machine, or riding a bicycle.

It is essential that the instructor make a careful analysis of a task to identify all the points he must cover in step two in establishing a complete pattern for the learner to follow. Without such a task analysis the instructor will omit some points, and the trainee will then have an incomplete pattern to follow.

The facts revealed by the analysis of a task can be written in narrative style, a word description of how the task is performed. Such a writeup requires considerable ability, is time-consuming, and is not too helpful as a guide for instruction. A simple, easy-to-use form has been developed to assist an instructor in making a quick task analysis, which permits him to record results in the form of short notes and provides him with a readily usable guide for teaching. Here is an illustration of the form and its use in analyzing a task—to identify what must be told, shown, and explained to a learner who has been assigned a routine clerical task:

TASK ANALYSIS

TASK: Opening and Sorting Incoming U.S. Mail

Step	Key Points
1. Arrange pile of envelopes	1. Place them face down, flap at right
2. Slit top envelope	2. Hold pile with left hand, slit flap edge away from body
3. Remove slit envelope	3. Remove slit envelope with left thumb to new pile at left, face down
4. Repeat operation on all envelopes	4. None
5. Capsize pile of slit envelopes	5. Turn them over in front of operator, flaps to the right
6. Remove contents of top envelope	6. Flatten out contents, staple or clip them together if necessary
7. Check for sender's address	7. If address is not on contents, staple envelope to contents to preserve sender's address
8. Stamp received date	8. Stamp date in upper right-hand corner
9. Pile contents at right	9. Place them face up, separate pile for each addressee
10. Discard envelope if not needed	10. None
11. Repeat operations 6-10 on each slit envelope	11. None

The analysis is made in two stages. First, the steps are listed in column one in the order in which they are to be performed. Second, opposite each step, in column two, notes are made of any points that may need emphasis or explanation when the work pattern is described. Column two is a finer breakdown. It outlines how the job is done. It is a list of the tricks of the trade and judgments involved in doing the job. It is a list of some of the minor details the instructor must be careful to explain when setting a pattern for the trainee to follow.

Making the analysis in two stages simplifies the task. It provides an orderly procedure which enables the analyst to avoid becoming confused and bogged down in a mass of minor details. However, it insures that each minor detail is recorded in the analysis at the exact point at which it should be presented and explained to the learner.

The instructor will seldom, if ever, hold an analysis sheet in his hand while instructing. He will, however, have the analysis in mind. After a little experience with written analyses an instructor can usually make an analysis mentally. He must, however, make an analysis of some kind before he attempts to teach the task.

The human mind cannot absorb too many new ideas at the same time. The instructor must arrange to teach the learner only a few things at a time. A general rule is that if the analysis of a task reveals more than ten or twelve steps, it is advisable to break that task up into two or more smaller tasks to be taught separately. For example, the job of a sales person in a retail hardware store involves several tasks:

1. Writing a cash sales slip.
2. Writing a charge sales slip.
3. Making change at the cash register.
4. Putting a new roll of paper into cash register.
5. Recording merchandise returned for credit.
6. Presenting various kinds of merchandise to customers.

Such tasks are simple but they can and probably should be taught one at a time. None of them will be difficult for the trainee to learn and they will be easy for the instructor to teach if a job analysis sheet is used.

The third step of the instruction procedure consists of providing the trainee an opportunity for practice under supervision. The learner here attempts to imitate the pattern set for him by the instructor in step two. He will make mistakes which should be detected promptly and corrected in a helpful, friendly way before they become habitual. It is important that the practice adhere to the correct, established work pattern.

Sufficient opportunity for practice must be provided in step three. In the early stages of this time-consuming step the instructor will have to watch the learner closely. After the learner demonstrates that he knows what he wants to do, less intensive supervision may be needed. The learner will get along with less and less supervision as proper habits gradually develop.

It is usually safe to let the trainee work on actual production tasks. He will make few serious errors if he has been properly instructed and is properly supervised. To assign him to practice work rather than actual work is almost always an expensive procedure. The learner, knowing that he is merely doing practice work, will not be properly concerned about errors. Further, the instructor may be inclined to take the attitude "it's only practice work" and may not hold the learner's workmanship up to standard.

It is a serious mistake to proceed on the theory that speed and accuracy cannot be learned at the same time. Many workers are low producers or produce excessive errors merely because both quality and quantity were not emphasized equally during the training period. The old saying "watch your accuracy, and speed will take care of itself" has been shown to be incorrect. The error ratios of rapid workers are almost always lower than those of slow workers.

Cross-training of employees for proficiency in several work operations provides an office work group with a considerable amount of flexibility. Cross-training also develops the individual employees. It prepares them for promotion and for greater responsibilities by increasing their overall knowledge of company operations and by allowing them to learn a variety of operations. Figure 28-2 shows a simple cross-training chart which enables the supervisor to keep up with the status of cross-training for each employee on various job operations. Obviously, the number of subordinates dictate the need for such a chart; in large work groups and in office situations where the employees usually perform a variety of tasks, a cross-training chart is extremely helpful for effective and efficient supervision. If desired, the chart could easily be expanded to include *planned* training as well as that already completed or in progress.

Supervisory Training and Development

There is no one method of training supervisors which can be pronounced best for everyone. Different situations demand different methods and combinations of methods. In this section, we shall present some of the techniques which may be employed in training and developing supervisors.

The conference method

Supervisory conferences or staff meetings require careful planning and

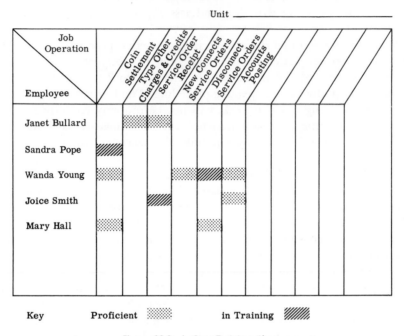

Figure 28-2. A Cross-Training Chart

skillful direction. The subject for each discussion must be carefully selected and a means must be provided for securing the maximum value from each discussion. Discussion must be directed and confined to the subject to achieve its purpose. The conference must not be a dry presentation of abstract material or a lecture, nor should it be allowed to become a bull-session or an aimless airing of personal gripes. The maximum thinking, participation, and contribution of each group member must be secured. The conference leader must have ability in planning and in stimulating, directing, and controlling the activity of the group members. He must be able to act as a master of ceremonies without becoming the speaker of the evening. He must be able to present information without assuming the role of teacher. He must know where to get information needed by the group and how to present such information. He should know when to bring in specially qualified staff members or outsiders to present necessary information on their special fields. He must be able to stimulate the group members to think and to participate actively in the discussion. A maximum of fifteen persons should participate in each session.

The conference leader may be the general manager, a member of top management or, if necessary, an especially qualified person employed to run the conferences as the plant manager's representative. The services of a regular member of the staff should be utilized if possible.

If the general manager does not personally conduct all the conferences, he should be careful to sit in as frequently as possible with each group to show his interest and to make group members realize that the conferences are, in fact, staff meetings.

The conference procedure requires much skill on the part of the discussion leader. His function is to provoke thought, draw out the ideas and contributions of the group, and induce the group to formulate a conclusion or decision. He acts as master of ceremonies and keeps the discussion confined to the matter under consideration. He attempts to get all the group members to contribute their ideas. He promotes thinking by asking thought-provoking questions, but he does not give out information or express his own opinion of the matters being discussed. Many excellent instructors experience difficulty in the use of the conference method if they must pump ideas from the group members.

In using the lecture or instructional procedure, the leader contributes the ideas and presents the information. In contrast to this, the conference method permits each group member to contribute ideas, and its aim is to obtain a summary of the thinking of the group.

To make the conferences or staff meetings interesting and to dramatize and effectively present information and points of view, use may be made of motion pictures, slides, film strips, and other visual aids. Films are available for rental or purchase at low cost, covering many of the basic principles of supervision. Many of these films have been developed by large corporations for use in their own plants. Their basic principles are equally applicable in other plants or offices. Minor points appearing to differ from a plant's current policies and practices can serve to provoke discussion of the policies and the underlying reasons for them.

Areas used for conferences should lend dignity to the program. The room should be quiet, well-lighted and ventilated, and equipped as a staff conference room with tables and comfortable chairs. Ample blackboards and wall areas for posters and charts are desirable. It will also be helpful if projection equipment, consisting of 16-mm sound motion picture projector, screen, sound-strip film projector, or slide projector, is provided.

The following are typical subjects for management development conferences. Each subject, of course, will require several sessions or conferences. Some can best be presented by an informational procedure; others are bona fide conference subjects.

Current office policies and regulations
New company or office policies and regulations as they are adopted
Supervisory and management techniques such as:
    Cost control through departmental budgets
    Job or work simplification
    Time study and standard setting
    Training, techniques of instruction
    Job evaluation
    Merit rating
    Directing personnel through leadership
    The company plan of organization
    Wage structure
    Employee morale and employee relations
    Economic facts of life a supervisor should know and teach
    State and federal labor laws
    Standardization practices
    Providing safe working conditions
    Medical programs
    Company accounting procedures
    Purchasing
    How to deal with problem employees

Conference sessions should, if possible, be held during the regular work hours of supervisors. In smaller offices where supervisors cannot be spared it may be necessary to hold sessions outside of working hours. Experience has shown that supervisors usually do not object to attending sessions conducted outside their usual working hours, provided such sessions are profitable for them. Conferences, however, should be conducted during working hours if possible. Time limits for conferences should be set so meetings will not carry on interminably and so those attending will be able to schedule their time. Conference sessions should be held from two to four times a month, and each session should last at least two hours.

Good morale on the part of all members of management is an absolute necessity for efficient management. Supervisors must have a will to do their jobs right and must have the necessary understanding. Supervisors will have high morale only if they are accepted as members of the management team, if there is a prompt flow of official information to them, if they are kept fully informed concerning changes, future plans, and so forth, if their ideas are sought in solving current problems, and if they have satisfaction in the kind of results they and other members of management are getting. The staff conference procedure has been found to be an excellent means of obtaining these greatly desired conditions.

On-the-job supervisory training

As in the case of employee training, most supervisory development is based upon on-the-job training and evaluation. This is a logical approach since with or without a formal training program, most supervisors must learn how to do their job while on the job. A few of the many advantages of on-the-job supervisory training are: the supervisor learns well under fire, the supervisor is free to demonstrate leadership potential, and on-the-job training is a normal process whereby authority and influence are earned by the supervisor. Obviously one disadvantage of on-the-job training for supervisors is that without close guidance, the supervisor must play his new role by ear and may consequently sink or swim. Another disadvantage, well known to most executives, is that on-the-job training is slow and does not permit much guidance for particular supervisory positions. Therefore, a more carefully planned approach to supervisory training and development is necessary.

Understudy or "assistant to" supervisory training

This is on-the-job training, where a supervisor is assigned an understudy who is charged with his regular duties and the responsibility of becoming familiar with the operations of his supervisor. This is a good system of training, but unfortunately, some superiors are reluctant to share their "secrets of success" with someone who may eventually replace them. This, too, has the connotation of "pre-selecting" supervisory talent, and some firms prefer to place promotion on an individual basis.

Job rotational supervisory training

Job rotational supervisory training has been accepted by many firms who realize that their management personnel need to be well grounded in various phases of the enterprise. The Consolidated Edison Company of New York uses job rotational supervisory training at both the supervisory and middle management levels. Assignments of supervisory training and progress evaluation are made by committees of department heads. Briefly, a few of the many advantages derived by Consolidated Edison Company from this type of supervisory training are:

1. Tests individuals under a variety of situations and responsibilities. Places emphasis on "leadership" rather than technical ability in any one department of the company.

2. Increases the supervisor's scope of acquaintances among other supervisors and executives, as well as providing a well-grounded background in other phases of the firm's operations.

3. Prevents "vested rights" or "empires" from being established by supervisors in a particular area of the firm.

Other types of supervisory training programs are multiple management, role playing training programs, simulation exercises, and special supervisory training programs developed for particular subjects, such as human relations in management, communications in management, talking with people, and company policies. These latter training programs are designed to improve the particular skills of supervisors and are applicable to the first line of supervision in an office type organization.

One of the most comprehensive supervisory and executive development programs in industry today is illustrated in Figure 28-3. The program is continually being changed and improved to reflect current needs of the industry, current trends in supervisory training, and to reflect the general "level" of the supervisory work force. Integration of the three courses is quite evident from analyzing the elements of study. While there is no definite hierarchial order applicable to the three training programs, ordinarily, new supervisors attend first the managerial development course, followed by periodic one to three day programs on special, timely subjects. Human relations in management is usually the second training course for supervisors and emphasizes the humanistic or behavioral science approach to leadership and motivation. The third training course is a "capstone" program designed to give the first level of supervision a basic

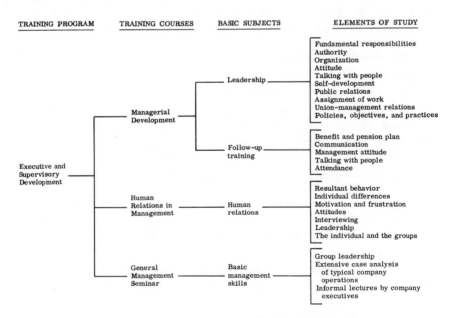

Figure 28-3. Schematic diagram of Integrated Industrial Training Programs

grounding in the management and policy concepts that present themselves in the particular industry.

Programmed Training for Industry

Programmed training for industry represents a logical, organized systematic approach to learning. The pioneering effort in the field of programmed learning was made by Professor S. L. Pressey of Ohio State University in the 1920's. It was revived and developed with respect to current research on learning by D. F. B. Skinner in the early 1950's, and it is largely through D. Skinner's efforts and foresight that programmed instruction is recognized and acclaimed today. R. W. Christian has referred to programmed instruction as the most exciting and potentially most significant development to appear on the business scene since digital computers.[3]

Programmed training makes maximum use of the participation concept. The information to be learned is broken down into "steps" or "units" called *frames*. A programmed course is a complete series of *frames*, with each frame building upon the last one. Programmed instruction also makes maximum use of "reinforcing" the participant's effort and responses. Comprehension is tested at each step or frame, and the learner's response is reinforced, whether right or wrong. If a wrong response is given, he is directed to repeat the frame, and a right response is reinforced through additional explanation, before proceeding to the next frame.

Although this section is not intended to be a complete review of programmed instruction,[4] it may be well to consider briefly two basic, although opposing schools of thought—commonly referred to as "mathetics" and "branching." Figure 28-4 illustrates a sample of a programmed lesson.

Mathetics. The mathetics concept of programmed learning breaks the material to be taught down into elements of discrimination, generalization, and sequences or chains. In a way, this resembles the army training concept of "key" words, which is used quite successfully. The advantages, say the experts, of mathetics are much fewer frames and a faster learning process.

Every subject is learned in a pattern which is most compatible to the

[3] R. W. Christian, "Guides to Programmed Learning," *Harvard Business Review*, Vol. 40, Nov.-Dec., 1962, 36.

[4] For further study of programmed instruction, see the following excellent references: Jerome P. Lysaught, ed., *Programmed Learning—Evolving Principles and Industrial Applications* (Ann Arbor: Foundation for Research on Human Behavior, 1961); Theodore B. Dolmatch, Elizabeth Marting, and Robert E. Finley, eds., *Revolution in Training; Programmed Instruction in Industry*, Management Report No. 72 (New York: American Management Association, 1962); Roger W. Christian, *op. cit.*

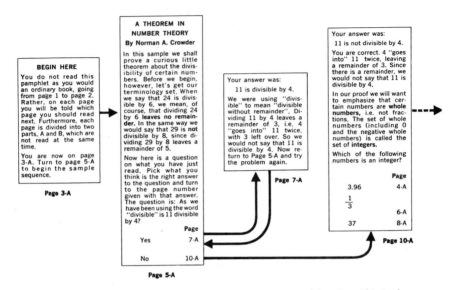

Figure 28-4. Sample branching instruction for programmed learning. This is the opening portion of a pamphlet created by Mr. Crowder (for U.S. Industries, Inc.) to demonstrate the format of the branching technique. Each block of programmed instruction you see represents a page in a "scrambled" textbook or a frame in a teaching machine.*

subject's content and facts. Goals and objectives are stressed by keeping them continually exposed to the learner in subsequent frames.

For example, a mathetics chain sequence of programmed learning for teaching a child to count to ten would begin with nine so that the goal can be easily reached and to develop a feeling of accomplishment. The next frame would begin with eight, and so on. Or, a new car salesman would be taught to "close a sale" before learning the other elements of the car salesmanship technique in a mathetics programmed instruction course.

Branching. Branching presents the material to be learned in larger segments than does mathetics and provides a means for rapid completion, as long as correct answers are given.

Branching is commonly referred to as the "tutor method" because if the student understands and knows the answer, he progresses right along, and if not, he receives a quick review. The remedial review is quite *flexible,* depending upon the difficulty of the material covered. That is, if the initial response is incorrect, the learner may be returned to the *original question* for further study, or he may be returned to a *different*

* Norman A. Crowder, "Programmed Instruction: Part II, The Case for Branching," *Administrative Management,* September, 1962, p. 27.

sequence of steps (frames) which repeat the original information in a more simplified elementary manner.

The branching technique can be applied through "scrambled" textbooks, also, which direct the student to turn to this page or that, depending upon his particular responses. Scrambled branching textbooks eliminate the need for intricate, costly, mechanical teaching machines. They are highly portable, and can be easily exchanged between different individuals.

Possibly the greatest benefit from the programmed branching training technique is that each learner can progress at his own rate and that the same program can be used by individuals with different levels of intelligence and skills.

Industrial applications of programmed training [5]

The IBM Corporation uses programmed training for a portion of its 7070 data processing system program. The pilot study of this programmed course included 719 frames. Response indicated that over 75% of the participants preferred the programmed method, comprehension was significantly improved, test results improved (only 11% below a grade of 90 was compared with 57% below 90 for a control group using the regular program method), and there was a drop of almost one-third in normal time required to present the data in the normal manner. As a result of this study, IBM has expanded the 7070 programmed instruction course to include 1,320 frames and is preparing to send this as a "packaged" training program to its branch offices.

General Telephone Company of California has used programmed tape training for its information operators quite successfully. The length of the training was reduced from ten days to six, which also meant a 40% reduction in costs. The quality of operator service during the three months' probation period exceeded that of operators trained under the regular ten-day training program.

Mead Johnson uses programmed training for its "detail men" or sales representatives. Four courses involving some 1,000 frames were developed to cover the company's entire product line and services.

The Schering Corporation used a 783 frame programmed instruction course to train its detail men on a new ethical drug introduced in 1960.

The Zenith Sales Corporation developed a 202 frame programmed instruction course covering the introduction of its line of color television sets. The course was divided into three sections covering: how color TV

---

[5] The following examples were summarized from: Dolmatch, Marting, and Finley, eds., *Revolution in Training: Programmed Instruction in Industry.* There are many additional examples of programmed instruction for industry discussed in this reference.

works, Zenith's superior dependability, and the model numbers and features of the entire Zenith line.

There are many other examples of programmed learning, but these few have been briefly cited to provide the reader with the broad implications of the almost endless potential that programmed training has for industrial use. The initial cost of developing and preparing a programmed training course is high, but the potential rewards and savings seem to warrant such a transition in industrial education.

Retraining Employees

Retraining is a significant aspect of managerial responsibility—possibly even more than initial training in view of today's dynamic business environment. Retraining involves planning for eventual employee changes necessitated by organizational changes, technological advancement, or simply *business evolution.* As discussed previously, the training process never ceases in a dynamic industry—particularly one that promotes from within, that provides for its employees whose jobs no longer exist, and that provides new jobs for its elderly or handicapped workers.

Retraining is, of course, a part of any formalized training program and one of the most important phases, for two reasons: [6]

1. Retraining programs are supported by sound economic motives since it pays to retain the services of older employees who have been faithful and loyal to the firm.

2. Retraining programs are soundly supported by society, particularly with respect to the older, somewhat handicapped employees who, without retraining, would become wards of society.

The importance of retraining and its impact upon our national economy is emphasized quite vividly in President Kennedy's program for "our major domestic challenge." This year, 1962, the Department of Labor initiated 100 retraining programs, involving some 8,500 unemployed persons in 30 states at a total cost of approximately $850,000. Congress is expected to appropriate upwards to $400 million for retraining programs during the next several years.[7]

Such a retraining program as this is obviously pointed toward a mass of people (typically the coal miner or the "blue collar" worker) whose jobs have been taken over by mechanization. But, we should not over-

[6] W. D. Scott, R. C. Clothier, and W. R. Spriegel, *Personnel Management: Principles, Practices, and Point of View* (New York: McGraw-Hill Book Company, Inc., 1954), p. 326.

[7] Robert L. Caleo, "Today's Retraining: What, Why, and How?" *Administrative Management,* Vol. XXIII, No. 6, June, 1962, 23.

look the fact that industry also has a responsibility for retraining. Creating new skills and finding new jobs for the jobless *is* a government responsibility, but *anticipating* such an event, planning for eventual changes in business operations, and making the most use of experienced and reliable employees is directly a responsibility of industry. Only company sponsored retraining programs can ward off more unemployment necessitated by automation in the office or in the white collar class.

Retraining of employees may be the result of several conditions. Two of the most logical and common are:

1. Certain highly skilled employees may have to be retrained when their particular operations are eliminated, changed, or combined. Then, too, a certain amount of retraining is necessary to maintain an "all around ability" of the general type of work performed in the firm.

2. As employees grow older, through no fault of their own they may become unable to continue working at their former assignments. Retraining is necessary to save the valuable employees and allow them to carry their share of the work in other job assignments where desirable.

There are many successful retraining programs in operation today. Most modern business enterprises recognize and accept their responsibility to society for maintaining a productive, useful employee in face of the dynamic technological changes. Two such programs, forerunners in the industry, are discussed below.[8]

International Telephone and Telegraph Federal Laboratories (ITTFL). ITTFL conducts two retraining programs, one on a daytime basis for individuals or groups of employees who have been replaced because of technological change. A particular case in point is the situation of eleven middle-aged women whose jobs were eliminated by technological change. These women were invited to attend a special retraining course—a special ITTFL electrical wiring course—to learn a new skill to prepare them for different job assignments in the same plant.

The second retraining course is on a tuition free, evening, college-like two-semester basis. The evening program is not a retraining program in the complete sense of the word. These employees voluntarily attend these programs to prepare themselves for a change in job assignment, promotion, or to prepare for whatever change may be required. This is retraining at its utmost—done voluntarily, individually, and with an eye to the future.

Morgan Guaranty Trust. This retraining program was necessitated by the merger of the J. P. Morgan and Company and the Guaranty Trust Company. Some 900 employees handling stock transfers were affected, 700 from the Guaranty Trust and 200 from the J. P. Morgan and Company.

The new stock transfer procedure was to be a little different from either of

[8] These case studies were adapted from: Robert L. Caleo, *op. cit.*, pp. 23-25.

the pre-merger procedures, requiring a complete new retraining program concurrent with normal operations. A formal retraining program using programmed instruction was designed which spelled out in detail exactly how the new stock transfer procedures were to be handled. The retraining program, other than preparation of the programmed instruction, took about five months, but when the merger officially took place, all workers in the stock transfer division were proficient in the new procedures.

Today the same volume of stock transfers is handled with some 200 fewer clerks (700 in total) with natural attrition accounting for the loss. The initial programmed instruction course has been revamped into an orientation and initial training program for new employees.

QUESTIONS FOR STUDY AND DISCUSSION

1. Relate performance appraisal to the training function within an organization. What justification is there for relating these two concepts?

2. Describe the self-appraisal technique of performance appraisal. What are its advantages? Its limitations?

3. Plan a simple training program for a large office-type organization. You might wish to consider subjects to be included, training approaches, sequence and timing, or other aspects which you consider essential.

4. Comment on the statement, "Business has a 'moral obligation' to train its employees." Do you agree? Why?

5. An analysis of training programs indicates that training is most prevalent when there is considerable economic prosperity and when the economy is growing. Comment on this approach to training. Do you agree that this is the best policy for the training of workers? Why? Discuss the recommendations that you would make, if any.

6. Training is rather expensive unless it is aimed at particular objectives and goals. That is to say, it is difficult to justify the funds for a training program unless some specific need is identified. What are some indicators of the need for training that might be found in an office-type organization?

7. It was stated in this chapter that on-the-job training is the most widely used of training for office workers. Does this necessarily mean that it is the best training plan for office workers? Why?

8. Discuss how you would go about evaluating a training program for office workers. Evaluate the training program that you recommended in question three above.

9. A typical statement regarding the training of industrial workers is: the average person may read and even memorize a statement without forming strong convictions as to the value of the ideas contained in it. To learn and develop a real understanding of proper work practices, we need the personal persuasion of a group and an interchange of ideas with others. Comment on this statement with respect to training of office workers. What type of training would you recommend to best meet this requirement? Why?

10. Basically, there are four alternatives when assigning responsibility for training an employee: the supervisor, a fellow employee who knows the particular job involved, a senior or lead worker within the department who has been "trained in how to train," or a staff specialist. Discuss the advantages and disadvantages of a training program administered and conducted by each.

11. What do you see as the main fields of usefulness for programmed instruction in office training?

12. How far does management's responsibility extend in the area of retraining office employees whose skills are made obsolete by new methods and equipment? At what point may governmental agencies need to step in, as you see it?

Case 28-1. Three Approaches to Training

A group of three supervisors recently had a discussion of training methods used by each.

Martin, the first supervisor, tries to have each new employee trained by the fellow employee who has the most experience on the particular job involved. Where possible, the person about to leave the job is given the responsibility of training the one who will replace him.

James, the second supervisor, has one experienced clerk—a sort of lead clerk, though without a special job title—who breaks in and trains all new employees and persons transferred to jobs within the unit.

Lowry, the third supervisor, attempts to do nearly all of his own training. He devotes a considerable portion of his time to training new employees, persons transferred in, and experienced employees who are being cross-trained or trained as understudies on higher jobs.

Problems and questions:

a. What are likely to be the advantages and disadvantages of each approach?

b. Can you state any general principles that might serve as guides in determining who should do the training in any given situation?

Case 28-2. The Randall Manufacturing Company

In the Randall Manufacturing Company, an engineer in the production division had complained loudly and bitterly about the "useless figures" which he was required to prepare and which were "wasting his time." The vice-president of production and the controller, who had high hopes for the young man, decided that this was an area of personal weakness for him, and that steps should be taken to remedy the deficiency. Accordingly, he was given a tour of duty in the controller's department where he assisted in the preparation of budgets and schedules involving use of the very data that he had formerly been requested to supply.

Problems and questions:

a. How can the earlier attitude of the engineer toward the office phases of his job be explained?

b. Is the approach followed likely to correct his deficiency? Discuss.

29

COMPENSATION METHODS; OFFICE UNIONS

Compensation methods · Job evaluation · Job pricing · Salary administration · Office unions

---

Two areas high in potential significance to motivation have not yet been dealt with directly; they are the financial compensation paid to employees, and the present and prospective role of unions. These areas will be considered briefly in this chapter, with special concern for office employees.

Compensation Methods

The salary a person receives is certainly not the *only* reward which is important to him. Earlier study of the priority of human needs and of those needs which can be largely, or even partly, satisfied by pay, indicated that the income a person receives is important chiefly in providing him with *subsistence* and *security*, plus having important *status* implications to the individual and to others.

Translated more specifically to salary expectations, the typical person desires (1) a level of pay which will support his desired standard of living, (2) stable income, and (3) equitable pay in relation to that paid for other jobs and to other people.

In this country, the combination of a generally high standard of living, a comparative abundance of job opportunities, increasingly responsible managements, increasingly influential unions, and increasingly active governmental concern for minimum income and aid to the unemployed

—has gone far toward providing adequate general levels and stability of income.

The most difficult problems of management, aside from being successful to the point where they can afford to create jobs and employ people, lie in the area of insuring equitable compensation. It is with this area that most compensation programs are predominantly concerned.

A typical salary plan consists of the following programs:

1. Job evaluation—to insure internal equity in salary paid for different jobs.

2. Job pricing—to insure external equity with salaries paid by other enterprises for comparable work.

3. Salary administration—to reward particular individuals in proportion to length of service, merit (including incentive arrangements) or another justifiable basis.

Each of these types of programs will now be considered briefly.

Job evaluation

The central purpose of job evaluation is to determine the relative worth of the different jobs in an enterprise. Relative worth is assumed to vary with the duties that must be performed, the conditions under which they are performed, and the qualifications required to perform them.

Evaluation of jobs, thus, begins with *job analysis.* Job analysis is the *process* of studying the duties and conditions of each job, and the qualifications which any person must possess in order to perform it. Such a study may be carried on by means of a *questionnaire* completed by either an employee who is experienced in a certain job under study, or his supervisor, or both. It may also be carried out by means of an *interview* between a trained job analyst and one or more holders of the job, with the supervisor usually consulted also. In many instances, particularly where clerical workers are involved, a *combination* of questionnaire and interview is found most successful. Completion of a well-designed questionnaire first, then careful verifying of job facts and qualifications by means of interview, can usually be made to produce satisfactory results.

The results of the job analysis are then written up as a *job description.* The analyst, or whoever is preparing the description, will go through a sifting and organizing process; he will present the essential details in a form which usually includes (1) the heading, made up of job title and other identifying information, (2) the job summary or purpose, (3) the duties performed, and (4) the personal requirements or specifications. Figure 29-1 presents an illustrative job description.

Actual evaluation of jobs is usually carried out by a rating committee,

STATE FARM INSURANCE COMPANIES
Homes Office
Bloomington, Illinois

Job Description and Specification

Date _January 15,1964_

Functional Job Title_ Field Claim _Representative Job No._061_Job Class _MA-2_
Name of Company ___Automobile___ Department or Division_Operating__
Section _Claims___ Location _Claim Service Office-Regional Offices_
   1. Supervision Received: _Claim Superintendent__ Type_____
   2 Functional Guidance Received: _Claim Superintendent_
   3. Supervision Given: Directly _____1_____ Indirectly_____

PURPOSE

To investigate, evaluate, negotiate and settle the claims in his area presented to
the State Farm Mutual Automobile Insurance Company and the automobile, medical
payment, and liability claims presented to the State Farm Fire and Casualty Company.

DUTIES, RESPONSIBILITIES, AND AUTHORITY

1. Checks, investigates and verifies questions of coverage, legal liability and extent
   of damage to persons and property
2. Takes statements of claimants and witnesses
3. Secures police reports, medical reports, photographs, diagrams and estimates
   (usually takes own photos, prepares own diagram and may make own estimate.)
4. Verifies wage losses, medical expense and other items of special damages
5. Determines legal liability and evaluates losses up to the extent of his discre-
   tionary authority---consults with Claim Superintendent on reserves and values
   in excess thereof.
6. Negotiates settlements with and secures releases from policyholders, claimants
   and their attorneys including such special interests as lienholders, contribution
   and subrogation.
7. Makes written reports covering investigations, evaluation, negotiation and
   settlements
8. Dictates correspondence and handles miscellaneous clerical and administrative
   work in connection with the management of his claim service office
9. Interviews and recommends legal representation in his area--collaborates with
   attorneys in preparation of lawsuits and in most cases controls negotiations and
   settlements.
10. Participates in agency meetings explaining claim policies and procedures--
    assists in training agents to handle claims promptly and properly
11. Exercises descretionary authority as outlined in General Claims Memo #152.

JOB REQUIREMENTS

Education
   College graduation normally required, however, equivalent exposure through
   experience may be acceptable.
   Completion of Home Office Claim School and Vale Technical Course.

Experience
   At least one year of satisfactory service as a State Farm Field Claim
   Representative Trainee.

Specific Knowledge Requirements
   Must have knowledge of company claim policies and procedures, company
   underwriting standards, automobile construction and repair costs, medical and
   anatomical terminology, types of personal injury and their prognosis, insurance
   contracts and endorsements, and at least a basic knowledge of law as it applies
   to the insurance industry and claims handling and verdicts in particular.

Working Conditions
   Is subject to continuous travel in a limited area by company automobile.
   Work hours irregular, but seldom has to be away overnight.

State Farm Insurance Companies

Figure 29-1. Illustration of job description and specification

consisting of members who, ideally, possess broad familiarity with jobs and with the organization, are well-grounded in the philosophy and techniques of job evaluation (usually justifying preliminary training), are objective, and have adequate time to devote to the work. Use of the committee approach, implying pooled judgment, is usually thought to produce more accurate results and to make acceptance more widespread.

Members of a rating committee ordinarily will benefit by careful formulation of basic policies. An illustrative set of guides is presented below; studying them will contribute to clearer understanding of the job evaluation process.

1. Rate the job—not the man on the job.

2. Strive to get the facts, get them accurately, and get them all.

3. Look especially for distinguishing features of jobs and for relationships to other jobs.

4. Study jobs independently and objectively, but then discuss views thoroughly and open-mindedly before reaching final decisions.

5. Remember that job evaluation is merely a systematic, carefully controlled type of judgment, based upon the best factual data obtainable.

6. Remember that the results of job evaluation not only must *be* fair, they must *seem* fair and rational to individuals affected.

The work of rating jobs requires development and use of a rating scale of some sort. There are four principal variations of rating scales in common use—(1) *ranking* all jobs from highest to lowest with respect to relative difficulty; (2) *classification* of jobs according to predetermined and defined grades; (3) *point rating* of jobs by comparing the characteristics of each with standard definitions of selected factors, broken down into degrees with point weightings attached; and (4) *factor comparison* of jobs by making direct job-to-job comparisons under each of a number of factors which have been selected and defined.[1] In most common use for clerical job evaluation is the point rating method, probably because it is somewhat easier to understand and to communicate than the factor comparison method (next in use) and is more thorough and systematic than either of the first two methods. A point rating plan which has been designed by the National Office Management Association, especially for

[1] Many sources are available to persons desiring fuller description and comparison of alternative job evaluation methods. Among these are John A. Patton, C. L. Littlefield, and S. A. Self, *Job Evaluation and Compensation Methods,* 3rd ed. (Homewood, Ill.: Richard D. Irwin, Inc.); Elizabeth Lanham, *Job Evaluation* (New York: McGraw-Hill Book Company, Inc.); Jay L. Otis, and Richard H. Leukart, *Job Evaluation* (Englewood Cliffs, N.J.: Prentice-Hall, Inc.); and Charles W. Lytle, *Job Evaluation Methods* (New York: The Ronald Press Company); and American Management Association, *The AMA Handbook of Wage and Salary Administration.*

clerical job evaluation, is outlined below. Definitions of factors and degrees, and suggestions for applying the plan are available from NOMA.

Clerical Job Evaluation Plan of the National Office Management Association

	Maximum Point Values	Percentage To Total
1. ELEMENTAL	250	25%
2. SKILL		
(a) General or special education 160		16
(b) Training time on job 40		4
(c) Memory 40		4
(d) Analytical 95		9.5
(e) Personal contact 35		3.5
(f) Dexterity 80		8
(g) Accuracy 50		5
Total	500	50%
3. RESPONSIBILITY		
(a) For company property 25		2.5
(b) For procedure 125		12.5
(c) Supervision 50		5
Total	200	20%
4. EFFORT		
(a) Place of work 5		.5
(b) Cleanliness of work 5		.5
(c) Position 10		1
(d) Continuity of work 15		1.5
(e) Physical or mental strain 15		1.5
Total	50	5%
Grand Total	1000	100%

The final step of job evaluation is that of grouping jobs into classes or grades, commonly about 7 to 12 in number for clerical jobs, although sometimes more. Jobs falling within each class are then treated alike for pay purposes; a rate range is assigned, and individual employees are paid salaries which fall within that range until promoted to a job in a higher grade.

Job pricing

The *general* pay scale of a firm is usually adjusted when salary surveys (comparing salaries paid to a sampling of comparable jobs) indicate that the general level is not in the desired relationship to competitive rates. Very common is a policy to "pay salaries equal to or better than those prevailing for comparable jobs"; carefully conducted salary surveys are the most reliable means of making the comparisons necessary.

Salary administration

The exact salary paid to an employee depends, first, upon the job grade into which his job falls. For each grade there will be a range, usually about 30% above the minimum salary for the grade, although this may vary. Some overlap of the range for one grade with that of the next higher is customary. It may be assumed that sufficient experience and outstanding performance in the lower of two job grades is of greater value than initial contribution in the higher one. Also, this may be a reward to a faithful, good-performing, old timer who does well in the lower-graded job but lacks certain qualifications, technical or other, for promotion to a higher job class.

Salary increases are of three main types: length-of-service, merit, and promotional. Length-of-service increases are automatic, usually a certain percentage or dollar increase once a year until a ceiling is reached. Merit increases are based upon some appraisal or measure of general suitability of performance. Promotional increases are given when an employee is moved from one job class to a higher one.

For clerical jobs, most firms attempt to base their salary programs chiefly on merit. An appraisal of the individual's performance during the period just completed is made; at the same time, other considerations such as his pay position within his rate range, his pay history, what his fellow employees are earning, and any limitations imposed by current salary budgets and controls are taken into account. While most managements subscribe to merit increase programs, making them work effectively is not easy. Most supervisors tend to try to get the maximum for their employees each time increases are to be considered, thus causing merit increases to approach the status of automatic increases, since employees come to expect them. In some plans, small differences in merit increase size are given; a legitimate question can be raised as to whether human judgment is sufficiently accurate to make more than three or four differentiations in quality of performance. It might work thus: poor performance: no increase, fair performance: automatic increases up to a ceiling of about 40% of the range; good performance: combination automatic and merit increases up to about 60% of the range; outstanding performance: combination increases up to the ceiling of the rate range.

Problems nearly always arise where appraisals for merit increases in salaries are used as the basic tools for developmental counseling at the same time. As was mentioned in the preceding chapter, best results in counseling are generally realized when appraisals are made separately and at a different time of the year, and with the entire focus being to help the person to develop. Where this effort is combined with salary determination, the latter tends to encourage preconceived notions as to what an employee's salary increase should be. The appraisal may be manipulated in such a manner that the final result will justify the increase—with most of the potential value of counseling likely to be lost in the process.

Controls over merit increase amounts are commonly exercised in the form of budget limits for merit increases, ratios of average salaries paid within each grade range to the midpoint salary for the range (preferably with some flexibility in application to small groups, which might tend to be strong or weak).

Promotions should usually be accompanied by immediate salary increases, to reflect the increase in responsibility assumed and to contribute to morale. Promotional increases must be considered in the light of merit increases recently given, however, and in the light of budget limits and perhaps other factors. Some firms have found that a combination limit, perhaps 20% of minimum of the lower job class for both merit and promotional increases within any one-year period, provides a satisfactory solution.

A special form of reward for merit is that of direct financial incentives. Such incentives may be either individual or group. Individual incentive plans usually start with base rates arrived at through job evaluation or some similar process, and with work standards indicating normal performance; a person is then paid an additional amount for each unit of work produced above standard. Group plans work similarly, with performance above the group standard (departmental average or other) rewarded by an amount which normally is apportioned as a percentage of the base salary of each employee in the group.

Use of direct financial incentives is a controversial topic. Particularly in the case of individual incentives, many managers feel that office employees will never develop the general sense of responsibility and awareness of all factors involved in effective service (not just quantity and accuracy), and that they will never achieve higher-level needs if their thinking is dominated by concern with financial incentives tied directly to current work. Group incentives seem to offer much more promise, since teamwork is encouraged; one particularly interesting variation is the Scanlon Plan, which shares the benefits of cost reduction with all employees in proportion to individual salaries.[2]

Office Unions

Of present significance to the motivation of office employees is the clerical unionization movement.

[2] Frederick G. Lesieur, ed., *The Scanlon Plan . . . A Frontier in Labor-Management Cooperation* (Industrial Relations Section, Massachusetts Institute of Technology, 1958).

A survey conducted by the National Office Management Association in 1960 revealed that about 6% of approximately 2,000 representative firms had office unions; not nearly all office employees in those having unions were members.[3]

Principal reasons listed in the survey by the large proportion of employees who *do not join* unions were (1) loss of prestige and status, (2) loss of employer-employee relationship, (3) same benefits usually received anyway, (4) opposition to paying dues, and (5) fear of strikes and lockouts. Principal reasons listed by those who *do join* were (1) unfair salary administration, (2) inadequate fringe benefits in comparison to unionized workers in same firms, (3) supervisors not well trained or informed, and (4) lack of firm promotion policies.

Despite frequently expressed union views that white-collar employees represent the principal frontier for organizational efforts in the future, and occasional instances of successful formation of office unions, the proportion of office employees who join unions seems to be growing slowly, if at all. In addition to the reasons cited in the NOMA survey, resistance to unionism among employees seems to be the result of rising educational levels and increasing proportions who attain or aspire to technical, professional, and managerial positions. There is also the large and increasing proportion of office employees who are women, and they have always been difficult to interest in the objectives of unionism, for a variety of reasons. Other reasons may be personal loyalties to supervisors, plans for limited work tenure, dislike of forceful or militant tactics, etc. Furthermore, managements have become increasingly alert to the possibility of office unionization and have taken deliberate steps to see that office employees are not placed at a disadvantage by gains won by factory unions; usually managements provide equivalent salary increases and other new programs to office and factory alike.

Most, although not all, office unions formed are in organizations where unions of factory or other operative employees already exist. Affiliation is most often with the AFL-CIO Industrial Union, the Office Employees-International Union, the United Automobile Workers of America, the United Steel Workers Union, or the Teamsters Union.

Certainly the shift in the white-collar, blue-collar ratio suggests the likelihood of stronger union attempts to organize office and other employees in the white-collar group. Many union leaders, and some impartial labor experts, predict that such efforts may achieve greater success in the future—pointing to the "production-line" nature of many office jobs today, the increased use of machines and need for machine operators, the diminishing status differences through improved working conditions

[3] Charles E. Ginder, "Unionization in the Office," *Office Executive*, January, 1961, pp. 11-14.

and rewards for factory employees, the decreasing use of the strike and other militant action by unions, and the possibility that depression or unstable economic conditions could cause many office employees to turn to unions.

Such a trend may materialize. It should be noted, however, that "production-line" types of office jobs are rapidly being automated; that the rise in educational levels and the need for technical, professional, and managerial personnel continues; that the proportion of women employees is still rising—including increasing numbers of women of middle-age, who have been particularly resistant to unionization. If the white-collar, blue-collar ratio reaches 3 to 1 by 1975, as frequently predicted, it becomes increasingly clear that any union successes will need to be based upon new and more potent appeals than those made in the past.

Viewed in the light of the human-needs concept, the form which these appeals might take is an interesting subject for speculation. Early union appeals were chiefly in terms of improved wages, hours, and working conditions—thus applying mainly to the two most basic levels of human needs: physiological and security. Since these major needs are now generally met to a rather full extent for office employees in the United States, it would seem that future union appeals will succeed in proportion to their contribution in filling social, egoistic, and self-fulfillment needs. Unions have undoubtedly contributed to fulfillment of certain social and egoistic needs for factory and other operative employees. Success in these areas with office employees has been more difficult to attain. Whether further office automation, unstable economic conditions, and other factors which might be favorable to unionization will be sufficiently strong in their influence to offset the forces working against office unionization—and whether unions can come up with a "new formula" which will have genuine appeal—will be interesting developments to follow in the years just ahead.

QUESTIONS FOR STUDY AND DISCUSSION

1. Assume that you have just completed college study and entered employment. Which is likely to be more important to you—your actual salary level or the relationship of your salary to that of fellow employees? Explain.

2. What contribution does each of the following make in an overall salary plan: (a) job evaluation, (b) job pricing, and (c) salary administration? Study the techniques suggested for each phase of an office salary plan, compare major alternatives, and raise questions about applying the techniques successfully.

3. Some businessmen feel that information about salaries should be regarded as strictly confidential. Others feel that to inform employees how their jobs are evaluated and on what basis pay increases are given will only make employees more "salary conscious" and may raise questions in employees' minds which

would not have arisen had the salary information been restricted. Comment on these viewpoints of management. Do you agree? Why? What advantages and disadvantages do you offer to support your position?

4. What is merit? How is it determined? If the compensation plan is established upon the basis of job evaluation, then merit rating brings the individual worker into the picture and may seem to confuse the issues. How are these two elements separated in a compensation program?

5. Why have incentive wage plans not found wide use in office organizations? What type of incentive plan would you recommend for an office organization, if any?

6. A large steel company made a comprehensive study of its salary plan and adjusted all salaries to a point where salaries in the firm were slightly higher than salaries being paid for comparable work in other firms in the area. Yet when a questionnaire was sent around a few months later and employees were asked to indicate whether they felt their pay was above average in the area, only five per cent indicated that they believed this to be so. What are some possible causes for the employees believing as they did? What do you recommend to the company to correct this situation?

7. Discuss the current status of the move toward unionization of office and white-collar workers. What, if any, have been the recent significant developments in this area?

8. Discuss several of the more important reasons why office and white-collar workers don't accept unionization more readily. What significant changes in these factors do you forecast for the future?

9. Miss Abbott and Miss Jennings have been with the company around 18 or 20 months. Both started as Class II employees and have since been promoted to Class III. Both are average or better than average employees. Mrs. Wilson has been with the company 13 months and started at a Class II which she still holds. She also is an average or better than average employee. Miss Abbott and Miss Jennings have found out that Mrs. Wilson is making more money than they are. How are you, the supervisor, going to keep them doing their best work since they have learned of Mrs. Wilson's salary?

Case 29-1. Ritz Department Store, Inc.

Soon after one particular payday, a supervisor noticed a growing uneasiness in his unit. However, the reason for this did not become apparent until one of his employees told him what was the matter. Since several people had received raises effective with this check, there had been some comparing. What appeared to be gross inequity had created dissension which might "explode" at any time.

Several of the employees of the unit had started work at the same time, and they are all of the same job classification. When the first raises came out, an idle word or statement led to a mass comparison of check stubs, with detrimental results. While they hesitated to ask the supervisor for clarifying information, they concluded the worst—that one of two "pet employees" were favored over the rest.

Problems and questions:

a. What factor or factors do you think led to this type of situation? Why?

b. What should the company have done to prevent such occurrences?

c. Should the supervisor discuss this matter before the entire unit, or should he let the matter lie dormant?

d. What other possible solutions do you recommend for this situation?

Case 29-2. The Case of Jennifer

Jennifer was one of two or three employees on whom Supervisor Arthur McClintock most heavily relied. The whole division was under a heavy workload, able employees were hard to find, and McClintock felt himself under particular pressure to secure and keep control of the difficult status situation.

About three months before Jennifer's next well-deserved raise was due, she came to him with the information that she had been offered a higher-paying job with another company, which carried with it the proviso that she start work for them immediately. Jennifer said that she had numerous personal responsibilities and felt she ought to take the proffered job. She did not especially wish to leave this company, however, and hoped that some adjustment in her salary might be made here.

McClintock realized that it would be highly irregular and unfair to other employees to grant this request, but due to the pressures of production, he took the problem to his superintendent. After several hours of deliberation, the superintendent and McClintock jointly reached a decision to grant the raise, and determined to instruct Jennifer to say nothing about it to any other employee. This was done, and Jennifer agreed to maintain silence.

About four o'clock of the same day, one of Jennifer's co-workers, Ann, confronted McClintock with the question as to why the raise was granted, pointing out to him that she had started with the company the same week as Jennifer, had received raises concurrently with her, and so far as she was able to determine, had produced as much and done as well as Jennifer.

All this was true. McClintock called Jennifer into the conference room immediately, where she admitted to having divulged the news of the raise because "it seemed too good to keep."

Some direct action was necessary. Ann was extremely hostile, though she had never been a troublemaker, and was clearly intent on seeing that her hostility was shared by the other employees, both within and outside the section.

Problems and questions:

a. Was the decision to give Jennifer the raise a justifiable one? Why?

b. Now that the action has been taken and the word leaked out, what should the supervisor and superintendent do?

Case 29-3. Roberts Real Estate Company

The Roberts Real Estate Company employs about 25 office workers below the level of supervisor. The company attempts to base salaries paid to the different employees upon a simple ranking plan of job evaluation. The plan merely involves asking each member of an evaluation committee to consider the duties of each job and the qualifications required by each, and then to give the separate jobs a numerical ranking from lowest to highest based upon the relative worth of the jobs. The rankings of the different committee members are then averaged, and salaries are brought into alignment with the rankings where possible.

The evaluation plan has just been initiated, and the first ranking shows that the committee members placed the receptionist's job near the bottom of the list—well below stenographers and operators of bookkeeping machines. One committee member commented in a discussion of the different jobs that "the receptionist doesn't have to have any skill. She just sits there, doing nothing most of the time."

Problems and questions:

Do you agree with the committee's evaluation of the receptionist's job? Explain fully your reactions in the matter and your general impression regarding the probable quality of reception service that is being provided in the Roberts Company.

30

PERSONNEL
ADMINISTRATION
AND CONTROL

*Personnel policies · Personnel records · Turnover · Attitudes
· Counseling · Suggestion systems · Safety · Employee benefits · Personnel research*

Personnel administration has been
unceremoniously defined as ". . . largely a collection of incidental techniques without much internal cohesion." [1] Another writer dispensed with
the subject briefly by terming it simply a program designed to promote
harmonious relations within an organization. A more respectful and
accurate definition is one which calls personnel administration a program
of activities relating to obtaining and maintaining a competent and
harmonious working group in which each individual is provided with
opportunities for personal development and is well utilized in the interests of the organization.

Any organization which has two or more employees has need for a
planned personnel program. Since it is the objective of management to
see that the necessary work is done efficiently, and since work must be
performed through people, it is clear that personnel management is a
tool of importance in the affairs of an organization. In some organizations the responsibilities connected with the personnel management program will be carried out largely by the personnel department. In other

---

[1] Peter F. Drucker, "Personnel Management—Its Assets and Liabilities," *Dun's Review and Modern Industry,* June, 1954, p. 42.

organizations, the responsibilities of personnel management will be carried out partially or fully by the office manager.

Personnel administration, which is synonymous with the term personnel management, is a relatively new area of study. There is no historical evidence which indicates that planned programs of personnel management, geared both to the interests of employee and employer, were in operation until comparatively recent times. Personnel management as we know it today began to develop following the Industrial Revolution of the nineteenth century. A new awareness was born in the minds of employees that they had certain rights which they had long been afraid to exercise. Almost simultaneously, management began to develop a clearer understanding of the rights of the individual and learned to view personnel as individuals not to be exploited but to be utilized to their mutual advantage. Gradually, employees came to be regarded as something more than chattel and commodities.

Many management historians credit Elton Mayo and F. W. Roethlisberger with bringing about the final turning point in management's attitude and in stating many of the principles on which programs of modern personnel management are based. The greatest contributions of these men were their comprehensive studies in employee behavior and productivity conducted in the 1930's at the Hawthorne Plant of the Western Electric Company in Chicago. These studies proved that management stands to gain when personnel are satisfied and contented in their jobs.

Programs of personnel management are designed to serve the interests of both management and employees. In carrying out this two-way responsibility the personnel department is in effect a neutral zone which, although it represents management, is nevertheless devoted to the interests of the employee and his adjustment and development in the organization. The tools of personnel management include the selection of personnel (see Chapter 27), job evaluation and compensation (see Chapter 29), and many other programs, including:

> Personnel policies, rules, and regulations
> Personnel records
> Controls on personnel turnover
> Personnel attitudes
> Personnel counseling
> Suggestion systems
> Personnel safety
> Employee benefits

Each of these tools will be discussed briefly in the succeeding pages.

Personnel Policies, Rules, and Regulations

It is valuable for management to have a written statement of personnel policy outlining the aims and objectives of the personnel program. A good statement of personnel policy outlines what employees may expect of management and what management in turn may expect of employees. Many administrators discount the necessity of putting these policies into written form. Yet, when they have done so, they frequently find that the process of writing the policies has crystallized in their minds the objectives of the program. The net result is usually of considerable value in giving both management and personnel a uniform understanding of the personnel policies which will be observed in the organization.

Frequently, a statement of personnel policy is included as a foreword to a personnel booklet on rules and regulations. Such a booklet has particular value in orienting new employees. It is also useful in standardizing rules and regulations and in serving as an authoritative source whenever questions arise concerning the personnel rules and regulations of the organization.

Personnel booklets outlining rules and regulations customarily include these headings:

> General statement of personnel policy
> Brief history of the company
> Hours of work
> Behavior and dress on the job
> What to do if unable to report for work
> Promotional policy
> Vacation policy
> Sick leave policy
> Leaves of absence
> Where to take grievances
> The pension plan
> Other employee benefits

Every company will have its own list of essential items to be included in the statement of personnel policies, rules, and regulations. See Figure 30-1 for an example of personnel policies as outlined in a booklet for employees.

Personnel Records

It is necessary that an organization maintain complete records on its personnel. The responsibility for keeping these records is ordinarily vested in the personnel officer, although in some cases this responsibility is decentralized to the office manager.

Personnel records ordinarily include the employee's original application form, data concerning comments made by those given as references, selection data such as physical examination reports and employment test scores, and any evaluations or merit ratings which supervisors have prepared relating to the employee's progress and development. It is customary for these records to be maintained in a manila folder and filed alphabetically in the personnel files.

In addition, larger offices will have a card index record on employees, located conveniently in the office. This card record will show such basic data as name, address, telephone number (office and home), age, education, wife's name and number of children, brief employment history, and date of employment. This record will be useful in enabling supervisors to furnish quickly such pertinent facts about employees as are frequently required.

Control of Personnel Turnover

Personnel turnover is a normal occurrence in healthy organizations. It is to be expected that some employees will leave the organization and will be replaced by others. Excessive turnover, however, is costly and it is a good idea to keep a record of monthly and annual turnover percentages, to maintain an awareness of the rate of turnover. The rate of turnover is usually computed simply by use of the following formula:

$$\frac{\text{Number of employees leaving the organization during the month}}{\text{Total employees in organization}} = \text{Turnover percentage}$$

The rate of turnover varies from one type of organization to another. For example, the rate of turnover among office employees in a large mail order house will usually be much greater than the rate of turnover among office employees in a bank. The reasons for the difference may be the stability of the employees selected, the degree to which employees are permanently established in the community, the prestige of the organization, and the wages being paid. As a general rule, normal turnover among office personnel in typical business organizations runs about one or two per cent per month.

Various estimates have been made of the cost of personnel turnover. Taken into consideration have been such factors as costs of recruiting, screening, interviewing, testing, orienting, and training the new employee. Other costs include those associated with the employee's low productivity at the beginning of his employment and the final costs

WAGE POLICY It is the policy of the company to pay wages which are:

1. Comparable to those paid for performing work requiring similar skill, either in the area in which the company operates plants or
2. Comparable to wages paid within our business-forms industry.

PAY DAY Pay in cash is issued each week on Wednesday. Your supervisor will explain to you in detail the procedure followed.

Your pay slip will indicate certain deductions that either you or your Government have decided upon. Old age benefits (Social Security) and Income Tax are two deductions which the Government requires us to make for all employees. In addition, you may decide to take advantage of our hospital plan and group insurance. If so, these also will be deducted from your weekly pay, and the deductions will be shown on your pay slip.

HOW MUCH IS YOUR JOB WORTH? All jobs are not alike in their requirements. Some require more skill, technical ability or training than others. In some jobs the responsibility for materials and equipment is far greater than in others. It is only reasonable then that wages and salaries should be in line with the requirements and responsibilities of the job.

As improvements are made in production and machinery, or as methods are changed, the working conditions of jobs and the jobs themselves may change. So it is necessary to make regular studies from time to time of all jobs in order to

keep the pay commensurate with the work being done. If new responsibilities are added to your job, you would naturally expect this change to be reflected in your pay. It is the function of job evaluation to insure this.

In making an evaluation, all the important parts of a job are studied. Some of the points considered are as follows:

Previous experience	Initiative
Education required	Cooperation & Personality
Training time required	Responsibility
Future Development	Application
Analytical ability needed	

HOLIDAYS UARCO regularly observes the following holidays: Christmas, New Year's Day, Memorial Day, Independence Day, Labor Day, and Thanksgiving.

You will receive full pay at your base day rate for these holidays, when they fall on a scheduled work day, providing you have worked your regularly scheduled shift both before and after the holiday.

VACATIONS WITH PAY None of us would argue with the old adage that "all work and no play makes Jack a dull boy." All of us need to get away from our work every now and then to relax and refresh ourselves. Uarco has long subscribed to this philosophy. And it has been a Company rule that all employees who meet certain service requirements receive vacations with pay. Here is how our vacation plan works:

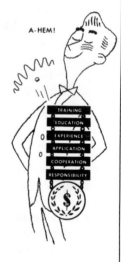

A-HEM!

Courtesy UARCO, Inc.

Figure 30-1. Sample statements from a booklet for employees describing personnel policies, rules, and regulations

associated with his termination. Most estimates indicate that these costs run between $100 and $500 per person.

What are the causes of high turnover? Studies conducted by the University of Illinois [2] indicate that the following causes contribute most to excessive turnover: reasons associated with family life, such as pregnancy, moving to a new locality, and caring for one's family; desire to get into different work or to seek better opportunities; low wages; dissatisfaction with supervisors or colleagues; poor working conditions.

Printed in U.S.A. REMINGTON RAND P-12425

12. If you have been dissatisfied with your job, was it the fault of Aldens?	1. Does your supervisor care about your welfare?
13. Does Aldens have a good vacation policy?	2. Is your supervisor fair with you?
14. Does Aldens have a good holiday policy?	3. Do you know what your supervisor considers a good day's work?
15. Does Aldens have a good promotion policy.	4. Does your supervisor tell you if your work is good?
16. Does Aldens have a good sick pay policy?	5. Are you reasonably sure of keeping your job as long as you do good work?
17. Does Aldens have a good life insurance policy?	6. When a better job is open, is the best qualified person promoted?
18. Does Aldens have a good hospital insurance policy?	7. When you have a problem, do you feel free to ask your supervisor for advice?
19. Does Aldens have a good employee discount plan?	8. Is your section the best to work in?
20. Does Aldens have a good training plan?	9. Is Aldens fair with you?
21. IF YOU HAVE A COMPLAINT, PLEASE LIST ON OTHER SIDE OF CARD.	10. When you have a complaint, are you able to get a fair hearing and a square deal?
	11. Is your pay fair in proportion to the amount of work you do?

Figure 30-2. A short-form attitude questionnaire in which employees are asked twenty questions, the answers to which provide an insight into the morale of personnel

Copyright, 1952, by Aldens, Inc.

The *exit interview,* which is a private interview conducted with the individual at the time of his departure, is an effort to elicit the employee's

_____

2 Based on a number of turnover studies conducted for various business organizations in Illinois by the Bureau of Business Management, University of Illinois.

real reasons for leaving the organization. The fruits of these interviews, however, have been shown to have only limited value. Most employees who are leaving an organization are intelligent enough to "keep the employment door open" should they desire to return to the organization in the future. Accordingly, they tend to give in the exit interview a reason which is logical and acceptable, but which is not necessarily the correct one. It appears that the best way for management to determine the real causes for turnover trends is to obtain the services of an independent agency, such as a consulting firm or the business research bureau of a university, and ask the agency to contact by letter or interview employees who have left the organization in an effort to learn their real reasons for leaving. If the agency stresses its impartial character and emphasizes that individual responses will be kept confidential, it is likely that accurate data on the causes for turnover trends can be determined. The agency can then tabulate the responses and furnish management with a summary report without violating the confidence of any given individual.

Personnel Attitudes

Since the attitude and morale of employees are so closely associated with productivity, it is essential that management keep abreast of trends in employee satisfaction. One of the simplest and most effective ways of determining the level of attitudes and morale is to distribute a questionnaire to employees, inviting them to complete and return the questionnaire without signing their names.

There are many different kinds of questionnaires available and it is not possible to say which type is best. The important factor is to make sure that the various questions are meaningful and have reference to the organization. See Figure 30-2.

It may be a good idea, particularly in smaller organizations where employees might feel management could determine who filled out a given questionnaire, that an outside, impartial agency administer the questionnaires and collect them. As in the case of turnover surveys, the presence of an impartial agency will encourage individuals to give truthful answers to the questions without fear of possible retaliation.

Merely conducting the survey, however, is not enough. Management should study the responses carefully and take steps to correct situations about which survey results indicate employees are concerned.

Personnel Counseling

Many personnel authorities regard counseling as a highly effective tool in motivating employees and in creating employee harmony. Many larger organizations have established formal programs of counseling in which employees are invited to confer whenever they wish with counselors trained in the art of listening and in the technique of helping people solve their own problems through "verbal catharsis." In addition to making counselors available, some companies schedule each employee for at least one annual, private talk with a counselor.

Counseling should always be conducted in complete privacy, in an atmosphere which is pleasant and relaxing. The counselor himself will, of course, be the most important factor in determining the success of the counseling program. A trained individual, who has a personality which is adaptable to people and whom employees instinctively like and trust, will prove very effective in counseling. One of the important requirements is that the counselor respect the confidences of employees and that he be adept at *helping* employees solve their own problems rather than in solving problems for them. There is currently a controversy raging over the relative merits of *directive counseling* (listening to the employee's problem and then giving him direct suggestions) and *non-directive counseling* (offering no direct suggestions but encouraging the employee to keep talking and probing at his own problem until he sees a solution himself). There are merits in both plans, and many counselors find that following a course somewhere between the two methods is most effective.

Suggestion Systems

Motivation is stimulated when employees are encouraged to think about their work and when they are made to feel that their ideas and recommendations have value in the eyes of management. Specialists on personnel management emphasize the role of suggestion programs not only in improving employee morale and in reducing turnover but also in finding new and better ways of doing things and in effecting economies for the organization. There are innumerable cases on record where employee suggestions have resulted in savings of many thousands of dollars.

Suggestion systems have failed in some companies, but there are many other organizations which have taken the trouble to develop effective programs and have found them to be of real value in achieving economies and higher worker morale. Suggestion plans usually fail when there are excessive delays in reviewing suggestions, when turndowns are handled ineptly, when there are inadequate rewards, when the program is ineffectively promoted, and when supervisors are indifferent. An effective program has a promotional plan which continuously stimulates employees to think about their jobs in order to discover new and better ways of doing required tasks. It is not enough that suggestion boxes be placed here and there in the hallways. An effective program also provides awards appropriately scaled to the value of the suggestion and provides suitable recognition to those whose suggestions are accepted. There is a great variance in different firms in the amount which is paid for acceptable suggestions. Figure 30-3 shows the method used in one firm for computing the award to be given for suggestions.

AWARDS

how much you may expect from your accepted ideas

SAMPLE AWARDS:

Your total award will be one-half of the first six months net cost reduction or, in any case, 3% of the first six months gross cost reduction.

WHERE NO EQUIPMENT IS REQUIRED	
Six months gross cost reduction	$500.00
Cost of equipment installed	$0.00
Net six months cost reduction	$500.00
One-half (½) of ($500.00) net cost reduction	
This is your TOTAL AWARD	$250.00

YOU WILL RECEIVE:

One-half of the first six months net cost reduction.

WHERE COST OF EQUIPMENT IS LESS THAN TWO YEARS COST REDUCTION	
Six months gross cost reduction	$500.00
Cost of equipment installed	$600.00
¼ of the cost of equipment installed	$150.00
Net six months cost reduction, $500.00 minus $150.00	$350.00
One-half (½) of ($350.00) net cost reduction	
This is your TOTAL AWARD	$175.00

YOU WILL RECEIVE:

One-half of the first six months net cost reduction, which is, the six months cost reduction minus one-quarter (¼) of the total cost of equipment, freight, and or installation.

WHERE COST OF EQUIPMENT EXCEEDS TWO YEARS COST REDUCTION	
Six months gross cost reduction	$500.00
Cost of equipment installed	$2000.00
3% of ($500.00) gross six months cost reduction	
This is your TOTAL AWARD	$ 15.00

YOU WILL RECEIVE:

A minimum award of 3% of the first six months gross cost reduction for any accepted idea.

The award will be presented to you in two payments:

(1) One-half of the award to be presented at time of installation.
(2) The balance of the award to be pre-

sented six months after installation and adjusted according to the actual cost reduction.

31

The Maytag Co., Newton, Iowa.

Figure 30-3. A page from an employee manual describing the method used in computing the amount of awards to be given for acceptable suggestions submitted by personnel

Occasionally there is supervisory opposition to employee participation in suggestion programs. This seems to stem from the fears of some supervisors that they may be criticized by their superiors for not having thought of the suggestions presented by their subordinates. In some cases the opposition is due to envy and jealousy. Such opposition can usually be overcome through supervisory indoctrination into the aims of the suggestion program. Another device is to give recognition to the supervisor as well whenever one of his employees submits a satisfactory suggestion. In some firms, suggestion clubs have been formed and all persons submitting at least one suggestion a month are invited to a monthly luncheon at company expense.

Personnel Safety

While industrial and plant accidents total up to a shocking loss of time in the course of a given year, the number of office accidents by comparison is negligible. Where factory and plant workers are frequently exposed to hazardous machines, slippery floors, moving belts, and overhead cranes, most office employees work in quarters considerably less hazardous than their own homes. Among the few office accidents on record are those resulting from tripping over electric cords and extended file drawers, combustion of flammable typewriter cleaning fluids, pulling file cabinets over on one, accidents resulting from practical jokes, and falling off chairs as a result of using them as ladders, or out of them as a consequence of reclining too far backwards.

The office manager should bear the responsibility for office safety and should instruct the various supervisors to correct conditions in the office which appear to be hazardous, and to admonish employees whose safety habits leave something to be desired. He should also see to it that there is in the office a well-equipped first aid kit and that employees are encouraged to utilize the contents of the kit whenever minor scratches or bruises occur on the job. Supervisors should also be urged to refer for immediate medical treatment employees who suffer accidents of possible severity.

Employee Benefits

Among the benefits most frequently available to personnel are vacation and sick leave, hospitalization and group insurance plans, and retirement and pension plans.

Vacation and sick leave

These benefits vary in different organizations. With reference to vacations, it appears that the majority of office workers receive a two week paid vacation annually. With reference to sick leave, most office workers are given paid time off for absences due to sickness, although there is usually a limit on the amount of paid sick leave which an employee may receive in any given year. Sick leave is often difficult to control. If employees are granted a specified number of days of sick leave annually, there is a tendency for employees to see to it that they are "sick" often enough to take the allotted time. Many firms have been successful in applying plans wherein employees are told they may have a certain number of days of paid sick leave annually, but that they will receive a cash bonus at the end of each year for each unused day of sick leave.

Hospitalization and group insurance plans

Many firms enter into arrangements with insurance firms under which hospitalization and life insurance plans are made available to employees, usually at a reduced rate. The premium may be paid by the employee, by both the employee and the employer, or by the employer. These plans provide a measure of security for employees by assuring them that in the event of hospitalization, the major part of the costs will be borne by the plan, and that in the event of death, funds will be available to their dependents.

Retirement and pension plans

More and more companies are establishing retirement and pension plans for employees. These plans are predicated on the basis that most employees are unable to save enough to provide for their support when they retire. Management, recognizing a continuing obligation to employees who have served the organization for many years, ordinarily develops the pension plan through a bank or an insurance company. Most pension plans in effect today require the retirement of the employee at 65, usually after at least twenty years of service, and the amount of the retirement pension is most often about fifty per cent of the average annual salary (up to a certain point) received by the individual during his last five years of employment.

Personnel Research

Research is a primary method of programming growth and orderly accomplishment. Growth cannot be allowed to wander aimlessly without control, guidance, and planned results. But, to a large extent, this is what will probably occur without adequate research to guide the efforts of many firms.

The past several decades have shown a marked increase in technological research: television, transistor, space age accomplishments, and synthetics. All are aimed at balancing our growing economy by maintaining employment and production, and stimulating consumption. Such technological accomplishments are notable, but the lack of emphasis upon *human research* is quite evident. The trends, the impact, and the ultimate effect upon the personnel of a business organization, as emphasized throughout this book, point out the increasing need for personnel research oriented toward the business environment.

As mentioned in the introduction to this section—management should be concerned also with the *human systems* of their organizations, as well as the *informational and operational systems.*

Responsibility for personnel research

The personnel department is usually assigned primary responsibility for personnel research within an organization. However, *all* managers or supervisors "manage personnel" in addition to their technical jobs, and each of these managers should participate in personnel development and growth through research. Personnel research does not have to be elaborately conceived and complicated to be effective. Simple acts of awareness and intellectual curiosity on the part of the managers and supervisors will do much toward identifying needed research, suggesting areas for study, questioning behavior of the employees, and questioning management's personnel policies.

The entire management and supervisory work force should be made aware of personnel research and its potential advantages in improving the productivity and general working environmental conditions. There must be an *innate curiosity* to learn the why's of personnel concepts and there must be continual research for methods to make the results of personnel management more effective.

Types of personnel research

Two basic types of personnel research are *operational* and *pure*. Operational personnel research is concerned with gaining knowledge which will have definite, tangible results. Ordinarily, operational research is aimed at a particular problem area where the results can be readily applied in the firm, with benefits realized rather quickly. Examples of operational personnel research are analysis of exit interviews, attitude surveys, and communication studies.

Pure personnel research resembles the clinical type of research usually associated with psychology and the social sciences. This type of personnel research may be described as exploratory or as "research for the sake of research." Pure personnel research is aimed at theories of personnel, worker motivation and satisfaction and similar intangibles. The results of pure personnel research are not readily recognizable, but such research does much to foster an environment of research and to provide the foundation necessary for much operational personnel research.

Research areas for personnel

It is impossible to set down all areas of a business organization which can benefit from personnel research. The following brief list indicates certain areas where personnel research may prove particularly productive. It is emphasized that the situation and particular circumstances as well as the initiative of managers will dictate basic areas of research likely to be investigated. Suggested areas are:

1. Patterns of job design which promote productivity and morale.
2. Participation in decision-making—opportunities and limitations.
3. Human response to controls.
4. Selection and placement—new skills requirements, improved techniques of selection.
5. Impact of integrated systems upon organization structure and personnel requirements.
6. Effect of and benefits from management development programs.
7. Leadership characteristics and the identification of the types of leadership particularly adaptable to administrative-type positions.
8. Effects of various salary plans upon employee morale and productivity.
9. Communication studies of all types regarding the effect on productivity, morale, safety, and informal relationships.
10. The effect of working environment upon office productivity.
11. Informal organization and the behavior of small groups in the office.
12. Exit interviews to analyze, study, and classify reasons, conditions and feelings behind employee terminations.

Who should perform personnel research?

Among those institutions and organizations most active in personnel research are (1) colleges and universities through faculty sponsored research grants and graduate theses, (2) private research organizations, and (3) company personnel departments. This does not exclude the individual line manager, but ordinarily he is in the position of being a "contributor" to personnel research sponsored by these agencies.

Staff members of personnel departments can benefit greatly from this research by keeping abreast of what research is conducted and by whom, applying the results to their organization where appropriate, and conducting similar studies on a smaller scale within their own organizations. There are many areas, too, in which the personnel managers and personnel departments are capable of initiating studies, but the management should recognize limitations in both knowledge and tools, and should not hesitate to enlist the help of psychologists, sociologists, consultants, and research agencies when and where needed to perform personnel research.

Participation by department heads, supervisors, and employees in improvement studies of numerous types—such as employee utilization, salary administration, and promotions policies—can often contribute to the effectiveness of personnel programs and can challenge and motivate the participants.

The nature and degree of direct participation in personnel research by managers and other line personnel will vary with circumstances. But on the question of awareness and familiarity with research findings, there is perhaps a lesser amount of latitude. Douglas McGregor has suggested that the manager of the future will need a degree of understanding of the social sciences which will enable him to read the literature and judge the adequacy of scientific findings and claims. The manager will need a depth of familiarity with psychology, sociology, and other social sciences comparable to that which a physician needs regarding biology and chemistry, in order to remain informed on current developments.[3]

QUESTIONS FOR STUDY AND DISCUSSION

1. What are the basic differences in personnel research as presented in this chapter and work simplification as presented in Chapters 9 and 10? What are the similarities? Can either exist without the other? Why?

2. Using the basic elements of personnel management presented in this part of the text and your own reasoning, plan a brief personnel program for an office-type organization. Indicate in your program those factors which you consider "essential" and those which you would consider "desirable but not essential." Would your program be any different if it were prepared for a manufacturing-type organization? How?

3. Explain the relationships that should exist between the social and civic obligation of a business organization and its personnel program.

4. What forces have provided the impetus for the changes in personnel management in the last decade or so? How have office workers been affected by these changes?

5. How can the relationships between company personnel policy and objectives be best explained to an employee? Should this be done during the orientation program? Why?

6. Excessive turnover is a serious problem for any business firm. Comment on the effect of turnover in an office situation. What part does the supervisor play in controlling turnover? How does this differ from the responsibilities for turnover of the personnel department as discussed in this chapter?

7. It is often said that the ability to recognize an area for personnel research is the most difficult step. After looking over the suggested areas for personnel re-

[3] Douglas McGregor, *The Human Side of Enterprise* (New York: McGraw-Hill Book Company, Inc.), Chapter 1.

search presented in this chapter, what other areas can you suggest which would lend themselves to research? Support your recommendations.

8. Are attitude and morale the same thing? What controls or influences attitude? How can these factors be manipulated by the supervisors? How should attitude surveys and studies be used in an office organization by the personnel management?

9. Is it necessary for an organization to have written personnel policies? What do you recommend in this respect? Why?

10. What are the basic purposes behind the suggestion system? What seem to be the most basic requirements for making such a system effective? Discuss the advantages of placing the suggestion program under the control of the personnel department.

11. Who in the firm should conduct personnel research? Why?

Case 30-1. The General Beverages Corporation

This large, national concern has 12 regional offices. Until about ten years ago, its management was quite highly centralized. Growth pressures, combined with further seasoning and maturing of field personnel, have led to a gradual extension of decentralization. During early stages of the decentralization program, corporate staff officers exercised what approached functional control over operations in their respective areas. Regional executives now have a degree of autonomy, subject to corporate objectives and broad policies and procedures.

Mr. E. B. Jackson was named two years ago to the position of Regional Vice-President of the Northeastern Region. Mr. Jackson had had extensive experience in different areas of the firm's operations and was highly respected by his superiors and associates for his leadership ability and his integrity.

During the first several months, Mr. Jackson devoted much study to the operations of the Northeastern Region, and he saw several areas in which he believed there was great opportunity for development. One of these was the area of personnel management.

Mr. Jackson decided to institute a Personnel Program Development Project in which he would include widespread line participation. He established a Steering Committee to head the study, naming a chairman who was known to be effective in getting results and selecting members mainly on the basis of their ability to contribute and promote the program actively. He made some effort to make the membership fairly representative of different departments but kept this consideration secondary. The Regional Personnel Manager and Assistant Personnel Manager were not to serve as members of the Steering Committee, but to act as advisors and to make studies as called for.

In his first meeting with the Steering Committee, Mr. Jackson laid out his general thinking regarding challenges and opportunities in the personnel area. He expressed his faith in the ability of line executives to think creatively within their areas and to contribute much more in the way of constructive ideas than they were usually capable of. He suggested that, even though many general personnel policies and procedures developed by staff specialists were sound, line experience in attempting to implement them was needed. He suggested that personnel specialists might contribute more "upward" in influencing regional policies and decisions of many sorts, and more "outward" in serving managers and employees at all levels. He assured the committee members of his strong interest in the project and of his full support in carrying on the work and in pushing for higher management acceptance of any idea having merit.

The first efforts of the Steering Committee members were directed to planning a general approach. In general, they decided that they should first gather pertinent material on company philosophy and policy in any specific area they might study. They would then pinpoint and define problem areas, clarify objectives in these areas, determine alternatives, decide what information was needed to arrive at courses of action (including staff research and counsel). They would then classify recommendations in terms of those (1) applicable regionally and without higher-management clearance, (2) applicable regionally with higher-management clearance, and (3) applicable company-wide and requiring higher-management clearance.

Members of the Steering Committee decided upon several areas of possible improvement in which they would begin study. These included Manager Selection and Development, Employee Education and Training, Performance Appraisal, Salary Administration, Promotions, and certain others. They decided that each area would be headed up by one of the members of the Steering Committee, who would name a sub-committee, again primarily on the basis of ability rather than widespread representation. In all, some 60 persons were named to the sub-committees. Sub-committees would make studies, come up with recommendations, and present these recommendations and evidence supporting them to the Steering Committee.

The members of the study teams approached their assignments with much enthusiasm. The general feeling was that Mr. Jackson would be receptive to any good idea and "go to bat" with the home office wherever needed. Some individuals who had been around for a good many years were somewhat skeptical regarding home office acceptance of very many suggestions coming up from the field. Some sub-committees required several weeks to get their studies well under way. There were situations in which uncertainty existed regarding staff support needed and obtainable.

But within a year, a partial list of specific accomplishments includes:

1. A carefully worked-out plan for recruiting potential managers and technical specialists.

2. A promotions policy (in what had been a "sore" area) which was recognized as being equitable, encouraging to merit, and well suited for communication and consistent application.

3. A performance appraisal program which encourages each person to assume the maximum degree of responsibility for his own development.

4. A salary administration program which has made policies in this area more workable and has cleared up misunderstanding and inconsistency on interpretations of merit as reflected in salary increases.

5. An orientation program for new employees which seems to be particularly effective, replacing one which had not worked well.

6. A work simplification program for supervisors and employees which is just getting started but is generating a great amount of interest.

Not all has gone smoothly, but the more than 60 people directly involved are more enthusiastic a year after the program was begun than they were at the start. And since they have been encouraged to look to other executives and employees for help, plus coming through with several well-accepted recommendations, the climate that pervades the entire regional operation has changed noticeably. Individuals in positions at all levels are getting the spirit of making suggestions, raising questions, and in general taking more interest in their jobs and in the company than was true before the program began.

Problems and questions:

a. Appraise the approach followed by Mr. Jackson in getting the program launched, the selection of participants, and the plan of attack developed.

b. Are the initial successes and enthusiasm likely to last? What factors are likely to determine these results?

c. Could such a program prove beneficial in many other firms? Discuss.

INDEX